Rick Steves®

PROVENCE &
THE FRENCH RIVIERA

Rick Steves & Steve Smith

CONTENTS

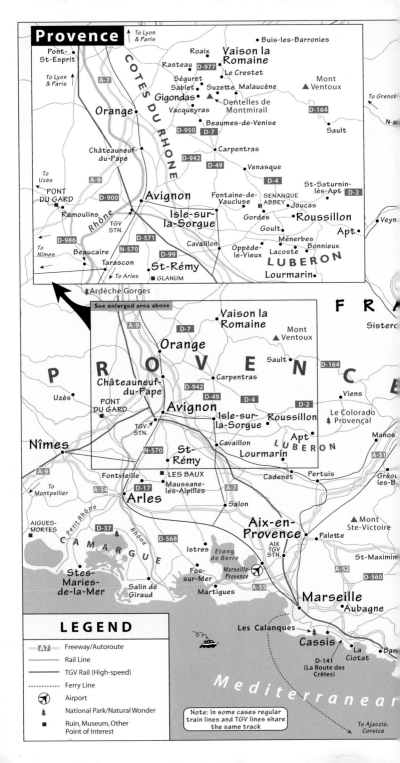

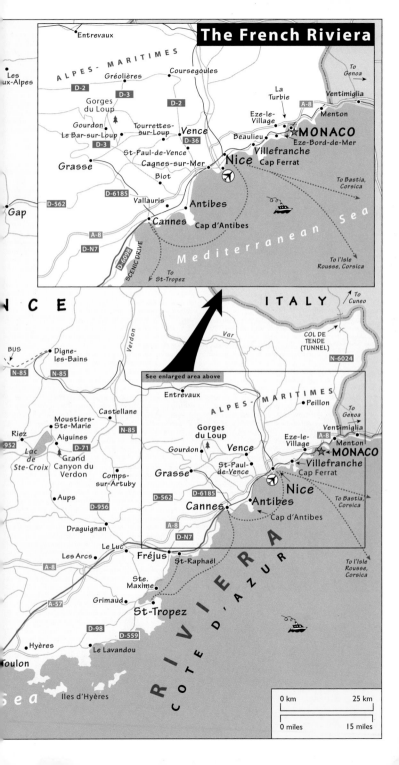

A sun-dappled café in the Luberon

Summer beach scene in Antibes

Nice's old port

Market day in Provence

Roussillon huddling atop its ochre cliffs

Rick Steves'

PROVENCE &
THE FRENCH RIVIERA

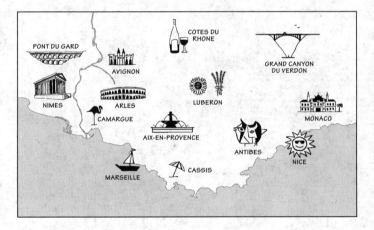

PONT DU GARD

COTES DU
RHONE

GRAND CANYON
DU VERDON

AVIGNON

NIMES

ARLES

CAMARGUE

LUBERON

AIX-EN-PROVENCE

MONACO

ANTIBES

NICE

MARSEILLE

CASSIS

AVALON
TRAVEL

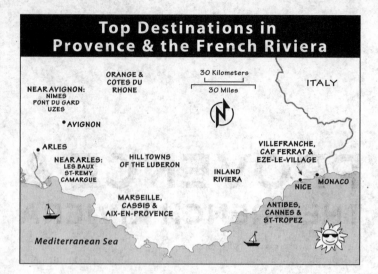

Top Destinations in Provence & the French Riviera

INTRODUCTION

Provence and the French Riviera are an intoxicating bouillabaisse of enjoyable cities, warm stone villages, Roman ruins, contemporary art, and breathtaking coastlines steaming with sunshine and stirred by the wind. There's something about the play of light in this region, where natural and man-made beauty mingle to dazzle the senses and nourish the soul. It all adds up to *une magnifique* vacation.

Provence and the Riviera stretch along France's southeast Mediterranean coast from the Camargue (south of Arles) to Monaco, and ramble north along the Rhône Valley into the Alps. The regions combined are about the same size as Massachusetts—you can take a train or drive from one end to the other in just three hours—yet they contain more sightseeing opportunities and let's-live-here villages than anywhere else in France. Marseille and Nice, the country's second- and fifth-largest cities, provide good transportation and an urban perspective to this otherwise laid-back region, where every day feels like a lazy Sunday.

In Provence, gnarled sycamores line the roads that twist their way through stone towns and between oceans of vineyards. France's Riviera is about the sea and money—it's populated by a yacht-happy crowd wondering where the next "scene" will be. Provence feels older and more *español* (with paella on menus and bullfights on Sundays), while the Riviera feels downright Italian—with fresh-Parmesan-topped pasta and red-orange, pastel-colored buildings. For every Roman ruin in Provence, there's a modern-art museum in the Riviera. Provence is famous for its wines and wind, while the bikini and ravioli were conceived on the Riviera. You can't go wrong.

This book covers the predictable biggies, from jet-setting beach resorts to famous museums, but it also mixes in a healthy

INTRODUCTION

Provence & the French Riviera

Ardèche Gorges

To Lyon & Paris

Nyons

FRA

A-7

D-977

Vaison la Romaine

To Lyon & Paris

Orange

TGV

Mont Ventoux ▲

Uzès

Châteauneuf-du-Pape

A-9

PONT DU GARD

Avignon

P R O V E N C E

Nîmes

Isle-sur-la-Sorgue

Le Colorado Provençal

To Montpellier

A-9

AVIGNON TGV STN.

Cavaillon

Roussillon

E-80

D-99

N-100

Apt

N-100

St-Rémy

LES BAUX

TGV

L U B E R O N

Petit Rhône

Aigues-Mortes

D-570

Arles

Lourmarin

C A M A R G U E

Rhône

A-7

D-543

A-51

Gréoux-les-Bains

Stes-Maries-de-la-Mer

AIX TGV STN.

Aix-en-Provence

A-51

Marseille Provence

A-8

A-55

A-52

Marseille

A-50

TGV

Cassis

The Calanques

A-50

Paris
FRANCE

Mediterranean Sea

Toulon

100 Miles

Note: In some cases regular train lines and TGV lines share the same track

dose of Back Door intimacy. Along with Pont du Gard, Nice, and Avignon, we'll introduce you to our favorite villages and scenic walks. You'll sample delicious wineries and find yourself alone at overlooked Roman ruins. You'll marvel at ancient monuments, take a canoe trip down the meandering Sorgue River, and settle into a shaded café on a made-for-movies square. Claim your favorite beach to call home, and at day's end dive headfirst into a southern France sunset. You'll enjoy tasty-yet-affordable wines while feasting on a healthy cuisine heavy on olives, tomatoes, and spices. Just as important, you'll get on a first-name basis with many of our Provençal friends—hoteliers, restaurateurs, vintners, and lots more.

This book is selective, including only the most exciting sights and romantic villages. There are *beaucoup de* Provençal hill towns...

but we cover only the most intriguing. And though there are scads of beach towns on the Riviera, we recommend our favorite three.

The best is, of course, only our opinion. But after spending more than half of our adult lives writing and lecturing about travel, guiding tours, and gaining an appreciation for all things French, we've developed a sixth sense for what touches the traveler's imagination.

About This Book

Rick Steves' Provence & the French Riviera is a personal tour guide in your pocket. Better yet, it's actually two tour guides in your pocket: The co-author of this book is Steve Smith. Steve, who has lived in France several times, now travels there annually (as he has since 1986) as a guide, a researcher, a homeowner, and a devout

Provence & the French Riviera Almanac

Official Name: Provence and the French Riviera are part of the Provence-Alpes-Côte-d'Azure (PACA), one of 27 administrative regions of France.

Capital: Marseille is the region's capital city.

Regional Population: Over 4.5 million.

Main Cities: Marseille (860,000), Nice (350,000), Aix-en-Provence (140,000), Antibes (80,000), Cannes (75,000), Avignon (13,000 people live within the walls), St-Tropez (5,700).

Language: French is the official language. More than 1.5 million people in the south of France speak one of two lesser-known dialects: Occitan, and specifically in the Provence region, Provençal (both dialects are closely related to Catalan, a dialect of Spanish).

Geography: Located in the southeast of France, the Provence-Alpes-Côte-d'Azure region spans over 71 miles of Mediterranean coastline, from Marseille and Toulon in the west, to Monaco and the Italian border in the east, where the Alps stretch to the north.

Climate: The Hautes-Alpes and Rhône-Alpes shield the region from severe weather and give Provence and the Riviera the highest average temperatures in France (a comfortable 72° F in summer, and around 43° F in winter). Locals enjoy more than 300 days of sun per year, but experience more storms (70-110 per year) than other parts of France.

Economy: The Provence-Alpes-Côte-d'Azure region is the third wealthiest in France and annually contributes nearly $158 billion (7%) to France's GDP. Tourism and service industries account

---

Francophile. He has restored an old farmhouse in Burgundy and today keeps one foot on each side of the Atlantic. Together, Steve and I keep this book up-to-date and accurate (though for simplicity, from this point "we" will shed our respective egos and become "I").

This book is organized by destinations. Each is a mini-vacation on its own, filled with exciting sights, strollable neighborhoods, affordable places to stay, and memorable places to eat. The content consists of two obvious parts: Provence and the Riviera (although almost everything covered in this book is officially considered part of the "Provence-Alpes-Côte d'Azur region" by the French government). The Provence half highlights Arles and Avignon, and their day-trip destinations; the photogenic hill towns of the Côtes du Rhône and Luberon; and the coastal towns of Marseille and Cassis, and nearby Aix-en-Provence. On the high-rolling French Riviera, I cover the waterfront destinations of Nice, Villefranche-sur-Mer, Cap Ferrat, Monaco, Antibes, Cannes, and St-Tropez—plus the best of the inland hill towns and the

for 80 percent of jobs, but the region is also a leading center for agriculture, biotechnology, and microelectronics.

Agriculture: Provence is known for its herbs (such as oregano, thyme, rosemary, and fennel), vegetables, and olive oil, and the region produces nearly two-thirds of France's olives. These ingredients, combined with elements of French, Spanish, and Italian cooking, make Provence's cuisine fresh, colorful, and flavorful.

Crafts: In the 17th century, Marseille began manufacturing expensive and colorful printed linens called "Indiennes," inspired by fabrics imported from India. Though most traditional textile factories are closed today, Provence still produces cotton fabrics (scarves, shawls) using original "Indienne" techniques and featuring the local cicada *(cigale)* in their designs.

Tourism: The Provence-Alpes-Côte-d'Azure region welcomes over 34 million tourists every year. Celebrities and wealthy Brits have vacationed on the French Riviera since the 19th century (giving the Promenade des Anglais in Nice its name). Nowadays, the Riviera attracts more than just celebrities: Over 5 million tourists visit every summer, with Nice at the center of the tourist commotion.

Famous Residents: The rich and famous have homes throughout Provence and the Riviera, including actors Brigitte Bardot, Mel Gibson, Brad Pitt, and Angelina Jolie; musicians Bono, Elton John, Tina Turner, Bill Wyman, and Rod Stewart; Formula One racing driver Michael Schumacher; and billionaire Bill Gates.

truly grand Grand Canyon du Verdon.

The introductions to **Provence** and **The French Riviera** acquaint you with the history, cuisine, and wine of the places you'll be visiting, and give practical advice on what to see, how to get around, and lots more. Don't overlook the valuable tips in these chapters.

In the destination chapters, you'll find these sections:

Planning Your Time suggests a schedule for how to best to use your limited time.

Orientation includes specifics on public transportation, helpful hints, local tour options, easy-to-read maps, and tourist information.

Sights describes the top attractions and includes their cost and hours.

Self-Guided Walks help you explore these fascinating towns and places on foot: Avignon, Nîmes, Arles, Aix-en-Provence, Les Baux, Isle-sur-la-Sorgue, Roussillon, Monaco, Antibes, Villefranche-sur-Mer, and Cannes. (A few of the in-depth walks

INTRODUCTION

Map Legend

⅃ Viewpoint	✈ Airport	)▨(Tunnel
↑ Entrance	Ⓣ Taxi Stand	Pedestrian Zone
✆ Tourist Info	+Ⓣ+ Tram & Stop	Railway
ⓦⓒ Restroom	Ⓑ Bus Stop	Ferry/Boat Route
⛫ Castle	Ⓟ Parking	Mtn. Pass
⌂ Church	Ⓡ RER Train	Stairs
▪ Statue/Point of Interest	Ⓣ Tourist Train	Walk/Tour Route
Park	Ⓑ Batobus Stop	Trail
◎ Fountain	Ⓜ Métro Stop	

Use this legend to help you navigate the maps in this book.

and tours get their own chapters: a stroll along Nice's Promenade des Anglais, a walk through Vieux Nice, and a guided visit to the Chagall Museum.) I also include a few **self-guided driving tours**, allowing you to explore the Côtes du Rhône wine road, the Grand Canyon du Verdon, and inland hill towns of the Riviera with the knowledge of a local.

Sleeping describes my favorite hotels, from good-value deals to cushy splurges.

Eating serves up a range of options, from inexpensive cafés to fancy restaurants.

Connections outlines your options for traveling to destinations by train and bus, plus route tips for drivers.

The book also includes detailed chapters on these key topics:

Traveling with Children offers general tips and destination-specific advice, like kid-friendly hotels and restaurants. Both co-authors have kids (from 12 to 26 years old), and we've used our substantial experience traveling with children to improve this book. Our kids have greatly enriched our travels, and we hope the same will be true for you.

Shopping has suggestions for this region's best souvenirs and bargains. My longtime friendships with shopkeepers, local guides, and vintners have contributed greatly to the savvy shopping advice.

France: Past and Present gives you a quick overview of the country.

The **appendix** is a traveler's tool kit, with telephone tips, useful phone numbers and websites, transportation basics (on trains, buses, car rentals, driving, and flights), recommended books and films, a festival list, climate chart, a handy packing checklist, and French survival phrases.

Browse through this book, choose your favorite destinations,

Key to This Book

Updates

This book is updated regularly—but once you pin down Provence, it wiggles. For the latest, visit www.ricksteves.com /update. For a valuable list of reports and experiences—good and bad—from fellow travelers, check www.ricksteves.com /feedback.

Abbreviations and Times

I use the following symbols and abbreviations in this book:

Sights are rated:

▲▲▲	**Don't miss**
▲▲	**Try hard to see**
▲	**Worthwhile if you can make it**
No rating	**Worth knowing about**

Tourist information offices are abbreviated as **TI**, and bathrooms are **WCs**. To categorize accommodations, I use a **Sleep Code** (described on page 28).

Like Europe, this book uses the **24-hour clock**. It's the same through 12:00 noon, then keeps going: 13:00, 14:00, and so on. For anything over 12, subtract 12 and add p.m. (14:00 is 2:00 p.m.).

When giving **opening times**, I include both peak season and off-season hours if they differ. So, if a museum is listed as "May-Oct daily 9:00-16:00," it should be open from 9 a.m. until 4 p.m. from the first day of May until the last day of October (but expect exceptions).

For **transit** or **tour departures**, I first list the frequency, then the duration. So, a train connection listed as "2/hour, 1.5 hours" departs twice each hour and the journey lasts an hour and a half.

and link them up. Then have a *très bon voyage!* Traveling like a temporary local, you'll get the absolute most out of every mile, minute, and dollar. As you visit places I know and love, I'm happy you'll be meeting my favorite French people.

Planning

This section will help you get started planning your trip—with advice on trip costs, when to go, and what you should know before you take off.

Travel Smart

Your trip to France is like a complex play—it's easier to follow and really appreciate on a second viewing. While no one does the same trip twice to gain that advantage, reading this book in its entirety

Provence and the French Riviera at a Glance

The following destinations are listed in the order they appear in this book.

Provence

▲▲**Arles** Once-important Roman outpost, now a bustling town famous for its ancient amphitheater and its artistic draw as a site that inspired Van Gogh.

▲▲**Near Arles** Several compelling sights: the cliff-topping castle ruins at Les Baux; St. Rémy with Roman ruins and a mental hospital that treated Van Gogh; and the Camargue—a nature lover's paradise, with flamingos, bulls, and white horses.

▲**Avignon** Fourteenth-century residence of the popes, today a youthful city with atmospheric cafés, lively squares, and a famous broken bridge.

▲▲▲**Near Avignon** Three worthy destinations, including the stunning Pont du Gard aqueduct; thriving Nîmes, with world-class Roman monuments; and pedestrian-friendly Uzès, a refreshing break from power monuments and busy cities.

▲▲▲**Orange and the Côtes du Rhône** Starring Orange's remarkably intact Roman theater, plus the sunny Côtes du Rhône wine road, cozy villages, and fields of lavender, anchored by charming Vaison la Romaine.

▲▲**Hill Towns of the Luberon** Boasting the sturdy market town of Isle-sur-la-Sorgue, delightful rock-top village of Roussillon,

before your trip accomplishes much the same thing.

Design an itinerary that enables you to visit sights at the best possible times. Note holidays, specifics on sights, and days when sights are closed. If you're using public transportation, read up on the tips for trains and buses (see pages 545 and 547 of the appendix). If you're renting a car, study my driving tips and the examples of road signs (see page 551). A smart trip is a puzzle—a fun, doable, and worthwhile challenge.

When you're plotting your itinerary, strive for a mix of intense and relaxed stretches. To maximize rootedness, minimize one-night stands. It's worth taking a long drive after dinner (or a train ride with a dinner picnic) to get settled in a town for two nights. Every trip—and every traveler—needs slack time (laundry, picnics, people-watching, and so on). Pace yourself. Assume you

crumbled castles, and meditative abbeys.

▲▲Marseille, Cassis, and Aix-en-Provence Gritty port of Marseille with art museums; the coastal town of Cassis, home of the *calanques* (Mediterranean fjords); and inland, genteel Aix-en-Provence.

The French Riviera

▲▲▲Nice The Riviera's metropolis, with a sun-drenched promenade, a delightful French-Italian old city, and museums dedicated to Chagall and Matisse.

▲▲▲Villefranche-sur-Mer, Cap Ferrat, and Eze-le-Village Small, Italianate beach town of Villefranche-sur-Mer, ritzy but woodsy Cap Ferrat, and little cliff-topping Eze-le-Village—linked by the panoramic roads known as the Three Corniches.

▲▲Monaco Tiny independent principality, known for its Grand Prix car race and classy casino.

▲Antibes, Cannes, and St-Tropez The Riviera's west: laid-back Antibes, with a medieval old town and Picasso Museum; glamorous Cannes, with sandy beaches and movie stars; and the luxurious port town of St-Tropez.

▲▲Inland Riviera Perfectly perched hill towns of St-Paul-de-Vence (France's most-visited village) and Vence, the perfume capital of Grasse, and the spectacular Grand Canyon du Verdon.

will return.

Reread this book as you travel, and visit local tourist information offices (abbreviated as TI in this book). Upon arrival in a new town, lay the groundwork for a smooth departure; get the schedule for the train or bus that you'll take when you depart. Drivers can study the best route to their next destination.

Get online at Internet cafés or your hotel, though I encourage you to disconnect from life back home and immerse yourself in the French experience. Carry a mobile phone (or use a phone card) to make travel plans: You can find tourist information, learn the latest on sights (special events, tour schedule, etc.), book tickets and tours, make reservations, reconfirm hotels, research transportation connections, and keep in touch with your loved ones.

Enjoy the friendliness of the French people. Connect with

Boules (Pétanque)

The game of *boules*—also called *pétanque*—is the horse-shoes of Provence and the Riviera. It's played in every village, almost exclusively by men, on level dirt areas kept specifically for this purpose. It was invented here in the early 1900s, and today every French boy grows up playing *boules* with Papa and *Ton-Ton* (Uncle) Jean. It's a social-yet-serious sport, and endlessly entertaining to watch—even more so if you understand the rules.

Boules is played with heavy metal balls (*boules*, about the size of baseballs) and a small wooden target ball (*le cochonnet*—"piglet," about the size of a table tennis ball). Whoever gets his *boule* closest to the *cochonnet* wins. It's most commonly played in teams of two, though individual competition and teams of three are not uncommon. (France has plenty of *boules* leagues and even professional players, who make little money but are national celebrities.) Most teams have two specialists, a *pointeur* and a *tireur*. The *pointeur* goes first and tries to lob his balls as close to the target as he can. The *tireur's* job is to blast away opponents' *boules*.

Here's the play-by-play: Each player gets three *boules*. A coin toss determines which team goes first. The starting team scratches a small circle in the dirt, in which players must stand (with both feet on the ground) when launching their *boules*. Next, the starting team tosses the *cochonnet* (about 6-10 yards)—that's the target. The *boule* must be tossed underhand, and can be rolled, thrown sky-high, or rocketed at its target. Most lob it like a slow pitch in softball, with lots of backspin. The starting team's *pointeur* shoots, then the other team's *pointeur* shoots until he gets closer. Once the second team lands a *boule* closer, it's the first team's turn. If the opposing team's *boule* is very near the *cochonnet*, the *tireur* will likely attempt to knock it away. If the team decides that they can lob one in closer, the *pointeur* shoots.

Once all *boules* have been launched, the tally is taken. This is where it gets tense, as the difference in distance often comes down to millimeters. Faces are drawn, lips are pursed, and eyes are squinted as teams try to sort through the who's-closer process. I've seen all kinds of measuring devices, from shoes to belts to tape measures. The team with the ball closest to the target receives 1 point, and the teams keep going until someone gets 13 points.

the culture. Learn a new French expression each day and practice it. Cheer for your favorite bowler at a *boules* match, leave no chair unturned in your quest for the best café, find that perfect hill-town view, and make friends with a waiter. Slow down and be open to unexpected experiences. Ask questions—most locals are eager to point you in their idea of the right direction. Keep a notepad in your pocket to organize your thoughts, confirm prices, and write down directions. Wear your money belt, learn the currency, and figure out how to estimate prices in dollars. Those who expect to travel smart, do.

Trip Costs

Five components make up your trip costs: airfare, surface transportation, room and board, sightseeing and entertainment, and shopping and miscellany.

Airfare: Nice is the handiest airport for Provence and the Riviera (though Marseille is becoming more convenient each year). A basic round-trip flight from the US to Nice or Paris can cost, on average, about $900-2,000 total, depending on where you fly from and when (cheaper in winter). Smaller budget airlines may provide bargain service from Paris and other European cities to places such as Marseille, Avignon, and Montpellier (see "Cheap Flights" on page 558 for details). If your trip covers a wide area, consider saving time and money in Europe by flying into one city and out of another; for instance into Nice and out of Paris.

Surface Transportation: Allow $30 per day per person for public transportation (trains, buses, and taxis), or $50 per day per person for a rental car (based on two people sharing), not including tolls, gas, and insurance. Leasing is worth considering for trips lasting three weeks or more. Car rentals and leases are cheapest if arranged from the US.

Railpasses only make sense if you are traveling to regions beyond Provence and the Riviera, as distances within this region are short, and point-to-point fares are reasonable. Train passes normally must be purchased outside Europe. Don't hesitate to consider flying, because flights offered by budget airlines can be cheaper than taking the train (check www.skyscanner.com for intra-European flights). For more on public transportation and car rental, see "Transportation" in the appendix.

Room and Board: You can thrive in Provence and the Riviera on $145 a day per person for room and board. This allows an average of $13 for breakfast, $18 for lunch, $44 for dinner with drinks, and $70 for lodging (based on two people splitting the cost of a $140 double room). That's definitely doable. Students and tightwads can enjoy Provence and the Riviera for as little as $60 a day ($30 per bed, $30 for meals and snacks).

Best Two-Week Trip of Provence & the French Riviera by Car

Day Plan

1 Fly into Nice. Settle in at your hotel, then take a walk along the Promenade des Anglais up to Castle Hill (see the Welcome to the Riviera Walk chapter). Sleep in or near Nice.

2 Start the morning with my self-guided tour of Vieux Nice (see the Vieux Nice Walk chapter). Take time to smell the *fougasse* and sample *un café.* Spend your afternoon at one or more of Nice's fine museums (see the Chagall Museum Tour chapter). Have dinner on the beach. Sleep in or near Nice.

3 Take the train or bus to nearby Villefranche-sur-Mer, explore, and have lunch. Consider my recommended seaside walks in Cap Ferrat, or the one-hour boat cruise from Nice's port. Everyone should spend the afternoon or evening in nearby Monaco. Sleep in or near Nice.

4 Pick up your rental car early as possible in Nice. Drive north to Vence or Grasse (you choose), then continue on to the Gorges du Verdon and sleep in tiny Aiguines or Moustiers-Ste-Marie.

5 Continue west into the Luberon and explore the villages of La Provence Profonde. Stay in or near Roussillon.

6 Spend your day sampling hill towns in the Luberon. Taste a village market, then drive over the hills to the valley of the Côtes du Rhône. Sleep in or near Vaison la Romaine (Mon arrival is ideal because market day is Tue). If you're here from late June to late July, when the lavender blooms, the drive to Vaison la Romaine via Sault is a must.

7 Explore Vaison la Romaine's upper medieval village and lower Roman city. Set sail along the Côtes du Rhône wine road (following my self-guided driving tour) and visit a winery or wine cooperative. Tour little Le Crestet and take a walk above Gigondas. Sleep in or near Vaison la Romaine.

8 Start your day touring the Roman Theater in Orange and consider a quick stop in Châteauneuf-du-Pape. Continue south and set up in Avignon. In the afternoon, take my self-guided Avignon walks and enjoy dinner on one of the town's many atmospheric squares. Sleep in Avignon.

9 Relax in Avignon this morning, then divide the rest of your day between Nîmes and Pont du Gard. If the weather's

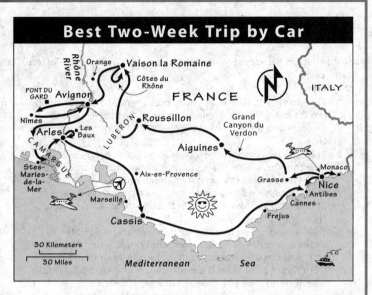

Best Two-Week Trip by Car

good, bring your swimsuit and float on your back with views of the 2,000-year-old Pont du Gard. Sleep in Avignon.

10 Take a joyride through the Camargue (but if it's summer, when flamingos are scarce and mosquitoes aren't, skip it and visit Les Baux this morning rather than tomorrow evening) and wind up in Arles (big market on Saturdays until 12:30). Sleep in Arles.

11 Spend your day in Arles. Drive to Les Baux for late afternoon sightseeing and dinner. Sleep in Arles.

12 Drive to Cassis, stopping for lunch and a midday visit to Aix-en-Provence or Marseille (Marseille is dicier by car). Set up in Cassis and watch the sun set from the old port while you savor a bouillabaisse dinner. Sleep in Cassis.

13 Spend all day in Cassis enjoying *la vie douce*. Take a boat trip or hike to the *calanques*, watch the *pétanque* balls fly, and end your day with a drive up Cap Canaille. Sleep in Cassis.

14 Fly out of Marseille today or, if leaving from Nice, drive to Antibes and spend your final day and evening here.

15 Trip over.

Best Two-Week Trip of Provence & the French Riviera by Train and Bus

Note that on Sundays, fewer trains run, and bus service often disappears.

Day Plan

1   Fly into Nice. Settle in at your hotel, then take a walk along the Promenade des Anglais and up to Castle Hill (see the Welcome to the Riviera Walk chapter). Sleep in or near Nice.

2   Start the morning with my self-guided tour of Vieux Nice (see the Vieux Nice Walk chapter). Take time to smell the *fougasse* and sample *un café*. Spend your afternoon at one or more of Nice's fine museums (see the Chagall Museum Tour chapter). Have dinner on the beach. Sleep in or near Nice.

3   Take a train or the bus to nearby Villefranche-sur-Mer, explore, and have lunch. Consider my recommended sea-side walks in Cap Ferrat, or take the one-hour boat cruise from Nice's port. Spend the afternoon or evening in almost-neighboring Monaco. Sleep in or near Nice.

4   Take a bus north to Vence and St-Paul-de-Vence. Stop for a stroll and visit the Fondation Maeght and/or Matisse's Chapel of the Rosary. Or link Vence with Grasse by bus (skipping St-Paul-de-Vence to save time). Sleep in Vence or back in Nice.

5   Take a train from Nice to Isle-sur-la-Sorgue via Marseille (best to arrive on Sat or Wed and awaken the next morning for market day). Wander and explore the town. Consider a canoe ride down the crystal-clear Sorgue River. Sleep in Isle-sur-la-Sorgue.

6   Enjoy market day this morning, then take a train to Avignon. Take my self-guided Avignon walks this afternoon and enjoy dinner on one of Avignon's many atmospheric squares. Sleep in Avignon.

7   Day-trip to Nîmes and the Pont du Gard aqueduct in the morning. If the weather's good, bring your swimsuit and

Sightseeing and Entertainment: Figure about $10 per major sight (Arles' Roman Arena-$9, Nice's Chagall Museum-$10, Avignon's Palace of the Popes-$14), around $6 for minor ones (e.g., climbing church towers), $30 for guided walks, and $40-70 for splurge experiences (such as bullfights or concerts). Arles and Avignon each offer a money-saving museum pass (details listed in this book)—and most of Nice's museums are free. An overall average of $25 a day works for most people. Don't skimp here. After all, this category is the driving force behind your trip—you came to sightsee, enjoy, and experience this wonderfully French region.

float on your back with views of the 2,000-year-old Pont du Gard. Explore Avignon in the afternoon and spend the night there.

8   Take a morning train to Orange (frequent departures) and connect to a less frequent bus to Vaison la Romaine (market day is Tue, so a Mon arrival is ideal). Set up in Vaison la Romaine for two nights. Explore Vaison la Romaine's upper medieval village and lower Roman city this afternoon.

9   Get to a wine village near Vaison la Romaine. Take a minivan tour of the wine road (see "Tours of Provence" on page 56), bike to Séguret and Gigondas, or hike to Le Crestet for lunch (taxi back). Check out Vaison la Romaine's wine cooperative. Sleep in Vaison la Romaine.

10   Take a morning bus to Orange, visit the theater, then hop a train to Arles (big market on Sat until 12:30) and explore the city this afternoon. Check into Arles for the next two nights.

11   Take a minivan tour or a taxi (or, in summer, a bus) to Les Baux and have breakfast with a view. Return to Arles by taxi or bus (minivan tours will probably include other destinations), and spend your afternoon there; or take a taxi from Les Baux to St. Rémy-de-Provence, explore there, then catch a bus back to Arles.

12   Hop the train to Marseille, check your bags, and take my walking tour of its ancient center. End your day in Cassis and watch the sunset from the old port while you savor a bouillabaisse dinner. Sleep in Cassis.

13   Spend all day in Cassis enjoying *la vie douce*. Take a boat trip or hike to the *calanques*, then watch the *pétanque* balls fly. Sleep in Cassis.

14   Fly out of Marseille or take a train back to Nice and savor a last night on the Promenade des Anglais. Sleep in Nice.

15   Trip over.

Shopping and Miscellany: Figure $5 per ice-cream cone, coffee, or soft drink. Shopping can vary in cost from nearly nothing to a small fortune. Good budget travelers find that this category has little to do with assembling a trip full of lifelong and wonderful memories.

Sightseeing Priorities
Depending on the length of your trip, and taking geographic proximity into account, here are my recommended priorities:

6 days:	Arles and day trips to Pont du Gard and Les Baux, a night in a Côtes du Rhône village, and Nice with a day trip to Monaco
9 days, add:	Avignon and Cassis
12 days, add:	Luberon, Grand Canyon du Verdon, and Antibes
14 days, add:	Nîmes, Marseille, Aix-en-Provence, and the Camargue

For a day-by-day itinerary of a two-week trip, see this chapter's two recommended routes (by car, and by train and bus).

When to Go

With more than 300 days of sunshine per year, Provence and the Riviera enjoy France's sunniest weather. Spring and fall are best, with generally comfortable weather—though crowds can be a problem, particularly during holiday weekends and major events (May is worst). April can be damp, and any month can be windy.

Summer means festivals, lavender, steamy weather, long hours at sights, and longer lines of cars along the Riviera. Europeans vacation in July and August, jamming the Riviera, the Gorges du Verdon, and Ardèche (worst from mid-July through mid-Aug), but leaving the rest of this region relatively calm. Though many French businesses close in August, the traveler hardly notices.

September brings the grape harvest, when small wineries are off-limits to taste-seeking travelers (for information on wine-tasting, see page 66). Late fall delivers beautiful foliage and a return to tranquility.

Although you can find mild, sunny weather in any season, Provence is famous for its bone-chilling temperatures when the wind blows (see page 68). Winter travel is OK in Nice, Aix-en-Provence, and Avignon, but you'll find smaller cities and villages buttoned up tight. Sights and tourist-information offices keep shorter hours, and some tourist activities (such as English-language castle tours) vanish altogether.

Thanks to Provence's temperate climate, fields of flowers greet the traveler much of the year:

May: Wild red poppies *(coquelicots)* sprout.

June: Lavender begins to bloom in the lower hills of Provence, generally during the last week of the month.

July: Lavender is in full swing in Provence, and sunflowers are awakening. If you can find adjacent fields with lavender and sunflowers, celebrate! Cities, towns, and villages everywhere overflow with carefully tended flowers.

August-September: Sunflowers flourish.

October: In the latter half of the month, the countryside glistens with fall colors (since most trees are deciduous). Vineyards go for the gold.

Know Before You Go

Your trip is more likely to go smoothly if you plan ahead. Check this list of things to arrange while you're still at home.

You need a **passport**—but no visa or shots—to travel in France. You may be denied entry into certain European countries if your passport is due to expire within three to six months of your ticketed date of return. Get it renewed if you'll be cutting it close. It can take up to six weeks to get or renew a passport (for more on passports, see www.travel.state.gov). Pack a photocopy of your passport in your luggage in case the original is lost or stolen.

Book rooms well in advance if you'll be traveling during peak season (mostly spring and summer) or any major holidays (see page 563).

Call your **debit- and credit-card companies** to let them know the countries you'll be visiting, to ask about fees, request your PIN code (it will be mailed to you), and more. See page 20 for details.

Do your homework if you want to buy **travel insurance.** Compare the cost of the insurance to the likelihood of your using it and your potential loss if something goes wrong. Also, check whether your existing insurance (health, homeowners, or renters) covers you and your possessions overseas. For more tips, see www.ricksteves.com/insurance.

Consider buying a **railpass** after researching your options, but keep in mind they only make sense if Provence is part of a larger trip (see page 540 and www.ricksteves.com/rail for all the specifics).

All **high-speed trains** (TGVs) in France require a seat reservation; book as early as possible, as these trains fill fast, and some routes use TGV trains almost exclusively. If you're using a railpass, it's especially important to reserve early—there's a tight limit on seat reservations for passholders. Traveling between Marseille and Nice can be tricky (most trains are TGV), so think about reserving that trip ahead. If you're taking an overnight train (especially to international destinations), and you need a *couchette* (overnight bunk) or sleeper—and you *must* leave on a certain day—consider booking it in advance through a US agent (such as www.raileurope.com), even though it may cost more. (For more on train travel, see the appendix.)

If you're planning on **renting a car** in France, bring your driver's license.

If you want to hire a **local guide,** reserve ahead by email. Popular guides can get booked up.

If you're bringing a **mobile device,** download any apps you might want to use on the road, such as translators, maps, and transit schedules. Check out **Rick Steves Audio Europe,** featuring hours of travel interviews and other audio content about France (via www.ricksteves.com/audioeurope, iTunes, Google Play, or the Rick Steves Audio Europe free smartphone app; for details, see page 559).

If you'll be **traveling with children,** read over the list of pretrip suggestions on page 502.

Check the **Rick Steves guidebook updates** page for any recent changes to this book (www.ricksteves.com/update).

Because **airline carry-on restrictions** are always changing, visit the Transportation Security Administration's website (www.tsa.gov) for an up-to-date list of what you can bring on the plane with you...and what you must check.

Practicalities

Emergency and Medical Help: In France, dial 17 for English-speaking police help. To summon an ambulance, call 15. If you get sick, do as the French do and go to a pharmacist for advice. Or ask at your hotel for help—they'll know the nearest medical and emergency services.

Theft or Loss: To replace a passport, you'll need to go in person to a US embassy or consulate (see page 535). If your credit and debit cards disappear, cancel and replace them (see "Damage Control for Lost Cards" on page 22). File a police report, either on the spot or within a day or two; you'll need it to submit an insurance claim for lost or stolen railpasses or travel gear, and it can help with replacing your passport or credit and debit cards. For more information, see www.ricksteves.com/help. Precautionary measures can minimize the effects of loss—back up your digital photos and other files frequently.

Time Zones: France, like most of continental Europe, is generally six/nine hours ahead of the East/West Coasts of the US. The exceptions are the beginning and end of Daylight Saving Time: Europe "springs forward" the last Sunday in March (two weeks after most of North America) and "falls back" the last Sunday in October (one week before North America). For a handy online time converter, see www.timeanddate.com/worldclock.

Business Hours: You'll find much of rural France closed weekdays from noon to 14:00 (lunch is sacred). On Sunday, most businesses are closed (family is sacred), though some small shops such as *boulangeries* (bakeries) are open until noon, special events and weekly markets pop up, and museums are open all day (but public transportation options are scant). On Mondays, some businesses are closed until 14:00 and possibly all day. Smaller towns are often quiet and downright boring on Sundays and Mondays, unless it's market day. Saturdays are virtually weekdays (without the rush hour).

Shopping: The Shopping chapter, near the end of this book, gives you tips on how to enjoy Provence's market days. For details on clothing-size conversions, see page 565 of the appendix. For customs regulations and VAT refunds (the tax refunded on large purchases made by non-EU residents), see page 23.

Watt's Up? Europe's electrical system is 220 volts, instead of North America's 110 volts. Most newer electronics (such as laptops, battery chargers, and hair dryers) convert automatically, so you won't need a converter, but you will need an adapter plug with two round prongs, sold inexpensively at travel stores in the US. Avoid bringing older appliances that don't automatically convert voltage; instead, buy a cheap replacement in Europe. You can buy low-cost hair dryers and other small appliances at Darty and Monoprix stores, which you'll find in major cities (ask at your hotel for the closest branch).

Discounts: Discounts aren't always listed in this book. However, many sights offer discounts for youths (up to age 18), students (with proper identification cards, www.isic.org), families, and groups of 10 or more. Always ask. Seniors (age 60 and over) may get the odd discount, though they may be limited to citizens of the European Union (EU). To inquire about a senior discount, ask, *"Réduction troisième âge?"* (ray-dook-see-ohn trwah-zee-ehm ahzh).

Online Translation Tip: You can use Google's Chrome browser (available free at www.google.com/chrome) to instantly translate websites. With one click, the page appears in (very rough) English translation. You can also paste the URL of the site into the translation window at www.google.com/translate.

Money

This section offers advice on how to pay for purchases on your trip (including getting cash from ATMs and paying with plastic), dealing with lost or stolen cards, VAT (sales tax) refunds, and tipping.

What to Bring

Bring both a credit card and a debit card. You'll use the debit card at cash machines (ATMs) to withdraw local cash for most purchases, and the credit card to pay for larger items. Some travelers carry a third card as a backup, in case one gets demagnetized or eaten by a temperamental machine.

For an emergency stash, bring €200 in hard cash in €20-50 bills (in euros; dollars can be hard to change).

Exchange Rate

1 euro (€) = about $1.30

To convert prices in euros to dollars, add about 30 percent: €20 = about $26, €50 = about $65. (Check www.oanda.com for the latest exchange rates.) Just like the dollar, one euro (€) is broken down into 100 cents. Coins range from €0.01 to €2, and bills from €5 to €500.

Cash

Cash is just as desirable in Europe as it is at home. Small businesses (hotels, restaurants, shops, etc.) prefer that you pay your bills with cash. Some vendors will charge you extra for using a credit card, and some won't take credit cards at all. Cash is the best—and sometimes only—way to pay for bus fare, taxis, and local guides.

Throughout Europe, ATMs are the standard way for travelers to get cash. But stay away from "independent" ATMs such as Travelex, Euronet, and Forex, which charge huge commissions and have terrible exchange rates.

To withdraw money from an ATM (known as a *distributeur;* dee-stree-bew-tur), you'll need a debit card (ideally with a Visa or MasterCard logo for maximum usability), plus a PIN code. Know your PIN code in numbers; there are only numbers—no letters— on European keypads. Although you can use a credit card for an ATM transaction, it only makes sense in an emergency, because it's considered a cash advance (borrowed at a high interest rate) rather than a withdrawal. Try to withdraw large sums of money to reduce the number of per-transaction bank fees you'll pay.

For increased security, shield the keypad when entering your PIN code, and don't use an ATM if anything on the front of the machine looks loose or damaged (a sign that someone may have attached a "skimming" device to capture account information). It's a good idea to monitor your account while traveling to detect any unauthorized transactions.

Pickpockets target tourists. To safeguard your cash, wear a money belt—a pouch with a strap that you buckle around your waist like a belt and tuck under your clothes. Keep your cash, credit cards, and passport secure in your money belt, and carry only a day's spending money in your front pocket.

Credit and Debit Cards

For purchases, Visa and MasterCard are more commonly accepted than American Express.

Just like at home, credit or debit cards work easily at larger hotels, restaurants, and shops. I typically use my debit card to withdraw cash to pay for most purchases. I use my credit card to cover major expenses (such as car rentals, plane tickets, and long hotel stays), and to pay for things near the end of my trip (to avoid another visit to the ATM). While you could use a debit card to make most large purchases, using a credit card offers a greater degree of fraud protection (because debit cards draw funds directly from your account).

Ask Your Credit- or Debit-Card Company: Before your trip, contact the company that issued your debit or credit cards.

• Confirm your **card will work overseas**, and alert them that you'll be using it in Europe; otherwise, they may deny transactions if they perceive unusual spending patterns.

• Ask for the specifics on transaction **fees.** When you use your credit or debit card—either for purchases or ATM withdrawals—you'll typically be charged additional "international transaction" fees of up to 3 percent (1 percent is normal) plus $5 per transaction. If your card's fees seem high, consider getting a different card just for your trip: Capital One (www.capitalone.com) and most credit unions have low-to-no international fees.

• If you plan to withdraw cash from ATMs, confirm your daily **withdrawal limit**, and if necessary, ask your bank to adjust it. Some travelers prefer a high limit that allows them to take out more cash at each ATM stop (saving on bank fees), while others prefer to set a lower limit in case their card is stolen. Note that foreign banks also set maximum withdrawal amounts for their ATMs.

• Get your bank's emergency **phone number** in the US (but not its 800 number, which isn't accessible from overseas) to call collect if you have a problem.

• Ask for your credit card's **PIN** in case you need to make an emergency cash withdrawal or encounter Europe's "chip-and-PIN" system; the bank won't tell you your PIN over the phone, so allow time for it to be mailed to you.

Chip and PIN: Europeans are increasingly using chip-and-PIN cards, which are embedded with an electronic security chip (in addition to the magnetic stripe on American-style cards). With this system, the purchaser punches in a PIN rather than signing a receipt. Your American-style card might not work at automated payment machines, such as those at train and subway stations, toll roads, parking garages, luggage lockers, and self-serve pumps at gas stations. If a machine won't take your card, find a cashier who can swipe your card and print out a receipt, or find a machine that takes cash.

And don't panic. Many travelers who use only magnetic-stripe cards never have a problem. Still, it pays to carry plenty of

Making Your Card Work

If you're using an American credit or debit card at a chip-and-PIN machine, there's no predicting whether—and how—your card might work. To be prepared, learn the PIN for your credit card (it's not the same as your debit-card PIN); get it from your bank before you leave on your trip, and memorize it.

Here's how to make your card work:

1. Swipe your credit card in the chip-and-PIN terminal.
2. When prompted for the PIN, ask the clerk (if one is nearby) to print out a receipt for you to sign instead.
3. If it's not possible to print out a receipt, try punching in your credit-card PIN.
4. If the PIN isn't accepted, try swiping your debit card and entering its PIN. Some chip-and-PIN machines accept debit cards but not credit cards.

If none of the above works, see if there's a machine that takes cash. Or you could ask a local person if you can pay them cash to run the transaction on their card. Or you could simply skip the purchase.

euros (you can always use an ATM with your magnetic-stripe debit card). Some chip-and-PIN machines will accept your US card if you are able to enter your PIN when prompted, so be sure you know it. For more tips, see "Making Your Card Work."

If you're still concerned, you can apply for a chip card in the US (though I think it's overkill). One option is the no-annual-fee GlobeTrek Visa, offered by Andrews Federal Credit Union in Maryland (open to all US residents; see www.andrewsfcu.org).

Dynamic Currency Conversion: If merchants offer to convert your purchase price into dollars (called dynamic currency conversion, or DCC), refuse this "service." You'll pay even more in fees for the expensive convenience of seeing your charge in dollars.

Damage Control for Lost Cards

If you lose your credit, debit, or ATM card, you can stop people from using your card by reporting the loss immediately to the respective global customer-assistance centers. Call these 24-hour US numbers collect: Visa (tel. 303/967-1096), MasterCard (tel. 636/722-7111), and American Express (tel. 336/393-1111). In France, to make a collect call to the US, dial 08 00 99 00 11; press zero or stay on the line for an English-speaking operator.

You can also reach the credit-card companies by calling their toll-free numbers in France: Visa (tel. 08 00 90 11 79) and MasterCard (tel. 08 00 90 13 87). American Express has a Paris office, but the call isn't free (tel. 01 47 77 72 00, greeting is in French only, dial 1 to speak with someone in English).

Providing the following information will allow for a quicker cancellation of your missing card: full card number, whether you are the primary or secondary cardholder, the cardholder's name exactly as printed on the card, billing address, home phone number, circumstances of the loss or theft, and identification verification (your birth date, your mother's maiden name, or your Social Security number—memorize this, don't carry a copy). If you are the secondary cardholder, you'll also need to provide the primary cardholder's identification-verification details. You can generally receive a temporary card within two or three business days in Europe (see www.ricksteves.com/help for more).

If you report your loss within two days, you typically won't be responsible for any unauthorized transactions on your account, although many banks charge a liability fee of $50.

Tipping

Tipping *(donner un pourboire)* in France isn't as automatic and generous as it is in the US, but for special service, tips are appreciated, if not expected. As in the US, the proper amount depends on your resources, tipping philosophy, and the circumstances, but some general guidelines apply.

Restaurants: At cafés and restaurants, a service charge is always included in the price of what you ordered *(service compris)*, but you won't see it listed on your bill. Unlike in the US, France pays servers a decent wage. Because of this, many locals never tip (credit-card receipts don't even have space to add a tip). If you feel the service was exceptional, it's kind to tip up to 5 percent extra. But never feel guilty if you don't leave a tip.

Taxis: To tip the cabbie, round up. For a typical ride, round up your fare a bit (for instance, if the fare is €13, pay €14); for a long ride, round to the nearest €10 (for a €58 fare, give €60). If the cabbie hauls your bags and zips you to the airport to help you catch your flight, you might want to toss in a little more. But if you feel like you're being driven in circles or otherwise ripped off, skip the tip.

Services: In general, if someone in the service industry does a super job for you, a small tip of a euro or two is appropriate...but not required. If you're not sure whether (or how much) to tip for a service, ask your hotelier or the TI.

Getting a VAT Refund

Wrapped into the purchase price of your French souvenirs is a Value-Added Tax (VAT) of about 19.6 percent. You're entitled to get most of that tax back if you purchase more than €175 (about $228) worth of goods at a store that participates in the VAT-refund scheme. Typically, you must ring up the minimum at a single retailer—you can't add up your purchases from various shops to reach the required amount.

Getting your refund is usually straightforward and, if you buy a substantial amount of souvenirs, well worth the hassle. If you're lucky, the merchant will subtract the tax when you make your purchase. (This is more likely to occur if the store ships the goods to your home.) Otherwise, you'll need to:

Get the paperwork. Have the merchant completely fill out the necessary refund document, *Bordereau de Vente a l'Exportation*, also called a "cheque." You'll have to present your passport. Get the paperwork done before you leave the store to ensure you'll have everything you need (including your original sales receipt).

Get your stamp at the border or airport. Process your VAT document at your last stop in the European Union (such as the airport) with the customs agent who deals with VAT refunds. Arrive an additional hour early before you need to check in for your flight, to give yourself time to find the local customs office—and to stand in line. Keep your purchases readily available for viewing by the customs agent (ideally in your carry-on bag—don't make the mistake of checking the bag with your purchases before you've seen the agent). You're not supposed to use your purchased goods before you leave. If you show up at customs wearing your chic new French ensemble, officials might look the other way—or deny you a refund.

Collect your refund. You'll need to return your stamped document to the retailer or its representative. Many merchants work with a service, such as Global Blue or Premier Tax Free, that has offices at major airports, ports, or border crossings (either before or after security, probably strategically located near a duty-free shop). These services, which extract a 4 percent fee, can refund your money immediately in cash or credit your card (within two billing cycles). If the retailer handles VAT refunds directly, it's up to you to contact the merchant for your refund. You can mail the documents from home, or more quickly, from your point of departure (using an envelope you've prepared in advance or one that's been provided by the merchant). You'll then have to wait—it can take months.

Customs for American Shoppers

You are allowed to take home $800 worth of items per person duty-free, once every 30 days. You can also bring in duty-free a liter of alcohol. As for food, you can take home many processed and packaged foods: vacuum-packed cheeses, dried herbs, jams, baked goods, candy, chocolate, oil, vinegar, mustard, and honey. Fresh fruits and vegetables and most meats are not allowed. However, canned goose, duck, and pork pâté can be imported to the US, but not beef. Any liquid-containing foods must be packed in checked luggage, a potential recipe for disaster. To check customs rules and duty rates, visit http://help.cbp.gov.

Sightseeing

Sightseeing can be hard work. Use these tips to make your visits to Provence's and the Riviera's finest sights meaningful, fun, efficient, and painless.

Plan Ahead

Set up an itinerary that allows you to fit in all your must-see sights. For a one-stop look at opening hours in the bigger cities, see the "At a Glance" sidebars for Arles, Avignon, Marseille, Nice, and Monaco. Most sights keep stable hours, but you can easily confirm the latest by checking with the TI or visiting museum websites.

Don't put off visiting a must-see sight—you never know when a place will close unexpectedly for a holiday, strike, or restoration. Many museums are closed or have reduced hours at least a few days a year, especially on holidays such as May 1 (Labor Day), Christmas, New Year's. A list of holidays is on page 563; check museum websites for possible closures during your trip. In summer, some sights may stay open late. Off-season, many museums have shorter hours.

Going at the right time helps avoid crowds and stress. This book offers tips on the best times to see specific sights. Try visiting the following villages and sights on weekdays, and arrive very early (for sights, at least 15 minutes before opening time) or very late: Les Baux, Pont du Gard, Séguret, Roussillon, Fontaine de Vaucluse, Nice's Chagall and Antibes' Picasso museums, St-Paul-de-Vence, Eze-le-Village, and St-Tropez. When sights are open late, visiting in the evening can be peaceful, with fewer crowds. Keep in mind that French monuments and cities (and some villages) are beautifully lit at night, making evening walks a joy. Some sights are best seen early, though, such as the *calanques*, the striking fjord-like inlets near Cassis.

Study up. To get the most out of the self-guided tours and sight descriptions in this book, read them before you visit. Several cities offer sightseeing passes that are worthwhile values for serious sightseers; plan ahead.

At Sights

Here's what you can typically expect:

Some important sights require you to check daypacks and coats. To avoid checking a small backpack, carry it under your arm like a purse as you enter. From a guard's point of view, a backpack is generally a problem while a purse is not. If you check a bag, the attendant may ask you if it contains anything of value—such as a camera, phone, money, passport—because these usually can't be checked.

At churches—which often offer interesting art (usually free) and a cool, welcome seat—a modest dress code (no bare shoulders or shorts) is encouraged.

Flash photography is often banned to prevent damage to delicate artworks, but taking photos without a flash is usually allowed (look for signs or ask a guard). Even without a flash, a handheld camera will take a decent picture (or buy postcards or posters at the museum bookstore).

Museums may show special exhibits in addition to their permanent collection. Some exhibits are included in the entry price, while others come at an extra cost (which you may have to pay even if you don't want to see the exhibit).

Expect changes—artwork can be on tour, on loan, out sick, or shifted at the whim of the curator. To adapt, pick up a floor plan as you enter, and ask museum staff if you can't find a particular item. Say the title or artist's name, or point to the photograph in this book, and ask for its location by saying, *"Où est?"* (oo ay).

Many sights rent audioguides, which generally offer useful recorded descriptions in English (about €3-6, sometimes included with admission). If you bring your own earbuds, you can enjoy better sound and avoid holding the device to your ear. To save money, bring a Y-jack and share one audioguide with your travel partner.

Important sights often have an on-site café or cafeteria (usually a handy place to rejuvenate during a long visit). The WCs at sights are usually free and generally clean.

Many places sell postcards that highlight their attractions. Before you leave a sight, scan the postcards and thumb through the biggest guidebook (or skim its index) to be sure you haven't overlooked something that you'd like to see.

Most sights stop admitting people 30 to 60 minutes before closing time, and some rooms may close early (often about 45 minutes before the actual closing time). Guards usher people out, so don't save the best for last.

Every sight or museum offers more than what is covered in this book. Use the information in this book as an introduction—not the final word.

Sleeping

Accommodations in Provence and the Riviera are a good value and generally easy to find. Choose from one- to five-star hotels (two and three stars are my mainstay), bed-and-breakfasts (*chambres d'hôte*, usually cheaper than hotels), hostels, campgrounds, and even homes (*gîtes*, rented by the week).

I favor hotels and restaurants that are handy to your sightseeing activities. Rather than list hotels scattered throughout a city, I describe two or three favorite neighborhoods and recommend the best accommodations values in each, from dorm beds to fancy doubles with all the comforts.

A major feature of this book is its extensive listing of good-value rooms. I like places that are clean, central, relatively quiet at night, reasonably priced, friendly, small enough to have a hands-on owner and stable staff, and run with a respect for French traditions. (In France, for me, five out of these seven criteria means it's a keeper.) I'm more impressed by a convenient location and a fun-loving philosophy than flat-screen TVs and a pricey laundry service.

Book your accommodations well in advance if you'll be traveling during busy times. Be ready for crowds during these holiday periods: Easter weekend; Ascension weekend; Pentecost weekend; Bastille Day and the week during which it falls; and the winter holidays (mid-Dec-early Jan). See page 563 for a list of major holidays and festivals in Provence and the French Riviera; for tips on making reservations, see page 34.

Rates and Deals

I've described my recommended accommodations using a Sleep Code (see sidebar). Prices listed are for one-night stays in peak season, do not include breakfast, and assume you're booking directly (not through a TI or online hotel-booking engine). Booking services extract a commission from the hotel, which logically closes the door on special deals. Book direct.

Given the economic downturn, hoteliers are often willing and eager to make a deal. I'd suggest emailing several hotels to ask for their best price. Comparison-shop and make your choice.

Many hotels use "dynamic pricing," which means room rates can change from day to day depending on demand. This makes it extremely difficult to predict what you'll pay. For many hotels, I list a range of prices. If the rate you're offered is at or near the bottom of my printed range, it's likely a good deal.

As you look over the listings, you'll notice that some accommodations promise special prices to Rick Steves readers who book directly with the hotel. To get these rates, you must mention this book when you reserve, and then show the book upon arrival. Rick Steves discounts apply to readers with ebooks as well as printed books. Because we trust hotels to honor this, please let me know if you don't receive a listed discount. Note, though, that discounts understandably may not be applied to promotional rates.

Sleep Code

(€1 = about $1.30, country code: 33)

Price Rankings

To help you easily sort through my listings, I've divided the accommodations into three categories based on the price for a double room with bath during high season:

$$$	**Higher Priced**
$$	**Moderately Priced**
$	**Lower Priced**

I always rate hostels as $, whether or not they have double rooms, because they have the cheapest beds in town. Prices can change without notice; verify the hotel's current rates online or by email. For the best prices, always book direct.

Abbreviations

To pack maximum information into minimum space, I use the following code to describe accommodations. Prices listed are per room, not per person. When a price range is given for a type of room (such as double rooms listing for €100-130), it means the price fluctuates with the season, size of room, or length of stay; expect to pay the upper end for peak-season stays.

- **S** = Single room (or price for one person in a double).
- **D** = Double or twin room.
- **T** = Triple (generally a double bed with a single).
- **Q** = Quad (usually two double beds; adding an extra child's bed to a T is usually cheaper).
- **b** = Private bathroom with toilet and shower or tub.
- **s** = Private shower or tub only (the toilet is down the hall).
- ***** = French hotel rating system, ranging from zero to five stars.

According to this code, a couple staying at a "Db-€90" hotel would pay a total of €90 (about $117) for a double room with a private bathroom. Unless otherwise noted, breakfast is not included, hotel staff speak basic English, and credit cards are accepted.

There's almost always Wi-Fi and/or a guest computer available, either free or for a fee.

In general, prices can soften if you do any of the following: travel off-season, stay at least three nights, or mention this book. You can also try asking for a cheaper room or a discount. To save money off-season, consider arriving without a reservation and dropping in at the last minute.

Types of Accommodations

Hotels

In this book, the price for a double room will range from €40 (very simple, toilet and shower down the hall) to €400-plus (grand lobbies, maximum plumbing, and the works), with most clustering at around €80-110 (with private bathrooms).

The French have a simple hotel rating system based on amenities and rated by stars (indicated in this book by asterisks, from * through *****). One star is modest, two has most of the comforts, and three is generally a two-star with a fancier lobby and more elaborately designed rooms. Four and five stars probably offer more luxury than you usually have time to appreciate. Two- and three-star hotels are required to have an English-speaking staff, though virtually all hotels I recommend have someone who speaks English (unless I note otherwise in the listing).

The number of stars does not generally reflect room size or guarantee quality. Some two-star hotels are better than many three-star hotels. One- and two-star hotels are inexpensive, but some three-star (and even a few four-star hotels) offer good value, justifying the extra cost. Unclassified hotels (no stars) can be bargains or depressing dumps.

Most hotels have lots of doubles and a few singles, triples, and the odd quad. Singles are usually doubles used by one person—so they cost about the same as a double. Room prices vary within each hotel depending on size, and whether the room has a bath or shower, and twin beds or a double bed (tubs and twins cost more than showers and double beds). A triple is often no bigger than a large double room, with a double or queen-size bed plus a sliver-size single bed. Quad rooms usually have two double beds. Hotels cannot legally allow more people in the room than what's shown on their price list. Some hotels have a few family-friendly rooms that open to each other *(chambres communiquantes)*.

Hotels in France must charge a daily tax *(taxe du séjour)* of about €1-2 per person per day. Some hotels include it in the price

Types of Rooms

Study the price list on the hotel's website or posted at the desk, so you know your options. Receptionists often don't mention the cheaper rooms—they assume you want a private bathroom or a bigger room. Here are the types of rooms and beds:

French	Pronounced	English
une chambre avec douche et WC	ewn shahm-bruh ah-vehk doosh ay vay-say	room with private shower and toilet
une chambre avec bain et WC	ewn shahm-bruh ah-vehk ban ay vay-say	room with private bathtub and toilet
une chambre avec cabinet de toilette	ewn shahm-bruh ah-vehk kah-bee-nay duh twah-leht	room with a toilet but no shower (some hotels charge for down-the-hall showers)
une chambre sans douche et WC	ewn shahm-bruh sahn doosh ay vay-say	room without a private shower or toilet (uncommon these days)
chambres communiquantes	shahm-bruh koh-mew-nee-kahnt	connecting rooms (ideal for families)
une chambre simple	ewn shahm-bruh san-pluh	a true single room (also called un single)
un grand lit	uhn grahn lee	double bed (55 inches wide)
deux petits lits	duh puh-tee lee	twin beds (30-36 inches wide)
un lit de cent-soixante	uhn lee duh sahn-swah-sahnt	queen-size bed (literally 160 centimeters, or 63 inches wide)
le king size	luh "king size"	a king-size bed (usually two twins pushed together)
un lit pliant	uhn lee plee-ahn	folding bed
un bérceau	uhn behr-soh	baby crib
un lit d'enfant	uhn lee dahn-fahn	child's bed

Keep Cool

If you're visiting southern France in the summer, the extra expense of an air-conditioned room can be money well spent. Most hotel rooms with air-conditioners come with a control stick (like a TV remote) that generally has similar symbols and features: fan icon (click to toggle through wind power, from light to gale); louver icon (choose steady airflow or waves); snowflake and sunshine icons (cold air or heat, depending on season); clock ("O" setting: run X hours before turning off; "I" setting: wait X hours to start); and the temperature control (20 or 21 degrees Celsius is comfortable; also see the thermometer diagram on page 566).

list, but most add it to your bill.

You can save as much as €20 by finding the rare room without a private shower or toilet. A room with a bathtub usually costs more than a room with a shower (and generally is larger). Hotels often have more rooms with tubs than showers and are inclined to give you a room with a tub (which the French prefer).

A double bed is usually cheaper than twins, though rooms with twin beds tend to be larger. Many hotels have rooms with queen-size beds (a bed that's 63 inches wide—most doubles are 55 inches). To learn if a hotel has queen-size beds, ask, *"Avez-vous des lits de cent-soixante?"* (ah-vay-voo day lee duh sahn-swah-sahnt). Some hotels push two twins together under king-size sheets and blankets to make *le king size*.

If you prefer a double bed (instead of twins) and a shower (instead of a tub), you need to ask for it—and you can save up to €20. If you'll take either twins or a double, ask generically for *une chambre pour deux* (room for two) to avoid being needlessly turned away.

Hotel elevators, while becoming more common, are often very small—pack light, or you may need to send your bags up separately.

Hotel lobbies, halls, and breakfast rooms are off-limits to smokers, though they can light up in their rooms. Still, I seldom smell any smoke in the hundreds of rooms I check each year. Some hotels have non-smoking rooms or floors—ask about them if this is important to you. If your room smells of smoke, ask for another one.

Most hotels offer some kind of breakfast, but it's rarely included in the room rates. The price of breakfast correlates with the price of the room: The more expensive the room, the more expensive the breakfast. This per-person charge, which increases with the number of stars the hotel has, can add up, particularly for families. While hoteliers hope that you'll buy their breakfast, it's optional unless otherwise noted (for more on breakfast, see "Eating," later in this chapter).

Some hoteliers, especially in resort towns, strongly encourage their peak-season guests to take *demi-pension* (half-pension)—that is, breakfast and either lunch or dinner. By law, they can't require you to take half-pension unless you are staying three or more nights, but, in practice, many do during summer. And though the food is usually good, it limits your ability to shop around. I've indicated where I think *demi-pension* is a good value.

Most hotel rooms have a TV, phone, and Internet access (usually Wi-Fi); some hotels have a computer for guests in the lobby. To turn on your TV, press the power button, or channel-up or channel-down button on the remote.

Towels aren't routinely replaced every day. Hang up your towel to dry. Extra pillows and blankets are often in the closet or available on request. To get a pillow, ask for *"Un oreiller, s'il vous plaît"* (un oh-ray-yay, see voo play).

If you're arriving early in the morning, your room probably won't be ready. You can drop your bag safely at the hotel and dive right into sightseeing.

Hoteliers can be a great help and source of advice. Most know their city well, and can assist you with everything from public transit and airport connections to calling an English-speaking doctor or finding a good restaurant, the nearest Internet café (*café internet*, kah-fay an-ter-net), or a self-service launderette (*laverie automatique*, lah-vay-ree oh-to-mah-teek).

Even at the best hotels, mechanical breakdowns occur: air-conditioning malfunctions, sinks leak, hot water turns cold, and toilets gurgle and smell. Report your concerns clearly and calmly at the front desk. For more complicated problems, don't expect instant results.

If you suspect night noise will be a problem, ask for a room in the back or on an upper floor. To guard against theft in your room, keep valuables out of sight. Some rooms come with a safe, and other hotels have safes at the front desk. I've never bothered using one.

Checkout can pose problems if surprise charges pop up on your bill. If you settle your bill the day before you leave, you'll have time to discuss and address any points of contention (before 19:00, when the night shift usually arrives).

Some hoteliers will ask you to sign their *Livre d'Or* (literally "Golden Book," for client comments). They take this seriously and enjoy reading your remarks.

Above all, keep a positive attitude. Remember, you're on vacation. If your hotel is a disappointment, spend more time out enjoying the place you came to see.

Modern Hotel Chains: France is littered with ultramodern hotels, often located on cheap land just outside of town, providing drivers with low-stress accommodations (though you'll find some in city centers as well). The antiseptically clean and cheap Ibis Budget chain (about €40-50/room for up to three people), the more attractive and spacious standard Ibis hotels (€80-110 for a double), and the cushier Mercure and Novotel hotels (€120-200 for a double) are all run by the same company, Accor (www.accor hotels.com). Though hardly quaint, these can be a good value (look for deals on their website), particularly when they're centrally located; I list many in this book. Another chain, Kyriad, offers moderate prices and good quality (from France, call 08 92 23 05 91, then 1 for reservations, www.kyriad.com; this telephone number also works for its affiliated chains). For a long listing of various hotels throughout France, see www.france.com.

Bed & Breakfasts

B&Bs (*Chambres d'hôte*, abbreviated "CH") generally are found in smaller towns and rural areas. They're usually a great deal, offering double the cultural intimacy for much less than most hotel rooms. While you may lose some hotel conveniences—such as lounges, in-room phones, daily bed-sheet changes, and credit-card payments—I happily make the trade-off for the personal touch and lower rates. You'll find B&Bs in this book and through local tourist offices often listed by the owner's family name. It's always OK to ask to see the room before you commit. And though some CHs post small *Chambres* or *Chambres d'hôte* signs in their front windows, many are found only through the local tourist office.

I recommend reliable CHs that offer a good value and/or unique experience (such as CHs in renovated mills, châteaux, and wine *domaines*). While *chambres d'hôte* have their own star-rating system, it doesn't correspond to the hotels' rating system. So, to avoid confusion, I haven't listed these stars for CHs. But virtually all of my recommended CHs have private in-room bathrooms, and some have common rooms with refrigerators. Doubles with breakfast generally cost €60-80 (€100-120 for the fancy ones; breakfast may or may not be included—ask). *Tables d'hôte* are CHs that offer an optional, reasonably priced, home-cooked dinner (usually a fine value, must be requested in advance). And though your hosts may not speak English, they will almost always be enthusiastic and pleasant.

Hostels

You'll pay about €20 per bed to stay at a hostel *(auberge de jeunesse)*. Travelers of any age are welcome if they don't mind dorm-style

Making Hotel Reservations

Reserve your rooms several weeks in advance—or as soon as you've pinned down your travel dates—particularly if you'll be traveling during peak times. Note that some national holidays jam things up and merit your making reservations far in advance (see "Holidays and Festivals" on 563).

Requesting a Reservation: It's usually easiest to book your room through the hotel's website. Many have a reservation-request form built right in. (For the best rates, be sure to use the hotel's official site and not a booking agency's site.) Simpler websites will generate an email to the hotelier with your request. If there's no reservation form, or for complicated requests, send an email (for a sample request, see below). Most recommended hotels are accustomed to guests who speak only English.

Sample Hotel Reservation Request

From: rick@ricksteves.com
Sent: Today
To: info@hotelcentral.com
Subject: Reservation request for 19-22 July

Dear Hotel Central,

I would like to reserve a double room for 2 people for 3 nights, arriving 19 July and departing 22 July. If possible, I would like a quiet room with a bathroom inside the room.

Please let me know if you have a room available and the price.

Thank you!
Rick Steves

The hotelier wants to know:
- the number and type of rooms you need
- the number of nights you'll stay
- your date of arrival
- your date of departure
- any special needs (such as bathroom in the room or down the hall, cheapest room, twin beds vs. double bed, crib,

air-conditioning, quiet, view, ground floor or no stairs, and so on)

If you request a room by email, use the European style for writing dates: day/month/year. For example, for a two-night stay in July of 2014, ask for "1 double room for 2 nights, arrive 16/07/14, depart 18/07/14." Make sure you mention any discounts—for Rick Steves readers or otherwise—when you make the reservation.

Confirming a Reservation: When the hotel replies with its room availability and rates, just email back to confirm your reservation. Most places will request a credit-card number to hold your room. While you can email it (I do), it's safer to share that confidential info via a phone call, two emails (splitting your number between them), or the hotel's secure online reservation form. On the small chance that a hotel loses track of your reservation, bring along a hard copy of their confirmation.

Canceling a Reservation: If you must cancel your reservation, it's courteous—and smart—to do so with as much notice as possible, especially for smaller family-run places. Simply make a quick phone call or send an email. Request confirmation of your cancellation in case you are accidentally billed.

Be warned that cancellation policies can be strict; read the fine print or ask about these before you book. For example, if you cancel on short notice, you could lose your deposit, or be billed for one night or even your entire stay. Internet deals may require prepayment, with no refunds for cancellations.

Reconfirming a Reservation: Call to reconfirm your room reservation a few days in advance. Smaller hotels and *chambres d'hôtes* appreciate knowing your estimated time of arrival. If you'll be arriving late (after 17:00), let them know.

Reserving Rooms as You Travel: You can make reservations as you travel, calling hotels and *chambres d'hôtes* a few days to a week before your arrival. If you'd rather travel without any reservations at all, you'll have greater success snaring rooms if you arrive at your destination early in the day. When you anticipate crowds (weekends are worst), call hotels at about 9:00 or 10:00 on the day you plan to arrive, when the receptionist knows who'll be checking out and which rooms will be available. If you encounter a language barrier, ask the fluent receptionist at your current hotel to call for you.

Phoning: For tips on how to call hotels overseas, see page 527.

accommodations and meeting other travelers. Most hostels offer kitchen facilities, guest computers, Wi-Fi, and a self-service laundry. Nowadays, concerned about bedbugs, hostels are likely to provide all bedding, including sheets. Family and private rooms may available on request.

Independent hostels tend to be easygoing, colorful, and informal (no membership required); www.hostelworld.com is the standard way backpackers search and book hostels these days, but also try www.hostelz.com, www.hostels.com, and www.hostelbookers.com.

Official hostels are part of Hostelling International and share an online booking site (www.hihostels.com). HI hostels typically require that you either have a membership card or pay extra per night.

Camping

In Europe, camping is more of a social than an environmental experience. It's a great way for American travelers to make European friends. Camping costs about €20 per campsite per night, and almost every destination recommended in this book has a campground within a reasonable walk or bus ride from the town center and train station. A tent, pillow, and sleeping bag are all you need. Many campgrounds have small grocery stores and washing machines, and some even come with cafés and miniature golf. Local TIs have camping information. You'll find more detailed information in the annually updated *Michelin Camping France*, available in the United States and at most French bookstores.

Gîtes and Apartments

Whether you're in a city or the countryside, renting an apartment, house, or villa can be a fun and cost-effective way to delve into Europe. Throughout France you can find reasonably priced rental homes, and nowhere are there more options than in Provence and the Riviera. Because this region is so small, you could rent one home in Provence and one in the Riviera, and day-trip to most of the sights described in this book.

Gîtes (pronounced "zheet") are homes in the countryside (usually urbanites' second homes) rentable by the week, from Saturday to Saturday. The objective of the *gîte* program was to save characteristic rural homes from abandonment and to make it easy and affordable for families to enjoy the French countryside. The government offers subsidies to renovate such homes, then coordinates rentals to make it financially feasible for the owner. Today, France has more than 9,000 *gîtes*. One of your co-authors restored a farmhouse a few hours north of Provence, and even though he and his wife are American, they received the same assistance that French owners get.

Gîtes are best for drivers (they're usually rural, with little public-transport access) and ideal for families and small groups (since they can sleep many for the same price). Homes range in comfort from simple cottages and farmhouses to restored châteaux. Most have at least two bedrooms, a kitchen, a living room, and a bathroom or two—but no sheets or linens (though you can usually rent them for extra). Like hotels, all *gîtes* are rated for comfort from one to four (using ears of corn—*épis*—rather than stars). Two or three *épis* generally indicate sufficient quality, but I'd lean toward three for more comfort. Prices generally range from €400-1,400 per week, depending on house size and amenities such as pools. If your owner does not speak English, be prepared for doing business in French—all the contracts are in French. For more information on *gîtes* in Provence, visit www.gites-de-france.com (with the most rentals), www.gite.com, or www.provence-guide.com.

Apartments, less common than *gîtes*, are available in cities and in towns along the Riviera (one-week minimum rentals). Avignon, Aix-en-Provence, Nice, and other Riviera towns have the biggest selection. It's usually more expensive to stay in an apartment than in a *gîte*.

You'll find homes and apartments for rent through TIs and on the Internet. Here are three good independent sources to consider: **VRBO** is an international network of apartment rentals (houses, apartments, gîtes) that cuts out the middleman by putting you directly in touch with the owners (www.vrbo.com). **France Homestyle** is run by Claudette, a service-oriented French woman from Seattle who handpicks every home and apartment she lists (US tel. 206/325-0132, www.francehomestyle.com, info@francehomestyle.com). Or try **Ville et Village,** which has a bigger selection of higher-end places (US tel. 510/559-8080, www.villeetvillage.com).

Other Options: Airbnb.com makes it reasonably easy to find a place to sleep in someone's home. Beds range from air-mattress-in-living-room basic to plush-B&B-suite posh. If you want a place to sleep that's free, Couchsurfing.com is a vagabond's alternative to Airbnb. It lists millions of outgoing members, who host fellow "surfers" in their homes.

Eating

The French eat long and well—nowhere more so than in the south. Relaxed and tree-shaded lunches with a chilled rosé, three-hour dinners, and endless afternoons at outdoor cafés are the norm. Local cafés, cuisine, and wines should become a highlight of any French adventure. It's sightseeing for your palate. Even if the rest of you is sleeping in cheap hotels, let your taste buds travel first class in France. (They can go coach in England.)

You can eat well without going broke—but choose carefully: You're just as likely to blow a small fortune on a mediocre meal as you are to dine wonderfully for €20. For specific suggestions on what to order where, see my cuisine suggestions in the introductions to Provence (page 61) and the Riviera (page 327).

When restaurant-hunting, choose a spot filled with locals, not the place with the big neon signs boasting, "We Speak English and Accept Credit Cards." Venturing even a block or two off the main drag leads to higher-quality food for less than half the price of the tourist-oriented places. Locals eat better at lower-rent locales.

All café and restaurant interiors are smoke-free. Today the only smokers you'll find are at outside tables, which—unfortunately—may be exactly where you want to be.

Waiters probably won't overwhelm you with friendliness (their tip is included in the bill, so there's less schmoozing than we're used to at home). Notice how hard they work. They almost never stop. Cozying up to clients (French or foreign) is probably the last thing on their minds. To get a waiter's attention, say, "*S'il vous plaît*" (see voo play)—"please."

Breakfast

You'll almost always have the option of breakfast at your hotel, which is usually pleasant and convenient. *Petit déjeuner* (puh-tee day-zhuh-nay) starts with café au lait, hot chocolate, or tea, and a roll with butter and marmalade. Some hotels offer only this classic continental breakfast for about €8, whereas others put out a buffet breakfast for about €10-13 (cereal, yogurt, fruit, cheese, croissants, juice, and hard-boiled eggs)—which I usually spring for.

If all you want is coffee or tea and a croissant, the local café offers travelers more atmosphere and is cheaper (though you get more coffee at your hotel). Go local at the café and ask for *une tartine* (oon tart-een; baguette slathered with butter or jam) with your café au lait. To keep it cheap, pick up some fruit at a grocery store and pastries at your favorite *boulangerie* (bakery), and have a picnic breakfast, then savor your coffee at the bar *(comptoir)* while standing, like the locals do.

Picnics and Snacks

Great for lunch or dinner, French picnics can be first-class affairs and adventures in high cuisine. Be daring. Try the smelly cheeses, ugly pâtés, sissy quiches, and minuscule yogurts. Shopkeepers are accustomed to selling small quantities of produce. Get a tasty salad-to-go, and ask for a plastic fork *(une fourchette en plastique)*. A small container is *une barquette*. A slice is *une tranche*. If you need a

Picnic Vocabulary

English	French	Pronounced
please	*s'il vous plaît*	see voo play
a plastic fork	*une fourchette en plastique*	ewn foor-sheht ahn plah-steek
a small box	*une barquette*	oon bar-keht
a knife	*un couteau*	uhn koo-toh
corkscrew	*tire-bouchon*	teer-boo-shohn
sliced	*tranché*	trahn-shay
a slice	*une tranche*	oon trahnsh
a small slice	*une petite tranche*	oon puh-teet trahnsh
more	*plus*	plew
less	*moins*	mwan (rhymes with man)
It's just right.	*C'est bon.*	say bohn
Thank you.	*Merci.*	mehr-see

knife *(couteau)* or corkscrew *(tire-bouchon),* ask to borrow one from your hotelier. And though wine is taboo in public places in the US, it's *pas de problème* in France.

Gather supplies early for a picnic lunch; you'll want to visit several small stores to assemble a complete meal, and many close at noon for their lunch break. Or visit open-air markets *(marchés),* which are fun and photogenic, but shut down around 13:00 (many are listed in this book; local TIs have complete lists). There's much more information about these wonderful Provençal experiences in the Shopping chapter (see "Market Day" on page 510).

Here are some ideas of what to look for, but don't hesitate if something unknown whets your appetite.

At the **boulangerie** (bakery), choose some bread. A baguette usually does the trick, or choose from the many square loaves of bread on display, such as *pain aux céréales* (whole grain with seeds), *pain de campagne* (country bread, made with unbleached bread flour), *pain complet* (wheat bread), or *pain de seigle* (rye bread). To ask to have it sliced, say, *"Tranché, s'il vous plaît."*

At the **pâtisserie** (pastry shop, usually the same place you bought the bread), choose a dessert that's easy to eat with your hands. My favorites are *éclairs* (*chocolat* or *café* flavored), individual fruit *tartes* (*framboise* is raspberry, *fraise* is strawberry, *citron* is lemon), and *macarons* (made of flavored cream sandwiched between two meringues, not coconut cookies like in the US).

At the *crémerie* or *fromagerie* (cheese shop), choose a sampling of cheeses. I usually get one hard cheese (like Comté, Cantal, or Beaufort), one soft cow's milk (like Brie or Camembert), one goat's milk cheese (anything that says chèvre), and one bleu cheese (Roquefort or Bleu d'Auvergne). Goat cheese usually comes in individual portions. For all other large cheeses, point to the cheese you want and ask for *une petite tranche* (a small slice). The shopkeeper will place a knife on the cheese indicating the size of the slice they are about to cut, then look at you for approval. If you'd like more, say *plus*. If you'd like less, say *moins*. If it's just right, say *"C'est bon!"*

At the **charcuterie** or *traiteur* (for deli items, prepared salads, meats, and pâtés), I like a slice of *pâté de campagne* (country pâté made of pork) and *saucissons sec* (dried sausages, some with pepper crust or garlic—you can ask to have it sliced thin like salami). I get a fresh salad, too. Typical choices are *carottes râpées* (shredded carrots in a tangy vinaigrette), *salade de betteraves* (beets in vinaigrette), and *céleri rémoulade* (celery root with a mayonnaise sauce).

At a *cave à vin*, you can buy chilled wines that the merchant is usually happy to open and re-cork for you. Note: Bottles of champagne don't require a corkscrew to open!

At a **supermarché, épicerie,** or **magasin d'alimentation** (small grocery store or minimart), you'll find plastic cutlery, paper plates, napkins, drinks, chips, and a small display of produce. Local *supermarchés* are less colorful than smaller stores, but cheaper, more efficient, and offer adequate quality. Department stores often have supermarkets in the basement. On the outskirts of cities, you'll find the monster *hypermarchés*. Drop in for a glimpse of hyper-France in action.

In stores, unrefrigerated soft drinks, bottled water, and beer are one-third the price of cold drinks. Wine is surprisingly affordable. Bottled water and boxed fruit juice are the cheapest drinks. Avoid buying drinks to go at streetside stands; you'll find them for far less in a shop. Try to keep a water bottle with you. Water quenches your thirst better and cheaper than anything you'll find in a store or café. I drink tap water throughout France, filling my bottle in hotel rooms as I go.

Sandwiches and Other Quick Bites

Everywhere in Provence and the Riviera, you'll find bakeries and small stands selling baguette sandwiches, quiche, and pizza-like items to go for about €4. Usually filling and tasty, they also streamline the picnic process. Here are some sandwiches you'll see:

   Fromage (froh-mahzh): Cheese (white on beige).

Jambon beurre (zhahn-bohn bur): Ham and butter (boring for most but a French classic).

Jambon crudités (zhahn-bohn krew-dee-tay): Ham with tomatoes, lettuce, cucumbers, and mayonnaise.

Pain salé (pan sah-lay) or *fougasse* (foo-gahs): Bread rolled up with salty bits of bacon, cheese, or olives.

Poulet crudités (poo-lay krew-dee-tay): Chicken with tomatoes, lettuce, maybe cucumbers, and always mayonnaise.

Saucisson beurre (saw-see-sohn bur): Thinly sliced sausage and butter.

Thon crudités (tohn krew-dee-tay): Tuna with tomatoes, lettuce, and maybe cucumbers, but definitely mayonnaise.

Anything served *à la provençale* has marinated peppers, tomatoes, and eggplant. A sandwich *à la italienne* is a grilled *panini*.

Typical **quiches** you'll see at shops and bakeries are *lorraine* (ham and cheese), *fromage* (cheese only), *aux oignons* (with onions), *aux poireaux* (with leeks—my favorite), *aux champignons* (with mushrooms), *au saumon* (salmon), or *au thon* (tuna).

Crêpes

The quintessentially French thin pancake called a crêpe (rhymes with "step," not "grape") is a good budget standby: It's filling, usually inexpensive, and generally quick. A place that sells them is a *crêperie* (krehp-eh-ree).

Crêpes generally come in two types: *sucrée* (sweet) and *salée* (savory). Technically, a savory crêpe should be made with a heartier buckwheat batter, and is called a galette (gah-leht). However, many cheap and lazy *crêperies* use the same sweet batter *(de froment)* for both their sweet-topped and savory-topped crêpes.

For savory crêpes, the standard toppings include *fromage* (cheese, usually Swiss-style Gruyère or Emmental), *jambon* (ham), *œuf* (an egg that's cracked and scrambled right on the hot plate), and *champignons* (mushrooms).

For sweet crêpes, common toppings include *chocolat* (chocolate syrup), Nutella (the delicious milk chocolate-hazelnut spread), jam/jelly, and powdered sugar.

During slow times, the *crêperie* chef might make several crêpes to be stacked up, then reheated later. Don't be surprised if he doesn't make a fresh one for you.

Café Culture

French cafés and brasseries provide user-friendly meals and a refuge from sightseeing overload. They're not necessarily cheaper than restaurants. Their key advantage is flexibility: they offer long serving hours, and you're welcome to order just a salad, a sandwich, or a bowl of soup, even for dinner. It's also OK to split starters and desserts, though not main courses.

Cafés and brasseries usually open by 7:00, but closing hours vary. Unlike restaurants, which open only for dinner and sometimes for lunch, some cafés and all brasseries serve food throughout the day (though with a more limited menu than at restaurants), making them the best option for a late lunch or an early dinner. (Note that many cafés in smaller towns close their kitchens from about 14:00 until 18:00.)

If you're a novice, it's easier to sit and feel comfortable when you know the system. Check the price list first, which by law must be posted prominently (if you don't see one, go elsewhere). There are two sets of prices: You'll pay more for the same drink if you're seated at a table *(salle)* than if you're seated or standing at the bar or counter *(comptoir)*. For tips on coffee and tea, see "Coffee and Tea Lingo" on page 46.

Standard Menu Items: A *salad, crêpe, quiche,* or *omelet* is a fairly cheap way to fill up. Each can be made with various extras like ham, cheese, mushrooms, and so on. Popular sandwiches, generally served day and night, are the *croque monsieur* (grilled ham-and-cheese) and *croque madame* (*croque monsieur* with a fried egg on top). Sandwiches are least expensive, but most are very plain (*boulangeries* serve better ones). To get more than a piece of ham *(jambon)* on a baguette, order a sandwich *crudité,* which means garnished with veggies. Omelets come lonely on a plate with a basket of bread. The daily special—*plat du jour* (plah dew zhoor), or just *plat*—is your fast, hearty, and garnished hot plate for €10-16. At most cafés, feel free to order only *entrées* (which in French means the starter course); many find these lighter and more interesting than a main course. A vegetarian can enjoy a tasty, filling meal by ordering two *entrées*. Regardless of what you order, bread is free but almost never comes with butter; to get more bread, just hold up your basket and ask, *"Encore, s'il vous plaît?"*

Salads: They're usually large—one is perfect for lunch or a light dinner. Here are some classics:

Salade niçoise (sah-lahd nee-swahz), a specialty from Nice, usually includes green salad topped with green beans, boiled potatoes, tomatoes, anchovies, olives, hard-boiled eggs, and lots of tuna.

Salade au chèvre chaud is a mixed green salad topped with warm goat cheese on small pieces of toast.

Salade composée is "composed" of any number of ingredients, such as *lardons* (bacon), Comté (a Swiss-style cheese), Roquefort (bleu cheese), *œuf* (egg), *noix* (walnuts), and *jambon* (ham, generally thinly sliced).

Salade paysanne generally comes with potatoes *(pommes de terre),* walnuts *(noix),* tomatoes, ham, and egg.

Salade aux gésiers includes chicken gizzards (and often slices of duck).

Dinner

Choose cafés and restaurants filled with locals. Consider my suggestions and your hotelier's opinion, but trust your instincts. If a restaurant or café doesn't post its prices outside, move along. Refer to my restaurant recommendations to get a sense of what a reasonable meal should cost.

Restaurants in the south open for dinner at 19:00 (cafés open earlier), and are most crowded about 20:30 (the early bird gets the table). Last seating is usually about 21:00 (22:00 in cities and on the French Riviera).

If a restaurant serves lunch, it generally begins at 12:00 and goes until 14:00, with last orders taken at about 13:30. If you're hungry when restaurants are closed (late afternoon), go to a brasserie or café; for more information, see "Café Culture," earlier.

At a *café* or a *brasserie*, if the table is not set, it's fine to seat yourself and just have a drink. However, if it's set with a placemat and cutlery, you should ask to be seated and plan to order a meal. If you're unsure, ask the server before sitting down.

This is the sequence of a typical restaurant experience: To get the waiter's attention, simply ask, *S'il vous plaît?* The waiter will give you a menu *(carte)* and then ask what you'd like to drink *(Vous voulez quelque choses à boire?)*, if you're ready to order *(Vous êtes prêts à commander?)* or what you'd like to eat *(Qu'est-ce que je vous sers?)*. Later the server will ask if everything is OK *(Tout va bien?)*, if you'd like dessert or coffee *(Vous voulez un dessert? Un café?)*, and if you're finished *(Vous avez terminé?)*. You ask for the bill *(L'addition, s'il vous plaît)*.

In French eateries, there are three ways to order food. First, you can order off the menu, which is called a *carte*. Second, you can order a multi-course, fixed-price meal, which is (confusingly) called a *menu*. Third, most places have a few special dishes of the day, called *plat du jour*, or simply *plat*.

So, if you ask for *un menu* (instead of *la carte*), you'll get a fixed-price meal. *Menus*, which usually include two or three courses, are generally a good value and will help you pace your meal like the locals. With a three-course menu, you'll get your choice of soup, appetizer, or salad; your choice of three or four main courses with vegetables; plus a cheese course and/or a choice of desserts. It sounds like a lot of food but portions are smaller in France and what we cram onto one large plate they spread out over several courses.

Service is included *(service compris)*, but wine and other drinks are generally extra. Certain premium items add a few euros to the price, clearly noted on the menu (*supplément* or *sup.*). Most restaurants offer less expensive and less filling, two-course *menus* sometimes called *formules*, featuring an *entrée et plat* (first course and main dish), or *plat et dessert* (main dish and dessert).

If you order à la carte (from what we would call the "menu"), you'll have a wider selection of food. It's traditional to order an *entrée* (which—again, confusingly—is a starter rather than a main dish) and a *plat principal* (main course). The *plats* are generally more meat-based, while the *entrées* usually include veggies. Multiple-course meals, while time-consuming (a positive thing in France), create the appropriate balance of veggies to meat. Elaborate meals may also have *entremets*—tiny dishes served between courses. Wherever you dine, consider the waiter's recommendations and anything *de la maison* (of the house), as long as it's not an organ meat (tripe, *rognons*, or andouillette).

Two people can split an *entrée* or a big salad (since small-size dinner salads are usually not offered á la carte) and then each get a *plat principal.* At restaurants, it's considered inappropriate for two diners to share one main course. If all you want is a salad or soup, go to a café or brasserie. Some restaurants (as well as other types of eateries) offer great-value lunch *menus*, and many restaurants have a reasonable *menu-enfant* (kid's meal).

In the south, I usually order *une entrée* and *un plat* from *la carte* (often as a fixed-price, two-course *menu* or *formule*), then find an ice-cream or crêpe stand and take a dessert stroll. If that sounds like too much, just order *un plat* (but don't skip the dessert stroll!).

Galloping gourmets should bring a menu translator. The most complete (and priciest) menu reader around is *A to Z of French Food* by G. de Temmerman. The *Marling Menu-Master* is also good. The *Rick Steves' French Phrase Book & Dictionary*, with a menu decoder, works well for most travelers.

Tune into the relaxed pace of French dining. The French don't do dinner and a movie on date nights; they just do dinner. Evening meals last a long time in restaurants, and once you've been seated, that table is yours for the night.

Vegetarians, Allergies, and Other Dietary Restrictions

Many French people think "vegetarian" means "no red meat" or "not much meat." If you're a strict vegetarian, be very specific: Tell your server what you don't eat—and it can be helpful to clarify what you do eat. Write it out on a card and keep it handy. Think of your meal (as the French do) as if it's a finely crafted creation by a trained artist. The chef knows what goes well together, and substitutions are considered an insult to his training. Picky eaters should just take it or leave it. However, French restaurants are willing to accommodate genuine dietary restrictions and other special concerns, or at least point you to an appropriate choice on the menu. These phrases can help: *Je suis végétarien* (zhuh swee vay-zhay-tah-ree-an). A female is a *végétarienne* (vay-zhay-tah-ree-ehn). For the following, fill in the blank with the food you need to avoid: "*Je ne peux pas manger de* ___" (zhuh nuh puh pah mahn-zhay duh) means "I cannot eat ___." "*Je suis allergique à* ___" (zhuh sweez ah-lehr-zheek ah) means "I am allergic to ___."

Beverages

Water: The French are willing to pay for bottled water with their meal (*eau minérale;* oh mee-nay-rahl) because they prefer the taste over tap water. Badoit is my favorite carbonated water (*l'eau gazeuse*; loh gah-zuhz). If you prefer a free pitcher of tap water, ask for *une carafe d'eau* (oon kah-rahf doh). Otherwise, you may unwittingly buy bottled water.

Wine and Beer: Wines are often listed in a separate *carte des vins*. House wine at the bar is cheap and good in this region (about €3-5/glass). At a restaurant, a bottle or carafe of house wine costs €8-18. To get inexpensive wine, order regional table wine (*un vin du pays;* uhn van duh pay) in a pitcher (*un pichet;* uhn pee-shay), rather than a bottle (only available when seated and when ordering food). Note, though, that finer restaurants usually offer only bottles of wine.

If all you want is a glass of wine, ask for *un verre de vin rouge* for red wine or *vin blanc* for white wine (uhn vehr duh van roozh/blahn). A half-carafe of wine is *un demi-pichet* (uhn duh-mee pee-shay); a quarter-carafe (ideal for one) is *un quart* (uh kar).

The local beer, which costs about €5 at a restaurant, is cheaper on tap (*une pression;* oon pres-yohn) than in the bottle (*bouteille;* boo-teh-ee). France's best beer is Alsatian; try Kronenbourg or the heavier Pelfort (one of your author's favorites). *Une panaché* (oon pah-nah-shay) is a tasty French shandy (beer and lemon soda).

Regional Specialty Drinks: For a refreshing before-dinner drink, order a *kir* (pronounced "keer")—a thumb's level of *crème de cassis* (black currant liqueur) topped with white wine. In Provence, try sweet wines such as Muscat de Beaumes de Venise or Rasteau (Vin Doux Naturel). Both should be served chilled (from the fridge, never with ice cubes) and are enjoyable before dinner or with certain desserts; they're terrific with foie gras, melons, peaches, or Roquefort cheese. Look also for sparkling wines, usually inexpensive versions of the pricey Champagne.

If you like brandy, try a *marc* (regional brandy) or an Armagnac, cognac's cheaper twin brother (which I prefer). *Pastis,* the standard southern France aperitif, is a sweet anise (licorice) drink that comes on the rocks with a glass of water. Cut it to taste

Coffee and Tea Lingo

By law, the waiter must give you a glass of tap water with your coffee or tea if you request it; ask for *"Un verre d'eau, s'il vous plaît"* (uhn vayr doh, see voo play).

Provence is known for its herbal and fruit teas. Look for *tilleul* (linden), *verveine* (verbena), or interesting blends such as *poire-vanille* (pear-vanilla).

Coffee

French	Pronounced	English
un café allongé (also called *café longue*)	uhn kah-fay ah-lohn-zhay (kah-fay lohn)	closest to an American cup of coffee
un express	uhn ex-press	shot of espresso
une noisette	oon nwah-zeht	espresso with a shot of milk
café au lait	kah-fay oh lay	coffee with lots of steamed milk (closest to an American latte)
un grand crème	uhn grahn krehm	big café au lait
un petit crème	uhn puh-tee krehm	small café au lait
un décaffiné	uhn day-kah-fee-nay	decaf—available for any of the above drinks

Tea

French	Pronounced	English
un thé nature	uhn tay nah-tour	plain tea
un thé au lait	uhn tay oh lay	tea with milk
un thé citron	uhn tay see-trohn	tea with lemon
une infusion	oon an-few-see-yohn	herbal tea

with lots of water.

Soft Drinks: For a fun, bright, nonalcoholic drink of 7-Up with mint syrup, order *un diabolo menthe* (uhn dee-ah-boh-loh mahnt). For 7-Up with fruit syrup, order *un diabolo grenadine* (think Shirley Temple). Kids love the local orange drink, Orangina, a carbonated orange juice with pulp and without caffeine. They also like flavored syrups mixed with bottled water (*sirops à l'eau;* see-roh ah loh). In France *limonade* (lee-moh-nahd) is Sprite or 7-Up.

Ordering Beverages: Be clear when ordering drinks—you

can pay €8 for an oversized Coke and €12 for a supersized beer at some cafés. When you order a drink, state the size in centiliters (don't say "small," "medium," or "large," because the waiter might bring a bigger drink than you want). For something small, ask for 25 *centilitres* (vant-sank sahn-tee-lee-truh; about 8 ounces); for a medium drink, order 33 cl (trahnt-twah; about 12 ounces—a normal can of soda); a large is 50 cl (san-kahnt; about 16 ounces); and a super-size is one liter (lee-truh; about a quart—which is more than I would ever order in France). The ice cubes melted after the last Yankee tour group left.

Cheese Course

In France the cheese course is served just before (or instead of) dessert. It not only helps with digestion, it gives you a great opportunity to sample the tasty regional cheeses—and time to finish up your wine. There are more than 400 different French cheeses to try. Some restaurants will offer a cheese platter, from which you select a few different kinds. A good platter has at least four cheeses: a hard cheese (such as Emmentaler—a.k.a. Swiss cheese), a flowery cheese (such as Brie or Camembert), a blue or Roquefort cheese, and a goat cheese.

If you'd like to sample several types of cheese from the cheese plate, say, *"Un assortiment, s'il vous plaît"* (uhn ah-sor-tee-mahn, see voo play). If you serve yourself from the cheese plate, observe French etiquette and keep the shape of the cheese. It's best to politely shave off a slice from the side or cut small wedges.

If you've run out of wine, consider ordering more. A glass of good red wine complements your cheese course in a heavenly way.

Desserts

If you order espresso, it will always come after dessert. To have coffee with dessert, ask for *"café avec le dessert"* (kah-fay ah-vehk luh day-sayr). See the list of coffee terms earlier in this chapter.

Here is a list of traditional French desserts you might find on any menu:

Baba au rhum (bah-bah oh room): Pound cake drenched in rum, served with whipped cream.

Café gourmand (kah-feh goor-mahn): An assortment of small desserts selected by the restaurant—a great way to sample several desserts and learn your favorite.

Crème brûlée (krehm broo-lay): A rich, creamy, dense, caramelized custard.

Crème caramel (krehm kah-rah-mehl): Flan in a caramel sauce.

Fondant au chocolat (fohn-dahnt oh shoh-koh-lah): A molten chocolate cake with a runny (not totally cooked) center. Also

INTRODUCTION

How Was Your Trip?

Were your travels fun, smooth, and meaningful? If you'd like to share your tips, concerns, and discoveries, please fill out the survey at www.ricksteves.com/feedback. I value your feedback. Thanks in advance—it helps a lot.

known as *moelleux* (meh-leh) *au chocolat.*

Fromage blanc (froh-mahzh blahn): A light dessert similar to plain yogurt (yet different), served with sugar or herbs.

Glace (glahs): Ice cream—typically vanilla, chocolate, or strawberry *(fraise).*

Île flottante (eel floh-tahnt): A light dessert consisting of islands of meringue floating on a pond of custard sauce.

Mousse au chocolat (moos oh shoh-koh-lah): Chocolate mousse.

Profiteroles (proh-fee-tuh-rohl): Cream puffs filled with vanilla ice cream, smothered in warm chocolate sauce.

Riz au lait (ree-zoh-lay): Rice pudding.

Sorbets: Light, flavorful, and fruity ices (known to us as sherbets), sometimes laced with brandy.

Tartes (tart): Narrow strips of fresh fruit, baked in a crust and served in thin slices (without ice cream).

Tarte tatin (tart tah-tan): Apple pie like grandma never made, with caramelized apples, cooked upside down, but served upright.

Traveling as a Temporary Local

We travel all the way to France to enjoy differences—to become temporary locals. You'll experience frustrations. Certain truths that we find "God-given" or "self-evident," such as cold beer, ice in drinks, bottomless cups of coffee, and bigger being better, are suddenly not so true. One of the benefits of travel is the eye-opening realization that there are logical, civil, and even better alternatives.

With a history rich in human achievement, France is an understandably proud country. To enjoy its people, you need to celebrate the differences. A willingness to go local ensures that you'll enjoy a full dose of French hospitality.

Europeans generally like Americans. But if there is a negative aspect to the French image of Americans, it's that we are loud, wasteful, ethnocentric, too informal (which can seem disrespectful), occasionally impolite, and a bit naive.

The French (and Europeans in general) place a high value on speaking quietly in restaurants and on trains. Listen while on the bus or in a restaurant—the place can be packed, but the decibel level is low. Try to adjust your volume accordingly to show respect for the culture.

While the French look bemusedly at some of our Yankee excesses—and worriedly at others—they nearly always afford us individual travelers all the warmth we deserve.

Judging from all the happy feedback I receive from travelers who have used this book, it's safe to assume you'll enjoy a great, affordable vacation—with the finesse of an independent, experienced traveler.

Thanks, and *bon voyage!*

INTRODUCTION

Back Door Travel Philosophy
From *Rick Steves' Europe Through the Back Door*

Travel is intensified living—maximum thrills per minute and one of the last great sources of legal adventure. Travel is freedom. It's recess, and we need it.

Experiencing the real Europe requires catching it by surprise, going casual..."Through the Back Door."

Affording travel is a matter of priorities. (Make do with the old car.) You can eat and sleep—simply and safely—anywhere in Europe for $120 a day plus transportation costs. In many ways, spending more money only builds a thicker wall between you and what you traveled so far to see. Europe is a cultural carnival, and time after time, you'll find that its best acts are free and the best seats are the cheap ones.

A tight budget forces you to travel close to the ground, meeting and communicating with the people. Never sacrifice sleep, nutrition, safety, or cleanliness to save money. Simply enjoy the local-style alternatives to expensive hotels and restaurants.

Connecting with people carbonates your experience. Extroverts have more fun. If your trip is low on magic moments, kick yourself and make things happen. If you don't enjoy a place, maybe you don't know enough about it. Seek the truth. Recognize tourist traps. Give a culture the benefit of your open mind. See things as different, but not better or worse. Any culture has plenty to share.

Of course, travel, like the world, is a series of hills and valleys. Be fanatically positive and militantly optimistic. If something's not to your liking, change your liking.

Travel can make you a happier American, as well as a citizen of the world. Our Earth is home to seven billion equally precious people. It's humbling to travel and find that other people don't have the "American Dream"—they have their own dreams. Europeans like us, but with all due respect, they wouldn't trade passports.

Thoughtful travel engages us with the world. In tough economic times, it reminds us what is truly important. By broadening perspectives, travel teaches new ways to measure quality of life.

Globetrotting destroys ethnocentricity, helping us understand and appreciate other cultures. Rather than fear the diversity on this planet, celebrate it. Among your most prized souvenirs will be the strands of different cultures you choose to knit into your own character. The world is a cultural yarn shop, and Back Door travelers are weaving the ultimate tapestry. Join in!

PROVENCE

PROVENCE

"There are treasures to carry away in this land, which has not found a spokesman worthy of the riches it offers."
—Paul Cézanne

This magnificent region is shaped like a giant wedge of quiche. From its sunburned crust, fanning out along the Mediterranean coast from the Camargue to Marseille, it stretches north along the Rhône Valley to Orange. The Romans were here in force and left many ruins—some of the best anywhere. Seven popes, artists such as Vincent van Gogh and Paul Cézanne, and author Peter Mayle all enjoyed their years in Provence. This destination features a splendid recipe of arid climate, oceans of vineyards, dramatic scenery, lively cities, and adorable hill-capping villages.

Explore the ghost town that is ancient Les Baux, and see France's greatest Roman ruins, the Pont du Gard aqueduct and the theater in Orange. Admire the skill of ball-tossing *boules* players in small squares in every Provençal village and city. Spend a few Van Gogh-inspired starry, starry nights in Arles. Youthful but classy Avignon bustles in the shadow of its brooding Palace of the Popes. Stylish and self-confident Aix-en-Provence lies 30 minutes from the sea and feels more Mediterranean. It's a short hop from Arles or Avignon into the splendid scenery and villages of the Côtes du Rhône and Luberon regions. To properly understand southern France, day-trip into gritty Marseille, and if you prefer a Provençal beach fix, find Cassis, just east of Marseille.

Choosing a Home Base

With limited time, make Arles or Avignon your sightseeing base—particularly if you have no car. Italophiles prefer smaller Arles, while poodles pick urban Avignon. Many enjoy nights in

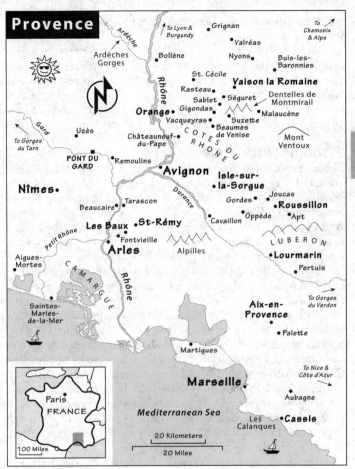

both cities. (With a car, head for St. Rémy or the hill towns.)

Arles has a blue-collar quality; the entire city feels like Van Gogh's bedroom. It also has this region's best-value hotels and is handy to Les Baux, St. Rémy, and the Camargue.

Avignon—double the size of Arles—feels sophisticated, with more nightlife and shopping. Avignon makes a good base for non-drivers thanks to its convenient public-transit options (within an hour, you can reach Pont du Gard, Uzès, and St. Rémy by bus, or Marseille by train; within a half-hour, you can reach Arles, Nîmes, Isle-sur-la-Sorgue, and Aix-en-Provence by train).

Or, for drivers who prefer a smaller-town base, **St. Rémy** is manageable and central. It offers a nice range of hotels with free and easy parking, good restaurants, and a few sights of its own. The towns of **Vaison la Romaine** (in the Côtes du Rhône region) and **Roussillon** (in the Luberon) are two good but remote hill-town options.

Aix-en-Provence works well as a base for Provence sights east of Arles and Avignon, with easy access to Marseille, Cassis, and some Luberon villages. About halfway between Arles and Nice, Aix-en-Provence also makes a convenient stopover, and if you're flying in or out of Marseille, Aix has quick access to the airport, making it a convenient first- or last-day stop.

Planning Your Time

The bare minimum you should spend in Provence is three days: one day for sightseeing in Arles and Les Baux (Arles is best on Wed or Sat, when it's market day); a day for Pont du Gard and Nîmes; and a full day for Orange and the Côtes du Rhône villages. Add two more days to explore Avignon; Uzès or St. Rémy; and more Provençal villages. Allow an additional two days in Cassis, using one of them for a day trip to Marseille or Aix-en-Provence (or both). Ideally, see the cities—Arles, Nîmes, Avignon, Aix-en-Provence, and Marseille—by train, then rent a car for the countryside.

To measure the pulse of rural Provence, spend at least a few nights in the smaller towns. (They come to life on market days, but can be quiet on Mondays, when shops are shuttered tight.) I've described many towns in the Côtes du Rhône and Luberon. The Côtes du Rhône is ideal for wine connoisseurs and an easy stop for those heading to or from the north. The Luberon was made for hill-town lovers and works well for travelers heading east, toward Aix-en-Provence or the Riviera. Avoid speeding through these areas. Provençal village evenings are what books are written about—spend the night, or two, or...

The small port town of Cassis is a marvelous Mediterranean meander between Provence and the Riviera (and more appealing than most Riviera resorts). It has easy day-trip connections to Marseille and Aix-en-Provence.

Depending on the length of your trip, here are my recommended priorities for Provence:

3-4 days:	Arles and Les Baux; Pont du Gard and Nîmes; and Orange and Côtes du Rhône villages
5-6 days, add:	Avignon and either St. Rémy or Uzès
7-8 days, add:	Cassis, Marseille, Aix-en-Provence
9-10 days, add:	Luberon hill towns, Camargue

Helpful Hints

Resources: Imagine Tours (near Avignon) offers free assistance to travelers. They can work with you to plan your itinerary, book hotels, or help you deal with problems that might arise during your trip (for contact information, see page 58).

Travel writer **Mary Dowey's** website reveals her favorite discoveries in Provence over many years of research—including restaurants, hotels, food and wine producers, shops, and markets (www.provencefoodandwine.com).

Cruise-Ship Sightseeing: Cruise lines that visit Provence call at either Marseille or Toulon (about 40 miles east of Marseille). Public-transit options are limited—with a short day, only Marseille, Cassis, and Aix-en-Provence are doable this way. (If docking at Marseille, it's possible to visit Avignon or Arles—but only if you have a long day in port.) If you want to journey beyond the immediate area and/or connect several worthwhile sights in one busy day, consider joining a cruise-line excursion, hiring a driver or guide (such as Mike Rijken's Wine Safari—listed in "Tours of Provence," later in this chapter), or renting a car. For more details on arriving in this region by cruise ship, see page 280. If your trip includes cruising beyond Provence, consider my guidebook, *Rick Steves' Mediterranean Cruise Ports*.

Getting Around Provence

By Bus or Train: Public transit is good between cities and decent to some towns, but marginal at best to the smaller villages. Frequent trains link Avignon, Arles, and Nîmes (no more than 30 minutes between each). Avignon has good train connections with Orange and adequate service to Isle-sur-la-Sorgue. Marseille is well-connected to all cities in Provence, with frequent service to Cassis (25 minutes) and Aix-en-Provence (45 minutes).

Buses connect many smaller towns, though service can be sporadic. From Arles you can catch a bus to Les Baux (high season only), Stes-Maries-de-la-Mer (in the Camargue), or St. Rémy. From Avignon, you can bus to Pont du Gard, St. Rémy, Uzès, Isle-sur-la-Sorgue (also by train), and to some Côtes du Rhône villages. St. Rémy, Isle-sur-la-Sorgue, and Uzès are the most accessible and interesting small towns. Vaison la Romaine—my favorite town—is a manageable bus ride from Orange (with fast and frequent train connections to Avignon). A visit here works well with a tour of Orange's Roman Theater.

While a tour of the villages of the Côtes du Rhône or Luberon is best on your own by car, a variety of minivan tours and basic bus excursions are available. (TIs in Arles and Avignon also have information on bus excursions to regional sights that are hard to reach *sans* car; see "Tours of Provence," later.)

By Car: The region is made to order for a car. Orange Michelin map #527 (1:275,000 scale) covers this book perfectly. Michelin maps #332 (Luberon and Côtes du Rhône) and #340

(Arles area) are also worth considering. I've described key sights and a variety of full-day drives deep into the countryside. Be wary of thieves: Park only in well-monitored spaces and leave nothing valuable in your car.

Avignon (pop. 110,000) is a headache for drivers. Arles (pop. 52,000) is easier but still challenging. Les Baux and St. Rémy work well from Arles or Avignon (or vice versa). Nîmes and Pont du Gard are a short hop west of Avignon and on the way to or from Languedoc. The town of Orange ties in tidily with a trip to the Côtes du Rhône villages and with destinations farther north. If you're heading north from Provence, consider a half-day detour through the spectacular Ardèche Gorges (see page 217). The Luberon villages are about halfway between Arles or Avignon and Aix-en-Provence (little Lourmarin works as a base for day trips to Aix-en-Provence). And if you're continuing on to the Riviera, let yourself be lured into the Grand Canyon du Verdon detour (✪ see the Inland Riviera chapter). Most drivers will prefer exploring congested Marseille on foot—take the train from Cassis or Aix-en-Provence (both towns have parking at their train stations with frequent trains and buses to the center of Marseille).

Tours of Provence

It's possible to take half-day or full-day excursions to most of the sights in Provence (best from Avignon). Most TIs have brochures on day trips and can help you make a reservation. Here are several top options to consider (in Avignon, most tours can pick you up at your hotel, the TI, or at either of the city's train stations):

Wine Safari

Dutchman Mike Rijken runs a one-man show, taking travelers through the region he adopted more than 20 years ago. Mike came to France to train as a chef, later became a wine steward, and has now found his calling as a driver/guide. His English is fluent, and though his focus is on wine and wine villages, Mike knows the region thoroughly and is a good teacher of its history (€75/half-day, €130/day, priced per person, group size varies from 2 to 6; pickups possible in Arles, Avignon, Lyon, Marseille, or Aix-en-Provence; tel. 04 90 35 59 21, mobile 06 19 29 50 81, www.wine safari.net, mikeswinesafari@orange.fr).

Local Guides

Celine Viany is a retired wine sommelier turned charming tour guide. She's an easy-to-be-with expert on her region and its chief product (from €75/half-day per person, from €90/day for up to 6 people, tel. 04 90 46 90 80, mobile 06 76 59 56 30, www.levina labouche.com, contact@degustation-levinalabouche.com).

Discover Provence is run by English-born Sarah Pernet, who has lived in Aix-en-Provence since 2001 and runs well-organized

PROVENCE

Top 10 Provençal Towns and Villages

1. **Roussillon,** a beautiful hill town sitting atop a huge ochre deposit, giving it a red-rock appeal, popular with American tourists; see page 232.
2. **Uzès,** a chic town with manicured pedestrian streets, popular with European tourists; see page 174.
3. **Joucas,** an adorable little village where flowers and stones are lovingly maintained, a magnet for artists; see page 240.
4. **Brantes,** a spectacularly situated cliff village literally at the end of the road, with few tourists; see page 217.
5. **Vaison la Romaine,** a bustling midsize town that spans both sides of a river and has Roman ruins, popular with tourists; see page 189.
6. **Lourmarin,** a lovely upscale village, busy during the day but quiet at night; see page 256.
7. **Le Crestet,** an overlooked village with a sensational hilltop location and one commercial enterprise; see page 204.
8. **Séguret,** a linear hillside village with memorable views, many day-trippers, but few overnighters; see page 201.
9. **Gigondas,** a world-famous wine village with a nice balance of commercial activity and quiet; see page 209.
10. **Nyons,** an overlooked midsize town with a few pedestrian streets, famous for its olive oil and ideal climate; see page 216.

and easygoing small-group tours of Provence with a focus on Aix-en-Provence and nearby villages (€80/half-day, €140/day, priced per person, private tours from €219/day for up to 6 people, tel. 0 6 16 86 40 24, www.discover-provence.net, discoverprovence@hotmail.com).

Art historian and photographer **Daniela Wedel** moved from Germany to Provence about 13 years ago after falling in love with southern France. She and her team of guides eagerly share their passion for the history, food, wine, and people of Provence (€170/half-day, €350/day, price varies depending on itinerary and number of people, tel. 06 43 86 30 83, daniela@treasure-europe.com).

Avignon Wine Tour
For a playful and distinctly French perspective on wines of the Côtes du Rhône region, contact François Marcou, who runs his tours with passion and energy, offering different itineraries every day (€110/person for all-day wine tours that include 4 tastings, €80/person for half-day tours, €350 for private groups, mobile 06 28 05 33 84, www.avignon-wine-tour.com, avignon.wine.tour@modulonet.fr).

Imagine Tours

Unlike most tour operators, this nonprofit organization focuses on cultural excursions, offering low-key, personalized tours that allow visitors to discover the "true heart of Provence and Occitania." The itineraries are adapted to your interests, and the guides will meet you at your hotel or the departure point of your choice (€190/half-day, €315/day, prices are for up to 4 people starting from the region around Avignon or Arles, mobile 06 89 22 19 87, www.imagine-tours.net, imagine.tours@gmail.com). They are also happy to help you plan your itinerary, book hotel rooms, or address other traveler issues.

Wine Uncovered

Passionate and engaging Englishman Olivier Hickman takes small groups on focused tours of selected wineries in Châteauneuf-du-Pape and in the villages near Vaison la Romaine. Olivier is serious about wine and knows his subject matter inside and out. His in-depth tastings include a half-day tour of two or three wineries—the Châteauneuf-du-Pape tour is especially popular. He also offers multiday tours with food and wine tastings, and can help arrange transportation (€35-70/person for half-day to full-day tours, prices subject to minimum tour fees, mobile 06 75 10 10 01, www.wine-uncovered.com, olivier.hickman@wine-uncovered.com).

Tours du Rhône

American Doug Graves, who owns a small wine domaine in the Côtes du Rhône, shares his passion for his adopted region, its people, and its wines on his custom tours of Châteauneuf-du-Pape, the villages of the Côtes du Rhône, and the Luberon Valley (€100/person, price is for up to 4 people, mobile 06 37 16 04 56, www.toursdurhone.com, doug@masdelalionne.com).

Promo Vinum

Experienced guide and wine connoisseur Joe McLean offers tours focused on the wines of Uzès, Châteauneuf-du-Pape, and the Côtes du Rhône. He also organizes custom tours at fair prices (€55-110/person, tel. 04 66 22 72 19, www.promo-vinum.com/gb/winetours, info@promo-vinum.com).

Visit Provence

This company runs day tours from Avignon and Arles (and one all-tour day option from Marseille and Aix-en-Provence). Tours from Avignon run year-round and include a great variety of destinations; tours from Arles run April through September only and are more limited in scope. While these tours provide introductory commentary to what you'll see, there is no guiding at the actual sights. They use eight-seat, air-conditioned minivans (about €60-80/half-day, €100-120/day; they'll pick you up at your hotel in Avignon, at the main TI in Arles, or at the TI in Marseille or Aix-en-Provence). Ask about their cheaper big-bus excursions, or

Top 10 Roman Sights in Provence

1. Pont du Gard aqueduct and its museum
2. Roman Theater in Orange
3. Maison Carrée in Nîmes
4. Ancient History Museum in Arles
5. Arena in Nîmes
6. Arena in Arles
7. Roman city of Glanum (in St. Rémy)
8. Ruined aqueduct near Fontvieille
9. Roman city of Vaison la Romaine
10. Julien Bridge (near Roussillon)

consider hiring a van and driver for your private use (plan on €220/half-day, €490/day, tel. 04 90 14 70 00, www.provence-reservation.com).

How About Them Romans?

Provence is littered with Roman ruins. Many scholars claim the best-preserved ancient Roman buildings are not in Italy, but in France. These ancient stones will compose an important part of your sightseeing agenda in this region, so it's worth learning about how they came to be.

Classical Rome endured from about 500 B.C. through A.D. 500—spending about 500 years growing, 200 years peaking, and 300 years declining. Julius Caesar conquered Gaul—which included Provence—during the Gallic Wars (58-51 B.C.), then crossed the Rubicon River in 49 B.C. to incite civil war within the Roman Republic. He erected a temple to Jupiter on the future site of Paris' Notre-Dame Cathedral.

The concept of one-man rule lived on with his grandnephew, Octavian (whom he had also adopted as his son). Octavian killed Brutus, eliminated his rivals (Mark Antony and Cleopatra), and united Rome's warring factions. He took the title "Augustus" and became the first in a line of emperors who would control Rome for the next 500 years—ruling like a king, with the backing of the army and the rubber-stamp approval of the Senate. Rome morphed from a Republic into an Empire: a collection of many diverse territories ruled by a single man.

Augustus' reign marked the start of 200 years of peace, prosperity, and expansion known as the *Pax Romana*. At its peak (c. A.D. 117), the Roman empire had 54 million people and stretched from Scotland in the north to Egypt in the south, as far west as Spain and as far east as modern-day Iraq. To the northeast, Rome was bounded by the Rhine and Danube Rivers. On Roman maps, the Mediterranean was labeled *Mare Nostrum* ("Our Sea").

At its peak, "Rome" didn't just refer to the city, but to the entire civilized Western world.

The Romans were successful not only because they were good soldiers, but also because they were smart administrators and businessmen. People in conquered territories knew they had joined the winning team and that political stability would replace barbarian invasions. Trade thrived. Conquered peoples were welcomed into the fold of prosperity, linked by roads, education, common laws and gods, and the Latin language.

Provence, with its strategic location, benefited greatly from Rome's global economy and grew to become an important part of

its worldwide empire. After Julius Caesar conquered Gaul, Emperor Augustus set out to Romanize it, building and renovating cities in the image of Rome. Most cities had a theater (some had several), baths, and aqueducts; the most important cities had sports arenas. The Romans also erected an elaborate infrastructure of roads, post offices, schools (teaching in Latin), police stations, and water-supply systems.

With a standard language and currency, Roman merchants were able to trade wine, salt, and olive oil for foreign goods. The empire invested heavily in cities that were strategic for trade. For example, the Roman-built city of Arles was a crucial link in the trade route from Italy to Spain, so they built a bridge across the Rhône River and fortified the town.

A typical Roman city (such as Nîmes, Arles, Orange, or Vaison la Romaine) was a garrison town, laid out on a grid plan with two main roads: one running north-south (the *cardus*), the other east-west (the *decumanus*). Approaching the city on your chariot, you'd pass by the cemetery, which was located outside of town for hygienic reasons. You'd enter the main gate and speed past warehouses and apartment houses to the town square (forum). Facing the square were the most important temples, dedicated to the patron gods of the city. Nearby, you'd find bathhouses; like today's fitness clubs, these served the almost sacred dedication to personal vigor. Also close by were businesses that catered to the citizens' needs: the marketplace, bakeries, banks, and brothels.

Aqueducts brought fresh water for drinking, filling the baths, and delighting the citizens with bubbling fountains. Men flocked to the stadiums in Arles and Nîmes to bet on gladiator games; eager couples attended elaborate plays at theaters in Orange,

Arles, and Vaison la Romaine. Marketplaces brimmed with exotic fruits, vegetables, and animals from the far reaches of the empire.

Some cities in Provence were more urban 2,000 years ago than they are today. For instance, Roman Arles had a population of 100,000—double today's size. Think about that when you visit.

In these cities, you'll see many rounded arches. These were constructed by piling two stacks of heavy stone blocks, connecting them with an arch (supported with wooden scaffolding), then inserting an inverted keystone where the stacks met. *Voilà!* The heavy stones were able to support not only themselves, but also a great deal of weight above the arch. The Romans didn't invent the rounded arch, but they exploited it better than their predecessors, stacking arches to build arenas and theaters, stringing them side by side for aqueducts, stretching out their legs to create barrel-vaulted ceilings, and building freestanding "triumphal" arches to celebrate conquering generals.

When it came to construction, the Romans' magic building ingredient was concrete. A mixture of volcanic ash, lime, water, and small rocks, concrete—easier to work than stone, longer-lasting than wood—served as flooring, roofing, filler, glue, and support. Builders would start with a foundation of brick, then fill it in with poured concrete. They would then cover important structures, such as basilicas, in sheets of expensive marble (held on with nails), or decorate floors and walls with mosaics—proving just how talented the Romans were at turning the functional into art.

Provence's Cuisine Scene

Provence has been called France's "garden market," featuring farm-fresh food (vegetables, fruit, and meats) prepared in a simple way, and meant to be savored with family and friends. Grilled foods are common, as are dishes derived from lengthy simmering—in part a reflection of long days spent in the fields. Colorful and lively, Provençal cuisine hammers the senses with an extravagant use (by French standards) of garlic, olive oil, and herbs. Order anything *à la provençal,* and you'll be rewarded with aromatic food heightened by rich and pungent sauces. Thanks to the proximity of the Riviera, many seafood dishes show up on Provençal menus (see "The Riviera's Cuisine Scene" on page 327).

Unlike other French regional cuisines, the food of Provence is inviting for nibblers. Appetizers (hors d'oeuvres) often consist of bowls of olives (try the plump, full-flavored black *tanche* or the green, buttery *picholine*), as well as plates of fresh vegetables served with lusty sauces ready for dipping. These same sauces adorn dishes of hard-boiled eggs, fish, or meat. Look for tapenade, a paste of pureed olives, capers, ancho-

vies, herbs, and sometimes tuna. True anchovy-lovers dig into *anchoïade* (a spread of garlic, anchovy, and parsley) or *bagna cauda* (a warm sauce of anchovies and melted butter or olive oil).

Aioli—a rich, garlicky mayonnaise spread over vegetables, potatoes, fish, or whatever—is another Provençal favorite. In the summertime, entire village festivals celebrate this sauce. Watch for signs announcing *aioli monstre* ("monster aioli") and, for a few euros, dive into a deeply French eating experience (pass the breath mints, please).

Despite the heat, soup is a favorite in Provence. *Soupe au pistou* is a thin yet flavorful vegetable soup with a sauce (called *pistou*) of basil, garlic, and cheese—pesto minus the pine nuts. Or try *soupe à l'ail* (garlic soup, called *aigo bouido* in the Provençal dialect). For details on seafood soups, see page 327.

Provençal main courses venerate fresh vegetables and meats. (Eat seafood on the Riviera and meat in Provence.) Ratatouille is a mixture of Provençal vegetables (eggplant, zucchini, onions, and peppers are the usual suspects) in a thick, herb-flavored tomato sauce. It's readily found in charcuteries and often served at room temperature, making it the perfect picnic food. Ratatouille veggies also show up on their own, stuffed and served in spicy sauces. Look for *aubergines* (eggplants), *tomates* (tomatoes), *poivrons* (sweet peppers), and *courgettes* (zucchini—especially *fleurs de courgettes*, stuffed and batter-fried zucchini flowers). *Tians* are gratin-like vegetable dishes named for the deep terra-cotta dish in which they are cooked and served. *Artichauts à la barigoule* are stuffed artichokes flavored with garlic, ham, and herbs (*barigoule* is from the Provençal word for thyme, *farigoule*). Also look for *riz de Camargue*—the reddish, chewy, nutty-tasting rice that has taken over the Camargue area, a marshy region that is otherwise useless for agriculture.

The famous herbs of Provence influence food long before it's cooked. The locally renowned lambs of the *garrigue* (shrub-covered hills), as well as rabbits and other small edible beasts in Provence, dine on wild herbs and spicy shrubs—preseasoning their delicate meat. Regional specialties include lamb (*agneau*, most often leg of lamb, *gigot d'agneau*), grilled and served no-frills, or the delicious *lapin à la provençale*—rabbit served with garlic, mustard, tomatoes, and herbs in white wine. Locals have a curious passion for quail *(caille)*. These tiny, bony birds are often grilled and served with any variety of sauces, including those sweetened with Provençal cherries or honey and lavender. *Daube*, named for the traditional cooking vessel *daubière*, is generally beef simmered in wine with spices and herbs—and perhaps a touch of orange zest—until it is spoon-tender; it's then served with noodles or the local rice. *Taureau* (bull's meat), usually raised in the marshy Camargue, melts in your mouth.

By American standards, the French undercook meats: *bleu* (bluh) is virtually raw (just flame-kissed); *saignant* (seh-nyahn) is close to raw; *à point* (ah pwahn)—their version of "medium"—is rare; and *bien cuit* (bee-yehn kwee, "well cooked") is medium. (Because French cows are raised on grass rather than corn, the beef is leaner than in the US, so limiting the cooking time keeps the meat tender.)

There are a few dishes to avoid: *Pieds et paquets* is a scary dish of sheep's feet and tripe (no amount of Provençal sauce can hide this flavor). *Tourte de blettes* is a confused "pie" made with Swiss chard; both savory and sweet, it can't decide whether it should be a first course or dessert (it shows up as both).

Eat goat cheese *(fromage de chèvre)* in Provence. Look for *banon de banon* or *banon à la feuille* (dipped in *eau-de-vie* to kill bad mold, then wrapped in a chestnut leaf), spicy *picodon* (the name means "spicy" in the old language), or the fresh, creamy *brousse du Rove* (often served mixed with cream and sugar for dessert). On Provençal cheese platters, you'll find small rounds of bite-size chèvres, each flavored with a different herb or spice—and some even rolled in chopped garlic (more breath mints, please).

Desserts tend to be light and fruit-filled, or traditionally French. Treat yourself to fresh tarts made with seasonal fruit, Cavaillon melons (served cut in half with a trickle of the sweet Rhône wine Beaumes de Venise), and ice cream or sorbet sweetened with honey and flavored with various herbs such as lavender, thyme, or rosemary.

Wines of Provence

Provence saw the first grapes planted in France, in about 600 B.C., by the Greeks. Romans built on what the Greeks started, realizing 2,000 years ago that Provence had an ideal climate for producing wine: mild winters and long, warm summers (but not too hot—thanks to the cooling winds).

This sun-baked, wine-happy region offers Americans a chance to sample wines blended from several grapes—resulting in flavors unlike anything we get at home (yes, we have good cabernet sauvignons, merlots, and pinot noirs, but Rhône wines are new to many of us). Provence's shorts-and-T-shirt climate and abundance of hearty, reasonably priced wines make for an enjoyable experience, particularly if you're patient and willing to learn. See "Provençal Wine-Tasting 101" (page 66) for the basics.

In France, wine production is strictly controlled by the government to preserve the overall quality. This ensures that vintners use specified grapes that grow best in that region and follow certain grape-growing procedures. The *Appellation d'Origine Controlée* (AOC) label found on many bottles is the government's seal of approval indicating that a wine has met various requirements. The type and percentages of grapes used, vinification methods, and taste are all controlled and verified.

Provençal vintners can blend wines using a maximum of 13 different types of grapes (five white and eight red)—unique in France. Only in Châteauneuf-du-Pape are all 13 grapes used; most vintners blend four or five types of grapes. (In Burgundy and Alsace, only one grape variety is used for each wine—so pinot noir, chardonnay, Riesling, Tokay, and pinot gris are each 100 percent from that grape.) This blending allows Provençal winemakers great range in personalizing their wine. The most prevalent types of red grapes are Grenache, Mourvèdre, Syrah, Carignan, and Cinsault. The white grapes include Grenache-Blanc, Roussanne, Marsanne, Bourboulenc, and Clairette.

There are three primary growing areas in Provence: Côtes du Rhône, Côtes de Provence, and Côteaux d'Aix-en-Provence. A few wines are also made along the Provençal Mediterranean coast. All regions produce rich, fruity reds and dry, fresh rosés. Only about five percent of wine produced here is white (the best of which comes from Cassis and Châteauneuf-du-Pape). Most Provençal whites are light, tart, with plenty of citrus and minerals, and work best as a pre-dinner drink or in a *kir*.

In Provence, I often drink rosé instead of white. Don't confuse these rosés with the insipid blush stuff sometimes found in the US; French rosé is often crisp and fruity, a perfect match to the hot days and Mediterranean cuisine. Rosé wines are made from red grapes. After the grapes are crushed, their clear juice is left in contact with their dark-red skins just long enough to produce the pinkish color (no more than 24 hours). Rosés from Tavel (20 minutes north and west of Avignon) are the darkest in color and best-known outside of Provence, but you'll find many good producers at affordable prices in other areas as well. If you're unaccustomed to drinking rosés, try one here.

French Wine Lingo

Here are the steps you should follow when entering any wine-tasting:

1. Greetings, Sir/Madam: *Bonjour, Monsieur/Madame.*

2. We would like to taste a few wines: *Nous voudrions déguster quelques vins* (noo voo-dree-ohn day-goo-stay kehl-kuh van).

3. We want a wine that is ___ and ___: *Nous voudrions un vin ___ et ___.* (noo voo-dree-ohn uhn van ___ ay ___).

Fill in the blanks with your favorites from this list:

English	French	Pronounced
wine	*vin*	van
red	*rouge*	roozh
white	*blanc*	blahn
rosé	*rosé*	roh-zay
light	*léger*	lay-zhay
full-bodied, heavy	*robuste*	roh-boost
fruity	*fruité*	frwee-tay
sweet*	*doux*	doo
tannic	*tannique*	tah-neek
jammy	*confituré*	koh-fee-tuh-ray
fine	*fin, avec finesse*	fan, ah-vehk fee-nehs
ready to drink (mature)	*prêt à boire*	preh tah bwar
not ready to drink	*fermé*	fair-may
oaky	*goût du fût de la chêne*	goo duh foo duh lah sheh-nuh
from old vines	*de vieille vignes*	duh vee-yay-ee veen-yah
sparkling	*pétillant*	pay-tee-yahn

*With the exception of the fortified white Beaumes de Venise (Muscat), few Provençal wines would be considered "sweet."

PROVENCE

Provençal Wine-Tasting 101

The American wine-tasting experience (I'm thinking Napa Valley) is generally informal, chatty, and entrepreneurial (logo-adorned baseball caps and golf shirts). Although Provençal vintners are welcoming and more easygoing than in other parts of France, it's still a serious, wine-focused experience. Your hosts are not there to make small talk, and they're likely to be "all business." For some people, it can be overwhelming to try to make sense of the vast range of options among Provençal wines, particularly when faced with a no-nonsense winemaker or sommelier. Take a deep breath, do your best to follow my instructions, and move on if you don't feel welcome (I've tried to identify which places are most accepting of wine novices). Visit several private wineries or stop by a *cave coopérative*—an excellent opportunity to taste wines from a number of local vintners in a single, less intimidating setting. You'll have a better experience at private wineries if you call ahead to let them know you're coming—even if the winery is open all day, it's good form to announce your visit (ask your hotelier for help).

Provençal winemakers are happy to work with you...*if* they can figure out what you want (which they expect you to know). When you enter a winery, it helps to know what you like (drier or sweeter, lighter or full-bodied, fruity or more tannic, and so on). The people serving you may know those words in English, but you're smart to learn and use these key words in French (see the "French Wine Lingo" sidebar). Avoid visiting places between noon and 14:00—many are closed then, and those that aren't would rather be at lunch.

French wines usually have a lower alcohol level than American or Australian wines. Whereas many Americans like a big, full-bodied wine, most French tend to prefer more subtle flavors. They judge a wine by virtue of how well it pairs with a meal—and a big, oaky wine would overwhelm most French cuisine. The French also enjoy sampling younger wines and divining how they will taste in a few years, allowing them to buy bottles at cheaper prices and stash them in their cellars. Americans want it now—for today's picnic.

Remember that the vintner is hoping you'll buy at least a bottle or two. If you don't, you may be asked to pay a small fee for the tasting. They understand that North Americans can't take much wine with them, and they don't expect to make a big sale, but they do hope you'll look for their wines in the US. Some shops and wineries can arrange shipping (about €15 per bottle to ship a case, though you save about 20 percent on the VAT tax when shipping—so expensive wines are worth the shipping cost).

PROVENCE

On the Wine Label

appellation	area in which a wine's grapes are grown
bouchonné	"corked" (spoiled from a bad cork)
bouquet	bouquet (the fragrance when first opened)
cave	cellar (or wine shop)
cépage	grape variety (Syrah, Chardonnay, etc.)
côte, côteaux	hillside or slope
domaine	wine estate
étiquette	label
fût, tonneau	wine barrel
grand vin	excellent wine
millésimé	wine from a given year
mis en bouteille au château / à la domaine	estate-bottled (bottled where it was made)
vin de table	table wine (can be a blend of several wines)
vin du pays	wine from a given area (a step up from vin de table)

Côtes du Rhône Wines

The Côtes du Rhône, which follows the Rhône River from just south of Lyon to near Avignon, is the king of Provençal wines. Our focus is on the southern section, roughly from Vaison la Romaine to Avignon (though wine-lovers should also try the big, complex reds found in the northern Rhône wines of St. Joseph, Hermitage, and Cornas, as well as the tasty whites of Condrieu). The wines of the southern Rhône are consistently good, sometimes exceptional, and usually inexpensive. The reds are full-bodied, rosés are dry and fruity, and whites are dry and fragrant, often with hints of flowers. Côtes du Rhône whites aren't nearly as good

PROVENCE

Le Mistral

Provence lives with its vicious mistral winds, which blow 30-60 miles per hour, about 100 days out of the year. Locals say it blows in multiples of threes: three, six, or nine days in a row. The mistral clears people off the streets and turns lively cities into ghost towns. You'll likely spend a few hours or days taking refuge. The winds are strongest between noon and 15:00.

When the mistral blows, it's everywhere, and you can't escape. Author Peter Mayle said it could blow the ears off a donkey (I'd include the tail). According to the natives, it ruins crops, shutters, and roofs (look for stones holding tiles in place on many homes). They'll also tell you that this pernicious wind has driven many people crazy (including young Vincent van Gogh). A weak version of the wind is called a mistralet.

The mistral starts above the Alps and Massif Central mountains and gathers steam as it heads south, gaining momentum as it screams over the Rhône Valley (which acts like a funnel between the Alps and the Cévennes mountains) before exhausting itself when it hits the Mediterranean. And though this wind rattles shutters everywhere in the Riviera and Provence, it's strongest over the Rhône Valley... so Avignon, Arles, and the Côtes du Rhône villages bear its brunt. While wiping the dust from your eyes, remember the good news: The mistral brings clear skies.

as the reds, though the rosés are refreshing and ideal for lunch on the terrace. For more on this wine region, including a self-guided driving tour of the area's villages and vintners, ✺ see the Côtes du Rhône chapter.

Many subareas of the southern Côtes du Rhône are recognized for producing outstandingly good wines, and have been awarded their own *appellations* (like Châteauneuf-du-Pape, Gigondas, Beaumes de Venise, Côtes de Ventoux, Tavel, and Côtes du Luberon). Wines often are named for the villages that produce them. The "Côtes du Rhône Villages" appellation is less prestigious, covering 20 villages on the eastern side of the Côtes du Rhône, including Séguret, Sablet, Rasteau, and Cairanne. Strict guidelines govern the production of these wines (called *appellation controllé*).

Here's a summary of what you might find on a Côtes du Rhône *carte des vins* (wine list):

Châteauneuf-du-Pape: Almost all wines from this famous village are reds (often blends; the most dominant grapes are Grenache, Mourvèdre, and Syrah). These wines have a velvety quality and can be spicy, with flavors of licorice and prunes. A few delicious whites are made here and worth sampling. Châteauneuf-du-Pape red wines merit lengthy aging. Considered among the best producers are Château de Beaucastel, Le Vieux Télégraphe, Clos des Papes, and Château la Nerthe. It's a breeze to find their wines in North America. It's also worth seeking out lesser-known names and smaller wineries (many of which are listed in this book).

Gigondas: These wines have many of the same qualities as Châteauneuf-du-Pape, but are lesser known and usually cheaper. Gigondas red wines are spicy, meaty, and can be pretty tannic. Again, aging is necessary to bring out the full qualities of the wine. Look for Domaine du Terme, Château de Montmirail, Domaine de Cassan, or Domaine de Coyeux for good quality.

Beaumes de Venise: While reds from this village are rich and flavorful, Beaumes de Venise is most famous for its Muscat—a sweet, fragrant wine usually served as an apéritif or with dessert. It often has flavors of apricots and peaches, and it should be consumed within two years of bottling. Try Domaine de Coyeux, Domaine de Durban, and Château Redortier.

Rasteau: This village sits across the valley from Gigondas and shares many of its qualities—at lower prices. Rasteau makes fine rosés, robust (at times "rough") and fruity reds, and a naturally sweet wine (Vin Doux Naturel). Their Côtes du Rhône Villages can be excellent. The cooperative in Rasteau is good, as are the wines from Domaine des Girasols.

Sablet: This village lies down in the valley below Gigondas and makes decent, fruity, and inexpensive reds and rosés.

Tavel: The queen of French rosés is 20 minutes north and west of Avignon, close to Pont du Gard. Tavel produces a rosé that is dry, crisp, higher in alcohol, darker, and more full-bodied than other rosés from the region. Look for any rosé from Tavel.

Côtes de Provence Wines

The lesser-known vineyards of the Côtes de Provence run east from Aix-en-Provence almost to St-Tropez. Typical grapes are Cinsault, Mourvèdre, Grenache, Carignan, and a little cabernet sauvignon and Syrah. The wines are commonly full-bodied and fruity, and are meant to be drunk when they're young. They cost less than Côtes du Rhônes and have similar characteristics. But the region is most famous for its "big" rosés that can be served with meat and garlic dishes (rosé accounts for 60 percent of production).

For one-stop shopping, make it a point to find the superb **La Maison des Vins Côtes de Provence** on RN-7 in Les Arcs-sur-Argens (a few minutes north of the A-8 autoroute, about halfway between Aix-en-Provence and Nice). This English-speaking wine shop and tasting center represents hundreds of producers, selling bottles at vineyard prices and offering free tastings of up to 16 wines (April-Sept daily 10:00-19:00; Oct-March Mon-Sat 10:00-18:00, Sun 10:00-17:00, tel. 04 94 99 50 20, www.maison-des-vins.fr).

Côteaux d'Aix-en-Provence Wines

This large wine region, between Les Baux and Aix-en-Provence, produces some interesting reds, whites, and rosés. Commonly used grapes are the same as in Côtes de Provence, though several producers (mainly around Les Baux) use a higher concentration of cabernet sauvignon, which helps distinguish their wines. The vintners around Les Baux produce some exceptionally good wines, and many of their vineyards are organic. Try Domaine d'Eole or Domaine Gourgonnier. The tiny wine-producing area of Palette houses only three wineries, all of which make exceptional rosés; one (Château Simone) also makes a delicious white wine. The Côtes de Provence-Sainte-Victoire wineries, with their beautiful views of Mont Ste-Victoire (famously painted by Cézanne), produce some excellent rosés.

Provençal Mediterranean Wines

Barely east of Marseille, Cassis and Bandol sit side by side, overlooking the Mediterranean. Though very close together, they are designated as separate wine-growing areas because of the distinctive nature of their wines. Cassis is one of France's smallest wine regions and is known for its strong, fresh, and very dry whites (made with the Marsanne grape)—arguably the best white wine in Provence. Bandol is known for its luscious, velvety reds. This wine, aged in old oak and made primarily from the Mourvèdre grape, is one of your author's favorites.

ARLES

By helping Julius Caesar defeat his archrival Gnaeus Pompey at Marseille, Arles (pronounced "arl") earned the imperial nod and was made an important port city. With the first bridge over the Rhône River, Arles was a key stop on the Roman road from Italy to Spain, the Via Domitia. After reigning as the seat of an important archbishop and a trading center for centuries, the city became a sleepy backwater of little importance in the 1700s. Vincent van Gogh settled here in the late 1800s, but left only a chunk of his ear (now long gone). American bombers destroyed much of Arles in World War II as the townsfolk hid out in its underground Roman galleries. But today Arles thrives again, with its evocative Roman ruins, an eclectic assortment of museums, made-for-ice-cream pedestrian zones, and squares that play hide-and-seek with visitors.

Workaday Arles is not a wealthy city, and compared to its neighbors Avignon and Nimes, it feels unpolished and even a little dirty. But to me, that's part of its charm.

Orientation to Arles

Arles faces the Mediterranean, turning its back on Paris. And though the town is built along the Rhône, it largely ignores the river. Landmarks hide in Arles' medieval tangle of narrow, winding streets. Virtually everything is close—but first-timers can walk forever to get there. Hotels have good, free city maps, and

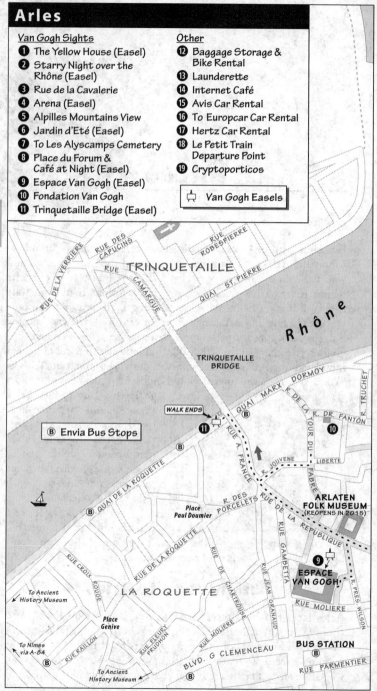

Arles

Van Gogh Sights

1. The Yellow House (Easel)
2. Starry Night over the Rhône (Easel)
3. Rue de la Cavalerie
4. Arena (Easel)
5. Alpilles Mountains View
6. Jardin d'Eté (Easel)
7. To Les Alyscamps Cemetery
8. Place du Forum & Café at Night (Easel)
9. Espace Van Gogh (Easel)
10. Fondation Van Gogh
11. Trinquetaille Bridge (Easel)

Other

12. Baggage Storage & Bike Rental
13. Launderette
14. Internet Café
15. Avis Car Rental
16. To Europcar Car Rental
17. Hertz Car Rental
18. Le Petit Train Departure Point
19. Cryptoporticos

Van Gogh Easels

ARLES

RUE DES CAPUCINS
RUE ROBESPIERRE
RUE DE LA VERRIERE
RUE CAMARGUE
TRINQUETAILLE
QUAI ST. PIERRE

Rhône

TRINQUETAILLE BRIDGE

WALK ENDS

QUAI MARX DORMOY
R. DE LA TOUR DU FABRE
R. TRUCHET
R. DR. FANTON

Ⓑ Envia Bus Stops

RUE A. FRANCE
R. JOUVENE
LIBERTE

QUAI DE LA ROQUETTE

R. DES PORCELETS
RUE DE LA REPUBLIQUE

ARLATEN FOLK MUSEUM
(REOPENS IN 2015)

Place Paul Doumier

RUE CROIX ROUGE
RUE DE LA ROQUETTE
RUE DE CHARTROUSE
RUE MOLIERE
RUE GAMBETTA
RUE JEAN GRANAUD

ESPACE VAN GOGH

R. PRES. WILSON

To Ancient History Museum

Place Genive

RUE RAILLON
RUE FLEURY PRUDHON
RUE MOLIERE

RUE MOLIERE

To Nîmes via A-84

BUS STATION

To Ancient History Museum

BLVD. G. CLEMENCEAU

RUE PARMENTIER

LA ROQUETTE

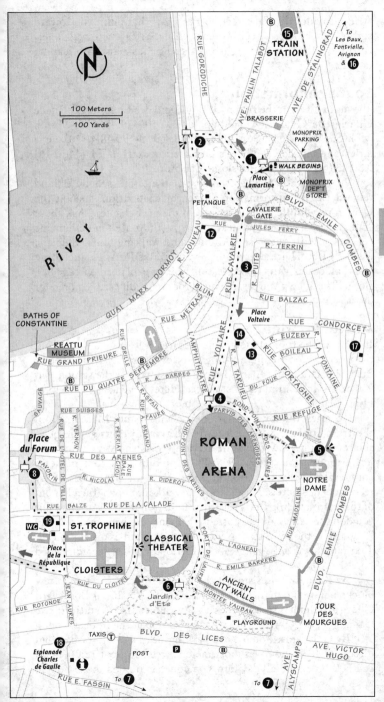

ARLES

N

100 Meters
100 Yards

River

TRAIN
STATION

To
Les Baux,
Fontvielle,
Avignon &

RUE GORODICHE

RUE PAULIN TALABOT

AVE. DE STALINGRAD

BRASSERIE

MONOPRIX
PARKING

WALK BEGINS

Place
Lamartine

MONOPRIX
DEP'T
STORE

PETANQUE

CAVALERIE
GATE

BLVD. EMILE COMBES

QUAI MARX DORMOY

RUE CAVALERIE

JULES FERRY

R. TERRIN

R. PUITS

RUE BALZAC

RUE JOUDEAU

RUE L. BLUM

RUE METRAS

Place
Voltaire

RUE CONDORCET

R. EUZEBY

R. LA FONTAINE

RUE BOILEAU

RUE VOLTAIRE

R. A TARDIEU

DU FOUR

ROND-POINT DES ARENES

RUE PORTAGNEL

RUE REFUGE

BATHS OF
CONSTANTINE

REATTU
MUSEUM

RUE GRAND PRIEURE

RUE GRILLE

RUE DU QUATRE SEPTEMBRE

R. A. BARBES

RUE RASPAIL

RUE FAURE

L'AMPHITHEATRE

PARVIS DES ARENOBES

ROMAN
ARENA

SAUVAGE

RUE SUISSES

RUE DE VERNON

R. PERRIAT

RUE DES ARENES

ACHOU

RUE BRIAND

R. NICOLAI

R. DIDEROT

Place
du Forum

FAVORIN

RUE DE L'HOTEL DE VILLE

NOTRE
DAME

RUE MADELEINE

RUE BALZE

RUE DE LA CALADE

WC

ST. TROPHIME

CLASSICAL
THEATER

Place de la
République

CLOISTERS

RUE DU CLOITRE

Jardin
d'Ete

PORTE DE LAURE

R. L'AGNEAU

R. EMILE BARRERE

ANCIENT
CITY WALLS

MONTEE VAUBAN

BLVD. EMILE COMBES

TOUR
DES
MOURGUES

RUE JEAN JAURES

RUE ROTONDE

TAXIS

POST

BLVD. DES LICES

PLAYGROUND

Esplanade
Charles
de Gaulle

RUE E. FASSIN

To

AVE. VICTOR
HUGO

AVE. ALYSCAMPS

To

Arles provides helpful street-corner signs that point you toward sights and hotels. Speeding cars enjoy Arles' medieval lanes, turning sidewalks into tightropes and pedestrians into leaping targets.

Tourist Information

The **main TI** is on the ring road Boulevard des Lices, at Esplanade Charles de Gaulle (April-Sept daily 9:00-18:45; Oct-March Mon-Sat 9:00-16:45, Sun 10:00-13:00; tel. 04 90 18 41 20, www .arlestourisme.com). There's also a **train station TI** (Mon-Fri 9:30-13:00 & 14:00-18:00, closed Sat-Sun).

At either TI, pick up the city map and bus schedules, and request English information on nearby destinations such as the Camargue wildlife area (described in the next chapter). Ask about "bullgames" in Arles and nearby towns (Provence's more humane version of bullfights—see page 92) and walking tours. Skip the useless €1 brochure describing several walks in Arles, including one that locates Van Gogh's "easels" (better explained on page 87). Both TIs can help you reserve hotel rooms (credit card required for deposit).

Arrival in Arles

By Train: The train station is on the river, a 10-minute walk from the town center. Before heading into town, get what you need at the train station TI. There's no baggage storage at the station, but you can walk 10 minutes to stow it at Hôtel Régence (see "Helpful Hints," later).

To reach the town center or Ancient History Museum from the train station, wait for the free **Envia minibus** at the glass shelter facing away from the station (cross the street and veer left, 3/hour Mon-Sat 7:00-19:00, none Sun). The bus makes a counterclockwise loop around Arles, stopping near most of my recommended hotels. It's a 15-minute **walk** into town (turn left out of the train station). **Taxis** usually wait in front of the station, but if you don't see any, call the posted telephone numbers, or dial 04 89 73 36 00. If the train station TI is open, you can ask them to call. Taxi rates are fixed—allow about €11 to any of my recommended hotels.

By Bus: All buses stop at the Centre-Ville bus station, a few blocks below the main TI, on the ring road at 16-24 Boulevard Georges Clemenceau. Buses to Avignon's TGV station, the Camargue, St-Rémy, and Les Baux also stop at the train station.

By Car: Most hotels have parking nearby—ask for detailed directions (€3/8 hours at most meters; free Mon-Sat 12:00-14:00 & 19:00-9:00, and all day Sun; some meters limited to 2.5 hours).

For most hotels, first follow signs to *Centre-Ville*, then *Gare SNCF* (train station). You'll come to a big roundabout (Place Lamartine) with a Monoprix department store to the right. You can park along the city wall and find your hotel on foot; the hotels I list are no more than a 10-minute walk away (best not to park here overnight due to theft concerns and markets on Wed and Sat). Fearless drivers can plunge into the narrow streets between the two stumpy towers via Rue de la Calade, and follow signs to their hotel. Again, theft is a problem—leave nothing in your car, and trust your hotelier's advice on where to park.

If you can't find parking near your hotel, Parking des Lices (Arles' only parking garage), near the TI on Boulevard des Lices, is a good fallback (€2.30/hour, €16/24 hours).

Helpful Hints

Market Days: The big markets are on Wednesdays and Saturdays. For details, see page 510.

Crowds: An international photo event jams hotels the second weekend of July. The let-'er-rip, twice-yearly Féria draws crowds over Easter and in mid-September (described on page 93).

Internet Access: A cyber café is near Place Voltaire at 31 Rue Augustin Tardieu (daily, tel. 04 90 18 87 40).

Baggage Storage and Bike Rental: The recommended Hôtel Régence will store your bags for €3 (daily 7:30-22:00 mid-March-mid-Nov, closed in winter, 5 Rue Marius Jouveau). They also rent bikes (€7/half-day, €14/day, one-way rentals within Provence possible, same hours as baggage storage) and may have electric bikes—ask. From Arles you can ride to Les Baux (20 miles round-trip). It's a darn steep climb going into Les Baux, so consider busing up there (regional buses have bike racks) and gliding back. Those in great shape can consider biking into the Camargue (40 miles round-trip, forget it in the wind).

Laundry: A launderette is at 12 Rue Portagnel (daily 7:00-21:30, you can stay later to finish if you're already inside, English instructions).

Car Rental: Avis is at the train station (tel. 08 20 05 05 05); **Europcar** and **Hertz** are downtown (Europcar is at 61 Avenue de Stalingrad, tel. 04 90 93 23 24; Hertz is closer to Place Voltaire at 10 Boulevard Emile Combes, tel. 04 90 96 75 23).

Local Guides: Charming **Agnes Barrier,** who knows Arles and nearby sights intimately, enjoys her work. Her tours cover Van Gogh and Roman history (€130/3 hours, mobile 06 11 23 03 73, agnes.barrier@hotmail.fr). **Alice Vallat** loves her native city and offers a variety of scheduled visits of its key sights (€10/person, otherwise €120/3 hours, tel. 06 74 01 22 54 or 04 90 47 75 68, www.guidearles.com, alice.vallat@voila.fr).

English Book Exchange: A small exchange is available at the recommended **Soleileis** ice-cream shop.

Public Pools: Arles has three pools (indoor and outdoor). Ask at the TI or your hotel.

Boules: The local "*boul*ing alley" is by the river on Place Lamartine. After their afternoon naps, the old boys congregate here for a game of pétanque (see page 10 for more on this popular local pastime).

Getting Around Arles

In this flat city, everything's within **walking** distance. Only the Ancient History Museum requires a healthy walk (or you can take a taxi or bus). The elevated riverside promenade provides Rhône views and a direct route to the Ancient History Museum (to the southwest) and the train station (to the northeast). Keep your head up for *Starry Night* memories, but eyes down for decorations by dogs with poorly trained owners.

Arles' **taxis** charge a set fee of about €11, but nothing except the Ancient History Museum is worth a taxi ride. To call a cab, dial 04 89 73 36 00 or 04 90 96 90 03.

The free **Envia minibus** circles the town, useful for access to the train station and the Ancient History Museum (see map on page 96, 3/hour, Mon-Sat 7:00-19:00, none Sun).

Le Petit Train d'Arles, a typical tourist train, gives you the lay of the land—if you prefer sitting to walking (€7, 35 minutes, stops in front of the main TI and at the Roman Arena).

Sights in Arles

Most sights cost €3.50-7, and though any sight warrants a few minutes, many aren't worth their individual admission price. The TI sells two different monument passes (called Passeports). **Le Passeport Avantage** covers almost all of Arles' sights (€13.50, under age 18-€12); **Le Passeport Liberté** (€9) lets you choose any five monuments (one must be a museum). Depending on your interests, the €9 Passeport is probably best.

Start at the Ancient History Museum (closed Tue) for a helpful overview (drivers should try to do this museum on their way into Arles), then dive into the city-center sights. Remember, many sights stop selling tickets 30-60 minutes before closing (both before lunch and at the end of the day). To make the most of Arles' Roman history, see page 59.

▲▲Ancient History Museum (Musée de l'Arles et de la Provence Antiques)

Begin your town visit here, for Roman Arles 101. Located on

the site of the Roman chariot racecourse (the arc of which is built into the parking lot), this air-conditioned, all-on-one-floor museum is just west of central Arles along the river. Models and original sculptures (with almost no posted English translations but a decent handout) re-create the Roman city, making workaday life and culture easier to imagine.

Cost and Hours: €8, Wed-Mon 10:00-18:00, closed Tue, Presqu'île du Cirque Romain, tel. 04 13 31 51 03, www.arles-antique.cg13.fr. Ask for the English booklet, which provides a helpful if not in-depth background on the collection.

Getting There: To reach the museum, take the free **Envia minibus** (stops at the train station and along Rue du 4 Septembre, then along the river, 3/hour Mon-Sat, none Sun). If you're coming **on foot** from the city center (a 20-minute walk), turn left at the river and take the scruffy riverside path under two bridges to the big, modern blue building (or better, consider strolling through Arles' enjoyable La Roquette neighborhood, described later). As you approach the museum, you'll pass the verdant Hortus Garden—designed to recall the Roman circus and chariot racecourse that were located here. A **taxi** ride costs €11 (museum can call a taxi for your return).

❍ Self-Guided Tour: The permanent collection is housed in two large rooms separated by dividers and exhibits.

A wall **map** of the region during the Roman era greets visitors and shows the geographic importance of Arles: Three important Roman trade routes—vias Domitia, Grippa, and Aurelia—all converged on or near Arles. In the next area, you'll see a model of a **pre-Roman** settlement (compare this hovel with the elegant buildings constructed during the Roman period). You'll then pass maps showing Roman Arles' expanding city limits.

Next, you'll see **models** of every Roman structure in (and near) Arles. These are the highlight for me, as they breathe life into the buildings as they looked 2,000 years ago. Start

Arles at a Glance

▲▲▲**Roman Arena** This big amphitheater, once used by gladiators, today hosts summer "bullgames" and occasional bullfights. **Hours:** Daily May-Sept 9:00-19:00, March-April and Oct 9:00-18:00, Nov-Feb 10:00-17:00. See page 85.

▲▲**Ancient History Museum** Filled with models and sculptures, this museum takes you back to Arles' Roman days. **Hours:** Wed-Mon 10:00-18:00, closed Tue. See page 77.

▲▲**Forum Square** Lively, café-crammed square that was once the Roman forum. **Hours:** Always open. See page 80.

▲▲**St. Trophime Church** Church with exquisite Romanesque entrance. **Hours:** Church—daily April-Sept 9:00-12:00 & 14:00-18:30, Oct-March 9:00-12:00 & 14:00-17:00; cloisters—daily May-Sept 9:00-19:00, March-April and Oct 9:00-18:00, Nov-Feb 10:00-17:00. See page 82.

▲**Arlaten Folk Museum** Shares the treasures and pleasures of Provençal life from the 18th and 19th centuries. Closed for renovation in 2014.

▲**Fondation Van Gogh** Small gallery with works by major contemporary artists paying homage to Van Gogh and at least one

with the model of Roman Arles and ponder the city's splendor over 2,000 years ago when Arles' population was double that of today. That's something to chew on. Find the forum—still the center of town today, though only two columns survive (the smaller section of the forum is where today's Place du Forum is built). Look at the space Romans devoted to their arena and huge racecourse—a reminder that an emphasis on sports is not unique to modern civilizations (the museum you're in is at the non-city end of the course). The model also illustrates how little Arles seems to have changed over two millennia, with its houses still clustered around the city center, and warehouses still located on the opposite side of the river.

Prowl the room for individual models of the major buildings shown in the city model: the elaborately elegant forum; the floating wooden bridge that gave Arles a strategic advantage (over the widest, and therefore slowest, part of the river); the theater (with its magnificent stage wall); the arena (with its movable stadium cover to shelter spectators from sun or rain); and the hydraulic mill of Barbegal (with its 16 waterwheels powered by water cascading down a hillside).

original piece painted during Van Gogh's time in the region. **Hours:** Daily 11:00-19:00 except likely closed Mon off-season. See page 86.

Cryptoporticos Underground support structure for Roman forum. **Hours:** Daily May-Sept 9:00-12:00 & 14:00-19:00, March-April and Oct 9:00-12:00 & 14:00-18:00, Nov-Feb 10:00-12:00 & 14:00-17:00. See page 84.

Classical Theater Ruined Roman theater, recently restored and still used for events. **Hours:** Daily May-Sept 9:00-19:00, March-April and Oct 9:00-18:00, Nov-Feb 10:00-17:00. See page 84.

Baths of Constantine Remains of Arles' Roman public baths. **Hours:** Daily, 9:00-12:00 & 14:00-18:00. See page 86.

Réattu Museum Decent, mostly modern art collection in a fine 15th-century mansion. **Hours:** Tue-Sun July-Sept 10:00-19:00, Oct-June 10:00-12:30 & 14:00-18:30, closed Mon year-round. See page 86.

La Roquette District Arles' little-visited western fringe, with cafés, bakeries, and bistros. **Hours:** Always open. See page 86.

ARLES

You'll also see displays of pottery, jewelry, metal, and glass artifacts, and well-crafted mosaic floors that illustrate how Roman Arles was a city of art and culture. The many **statues** are all original, except for the greatest—the *Venus of Arles*, which Louis XIV took a liking to and had moved to Versailles. It's now in the Louvre—and, as locals say, "When it's in Paris...bye-bye."

The statue of Caesar Augustus stood in the center of Arles' theater stage wall. Throughout the hall you'll come across expertly carved pagan and early-Christian **sarcophagi** (from the second to fifth centuries A.D.). These would have lined the Via Aurelia outside the town wall. In the early days of the Church, Jesus was often portrayed beardless and as the good shepherd, with a lamb over his shoulder.

The museum's newest and most exciting exhibit is the **Gallo-Roman vessel** and much of its cargo. This almost-100-foot-long Roman barge was pulled out of the Rhône in 2010, along with some 280 amphorae and 3,000 ceramic artifacts (you'll pass a worthwhile video—just before entering the room—describing how the barge was removed from the river). It was typical of flat-bottomed barges used to shuttle goods between Arles and ports

A Day in the Life of an Arles Citizen in the Roman Era

Ancient Rome has often been compared to America...without cars or electricity, but with slaves to make up for it. Rome's wealth made a lifestyle possible that was the envy of the known world. Let's look at a typical well-to-do Arles citizen and his family in the era of Roman rule over the course of a day.

In the morning, Nebulus reviews the finances of the country farm with his caretaker/accountant/slave. He's interrupted by a "client," one of many poorer people dependent upon him for favors. The client, a shoemaker, wants permission from the government to open a new shop. He asks Nebulus to cut through the red tape. Nebulus promises to consult a lawyer friend in the basilica, or legal building.

Hungry, Nebulus stops at Burger Emp to grab a typical fast-food lunch. Most city dwellers don't cook in their cramped, wooden apartments because of the fire hazard. After a siesta, he walks to the baths for a workout and a little business networking. He discusses plans for donating money to build a new aqueduct for the city.

The children, Raucous and Ubiquitous, say good-bye to the pet dog and head off to school in the Forum. Nothing funny happens on the way. At school, it's down to business. They learn the basic three Rs. When they get older, they'll study literature, Greek, and public speaking. (The saving grace of this dreary education is that they don't have to take Latin.)

Work done, Nebulus heads for the stadium. The public is crazy about the chariot races. There are 12 per day, 240 days a year. Four teams dominate the competition (Reds, Whites, Blues, and Greens), and Nebulus has always been a die-hard Blue.

Back home, Nebulus' wife, Vapid, tends to the household affairs. She pauses in the bedroom to offer a prayer to her per-

along the Mediterranean (vessels were manually towed upriver). The same hall shows a large model of the chariot racecourse. Part of the original racecourse was just outside the windows, and though long gone, it must have resembled Rome's Circus Maximus in its day.

From Forum Square to the Roman Arena

Ideally, visit these sights in the order listed below. I've included some walking directions to connect the dots (see the Arles map on pages 72-73).

▲▲Forum Square (Place du Forum)

Named for the Roman forum that once stood here, Place du Forum was the political and religious center of Roman Arles. Still lively, this café-crammed square is a local watering hole and popular for

sonal goddess for good weather for tonight. Meanwhile, the servants clean the house and send clothing to the laundry. A typical outfit is a simple woolen tunic: two pieces of cloth, front and back, sewn together at the sides. But tonight they'll dress up for a dinner party. She'll wear silk, with a wreath of flowers, and Nebulus will wear his best toga, a 20-foot-long white cloth. It's heavy and hard to put on, but it's all the rage. Nebulus dons his phallic-shaped necklace, which serves as an amulet against the evil eye and as a symbol of good luck in health, business, and bed.

At the dinner party, Vapid marvels over the chef's creation: ham soaked with honey, pasted in flour and baked. The guests toast each other with clay goblets bearing inscriptions like "Fill me up," and "Love me, baby!" Reclining on a couch, waited on by slaves, Nebulus orders a bowl of larks' tongues and a roast pig stuffed with live birds, then washes it down with wine. He calls for a feather, vomits, and starts all over. He catches the eye of a dark-skinned slave dancer from Egypt, and he takes her to the bedroom just down the hall...

...Or so went the stories. In fact, the legendary Roman orgy was just that—legendary. Romans advocated moderation and fidelity. Stuffiness and business sense were the rule. The family unit was considered sacred. If anything, the decadence of Roman life was confined to the upper classes in the later years of the empire.

ARLES

---

a *pastis* (anise-based apéritif). The bistros on the square, though no place for a fine dinner, can put together a good-enough salad or *plat du jour*—and when you sprinkle on the ambience, that's €12 well spent.

At the corner of Grand Hôtel Nord-Pinus (a favorite of Pablo Picasso), a plaque shows how the Romans built a foundation of galleries to make the main square level in order to compensate for Arles' slope down to the river. The two columns are all that survive from the upper story of the entry to

the forum. Steps leading to the entrance are buried—the Roman street level was about 20 feet below you (you can get a glimpse of it by peeking through the street-level openings under the Hôtel d'Arlatan, two blocks below Place du Forum on Rue du Sauvage; find information panels above the openings).

The statue on the square is of **Frédéric Mistral** (1830-1914). This popular poet, who wrote in the local dialect rather than in French, was a champion of Provençal culture. After receiving the Nobel Prize in Literature in 1904, Mistral used his prize money to preserve and display the folk identity of Provence. He founded the regional folk museum (the Arlaten Folk Museum, described later) at a time when France was rapidly centralizing. (The local mistral wind—literally "master"—has nothing to do with his name.)

The **bright-yellow café**—called Café la Nuit—was the subject of one of Vincent van Gogh's most famous works in Arles. Although his painting showed the café in a brilliant yellow from the glow of gas lamps, the facade was bare limestone, just like the other cafés on this square. The café's current owners have painted it to match Van Gogh's version...and to cash in on the Vincent-crazed hordes who pay too much to eat or drink here.

• *With your back to Café la Nuit, walk left one block (past Grand Hôtel Nord Pinus) and turn left. Walk through Hôtel de Ville's vaulted entry (or take the next right if it's closed), and pop out onto the big...*

Republic Square (Place de la République)
This square used to be called "Place Royale"...until the French Revolution. The obelisk was the former centerpiece of Arles' Roman Circus. The lions at its base are the symbol of the city, whose slogan is (roughly) "the gentle lion." Find a seat and watch the peasants—pilgrims, locals, and street musicians. There's nothing new about this scene.

• *Find the exquisitely carved facade of...*

▲▲St. Trophime Church
Named after a third-century bishop of Arles, this church sports the finest Romanesque main entrance I've seen anywhere. The Romanesque-and-Gothic interior, with tapestries and relics, is worth a wander. The cloisters are skippable.

Cost and Hours: Church—free, daily April-Sept 9:00-12:00 & 14:00-18:30, Oct-March 9:00-12:00 & 14:00-17:00; cloisters—€3.50, similar hours as church, but open all day (no lunch break).

◆ Self-Guided Tour: Like a Roman triumphal arch, the church facade trumpets the promise of Judgment Day. The tympanum (the semicircular area above the door) is filled with Christian symbolism. Christ sits in majesty, surrounded by symbols of the four evangelists: Matthew (the winged man), Mark (the winged lion), Luke (the ox), and John (the eagle). The

12 apostles are lined up below Jesus. It's Judgment Day...some are saved and others aren't. Notice the condemned (on the right)—a chain gang doing a sad bunny-hop over the fires of hell. For them, the tune trumpeted by the three angels above Christ is not a happy one. Below the chain gang, St. Stephen is being stoned to death, with his soul leaving through his mouth and instantly being welcomed by angels. Ride the exquisite detail back to a simpler age. In an illiterate medieval world, long before the vivid images of our Technicolor time, this was a neon billboard over the town square.

Interior: Just inside the door on the right, a chart locates the interior highlights and helps explain the carvings you just saw on the tympanum.

Tour the church counterclockwise. The tall 12th-century Romanesque nave is decorated by a set of tapestries showing scenes from the life of Mary (17th century, from the French town of Aubusson). Amble around the Gothic apse. Two-thirds of the way around, find the relic chapel behind the ornate wrought iron gate, with its fine golden boxes that hold long-venerated bones of obscure saints. The next chapel houses the skull of St. Anthony of the Desert, with good English explanations. Several chapels down, look for the early-Christian sarcophagus from Roman Arles (dated about A.D. 300) under the black columns. The heads were lopped off during the French Revolution.

This church is a stop on the ancient pilgrimage route to Santiago de Compostela in northwest Spain. For 800 years pilgrims on their way to Santiago have paused here...and they still do today. Notice the modern-day pilgrimages advertised on the far right near the church's entry.

Cloisters: Leaving the church, turn left, then left again through a courtyard to enter the adjacent cloisters. The cloisters are worth a look only if you have a pass (big cleaning underway, enter at the far end of the courtyard). The many small columns were scavenged from the ancient Roman theater. Enjoy the sculpted capitals, the rounded 12th-century Romanesque arches, and the pointed 14th-century Gothic ones. The pretty vaulted hall exhibits 17th-century tapestries showing scenes from the First Crusade to the Holy Land. On the second floor, you'll walk along an angled rooftop designed to catch rainwater—notice the slanted gutter that channeled the water into a cistern and the heavy roof slabs covering the tapestry hall below.

• Return to the square and walk into the Hôtel de Ville to find the entrance to...

Cryptoporticos (Cryptoportiques)

This dark, drippy underworld of Roman arches was constructed to support the upper half of Forum Square. Two thousand years ago, most of this gallery of arches was at or above street level; modern Arles has buried about 20 feet of its history over the millennia. Pick up the minimalist English flier and read it before you descend into the dark.

Cost and Hours: €3.50, daily May-Sept 9:00-12:00 & 14:00-19:00, March-April and Oct 9:00-12:00 & 14:00-18:00, Nov-Feb 10:00-12:00 & 14:00-17:00.

• Walk up Rue de la Calade to reach the...

Classical Theater (Théâtre Antique)

This first-century B.C. Roman theater once seated 10,000...just like the theater in Orange. But unlike Orange, here in Arles there was no hillside to provide support.
This theater was an elegant, three-level structure with 27 arches radiating out to the street level. From the outside, it looked much like a halved version of Arles' Roman Arena. For more on Roman theaters, read about the theater in
Orange (see page 181) and spring for the helpful €3 brochure.

Cost and Hours: €6.50, daily May-Sept 9:00-19:00, March-April and Oct 9:00-18:00, Nov-Feb 10:00-17:00. Budget travelers can peek over the fence from Rue du Cloître and see just about everything for free.

Visiting the Theater: Start with the video outside, which provides helpful background information and images that make it easier to put the scattered stones back in place (crouch in front to make out the small English subtitles). You'll also find a large information panel nearby on the grass that adds more context. Walk into the theater and pull up a stone seat in a center aisle. To appreciate the theater's original size, look left (about 9:00) to the upper-left side of the tower and find the protrusion that supported the highest seating level. The structure required 33 rows of seats covering three levels to accommodate demand. During the Middle Ages, the old theater became a convenient town quarry—St. Trophime Church was built from theater rubble. Precious little of the original theater survives—though it still is used for events, with seating for 3,000 spectators.

Two lonely Corinthian columns are all that remain of a three-story stage wall that once featured more than 100 columns and statues painted in vibrant colors. Actors with main roles entered through the central arch, over which a grand statue of Caesar Augustus stood (on display at the Ancient History Museum). Bit players entered through side arches. The orchestra section is defined by a semicircular pattern in the stone in front of you. Stepping up onto the left side of the stage, look down to the slender channel that allowed the brilliant-red curtain to disappear below, like magic. The stage, which was built of wood, was about 160 feet across and 20 feet deep. The actors' changing rooms are backstage, down the steps.

• *A block uphill is the...*

▲▲▲Roman Arena (Amphithéâtre)

Nearly 2,000 years ago, gladiators fought wild animals here to the delight of 20,000 screaming fans. Today local daredevils still fight

wild animals here—"bullgame" posters around the arena advertise upcoming spectacles (see page 92). A lengthy restoration process is now complete, giving the amphitheater an almost bleached-teeth whiteness.

Cost and Hours: €6.50, daily May-Sept 9:00-19:00, March-April and Oct 9:00-18:00, Nov-Feb 10:00-17:00, Rond-point des Arènes, tel. 08 91 70 03 70, www.arenes-arles.com.

Visiting the Arena: After passing the ticket kiosk, find the helpful English information display that describes the arena's history and renovation, then take a seat in the upper deck. In Roman times, games were free (sponsored by city bigwigs), and fans were seated by social class. Thirty-four rows of stone bleachers extended all the way to the top of those vacant arches that circle the arena. All arches were numbered to help distracted fans find their seats. The many passageways you'll see (called vomitoires) allowed for rapid dispersal after the games—fights would break out among frenzied fans if they couldn't leave quickly. During medieval times and until the early 1800s, the arches were bricked up and the stadium became a fortified town—with 200 humble homes crammed within its circular defenses. Parts of three of the medieval towers survive (the one above the ticket booth is open and rewards those who climb it with terrific views). To see two still-sealed arches—complete with cute medieval window frames—turn right as you leave, walk to the L'Andaluz Restaurant, and look back to the second floor.

For more on Roman amphitheaters, see the description of Nîmes' amphitheater on page 160.

ARLES

More Sights in Arles

▲Fondation Van Gogh

This art foundation delivers a refreshing stop for modern-art lovers and Van Gogh fans with temporary exhibits where artists pay homage to Vincent through thought-provoking interpretations of his works (for more on Vincent, see "Van Gogh Sights in Arles," later). You'll also see at least one original work by Van Gogh (painted during his time in the region) and Japanese prints that were so influential to his work.

The second-floor terrace offers a good view of the kaleidoscope-roof by Raphael Hefti (whose works strive to combine art, science, and manufacturing processes); the fourth-floor terrace offers expansive panoramas over Arles' rooftops. There's a good variety of Van Gogh souvenirs, prints, and postcards in the gift shop.

Cost and Hours: €9, daily 11:00-19:00, except likely closed Mon off-season, may close in between temporary exhibits, audioguide-€3; Hôtel Leautaud de Donines, 35 Rue du Docteur Fanton, tel. 04 90 49 94 04, www.fondation-vincentvangogh -arles.org.

La Roquette District

To escape the tourist beat in Arles, take a detour into Arles' little-visited western fringe. Find Rue de la Roquette near the Trinquetaille Bridge and stroll several blocks into pleasing Place Paul Doumier, where you'll find a lively assortment of cafés, bakeries, and inexpensive bistros with nary a tourist in sight (see map on page 72). Continue along Rue de la Roquette and turn right on charming Rue Croix Rouge to reach the river. Those walking to or from the Ancient History Museum can use this appealing stroll as a shortcut.

Baths of Constantine (Thermes de Constantin)

These partly intact Roman baths were built in the early fourth century when Emperor Constantine declared Arles an imperial residence. Roman cities such as Arles had several public baths like this, which were used as much for exercising, networking, and chatting with friends as for bathing. These baths were located near the Rhône River for easy water access. You can get a pretty good look at the baths through the fence (€3, daily 9:00-12:00 & 14:00-18:00).

Réattu Museum (Musée Réattu)

Housed in the former Grand Priory of the Knights of Malta, this modern-art collection is always changing. The permanent collection usually includes a series of works by homegrown Neoclassical artist Jacques Réattu, along with at least one Picasso painting and a roomful of his drawings (donated by the artist, some two-sided and all done in a flurry of creativity). The museum shuffles its large Picasso collection around regularly (they have more works than space to display them). Most of the three-floor museum houses (usually worthwhile) temporary exhibits of modern artists; check the website to see who's playing.

Cost and Hours: €8, free first Sun of each month, July-Sept Tue-Sun 10:00-19:00, Oct-June Tue-Sun 10:00-12:30 & 14:00-18:30, closed Mon year-round, last entry 30 minutes before closing for lunch or at end of day, 10 Rue du Grand Prieuré, tel. 04 90 96 37 68, www.museereattu.arles.fr.

▲Arlaten Folk Museum (Musée Arlaten/Museon Arlaten)

This museum, which explains the ins and outs of daily Provençal life, is closed for renovation until 2015. Ask at the TI or check the museum's website for the latest (www.museonarlaten.fr, French only).

Van Gogh Sights in Arles

In the dead of winter in 1888, 35-year-old Dutch artist Vincent van Gogh left big-city Paris for Provence, hoping to jump-start his floundering career and personal life. He was as inspired as he was lonely. Coming from the gray skies and flat lands of the north, Vincent was bowled over by everything Provençal—the sun, bright colors, rugged landscape, and raw people. For the next two years he painted furiously, cranking out a masterpiece every few days.

None of the 200-plus paintings that Van Gogh did in the south can be found today in the city that so moved him. But you can walk the same streets he knew and see places he painted, marked by about a dozen steel-and-concrete "**easels**," with photos of the final paintings for then-and-now comparisons. The TI has a €1 brochure that locates all the easels (those described in this book are easily found without the brochure). Small stone markers with yellow accents embedded in the pavement lead to the easels.

• *Take a walk in Vincent's footsteps (roughly north to south through Arles' center) and watch his paintings come to life by putting yourself in his shoes (use the map on pages 72-73). Start at **Place Lamartine** and find the stone easel by the grass with the big Monoprix to your right.*

❶ The Yellow House Easel: Vincent arrived in Arles on February 20, 1888, to a foot of snow. He rented a small house on the north side of Place Lamartine. The house was destroyed in 1944 by an errant bridge-seeking bomb, but the four-story building behind it—where you see the brasserie—still stands (find it in the painting). The

house had four rooms, including a small studio and the cramped trapezoid-shaped bedroom made famous in paintings. It was painted yellow inside and out, and Vincent named it..."The Yellow House." In the distance, the painting shows the same bridges you see today, as well as a steam train—which was a rather recent invention in France, allowing people like Vincent to travel greater distances and be jarred by new experiences. (Today's TGV system continues that trend.)

Freezing Arles was buttoned up tight when Vincent arrived, so he was forced to work inside, where he painted still lifes and self-portraits—anything to keep his brush moving. In late March, spring finally arrived. In those days, a short walk from Place Lamartine led to open fields. Donning his straw hat, Vincent set up his easel outdoors and painted quickly, capturing what he saw and felt—the blossoming fruit trees, gnarled olive trees, peasants sowing and reaping, jagged peaks, and windblown fields, all lit by a brilliant sun that drove him to use ever-brighter paints.

• *Walk to the river, passing a monument in honor of two WWII American pilots killed in action during the liberation of Arles. The monument was erected in 2002 as a post-9/11 sign of solidarity with Americans. Find the easel in the wall where ramps lead down to the river (this is also about where the Roman bridge would have crossed the Rhône).*

❷ **Starry Night over the Rhône Easel:** One night, Vincent set up shop along the river and painted the stars boiling above the city skyline. Vincent looked to the night sky for the divine and was the first to paint outside after dark, adapting his straw hat to hold candles (which must have blown the minds of locals back then). As his paintings progressed, the stars became larger and more animated (like Vincent himself). The lone couple in the painting pops up again and again in his work. Experts say that Vincent was desperate for a close relationship with another being...someone to stroll the riverbank with under a star-filled sky. (Note: This painting is not the *Starry Night* you're thinking of—that one was painted later in St-Rémy; described on page 118.)

To his sister Wilhelmina, Van Gogh wrote, "At present I absolutely want to paint a starry sky. It often seems to me that night is still more richly colored than the day; having hues of the most intense violets, blues, and greens. If only you pay attention to it, you will see that certain stars are lemon-yellow, others pink or a green, blue, and forget-me-not brilliance." Vincent painted this scene on his last night in Arles. Come back at night to match his painting with today's scene.

• *Turn around and walk through the small park, then go into town between the stumpy stone towers along* ❸ *Rue de la Cavalerie, which becomes Rue Voltaire.*

Van Gogh walked into town the same way. Arles' 19th-century red light district was just east of Rue de la Cavalerie, and the far-from-home Dutchman spent many lonely nights in its bars and brothels. The street retains a certain local color—drop in to the down-and-dirty café at Hôtel de Paris for a taste.

• *Keep straight through Place Voltaire, continue walking up Rue Voltaire to the Roman Arena, and then find the easel at the top of the arena steps, to the right.*

❹ **Arena Easel:** All summer long, fueled by sun and alcohol, Vincent painted the town. He loved the bullfights in the arena and sketched the colorful surge of the crowds, spending more time studying the people than watching the bullfights (notice how the bull is barely visible). Vincent had little interest in Arles' antiquity—it was people and nature that fascinated him.

• *Walk clockwise around the arena, then up the cobbled lane next to L'Andaluz Restaurant. Keep left in the parking lot to find a viewpoint.*

❺ **Alpilles Mountains View:** This view (no easel) pretty much matches what Vincent would have seen (be here late in the day for the best light). Vincent was an avid walker. Imagine him hauling his easel into those fields under intense sun, leaning against a ferocious wind, struggling to keep his hat on. He did this about 50 times during his stay in Arles, just to paint the farm workers. Vincent venerated but did not glorify peasants. Wanting to show their lives and their struggles, he reproached Renoir and Monet for elevating them in their works.

Vincent carried his easel as far as the medieval abbey of Montmajour, that bulky structure three miles straight ahead on the hill. The St. Paul Hospital, where he was eventually treated in St-Rémy, is on the other side of the Alpilles mountains, several miles beyond Montmajour. On a clear day, you can make out the hill town of Les Baux at about two o'clock (with Montmajour at high noon).

• *Continue along the upper end of the arena, turn left before the Classical Theater, and walk out Rue de Porte de Laure. Just after the street turns left, go right, down the curved staircase into the park and find the easel on the second path to the right.*

❻ **Jardin d'Eté Easel:** Vincent spent many a sunny day painting the leafy Jardin d'Eté. In another letter to his sister, Vincent wrote, "I don't know whether you can understand that one may make a poem by arranging colors...In a similar manner, the bizarre lines, purposely selected and multiplied, meandering all through the picture may not present a literal image of the garden, but they may present it to our minds as if in a dream."

Vincent never made real friends, though he desperately wanted to. The son of disinterested parents, he never found the social skills necessary to sustain close friendships. He palled around with (and painted) his mailman and a Foreign Legionnaire. (The fact that locals pronounced his name "vahn-saw van gog" had nothing to do with his psychological struggles here.)

Packing his paints and a picnic in a rucksack, he day-tripped to the old Roman cemetery of ❼ **Les Alyscamps,** a 10-minute detour from this route (across the busy street and to the left).

• *Continue through the gardens, walking toward the arches of the Classical Theater and exit the park at the upper-right corner. Turn right on Rue du Cloître, then turn left on Rue de la Calade and stroll downhill for several blocks. Turn right on Rue du Palais to find* **Place du Forum;** *locate an easel one café down from the yellow Café la Nuit.*

ARLES

❽ *Café at Night* **Easel:** In October, lonely Vincent—who dreamed of making Arles a magnet for fellow artists—persuaded his friend Paul Gauguin to come. He decorated Gauguin's room with several humble canvases of sunflowers (now some of the world's priciest paintings), knowing that Gauguin had admired a similar painting he'd done in Paris. Their plan was for Gauguin to be the "dean" of a new art school in Arles, and Vincent its instructor-in-chief. At first, the two got along well. They spent days side by side, rendering the same subject in their two distinct styles. At night they hit the bars and brothels. Van Gogh's well-known *Café at Night* captures the glow of an absinthe buzz at Café la Nuit on Place du Forum.

After two months together, the two artists clashed over art and personality differences (Vincent was a slob around the house, whereas Gauguin was meticulous). The night of December 23, they were drinking absinthe at the café when Vincent suddenly went ballistic. He threw his glass at Gauguin. Gauguin left. Walking through Place Victor Hugo, Gauguin heard footsteps behind him and turned to see Vincent coming at him, brandishing a razor. Gauguin quickly fled town. The local paper reported what happened next: "At 11:30 p.m., Vincent Vaugogh [*sic*], painter from Holland, appeared at the brothel at no. 1, asked for Rachel, and gave her his cut-off earlobe, saying, 'Treasure this precious object.' Then he vanished." He woke up the next morning at home with his head wrapped in a bloody towel and his earlobe missing. Was Vincent emulating a successful matador, whose prize is cutting off the bull's ear?

• *From here retrace your steps and walk into Place de la République, turn right in the square's far corner (Rue de la République), and walk to the Arlaten Folk Museum. Turn left on Rue Président Wilson, and find*

Espace Van Gogh (on the right through the arch). There's an easel in the courtyard near the postcard racks.

❾ Espace Van Gogh Easel: Vincent was checked into the local hospital—today's Espace Van Gogh cultural center (the Espace is free, but only the courtyard is open to the public). It surrounds a flowery courtyard that the artist loved and painted, when he was being treated for blood loss, hallucinations, and severe depression that left him bedridden for a month. The citizens of Arles circulated a petition demanding that the mad Dutchman be kept under

medical supervision. Félix Rey, Vincent's kind doctor, worked out a compromise: The artist could leave during the day so that he could continue painting, but he had to sleep at the hospital at night. Look through the postcards sold in the courtyard and find a painting of Vincent's ward showing nuns attending to patients in a gray hall *(Ward of Arles Hospital).*

In the spring of 1889, the bipolar genius (a modern diagnosis) admitted himself to the St. Paul Monastery and Hospital in

St-Rémy-de-Provence (see page 118), where he spent a year, thriving in the care of nurturing doctors and nuns. Painting was part of his therapy, so they gave him a studio to work in, and he produced more than 100 paintings. Alcohol-free and institutionalized, he did some of his wildest work. With thick, swirling brushstrokes and surreal colors, he made his placid surroundings throb with restless energy. Today, at the hospital in St-Rémy, you can see a replica of his room and his studio, plus many scenes he painted *in situ* like these in Arles—the courtyard, the plane trees, the view out the upstairs window of nearby fields, and the rugged Alpilles mountains.

In the spring of 1890, Vincent left Provence to be cared for by a sympathetic doctor in Auvers-sur-Oise, north of Paris. On July 27, he wandered into a field and shot himself. He died two days later.

• *To see paintings by artists inspired by Van Gogh,* find the **Fondation Van Gogh** on your map ❿ *(should reopen in spring of 2014; described on page 86). The easels below are less central, but easily located and worth the effort for Van Gogh fans.*

Bridge Easels: The ⓫ **Trinquetaille Bridge** is on the river walkway toward the Ancient History Museum (the current bridge is a 1951 replacement). Most famous, the **Langlois Drawbridge** is 1.5 miles south of town, along a Rhône canal (today's bridge is a 1926 duplicate of the original).

Experiences in Arles

▲▲Markets

On Wednesday and Saturday mornings, Arles' ring road erupts into an open-air festival of fish, flowers, produce...and everything Provençal. The main event is on Saturday, with vendors jamming the ring road from Boulevard Emile Combes to the east, along Boulevard des Lices near the TI (the heart of the market), and continuing down Boulevard Georges Clemenceau to the west. Wednesday's market runs only along Boulevard Emile Combes, between Place Lamartine and bis Avenue Victor Hugo; the segment nearest Place Lamartine is all about food, and the upper half features clothing, tablecloths, purses, and so on. On the first Wednesday of the month, a flea market doubles the size of the usual Wednesday market along Boulevard des Lices near the main TI. Join in: Buy some flowers for your hotelier, try the olives, sample some wine, and swat a pickpocket. Both markets are open until 12:30.

Part of the market has a North African feel, thanks to the Algerians and Moroccans who live in Arles. They came to do the lowly city jobs that locals didn't want, and now they mostly do the region's labor-intensive agricultural jobs (picking olives, harvesting fruit, and working in local greenhouses; see sidebar on page 263).

▲▲Bullgames *(Courses Camarguaises)*

Provençal "bullgames" are held in Arles and in neighboring towns. Those in Arles occupy the same seats that fans have used for nearly 2,000 years, and take in the city's most memorable experience—the *courses camarguaises* in the ancient arena. The nonviolent "bullgames" are more sporting than bloody bullfights (though traditional Spanish-style bullfights still take place on occasion). The bulls of Arles (who, locals stress, "die of old age") are promoted in posters even more boldly than their human foes. In the bullgame, a ribbon *(cocarde)* is laced between the bull's horns. The *razeteur,* with a special hook, has 15 minutes to snare the ribbon. Local businessmen encourage a *razeteur*

(dressed in white, with a red cummerbund) by shouting out how much money they'll pay for the *cocarde*. If the bull pulls a good stunt, the band plays the famous "Toreador" song from *Carmen*. The following day, newspapers report on the games, including how many *Carmens* the bull earned.

Three classes of bullgames—determined by the experience of the *razeteurs*—are advertised in posters: The *course de protection* is for rookies. The *trophée de l'Avenir* comes with more experience. And the *trophée des As* features top professionals. During Easter and the fall rice-harvest festival *(Féria du Riz)*, the arena hosts traditional Spanish bullfights (look for *corrida*) with outfits, swords, spikes, and the whole gory shebang.

Don't pass on a chance to see *Toro Piscine*, a silly spectacle for warm summer evenings where the bull ends up in a swimming pool (uh-huh...get more details at the TI or check online at www.ffcc.info—French only, click on *Calendrier des Courses* for schedules). Nearby villages stage *courses camarguaises* in small wooden bullrings nearly every weekend; TIs have the latest schedule.

Cost and Hours: Arles' bullgame tickets usually run €5-15; bullfights are pricier (€34-85). Schedules vary (usually July-Aug on Wed and Fri)—ask at the TI or check online at www.arenes-arles.com.

Easter and Fall Fairs (*Féria du Pâques* and *Féria du Riz*)

For 150 years, Arles has thrown citywide parties to celebrate the arrival of spring and fall. During the four days that each event lasts, more than 500,000 people come to Arles for bullfights, street concerts, piles of paella, and parties *(Feria du Pâques* is Fri-Mon of Easter weekend, and *Feria du Riz* is Fri-Mon on the second weekend of Sept). The Easter event kicks off the bullfighting season, while the September event celebrates the land and traditions of Arles. Only during these fairs are bulls killed in the bullfights and only during these events does Arles feel overrun.

Sleeping in Arles

Hotels are a great value here—many are air-conditioned, though few have elevators. The Calendal, Musée, and Régence hotels offer exceptional value.

$$$ Hôtel le Calendal*** is a seductive place located between the Roman Arena and Classical Theater. Enter an expertly run hotel with airy lounges and a lovely palm-shaded courtyard. Enjoy the elaborate €12 buffet breakfast, have lunch in the courtyard or at the inexpensive sandwich bar (daily 12:00-15:00), and take advantage of their four free laptops for guests. You'll also find a Jacuzzi and a spa with a Turkish bath, hot pool, and massages at good rates. The comfortable rooms sport Provençal decor and

ARLES

Sleep Code

(€1 = about $1.30, country code: 33)
S = Single, **D** = Double/Twin, **T** = Triple, **Q** = Quad, **b** = bathroom,
s = shower only, * = French hotel rating system (0-5 stars).
Unless otherwise noted, credit cards are accepted and English is spoken.

To help you sort easily through these listings, I've divided the accommodations into three categories based on the price for a standard double room with bath:

$$$ Higher Priced—Most rooms €90 or more.
  $$ Moderately Priced—Most rooms between €65-90.
    $ Lower Priced—Most rooms €65 or less.

Prices can change without notice; verify the hotel's current rates online or by email. For the best prices, always book direct.

---

come in all shapes and sizes (standard Db-€119, larger or balcony Db-€139, spacious Db-€169, Tb/Qb-€169, air-con, Wi-Fi, reserve ahead for parking-€8, just above arena at 5 Rue Porte de Laure, tel. 04 90 96 11 89, www.lecalendal.com, contact@lecalendal.com). Ask about their studio apartments. They also run the nearby, budget La Maison du Pelerin, described later.

$$$ Hôtel d'Arlatan*, built on the site of a Roman basilica, offers faded elegance in a classy shell. It has comfy public spaces, a tranquil terrace, a designer pool, and a range of rooms, many with high, wood-beamed ceilings and stone walls (a newer wing has more modern rooms). In the lobby of this 15th-century building, a glass floor looks down into Roman ruins. Hallway carpets are worn, and some rooms could use a little TLC, but the place is still a fair value if Old World charm trumps updated amenities (standard Db-€85-137, bigger Db with terrace or Tb-€157, Db/Qb suites-€180, family rooms-€200-250, killer last-minute deals, excellent buffet breakfast/brunch-€15 served until 11:00, air-con, ice machines, elevator, Wi-Fi, parking garage-€14, closed Nov-April, 1 block below Place du Forum at 26 Rue du Sauvage—tough by car, tel. 04 90 93 56 66, www.hotel-arlatan.fr, hotel-arlatan@wanadoo.fr).

$$ Hôtel du Musée is a quiet, affordable manor-home hideaway tucked deep in Arles (difficult to find by car). This delightful refuge comes with 28 air-conditioned and wood-floored rooms, a flowery two-tiered courtyard, and comfortable lounges. Lighthearted Claude and English-speaking Laurence, the gracious owners, are eager to help (Sb-€65, Db-€70-85, Tb-€90-

100, Qb-€140, buffet breakfast-€8.50, no elevator, Wi-Fi, laptop available for guests, garage-€10, follow signs to *Réattu Museum* to 11 Rue du Grand Prieuré, tel. 04 90 93 88 88, www.hoteldumusee .com, contact@hoteldumusee.com).

$$ Hôtel de la Muette**, with reserved owners Brigitte and Alain, is another good choice. Located in a quiet corner of Arles, this low-key hotel is well-kept, with stone walls, brown tones, and a small terrace in front. You'll pay a bit more for the upgraded rooms, but it's money well-spent (most Db-€66, bigger Db-€75, Tb-€77, Qb-€92, buffet breakfast-€8, air-con, no elevator, guest computer and Wi-Fi, private garage-€10, 15 Rue des Suisses, tel. 04 90 96 15 39, www.hotel-muette.com, hotel.muette@wanadoo.fr).

$ Hôtel Régence**, a top budget deal, has a riverfront location, immaculate and comfortable Provençal rooms, safe parking, and easy access to the train station (Db-€55-70, Tb-€70-85, Qb-€80-100, choose river view or quieter courtyard rooms, most rooms have showers, good buffet breakfast-€6, air-con, no elevator but only two floors, guest computer and Wi-Fi, garage-€6; from Place Lamartine, turn right immediately after passing between towers to reach 5 Rue Marius Jouveau; tel. 04 90 96 39 85, www.hotel -regence.com, contact@hotel-regence.com). The gentle Nouvions speak some English.

$$ Hôtel Acacias**, just off Place Lamartine and inside the old city walls, is a modern hotel selling reliable comfort at fair prices. The pretty pastel rooms are on the small side, but the modern elevator makes this a find in Arles (standard Sb-€55, Db-€65-74, extra bed-€15, breakfast-€8, air-con, Wi-Fi, 2 Rue de la Cavalerie, tel. 04 90 96 37 88, www.hotel-acacias.com, contact @hotel-acacias.com).

$ Hôtel Voltaire* rents 12 small, spartan rooms with ceiling fans and nifty balconies overlooking a fun square. A block below the arena, it's good for starving artists who aren't particular about cleanliness. Smiling owner "Mr." Ferran (fur-ran) loves the States, and hopes you'll add to his postcard collection (D-€30, Ds-€35, Db-€40, 1 Place Voltaire, tel. 04 90 96 49 18, levoltaire13@aol .com). They also serve a good-value lunch and dinner in their recommended restaurant.

$ La Maison du Pelerin offers spotless dorm rooms with three to six beds per room. It's a great value, just above the Roman Arena and Classical Theater, with a shared kitchen and homey living area. Book in advance by phone or email and get the door code. You can also check in next door at the recommended Hôtel le Calendal (they own the place). Sheets are included (€25/person, shared bath, must pay in advance, Wi-Fi, 26 Place Pomme, tel. 06 99 71 11 89, www.arles-pelerins.fr).

ARLES

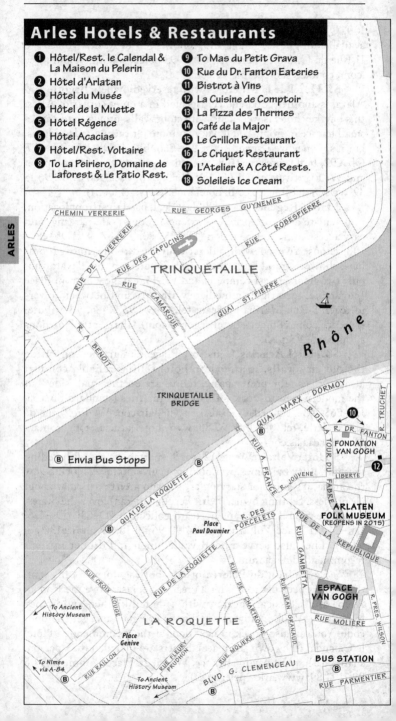

Arles Hotels & Restaurants

1. Hôtel/Rest. le Calendal & La Maison du Pelerin
2. Hôtel d'Arlatan
3. Hôtel du Musée
4. Hôtel de la Muette
5. Hôtel Régence
6. Hôtel Acacias
7. Hôtel/Rest. Voltaire
8. To La Peiriero, Domaine de Laforest & Le Patio Rest.
9. To Mas du Petit Grava
10. Rue du Dr. Fanton Eateries
11. Bistrot à Vins
12. La Cuisine de Comptoir
13. La Pizza des Thermes
14. Café de la Major
15. Le Grillon Restaurant
16. Le Criquet Restaurant
17. L'Atelier & A Côté Rests.
18. Soleileis Ice Cream

CHEMIN VERRERIE

RUE GEORGES GUYNEMER

RUE DE LA VERRERIE

RUE DES CAPUCINS

RUE ROBESPIERRE

TRINQUETAILLE

RUE CAMARGUE

RUE

QUAI ST. PIERRE

R. A. BENOIT

Rhône

TRINQUETAILLE BRIDGE

QUAI MARX DORMOY

R. DE LA TOUR DU FABRE

R. TRUCHET

R. DR. FANTON

FONDATION VAN GOGH

LIBERTE

B Envia Bus Stops

RUE A. FRANCE

R. JOUVENE

ARLATEN FOLK MUSEUM
(REOPENS IN 2015)

QUAI DE LA ROQUETTE

R. DES PORCELETS

Place Paul Doumier

RUE DE LA REPUBLIQUE

RUE GAMBETTA

ESPACE VAN GOGH

R. PRES. WILSON

RUE CROIX ROUGE

RUE DE LA ROQUETTE

RUE DE CHARTROUSE

RUE JEAN GRANAUD

RUE MOLIÈRE

To Ancient History Museum

LA ROQUETTE

Place Genive

RUE MOLIÈRE

BUS STATION

B

To Nîmes via A-54

RUE RAILLON

RUE FLEURY PRUDHON

BLVD. G. CLEMENCEAU

RUE PARMENTIER

To Ancient History Museum

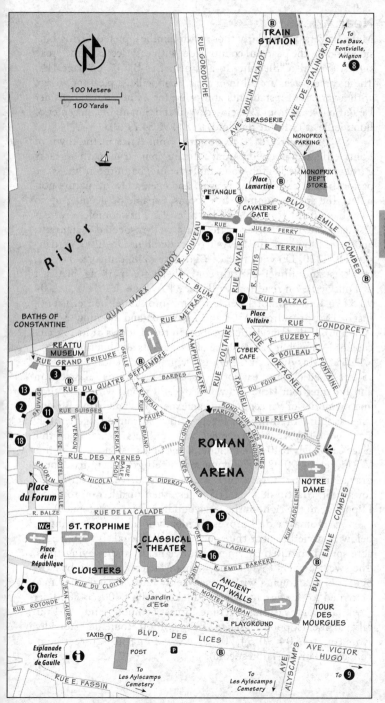

ARLES

Near Arles

Many drivers, particularly those with families, prefer staying outside Arles in the peaceful countryside, with easy access to the area's sights. (See also "Sleeping in and near Les Baux," on page 111.) These three places are all in or near Fontvieille, a pleasant village with a variety of restaurants and cafés; for a fine dinner, consider **Le Patio** (*menus* from €29, closed Wed and Sun nights, in center of Fontvieille at 19 Route du Nord, tel. 04 90 54 73 10).

$$$ La Peiriero***, 15 minutes from Arles in the town of Fontvieille, is a pooped parent's dream come true, with a grassy garden, massive heated pool, table tennis, badminton, massage parlor, indoor children's play area, and even a few miniature golf holes. The spacious family-loft rooms, capable of sleeping up to five, have full bathrooms on both levels. This complete retreat also comes with a terrace café and a well-respected restaurant, and helpful owners, the Levys (streetside Sb or Db-€100, garden-side Db-€120, Db with terrace-€141, loft-€218, dinner *menu*-€31, breakfast and dinner-€38, air-con, Wi-Fi, free parking, just east of Fontvieille on road to Les Baux, 34 Avenue des Baux, tel. 04 90 54 76 10, www.hotel-peiriero.com, info@hotel-peiriero.com). Just a short drive from Arles and Les Baux (and 20 minutes from Avignon), little Fontvieille slumbers in the shadows of its big-city cousins—though it has its share of restaurants and boutiques.

$$$ Mas du Petit Grava is a vintage Provençal farmhouse 15 tree-lined minutes east of Arles. Here California refugees Jim and Ike offer four large and well-cared-for rooms with tubs, tiles, and memories of Vincent (Jim is an expert on Van Gogh's life and art—ask him anything). A lovely garden surrounds a generously sized pool, but what draws most here are Jim and Ike. Book this place early (Db-€110-130, includes a fine breakfast, no air-con, free Wi-Fi, tel. 04 90 98 35 66, www.masdupetitgrava.net, masdupetitgrava@masdupetitgrava.net). From Arles, drive east on D-453 toward St. Martin de Crau (1.5 miles), then turn left on route St. Hippolyte to the right of the large building (Massa Autopneu).

$$ Domaine de Laforest is ideally located a few minutes below Fontvieille, near the aqueduct of Barbegal. It's a big 320-acre spread engulfed by vineyards, rice fields, and swaying trees. The sweet owners (Sylvie and mama Mariette) have eight two-bedroom apartments with great weekly rates, though they may be rented for fewer days when available (€310, €400, or €800 per week, air-con, washing machines, guest computer and Wi-Fi in all apartments, pool, big lawn, swings, 1000 Route de l'Aqueduc Romain, tel. 04 90 54 70 25, www.domaine-laforest.com, contact@domaine-laforest.com).

Eating in Arles

You can dine well in Arles on a modest budget—in fact, it's hard to blow a lot on dinner here (most of my listings have *menus* for under €25). Before dinner, go local on Place du Forum and enjoy a *pastis*. This anise-based apéritif is served straight in a glass with ice, plus a carafe of water—dilute to taste. Sunday is a quiet night for restaurants, though most eateries on Place du Forum are open.

For **picnics,** a big, handy Monoprix supermarket/department store is on Place Lamartine (Mon-Thu 8:30-19:30, Fri-Sat 8:30-20:00, closed Sun).

On or near Place du Forum

Great atmosphere and mediocre food at fair prices await on Place du Forum. By all accounts, the garish yellow Café la Nuit is worth avoiding. Most other cafés on the square deliver acceptable quality and terrific ambience. For better cuisine, wander away from the square.

On Rue du Dr. Fanton

A half-block below the Forum, on Rue du Dr. Fanton, lies a terrific lineup of restaurants. Come here to peruse your options side by side. You can't go wrong—all offer good value and have appealing indoor and outdoor seating.

Le 16 is a warm, affordable place to enjoy a fresh salad (€10), or a fine two- or three-course dinner (€20-€25). The choices are limited, so check the selection before sitting down. The goat cheese *croustillant* salad and *taureau* (bull's meat) in a tasty sauce make a fine combination (closed Sat-Sun, 16 Rue du Dr. Fanton, tel. 04 90 93 77 36, www.le16restaurant.com).

Au Brin de Thym, a few doors down, offers a reliable blend of traditional French and Provençal cuisine at very fair prices. Arrive early for an outdoor table or call ahead, and let hardworking and formal Monsieur and Madame Colombaud and their daughter take care of you. Monsieur does *le cooking* while *les filles* do *le serving* (€14 lunch *menu*, excellent à la carte choices: €9 starters, €16 *plats;* closed Tue, 22 Rue du Dr. Fanton, tel. 04 90 49 95 96, www.aubrindethym.com).

Le Plaza, next to Au Brin, is run by a young couple (Stéphane cooks while Graziela serves) and features tasty Provençal cuisine in a fine setting—inside or out—at good prices (€22 *menu,* closed Wed, 28 Rue du Dr. Fanton, tel. 04 90 96 33 15).

Le Galoubet is a popular local spot, blending a cozy interior, traditional French cuisine, and service with a smile, thanks to owner Frank. It's the most expensive of the places I list on this street and the least flexible, serving a €29 *menu* only. If it's cold,

ARLES

a roaring fire keeps you toasty (closed Sun-Mon, great fries and desserts, 18 Rue du Dr. Fanton, tel. 04 90 93 18 11).

Bistrot à Vins suits wine-lovers who enjoy pairing food and drink, and those in search of a good glass of *vin*. Sit at a convivial counter or at one of five tables while listening to light jazz (book ahead for a table). Affable Ariane speaks enough English and offers a limited selection of simple, tasty dishes, though she talks of retiring (you may meet new owners and a new *menu*). Her savory *tartes* and fresh green salad make a great meal (€10-16), and the wines—many available by the glass—are well priced (indoor dining only from 18:30 to 22:00, closed Mon-Tue, 2 Rue du Dr. Fanton, tel. 04 90 52 00 65).

And for Dessert: Soleileis has Arles' best ice cream, with all-natural ingredients and unusual flavors such as *fadoli*—olive oil mixed with nougatine. There's also a shelf of English books for exchange (daily 14:00-18:30, across from recommended Le 16 restaurant at 9 Rue du Dr. Fanton).

Other Places near Place du Forum

At **La Cuisine de Comptoir,** welcoming owners Alexandre and Vincent offer light *tartine* dinners—a delicious cross between pizza and bruschetta, served with soup or salad for just €10 (a swinging deal—the *brandada* is tasty and filling). Watch *le chef* at work as you sip your €2 glass of rosé in fine glassware and enjoy the lively ambience of this cool little bistro (closed Sun, mostly indoor dining, just off Place du Forum's lower end at 10 Rue de la Liberté, tel. 04 90 96 86 28).

La Pizza des Thermes, an inviting eatery a few blocks north of Place du Forum, serves good pizza and pasta for €10-13 and has comfortable indoor and outdoor seating (daily, 6 Rue du Sauvage, tel. 04 90 49 60 64).

Café de la Major is *the* place to go to recharge with some serious coffee or tea (closed Sun, 7 bis Rue Réattu, tel. 04 90 96 14 15).

Near the Roman Arena

For about the same price as on Place du Forum, you can enjoy regional cuisine with a point-blank view of the arena. Because they change regularly, the handful of (mostly) outdoor eateries that overlook the arena are pretty indistinguishable.

Le Grillon, with the best view above the arena, offers friendly service (say *bonjour* to smiling Nordine) and good-enough salads (the *camarguaise* is a riot of color), pizza and tasty *tartines* for €10 (including small salad), and *plats du jour* for €10-14 (closed all day Wed and Sun night, at the top of the arena on Rond-point des Arènes, tel. 04 90 96 70 97).

Le Criquet, a sweet little place two blocks above the arena, serves Provençal classics with joy at good prices. If you're really hungry, try the €25 *bourride*—a creamy fish soup thickened with aioli and garlic and stuffed with mussels, clams, calamari, and more (good €19-26 three-course *menus,* indoor and outdoor dining, 21 Rue Porte de Laure, tel. 04 90 96 80 51).

For details on the next two places, see their listings under "Sleeping in Arles," earlier. **Hôtel le Calendal** serves lunch in its lovely courtyard (€12-18, daily 12:00-15:00) or delicious little sandwiches for €2.50 each at its small café. **Hôtel Voltaire,** well-situated on a pleasing square, serves simple three-course lunches and dinners at honest prices to a loyal clientele (€13 *menus*; hearty *plats* and filling salads for €10—try the *salade fermière, salade Latine,* or the filling *assiette Provençale;* closed Sun evening).

A Gastronomic Dining Experience

One of France's most recognized chefs, Jean-Luc Rabanel, has created a sensation with two very different options 50 yards from Place de la République (at 7 Rue des Carmes). They sit side by side, both offering indoor and terrace seating.

L'Atelier is so intriguing that people travel great distances just for the experience. Diners fork over €110 (at lunch, you'll spoon out €60) and trust the chef to create a memorable meal...which he does—and Monsieur Michelin agrees, having just awarded him a second star. There is no menu, just an onslaught of delicious taste sensations served in artsy dishes. Don't plan on a quick dinner, and don't come for a traditional setting; rooms are *très* contemporary. Several outdoor tables are also available. You'll probably see or hear the famous chef. Hint: He has long salt-and-pepper hair and a deep voice (closed Mon-Tue, best to book ahead, friendly servers will hold your hand through this palate-widening experience, tel. 04 90 91 07 69, www.rabanel.com).

A Côté saddles up next door, offering a smart wine bar/bistro ambience and top-quality cuisine for far less. Here you can sample the famous chef's talents for as little as €18 (daily *plat*) or as much as €38 (three-course *menu,* smallish servings, reasonably priced wines, open daily, tel. 04 90 47 61 13, www.bistro-acote.com).

Arles Connections

By Train

Some trains in and out of Arles require a **reservation.** These include connections with Nice to the east and Bordeaux to the west (including intermediary stops). Ask at the station.

From Arles by Train to: Paris (11/day, 2 direct TGVs—4 hours, 9 more with transfer in Avignon—5 hours), **Avignon Centre-Ville** (roughly hourly, 20 minutes, less frequent in the afternoon), **Nîmes** (9/day, 30 minutes), **Orange** (4/day direct, 35 minutes, more frequent with transfer in Avignon), **Aix-en-Provence Centre-Ville** (10/day, 2.25 hours, transfer in Marseille, train may separate midway—be sure you're in section going to Aix-en-Provence), **Marseille** (11/day, 1.5 hours), **Cassis** (7/day, 2 hours), **Carcassonne** (8/day, 2.5-3.75 hours, most with transfer in Nîmes or Narbonne, direct trains may require reservations), **Beaune** (10/day, 4.5-5 hours, 9 with transfer in Lyon and Nîmes or Avignon), **Nice** (11/day, 3.75-4.5 hours, most require transfer in Marseille), **Barcelona** (2/day, 6 hours, transfer in Montpellier), **Italy** (3/day, transfer in Marseille and Nice; from Arles, it's 4.5-5 hours to Ventimiglia on the border, 8 hours to Milan, 9.5 hours to Cinque Terre, 11-12 hours to Florence, and 13 hours to Venice or Rome).

By Bus

The bus station is at 16-24 Boulevard Georges Clemenceau (2 blocks below main TI, next to Café le Wilson). Cartreize buses to St-Rémy, Les Baux, and the Camargue depart from the train station and from the downtown bus station. The downtown station is labeled on schedules as Rue Georges Clemenceau (see timetables at www.cg13.fr/cartreize/lignes.php). Bus info: Tel. 08 10 00 13 26.

From Arles Train Station to Avignon TGV Station: The direct SNCF bus is easier than the train and leaves only from Arles' train station (8/day, 1 hour, €7, included with railpass). You can also take the train from Arles to Avignon's Centre-Ville Station, then catch the *navette* (shuttle bus) to the TGV station (2-block walk, see page 128).

From Arles by Bus to: Nîmes (bus #C30, 6/day, 1 hour, €1.50), **Aix-en-Provence** (faster than trains, 5/day Mon-Sat, 2/day Sun, 1.5 hours), **St-Rémy-de-Provence** (bus #54, 3/day Mon-Sat, none on Sun, 50 minutes; bus #59 also goes to St-Rémy via Les Baux in summer—see below), **Fontvieille** (6/day, 10 minutes), **Camargue/Stes-Maries-de-la-Mer** (bus #20, 6/day including Sun, 1 hour).

From Arles by Bus to Les Baux and St-Rémy: Bus #59 connects Arles to **Les Baux** and **St-Rémy** (6/day daily July-Aug, Sat-Sun only in June and Sept; 35 minutes to Les Baux, 50 minutes to St-Rémy, then runs between St-Rémy and Avignon as bus #57). Bus #54 (see above) also goes to St-Rémy but not via Les Baux.

For other ways to reach Les Baux and St-Rémy, see page 104.

NEAR ARLES

*Les Baux • St-Rémy •
The Camargue*

The diverse terrain around Arles harbors many worthwhile and easy day trips. The medieval ghost town of Les Baux haunts the eerie Alpilles mountains, while chic and compact St-Rémy-de-Provence awaits just over the hills, offering Roman ruins and memories of Vincent van Gogh. For an entirely different experience, the flat Camargue knocks on Arles' southern door with sandy beaches, saltwater lakes, rice paddies, flamingos, wild horses, and wild black bulls.

Planning Your Time

Because public transportation in this area is sparse, these sights are easiest to reach by car, taxi, or minivan tour. For a memorable one-day road trip from Arles or Avignon, spend the morning in Les Baux (before the crowds), have lunch in St-Rémy and explore its sights, then finish at the Roman aqueduct of Barbegal. Non-drivers can do the same day trip (without the aqueduct) by bus and taxi. If you have more time or are a nature or bird-watching buff, head for the Camargue. A good market pops up on Friday mornings in little Eyguières (near Les Baux and St-Rémy).

Les Baux

The hilltop town of Les Baux crowns the rugged Alpilles (ahl-pee) mountains, evoking a tumultuous medieval history. Here, you can imagine the struggles of a strong community that lived a rough-and-tumble life—thankful more for their top-notch fortifications than for their dramatic views. It's mobbed with tourists most of the day, but Les Baux rewards those who arrive by 9:00 or after 17:30. (Although the hilltop citadel's entry closes at the end of the day, once you're inside, you're welcome to live out your medieval fantasies all night long, even with a picnic.) Sunsets are dramatic, the castle is brilliantly illuminated after dark, and nights in Les Baux are pin-drop peaceful. (If you like what you see here, but want a more off-the-beaten-path experience, head for the Luberon and find Fort de Buoux—see page 255).

Getting to Les Baux

By Car: Les Baux is a 20-minute drive from Arles: Follow signs for *Avignon,* then *Les Baux.* Drivers can combine Les Baux with St-Rémy (15 minutes away) and the ruined Roman aqueduct of Barbegal.

By Bus: From Arles, **Cartreize** bus #59 runs to Les Baux (daily July-Aug, in June and Sept Sat-Sun only, €2.20 one-way, 6/day, 35 minutes, via Abbey of Montmajour, Fontvieille, and Le Paradou, destination: St-Rémy, see timetables at www.cg13.fr/cartreize/lignes.php).

It's possible to combine Les Baux and St-Rémy into a worthwhile day trip from Arles or Avignon: From either city, take the bus to St-Rémy (about 45 minutes from each, see the "Connections" sections in those chapters for frequency).

St-Rémy, about seven miles north of Les Baux, is a workable transit point for those home-basing in Avignon: Ride the Cartreize #57 bus from Avignon to St-Rémy (6/day, 45 minutes); on weekends in June or September or daily July-August, you can continue to Les Baux on the same bus, renumbered as #59 (see above website for timetables). Or travel from St-Rémy to Les Baux by taxi (see next).

By Taxi: If buses aren't running to Les Baux, you can taxi there from St-Rémy, then take another taxi to return to St-Rémy or to your home base. Figure €40 for a taxi one-way from Arles to Les Baux (€50 after 19:00), and allow €18 one-way from St-Rémy (mobile 06 80 27 60 92).

By Minivan Tour: The best option for many is a minivan tour, which can be both efficient and economical (easiest from Avignon; see page 133).

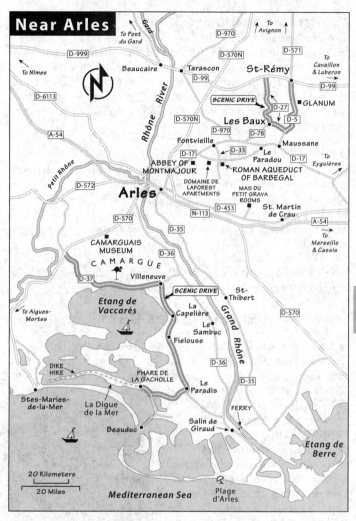

Orientation to Les Baux

Les Baux is actually two visits in one: castle ruins perched on an almost lunar landscape, and a medieval town below. Savor the castle, then tour—or blitz—the lower streets on your way out. While the town, which lives entirely off tourism, is packed with shops, cafés, and tourist knickknacks, the castle above stays manageable because crowds are dispersed over a big area. The lower town's polished-stone gauntlet of boutiques is a Provençal dream come true for shoppers.

Tourist Information

The TI is immediately on the left as you enter the village (Mon-Fri 9:30-17:00, Sat-Sun 10:00-17:30, closed Sun off-season, tel. 04 90 54 34 39, www.lesbauxdeprovence.com). Consider purchasing their "Passes," which can save you money if you visit all the sights. You'll also see deals combining Les Baux with other sights in the region (such as the theater in Orange). The TI has free Wi-Fi and can call a cab for you.

Arrival in Les Baux

Drivers pay €5 to park at the foot of the village (behind the barrier), or €4 to park several blocks below (you'll pass the parking lot on your way in; the ticket is good for the day). Pay at the machine just below the town entry (next to the pay phone, WC, and bakery) before you return to your car—you'll need the validated ticket to exit the lot.

Walk up the cobbled street into town, where you're greeted first by the TI. From here the main drag leads directly to the castle—just keep going uphill (a 10-minute walk).

Sights in Les Baux

▲▲▲The Castle Ruins (The "Dead City")

The sun-bleached ruins of the "dead city" of Les Baux are carved into, out of, and on top of a rock 650 feet above the valley floor.

Many of the ancient walls of this striking castle still stand as a testament to the proud past of this once-feisty village.

Cost and Hours: €8, €9.50 if there's "entertainment," described next, ask about family rates), includes excellent audioguide available up to one hour before closing, daily Easter-June and Sept 9:00-19:00, July-Aug 9:00-20:00, March and Oct 9:30-18:30, Nov-Feb 10:00-17:00. If you're inside the castle when the entry closes, you can stay as long as you like (free Wi-Fi throughout the site).

Entertainment: On weekends from April through September, the castle presents medieval pageantry, tournaments, demonstrations of catapults and crossbows, and jousting matches (schedule in English at www.chateau-baux-provence.com). If you bring lunch, enjoy the picnic tables.

Background: Imagine the importance of this citadel in the Middle Ages, when the Lords of Baux were notorious warriors.

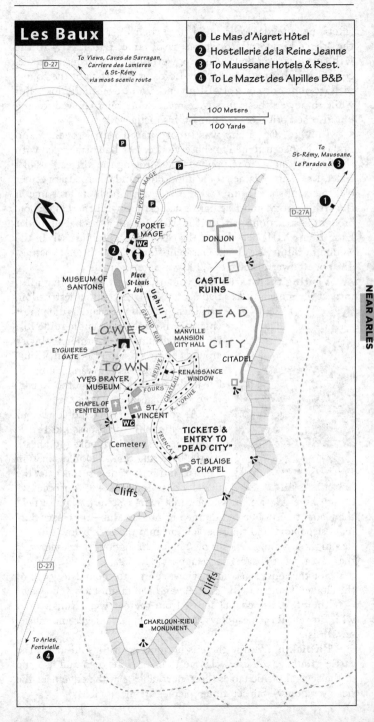

Les Baux

1. Le Mas d'Aigret Hôtel
2. Hostellerie de la Reine Jeanne
3. To Maussane Hotels & Rest.
4. To Le Mazet des Alpilles B&B

100 Meters

100 Yards

D-27

To Views, Caves de Sarragan,
Carriere des Lumieres
& St-Rémy
via most scenic route

To
St-Rémy, Maussane,
Le Paradou & 3

D-27A

1

2

P

P

P

RUE PORTE MAGE

PORTE
MAGE

WC

i

DONJON

CASTLE
RUINS

DEAD

CITY

MUSEUM OF
SANTONS

Place
St-Louis
Jou

Uphill!

GRAND RUE

LOWER

MANVILLE
MANSION
CITY HALL

EYGUIERES
GATE

TOWN

YVES BRAYER
MUSEUM

NEUVE

CITADEL

RENAISSANCE
WINDOW

FOURS

CHATEAU

R. L'ORINE

CHAPEL OF
PENITENTS

ST.
VINCENT

WC

Cemetery

TRENCAT

TICKETS &
ENTRY TO
"DEAD CITY"

ST. BLAISE
CHAPEL

Cliffs

D-27

Cliffs

CHARLOUN-RIEU
MONUMENT

To Arles,
Fontvielle
& 4

NEAR ARLES

(How many feudal lords could trace their lineage back to one of the "three kings" of Christmas-carol fame, Balthazar?) In the 11th century, Les Baux was a powerhouse in southern France, controlling about 80 towns. The Lords of Baux fought the counts of Barcelona for control of Provence...and eventually lost. But while in power, these guys were mean. One ruler enjoyed forcing unransomed prisoners to jump off his castle walls.

In 1426, Les Baux was incorporated into Provence and France. Not accustomed to subservience, Les Baux struggled with the French king, who responded by destroying the fortress in 1483. Later, Les Baux regained some importance and emerged as a center of Protestantism. Arguing with Rome was a high-stakes game in the 17th century, and Les Baux's association with the Huguenots brought destruction again in 1632 when Cardinal Richelieu (under King Louis XIII) demolished the castle. Louis rubbed salt in the wound by billing Les Baux's residents for his demolition expenses. The once-powerful town of 4,000 was forever crushed.

Visiting the Castle: Buy your ticket in the old olive mill, inspect the models of Les Baux before its 17th-century destruction,

and then pick up your audioguide after entering the sight. The audioguide follows posted numbers counterclockwise around the rocky spur. Take full advantage of this tool—as you wander around, key in the number for any of the 30 narrated stops that interest you.

As you walk on the windblown spur (*baux* in French), you'll pass kid-thrilling medieval siege weaponry (go ahead, try the battering ram). Good displays in English and images help reconstruct the place. Try to imagine 4,000 people living up here. Notice the water-catchment system (a slanted field that caught rainwater and drained it into cisterns—necessary during a siege) and find the reservoir cut into the rock below the castle's highest point. Look for post holes throughout the stone walls that reveal where beams once supported floors.

For the most sensational views, climb to the blustery top of the citadel. Hang on. The mistral wind just might blow you away.

The St. Blaise chapel across from the entry/exit runs videos with Provençal themes (plays continuously; just images and music, no words).

Picnicking: While there is no food or drink sold inside the castle grounds, you are welcome to bring your own and use one of the several picnic tables (best view table is at the edge near the siege weaponry). Sunset dinner picnics are memorable.

▲Lower Town

After your castle visit, you can shop and eat your way back through the new town. Or you can escape some of the crowds by following my short walking tour, below, which covers these minor but worthwhile sights as you descend (all stay open at lunch except the Yves Brayer Museum).

• *Follow the main drag (grand Rue Frédéric Mistral) downhill. On the right a few short blocks below the castle exit, find the flags.*

Manville Mansion City Hall

The 15th-century city hall occasionally flies the red-and-white flag of Monaco amid several others, a reminder that the Grimaldi family (which has long ruled the tiny principality of Monaco) owned Les Baux until the French Revolution (1789). In fact, in 1982, Princess Grace Kelly and her royal husband, Prince Rainier Grimaldi, came to Les Baux to receive the key to the city.

Exit left out of the city hall and walk uphill to the empty 1571 **Renaissance window frame**, marking the site of a future Calvinist museum. This beautiful stone frame stands as a reminder of this town's Protestant history. This was probably a place of Huguenot worship—the words carved into the lintel, *Post tenebras lux,* were a popular Calvinist slogan: "After the shadow comes the light."

• *Continue walking uphill, and turn right on Rue des Fours to find the...*

Yves Brayer Museum (Musée Yves Brayer)

This enjoyable museum lets you peruse three floors of paintings (Van Gogh-like Expressionism, without the tumult) by Yves Brayer (1907-1990), who spent his final years here in Les Baux. Like Van Gogh, Brayer was inspired by all that surrounded him, and by his travels through Morocco, Spain, and the rest of the Mediterranean world. Pick up the descriptive English sheet at the entry.

Cost and Hours: €5, daily April-Sept 10:00-12:30 & 14:00-18:30, Oct-Dec and March Wed-Mon 11:00-12:30 & 14:00-17:00, closed Jan-Feb, tel. 04 90 54 36 99, www.yvesbrayer.com.

• *Next door is...*

St. Vincent Church

This 12th-century Romanesque church was built short and wide to fit the terrain. The center chapel on the right (partially carved out of the rock) houses the town's traditional Provençal processional chariot. Each Christmas Eve, a ram pulled this cart—holding a lamb, symbolizing Jesus, and surrounded by candles—through town to the church.

• *As you leave the church, WCs are to the left and up the stairs. Directly in front of the church is a vast view, making clear the strategic value of this rocky bluff's natural fortifications. A few steps away is the...*

Chapel of Penitents

Inside, notice the nativity scene painted by Yves Brayer, illustrating the local legend that says Jesus was born in Les Baux. On the opposite wall, find his version of a starry night. Leaving the chapel, turn left.

• *As you leave the church, wash your shirt in the old town "laundry" —with a pig-snout faucet and 14th-century stone washing surface designed for short women.*

Continue down steep Rue de la Calade, passing cafés with wonderful views, the town's fortified wall, and one of its two gates. Before long, you'll run into the...

Museum of Santons

This free and worthwhile "museum" displays a collection of *santons* ("little saints"), popular folk figurines that decorate local Christmas mangers. Notice how the nativity scene "proves" once again that Jesus was born in Les Baux. These painted clay dolls show off local dress and traditions (with good English descriptions). Find the old couple leaning heroically into the mistral.

Near Les Baux

A half-mile beyond Les Baux, D-27 (toward Maillane) leads to dramatic views of the hill town. There are pullouts with great vistas, and cavernous caves in former limestone quarries dating back to the Middle Ages. (The limestone is easy to cut, but gets hard and nicely polished when exposed to the weather.) Speaking of quarries, in 1821, the rocks and soil of this area were found to contain an important mineral for making aluminum. It was named after the town: bauxite.

You'll enjoy superb views of Les Baux from the Caves de Sarragan parking lot, once occupied by the Sarragan Winery. For still better views, continue driving up. After several switchbacks you'll reach the top—turn right on the paved lane where you see a red kilometer marker and find the views. You'll see walking trails nearby (ask at TIs for info on hikes in the Alpilles; Les Baux to St-Rémy is a 2.5-hour hike).

D-27 continues to St-Rémy, allowing for a handy loop trip (to complete the loop, return from St-Rémy to Les Baux via D-5). For more details, see "Getting to St-Rémy" on page 114.

▲▲Carrière des Lumières

This nearby cave offers a mesmerizing sound-and-slide show, with 48 projectors flashing countless images on expansive quarry walls, accompanied by music. The show lasts 40 minutes (dress warmly, as the cave is cool), and there's a different program every year (announced in Sept, check website).

Cost and Hours: €9.50, daily April-Sept 9:30-19:30, March and Oct-Dec 10:00-18:00, closed Jan-Feb, tel. 04 90 54 47 37, www.carrieres-lumieres.com.

Sleeping in and near Les Baux

In Les Baux

$$$ Le Mas d'Aigret*, a 10-minute walk east of Les Baux on the road to St-Rémy (D-27), is a lovely refuge that crouches under

Les Baux. Lie on your back and stare up at the castle walls rising beyond the heated swimming pool, or enjoy valley views from the groomed terraces. The rooms are simple and slightly worn, but you can't beat the location (viewless Db-€120-145, larger Db with balcony and view-€150-180, Tb/Qb-€230-290, two cool troglodyte rooms-€240, convenient half-pension dinner option-€33/person, air-con, Wi-Fi, rooms have some daytime road noise, tel. 04 90 54 20 00, www.masdaigret.com, contact@masdaigret.com, Dutch Marieke and French Eric are wonderful hosts).

$$ Hostellerie de la Reine Jeanne, warmly run by Gaelle (speaks English) and Marc (speaks French), offers a handful of rooms above a busy, good-value restaurant. The rooms are scheduled to be renovated, so these prices may change (standard Db-€56, Db with view deck-€70, Tb-€80, cavernous family suite-€100, air-con in half the rooms, for view deck ask for *chambre avec terrasse,* good *menus* from €16, 150 feet to your right after entry to the village of Les Baux, tel. 04 90 54 32 06, www.la-reinejeanne.com, marc.braglia@wanadoo.fr).

In Maussane

The appealing village of Maussane lies a few minutes' drive south of Les Baux. It has some hotels, a handful of restaurants, and an atmospheric square lined with cafés. There's also bike rental and a small TI (tel. 04 90 54 33 60, www.maussane.com). These two accommodations are well worth considering.

$$ Hôtel les Magnanarelles, in the center of Maussane, gives solid two-star value in its 18 tastefully designed rooms above a handsome restaurant. Enjoy the generously sized pool (Db-€68-78, extra person-€17, ask for a room off the street, no air-con, 104 Avenue de la Vallée des Baux, tel. 04 90 54 30 25, www.hotel-magnanarelles.com).

$$ Le Mas de l'Esparou *chambres d'hôte* is welcoming and kid-friendly, with four simple-yet-spacious rooms, a big swimming

---

Sleep Code

(€1 = about $1.30, country code: 33)
S = Single, **D** = Double/Twin, **T** = Triple, **Q** = Quad, **b** = bathroom,
s = shower only, * = French hotel rating system (0-5 stars).
Unless otherwise noted, credit cards are accepted and
English is spoken.

To help you easily sort through these listings, I've divided
the accommodations into three categories, based on the
price for a standard double room with bath:

$$$ **Higher Priced**—Most rooms €80 or more.
$$ **Moderately Priced**—Most rooms between €60-80.
$ **Lower Priced**—Most rooms €60 or less.

Prices can change without notice; verify the hotel's current rates online or by email. For the best prices, always book
direct.

---

pool, table tennis, swings, and distant views of Les Baux.
Jacqueline loves her job, and her lack of English only makes her
more animated. She dislikes email though, so you'll have to call
(Db-€74, Tb/Qb-€120-145, includes breakfast, cash only, no air-
con, between Les Baux and Maussane on D-5, look for white sign
with green lettering, tel. 04 90 54 41 32).

In Le Paradou

$ Le Mazet des Alpilles is a small home with three tidy, air-
conditioned rooms around a lovely garden, located just outside
the sleepy village of Le Paradou (five minutes south of Les Baux).
Sweet Annick is happy to share her knowledge of the area with
you (Db-€65, ask for largest room, includes breakfast, cash only,
air-con, child's bed available, drive into Le Paradou and look for
signs, Route de Brunelly, tel. 04 90 54 45 89, www.alpilles.com
/mazet.htm, lemazet@wanadoo.fr).

Eating in and near Les Baux

You'll find quiet cafés with views along my self-guided tour route.

The recommended **Hostellerie de la Reine Jeanne** offers
friendly service and good-value meals indoors or out (€12 salads,
€16 *menus*, try the *salade Estivale*, open daily).

You'll also find several worthwhile places in Maussane, south
of Les Baux. Place de la Fontaine, the town's central square, makes
a good stop for café fare. **Pizza Brun** has the region's best pizza

(closed Mon-Tue, 1 Rue Edouard Foscalina; with your back to Place de la Fontaine, walk to the right for about 10 minutes and look for colored tables in an alleyway; tel. 04 90 54 40 73). **La Place** is a good choice for a real restaurant (*menus* from €24-37, closed Wed, indoor seating only, 65 Avenue de la Vallée des Baux, tel. 04 90 54 23 31).

Sights Between Les Baux and Arles

The following stops are easiest for drivers.

Abbey of Montmajour

This brooding hulk of a ruin, just a few minutes' drive from Arles toward Les Baux, was once a thriving abbey and a convenient papal retreat (c. A.D. 950). Today, the vacant abbey church is a massive example of Romanesque architecture that comes with great views from its tower. Film buffs will appreciate this sight as the setting for *The Lion in Winter,* where Eleanor of Aquitaine (played by Katharine Hepburn) battled with her husband, Henry II (Peter O'Toole). For more on abbeys, see the sidebar on page 244.

The surrounding fields were a favorite of Van Gogh, who walked here from Arles to paint his famous wheat fields.

Cost and Hours: €7; May-Aug daily 10:00-18:30, Sept-April Tue-Sun 10:00-17:00, closed Mon; tel. 04 90 54 64 17.

▲Roman Aqueduct of Barbegal

To be all alone with evocative Roman ruins, drivers can take a quick detour to the crumbled arches of ancient Arles' principal aqueduct.

From the parking area, follow the dirt path through the olive grove and along the aqueduct ruins for 200 yards. Approaching the bluff with the grand view, you'll see that the water canal is split into two troughs: One takes a 90-degree right turn and heads for Arles; the other goes straight to the bluff and over, where it once sent water cascading down to power eight grinding mills. Romans grew wheat on the vast fields you see from here, then brought it down to the mega-watermill of Barbegal. Historians figure that this mill produced enough flour each day to feed 12,000 hungry Romans. If you saw the model of this eight-tiered mill in Arles' Ancient History Museum (see page 77), the milling is easy to

NEAR ARLES

visualize—making a visit here quite an exciting experience.

Returning to your car, find the broken bit of aqueduct—it's positioned like a children's playground slide—and take a look at the waterproofing mortar that lined all Roman aqueducts.

Getting There: Coming from Arles, take D-17 toward Fontvieille; a little less than two miles before Fontvieille, look for signs for *L'Aqueduc Romain* on D-82 (it's signed coming from Fontvieille to Arles as well, on the left). In less than two miles, park at the dirt pullout (no sign—it's just after the *Los Pozos Blancos* sign, where the ruins of the aqueduct cross the road). Leave no valuables visible in your car; the gravel twinkles with the remains of broken car windows.

St-Rémy-de-Provence

Sophisticated and sassy, St-Rémy (sahn ray-mee) gave birth to Nostradamus and cared for a distraught artist. Today, it caters to

shoppers and Van Gogh fans. A few minutes from the town center, you can visit the once-thriving Roman city called Glanum and the mental ward where Vincent van Gogh was sent after lopping off his lobe. Best of all is the chance to elbow your way through St-Rémy's raucous Wednesday market (until 12:30). A ring road—which local drivers mistake for a racecourse—hems in a pedestrian-friendly center that's well-stocked with fine foods, estheticians, pottery boutiques, art galleries, and the latest Provençal fashions.

Getting to St-Rémy

By Car: From Les Baux, St-Rémy is a spectacular 15-minute drive over the hills and through the woods. Roads D-5 and D-27 each provide scenic routes between these towns, making a loop drive between them worthwhile. The most scenic approach is on D-27; from Les Baux, take the road toward Maillane that passes the Carrière des Lumières. Take advantage of the many good pullouts and get out of your car for the view.

Parking in St-Rémy is tricky; it's easiest at the TI lot (€1.30/hour, free Mon-Sat 12:30-14:30 and all day Sun). Parking on Place Charles de Gaulle is always free, but farther from the center (leave the ring road on Avenue Frédéric Mistral).

By Bus: It's 50 minutes from Arles via bus #54 (3/day Mon-Sat, none on Sun, €2.20 one-way) or bus #59 (6/day daily July-Aug, Sat-Sun only in June and Sept) and 45 minutes from Avignon via bus #57 (6/day). If arriving at St-Rémy by bus, get off on the ring road at the République stop and continue uphill. The TI is a block up Avenue Durand Maillane (to the right).

By Taxi: From Les Baux, allow €18 one-way; from Avignon, count on €40 (mobile 06 80 27 60 92 or 06 09 52 71 54). St-Rémy's four taxis park on Place de la République, next to the bus stop, but it's best to have the TI call for you.

Orientation to St-Rémy

From St-Rémy's circular center, it's a 15-minute walk along a busy road with no sidewalk to Glanum and the St. Paul Monastery (Van Gogh's mental hospital).

Tourist Information

The TI is two blocks toward Les Baux from the ring road (Mon-Sat 9:00-12:30 & 14:00-18:30, Sun 10:00-12:30—except closed Sun Oct-April; free Wi-Fi which you can access from the terrace after hours; tel. 04 90 92 05 22, www.saintremy-de-provence .com). At the TI, pick up a town map, bus schedules, and a map tracing Van Gogh's favorite painting locations with *in situ* copies of the painted scenes (the *Starry Night* panel is just outside the TI). Hikers may want to pick up the good trail map (€2, the hike to Les Baux is about 10 miles and 5 hours). Ask about the **St-Rémy pass,** which offers discounts at some sights. The TI runs English "In the Footsteps of Van Gogh" walking tours (€8, 1.5 hours; departs TI at 10:00—usually Tue, Thu, Fri, and Sat; also gives occasional afternoon tours of the town, 8-person minimum, call ahead to confirm).

Each year during the last week of September, St-Rémy celebrates *les fêtes votives*, a tradition in the Camargue region honoring the town's patron saint. The carnival-like festivities include bullfights, parades, and *boules* competitions. Some enjoy the chance to party with the locals, while others find the town noisy and crowded.

Sights in St-Rémy

St-Rémy's best attractions are outside the town center: the ruins at Glanum and the hospital where Vincent van Gogh was treated. This cluster of sights is an unappealing 15-minute walk south of the TI. If you're driving, you can park for free at the St. Paul Monastery (coming from Les Baux, it's the first right after passing Glanum) and walk five minutes to Glanum from there (or pay €2.50 to park at the Glanum site). Theft is a problem, so leave absolutely nothing in your car.

▲Glanum Ruins

These crumbling stones are the foundations of a Roman market town, located at the crossroads of two ancient trade routes between Italy and Spain.

Cost and Hours: €7.50, under age 18-free, daily April-Sept 9:30-18:30, Oct-March 10:00-17:00, parking-€2.60, tel. 04 90 92 23 79.

Information: The free English handout, the exhibits in the entry, and the helpful information panels scattered about the site all help put this picture together. Still, eager Romanophiles will want to spring for the well-done "Itineraries" book (€7). A pleasant on-site café serves Roman specialties and classic snack fare.

Lunch: La Taverne Romaine just past Glanum's entry serves an "authentic" Roman meal with good seating in the site (allow €12 for a *plat*, open same hours as the site).

Touring the Ruins: While the ruins are, well...ruined, their setting at the base of the rocky Alpilles is lovely. It's also unshaded, so if it's hot, come early or late.

About 2,500 people lived in Glanum at its zenith. And though this was an important town, with grand villas, temples, a basilica, a forum, a wooden dam, and aqueducts, it was not important enough to justify an arena or a theater (such as those in Arles, Nîmes, and Orange).

A heavy Roman arch and tower stand across the road as proud reminders of the town's glory days, and indicate how much larger the town was back then (the Roman city was about seven times bigger than the visible ruins). The arch marked the entry into Glanum, and the tower is a memorial to the grandsons of Emperor Augustus Caesar.

Stroll up Glanum's main street and see remains of a market hall, a forum, thermal baths, reservoirs, and more. The view from the belvedere justifies the effort. These ruins highlight the range and prosperity of the Roman Empire. Taken together with other Roman monuments in Provence, they paint a more complete picture of Roman life. For more on Roman history, see page 59.

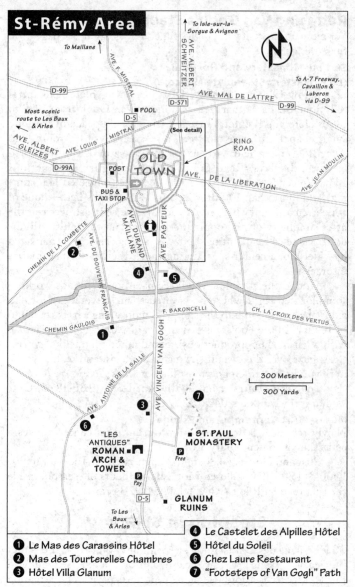

St-Rémy Area

To Maillane ↑

To Isle-sur-la-Sorgue & Avignon ↑

AVE. ALBERT SCHWEITZER

N

AVE. F. MISTRAL

D-99

■ POOL

D-5

D-571

AVE. MAL DE LATTRE

D-99

To A-7 Freeway, Cavaillon & Luberon via D-99 →

Most scenic route to Les Baux & Arles ←

AVE. ALBERT GLEIZES

AVE. LOUIS MISTRAL

(See detail)

RING ROAD

OLD TOWN

D-99A

POST

AVE. DE LA LIBERATION

AVE. JEAN MOULIN

BUS & TAXI STOP

AVE. DURAND MAILLANE

AVE. PASTEUR

CHEMIN DE LA COMBETTE

AVE. DU SOUVENIR FRANCAIS

2

4

5

F. BARONCELLI

CH. LA CROIX DES VERTUS

CHEMIN GAULOIS

1

AVE. ANTOINE DE LA SALLE

AVE. VINCENT VAN GOGH

300 Meters

300 Yards

7

3

6

"LES ANTIQUES" ROMAN ARCH & TOWER ■

■ ST. PAUL MONASTERY

P Free

P Pay

D-5

GLANUM RUINS ■

To Les Baux & Arles ↓

1 Le Mas des Carassins Hôtel
2 Mas des Tourterelles Chambres
3 Hôtel Villa Glanum
4 Le Castelet des Alpilles Hôtel
5 Hôtel du Soleil
6 Chez Laure Restaurant
7 "Footsteps of Van Gogh" Path

NEAR ARLES

Retracing Van Gogh's Steps

For more on Vincent van Gogh's time in this region, see page 87 in the Arles chapter.

St. Paul Monastery and Hospital
(Le Monastère St. Paul de Mausole)

Just below Glanum is the still-functioning mental hospital (Clinique St. Paul) that treated Vincent van Gogh from 1889 to 1890. Here you'll enter Vincent's temporarily peaceful world: a small chapel, intimate cloisters, a re-creation of his room, and a small lavender field with six (of my favorite) paintings copied on large displays. Read the thoughtful English explanations about Vincent's tortured life. Amazingly, he completed 143 paintings and more than 100 drawings in his 53 weeks here—none of which remains anywhere nearby today. The contrast between the utter simplicity of his room (and his life) and the multimillion-dollar value of his paintings today is jarring. The site is managed by Valetudo, a center specializing in art therapy for psychiatric disorders.

Around the complex, you'll see panels of Vincent's works—some located right where he painted them. Several are located along the short road into the site, with more along a back road into St-Rémy ("In the Footsteps of Van Gogh" path; the TI has a map with a list of the reproductions). Stand among flamelike cypress trees, gaze over the distant skyline of St-Rémy, and realize you're in the midst of Van Gogh's most famous work, *The Starry Night*.

Cost and Hours: €4.50, daily April-Sept 9:30-18:45, Oct-March 10:15-17:00, tel. 04 90 92 77 00.

Musée d'Art Contemporain Estrine

Newly reopened after a long renovation, this center houses a collection of contemporary art.

Cost and Hours: €4.80, mid-March-mid Oct Tue-Sun 10:00-13:00 & 15:00-19:00, closed Mon, shorter hours off-season, inside the ring road on Rue Estrine, tel. 04 90 92 34 72.

Sleeping in St-Rémy

$$$ Le Mas des Carassins*,** a 15-minute walk from the center (but easy parking), is impeccably run by friendly Michel and Pierre. Luxury is affordable here. Your hosts pay careful attention to every detail, from the generously sized pool, gardens, and outdoor lounging spaces to the muted room decor and optional €34 home-cooked dinner. Reservations are smart—its 22 rooms fill fast (standard Db-€140, superior Db-€170, deluxe Db with terrace-€180-205, Db suite-€230, extra bed-€36, includes American-style breakfast, air-con, Wi-Fi, table tennis, look for signs 200 yards toward Les Baux from TI, 1 Chemin Gaulois, tel.

NEAR ARLES

04 90 92 15 48, www.masdescarassins.com, info@masdescarassins
.com).

$$$ Mas des Tourterelles Chambres, a converted Provençal
farmhouse, hides behind a walled garden just a five-minute walk
from the center of St-Rémy. Restored by friendly Brits Richard
and Carrie, it has four well-appointed rooms with top-quality
English beds and good showers (Db-€110-125, 2-night minimum,
includes breakfast, Wi-Fi, pool, 21 Chemin de la Combette, tel.
04 32 60 19 93, www.masdestourterelles.com, richard.ahern@sfr
.fr). Turn right at the top of Place de la République onto Chemin
de la Combette; after 400 yards look for the entrance on the left
(past the speed bumps).

$$$ Hôtel Villa Glanum*** is a pleasant hotel on the main
road (some traffic noise) across from the St. Paul Monastery and
the Glanum ruins. It's a 15-minute walk from the town center, with
tight but well-maintained rooms. The rooms in the main building
are larger, but I prefer the smaller *bastide* rooms with private
terraces around the pretty pool (*bastide* Db-€100-130 depending
on size; main building Db-€120, Tb-€140; cheaper off-season,
46 Avenue Van Gogh, tel. 04 90 92 03 59, www.villaglanum.com,
contact@villaglanum.com).

$$ Le Castelet des Alpilles*** is way Old World, but the
location is good (halfway between St-Rémy's old town and the
Roman ruins), the terrace is big, the price is fair, and the rooms
are plenty comfortable. Most are big and airy, and some have
views of the Alpilles (Db-€82-89, Db with air-con and view
balcony-€107, Tb-€120, Wi-Fi, easy parking, 6 Place Mireille,
tel. 04 90 92 07 21, www.castelet-alpilles.com, hotel.castel.alpilles
@wanadoo.fr).

$$ Hôtel du Soleil**, a quick walk from St-Rémy's center,
is a modern air-conditioned refuge, with newly renovated
white stone and beige decor throughout. Its spotless rooms
cluster around a pleasant, flowery courtyard and pool (standard
Db-€100-110, bigger Db-€120-130, Tb-€165-180, 3 rooms have
small terraces, 2-room apartment-€140-165, guest computer and
Wi-Fi, easy parking, indifferent owners, a block above the TI at
35 Avenue Pasteur, tel. 04 90 92 00 63, www.hotelsoleil.com, info
@hotelsoleil.com).

Eating in St-Rémy

The town is packed with fine restaurants, each trying to outdo the
other. Join the evening strollers and compare.

Crêperie Lou Planet, on pleasant Place Favier, is cheap and
peaceful, with outdoor seating in summer, delicious crêpes, good
salads, and inexpensive fine house wine. Owner Jean has been here

NEAR ARLES

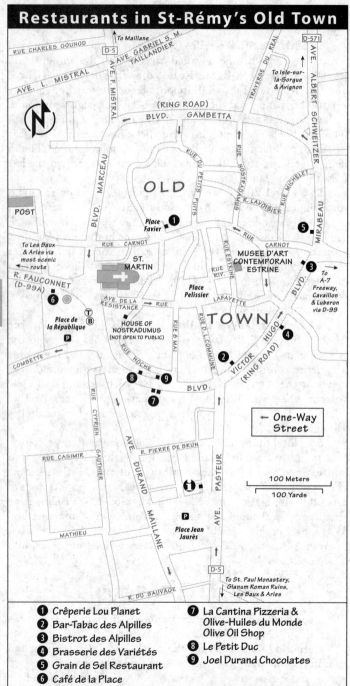

Restaurants in St-Rémy's Old Town

NEAR ARLES

1. Crêperie Lou Planet
2. Bar-Tabac des Alpilles
3. Bistrot des Alpilles
4. Brasserie des Variétés
5. Grain de Sel Restaurant
6. Café de la Place

7. La Cantina Pizzeria & Olive-Huiles du Monde Olive Oil Shop
8. Le Petit Duc
9. Joel Durand Chocolates

Food-Lovers' Guide to St-Rémy

Wednesday is market day in St-Rémy, but you don't have to fast until then. Foodies will appreciate the three shops gathered on the ring road in St-Rémy, near the turnoff to Les Baux.

Start at **Olive-Huiles du Monde,** where you can sample the best olive oil and vinegar in the area in a wine bar-like setting. The friendly staff speaks English and is happy to spoon up samples of three olive oils and two surprisingly tasty vinegars. Check out the impressive display of other products made from olive oil, and the good truffle display (daily 10:00-12:30 & 15:00-19:00, 16 Boulevard Victor Hugo, tel. 04 90 15 02 33).

Le Petit Duc, across the road, offers a remarkable introduction to traditional cookies (Tue-Sat 10:00-13:00 & 15:00-19:00, closed Sun-Mon, 7 Boulevard Victor Hugo, tel. 04 90 92 08 31).

Just one whiff from **Joel Durand Chocolates** will lure chocoholics inside. Ask for a sample and learn the letter-coded system. The lavender is surprisingly good (Mon-Sat 9:30-19:30, Sun 10:00-13:00 & 14:30-19:30, a few doors down from Le Petit Duc at 3 Boulevard Victor Hugo, tel. 04 90 92 38 25).

for more than 30 years and still hasn't changed the menu (daily April-Sept 12:00-22:00, behind Hôtel de Ville at Place Favier, next to Musée des Alpilles).

Bar-Tabac des Alpilles, a favorite among locals, sits on the ring road. It offers a great salad selection and good standard café fare, including pasta dishes for €10 (open daily for lunch and dinner, 21 Boulevard Victor Hugo, tel. 04 90 92 0 17). Don't confuse this with my next recommendation...

At **Bistrot des Alpilles**, the America-loving owner Jean-Claude will offer a free plate of foie gras to anyone with an ID from California, the state that outlawed the liver delicacy. The rest of us will find Provençal specialties and a good wine selection (closed Tue, on the ring road at 15 Boulevard Mirabeau, tel. 04 90 92 09 17).

Brasserie des Variétés has good kids' menus, along with computers and Wi-Fi (daily, #32 on the ring road, tel. 04 90 92 42 61).

Grain de Sel is a modern place with a Baroque touch, where nouvelle cuisine blends with local specialties (open daily for dinner, closed Tue-Thu for lunch, €24-40 *plats,* look for daily specials, on ring road, tel. 04 90 92 00 89, www.graindesel-resto.com).

Café de la Place, on Place de la République behind the parking lot, is a hit with the young, local crowd. With funky decor, a huge terrasse, and free Wi-Fi, it's good for a meal or just a drink (*plats*-€18-24, salads-€14-16, open daily, tel. 04 90 92 02 13).

La Cantina Pizzeria, next to the olive oil shop on Boulevard Victor Hugo, serves fine pizzas in a laid-back setting (€10-15, takeaway no problem, closed Wed, tel. 04 90 90 90 60).

Chez Laure is a simple, local, and relaxed outdoor restaurant. It's located a mile from St-Rémy in a park-like setting with toys available for kids (salads, €13 *plats,* €18-24 lunch *menu,* €20-24 dinner *menu,* closed Mon, Sun evening concerts run June-Aug and range from jazz to area folk music, on Route du Lac, tel. 04 90 92 51 99). To find the restaurant, look for signs between the Glanum ruins and the TI.

The Camargue

The Camargue region, occupying the vast delta of the Rhône River, is one of Europe's most important wetlands. This marshy area exists where the Rhône splits into two branches (big and little), just before it flows into the Mediterranean. Over the millennia, a steady flow of sediment has been deposited at the mouth of the rivers—thoroughly land-locking villages that once faced the sea.

Since World War II, farmers have converted large northern tracts of the Camargue to rice fields, making the delta a major producer of France's rice. Salt is the other key industry in the Camargue: You can see vast salt marshes and evaporation beds around the town of Salin de Giraud. Because the salt marshes were long considered useless, the land has remained relatively untouched, leaving it a popular nature destination today.

Today the Camargue Regional Nature Park is a protected and "wild" area, where pink flamingos, wild bulls, nasty boars, nastier mosquitoes (in every season but winter—come prepared), and the famous white horses wander freely through lagoons and tall grass. For more on these animals, see the sidebar.

The Camargue's subtle wetlands beauty makes it a worthwhile joyride for naturalists, but it's a take-it-or-leave-it sight for many (unless it's spring and you've never seen a flamingo in flight). The Everglades-like scenery is a birder's paradise, and occasional bulls and wild horses add to the enjoyment. But for avid city sightseers, this can feel like a big swamp—interesting to drive through, but where's the excitement? Read ahead and decide for yourself (tel. 04 90 97 86 32, French only website: www.parc-camargue.fr,

The Wildlife of the Camargue

In this nature reserve, amusing flamingos and countless other bird species flourish—attracting birdwatchers from all over the world. Once an endangered species, the flamingos flock here because of all that salt—which is why they come to the Camargue rather than to, say, the sandy beaches of the Riviera. Ten thousand flamingos leave here each fall, heading to warmer climates, and then return in March to pink up the Camargue (a visit here in the spring reaps big, pink rewards). To see a formation of these long, clumsy-looking birds in flight is an experience you won't soon forget.

The black bulls are raised for bullfights (by local cowboys called *gardians*) and eventually end up on plates in Arles' restaurants (you may have met one already). The *gardians*, who have patrolled the Camargue on local horses for centuries, give the area a Wild West aura. The region's unique small horses—born brown or black, later turning light gray or white—are one of the oldest breeds in the world, and may have existed in the area since prehistoric times.

With the continual loss of wetlands throughout the world, it's critical that places like this remain preserved and that we understand their significance.

info@parc-camargue.fr). The birds are fewest and the mosquitoes are greatest in summer, so I'd pass on the Camargue at that time.

However, if you have children who can't take the city anymore, a picnic on the long sandy beach at Plage d'Arles may be just what the doctor ordered. Also called Plage de Piemanço, this public beach is 10 kilometers (6 miles) after Salin de Giraud (see map on page 105). Bring everything you might need, as there are no vendors, but the sand is soft and the sea is warm.

Getting to the Camargue

There are several ways aside from a car to experience the Camargue: horseback, mountain bikes, and jeep safaris. All three options are available in Stes-Maries-de-la-Mer, and jeep safaris are also offered from Arles (ask at TI). Hiking is not good in the Camargue, as there are few decent trails (check www.kustgids.nl /camargue-en). The best biking is across the Digue (dike) to Phare de la Gacholle.

By Scenic Drive: There are two primary driving routes from Arles through the Camargue: to Stes-Maries-de-la-Mer, and toward Salin de Giraud.

My favorite route is toward **Salin de Giraud** (see map on page 105): Leave Arles toward Stes-Maries-de-la-Mer and find the D-570. Skip the D-36 turnoff to Salin de Giraud (you'll return along this route). After about 10 kilometers (6 miles), consider a stop at the **Camarguais Museum** (described later). Next, continue along D-570, then turn left on D-37 and follow it as it skirts the Etang de Vaccarès lagoon. The lagoon itself is off-limits, but this area has views and good opportunities to get out of the car and smell the marshes (look for viewing stands, but any dirt turnoff works). Turn right off D-37 onto the tiny road at Villeneuve, following signs for C-134 to La Capelière and La Fiélouse.

Make time for a stop at **La Capelière** (headquarters for Camargue sightseers), where you can pick up an excellent map, ask the eager staff questions, and enjoy a small exhibit (hand-held English explanations) and one-mile walking trail with some English information on the Camargue (modest trail fee, daily 9:00-13:00 & 14:00-18:00). Birders can look at the register to see what birds have been spotted recently (observations in English are in red), and enthusiasts can buy the €5 Camargue booklet, *Fiches Camargue*, in English.

The best part of this drive (particularly in spring) is the next stretch to and around **La Digue de la Mer,** about six scenic miles past La Capelière. At La Digue de la Mer, a rough dirt road greets travelers; it's time to get out of your car and stroll (though you can drive on for about three miles to Phare de la Gacholle). This is a critical reproduction area for flamingos (about 13,000 couples produce 5,000 offspring annually), so it's your best chance to see groups of mamas and papas up close and personal. If you rented a mountain bike, now would be the right time to use it: It's about eight bumpy but engaging miles between water and sand dunes to Stes-Maries-de-la-Mer.

For the fastest way back to Arles, backtrack north to D-37 at Villeneuve, then follow D-36. If continuing to Stes-Maries-de-la-Mer, you'll find several parking lots and plenty of on-street parking.

By Bus: Buses serve the Camargue (stopping at Camarguais Museum and Stes-Maries-de-la-Mer) from Arles' bus or train station (bus #20, 6/day including Sun, 1 hour, tel. 08 10 00 13 26, www.cg13.fr/cartreize/lignes.php).

Sights in the Camargue

Camarguais Museum (Musée Camarguais)

Located in a traditional Camargue barn on the road to Stes-Maries-de-la-Mer, this well-designed folk museum does a good job of describing the natural features and cultural traditions of the Camargue. The costumes, tools, and helpful exhibits come with some English explanations (look for handouts and small screens). The entire museum was closed for renovation in 2013 with promises of new projects in and around the museum. A two-mile nature trail, picnic tables, and a WC round out the amenities.

Cost and Hours: €5; April-Sept daily 9:00-12:30 & 13:00-18:00, Oct-March Wed-Mon 10:00-12:30 & 13:00-17:00, closed Tue; 8 miles from Arles on D-570 toward Stes-Maries-de-la-Mer, at Mas du Pont de Rousty farmhouse; tel. 04 90 97 10 82, www.parc-camargue.fr.

Stes-Maries-de-la-Mer

At the western end of the Camargue lies this whitewashed, Spanish-feeling seafront town with acres of flamingos, bulls, and horses at its doorstep. From the bus stop, walk to the church (10 minutes) to get oriented. The place is so popular that it's best avoided on weekends and during holidays. It's a French Coney Island—a trinket-selling, perennially windy place.

The town is also famous as a mecca for the Roma (also known as Gypsies). Every May, Roma from all over Europe pile in their caravans and migrate to Stes-Maries-de-la-Mer to venerate the town's statue of Saint Sarah. Legend has it that Mary Magdalene made landfall here in a boat with no oars after an epic journey across the Mediterranean from Egypt. Fleeing persecution for practicing the new and unpopular Christian faith, she was accompanied by two other "Stes-Maries": Mary Jacobe, the mother of the apostle James, and Mary Salome, the mother of the apostles James and John. Also in the boat was "Black Sarah," an Egyptian servant. Sarah collected alms for the poor; over time, her request for handouts became associated with the Roma people, who embrace her as their patron saint (the name Gypsy comes from the label Europeans gave those who came across from Egypt—*Gyptians*). Today's impressive spectacle to honor Sarah is like a sprawling flea market spilling out from the town.

Tourist Information: Stes-Maries-de-la-Mer's TI is located along its waterfront promenade (daily April-Sept 9:00-19:00, until 20:00 in summer, Oct-March 10:00-17:00, 5 Avenue Van Gogh, tel. 04 90 97 82 55, www.saintesmaries.com).

Sights and Activities: Outside of May, when the celebration for Saint Sarah takes place, the town of Stes-Maries-de-la-Mer has little to offer except its beachfront promenade, bullring, and towering five-belled fortified church. The **church** interior is worth a look for its unusual decorations and artifacts, including the statue of Saint Sarah (free, €2 to climb to roof for Camargue and sea views). Avoid the women with flowers and the assertive palm readers, who often cluster near the church—they want your money, not your friendship.

Most tourists come to take a horse, a jeep, or a bike into the Camargue—and there's no lack of outfits ready to take you for a ride. The TIs in Arles and Stes-Maries-de-la-Mer have long lists. Rental bikes (for the ride out to La Digue de la Mer) and advice on the best routes are available at Le Vélo Saintois (€18/day, 19 Rue de la République in Stes-Maries-de-la-Mer, tel. 04 90 97 74 56, www.levelosaintois.camargue.fr). Book jeep excursions with Jerry Perkins at Nature et Découverte (2-hour trips from €40, on route d'Aigues-Mortes near Stes-Maries-de-la-Mer, tel. 06 12 44 64 74, www.visite-camargue.com) or at one of the many outfits based in Arles. Les Cabanes de Cacharel gives top-notch horseback tours (€18/hour—plan on at least 2 hours, Route de Cacharel near Stes-Maries-de-la-Mer, tel. 04 90 97 84 10, www.cabanesdecacharel .com, info@camargueacheval.com).

Aigues-Mortes

This strange walled city, on the western edge of the Camargue (20 miles from Nîmes), was built by Louis IX as a jumping-off point for his Crusades to the Holy Land. Although Aigues-Mortes was a strategically situated royal port city, it was actually never near the sea—ships reached it via canals that were dug through an immense lagoon. Today its tall towers and thick fortifications seem oddly out of place, surrounded by nothing but salt marshes and flamingos. The name "Aigues-Mortes" means "Dead Waters," which says it all. Skip it unless you need more souvenirs and crowded streets, although drivers going between Nîmes and Arles can detour to Aigues-Mortes for a quick-and-easy taste of the Camargue. Aigues-Mortes and Nîmes are linked by buses (6/day, 50 minutes) and trains (6/day, 45 minutes).

AVIGNON

Famous for its nursery rhyme, medieval bridge, and brooding Palace of the Popes, contemporary Avignon (ah-veen-yohn) bustles and prospers behind its mighty walls. During the 94 years (1309-1403) that Avignon starred as the *Franco Vaticano* (the temporary residence of the popes) and hosted two antipopes, it grew from a quiet village into a thriving city. With its large student population and fashionable shops, today's Avignon is an intriguing blend of medieval history, youthful energy, and urban sophistication. Street performers entertain the international throngs who fill Avignon's ubiquitous cafés and trendy boutiques. If you're here in July, be prepared for big crowds and higher prices, thanks to the rollicking theater festival. (Reserve your hotel far in advance.) Clean, lively, and popular with tourists, Avignon is more impressive for its outdoor ambience than for its museums and monuments.

Orientation to Avignon

Cours Jean Jaurès, which turns into Rue de la République, runs straight from the Centre-Ville train station to Place de l'Horloge and the Palace of the Popes, splitting Avignon in two. The larger eastern half is where the action is. Climb to the Jardin du Rochers des Doms for the town's best view, consider touring the pope's immense palace, lose yourself in Avignon's back streets (you can follow my "Discovering Avignon's Back Streets" self-guided walk), and find a shady square to call home. Avignon's shopping district fills the traffic-free streets near where Rue de la République meets Place de l'Horloge. As you wander, look for signs in Occitan—the language of the Occitania region; you might see the name of the city written as "Avinhon" or "Avignoun."

Tourist Information

The **main TI** is between the Centre-Ville train station and the old town, at 41 Cours Jean Jaurès (April-Oct Mon-Sat 9:00-18:00—until 19:00 in July, Sun 9:45-17:00; Nov-March Mon-Fri 9:00-18:00, Sat 9:00-17:00, Sun 10:00-12:00; tel. 04 32 74 32 74, www.avignon-tourisme.com). From April through mid-October, a branch TI office is open inside **Les Halles market** (Fri-Sun 10:00-13:00, closed Mon-Thu). At any TI, get the helpful map. If you're staying awhile, pick up the free *Guide Touristique* (info on bike rentals, hotels, apartment rentals, events, and museums).

Sightseeing Pass: Everyone should pick up the free **Avignon Passion Pass** (valid 15 days, for up to 5 family members). Get the pass stamped when you pay full price at your first sight, and then receive reductions at the others (for example, €2 less at the Palace of the Popes and €3 less at the Petit Palais). The discounts add up—always show your Passion Pass when buying a ticket. The pass comes with the Avignon "Passion" map and guide, which includes several good (but tricky-to-follow) walking tours.

Arrival in Avignon
By Train

Avignon has two train stations: TGV (linked to downtown by frequent shuttle buses) and Centre-Ville. While most TGV trains serve only the TGV Station, some also stop at Centre-Ville—verify your station in advance.

TGV Station (Gare TGV): This shiny new station, on the outskirts of town, has no baggage storage (bags can be stored only at the Centre-Ville train station). Car rental, buses, and taxis are all out the north exit *(sortie nord)*.

To get to the city center, take the **TER local train** from the TGV Station to the Avignon Centre-Ville Station (€1.60, 2/hour, 5 minutes). From there, cross the street in front of the Centre-Ville Station and walk through the city walls onto Cours Jean Jaurès. The TER train was supposed to replace the existing shuttle bus service between the TGV Station and the city. But, should there still be bus service, you'll likely find it by walking out the TGV Station's north entrance—look for bus #10 (€1.30, 3/hour, 20 minutes).

A **taxi** ride between the TGV station and downtown Avignon costs about €20 (more on Sunday and from 19:00 to 6:00).

Buses to **Arles' Centre-Ville train station** stop at the next shelter down from the Avignon buses (8/day, 1 hour, €7, included with railpass, schedule posted on the shelter and available at info booths inside the TGV Station).

Rental car offices are straight out the north exit and down the steps. If you're driving directly to Arles, St-Rémy-de-Provence, Les Baux, or the Luberon, leave the station, following signs to *Avignon Sud*, then *La Rocade*. You'll soon see exits to Arles (best for St-Rémy and Les Baux) and Cavaillon (for Luberon villages).

Centre-Ville Station (Gare Avignon Centre-Ville): All non-TGV trains (and a few TGV trains) serve the central station. The Centre-Ville Station has car rental agencies (open Mon-Sat 9:00-12:00 & 14:00-18:00, closed Sun) but doesn't have any baggage storage. To reach the town center, cross the busy street in front of the station and walk through the city walls onto Cours Jean Jaurès. The TI is three blocks down, at #41.

By Bus

The grimy bus station *(gare routière)* is 100 yards to the right as you leave the Centre-Ville train station, beyond and below Hôtel Ibis (info desk open Mon-Sat 8:00-19:30, closed Sun, tel. 04 90 82 07 35, staff speaks a little English).

By Car

Drivers entering Avignon follow *Centre-Ville* and *Gare SNCF* (train station) signs. You'll find central pay lots (about €10/half-day, €15/day) in the garage next to the Centre-Ville train station, at the Parking Jean Jaurès under the ramparts across from the station. Two less pricey options are Parking Les Halles in the center of town, on Place Pie ("pee"), and Parking Palais des Papes. Hotels have advice for smart overnight parking, and some offer small discounts in the municipal parking garages. No matter where you park, leave nothing in your car.

Free or Cheap Parking: Two free lots have complimentary shuttle buses to the center except on Sunday (follow *P Gratuit* signs): One is just across Daladier Bridge (Pont Daladier) on Ile de la Barthelasse, with shuttles to Place Crillon; the other is along the river east of the Palace of the Popes, with shuttles to Place Carnot (both lots are within a long walk of the city center if need be). Parking on the street is free in the *bleu* zones 12:00-14:00 and 19:00-9:00. It's €2 for about three hours 9:00-12:00 and 14:00-19:00 (hint: If you put €2 in the meter after 19:00, it's good until 14:00 the next day, or if you put €2 in at 9:00, you're good until 14:00).

Helpful Hints

Book Ahead for July: During the July theater festival, rooms are sparse—reserve very early, or stay in Arles or St-Rémy.

Local Help: David at **Imagine Tours,** a nonprofit group whose

AVIGNON

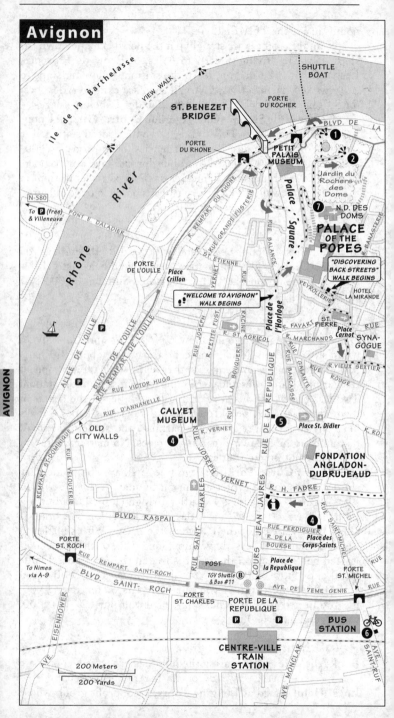

Avignon

AVIGNON

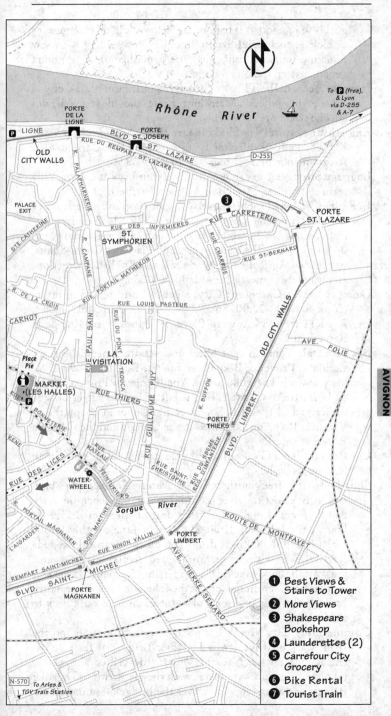

To P (free), & Lyon via D-255 & A-7

Rhône River

PORTE DE LA LIGNE

P LIGNE

OLD CITY WALLS

BLVD ST. JOSEPH

PORTE ST. JOSEPH

RUE DU REMPART ST. LAZARE

RUE ST. LAZARE

D-255

PORTE ST. LAZARE

PALACE EXIT

STE CATHERINE

R. PALAPHARNERIE

R. CAMPANE

RUE DES INFIRMIERES

ST. SYMPHORIEN

❸

RUE CARRETERIE

RUE CHARRUE

RUE ST-BERNARD

RUE PORTAIL MATHERON

R. DE LA CROIX

RUE PAUL SAIN

RUE LOUIS PASTEUR

CARNOT

RUE DU PONT

OLD CITY WALLS

AVE. FOLIE

Place Pie

ℹ️

LA VISITATION

TROUCA

R. BUFFON

MARKET (LES HALLES)

P

RUE THIERS

RUE GUILLAUME PUY

PORTE THIERS

BLVD. LIMBERT

BONNETERIE

RENE

RUE RATEAU

RUE SAINT-CHRISTOPHE

RUE DU 58EME REG. D'INFANTERIE

RUE DES LICES

R. TEINTURIERS

WATER-WHEEL

Sorgue River

ROUTE DE MONTFAVET

R. PORTAIL MAGNANEN

R. BON MARTINET

L'AIGARDEN

RUE NINON VALLIN

PORTE LIMBERT

REMPART SAINT-MICHEL

MICHEL

AVE. PIERRE SEMARD

BLVD. SAINT-

PORTE MAGNANEN

N-570 To Arles & TGV Train Station

AVIGNON

❶	Best Views & Stairs to Tower
❷	More Views
❸	Shakespeare Bookshop
❹	Launderettes (2)
❺	Carrefour City Grocery
❻	Bike Rental
❼	Tourist Train

goal is to promote this region, can help with hotel emergencies or tickets to special events (mobile 06 89 22 19 87, www.imagine-tours.net, imagine.tours@gmail.com). If you don't get an answer, leave a message.

Internet Access: The TI has a current list of Internet cafés, or you can ask your hotelier. Many bigger cafés provide free Wi-Fi to anyone who buys a drink.

English Bookstore: Try **Shakespeare Bookshop** (Tue-Sat 9:30-12:00 & 14:00-18:30, closed Sun-Mon, 155 Rue Carreterie, in Avignon's northeast corner, tel. 04 90 27 38 50).

Baggage Storage: You can usually leave your bags at Centre-Ville train station (see "Arrival in Avignon," earlier).

Laundry: At **La Blanchisseuse,** you can drop off your laundry and pick it up the same day for about €12 a load (daily 7:00-21:00, a few blocks west of main TI at 24 Rue Lanterne, tel. 04 90 85 58 80). The launderette at 66 Place des Corps-Saints, where Rue Agricol Perdiguier ends, has English instructions and is handy to most hotels (daily 7:00-20:00).

Grocery Store: Carrefour City is central and has long hours (Mon-Sat 7:00-22:00, Sun 9:00-12:00, next to McDonald's, 2 blocks from TI, toward Place de l'Horloge on Rue de la République).

Bike Rental: You can rent bikes and scooters near the train station at **Provence Bike** (7 Avenue St. Ruf, tel. 04 90 27 92 61, www.provence-bike.com). You'll enjoy riding on the Ile de la Barthelasse, but biking is better in Isle-sur-la-Sorgue (described in the Hill Towns of the Luberon chapter) and Vaison la Romaine (described in the Orange and the Côtes du Rhône chapter).

Car Rental: The TGV train station has car-rental agencies (open long hours daily).

Shuttle Boat: A free shuttle boat, the *Navette Fluviale,* plies back and forth across the river (as it did in the days when the town had no functioning bridge) from near St. Bénezet Bridge (3/hour, daily July-Aug 11:00-21:00, Sept-June roughly 10:00-12:30 & 14:00-18:00). It drops you on the peaceful Ile de la Barthelasse, with its recommended riverside restaurant, grassy walks, and bike rides with terrific city views. If you stay on the island for dinner, check the schedule for the last return boat—or be prepared for a pleasant 25-minute walk back to town.

Commanding City Views: For great views of Avignon and the river, walk or drive across Daladier Bridge, or ferry across the Rhône on the *Navette Fluviale* (described above). I'd take the boat across the river, walk the view path to Daladier Bridge, and then cross back over the bridge (45-minute walk

Festival d'Avignon

The last thing Avignon needs is an excuse to party. Still, as it has every July since 1947, a theater festival crashes the city, creating a Mardi Gras-like atmosphere. Contemporary theater groups come from throughout Europe, and each year the festival showcases a different theater director or artist. The program is announced in May, and most tickets are booked immediately—hotels are 80 percent full by March. The festival is indoors, but venues overflow onto the streets. The organizers need 20 different locations for the performances, from actual theater spaces to small chapels to the inner courtyard of the Palace of the Popes, which seats 2,000. There's also a "fringe festival," called Avignon-Off, which adds another 100 venues and countless amateur performances, as well as a children's theater festival, with storytellers, dance, musicals, and marionettes. In July the entire city is a stage, with mimes, fire-breathers, singers, and musicians filling the streets. Most of the performances are in French, some are in English, and many dance performances don't require language at all (www.festival-avignon.com and www.avignonleoff.com).

over mostly level ground). You can enjoy other impressive vistas from the top of the Jardin du Rochers des Doms, from the tower in the Palace of the Popes, from the end of the famous, broken St. Bénezet Bridge, and from the entrance to Fort St. André, across the river in Villeneuve-lès-Avignon.

Tours in Avignon

Walking Tours

On mid-season Mondays and Saturdays, the TI offers informative English walking tours of Avignon, which include a visit to the Palace of the Popes (€19, discounted with Avignon Passion Pass, April-June and Aug-Oct Mon at 15:00, no tours in July or Nov-March). Behind-the-scenes tours in English of the Palace of the Popes are also possible; ask at the TI.

Tourist Trains

The little train leaves regularly from in front of the Palace of the Popes and offers a decent overview of the city, including the Jardin du Rochers des Doms and St. Bénezet Bridge (€7, 2/hour, 40 minutes, mid-March-mid-Oct daily 10:00-18:00, until 19:00 July-Aug, English commentary).

Guided Excursions

Several minivan tour companies based in Avignon offer transportation to destinations described in this book, including Pont du Gard, the Luberon, and the Camargue (about €65-80/

Avignon at a Glance

▲▲**Jardin du Rochers des Doms** Park and ramparts at the hilltop where Avignon was first settled, with great views of the Rhône River Valley and the famous broken bridge. **Hours:** Daily April-Sept 7:30-20:00, Oct-March 7:30-18:00. See page 137.

▲▲**St. Bénezet Bridge** The "Pont d'Avignon" of nursery-rhyme fame, once connecting the pope's territory to France. **Hours:** Daily mid-March-Oct 9:00-19:00, until 20:00 July and Sept, until 21:00 in Aug, Nov-mid-March 9:30-17:45. See page 138.

▲▲**Scenic Squares** Numerous hide-and-seek squares ideal for postcard-writing and people-watching—pick your favorite: Place des Corps-Saints, Place St. Pierre, Place des Châtaignes (adjacent to Place St. Pierre), Place Crillon, Place St. Didier (near the recommended Caveau du Théâtre restaurant), and the big Place Pie (see map on page 130). **Hours:** Always open.

▲**Palace of the Popes** Fourteenth-century Gothic palace built by the popes who made Avignon their home. **Hours:** Daily March-June and Sept-Oct 9:00-19:00, July-Aug 9:00-20:00, Nov-Feb 9:30-17:45. See page 139.

▲**Tower of Philip the Fair** Massive tower across St. Bénezet Bridge, featuring the best view over Avignon and the Rhône basin. **Hours:** March-April Tue-Sun 10:00-12:00 & 14:00-17:00, closed Mon; May-Oct daily 10:00-12:00 & 14:00-18:00; closed Nov-Feb. See page 143.

Petit Palais Museum "Little palace" displaying the Church's collection of medieval Italian painting and sculpture. **Hours:** Wed-Mon 10:00-13:00 & 14:00-18:00, closed Tue. See page 136.

Synagogue Thirteenth-century synagogue rebuilt in a Neoclassical Greek-temple style (requires advance notice, closed Sat-Sun). See page 141.

Fondation Angladon-Dubrujeaud Museum with a small but enjoyable Post-Impressionist collection, including art by Cézanne, Van Gogh, Daumier, Degas, and Picasso. **Hours:** Tue-Sun 13:00-18:00, closed Mon. See page 143.

Calvet Museum Fine-arts museum with a good collection and English audioguide. **Hours:** Wed-Mon 10:00-13:00 & 14:00-18:00, closed Tue. See page 143.

AVIGNON

person for all-day tours). See "Tours of Provence" on page 56 (note that Imagine Tours and guides François Marcou and Daniela Wedel are all based in Avignon).

Self-Guided Walks

For a fine overview of the city, combine these two walks. "Welcome to Avignon" covers the major sights, while "Discovering Avignon's Back Streets" leads you along the lanes less taken, delving beyond the surface of this historic city.

▲▲Welcome to Avignon

Before starting this walk—which connects the city's top sights—be sure to pick up the Avignon Passion Pass at the TI, then show it when entering each attraction to receive discounted admission (explained earlier, under "Tourist Information").

• *Start your tour where the Romans did, on Place de l'Horloge, in front of City Hall (Hôtel de Ville).*

Place de l'Horloge

This café square was the town forum during Roman times and the market square through the Middle Ages. (Restaurants here offer good people-watching, but they also have less ambience and low-quality meals—you'll find better squares elsewhere to hang your beret in.) Named for a medieval clock tower mostly hidden behind City Hall (find plaque in English), this square's present popularity arrived with the trains in 1854. Walk a few steps to the center of the square, and look down the main drag, Rue de la République. When the trains came to Avignon, proud city fathers wanted a direct, impressive way to link the new station to the heart of the city (just like in Paris)—so they plowed over homes to create Rue de la République and widened Place de l'Horloge. This main drag's Parisian feel is intentional—it was built not in the Provençal manner, but in the Haussmann style that is so dominant in Paris (characterized by broad, straight boulevards lined with stately buildings).

• *Walk slightly uphill past the carousel (public WCs behind). Veer right at the Hôtel des Palais des Papes and continue into...*

Palace Square (Place du Palais)

Pull up a concrete stump just past the café. Nicknamed *bites* (slang for the male anatomy), these stumps effectively keep cars from double-parking in areas designed for people. Many of the metal ones slide up and down by remote control to let privileged cars come and go.

Now take in the scene. This grand square is lined with the

Palace of the Popes, the Petit Palais, and the cathedral. In the 1300s the entire headquarters of the Catholic Church was moved to Avignon. The Church bought Avignon and gave it a complete makeover. Along with clearing out vast spaces like this square and building this three-acre palace, the Church erected more than three miles of protective wall (with 39 towers), "appropriate" housing for cardinals (read: mansions), and residences for its entire bureaucracy. The city was Europe's largest construction zone. Avignon's population grew from 6,000 to 25,000 in short order. (Today, 13,000 people live within the walls.) The limits of pre-papal Avignon are outlined on your city map: Rues Joseph Vernet, Henri Fabre, des Lices, and Philonarde all follow the route of the city's earlier defensive wall.

The Petit Palais (Little Palace) seals the uphill end of the square and was built for a cardinal; today it houses medieval paintings (museum described later). The church just to the left of the Palace of the Popes is Avignon's cathedral. It predates the Church's purchase of Avignon by 200 years. Its small size reflects Avignon's modest, pre-papal population. The gilded Mary was added in 1854, when the Vatican established the doctrine of her Immaculate Conception. Mary is taller than the Palace of the Popes by design: The Vatican never accepted what it called the "Babylonian Captivity" and had a bad attitude about Avignon long after the pope was definitively back in Rome. There hasn't been a French pope since the Holy See returned to Rome—over 600 years ago. That's what I call a grudge.

Right behind you, across the square from the palace's main entry stands a cardinal's residence, built in 1619 (now the Conservatoire National de Musique). Its fancy Baroque facade was a visual counterpoint to the stripped-down Huguenot aesthetic of the age. During this time, Provence was a hotbed of Protestantism—but, buried within this region, Avignon was a Catholic stronghold.

• You can visit the massive **Palace of the Popes** (described on page 139) now, but it works better to visit that palace at the end of this walk, then continue directly to the "Back Streets" walk, described later.

Now is a good time to take in the...

Petit Palais Museum (Musée du Petit Palais)

This former cardinal's palace now displays the Church's collection of mostly medieval Italian painting (including one delightful Botticelli) and sculpture. All 350 paintings deal with Christian themes. A visit here before going to the Palace of the Popes helps furnish and populate that otherwise barren building, and a quick peek into its courtyard (even if you don't tour the museum) shows the importance of cardinal housing. The museum's garden café provides a shady, peaceful refuge.

Cost and Hours: €6, €3 English brochure, some English explanations posted; Wed-Mon 10:00-13:00 & 14:00-18:00, closed Tue; at north end of Palace Square, tel. 04 90 86 44 58.

• *From Palace Square we'll head up to the rocky hilltop where Avignon was first settled, then drop down to the river. With this short loop, you can enjoy a small park, hike to a grand river view, and visit Avignon's beloved broken bridge.*

Start by climbing to the church level (you can fill your bottle with cold water here), then take the central switchback ramps up to...

▲▲Jardin du Rochers des Doms

Though the park itself is a delight—with a sweet little café (good prices for food and drinks) and public WCs—don't miss the

climax: a panoramic view of the Rhône River Valley and the broken bridge. For the best views (and the favorite make-out spot for local teenagers later in the evening), find the small terrace behind the odd zodiac display across the grass from the pond-side park café. If the green fence is ruining it for you, stand on the short wall behind you, or detour a few minutes through the park (to the right, with the river on your left) to find a bigger terrace.

On a clear day, the tallest peak you see, with its white limestone cap, is Mont Ventoux ("Windy Mountain"). Below and just to the right, you'll spot free passenger ferries shuttling across the river (great views from path on other side of the river), and—tucked amidst the trees on the far side of the river—a fun, recommended restaurant, Le Bercail. The island in the river is the Ile de la Barthelasse, a lush nature preserve where Avignon can breathe. To the left in the distance, the TGV rail bridge floats gracefully above the valley.

Fort St. André (across the river on the hill; see the info plaque to the left) was built by the French in 1360, shortly after the pope moved to Avignon, to counter the papal incursion into this part of Europe. The castle was across the border, in the kingdom of France. Avignon's famous bridge was a key border crossing, with towers on either end—one was French, and the other was the pope's. The French one, across the river, is the Tower of Philip the Fair (described later, under "More Sights in Avignon").

Cost and Hours: Free, park gates open daily April-Sept 7:30-20:00, Oct-March 7:30-18:00.

AVIGNON

• *Take the walkway down to the left and find the stairs (closed at dusk) leading down to the tower. You'll catch glimpses of the...*

Ramparts

The only bit of the rampart you can walk on is accessed from St. Bénezet Bridge (pay to enter—see next). Just after the papacy took control of Avignon, the walls were extended to take in the convents and monasteries that had been outside the city. What you see today was restored in the 19th century.

• *When you come out of the tower on street level, exit out of the walls, then turn left along the wall to the old bridge. Pass under the bridge to find its entrance shortly after.*

▲▲St. Bénezet Bridge (Pont St. Bénezet)

This bridge, whose construction and location were inspired by a shepherd's religious vision, is the "Pont d'Avignon" of nursery-

rhyme fame. The ditty (which you've probably been humming all day) dates back to the 15th century: *Sur le Pont d'Avignon, on y danse, on y danse, sur le Pont d'Avignon, on y danse tous en rond* ("On the bridge of Avignon, we will dance, we will dance, on the bridge of Avignon, we will dance all in a circle").

But the bridge was a big deal even outside of its kiddie-tune fame. Built between 1171 and 1185, it was the only bridge crossing the mighty Rhône in the Middle Ages—important to pilgrims, merchants, and armies. It was damaged several times by floods and subsequently rebuilt. In 1668 most of it was knocked out for the last time by a disastrous icy flood. Lacking a government stimulus package, the townsfolk decided not to rebuild this time, and for more than a century, Avignon had no bridge across the Rhône. While only four arches survive today, the original bridge was huge: Imagine a 22-arch, 3,000-foot-long bridge extending from Vatican territory across the island to the lonely Tower of Philip the Fair, which marked the beginning of France (see displays of the bridge's original length).

Cost and Hours: €4.50, includes audioguide, €13 combo-ticket includes Palace of the Popes, same hours as Palace of the Popes (described next), tel. 04 90 27 51 16.

Visiting the Bridge: The ticket booth is housed in what was a medieval hospital for the poor (funded by bridge tolls). Admission includes a small room dedicated to the song of Avignon's bridge and your only chance to walk a bit of the ramparts (enter both from the tower). A Romanesque chapel on the bridge is dedicated to St. Bénezet. Though there's not much to see on the bridge, the audioguide included with your ticket tells a good enough story. It's also fun to be in the breezy middle of the river with a sweeping city view.

• *To get to the Palace of the Popes from here, leave via the riverfront exit, turn left, then turn left again back into the walls. Walk to the end of the short street, then turn right following signs to Palais des Papes. Next, look for brown signs leading left under the passageway, then stay the course up the narrow steps to Palace Square.*

▲Palace of the Popes (Palais des Papes)

In 1309 a French pope was elected (Pope Clément V). At the urging of the French king, His Holiness decided that dangerous Italy was

no place for a pope, so he moved the whole operation to Avignon for a secure rule under a supportive king. The Catholic Church literally bought Avignon (then a two-bit town), and popes resided here until 1403. Meanwhile, Italians demanded a Roman pope, so from 1378 on, there were twin popes—one in Rome and one in Avignon—causing a schism in the Catholic Church that wasn't fully resolved until 1417.

AVIGNON

Cost and Hours: €10.50 (more for special exhibits), essential audioguide-€2, €13 combo-ticket includes St. Bénezet Bridge, daily March-June and Sept-Oct 9:00-19:00, July-Aug 9:00-20:00, Nov-Feb 9:30-17:45, last entry one hour before closing, tel. 04 90 27 50 74, www.palais-des-papes.com.

Visiting the Palace: Spring for the slick multimedia audioguide, which leads you along a one-way route and does a decent job of overcoming the palace's complete lack of furnishings. It teaches the basic history while allowing you to tour at your own pace. A small museum inside the palace also adds context. Still, touring the palace is pretty anticlimactic, given its historic importance.

As you wander, ponder that this palace—the largest surviving Gothic palace in Europe—was built to accommodate 500 people as the administrative center of the Holy See and home of the pope. This was the most fortified palace of the age (remember, the pope left Rome to be more secure). Nine popes ruled from here, making this the center of Christianity for nearly 100 years. You'll walk through the pope's personal quarters (frescoed with happy hunting scenes), see many models of how the various popes added to the building, and learn about its state-of-the-art plumbing. The rooms are huge. The "pope's chapel" is twice the size of the adjacent Avignon cathedral.

The last pope (or, technically, antipope, since by then Rome also had its own rival pope) checked out in 1403 (escaping a siege), but the Church owned Avignon until the French Revolution in 1789. During this interim period, the pope's "legate" (official representative, normally a nephew) ruled Avignon from this palace. Avignon residents, many of whom had come from Rome, spoke Italian for a century after the pope left, making it a linguistic ghetto within France. In the Napoleonic age, the palace was a barracks, housing 1,800 soldiers. You can see cuts in the wall where high ceilings gave way to floor beams. Climb the tower (Tour de la Gâche) for grand views and a rooftop café with surprisingly good food at very fair prices.

Wine Room: A room at the end of the tour (called *la boutellerie*) is dedicated to the region's wines, of which they claim the pope was a fan. Sniff "Le Nez du Vin"—a black box with 54 tiny bottles designed to develop your "nose." (Blind-test your travel partner.) The nearby village of Châteauneuf-du-Pape is where the pope summered in the 1320s. Its famous wine is a direct descendant of his wine. You're welcome to taste here (about €6 for three to five fine wines and souvenir tasting cup). If it's only wine you want, go directly to the back entrance of the palace and enter the boutique.

• *You'll exit at the rear of the palace, where my "Back Streets" walking tour begins (described next). Or, to return to Palace Square, make two rights after exiting the palace.*

▲▲Discovering Avignon's Back Streets

Use the map in this chapter or the TI map to navigate this easy, level, 30-minute walk. This self-guided tour begins in the small square (Place de la Mirande) behind the Palace of the Popes. If you've toured the palace, this is where you exit. Otherwise, from the front of the palace, follow the narrow, cobbled Rue de la Peyrollerie—carved out of the rock—around the palace on the right side as you face it.

• *Our walk begins at the...*

Hôtel La Mirande: Located on the square, Avignon's finest hotel welcomes visitors. Find the atrium lounge and consider a coffee break amid the understated luxury (€12 afternoon tea served daily 15:00-18:00, includes a generous selection of pastries). Inspect the royal lounge and dining room; cooking demos are offered in the basement below. Rooms start at about €425 in high season.

• *Turn left out of the hotel and left again on Rue de la Peyrollerie ("Coppersmiths' Street"), then take your first right on Rue des Ciseaux d'Or. On the small square ahead you'll find the...*

Church of St. Pierre: The original chestnut doors were carved in 1551, when tales of New World discoveries raced across Europe. (Notice the Indian headdress, top center of left-side door.) The fine Annunciation (eye level on right-side door) shows Gabriel giving Mary the exciting news in impressive Renaissance 3-D. Now take 10 steps back from the door and look way up. The tiny statue breaking the skyline of the church is the pagan god Bacchus, with oodles of grapes. What's he doing sitting atop a Christian church? No one knows. The church's interior holds a beautiful Baroque altar. (For recommended restaurants near the Church of St. Pierre, see "Eating in Avignon," later.)

• *Facing the church door, follow the alley to the left, which was covered and turned into a tunnel during the town's population boom. It leads into...*

Place des Châtaignes: The cloister of St. Pierre is named for the chestnut *(châtaigne)* trees that once stood here (now replaced by plane trees). The practical atheists of the French Revolution destroyed the cloister, leaving only faint traces of the arches along the church side of the square.

• *Continue around the church and cross the busy street to the Banque Chaix. Across little Rue des Fourbisseurs find the classy...*

15th-Century Building: With its original beamed eaves showing, this is a rare vestige from the Middle Ages. Notice how this building widens the higher it gets. A medieval loophole based taxes on ground-floor square footage—everything above was tax-free. Walking down Rue des Fourbisseurs ("Street of the Animal Furriers"), notice how the top floors almost meet. Fire was a constant danger in the Middle Ages, as flames leapt easily from one home to the next. In fact, the lookout guard's primary responsibility was watching for fires, not the enemy. Virtually all of Avignon's medieval homes have been replaced by safer structures.

• *Walk down Rue des Fourbisseurs and turn left onto the traffic-free Rue du Vieux Sextier ("Street of the Old Balance," for weighing items); another left under the first arch leads 10 yards to Avignon's...*

Synagogue: Jews first arrived in Avignon with the Diaspora (exile) of the first century. Avignon's Jews were nicknamed "the Pope's Jews" because of the protection that the Vatican offered to Jews expelled from France. Although the original synagogue dates from the 1220s, in the mid-19th century it was completely rebuilt in a Neoclassical Greek-temple style by a non-Jewish architect. This is the only synagogue under a rotunda that you'll see anywhere. It's an intimate, classy place dressed with white colonnades and walnut furnishings. To enter the synagogue, you'll have to email in advance of your visit (free, closed Sat-Sun, 2 Place Jerusalem, tel. 04 90 55 21 24, rabinacia@hotmail.fr).

• *Retrace your steps to Rue du Vieux Sextier and turn left, then continue to the big square and find the big, boxy...*

Market (Les Halles): In 1970, the town's open-air market was replaced by this modern one. The market's jungle-like green

wall reflects the changes of seasons and helps mitigate its otherwise stark exterior (open Tue-Sun until 13:00, closed Mon, small TI inside open April-mid-Oct Fri-Sun). Step inside for a sensual experience of organic breads, olives, and festival-of-mold cheeses. The Rue des Temptations cuts down the center. Cafés and cheese shops are on the right—as far as possible from the stinky fish stalls on the left. Follow your nose away from the fish and have a coffee with the locals.

• *Exit out the back door of Les Halles, turn left on Rue de la Bonneterie ("Street of Hosiery"), and track the street for five minutes to the plane trees, where it becomes...*

Rue des Teinturiers: This "Street of the Dyers" is a tie-dyed, tree- and stream-lined lane, home to earthy cafés and galleries. This was the cloth industry's dyeing and textile center in the 1800s. The stream is a branch of the Sorgue River. Those stylish Provençal fabrics and patterns you see for sale everywhere were first made here, after a pattern imported from India.

About three small bridges down, you'll pass the Grey Penitents chapel on the right. The upper facade shows the GPs, who dressed up in robes and pointy hoods to do their anonymous good deeds back in the 13th century (long before the KKK dressed this way). As you stroll on, you'll see the work of amateur sculptors, who have carved whimsical car barriers out of limestone.

Fun restaurants on this atmospheric street are recommended later, under "Eating in Avignon."

• *Farther down Rue des Teinturiers, you'll come to the...*

Waterwheel: Standing here, imagine the Sorgue River—which hits the mighty Rhône in Avignon—being broken into several canals in order to turn 23 such wheels. In about 1800, waterwheels powered the town's industries. The little cogwheel above the big one could be shoved into place, kick-

ing another machine into gear behind the wall. (For more on the Sorgue River and its waterwheels, see my self-guided walk of Isle-sur-la-Sorgue on page 223.)

• *To return to the real world, double back on Rue des Teinturiers and turn left on Rue des Lices, which traces the first medieval wall. (*Lice *is the no-man's-land along a protective wall.) After a long block you'll pass a striking four-story building that was a home for the poor in the 1600s, an army barracks in the 1800s, a fine-arts school in the 1900s, and is a deluxe condominium today (much of this neighborhood is going high-class residential). Eventually you'll return to Rue de la République, Avignon's main drag.*

More Sights in Avignon

Most of Avignon's top sights are covered earlier by my self-guided walks. With more time, consider these options.

Fondation Angladon-Dubrujeaud
Visiting this museum is like being invited into the elegant home of a rich and passionate art collector. It mixes a small but enjoyable collection of art from Post-Impressionists to Cubists (including Paul Cézanne, Vincent van Gogh, Honoré Daumier, Edgar Degas, and Pablo Picasso), with re-created art studios and furnishings from many periods. It's a quiet place with a few superb paintings.

Cost and Hours: €6, Tue-Sun 13:00-18:00, closed Mon, 5 Rue Laboureur, tel. 04 90 82 29 03, www.angladon.com.

Calvet Museum (Musée Calvet)
This fine-arts museum impressively displays its collection, highlighting French Baroque works. This museum goes ignored by most, but you'll find a few diamonds in the rough upstairs: Géricault, Soutine, and one painting each from Manet, Sisley, Bonnard, Dufy, and Vlamnick.

Cost and Hours: €6, includes audioguide, Wed-Mon 10:00-13:00 & 14:00-18:00, closed Tue, in the quieter western half of town at 65 Rue Joseph Vernet, antiquities collection a few blocks away at 27 Rue de la République—same hours and ticket, tel. 04 90 86 33 84, www.musee-calvet.org.

Near Avignon, in Villeneuve-lès-Avignon
▲Tower of Philip the Fair (Tour Philippe-le-Bel)
Built to protect access to St. Bénezet Bridge in 1307, this hulking tower offers a terrific view over Avignon and the Rhône basin. It's best late in the day.

Cost and Hours: €2.30; March-April Tue-Sun 10:00-12:00 & 14:00-17:00, closed Mon; May-Oct daily 10:00-12:00 & 14:00-18:00; closed Nov-Feb.

Getting There: To reach the tower from Avignon, drive five minutes (cross Daladier Bridge, follow signs to *Villeneuve-lès-Avignon*), or take bus #11 (2/hour, catch bus in front of post office on Cours Président Kennedy—see map on pages 130-131).

Sleeping in Avignon

Hotel values are better in Arles, though I've found some pretty good deals in Avignon. Avignon is crazy during its July festival (see sidebar on page 133), when you must book long ahead (expect inflated prices). Drivers should ask about parking deals as most hotels offer 20 percent off on pay lots.

Near Avignon's Centre-Ville Station

These listings are a five-to-ten-minute walk from the Centre-Ville train station.

$$$ Hôtel Bristol*** is a big, professionally run place on the main drag, offering predictable "American" comforts, including spacious public spaces, large rooms decorated in neutral tones, duvets on the beds, a big elevator, air-conditioning, and a generous buffet breakfast (standard Db-€116, bigger Db-€140, Tb/Qb-€170, breakfast-€12, parking-€12, 44 Cours Jean Jaurès, tel. 04 90 16 48 48, www.bristol-hotel-avignon.com, contact@bristol-avignon.com).

$$ Hôtel Colbert** is a solid two-star hotel and a good mid-range bet, with richly colored, comfortable rooms in many sizes. Your hardworking hosts—Patrice, Annie, and *le chien* Brittany—care for this restored manor house, with its warm public spaces and sweet little patio. It's a popular place, so it's best to book in advance (Sb-€72, small Db-€78, bigger Db-€92, some tight bathrooms, no triples, rooms off the patio can be musty, air-con, Wi-Fi, no elevator, closed Nov-mid-March, turn right off Cours Jean Jaurès on Rue Agricol Perdiguier to #7, tel. 04 90 86 20 20, www.lecolbert-hotel.com, contact@avignon-hotel-colbert.com).

$$ Hôtel Ibis Centre Gare** offers no surprises—just predictable two-star comfort at the central train and bus stations. This well-priced place offers generous public spaces, a big café, an elevator, and a bar (Db-€75-90, guest computer and Wi-Fi, 42 Boulevard St. Roch, tel. 04 90 85 38 38, www.ibishotel.com, h0944@accor.com).

$$ Hôtel le Splendid* rents 17 acceptable rooms with faux-wood floors, most of which could use a little attention (Sb-€52, Db-€72, bigger Db with air-con-€82, Tb with air-con-€90, three Db apartments-€98, continental breakfast-€9, guest computer and Wi-Fi, no elevator, turn right off Cours Jean Jaurès on Rue Agricol Perdiguier to #17, tel. 04 90 86 14 46, www.avignon-splendid-hotel.com, splendidavignon@gmail.com).

Sleep Code

(€1 = about $1.30, country code: 33)
S = Single, **D** = Double/Twin, **T** = Triple, **Q** = Quad, **b** = bathroom,
s = shower only, * = French hotel rating system (0-5 stars).
Unless otherwise noted, credit cards are accepted and
English is spoken.

To help you easily sort through these listings, I've divided
the accommodations into three categories, based on the
price for a standard double room with bath:

$$$ Higher Priced—Most rooms €90 or more.
$$ Moderately Priced—Most rooms between €65-90.
$ Lower Priced—Most rooms €65 or less.

Prices can change without notice; verify the hotel's current rates online or by email. For the best prices, always book
direct.

$ Hôtel Boquier**, run by engaging managers Madame
Sendra and husband Pascal, has 12 quiet, good-value, and homey
rooms under wood beams in a central location (small Db-€62,
bigger Db-€73, Tb-€81, Qb-€94, air-con, guest computer and
Wi-Fi, steep and narrow stairways to some rooms, no elevator,
parking-€12, near the TI at 6 Rue du Portail Boquier, tel. 04 90 82
34 43, www.hotel-boquier.com, contact@hotel-boquier.com).

$ Hôtel Innova is a shy little place with 11 spotless rooms
at good rates (Db-€50-60, €8 less for rooms *sans* WC, extra
person-€7, no air-con, no elevator, 100 Rue Joseph Vernet, tel. 04
90 82 54 10, www.hotel-innova.fr, innova.hotel@wanadoo.fr).

In the Center, near Place de l'Horloge

$$$ Hôtel d'Europe****, with Avignon's most prestigious address,
lets peasants sleep royally without losing their shirts—but only if
they land one of the 14 surprisingly reasonable "classique" rooms.
Enter through a shady courtyard, linger in the lounges, and savor
every comfort. The hotel is located on the handsome Place Crillon,
near the river (standard Db-€195-220, large Db-€365-€550, view
suites-€900, breakfast-€21, guest computer, elevator, garage-€18,
near Daladier Bridge at 12 Place Crillon, tel. 04 90 14 76 76, www
.heurope.com, reservations@heurope.com). The hotel's fine restau-
rant is described in "Eating in Avignon," later.

$$$ Hôtel de l'Horloge****, a top four-star choice, is as
central as it gets—right on Place de l'Horloge. It offers 66 well-
appointed rooms, some with terraces and views of the city and
the Palace of the Popes (standard Db-€100-120, bigger Db with

AVIGNON

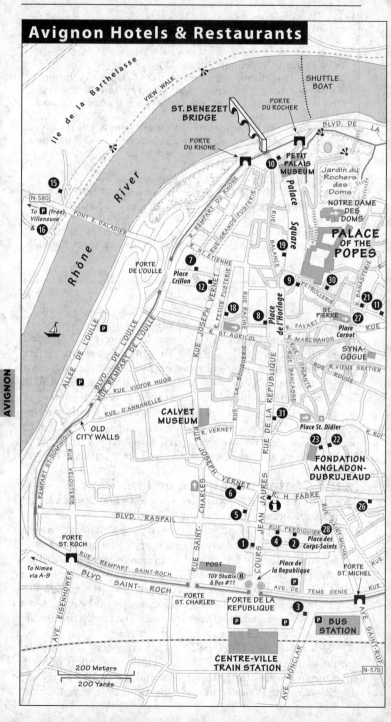

Avignon Hotels & Restaurants

AVIGNON

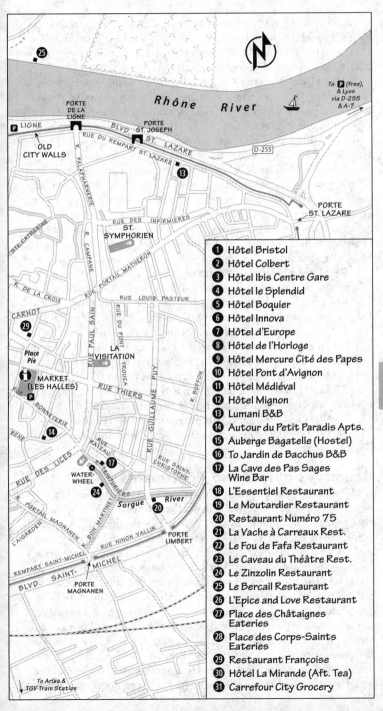

AVIGNON

1 Hôtel Bristol
2 Hôtel Colbert
3 Hôtel Ibis Centre Gare
4 Hôtel le Splendid
5 Hôtel Boquier
6 Hôtel Innova
7 Hôtel d'Europe
8 Hôtel de l'Horloge
9 Hôtel Mercure Cité des Papes
10 Hôtel Pont d'Avignon
11 Hôtel Médiéval
12 Hôtel Mignon
13 Lumani B&B
14 Autour du Petit Paradis Apts.
15 Auberge Bagatelle (Hostel)
16 To Jardin de Bacchus B&B
17 La Cave des Pas Sages Wine Bar
18 L'Essentiel Restaurant
19 Le Moutardier Restaurant
20 Restaurant Numéro 75
21 La Vache à Carreaux Rest.
22 Le Fou de Fafa Restaurant
23 Le Caveau du Théâtre Rest.
24 Le Zinzolin Restaurant
25 Le Bercail Restaurant
26 L'Epice and Love Restaurant
27 Place des Châtaignes Eateries
28 Place des Corps-Saints Eateries
29 Restaurant Françoise
30 Hôtel La Mirande (Aft. Tea)
31 Carrefour City Grocery

terrace-€150-215, terrace rooms also work as Tb or Qb, elaborate buffet breakfast/brunch-€17, served until 11:00, 1 Rue Félicien David, tel. 04 90 16 42 00, www.hotel-avignon-horloge.com, hotel.horloge@hotels-ocre-azur.com).

$$$ Hôtel Mercure Cité des Papes***, within spitting distance of the Palace of the Popes, has 89 smartly designed rooms with every comfort (Sb-€135-150, standard Db-€170, large Db-€200, breakfast-€13, look for Internet deals, many rooms have views over Place de l'Horloge, air-con, elevator, 1 Rue Jean Vilar, tel. 04 90 80 93 00, www.mercure.com, h1952@accor.com).

$$$ Hôtel Pont d'Avignon***, just inside the walls near St. Bénezet Bridge, is part of the same chain as Hôtel Mercure Cité des Papes, with the same prices for its 87 rooms. There's a smart atrium breakfast room and small garden terrace (direct access to a garage makes parking easier than at the other Mercure hotel, elevator, on Rue Ferruce, tel. 04 90 80 93 93, www.mercure.com, h0549@accor.com).

$$ Hôtel Médiéval** is burrowed deep a few blocks from the Church of St. Pierre. Built as a cardinal's home, this stone mansion has a small garden and 35 pastel, air-conditioned rooms, with helpful Régis and Mike manning the ship (Sb-€60, Db-€75-92, Tb-€110, kitchenettes available but require 3-night minimum stay, Wi-Fi, no elevator, 5 blocks east of Place de l'Horloge, behind Church of St. Pierre at 15 Rue Petite Saunerie, tel. 04 90 86 11 06, www.hotelmedieval.com, hotel.medieval@wanadoo.fr).

$$ Hôtel Mignon* is a good-enough, one-star place with fair comfort, air-conditioning, and tiny bathrooms (Sb-€60, Db-€70-75, Tb-€87, Qb-€116, guest computer and Wi-Fi, 12 Rue Joseph Vernet, tel. 04 90 82 17 30, www.hotel-mignon.com, reservation @hotel-mignon.fr).

Chambres d'Hôte and Apartments

$$$ Lumani provides the ultimate urban refuge just inside the city walls, a 15-minute walk from the Palace of the Popes. In this graceful old manor house, gentle Elisabeth and Jean welcome guests to their art-gallery-cum-bed-and-breakfast that surrounds a fountain-filled courtyard with elbow room. She paints, he designs buildings, and both care about your experience in Avignon. The five rooms are decorated with flair; no two are alike, and all overlook the shady garden (small Db-€100, big Db-€140, Db suites-€170, extra person-€30, includes organic breakfast, guest computer and Wi-Fi, music studio, parking-€10 or easy on street, 37 Rue de Rempart St. Lazare, tel. 04 90 82 94 11, www .avignon-lumani.com, lux@avignon-lumani.com).

$$$ Autour du Petit Paradis Apartments, run by Sabine and Patrick, offer four well-furnished apartments conveniently located in the city center (€750-1,000/week, 5 Rue Noel Biret, tel. 04 90 81 00 42, www.autourdupetitparadis.com, contact@autour dupetitparadis.com).

On the Outskirts of Town

$ Auberge Bagatelle offers dirt-cheap beds in two buildings—a budget hotel and a youth hostel—and has a young and lively vibe, café, grocery store, launderette, great views of Avignon, and campers for neighbors (Ds-€46, Db-€66, Tb-€95, Qb-€100, dorm bed-€18, includes breakfast, across Daladier Bridge on Ile de la Barthelasse, bus #10 from main post office, tel. 04 90 86 30 39, www.campingbagatelle.fr, auberge.bagatelle@wanadoo.fr).

Near Avignon

$$$ At Jardin de Bacchus, just 15 minutes northwest of Avignon and convenient to Pont du Gard, enthusiastic and English-speaking Christine and Erik offer three double rooms in their rural farmhouse, which overlooks the famous rosé vineyards of Tavel (Db-€90-120, includes breakfast, fine dinner possible, Wi-Fi, swimming pool, tel. 04 66 90 28 62, www.jardindebacchus .fr, jardindebacchus@free.fr). For details on their cooking classes, see page 537. Check their website to learn about their small-group food and wine tours. For bus connections, see www.edgard -transport.fr.

Eating in Avignon

Avignon offers a good range of dining experiences and settings from lively squares to atmospheric streets. Skip the overpriced, underwhelming restaurants on Place de l'Horloge and find a more intimate location for your dinner. Avignon is riddled with delightful squares and backstreets with tables ready to seat you.

Wherever you dine, start or end your evening on atmospheric Rue des Teinturiers at **La Cave des Pas Sages** for a cheap glass of regional wine. Choose from the blackboard by the bar that lists all the open bottles, then join the gang outside by the canal. In the evening, this place is a hit with the young local crowd for its wine and weekend concerts (Mon-Sat 10:00-1:00 in the morning, closed Sun, no food in evening, across from waterwheel at 41 Rue des Teinturiers).

Worthwhile for a Splurge

Book a few days ahead for these places:

L'Essentiel is where in-the-know locals go for a fine meal at reasonable prices. The setting is classy-contemporary, the wine list is extensive, the cuisine is classic French, and gentle owner Dominique makes timid diners feel at ease (inside only, €32-45 *menus*, closed Sun-Mon, 2 Rue Petite Fusterie, tel. 04 90 85 87 12, www.restaurantlessentiel.com).

Le Moutardier serves fine meals with a mesmerizing, full-monty view of the floodlit Palace of the Popes. Book ahead for the terrace tables, but skip it if you can't dine outside (€36-50 *menus*, daily, 15 Place du Palais, tel. 04 90 85 34 76).

Hôtel d'Europe's restaurant earned a Michelin star and serves a surprisingly reasonable menu in its lovely dining room and courtyard terrace (€48 *menu*, inexpensive champagne, see "Sleeping in Avignon," earlier, for details).

Restaurant Numéro 75 is worth the walk (just past where the cobbles end on Rue des Teinturiers). It fills the Pernod mansion (of *pastis* liquor fame) and a large, romantic courtyard with outdoor tables. The selection is limited to Mediterranean cuisine, but everything's *très* tasty (€30 lunch *menu*, dinner *menus*: €29 two-course and €35 three-course, Mon-Sat 12:00-14:00 & 20:00-22:00, closed Sun, 75 Rue Guillaume Puy, tel. 04 90 27 16 00, www.numero75.com).

Good for Moderate Budgets

Rue des Teinturiers has a fun concentration of mid-range eateries popular with the locals, and justifies the long walk. It's a trendy, youthful area, spiffed up with a canalside ambience and little hint of tourism. (Note that Restaurant Numéro 75 and La Cave des Pas Sages, both listed earlier, are on this street.)

La Vache à Carreaux venerates cheese and wine, while offering a full range of cuisine. It's a lively place to spend an evening, with colorful decor and an extensive and reasonable wine list. This place is a hit with locals, who gather around outside, sipping €4 glasses of good wine, reluctant to leave. Try the *poulet au Comté* (chicken with *Comté* cheese) or a *tartiflette* (tasty scalloped potatoes with melted cheese), and say *bonsoir* to welcoming owner Ludovic (inside dining only, €9 starters, €12-16 *plats*, open daily, just off atmospheric Place des Châtaignes at 14 Rue de la Peyrollerie, tel. 04 90 80 09 05).

Le Fou de Fafa's friendly British owners are making a splash with locals, serving tasty, fresh, creative cuisine at good prices. Delightful Antonia runs the entire room alone while her husband cooks (inside dining only, book ahead or arrive early, open at

18:30, closed Mon, €22-27 *menus*, 17 Rue des Trois Faucons, tel. 04 32 76 35 13).

Le Caveau du Théâtre is a convivial place where Richard invites diners to have a glass of wine or dinner at a sidewalk table, or inside in one of two carefree rooms (€15 *plats*, €22-28 *menus*, fun ambience for free, closed for lunch Sat and all day Sun, 16 Rue des Trois Faucons, tel. 04 90 82 60 91).

Le Zinzolin, enjoyable and artsy, serves international cuisine to a younger crowd at fair prices with good vegetarian options (meal-size salads-€12, *plats*-€14, desserts-€4, closed Sun-Mon, 22 Rue des Teinturiers, tel. 04 90 82 41 55).

Le Bercail offers a fun opportunity to get out of town (barely) and take in *le fresh air* with a terrific riverfront view of Avignon, all while enjoying big portions of Provençal cooking (*menus* from €26, daily April-Oct, serves late, tel. 04 90 82 20 22). Take the free shuttle boat (located near St. Bénezet Bridge) to the Ile de la Barthelasse, turn right, and walk five minutes. As the boat usually stops running at about 18:00 (except in July-Aug, when it runs until 21:00), you can either taxi home or walk 25 minutes along the pleasant riverside path and over Daladier Bridge.

Good Budget Places

At **L'Epice and Love** (the name is a fun French-English play on words, pronounced "lay peace and love"), English-speaking owner Marie creates a playful atmosphere in her inviting restaurant, where the few colorfully decorated tables (inside only) greet the hungry traveler. The limited selection changes daily, and Marie cooks it all: tasty meat, fish, and vegetarian dishes, some with a North African touch, all served at good prices (€16 *menus*, closed Sun, 30 Rue des Lices, tel. 04 90 82 45 96).

Place des Châtaignes: This square offers cheap meals and a fun commotion of tables. The intimate **Chez Lulu** is the best of the lot, with a handful of tables inside and out and a limited menu that assures quality cuisine. Their gourmet burger is a treat (€15 *plats*, closed Tue-Wed, 6 Place des Châtaignes, tel. 04 90 85 69 44). The **Crêperie du Cloître** makes cheap, mediocre dinner crêpes and salads, but has the best seating on the square (daily, cash only).

Place des Corps-Saints: This untouristy yet welcoming square is my favorite place for simple outdoor dining in Avignon. You'll find several reasonable eateries with tables sprawling under big plane trees. **Bistrot à Tartines** specializes in—you guessed it— *tartines* (big slices of toast smothered with toppings), and has the coziest interior and best desserts on the square (€8 *tartines* and salads, €10 lunch *menu*, daily, tel. 04 90 85 58 70). **Zeste** is a friendly, modern deli offering fresh soups, pasta salads, wraps,

AVIGNON

smoothies, and more. Get it to go, or eat inside or on the scenic square—all at unbeatable prices (closed Sun, tel. 09 51 49 05 62). **Boulangerie Olivero** makes a fine setting for a budget breakfast, lunch, or a light (and early) dinner. Monsieur Olivero makes a mean baguette and offers anyone showing this book a free croissant with any purchase. Enjoy your coffee, croissant, sandwich, or quiche at the outside tables (on the square near Rue des Lices, daily until 20:00).

Place Pie: On this big square filled with cafés, Avignon's youth make their home. **Restaurant Françoise** is a pleasant café and tea salon, where fresh-baked tarts—savory and sweet—and a variety of salads and soups make a healthful meal, and vegetarian options are plentiful (€7-12 dishes, Mon-Sat 8:00-19:00, closed Sun, free Wi-Fi, a block off Place Pie at 6 Rue Général Leclerc, tel. 04 32 76 24 77).

Avignon Connections

By Train

Remember, there are two train stations in Avignon: the suburban TGV Station and the Centre-Ville Station in the city center (€1.60 local TER shuttle train connects both stations, 2/hour, 5 minutes). TGV trains usually serve the TGV Station only, though a few depart from Centre-Ville Station (check your ticket). The Centre-Ville station and the TGV station both have car rental agencies (open long hours), but neither has baggage storage. Some cities are served by slower local trains from Centre-Ville Station as well as by faster TGV trains from the TGV Station; I've listed the most convenient stations for each trip.

From Avignon's Centre-Ville Station to: Arles (roughly hourly, 20 minutes, less frequent in the afternoon), **Orange** (15/day, 15 minutes), **Nîmes** (12/day, 30 minutes), **Isle-sur-la-Sorgue** (10/day on weekdays, 5/day on weekends, 30 minutes), **Lyon** (10/day, 2 hours, also from TGV Station in 1.5 hours—see below), **Carcassonne** (8/day, 7 with transfer in Narbonne, 3 hours), **Barcelona** (2/day, 5.75 hours with changes in Nîmes and Figueres-Vilafant; more frequent but slower, with a change in Cerbère).

From Avignon's TGV Station to: Nice (20/day, most by TGV, 4 hours, most require transfer in Marseille), **Marseille** (10/day, 35 minutes), **Cassis** (7/day, 2 hours), **Aix-en-Provence TGV** (10/day, 25 minutes), **Lyon** (12/day, 1.5 hours, also from Centre-Ville Station—see above), **Paris'** Gare de Lyon (9/day direct, 2.5 hours; more connections with transfer, 3-4 hours), **Paris'** Charles de Gaulle airport (7/day, 3 hours).

By Bus

The bus station *(gare routière)* is just past and below Hôtel Ibis, to the right as you exit the train station. Nearly all buses leave from this station (a few leave from the ring road outside the station—ask, buy tickets on bus, small bills only). Service is reduced or nonexistent on Sundays and holidays. Check your departure time beforehand, and make sure to verify your destination with the driver.

From Avignon to Pont du Gard: Buses go to this famous Roman aqueduct (3/day, 50 minutes, departs from bus station and possibly from TGV station in high season, ask about round-trip ticket that includes Pont du Gard entry, see page 155); I'd also consider a taxi one-way and bus back. For a more worthwhile day trip, see my suggested train/bus excursion that combines Nîmes and Pont du Gard (see "Planning Your Time," next chapter).

By Bus to Other Regional Destinations: Arles (8/day, 1 hour, leaves from TGV Station); **Aix-en-Provence** (6/day Mon-Sat, 2/day Sun, 75 minutes, faster and easier than train), **Uzès** (3-5/day, 60-80 minutes, stops at Pont du Gard); **St-Rémy-de-Provence** (Cartreize #57 bus, 6/day, 45 minutes, stall #2, handy way to visit its Wed market); **Orange** (Mon-Sat hourly, none Sun, 45 minutes—take the train instead); **Isle-sur-la-Sorgue** (6-8/day Mon-Sat, 3-4/day Sun, 45 minutes, stall #13, some leave from ring road); **Châteauneuf-du-Pape** (2/day Mon-Sat, none Sun, 45 minutes). For the **Côtes du Rhône** area, the bus runs to **Vaison la Romaine, Nyons, Sablet,** and **Séguret** (5/day during the school year—called *période scolaire,* 3/day otherwise, and 1/day from TGV Station; 1.5 hours, all buses pass through Orange—faster to take train to Orange, and transfer to bus there). For the **Luberon** area—including **Lourmarin, Roussillon,** and **Gordes**—take the bus to Cavaillon, then take bus #8 toward Pertuis for Lourmarin (3/day) or bus #15 for Gordes/Roussillon (only 1/day).

AVIGNON

NEAR AVIGNON

Nîmes • Pont du Gard • Uzès

Although Avignon lacks Roman monuments of its own, some of Europe's greatest Roman sights are an easy, breezy day trip away. (To get the most out of these sights, read "How About Them Romans?" on page 59 before you visit.) The Pont du Gard aqueduct is a magnificent structure to experience, as is the city it served 2,000 years ago, Nîmes, which wraps a handful of intriguing Roman monuments together in a bigger-city package. The pedestrian-friendly town of Uzès, between Nîmes and Pont du Gard, offers a refreshing break from power monuments and busy cities. Combining these three sights makes a memorable (if busy) day trip into the Languedoc region. Traveling by car, you'll drive scenic roads between Uzès and Nîmes that show off the rugged *garrigue* landscape that this area is famous for.

Planning Your Time

Consider getting away from the tourists and spending a night in classy Nîmes or cozy Uzès. If you're on a tighter schedule, no worries—this region's sights are easy to cover in a day trip from Avignon, even without a car.

By Bus, Train, or Taxi: With only a few buses a day connecting Avignon with Pont du Gard and Uzès (3-5/day), you need to plan carefully—particularly off-season when weekend service almost vanishes. If you have the time and patience, public transit is a good option. Double-check all schedules at Avignon's bus station (tel. 04 90 82 07 35, some English usually spoken, Mon-Sat 8:00-19:30, closed Sun). Arrive at bus stops at least five minutes early, pay the driver (no big bills), and always verify your stop and direction with the driver. Here are three plans to consider (connections for these trips are for Mon-Fri—buses run less frequently on weekends; I've listed bus times as they were in

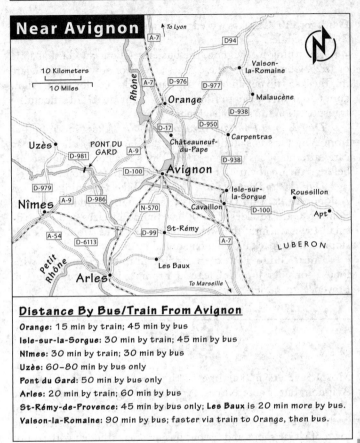

Near Avignon

To Lyon

Vaison-la-Romaine

Orange

Malaucène

Châteauneuf-du-Pape

Carpentras

Uzès

PONT DU GARD

Avignon

Isle-sur-la-Sorgue

Roussillon

Nîmes

Cavaillon

Apt

St-Rémy

LUBERON

Petit Rhône

Les Baux

Arles

To Marseille

10 Kilometers
10 Miles

Rhône

Distance By Bus/Train From Avignon

Orange: 15 min by train; 45 min by bus

Isle-sur-la-Sorgue: 30 min by train; 45 min by bus

Nîmes: 30 min by train; 30 min by bus

Uzès: 60–80 min by bus only

Pont du Gard: 50 min by bus only

Arles: 20 min by train; 60 min by bus

St-Rémy-de-Provence: 45 min by bus only; **Les Baux** is 20 min more by bus.

Vaison-la-Romaine: 90 min by bus; faster via train to Orange, then bus.

2013, so confirm these locally when planning your day). Buses cost about €1.50 and take about 40-50 minutes to get to Pont du Gard from Avignon and from Nîmes; trains take 30 minutes to connect Avignon and Nîmes and cost about €10. Allow €55 for a taxi each way from Avignon or Nîmes to Pont du Gard.

Day Trip to Pont du Gard: Take a morning bus from Avignon's bus station (8:45 or 11:40), then hop on the early-afternoon (13:16) or evening (17:25) bus back to Avignon. To save time and have more flexibility, catch a cab from Avignon (25 minutes, €55 one-way), then ride the bus back. Allow about two hours for visiting Pont du Gard (see page 169 for more details on getting to Pont du Gard). From May through September, buses bound for Pont du Gard may begin at Avignon's TGV station (leaving there 20 minutes before and arriving back 20 minutes later than the times listed below). The bus company (Edgard) sells a good-deal combo-ticket, including round-trip bus fare and entry to the Pont du

Gard, for €10. Check www.edgard-transport.fr or call 08 10 33 42 73 for schedules.

Returning to Avignon, the bus leaves Pont du Gard at 13:16 or 17:25. Confirm all of these times at a TI or at www.pontdugard .fr. The 8:45 trip out and 13:16 trip back works best for most. Allow about four or five hours for visiting Pont du Gard, including transportation time from Avignon.

Day Trip to Pont du Gard and Nîmes: Take a morning bus from Avignon's bus station to Pont du Gard (8:45), then take an early-afternoon bus to Nîmes (13:50) for a few hours of sightseeing before returning by train to Avignon (trains almost hourly).

Day Trip to Pont du Gard and Uzès: Take a morning bus from Avignon to Pont du Gard (8:45), then catch a midday bus from Pont du Gard to Uzès (12:16), have lunch in Uzès and enjoy its small-town warmth, then return on the 17:10 bus (from Esplanade stop) to arrive back in Avignon around 18:15.

Local Guide: For expert guiding in this region with a wine focus, consider Joe McClean at Promo Vinum (see "Tours of Provence," page 56).

Nîmes

Most travelers make time in their schedules for Arles and Avignon, but ignore Nîmes. Arles and Avignon may have more touristic appeal, but Nîmes—which feels richer and surer of itself—is refreshingly lacking in overnight tourists. This thriving town of classy shops and serious businesses is studded with world-class Roman monuments and laced with traffic-free lanes. (And if you've visited the magnificent Pont du Gard, you gotta be curious where all that water went.)

Since the Middle Ages, Nîmes has exported a famous fabric: The word "denim" actually comes from here (*de Nîmes* = "from Nîmes"). Denim caught on in the United States in the 1800s, when a Bavarian immigrant, Levi Strauss, popularized its use in the American West.

Today, Nîmes is officially in the Languedoc region (for administrative purposes only), yet historically the town has been a key player in the evolution of Provence. Only 30 minutes by train from Arles or Avignon (about €10 one-way to either), and three hours from Paris on the TGV, Nîmes is worth a visit if you want a taste of today's urban Provence. The city keeps its clean and tranquil old center a secret for its well-heeled residents. (Locals admit they don't need the tourism money as much as other Provençal towns.) While most visitors understandably prefer sleeping in Arles or Avignon, a night here provides a good escape from tourist crowds and a truer taste of a Provençal city.

Orientation to Nîmes

Nîmes ("neem") has no river or natural landmark to navigate by, so it's easy to become disoriented. For a quick visit, limit yourself to the manageable triangle within the ring of roads formed by boulevards Victor Hugo, Amiral Courbet, and Gambetta.

The town's landmarks are connected by 10-minute walks: It's 10 minutes from the train station to the arena, 10 minutes from the arena to the Roman temple of Maison Carrée, and 10 minutes from Maison Carrée to either the Castellum or the Fountain Garden. Apart from seeing this handful of ancient monuments, appreciate the city's traffic-free old center—a delight for browsing, strolling, sipping coffee, and people-watching.

Tourist Information

The helpful TI, across the street and a half-block up from Maison Carrée, is a 20-minute walk from the train station (Mon-Sat 8:30-19:00, Sun 10:00-18:00, 6 Rue Auguste, tel. 04 66 58 38 00, www.ot-nimes.fr). Pick up the *Discovering Nîmes* pamphlet, which includes a map with a description of the city's sights and museums, and a worthwhile old-town walk. You can also rent an MP3-player audioguide for a walking tour of Old Nîmes (€8, €10/2 people, leave ID as deposit).

Arrival in Nîmes

By Train and Bus: Trains and buses use the same station (handy if you're combining Pont du Gard with Nîmes). There is no baggage storage. Confirm return schedules before leaving the station. The bus station and information office are at the rear of the train station (look for bright yellow *Edgard* logo, Mon-Fri 8:00-12:30 & 14:00-18:00, Sat 8:00-12:30, closed Sun). Ask in the office which stall your bus leaves from (usually between 8 and 14); the shelters are to the right out the rear exit of the train station).

The arena is a 10-minute walk out the front of the train station (see map on page 158). Head up the left side of Avenue Feuchères, go left at the big plaza, curve right, and you'll see the arena (to find its entrance, walk counterclockwise around it). The Maison Carrée and TI are an enjoyable stroll from the arena through Nîmes' traffic-free old town.

By Car: Follow signs for *Centre-Ville* and *TI*, then *Arènes Parking*, and pay to park underneath the arena. In this huge garage, make a note of where you parked. If it's full, Parking des Feuchères

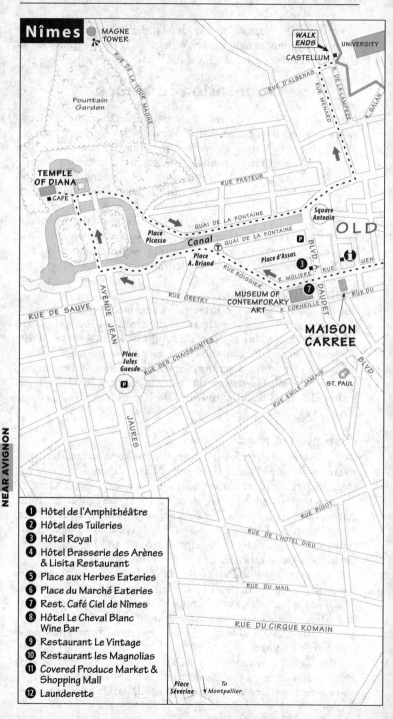

Nîmes

MAGNE TOWER

WALK ENDS

UNIVERSITY

CASTELLUM

RUE DE LA TOUR MAGNE

RUE D'ALBENAS

R. DE LA LAMPEZE

RUE MENARD

R. SALAN

Fountain Garden

TEMPLE OF DIANA

CAFE

RUE PASTEUR

QUAI DE LA FONTAINE

Square Antonin

OLD

Place Picasso

Canal

QUAI DE LA FONTAINE

Place d'Assas

BLVD. A.

GEN.

Place A. Briand

RUE BOISSIER

R. MOLIERE

RUE

DAUDET

RUE DE SAUVE

RUE GRETRY

MUSEUM OF CONTEMPORARY ART

R. CORNEILLE

RUE DU

AVENUE JEAN

MAISON CARREE

BLVD.

Place Jules Guesde

RUE DES CHAISSAINTES

RUE EMILE JAMAIS

ST. PAUL

JAURES

RUE BIGOT

RUE DE L'HOTEL DIEU

RUE DU MAIL

RUE DU CIRQUE ROMAIN

Place Séverine

To Montpellier

1 Hôtel de l'Amphithéâtre
2 Hôtel des Tuileries
3 Hôtel Royal
4 Hôtel Brasserie des Arènes & Lisita Restaurant
5 Place aux Herbes Eateries
6 Place du Marché Eateries
7 Rest. Café Ciel de Nîmes
8 Hôtel Le Cheval Blanc Wine Bar
9 Restaurant Le Vintage
10 Restaurant les Magnolias
11 Covered Produce Market & Shopping Mall
12 Launderette

NEAR AVIGNON

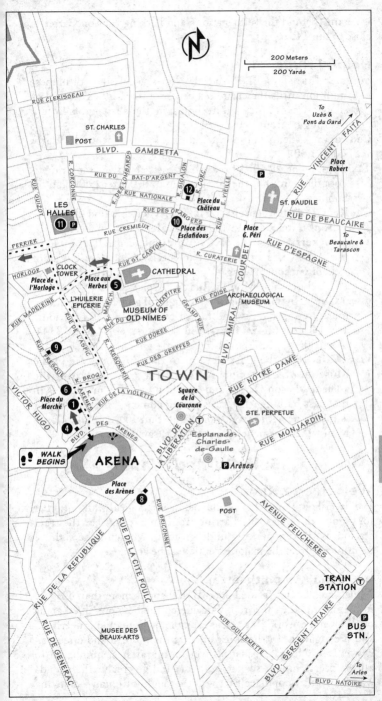

To Uzès &
Pont du Gard

RUE CLERISSEAU

ST. CHARLES
POST

BLVD. GAMBETTA

Place
Robert

RUE DU BAT-D'ARGENT

RUE NATIONALE

R. DES LOMBARDS

R. SIGALON

R. CORC.

R. VIEILLE

RUE VINCENT FAÏTA

RUE CORCONNE

Place du
Château **12**

ST. BAUDILE

RUE GUIZOT

LES HALLES
11 P

RUE DES ORANGERS

RUE CREMIEUX

Place des
Esclafidous **10**

Place
G. Péri

RUE DE BEAUCAIRE

To
Beaucaire &
Tarascon

FERRIER

HORLOGE

Place de
l'Horloge

CLOCK
TOWER

RUE ST. CASTOR

Place aux
Herbes **5**

CATHEDRAL

R. CURATERIE

RUE D'ESPAGNE

BLVD. AMIRAL COURBET

L'HUILERIE
EPICERIE

RUE MADELEINE

RUE DE L'ASPIC

RUE MARCH

R. CHAPITRE

MUSEUM OF
OLD NÎMES

RUE FOISE

ARCHAEOLOGICAL
MUSEUM

GRAND RUE

RUE FRESQUE

9

RUE DOREE

RUE DES GREFFES

R. TRESORERIE

R. BROG.

TOWN

RUE NOTRE DAME

R. D. ARENES

RUE DE LA VIOLETTE

6

Place du
Marché **1**

4

Square
de la
Couronne

2

STE. PERPETUE

RUE MONJARDIN

VICTOR HUGO

BLVD. DES ARENES

WALK
BEGINS

ARENA

BLVD. DE LA LIBERATION

Esplanade
Charles-
de-Gaulle

P Arènes

Place
des Arènes **8**

RUE BRICONNET

POST

AVENUE FEUCHERES

RUE DE LA REPUBLIQUE

RUE DE LA CITE FOULC

MUSEE DES
BEAUX-ARTS

TRAIN
STATION

BUS
STN.

RUE GUILLEMETTE

RUE SERGENT TRIAIRE

To
Arles

RUE DE GENERAC

BLVD. NATOIRE

N

200 Meters
200 Yards

NEAR AVIGNON

is nearby (behind the train station), and Parking Maison Carrée is close to the TI.

Helpful Hints

Summer Thursdays: The "Jeudi de Nîmes" (Thursdays of Nîmes) tradition turns the entire old center of town into a festival of shops, street music, and liveliness on Thursday nights in July and August from 18:00 until late.

Laundry: A clean launderette is at 14 Rue Nationale (daily 7:00-21:00).

Taxi: Call 04 66 29 40 11 for a cab. It costs about €55 for a ride to Pont du Gard, but the fare goes up to €70 after 19:00 and on Sundays.

Car Rental: At the station, you'll find **Avis** (tel. 04 66 29 66 36), **Europcar** (tel. 04 66 29 07 94), and **Hertz** (tel. 04 66 76 25 91).

Train Tickets: The small **SNCF Boutique,** centrally located in the old town, is an easy place to check schedules or buy train tickets without having to go to the station (Tue-Sat 8:30-18:50, closed Sun-Mon, 11 Rue de l'Aspic).

Local Guide: Sylvie Pagnard is a delightful guide whose walking tours are top-quality and top-price. She does regional tours and has a car (€145/3 hours, €360/8 hours, tel. 04 66 20 33 14, mobile 06 03 21 37 33, sylviepagnard@gmail.com).

View Café: Ride the glass elevator to the top-floor café of the Museum of Contemporary Art for a great view over the ancient Maison Carrée and a quiet break. The museum is in the glass building that faces the monument, and the elevator is inside near the front door (Tue-Sun 10:00-18:00, closed Mon). The basement has good WCs (same hours as café).

Self-Guided Walk

Welcome to Nîmes

I've described Nîmes' best sights below in a logical walking order for a good daylong visit, starting from the arena (near the train station, with easy parking underground). Many of the sights I mention are free; the major exception is the arena.

▲▲Arena (Amphithéâtre)

Nîmes' arena dates from about A.D. 100 and is more than 425 feet in diameter and 65 feet tall. Considered the best-preserved arena of the Roman world, it's a fine example of Roman engineering... and propaganda. In the spirit of "give them bread and circuses," it was free. No gates, just 60 welcoming arches, numbered to allow entertainment-seekers to come and go freely. The agenda was to create a populace that was thoroughly Roman—enjoying

the same activities and entertainment, all thinking as one (not unlike Americans' nationwide obsession with the same reality-TV shows). The 24,000 seats could be filled and emptied in minutes (through passageways called *vomitoires*).

Cost and Hours: €9, includes great audioguide, daily March-Oct 9:00-18:00, June-Aug until 19:00, Nov-Feb 9:00-17:00, last ticket sold 30 minutes before closing, may close for special events—check at TI. Buy the €11 combo-ticket if you plan to visit the Maison Carrée and/or the Tour Magne (tower in the Fountain Garden—not worth the climb). Tel. 04 66 21 82 56, www.arenes-nimes.com.

◆ Self-Guided Tour: Pick up the helpful plan of the arena. It follows the audioguide route and gives brief background descriptions (handy for referring back to). You'll find helpful English information panels as you tour the arena, which, combined with the excellent audioguide, give a thorough and enjoyable history lesson. Don't miss the panels describing the different types of gladiators.

Climb to the very top—it's a rare opportunity to enjoy the view from the nosebleed seats of a Roman arena. An amphitheater is literally a double theater: two theaters facing each other, designed so that double the people could view a *Dirty Harry* spectacle (without the acoustics provided by the back wall of a theater stage). You may think of this as a "colosseum," but that's not a generic term. Rome's Colosseum was a one-of-a-kind arena—named for a colossal statue of Nero that stood nearby.

The floor where the action took place was the *arena* (literally, "sand," which absorbed the blood, as in bullfights today). The arena's floor, which covered passages and storage areas underneath, came with the famous elevator for surprise appearances of wild animals. (While Rome could afford exotic beasts from the tropics, places like Nîmes made do with snarling local beasts...bulls, wild boars, lots of bears, and so on.) The standard fight was as real as professional wrestling is today—mostly just crowd-pleasing. Thumbs down and kill the guy? Maybe in Rome, but only rarely (if ever) here.

After Rome fell, and stability was replaced by Dark Age chaos, a huge structure like this was put to good use—bricked up and made a fortress (just like the Roman Arena in Arles). In the 13th century, after this region was incorporated into France, the arena became a gated community housing about 700 people—with

Roman Nîmes

Born a Celtic city (about 500 B.C.), Nîmes joined the Roman Empire in the first century B.C. Because it had a privileged status within the Roman Empire, Nîmes was never really considered part of the conquered barbarian world. It rated highly enough to merit one of the longest protective walls in the Roman world and to have a 30-mile-long aqueduct (Pont du Gard) built to serve its growing population.

Today, the physical remains of Roman Nîmes testify to its former importance. The city's emblem—a crocodile tied to a palm tree—is a reminder that Nîmes was a favorite retirement home for Roman officers who conquered Egypt. (The crocodile is Egypt, and the palm tree symbolizes victory.) All over town, little bronze croc-palm medallions shine on the sidewalks. In the City Hall, 400-year-old statues of crocodiles actually swing from the top of a monumental staircase.

streets, plumbing, and even gardens on the top level. Only in 1809 did Napoleon decide to scrape away the people and make this a historic monument, thus letting the ancient grandeur of Roman France shine.

Two **multimedia exhibits** on the arena's ground floor in the *Quartiers des Gladiateurs* (gladiators' locker room) bring bullfighting and gladiating to life (was that Kirk Douglas in those tight shorts?). Since 1850, Nîmes' arena has been a venue for spectacles, including Spanish-style bullfights and rock concerts featuring musical gladiators like Sting and Santana.

▲▲Old City

Those coming to Nîmes only for its famous Roman sights are enchanted by its carefully preserved old center. Here, you can study how elements in the buildings from the medieval and Renaissance times artfully survive: Shop interiors incorporate medieval brick with stone arches; windows expose Gothic finery; and Renaissance staircases grace peaceful courtyards.

• *From the arena, enter Nîmes' "conservation zone"—the Old City. With your back to the arena's ticket office, follow Rue des Arènes into...*

Place du Marché

With an inviting café ambience, including a wispy palm-tree-and-crocodile fountain (Nîmes' emblem in Roman times—see sidebar), this fine square is ideal for lunch or a coffee break. **Le Courtois Café/Pâtisserie** is the class act of the square—check out its old-time interior. It's been family-run since 1892. If you have a sweet tooth, let the sweet women serve you the house specialty, a chocolate-dipped *nélusko;* it's like a cross between a cake and a cookie, and the oldest recipe of the house. Or try a Nîmes specialty, *caladon*—literally "cobble," like on the street—a hard honey-and-almond cookie (daily May-Oct; Nov-April 8:00-19:30, closed Wed, tel. 04 66 67 20 09).

• *Leave the square passing the croc on your right (on Rue des Broquiers), then turn left on Rue de l'Aspic, the town's primary shopping spine. Rue de l'Aspic leads to Place de l'Horloge, the center of the old town. From here pedestrian-friendly streets fan out in all directions, including directly to Maison Carrée (described later). Take unsigned Rue de la Madeleine, the first street to the right as you enter Place de l'Horloge, to the...*

▲Place aux Herbes

This inviting square is the site of Nîmes' oldest market. At the center of the old town, it's a good hub for a bit of sightseeing and café lounging (see "Eating in Nîmes," later). The next three sights are on or within a block of this square:

Nîmes Cathedral: While its Romanesque facade survives from the 12th century, the cathedral's interior—gutted over centuries of dynastic squabbles, Reformation, and Revolution—is unremarkable Neo-Romanesque, mostly from the 19th century. But it's a cool place for a break if you need to lower your temperature.

Museum of Old Nîmes: Taking a left out of the cathedral leads to this humble museum, inhabiting a 17th-century bishop's palace. The only reason to enter is to learn the story of indigo, 19th-century denim wear, and early Levi's (free, no English but basics are easy to understand, Tue-Sun 10:00-18:00, closed Mon, tel. 04 66 76 73 70).

Old-Time Spice Shop: L'Huilerie Epicerie is a charming time warp displaying spices and herbs, oils, and candy (Tue-Sun 9:00-12:00 & 15:00-19:00, closed Mon; a block off Place aux Herbes, down the small lane past Le Petit Moka café at 10 Rue des Marchands). To revel in more of Nîmes' medieval atmosphere, find the nearby Passage du Vieux Nîmes.

• *When you're ready to move on, return to Place de l'Horloge, turn right, and follow Rue de Gazan past the clock tower to the...*

Covered Produce Market

Les Halles Centre Commerciale looks big, black, and ugly on the outside, but inside its ground floor is a thriving, colorful market hall, well worth exploring (daily until 13:00). If it's hot, and/or you need to shop, escalate a floor up to the air-conditioned mall.

• *Take a right out of the covered market on Rue Général Perrier, and walk several blocks to the...*

NEAR AVIGNON

▲▲▲Maison Carrée

This stunning temple rivals Rome's Pantheon as the most complete and splendid building that survives from the Roman Empire. The

temple radiates beauty today thanks to a two-year cleaning process. (There's nothing inside but a tacky 3-D history movie, so we'll focus on its exterior.)

The temple survived in part because it's been in constant use for the last thousand years—as a church, a City Hall, a private stable, archives during the Revolution, a people's art gallery after the Revolution (like Paris' Louvre), and finally as the monument you visit today. It's a textbook example of a "pseudo-peripteral temple" (surrounded by columns, half of which support the roof over a porch, and half of which merely decorate the rest of the building) and a "six-column temple" (a standard proportion—if it's six columns wide, it must be eleven columns deep).

The lettering across the front is long gone (though there is talk of replacing it), but the tiny surviving "nail holes" presented archaeologists with a fun challenge: Assuming each letter would leave a particular series of nail holes as evidence, derive the words. Archaeologists agree that this temple was built to honor Caius and Lucius, the grandsons (and adopted sons) of Emperor Augustus. And from this information, they date the temple from the year A.D. 4.

Maison Carrée ("Square House"—named before they had a word for "rectangle") was the centerpiece of a fancy plaza surrounded by a U-shaped commercial, political, and religious forum. This marked the core of Roman Nîmes. As was the case in all Roman temples, only the priest went inside. Worshippers gathered for religious rituals at the foot of the steps. Climb the steps as a priest would—starting and ending with your right foot...*dexter* (from the Latin for "right") rather than *sinister* ("left"). Put your right foot forward for good karma.

Inside, the *Heroes of Nîmes* **movie** tells the story of six locals, each vying to be "the most heroic citizen of noble Nîmes." Though entertaining, this 3-D film—covering 2,000 years in 20 minutes—insults the building it fills (€5, every 30 minutes, daily 10:00-19:00, soundtrack in Latin and French with English subtitles).

Nearby: The modern building facing the temple is Nîmes' **Carrée d'Art** ("Square of Art"), designed by British architect Lord Norman Foster. It's home to the city's Museum of Contemporary

Art (Tue-Sun 10:00-18:00, closed Mon, WCs, good view café—see "Helpful Hints," earlier). Nîmes' TI is across the street and a few steps up from Maison Carrée at 6 Rue Auguste.

• *To reach the next sight, walk down Rue Molière with the Museum of Contemporary Art on your left. Dogleg right until you hit the tree-lined canal, then follow the canal left until you reach the...*

▲Fountain Garden (Jardin de la Fontaine)

Centuries before the Romans arrived in Nîmes, the Spring of Nemo was here (named, like the town itself, for a Celtic god). When the Romans built a shrine to Emperor Augustus around the spring, rather than bulldoze the Nemo temple, they built alongside it and welcomed Nemo into their own pantheon (as was their more-gods-the-merrier tradition). Today, the spring remains, though the temple is gone.

Walk into the center of the Fountain Garden and look into the canal. In the early 1700s, Nîmes needed a reliable source of water for its textile industry—to power its mills and provide water for the indigo dyes for the fabric *serge de Nîmes* (denim). In about 1735, the city began a project to route a canal through the city and discovered a Roman temple. The city eventually agreed to fund a grander project that resulted in what you see today: a lavish Versailles-type park, complete with an ornate network of canals and boulevards. This was just 50 years after the construction of Versailles, and to the French, this place has a special significance. These were the first grand public gardens not meant for a king, but for the public. The industrial canals built then still wind throughout the city.

• *Hiding behind trees in the back-left corner of Fountain Garden, find the...*

▲Temple of Diana

This first-century "temple," which modern archaeologists now believe was more likely a Roman library, has long been considered one of the best examples of ancient stonework. Its roof—a round Roman barrel vault laced together with still-visible metal pegs (find the panel with a drawing of the temple before entering)—survived until it was hit by a blast in the 1500s, during the Catholic-Protestant Wars of Religion.

At first glance, all the graffiti seems odd. But it's actually part of the temple's story. For centuries, France had a highly esteemed guild of stone-, metal-, and woodworkers called the Compagnons, founded by Gothic-church builders in the Middle Ages. As part of their almost mystic training, these craftsmen would visit many buildings—including the great structures of antiquity (such as this one)—for inspiration. Walk through the side aisle for a close look at the razor-accurate stonework and the 17th-, 18th-, and 19th-century signatures of the Compagnon craftsmen inspired by this building. Notice how their signatures match their era—no-nonsense "Enlightened" chiseling of the 18th century gives way to ornate script in the Romantic 19th century.

Skip the hike up to Tour Magne (at top of gardens), which has two remaining levels of a Roman tower; the view is worth neither the sweat nor the €3 fee. Instead, have a coffee break or snack at the park's café, located next to the Temple of Diana.

Cost and Hours: The park and temple are free, open daily April-mid-Sept 7:30-22:00, mid-Sept-March 7:30-18:30.

• *To reach the next sight (about a 10-minute walk), angle back across the park, turning left at the canal (Quai de la Fontaine). At the busy ring road, swim upstream against traffic, along busy Boulevard Gambetta. Just after the tiny park, turn left onto Rue Ménard. Follow it uphill for three blocks, and head right on Rue d'Albenas, following the sign that leads to the...*

▲Castellum

This small excavation site, sitting next to the street, shows a modest-looking water distribution tank that was the grand finale

of the 30-mile-long Pont du Gard aqueduct.

Discovered in the 1850s, this is one of only two known Roman distribution tanks (the other is in Pompeii). The water needs of Roman Nîmes grew beyond the capacity of its local springs. Imagine the jubilation on the day (in A.D. 50) that this system was finally operational. Suddenly, the town had an abundance of water—for basic needs as well as for cool extras like public fountains. Notice the square plugged hole marking the end of the aqueduct, a pool, a lower water channel, and the water-distribution holes. The lower channel, which runs under you, served top-priority needs, providing water via stone and lead pipes to the public wells that graced neighborhood squares. The higher holes—which got wet only when the supply was plentiful—routed water to the homes of the wealthy, to public baths, and to nonessential fountains. (For more on this impressive example of Roman engineering, see the "Pont du Gard" section, later.)

Cost and Hours: The excavation site is free to see and always open.

Sleeping in Nîmes

$$$ Hôtel de l'Amphithéâtre*** is ideally located on a pedestrian street a spear's toss from the arena. Run by gracious Ghislaine and Marcus, this is a top Nîmes value, with quiet, spacious, and very sharp rooms at good rates (Sb-€70, Db-€90, Tb-€100, air-con in most rooms, no elevator, Wi-Fi, 4 Rue des Arènes, tel. 04 66 67 28 51, www.hoteldelamphitheatre.com, contact @hoteldelamphitheatre.com).

$$ Hôtel des Tuileries** is a good value, with helpful English hosts (Andrew and Karen) and a central location 10 minutes on foot from the train station. Rooms are large, and some have balconies (Sb/Db-€75-90, air-con, elevator, Wi-Fi, 22 Rue de Roussy, tel. 04 66 21 31 15, www.hoteldestuileries.com, les-tuileries@wanadoo.fr).

$$ Hôtel Royal*** rents comfortable, good-enough rooms at two- and three-star prices and makes a fair fallback if other hotels are full. It's an artsy place well-located on a main street near Maison Carrée (Db-€70-120, cheaper rooms are smaller and lack air-con, 3 Boulevard Alphonse Daudet, tel. 04 66 58 28 27, www.royalhotel-nimes.com, rhotel@wanadoo.fr).

$ Hôtel Brasserie des Arènes* occupies a privileged location facing the arena. Its 11 basic rooms above a modern café—some rooms with kitchenettes—provide one-star comfort at fair rates (Sb-€40, Db-€45, Tb-€52, no air-con or elevator, 4 Boulevard des Arènes, tel. 04 66 67 23 05, www.brasseriedesarenes.fr, contact @brasserie-arenes.fr).

Sleep Code

(€1 = about $1.30, country code: 33)
S = Single, **D** = Double/Twin, **T** = Triple, **Q** = Quad, **b** = bathroom, **s** = shower only, * = French hotel rating system (0-5 stars). Unless otherwise noted, credit cards are accepted and English is spoken.

To help you easily sort through these listings, I've divided the accommodations into three categories, based on the price for a standard double room with bath:

  $$$ Higher Priced—Most rooms €85 or more.
    $$ Moderately Priced—Most rooms between €60-85.
      $ Lower Priced—Most rooms €60 or less.

Prices can change without notice; verify the hotel's current rates online or by email. For the best prices, always book direct.

Eating in Nîmes

For Lunch

Enjoy the elegance of Nîmes by eating lunch on one of its charming squares. Sadly, most of these cafés close for dinner.

Place aux Herbes: This square, beautifully situated in the shadow of the cathedral, boasts several popular bistros. **Restaurant ô Délices** (open daily) and **Le Petit Moka** (closed Sun) both serve fresh salads, crêpes, and *tartines* for €9 or less.

Place du Marché: A block from the arena, this square is home to **Mogador Café,** serving tasty, light lunches (salads, crêpes, and lots of veggies), and **Le Courtois Café/Pâtisserie,** with its trademark desserts (described under my self-guided walk—see page 162).

Overlooking the Maison Carrée: **Restaurant Café Ciel de Nîmes** fills a terrace atop the city's Norman Foster-designed contemporary art gallery, offering diners great views of the Roman temple (€10 *plats du jour,* €12 salads, €16 three-course workday lunch special, Tue-Sun 10:00-18:00, closed Mon, Place de la Maison Carrée, tel. 04 66 36 71 70). Facing the temple, you'll see the terrace atop the modern building on your right.

For Dinner

Many places close on Sunday and Monday, making evening meals a challenge. Diners can start, end, or spend their entire evening at the cozy wine bar at **Hôtel Le Cheval Blanc,** where good wines, appetizers, and meals are served at fair prices (€16 *plats,* closed Sun, 1 Place des Arènes, tel. 04 66 76 19 59).

Restaurant Le Vintage, a cool and contemporary wine bar/bistro, offers local cuisine and wines in an easygoing ambience inside or out, on a sweet little terrace (€26 *menus,* €15 *plats,* reasonable wine prices, closed Sun-Mon, a few blocks up Rue Fresque from Place du Marché at 7 Rue de Bernis, tel. 04 66 21 04 45, www.restaurant-levintage-nimes.com).

Stylish **Lisita,** a few steps from the arena, serves fine cuisine with a Spanish accent, and has good interior and terrific exterior seating (€30 *menu,* closed Sun-Mon, 2 Boulevard des Arènes, tel. 04 66 67 29 15, www.lelisita.com).

At **Restaurant les Magnolias,** on cute Place des Esclafidous, you'll dine in the cozy interior or on their peaceful terrace. Meals are reasonable, the service is friendly, and it's open on weekends (*menus* from €19, big salads for €10, daily for dinner, two blocks behind the cathedral—find the post office on Rue Crémieux and walk behind it, tel. 04 66 21 64 01).

Nîmes Connections

Trains and buses depart from the same station in Nîmes (see "Arrival in Nîmes," earlier). If traveling by bus, plan to arrive early at the station to double-check your schedule. Ask at the bus-information office in the rear of the train station (find yellow *Edgard* logo on glass door) for the next bus to your destination and which stall it leaves from (most likely stalls 8-14, look for shelters to your right as you walk outside). Buy your ticket from the driver (about €1.50 one-way to Pont du Gard, avoid big bills). Route numbers posted on the buses themselves usually do not correspond to those on paper timetables, so verify your destination with the driver.

From Nîmes by Train to: Arles (9/day, 30 minutes), **Avignon** (12/day, 30 minutes), **Aigues-Mortes** in the Camargue (6/day, 45 minutes), **Carcassonne** (8/day, 2.5 hours, transfer in Narbonne), **Paris** (10/day, 3 hours).

By Bus to: Uzès (7/day Mon-Fri, 3/day Sat, 2/day Sun, 40 minutes, €1.50), **Pont du Gard** (6/day Mon-Fri, none on weekends Nov-April, 4/day Sat, 2/day Sun May-Oct, 40 minutes; check return times before you leave, tel. 08 10 33 42 73, www.edgard -transport.fr), **Aigues-Mortes** in the Camargue (6/day, 50 minutes), **Arles** (6/day, 1 hour).

Pont du Gard

Throughout the ancient world, aqueducts were like flags of stone that heralded the greatness of Rome. A visit to this sight still works to proclaim the wonders of that age. This perfectly preserved Roman aqueduct was built in about 19 B.C. as the critical link of a 30-mile canal that, by dropping one inch for every 350 feet, supplied nine million gallons of water per day (about 100 gallons per second) to Nîmes—one of ancient Europe's largest cities. Though most of the aqueduct is on or below the ground, at Pont du Gard it spans a canyon on a massive bridge—one of the most remarkable surviving Roman ruins anywhere. Wear sturdy shoes if you want to climb around the aqueduct (footing is tricky), and bring swimwear and flip-flops if you plan to backstroke with views of the monument.

Getting to Pont du Gard

The famous aqueduct is between Remoulins and Vers-Pont du Gard on D-981, 17 miles from Nîmes and 13 miles from Avignon.

By Car: Pont du Gard is a 25-minute drive due west of Avignon (follow N-100 from Avignon, tracking signs to *Nîmes* and

NEAR AVIGNON

Not to scale:
Roundabout to Museum is a 10-minute walk
Museum to Pont du Gard is a 5-minute walk

Remoulins, then *Pont du Gard* and *Rive Gauche*), and 45 minutes northwest of Arles (via Tarascon on D-6113). If going to Arles from Pont du Gard, follow signs to *Nîmes* (not *Avignon*), then D-6113, or A-54 (autoroute) to Arles.

By Bus: Buses run to Pont du Gard (on the Rive Gauche side) from Nîmes, Uzès, and Avignon. Combining Pont du Gard with Nîmes and/or Uzès makes a good day-trip excursion from Avignon (see "Planning Your Time" at the beginning of this chapter).

Buses stop at the traffic roundabout 300 yards from the aqueduct (stop name: Rond Point Pont du Gard; see Pont du Gard map). In summer and on weekends, however, buses usually drive into the Pont du Gard site and stop at the parking lot's ticket booth. Confirm where the bus stops at the parking booth inside the Pont du Gard site.

At the roundabout, the stop for buses coming from Avignon and Nîmes (and going to Uzès) is on the side opposite Pont du Gard; the stop for buses to Nîmes and to Avignon is on the same side as Pont du Gard (a block to your left as you exit Pont du Gard onto the main road). Make sure you're waiting for the bus on the correct side of the traffic circle (stops have schedules posted), and wave your hand to signal the bus to stop for you (otherwise, it'll chug on by). Buy your ticket when you get on and verify your destination with the driver.

By Taxi: From Nîmes or Avignon it's about €55 for a taxi to Pont du Gard (allow €70 after 19:00 and on Sun). If you're staying in Avignon and only want to see Pont du Gard (and not Nîmes or Uzès), consider splurging on a taxi to the aqueduct in the morning, then take the early-afternoon bus back.

Orientation to Pont du Gard

There are two riversides to Pont du Gard: the Left Bank (Rive Gauche) and Right Bank (Rive Droite). Park on the Rive Gauche, where you'll find the museums, ticket booth, ATM, cafeteria, WCs, and shops—all built into a modern plaza. You'll see the aqueduct in two parts: first the fine museum complex, then the actual river gorge spanned by the ancient bridge.

Cost and Hours: €18 per car (for up to five; €12 for a motorcycle, €23 for an annual pass). If arriving on foot, by bus, or by bike, you'll pay €10 per person. This gives you access to the aqueduct, museum, film, and outdoor *garrigue* nature area. The museum is open daily May-Sept 9:00-19:00, Oct-April 9:00-17:00, closed two weeks in Jan. The aqueduct itself is open until 1:00 in the morning, as is the parking lot. The *garrigue* is always open. Tel. 04 66 37 99, www.pontdugard.fr.

Tours: Call ahead or visit the website for information on infrequent guided walks on top of the aqueduct (about €10).

Canoe Rental: Floating under Pont du Gard by canoe is an experience you won't soon forget. Collias Canoes will pick you up at Pont du Gard (or elsewhere, if pre-arranged) and shuttle you to the town of Collias. You'll float down the river to the nearby town of Remoulins, where they'll pick you up and take you back to Pont du Gard (€21/person, €12/child under 12, usually 2 hours, though you can take as long as you like, good idea to reserve the day before in July-Aug, tel. 04 66 22 85 54).

Plan Ahead for Swimming and Hiking: Pont du Gard is perhaps best enjoyed on your back and in the water—bring along a swimsuit and flip-flops for the rocks. The best Pont du Gard viewpoints are up steep hills with uneven footing—bring good shoes.

Sights at Pont du Gard

▲Museum
In this state-of-the-art museum (well-presented in English), you'll enter to the sound of water and understand the critical role fresh water played in the Roman "art of living." You'll see examples of

NEAR AVIGNON

lead pipes, faucets, and siphons; walk through a mock rock quarry; and learn how they moved those huge rocks into place and how those massive arches were made. While actual artifacts from the aqueduct are few, the exhibit shows the immensity of the undertaking as well as the payoff. Imagine the excitement as this extravagant supply of water finally tumbled into Nîmes. A relaxing highlight is the scenic video of a helicopter ride along the entire 30-mile course of the structure, from its start at Uzès all the way to the Castellum in Nîmes.

Other Activities

Several additional attractions are designed to give the sight more meaning—and they do (but for most visitors, the museum is sufficient). A corny, romancing-the-aqueduct 25-minute film plays in the same building as the museum and offers good information in a flirtatious French-Mediterranean style...and a cool, entertaining, and cushy break. The nearby kids' museum, called *Ludo*, offers a scratch-and-sniff teaching experience (in English) of various aspects of Roman life and the importance of water. The extensive outdoor *garrigue* natural area, closer to the aqueduct, features historic crops and landscapes of the Mediterranean.

▲▲▲Viewing the Aqueduct

A park-like path leads to the aqueduct. Until a few years ago, this was an actual road—adjacent to the aqueduct—that had spanned the river since 1743. Before you cross the bridge, pass under it and hike about 300 feet along the riverbank for a grand viewpoint from which to study the world's second-highest standing Roman structure. (Rome's Colosseum is only 6 feet taller.)

This was the biggest bridge in the whole 30-mile-long aqueduct. It seems exceptional because it is: The arches are twice the width of standard aqueducts, and the main arch is the largest the Romans ever built—80 feet (so it wouldn't get its feet wet). The bridge is about 160 feet high and was originally about 1,100 feet long. Today, 12 arches are missing, reducing the length to 790 feet.

Though the distance from the source (in Uzès) to Nîmes was only 12 miles as the eagle flew, engineers chose the most economical route, winding and zigzagging 30 miles. The water made the trip in 24 hours with a drop of only 40 feet. Ninety percent of the aqueduct is on or under the ground, but a few river canyons like this required bridges. A stone lid hides a four-foot-wide, six-foot-tall chamber lined with waterproof mortar that carried the stream for more than 400 years. For 150 years, this system provided Nîmes with good drinking water. Expert as the Romans were, they miscalculated the backup caused by a downstream corner, and had to add the thin extra layer you can see just under the lid to make the channel deeper.

The bridge and the river below provide great fun for holiday-goers. While parents suntan on rocks, kids splash into the gorge from under the aqueduct. Some daredevils actually jump from the aqueduct's lower bridge—not knowing that crazy winds scrambled by the structure cause painful belly flops (and sometimes even accidental deaths). For the most refreshing view, float flat on your back underneath the structure.

The appearance of the entire gorge changed in 2002, when a huge flood flushed lots of greenery downstream. Those floodwaters put Roman provisions to the test. Notice the triangular-shaped buttresses at the lower level—designed to split and divert the force of any flood *around* the feet of the arches rather than *into* them. The 2002 floodwaters reached the top of those buttresses. Anxious park rangers winced at the sounds of trees crashing onto the ancient stones...but the arches stood strong.

The stones that jut out—giving the aqueduct a rough, unfinished appearance—supported the original scaffolding. The protuberances were left, rather than cut off, in anticipation of future repair needs. The lips under the arches supported wooden templates that allowed the stones in the round arches to rest on something until the all-important keystone was dropped into place. Each stone weighs four to six tons. The structure stands with no mortar (except at the very top, where the water flowed)—taking full advantage of the innovative Roman arch, made strong by gravity.

Hike over the bridge for a closer look and the best views.

Steps lead up a high trail (marked *panorama*) to a superb viewpoint (go right at the top; best views are soon after the trail starts descending). You'll also see where the aqueduct meets a rock tunnel. Walk through the tunnel and continue for a bit, following a trail that meanders along the canal's path.

Back on the museum side, steps lead up to the Rive Gauche side of the aqueduct, where you can follow the canal path along a trail (marked with red-and-white horizontal lines) to find some remains of the Roman canal. You'll soon reach another *panorama* with more great views of the aqueduct. Hikers can continue along the path, following the red-and-white markings that lead through a forest, after which you'll come across more remains of the canal (much of which are covered by vegetation). There's not much left to see because of medieval cannibalization—frugal builders couldn't resist the precut stones as they constructed area churches (stones along the canal were easier to retrieve than those high up on the aqueduct). The path continues for about 15 miles, but there's little reason to go farther. However, there is talk of opening the ancient quarry...someday.

Uzès

Like Nîmes and Pont du Gard, this intriguing, less-trampled town is officially in Languedoc, not Provence. Uzès (oo-zehs) feels like it must have been important once—and it was, as a bishopric from the fifth century until 1789. It's best seen slowly on foot, with a loooong coffee break in its arcaded and mellow main square, Place aux Herbes (not so mellow during the colorful Wednesday morning market and even bigger all-day Saturday market).

By car, Uzès is 10 minutes from Pont du Gard and 30 minutes from Nîmes and Avignon. It offers a refreshing small-town break from serious sightseeing. Go local and stay overnight here. Arrive on Tuesday or Friday nights to enjoy the next morning's market.

Getting to Uzès

Uzès is a short hop west of Pont du Gard. It's well-served by **bus** from Nîmes (Edgard bus #E52, direction Saint-Quentin-la-Poterie, 7/day Mon-Fri, 3/day Sat, 2/day Sun, 40 minutes, €1.50), but less so from Avignon (Edgard bus #A15, direction Alès, 3-5/day, 60-80 minutes, stops near Pont du Gard, €1.50). Check www.edgard-transport.fr or call 08 10 33 42 73 for schedules.

Drivers will circle the old town on the busy ring road. The TI and one hotel that I list are on this ring road.

Orientation to Uzès

Tourist Information

The unhelpful TI sits at the top of the ring road on Place Albert 1er. Pick up the brief self-guided tour brochure in English (June-

Sept Mon-Fri 9:00-18:00, Sat-Sun 10:00-13:00 & 14:00-17:00; Oct-May Mon-Fri 10:00-12:30 & 14:00-18:00, Sat 10:00-13:00, closed Sun; tel. 04 66 22 68 88, www.uzes-tourisme.com).

Sights in Uzès

Strolling the Town
The traffic-free, tastefully restored town itself is the sight. In spite of all those bishops, there are no important sights to visit in Uzès. You can follow the TI's self-guided walking tour, but skip their sad audioguide tour and avoid the dull, overpriced Palace of the Duché de Uzès (€18, French-only tour). The town's trendy boutiques are as numerous as English-speaking visitors, which give the place an upscale, international feel. (The toy shop Au Bois de mon Coeur, under the arcade at 8 Place aux Herbes, has special treats for kids.) The unusual circular tower called Tour Fenestrelle is all that remains of a 12th-century cathedral.

Medieval Garden
Even if you're not a plant enthusiast, pop into the Medieval Garden, a "living herbarium" with plants thought to have curative qualities. The garden is at the foot of the King's and Bishop's towers. The entrance fee includes a little shot of lemongrass tea lovingly delivered by the volunteers who care for this sight.

Cost and Hours: €6, April-Sept daily 14:00-18:00 plus 10:30-12:30 on Sat-Sun and daily in July-Aug, Oct 14:00-17:00 daily; closed Nov-March, English handout and some information posted, tel. 04 66 22 38 21.

Musée du Bonbon
This candy museum, just outside Uzès, explains the history and manufacturing process of Haribo (of Gummi Bears fame). It's interactive and makes a worthwhile detour for the kids.

Cost and Hours: Adults-€7.50, kids ages 5-15-€4.50, kids under 5 free, July-Aug daily 10:00-19:00; Sept-June Tue-Sun 10:00-13:00 & 14:00-18:00, closed Mon; last entry one hour before closing, 1.5 miles from Uzès on the road to Avignon and Pont du Gard, tel. 04 66 22 74 39, www.museeharibo.fr.

Sleeping in Uzès

Hotels in Uzès mirror the upscale flavor of the town. Pale-green signs direct drivers to hotels from the ring road.

$$$ La Maison d'Uzès**, in the heart of the old town, is filled with modern luxury and nestled in the charm of a beautifully restored 17th-century building. In this boutique hotel, you'll find sumptuous lounges, a gastronomic restaurant, a full-service spa complete with a waterfall Roman bath, and nine well-designed rooms with every amenity (Db-€220-275, bigger "deluxe" Db-€295-355, suites-€440-530, half of the rooms lack elevator access, 18 Rue du Docteur Blanchard, tel. 04 66 20 07 00, www .lamaisonduzes.fr).

$$$ L'Hostellerie Provençale**, charming if slightly overpriced, has nine comfortable rooms just off the ring road, a few blocks after the TI. Breakfast and dinner can be served on their splendid rooftop terrace or downstairs in the cozy restaurant (standard Db-€101-121, larger Db-€131-151, pricey breakfast-€14 or €17 on terrace, air-con, Wi-Fi, parking garage-€15, restaurant closed Sun, 1 Rue de la Grande Bourgade, tel. 04 66 22 11 06, www.hostellerieprovencale.com, contact@hostellerieprovencale .com).

Eating in Uzès

When the weather cooperates, it's hard to resist meals on Place aux Herbes, which is lined with appealing café options.

The creative **Resto Burger** serves gourmet Charolais burgers and great salads, each for about €13. It has good wines by the glass. Beware: Only Americans eat their burgers with their hands—the French use a knife and fork (many options including kids' and vegetarian *menus,* July-Aug daily 12:00-22:00, Nov-March closed Mon-Tue, 19 Place aux Herbes, tel. 04 66 20 21 03).

Le Bec à Vin is one of the most atmospheric places in town. Owner Frédéric offers delicious beef dishes served inside a 14th-century vaulted room or in shady interior courtyards surrounded by medieval walls (*plats* from €18, *menus* from €29, open daily, 6 Rue Entre-les-Tours, tel. 04 66 22 41 20, www .lebecavin.com).

Le Zanelli Italian, dishing up pizzas and more, is located on the most prized, tucked-away terrace in the center of Uzès. Leave the Place aux Herbes through the passage left of Resto Burger (allow €8-18, daily July-Aug, otherwise closed Tue-Wed, Place Nicolas Froment, tel. 04 66 03 01 93).

To dine well indoors or high above the town on their rooftop terrace, find the restaurant **La Parenthèse** (four-course dinner *menus* from €36, closed Sun) in the recommended **L'Hostellerie Provençale** (described earlier).

ORANGE and the COTES DU RHONE

Orange • Châteauneuf-du-Pape • Vaison la Romaine • Best of the Côtes du Rhône Villages • More Côtes du Rhône Drives

The sunny Côtes du Rhône wine road—one of France's best—starts at Avignon's doorstep. It winds north through a mountainous landscape carpeted with vines, studded with warm stone villages, and presided over by the Vesuvius-like Mont Ventoux. The wines of the Côtes du Rhône (grown on the *côtes*, or hillsides, of the Rhône River Valley) are easy on the palate and on your budget. But this hospitable place offers more than famous wine—its hill-capping villages inspire travel posters, its Roman ruins inspire awe, and the people you'll meet are welcoming...and, often, as excited about their region as you are. Yes, you'll have good opportunities for enjoyable wine-tasting, but there is also a soul to this area...if you take the time to look.

Located 30 minutes north of Avignon, the ancient town of Orange has vineyards on its outskirts. But it's because of its well-preserved Roman Theater that Orange gets (and deserves) attention.

Planning Your Time

Vaison la Romaine is the small hub of this region, offering limited bus connections with Avignon and Orange, bike rental, and a mini-Pompeii in the town center. Nearby, you can visit the impressive Roman Theater in Orange, drive to the top of Mont Ventoux, follow my self-guided driving tour of Côtes du Rhône villages and wineries, or pedal to nearby towns for a breath of fresh air. The vineyards' centerpiece, the Dentelles de Montmirail mountains, are laced with a variety of trails ideal for hikers.

To explore this area, allow two nights for a good start. Drivers should head for the hills (read this chapter's self-guided driving tour before deciding where to stay). Those without wheels find that

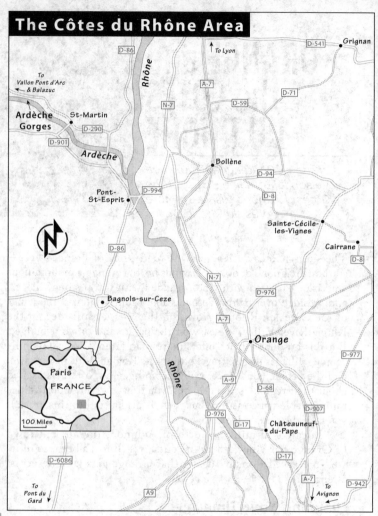

Vaison la Romaine or Orange make the only practical home bases (or, maybe better, consider a minivan tour for this area).

Getting Around the Côtes du Rhône

By Car: Pick up Michelin Local maps #332 or #527 to navigate your way around the Côtes du Rhône. (Landmarks like the Dentelles de Montmirail and Mont Ventoux make it easy to get your bearings.) I've described my favorite driving route in a self-guided driving tour on page 199.

If your plan is to connect the Côtes du Rhône with the scenic **Luberon** (next chapter), you can do it via Mont Ventoux between

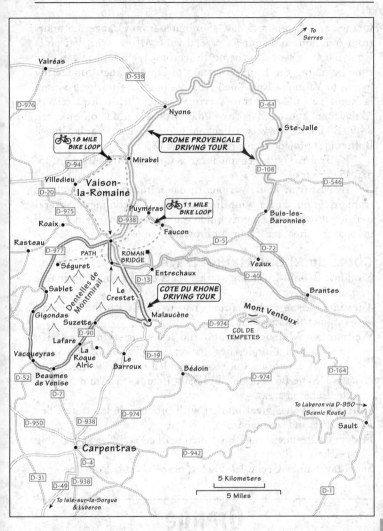

mid-April and mid-November—check with the TI beforehand to make sure the summit is open (follow signs to *Malaucène,* then to *Mont Ventoux,* allowing 2 hours to Roussillon). This route is one of the most spectacular in Provence. But if the summit is closed (in bad weather years, the reopening can be delayed through May), skip the long, underwhelming alternative route through Bédoin. Instead, zip to the Luberon by taking the autoroute via Orange and Cavaillon. A third more direct route takes you through the traffic-snarled, difficult-to-navigate city of Carpentras, which should be avoided. Get advice from your hotelier.

By Bus: Lieutaud buses run to Vaison la Romaine from

Orange and Avignon (5/day, 45 minutes from Orange, 1.5 hours from Avignon) and connect several wine villages with Vaison la Romaine and Nyons to the north. (From Avignon, you can save time by taking the 15-minute train to Orange, then connecting by bus to Vaison la Romaine.) Another bus line runs from Vaison la Romaine to Carpentras, serving Crestet (below Le Crestet), Malaucène, and Le Barroux (3/day Mon-Sat, none on Sun, tel. 04 90 36 09 90, www.cars-lieutaud.fr/provence/en/regular-lines). Both routes provide scenic rides through this area.

By Train: Trains get you as far as Orange (from Avignon: 15/day, 15 minutes).

By Minivan Tour: Various all-day minivan excursions leave from Avignon. For a wine-focused tour, I recommend several individuals who can expertly guide you through the region. For all tours to this area, see "Tours of Provence" on page 56.

Côtes du Rhône Market Days

Monday: Bédoin (intimate market, between Vaison la Romaine and Mont Ventoux)

Tuesday: Vaison la Romaine (great market with produce and antiques/flea market)

Wednesday: Malaucène (good and less-touristy market with produce and antiques/flea market, near Vaison la Romaine), Buis-les-Barronies (on recommended loop drive north into the Drôme Provençale), and Sault (handy if you're driving to the Luberon area)

Thursday: Nyons (great market with produce and antiques/flea market) and Vacqueyras

Friday: Châteauneuf-du-Pape (small market) and Carpentras (big market)

Saturday: Sainte-Cécile-les-Vignes, near Vaison la Romaine

Orange

Orange, called *Arausio* in Roman times, is notable for its Roman arch and grand Roman Theater. Orange was a thriving city in ancient times—strategically situated on the Via Agrippa, connecting the important Roman cities of Lyon and Arles. It was actually founded as a comfortable place for Roman army officers to enjoy their retirement. Even in Roman times, professional military men retired with time for a second career. Did the emperor want thousands of well-trained, relatively young guys hanging around Rome? No way. What to do? "How about a nice place in the south of France...?"

Today's Orange (oh-rahnzh) is a busy, workaday city with considerably less charm than smaller towns I describe, and little urban energy compared to other cities I list. Still, it works as a base for some non-drivers, thanks to its quick rail link to Avignon and just enough bus service to the wine villages of the Côtes du Rhône.

Orientation to Orange

Tourist Information

The unnecessary TI is located next to the fountain and parking area at 5 Cours Aristide Briand (April-Sept Mon-Sat 9:00-18:30, Sun 10:00-13:00 & 14:00-18:30; Oct-March Mon-Sat 10:00-13:00 & 14:00-17:00, closed Sun; tel. 04 90 34 70 88, www.otorange.fr).

Arrival in Orange

By Train: Orange's **train station** is a level 20-minute walk from the Roman Theater (or an €8 taxi ride, mobile 06 09 51 32 25). The recommended Hôtel de Provence, across from the station, will keep your bags (see "Sleeping in Orange," later). To walk into town from the train station, head straight out of the station (down Avenue Frédéric Mistral), merge left onto Orange's main shopping street (Rue de la République), then turn left on Rue Caristie; you'll run into the Roman Theater's massive stage wall.

By Bus: Lieutaud buses stop at the train station (Gare SNCF) and at Place Pourtoules, two blocks from the Roman Theater (walk to the hill and turn right to reach the theater, bus station tel. 04 90 34 15 59, www.cars-lieutaud.fr/provence/en/regular-lines).

By Car: Follow *Centre-Ville* signs, then *Théâtre Antique* signs, and park as close to the Roman Theater's huge wall as possible—the easiest option is labeled *Parking Office du Tourisme* (by the fountain and the TI). Those coming from the autoroute will land here by following *Centre-Ville* signs; others should follow *Centre-Ville* signs, then *Office du Tourisme* signs, to find this parking lot. To reach the theater, walk to the hill and turn left.

Sights in Orange

▲▲Roman Theater (Théâtre Antique)

Orange's ancient theater is the best-preserved in existence, and the only one in Europe with its acoustic wall still standing. (Two others in Asia Minor also survive.)

Cost and Hours: €9, drops to €7.50 one hour before closing; ticket includes film, multimedia show, good audioguide, and entry to small museum across the street; daily April-Sept 9:00-18:00, until 19:00 June-Aug; Oct-March 9:30-17:30 except Nov-Feb until 16:30, closing times can sometimes be changed for evening

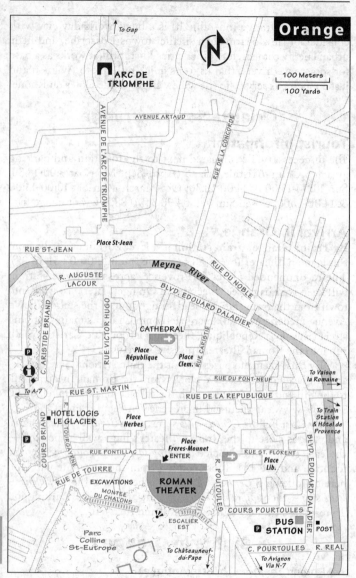

performance or rehearsals, tel. 04 90 51 17 60, www.theatre
-antique.com.

Cheap Trick: Vagabonds wanting a partial but free view of
the theater can see it from the bluff high above in the Parc de la
Colline St-Eutrope. Find the *escalier est* (east staircase) off Rue
Pourtoules and start climbing—it's several hundred steps to the
top. At the sign for *Promenade Botanique*, keep left, and at the

next fork, follow the stairs up to the right. When you see the playground, head to the right to find the view. Benches and grassy areas make this a good picnic spot (no WCs).

Museum: Pop into the museum across the street (Musée d'Art et d'Histoire, included with ticket) to see a few theater details and a rare grid used as the official property-ownership registry—each square represented a 120-acre plot of land.

Eating: The café in the theater, La Grotte d'Auguste, has reasonably priced snacks and lunches and great views (closed Sun year-round, closed Mon off-season, tel. 04 90 60 22 54). A shaded, café-filled square, Place de la République, is two blocks from the theater up Rue Ségond Weber.

◑ Self-Guided Tour: After you enter (to the right of the actual theater), you'll see a huge dig—the site of the Temple to the Cult of the Emperor (English explanations posted). *Arausio* is the Roman name for the town.

Look for signs to the worthwhile film and multimedia show (near the ticket office). The 15-minute **film** is in French with English subtitles (ask at front desk if subtitles aren't on). *The Ghosts of the Theatre* **multimedia show** covers four different periods of performance history. Both run continuously and can help you gain a good visual sense of how the theater looked to the Romans.

Next, enter the theater, then climb the steep stairs to find a seat high up to appreciate the acoustics (eavesdrop on people by the stage). Contemplate the idea that 2,000 years ago, Orange residents enjoyed grand spectacles with high-tech sound and lighting effects—such as simulated thunder, lightning, and rain.

A grandiose **Caesar** overlooks everything, reminding attendees of who's in charge. If it seems like you've seen this statue before, you probably have. Countless sculptures identical to this one were mass-produced in Rome and shipped throughout the empire to grace buildings like this theater for propaganda purposes. To save money on shipping and handling, only the heads of these statues were changed with each new ruler. The permanent body wears a breastplate emblazoned with the imperial griffon (body of a lion, head and wings of an eagle) that only the emperor could wear. When a new emperor came to power, new heads  were made in Rome and shipped off throughout the empire to replace the pop-off heads on all these statues. (Imagine Barack Obama's head on George W. Bush's body.)

Archaeologists believe that a puny, vanquished Celt was included at the knee of the emperor, touching his ruler's robe respectfully—a show of humble subservience to the emperor. It's interesting to consider how an effective propaganda machine can con the masses into being impressed by their leader.

The horn has blown. It's time to find your **seat:** row 2, number 30. Sitting down, you're comforted by the "EQ GIII" carved into the seat (*Equitas Gradus* #3...three rows for the Equestrian order). You're not comforted by the hard limestone bench (thinking it'll probably last 2,000 years). The theater is filled with 10,000 people. Thankfully, you mix only with your class, the nouveau riche—merchants, tradesmen, and city big shots. The people seated above you are the working class, and way up in the "chicken roost" section is the scum of the earth—slaves, beggars, prostitutes, and youth hostellers. Scanning the orchestra section (where the super-rich sit on real chairs), you notice the town dignitaries hosting some visiting VIPs.

OK, time to worship. They're parading a bust of the emperor from its sacred home in the adjacent temple around the **stage.** Next is the ritual animal sacrifice called *la pompa* (so fancy, future generations will use that word for anything full of such... pomp). Finally, you settle in for an all-day series of spectacles and dramatic entertainment. All eyes are on the big stage door in the middle—where the Angelina Jolies and Brad Pitts of the day will appear. (Lesser actors come out of the side doors.)

The play is good, but many come for the halftime shows—jugglers, acrobats, and striptease dancers. In Roman times, the theater was a festival of immorality. An ancient writer commented, "The vanquished take their revenge on us by giving us their vices through the theater."

With an audience of 10,000 and no amplification, **acoustics** were critical. A roof made of linen (called the velarium) originally covered the stage, somewhat like the glass-and-iron roof you see today (installed to protect the stage wall). The original was designed not to protect the stage from the weather, but to project the voices of the actors into the crowd. For further help, actors wore masks with leather caricature mouths that functioned as megaphones. The theater's side walls originally rose as high as the stage wall and supported a retractable roof that gave the audience some protection from the sun or rain. After leaving the theater, look up to the stage wall from the outside and notice the supports for poles that held the velarium in place, like the masts and sails of a ship.

The Roman Theater was all part of the "give them bread and circuses" approach to winning the support of the masses (not unlike today's philosophy of "give them tax cuts and *American Idol*"). The spectacle grew from 65 days of games per year when the theater was first built (and when Rome was at its height) to about 180 days each year by the time Rome finally fell.

In the fourth century (under Christian emperor Constantine), the church forced many theaters to close their doors. Later, during the barbarian invasions, the stage wall became a protective wall and the theater became a secure residence for many. Amazingly, people squatted here until the 19th century. You can still see traces of some buildings within the theater.

▲Roman "Arc de Triomphe"

Technically the only real Roman arches of triumph are in Rome's Forum, built to commemorate various emperors' victories. The great Roman arch of Orange is actually a municipal arch erected (in about A.D. 19) to commemorate a general named Germanicus, who protected the town. The 60-foot-tall arch is on a noisy traffic circle (north of city center, on Avenue Arc de Triomphe).

Sleeping in Orange

$$ Hôtel de Provence**, at the train station, is air-conditioned, quiet, comfortable, and affordable. Friendly Madame Verbe runs this traditional place with grace (Db-€65-85, Tb-€75-110, family rooms available, small rooftop pool, café, 60 Avenue Frédéric Mistral, tel. 04 90 34 00 23, www.hotelprovence-orange.com, hoteldeprovence84@orange.fr).

$$ Hôtel Logis Le Glacier** is a sweet hotel with nice touches in the center of town, a few blocks from the Roman Theater. It has easy parking and very fair rates (small Db-€56,

---

Sleep Code

(€1 = about $1.30, country code: 33)
S = Single, **D** = Double/Twin, **T** = Triple, **Q** = Quad, **b** = bathroom, **s** = shower only, * = French hotel rating system (0-5 stars). Unless otherwise noted, credit cards are accepted and English is spoken.

To help you sort easily through these listings, I've divided the accommodations into three categories based on the price for a standard double room with bath:

  $$$ Higher Priced—Most rooms €85 or more.
    $$ Moderately Priced—Most rooms between €55-85.
      $ Lower Priced—Most rooms €55 or less.

Prices can change without notice; verify the hotel's current rates online or by email. For the best prices, always book direct.

standard Db-€76, bigger Db-€110-130, 46 Cours Aristide Briand, tel. 04 90 34 02 01, www.le-glacier.com, info@le-glacier.com).

Orange Connections

From Orange by Train to: Avignon (15/day, 15 minutes), **Arles** (4/day direct, 35 minutes, more frequently with transfer in Avignon), **Lyon** (16/day, 2 hours).

By Bus to: Châteauneuf-du-Pape (2/day, none Sun, 30 minutes), **Vaison la Romaine** (3-5/day, 45 minutes), **Avignon** (Mon-Sat hourly, none Sun, 45 minutes—take the train instead). Buses to Vaison la Romaine and other wine villages depart from the gare SNCF and from Place Pourtoules (turn right out of the Roman Theater, and right again onto Rue Pourtoules).

Near Orange: Châteauneuf-du-Pape

This most famous of the Côtes du Rhône wine villages is busy with tourists eager to sample its famous product and stroll its climbing

lanes. While I prefer the less-famous wine villages farther north (described later, under "The Best of the Côtes du Rhône Villages"), this welcoming wine-drenched town makes an easy day trip from Avignon and works well with a visit to nearby Orange.

Châteauneuf-du-Pape means "New Castle of the Pope," named for the pope's summer retreat—now a ruin capping the beautiful-to-see but little-to-do hill town (more interesting during the Friday market). Wine-loving popes planted the first vines here in the 1300s. The pope's crest is embossed on all bottles of this deservedly famous wine.

Approaching from Avignon, signs announce, "Here start the vineyards of Châteauneuf-du-Pape." Pull over and stroll into a vineyard with a view of the hill town. Notice the rocky soil—perfect for making a good wine grape. Those stones retain the sun's heat (plentiful here) and force the vines to struggle, resulting in a lean grape—lousy for eating, but ideal for producing big wines (see "Côtes du Rhône Wines" on page 67). Eight different grapes are blended to make the local specialty, which has been strictly controlled for 80 years. Grenache dominates the blend, accounting for about 75 percent of the grapes grown. Syrah and Mourvèdre are the other two most-used grapes, each contributing about 10 percent to the final blend. The most interesting white wines in Provence are also made here (a blend of up to five grapes), but the reds are what attract most visitors. For more information on the area's wines, look for the Wine Museum (described later) at the start of the village as you come from Avignon.

Orientation to Châteauneuf-du-Pape

To visit Châteauneuf-du-Pape you can take a bus from Avignon or Orange (no buses on Sun) or drive. If you're coming by car, park below the town. Follow *Château* signs up the hill to the main square, Place du Portail. The helpful **TI** on Place du Portail has a long list of wineries that you can visit and good documentation on the area (July-Sept Mon-Sat 9:30-18:00, closed Sun; Oct-June Mon-Tue and Thu-Sat 9:30-12:30 & 14:00-18:00, closed Wed and Sun; tel. 04 90 83 71 08). Appealing streets fan out from here, most with cellars selling the famous wine.

Sights in Châteauneuf-du-Pape

Wine Museum (Musée du Vin)
Located at the Brotte Winery, this museum provides useful background for your Côtes du Rhône exploration. After a brief tour of the winemaking process and the work of a *vigneron* (audioguides available), enjoy a tasting. You'll need to tell them what you want; see "French Wine Lingo" on page 65. For a clear contrast, taste a "ready-to-drink" wine (*prêt à boire;* preh tah bwar), then a wine from "old vines" (*vieille vignes;* vee-yay-ee veen-yuh).

Cost and Hours: Free, daily April-Oct 9:00-13:00 & 14:00-19:00, Nov-March 9:00-12:00 & 14:00-18:00, on Avenue Pierre de Luxembourg, at start of village if coming from Avignon, tel. 04 90 83 70 07, www.brotte.com.

Wine Tasting
The town offers many places to taste wine, including these four cellars.

Near the TI: These two cellars are central. With your back to the TI, walk on the level road to the right to find Daniele Brunel's **The Best Vintage Cave,** a top place to sample Châteauneuf-du-Pape wines. Speaking fluent English and offering wines from 25 different producers (including her own), charismatic Daniele provides a good introduction to area wines. The youngest member of the famous Brunel wine family, Daniele represents a new generation of winemakers who combine traditional values and modern techniques (daily March-Oct 10:30-12:30 & 13:30-18:30, Nov-Dec 11:00-12:30 & 13:30-17:30, closed Jan-Feb, near Place du Portail at 7 Rue de la République, tel. 04

COTES DU RHONE

90 83 31 75, www.the-best-vintage.com). A free WC is next door.

Continuing along this street (and up the staircase), you'll find **Vinadéa Maison des Vins,** where you can taste and buy more than 200 kinds of Châteauneuf-du-Pape appellation wines from 90 different producers. Marie speaks English (daily June-Sept 10:00-13:00 & 14:00-19:00, Oct-May 10:00-12:00 & 14:00-18:00, 8 Rue Maréchal Foch, tel. 04 90 83 70 69, www.vinadea.com).

Uphill from Place du Portail: These two cellars are best suited for serious tasters.

Les Caves St. Charles offers tastings inside a 13th-century cellar, surrounded by barrels and *beaucoup* ambience. Helpful Guy Brémond answers all your questions in superb English (May-Oct Mon-Sat 10:00-19:00, closed Sun, 10 Rue des Papes, tel. 04 90 39 13 85, www.cave-saint-charles.com).

You can huff and puff (or drive) to the fancy restaurant **Cave du Verger des Papes,** which recently opened its Gallo-Romaine cellar for tastings (free, rotating selection of 3-4 wines, Mon-Sat July-Aug 10:00-19:00, closed Sun; Sept-June Tue-Sat 10:00-18:00, Sun 10:00-16:00, closed Mon, 2 Rue Montée du Château, tel. 04 90 83 58 08, www.caveduverger.com).

Near Châteauneuf-du-Pape

Mas de Lionne

Lying on the fringe of Châteauneuf-du-Pape, Mas de Lionne winery is where American Doug Graves is following his retirement dream. Doug bought this small vineyard in 2008 and has been living and working it nonstop since. He does just about everything by himself, but still has time to greet travelers and explain how his wines are made. Because his vineyard is across a tiny road from the officially designated Châteauneuf-du-Pape area, he can't label his wine with this prestigious name. Instead, his wines are designated Côtes du Rhône, even though they share much in common with Châteauneuf-du-Pape (notice the rocky soil). Doug makes a light rosé (€3.50) and velvety red wines (€5-9) using 100 percent Grenache grapes (unusual in this area, where typically several grapes are blended). His interesting story and ability to explain winemaking to Anglophones make this a worthwhile stop for aficionados.

Cost and Hours: Price varies by glass, Tue-Sat 14:00-18:00, closed Sun-Mon; find the town of Sorgues and look for *Mas de Lionne* signs off N-7, pass the first house with the small *Mas de Lionne* sign—the winery is 100 yards up the road at 948 Chemin de la Lionne, mobile 06 37 16 04 56, www.masdelalionne.com.

Sleeping and Eating in Châteauneuf-du-Pape

To bed down in Châteauneuf-du-Pape, try the traditional **Hotel-Restaurant La Garbure**, ideally located one door up the (mostly) pedestrian street from the TI (Db-€75-95, classy restaurant, 3 Rue Joseph Ducos, tel. 04 90 83 75 08, www.la-garbure.com).

You'll find several appealing eateries around Place du Portail on Rue Joseph Ducos. **Le Pistou** serves salads and *menus* from €13 (closed Sun evening and all day Mon, #15, tel. 04 90 83 71 75). **La Maisouneta,** at #7, is good for fresh pasta dishes (*menus* from €15, closed Tue evenings and all day Wed, tel. 04 90 32 55 03). **La Côté de l'Ange** serves small plates of food while you wine-taste (#22, tel. 04 90 89 15 86).

If you have the energy, follow signs up the hill to **Le Verger des Papes,** a fine restaurant where you can feast both on the terrace views and on their traditional and sophisticated cuisine (€19 lunch *menu,* €30 dinner *menu,* closed Sun evening, 4 Rue Montée du Château—drivers can follow *Château* signs and park at the top to skip the climb, tel. 04 90 83 50 40, www.vergerdespapes.com).

Picnics: The **three cafés** that surround the TI can all make their sandwiches to go, or find the small grocery, **Le Cigalou,** halfway up Rue Joseph Ducos (Tue-Fri 8:00-12:30 & 15:30-19:30, hours vary on weekends, open only in afternoon on Mon).

Côtes du Rhône

The Côtes du Rhône region features classic Provençal scenery, characteristic villages, cozy wineries, fields of fragrant lavender, and excellent restaurants. If you're sleeping in this area, Vaison la Romaine is a handy home base. Then delve into the region's highlights by following my self-guided driving tour. With more time, dig deeper into the Côtes du Rhône with a drive up Mont Ventoux, a spin around the Drôme Provençale, or a visit to the Ardèche Gorges.

Vaison la Romaine

With quick access to vineyards, villages, and Mont Ventoux, this lively little town of 6,000 makes a handy base for exploring the Côtes du Rhône region by car, by bike, or on foot. You get two villages for the price of one: Vaison la Romaine's "modern" lower city has worthwhile Roman ruins, a lone pedestrian street, and

a lively main square—café-studded Place Montfort. The car-free medieval hill town looms above, with meandering cobbled lanes, art galleries and cafés, and a ruined castle with a fine view from its base. (Vaison la Romaine is also a good place to have your hair done, since there are more than 20 hairdressers in this small town.)

Orientation to Vaison la Romaine

The city is split in two by the Ouvèze River. The Roman Bridge connects the more modern lower town (Ville-Basse) with the hill-capping medieval upper town (Ville-Haute).

Tourist Information

The superb TI is in the lower city, between the two Roman ruin sites, at Place du Chanoine Sautel (June-Aug Mon-Fri 9:00-18:45,

Sat-Sun 9:00-12:30 & 14:00-18:45; Sept-May Mon-Sat 9:30-12:00 & 14:00-17:45, Sun 9:00-12:00—except closed Sun mid-Oct-March; tel. 04 90 36 02 11, www.vaison-ventoux-tourisme .com). Say *bonjour* to *charmante* and ever-so-patient Valerie. Get bus schedules, ask about festivals and evening programs, and pick up information on walks from Vaison la Romaine. Find the big wall map showing hiking trails, and try the slick computer terminals that allow you to download hikes and bike rides with English instructions. You can also pick up English pamphlets on biking and hiking with instructions for several loop trails, ranging from easy half-day trips to all-day affairs.

Arrival in Vaison la Romaine

By Bus: The unmarked bus stop to Orange and Avignon is in front of the Cave la Romaine winery (by the driveway closer to the roundabout). Buses from Orange or Avignon drop you across the street (3-5/day, 45 minutes from Orange, 1.5 hours from Avignon, best from Orange and just €3). Tell the driver you want the stop for the *Office de Tourisme*. When you get off the bus, walk five minutes down Avenue Général de Gaulle to reach the TI and

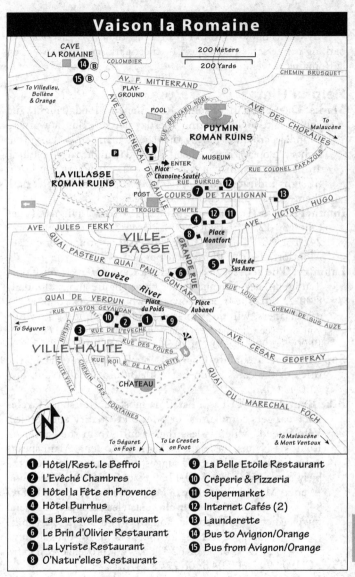

Vaison la Romaine

200 Meters
200 Yards

1 Hôtel/Rest. le Beffroi
2 L'Evêché Chambres
3 Hôtel la Fête en Provence
4 Hôtel Burrhus
5 La Bartavelle Restaurant
6 Le Brin d'Olivier Restaurant
7 La Lyriste Restaurant
8 O'Natur'elles Restaurant
9 La Belle Etoile Restaurant
10 Crêperie & Pizzeria
11 Supermarket
12 Internet Cafés (2)
13 Launderette
14 Bus to Avignon/Orange
15 Bus from Avignon/Orange

COTES DU RHONE

recommended hotels.

By Car: Follow signs to *Centre-Ville,* then *Office de Tourisme;* parking is free across from the TI—most parking is free in Vaison la Romaine as well.

Helpful Hints

Market Day: Sleep in Vaison la Romaine on Monday night, and you'll wake to an amazing Tuesday market. But be warned: Mondays are quiet during the day, as many shops close (but sights are open). If you spend a Monday night, avoid parking at market sites, or you won't find your car where you left it (if signs indicate *Stationnement Interdit le Mardi,* don't park there—ask your hotelier where you can park).

Internet Access: Try **Vaison 2 Mils** at 51 Cours Taulignan (Tue-Sun 8:30-12:30 & 15:00-19:00, closed Mon, tel. 04 90 36 23 24). For Wi-Fi, head to **Café Universal** on atmospheric Place Montfort. See the TI for more options.

Laundry: The self-service **Laverie la Lavandière** is on Cours Taulignan, near Avenue Victor Hugo (figure about €10, daily 8:00-22:00). The friendly owners, who work next door at the dry cleaners, will do your laundry—for around €20—while you sightsee (dry cleaners open Mon-Fri 9:00-12:00 & 15:00-19:00, Sat 9:00-12:00, closed Sun).

Supermarket: A handy **Casino** is on Place Montfort in the thick of the cafés (Mon-Sat 7:30-13:00 & 15:30-19:30, Sun 9:00-13:00).

Bike Rental: The TI has a list. The most central shop, **Cycles Chaves**, gets complaints for poor bike quality and service. **Vélo Speed,** which is less than a mile from the center on Route de Nyons, has eight racing bikes to rent; Alain speaks some English and has good suggestions for routes to avoid the busy roads (Mon-Sat 8:30-12:30 & 14:00-19:00, closed Sun, Avenue Marcel Pagnol near Point S store, tel. 04 90 28 17 84, www.velospeed.fr). **E-cyclo** rents electric bikes in several towns (including Vaison la Romaine) and offers tours (bike rental-€25/day, see website for tours and up-to-date address, tel. 04 75 27 12 97 or 06 08 62 43 86, www.provence-ecyclo.fr).

Taxi: Call 04 90 36 00 04 or 06 22 28 24 49.

Car Rental: You can rent cars by the day, though they must be returned to Vaison la Romaine; ask at the TI for locations.

Local Guide: Let sincere and knowledgeable **Anna-Marie Melard** bring those Roman ruins to life for you (tel. 04 90 36 50 48). Scottish by birth and an attorney by profession, **Janet Henderson** offers in-depth historic walks of Vaison la Romaine for €25 per person (allow 2 hours, 3-person or €75 minimum, janet.henderson@wandoo.fr).

COTES DU RHONE

Cooking Classes: Charming **Barbara Schuerenberg** offers reasonably priced cooking classes from her view home in Vaison la Romaine, where you'll pick herbs from the garden to use in the recipes (€80, includes lunch, 4-person maximum, tel. 04 90 35 68 43, www.cuisinedeprovence.com, barbara@cuisine deprovence.com).

Sights in Vaison la Romaine

Roman Ruins

Ancient Vaison la Romaine had a treaty that gave it the preferred "federated" relationship with Rome (rather than simply being a colony). This, along with a healthy farming economy (olives and vineyards), made it a most prosperous place... as a close look at its sprawling ruins demonstrates. About 6,000 people called Vaison la Romaine home 2,000 years ago. When the barbarians arrived, the Romans were forced out, and the townspeople fled into the hills (see the sidebar on page 202). The town has only recently reached the same population it had during its Roman era.

Cost and Hours: €8 Roman ruins combo-ticket includes both ruins and helpful audioguide; daily April-May 9:30-18:00, June-Sept 9:30-18:30, Oct-March 10:00-12:00 & 14:00-17:00, Oct and March until 17:30.

Visiting the Ruins: Vaison la Romaine's Roman ruins are split by a modern road into two sites: Puymin and La Villasse. Each is well-presented, thanks to the audioguide and occasional English information panels, offering a good look at life during the Roman Empire. The Roman town extended all the way to the river, and its forum still lies under Place Montfort. What you can see is only a small fraction of the Roman town's extent—most is still buried under today's city.

Visit **Puymin** first. Nearest the entry are the scant but impressive ruins of a sprawling mansion. Find the faint remains of a colorful frescoed wall. Climb the hill to the good little **museum** (pick up your audioguide here; exhibits also explained in English loaner booklet). Be sure to see the **3-D**

film that takes you inside the home of a wealthy Vaison resident and explores daily life some 2,000 years ago. Behind the museum is a still well-used, 6,000-seat theater, with just enough seats for the whole town (of yesterday and today).

Back across the modern road in **La Villasse,** you'll explore a "street of shops" and the foundations of more houses. You'll also see a few wells, used before Vaison's two aqueducts were built.

Lower Town (Ville-Basse)

Vaison la Romaine's modern town centers on café-friendly Place Montfort. Tables grab the north side of the square, conveniently sheltered from the prevailing mistral wind while enjoying the generous shade of the ubiquitous plane *(platane)* trees. The trees are cut back each year to form a leafy canopy (see sidebar on page 303).

A 10-minute walk below Place Montfort, the stout **Notre-Dame de Nazareth Cathedral**—with an evocative cloister—is a good example of Provençal Romanesque (free, daily April-Sept 10:00-12:00 & 14:00-17:00, closed Oct-March). The pedestrian-only Grand Rue is a lively shopping street leading to the small river gorge and the Roman Bridge.

Roman Bridge

The Romans cut this sturdy, no-nonsense vault into the canyon rock 2,000 years ago, and it has survived ever since. Find the information panel at the new town end of the bridge. Until the 20th century, this was the only way to cross the Ouvèze River. The stone plaque on the rock wall *(Septembre 22-92...)* shows the high-water mark of the record flood that killed 30 people and washed away the valley's other bridges. The flood swept away the modern top of this bridge...but couldn't budge the 55-foot Roman arch.

Upper Town (Ville-Haute)

Although there's nothing of particular importance to see in the fortified medieval old town atop the hill, the cobbled lanes and enchanting fountains make you want to break out a sketchpad. Vaison la Romaine was ruled by a prince-bishop starting in the fourth century. He came under attack by the Count of Toulouse in the 12th century. Anticipating a struggle, the prince-bishop abandoned the lower town and built a château on this rocky outcrop (about 1195). Over time, the rest of the townspeople followed, vacating the lower town and building their homes at the base of the château behind the upper town's fortified wall.

To reach the upper town, hike up from the Roman Bridge (passing memorials for both world wars) through the medieval gate, under the lone tower crowned by an 18th-century wrought iron bell cage. The château is closed, but a steep, uneven trail to its base rewards hikers with a sweeping view.

▲▲Market Day

In the 16th century, the pope gave Vaison la Romaine market-town status. Each Tuesday morning since then, the town has hosted a farmers' market. Today merchants turn the entire place into a festival of produce and Provençal products. This market is one of France's best, but it can challenge claustrophobes. Be warned that parking is a real headache unless you arrive early (see "Helpful Hints," earlier; for tips on enjoying market day, see the Shopping chapter).

Wine Tasting

Cave la Romaine, a five-minute walk up Avenue Général de Gaulle from the TI, offers a big variety of good-value wines from nearby villages in a pleasant, well-organized tasting room (free tastes, Mon-Sat 8:30-18:30, Sun 9:00-12:00, Avenue St. Quenin, tel. 04 90 36 55 90, www.cave-la-romaine.com).

▲Hiking

The TI has good information on relatively easy hikes into the hills above Vaison la Romaine. It's about 1.25 hours to the quiet hill town of Le Crestet, though views begin immediately. To find this trail, drive or walk on the road past the upper town (with the rock base and castle just on your left), continue on Chemin des Fontaines (blue signs), and stay the course as far as you like (follow yellow Crestet signs). Cars are not allowed on the road after about a mile. To find the 8.5-mile walk to Séguret (allow 2.5 hours), take the same road above Vaison la Romaine and look for a yellow sign. For either hike, consider the value of hiking one way and taking a taxi back (see "Helpful Hints," earlier, for taxi contact info).

Biking

This area is not particularly flat, and if it's hot and windy, bike-riding is a dicey option. But if the air's calm and cool, the five-mile ride to cute little Villedieu (with the recommended La Maison Bleue restaurant, listed on page 213) is a delight. Electric bike rental options make this a more appealing option for many (see "Helpful Hints," earlier). The bike route is signed along small roads; you'll find signs from Vaison la Romaine to Villedieu at the roundabout past Cave La Romaine toward Orange (see map on page 191). With a bit more energy, you can pedal beyond Villedieu on the lovely road to Mirabel (from Villedieu, follow signs to *Nyons*) and make a loop back on a busier road to Vaison (figure about 18 miles total). Or get a good map and connect the following villages for an enjoyable 11-mile loop ride: Vaison la Romaine,

St. Romain-en-Viennois, Puyméras (with the recommended La Girocedre restaurant—see page 213), Faucon, and St. Marcellin-lès-Vaison. The TI and bike shops have good information on mountain-biking trails.

Stream-Walking in the Valley of Toulauranc

For a refreshing experience and a breath of cool air, drive about 15 minutes from Vaison la Romaine to the valley of Toulauranc, where you can literally wander upstream into a beautiful canyon. You'll need shoes that work in water and a bathing suit. Leave Vaison la Romaine toward Malaucène, then follow *Entrechaux* signs and join D-5. Follow D-5, then signs to *Veaux*. Be alert as you near the tiny village of Veaux—just before reaching the village, you'll cross the river. Stop and park at the bridge, then walk upstream as far as you feel comfortable. River levels vary by season.

Sleeping in Vaison la Romaine

Hotels in Vaison la Romaine are a good value and are split between the lower, main town (with all the services) and the upper medieval village. Those in the upper town (Ville-Haute) are quieter, cozier, cooler, and give you the feeling of sleeping in a hilltop (some come with views), with all the services of a real town steps away. But they require a 10-minute walk to the town center and Roman ruins. If staying at one of the first three places, follow signs to Cité Médiévale and park just outside the upper village entry (driving into the Cité Médiévale itself is a challenge, with tiny lanes and nearly impossible parking). If you have a car, consider staying in one of the Côtes du Rhône villages near Vaison la Romaine (see "Sleeping and Eating Near Vaison la Romaine" on page 210).

$$$ Hôtel le Beffroi*** hides deep in the upper town, just above a demonstrative bell tower (you'll hear what I mean). It offers 16th-century red-tile-and-wood-beamed-cozy lodgings with nary a level surface. The rooms—split between two buildings a few doors apart—are Old World comfy, and some have views. You'll also find tasteful public spaces, a garden with view tables (light meals available in the summer), a small pool with more views, and animated Nathalie at the reception (standard Db-€95-120, superior Db-€160, Tb-€180, Rue de l'Evêché, tel. 04 90 36 04 71, www.le-beffroi.com, info@le-beffroi.com). The hotel's restaurant offers *menus* from €28 (closed for lunch weekdays and all day Tue).

$$$ L'Evêché Chambres, almost next door to le Beffroi in the upper town (look for the ivy), is a five-room melt-in-your-chair B&B. The owners (the Verdiers) have an exquisite sense of interior design and are passionate about books, making this place feel like a cross between a library and an art gallery (Sb-€78-85, standard Db-€93, Db suite-€120-140, the *solanum* suite is worth every euro,

Tb-€120-160, guest computer and Wi-Fi, Rue de l'Evêché, tel. 04 90 36 13 46, http://eveche.free.fr, eveche@aol.com).

$$ Hôtel la Fête en Provence, conveniently located for drivers at the entry to the medieval upper town, has a variety of room shapes and sizes. All the 15 rooms are chiffon-comfortable, and several have small kitchenettes. Rooms are located around a courtyard, with noise from the restaurant in summer (except Tue and Wed when it's closed), and there's an outdoor pool and Jacuzzi next door (standard Db-€75, bigger Db with king-size bed and bath-€105, Tb-€135, extra person-€15, Cité Médiévale, tel. 04 90 36 36 43, www.hotellafete-provence.com, fete-en-provence @wanadoo.fr). Their apartments (€180) sleep up to six people, and come with a kitchenette and sitting area.

$$ Hôtel Burrhus** is part art gallery, part simple, funky hotel—and the best value in the lower town. It's a central, laid-back, go-with-the-flow place, with a broad terrace over the raucous Place Montfort (the double-paned windows are effective, but for maximum quiet, request a back room). Its floor plan will confound even the ablest navigator (Db-€63-78, larger Db-€86-95, Qb apartment-€145, extra bed-€15, air-con, guest computer and Wi-Fi, 1 Place Montfort, tel. 04 90 36 00 11, www.burrhus.com, info@burrhus.com).

Eating in Vaison la Romaine

Vaison la Romaine offers a handful of excellent places—arrive by 19:30 or reserve ahead, particularly on weekends. And while you can eat very well on a moderate budget in Vaison, it's well worth venturing to nearby Côtes du Rhône villages to eat (see "Sleeping and Eating Near Vaison la Romaine" on page 210). Wherever you dine, begin with a fresh glass of Muscat from the nearby village of Beaumes de Venise.

La Bartavelle is a good place to savor traditional French cuisine in the lower town, with a tourist-friendly mix-and-match choice of local options. The €29 *menu* gets you four courses; the €22 *menu* gives you access to all the top-end selections but fewer courses. Be sure to reserve ahead (closed Mon, Fri at lunch, and off-season on Sun; small terrace outside, air-con interior, 12 Place de Sus Auze, tel. 04 90 36 02 16, www.restaurant-bartavelle.fr).

Le Brin d'Olivier is the most romantic place I list, with soft lighting, hushed conversations, earth tones, and a semi-gastronomic range of food that celebrates Provence (no-choice €29 and €36 *menus*, €22-26 à la carte *plats*, closed Wed except July-Aug, 4 Rue du Ventoux, tel. 04 90 28 74 79, www.restaurant -lebrindolivier.com, owner Patrick speaks a little English).

La Lyriste, named for the loudest "singing" *cigale* (cicada), puts cuisine above decor. Marie serves what hubby Benoît cooks. Both are shy, yet proud of their restaurant. There's a fine *menu* for €19, but go for the slightly pricier €29 *menus,* which are inventive and *très delectable* (closed Mon, vegetarian options, indoor and outdoor seating, 45 Cours Taulignan, tel. 04 90 36 04 67).

O'Natur'elles is ideal for vegetarians; the all-organic dishes can be served with or without meat. Locals love this place and it's small, so reservations are smart (€14-20 *plats,* daily, 36 Place Montfort, tel. 04 90 65 81 67).

Eating in the Upper Town: The recommended **Hôtel le Beffroi's** garden is just right for a light dinner in the summer (*menus* from €28, closed at lunch weekdays, and all day Tue).

La Belle Etoile is where locals go for simple, fresh, and good-value meals (open irregular days April-Sept, closes when they run out of food, tel. 04 90 37 31 45).

You'll also find a simple *crêperie* and a **pizzeria** on the main street leading up to the old town. Both have decks with views over the river, plastic chairs, and cheap food (good for families).

Vaison la Romaine Connections

The most central **bus stop** is a few blocks up Avenue Général de Gaulle from the TI at the main winery, Cave la Romaine.

From Vaison la Romaine by Bus to: Avignon (5/day during school year—called *période scolaire,* otherwise 3/day, all buses pass through Orange, 1.5 hours; faster to bus to Orange and train from there), **Orange** (3-5/day, 45 minutes), **Nyons** (3-5/day, 45 minutes), **Crestet** (lower village below Le Crestet, 2/day, 5 minutes), **Carpentras** (2/day, 45 minutes).

The Best of the Côtes du Rhône Villages

CÔTES DU RHÔNE

Officially, the Côtes du Rhône vineyards follow the Rhône River from just south of Lyon to Avignon. Our focus is the southern section of the Côtes du Rhône, centering on the small area between Châteauneuf-du-Pape and Vaison la Romaine. This area is best toured by car or bike. My self-guided driving tour starts in the village of Séguret, then returns to Vaison la Romaine and winds clockwise around the Dentelles de Montmirail, visiting the mountaintop village of Le Crestet, adorable little Suzette, and the renowned wine villages of Beaumes de Venise and Gigondas. I've listed several wineries *(domaines)* along the way. Before you go, study up with "Provençal Wine-Tasting 101" on page 66. Even if wine isn't your style, don't miss this scenic drive. Theft is a problem in this beautiful area—leave absolutely nothing in your car.

Planning Your Time

Although seeing the Côtes du Rhône is possible as a day trip by car from Arles or Avignon, you'll have a more enjoyable and intimate experience if you sleep in one of the villages (my favorite accommodations are listed under "Sleeping and Eating Near Vaison la Romaine" on page 210).

With a car, the best one-day plan is to take the driving tour described below (allow an entire day for the 80-mile round-trip from Avignon). Try to get the first two stops done before lunch (most wineries are closed 12:00-14:00; call ahead if possible), then complete the loop in the afternoon. Some wineries are closed on Sundays, holidays, and during the harvest (mid-Sept). This route is picnic-friendly, but there are few shops along the way—stock up before you leave.

Getting Around the Côtes du Rhône Villages

This area is clearly easiest if you have four wheels. Without a car, it's tougher, but a representative sampling is doable by **bike** (for ideas, see "Biking" on page 195) or by **bus** (3-5 buses/day from Avignon and Orange stop at several Côtes du Rhône villages; consider taking the bus one-way, then returning by taxi). For less effort and more expense, several of the local guides and minivan tour companies I list are happy to follow this route (see "Tours of Provence" on page 56).

Self-Guided Driving Tour

The Côtes du Rhône Wine Road

This tour introduces you to the characteristic best of the Côtes du Rhône wine road. While circling the rugged Dentelles de Montmirail mountain peaks, you'll experience all that's unique about this region: its natural beauty, glowing limestone villages, inviting wineries, and rolling hills of vineyards. As you drive, notice how some vineyards grow at angles—they're planted this way to compensate for the strong effect of the mistral wind. One hundred million years ago, the Mediterranean Sea extended this far north, leaving behind a sandy soil base for today's farmers (the wine town of Sablet's name comes from the French word *sable*, meaning sand).

This trip provides a crash course in Rhône Valley wine, an excuse to meet the locals who make the stuff, and breathtaking scenery—especially late in the day, when the famous Provençal sunlight causes colors to absolutely pop. This region is not only

CÔTES DU RHÔNE

Côtes du Rhône Driving Tour

1 Séguret
2 Domaine de Mourchon Winery
3 Le Crestet
4 Le Col de la Chaîne Mountain Pass

5 Suzette
6 Domaine de Coyeux Winery
7 Domaine de Durban Winery
8 Gigondas

about wine; you'll pass orchards of apricots, figs, cherries, and table grapes as well.

Remember that the wineries you'll visit are serious about their wines—and hope that you'll take them seriously, too. At private wineries, tastings are not happy-go-lucky chances to knock back a few glasses and buy a T-shirt with the property's label on it. Show genuine interest in the wines, and buy some if you enjoyed your tastes. Don't expect to be served immediately and simultaneously with other customers: Here it's done one at a time so that the client gets the server's full attention. And remember that those pouring your wine are hoping you'll buy (especially more than one bottle) if you are tasting for free.

The many fine restaurants along the way are another highlight of the route. I've mentioned some of my favorites; you'll find much more detail about these later, under "Sleeping and Eating Near Vaison la Romaine."

The Drive Begins

Our tour starts just south of Vaison la Romaine in little Séguret. This town is best for a visit early or late, when it's quieter. (If you get a late start or prefer ending your tour here, begin the tour in Le Crestet—stop #3—and save the first two stops for last.)

• *From Vaison la Romaine, the easiest way to reach Séguret is to follow signs for Orange, then look for the turnoff to Séguret in a few minutes. By bike, or for a more scenic drive, cross to the Cité Médiévale side of the river in Vaison la Romaine, then follow D-977 signs downriver to Séguret. A hiking trail from above Vaison la Romaine's castle leads to Séguret in 8.5 miles (see page 195).*

❶ Séguret

Blending into the hillside with a smattering of shops, two cafés, made-to-stroll lanes, and a natural spring, this hamlet is understandably popular. Séguret makes for a good coffee or ice cream stop.

Séguret's name comes from the Latin word *securitas* (meaning "security"). The bulky entry arch came with a massive gate, which drilled in the message of the village's name. In the Middle Ages, Séguret was patrolled 24/7—they never took their *securitas* for granted. Walk through the arch. To appreciate how the homes' outer walls provided security in those days, drop down the first passage on your right (near the fountain). These exit passages, or *poternes,* were needed in periods of peace to allow the town to expand below.

Find Séguret's open washbasin *(lavoir),* a hotbed of social activity and gossip over the ages. The basins behind the fountain (now planted) were reserved for washing animals (which outnumbered residents in the Middle Ages); the larger ones (on the left) were for laundry only. Public washbasins like this were used right up until World War II. Farther on, take a left at the fork. The community bread oven *(four banal)* was used for festivals and celebrations. Rue Calade leads up to the unusual 12th-century St. Denis church for views (the circular village you see below is Sablet). This rock-sculpted church is usually closed, but it's worth a look from the outside. High above, a castle once protected Séguret, but all that's left today is a tower that you can barely make out

The Life of a Hill Town in Provence

Heat-seeking northerners have made Provence's hill towns prosperous and worldly. But before the 1960s, few wanted to live in these sun-drenched, rock-top settings. Like lost ships in search of safe harbor, the people of long ago took refuge here only out of necessity.

When the Romans settled Provence (125 B.C.), they brought stability to the warring locals, and hill-towners descended en masse to the Roman cities (such as Arles, Orange, Nîmes, and Vaison la Romaine). There they enjoyed theaters, fresh water from aqueducts, and commercial goods brought via the Roman road that stretched from Spain to Italy (passing along the northern edge of the Luberon).

When Rome fell (A.D. 476), barbarians swept in to rape and pillage, forcing locals back up into the hills, where they'd stay for almost 1,000 years. These "Dark Ages" were when many of the villages we see today were established. Most grew up around castles, since peasants depended on their lord for security. The hill-towners gathered stones from nearby fields and built their homes side by side to form a defensive wall, terracing the hillsides to maximize the scarce arable land. They would gather inside heavy-stone Romanesque churches to pray for salvation. Medieval life was not easy behind those walls—there were barbarians, plagues, crop failures, droughts, thieves, wars, and the everyday battle with gravity.

As the Renaissance approached, and Provence came under the protection of an increasingly centralized French nation, barbarian invasions dwindled. Just when the hill-towners thought the coast was clear to relocate below, France's religious wars (1500s) chased them back up. As Protestants and Catholics duked it out, hilltop villages prospered, welcoming refugees. Little Séguret (pop. 100 today) had almost 1,000 residents; the village of Mérindol (near Avignon) sprouted from nowhere; and Fort de Buoux (near Apt, nothing but ruins today—see page 255) was an impregnable fortress. The turmoil of the Revolution (1789) continued to make the above-the-fray hill towns desirable.

Over the next century, hill towns slept peacefully as the rest of France modernized. Most of the hill towns you'll visit housed between 200 and 600 people and were self-sufficient, produc-

(trails provide access). At Christmas, this entire village transforms itself into one big crèche scene—a Provençal tradition that has long since died out in other villages.

• *Signs near Séguret's parking will lead you up, up, and away to our next stop, Domaine de Mourchon.*

❷ Domaine de Mourchon

This high-flying winery has become the buzz of the Côtes du

ing just what was needed (farmers, lawyers, and telemarketers were at equilibrium). Many town fountains and communal washrooms date from this time. Animals were everywhere, outnumbering humans four to one.

But 20th-century life down below required fewer stairs—and was closer to the convenience of trains, planes, and automobiles. So after World War I, down the hill-towners moved. To build in the flatlands, they pillaged the hill towns' stones, roof tiles, you name it, leaving those villages in ruin. By mid-century, most of these lovely villages became virtual ghost towns (in 1965, Le Crestet had but 15 residents—less than a third of its current population).

In recent years, hill towns have bounced back. Lavender production took off, and the government launched irrigation projects. But most of all, real estate boomed as Parisians, northern Europeans, and (to a lesser extent) North Americans discovered the rustic charm of hill-town life. They invested huge sums—far more than most locals could afford—to turn ancient stone structures into modern vacation homes (in many cases, buying several houses and combining them into one). Today's hill towns survive in part thanks to these outsiders' deep pockets.

Today, many villages have organizations to preserve their traditions and buildings (such as Les Amis de Séguret, or "Friends of Séguret"). Made up of older residents, groups like these raise money, sponsor festivals and dances, and even write collective histories of their villages. Many fear that younger folks won't have the motivation to carry on this tradition.

But hope springs eternal, as there may be a movement of locals back to these villages. Some northerners are finding hill-town life less romantic as their knee replacements fail. Meanwhile, the popularity of organic produce is making it financially viable for hill-town farmers with smaller plots to pursue their healthy dreams of living off the land. Finally, the Internet age has allowed some hill-towners to live in remote villages and telecommute, rather than move into bigger cities. Could the cycle be restarting? Armed with laptops, smart phones, and tablets, will hill-towners once again prosper when the next wave of barbarians comes?

Rhône by blending state-of-the-art technology with traditional winemaking methods (a dazzling ring of stainless-steel vats holds wines grown on land plowed by horses). The wines are winning the respect of international critics, yet the (Scottish) owners seem eager to help anyone understand Rhône Valley wines. Language is not an issue here, nor is a lack of stunning views. Free and informative English tours of the vineyards are offered once a week.

Cost and Hours: Winery open Mon-Sat 8:00-12:00 & 14:00-18:00, Sun by appointment only; from Easter-Sept, free English tour and tasting offered only on Wed at 17:00, check website or call to verify; tel. 04 90 46 70 30, www.domainede mourchon.com.

• *Next, return to Vaison la Romaine and follow signs toward Carpentras/ Malaucène. After passing through Crestet, you'll come to Le Crestet (on D-938). Look for signs leading up to Le Village and use the Parking Visiteurs lot at its entry.*

❸ Le Crestet

This village—founded after the fall of the Roman Empire, when people banded together in high places like this for protection from marauding barbarians—followed the usual hill-town evolution (see sidebar). The outer walls of the village did double duty as ramparts and house walls. The castle above (from about A.D. 850) provided a final safe haven when the village was attacked.

The Bishop of Vaison la Romaine was the first occupant, lending little Le Crestet a certain prestige. With about 500 residents in 1200, Le Crestet was a big deal in this region, reaching its zenith in the mid-1500s, when 660 people called it home. Le Crestet's gradual decline started when the bishop moved to Vaison la Romaine in the 1600s, though the population remained fairly stable until World War II. Today, about 35 people live within the walls year-round (about 55 during the summer boom).

Wander the peaceful lanes and appreciate the amount of work it took to put these stones in place. Notice the elaborate water channels. Le Crestet was served by 18 cisterns in the Middle Ages, and disputes over water were a common problem. The peaceful church (might be closed, €0.50 turns the lights on) has a beautiful stained-glass window behind the altar. Imagine hundreds of people living here and animals roaming everywhere. Get to the top of town. The village's only business, the recommended café-restaurant **Le Panoramic,** has an upstairs terrace with a view that justifies the name...even if the food is mediocre.

Walkers can return to Vaison la Romaine along a scenic footpath. The trail leaves from Chemin de la Verrière at the very top of the village (by the intersection with the road from below). Look for the brown sign, which indicates that it's 8 kilometers (about 5 miles) to Vaison la Romaine, and—in a few steps—turn right, following the yellow sign that shows it's 5.1 kilometers (3

The Phoenicians' Wine-Growing Almanac

Phoenicians brought about five grape varieties with them to southern Europe approximately 3,000 years ago. Today there

are more than 2,000 different grape varieties in the world, of which 150 are in France and 14 are in the Côtes du Rhône.

But some things have changed very little over the past three millennia: Today's Provençal farmers tend their grapes following much the same rhythm as did their Phoenician forerunners.

After a quiet winter, the plants begin waking up in March, pushing out new growth. By about mid-May, the plants are growing at a very fast pace, requiring farmers to do their first pruning of the year. Often working by hand, they pull off sucker plants and prune back new shoots, focusing the plant's energy on four to five main stalks.

Over the next three months, the farmers plow the soil, encouraging moisture to reach the plants. Every few weeks they spray for mildew (not a big problem in this dry area).

Next comes the harvest. Its precise date is dictated by how much sun and warmth the vines absorbed through the spring and summer: The hotter and drier the weather, the earlier the harvest.

In France, the grape harvest starts in the south and rolls north, ending about six weeks later in the country's northern-most vineyards, in Champagne. During the harvest, grapes are picked from the vines—either by hand or by machine—then separated from their stems. Pressing comes 2-3 weeks later, and the winemaking process is under way.

In the fall, farmers are busy watching and tweaking their wines. By December it's time for heavy pruning, when the plants are cut way back for the winter hibernation. Farmers spend the winter months catching up on maintenance, reading...and sleeping.

miles) to Vaison la Romaine (via Chemin des Fontaines).

• *Drivers should carry on and reconnect with the road below, following signs to Malaucène. As you near Malaucène, look for the huge* boules courts *separated by logs (on your left). Entering Malaucène, turn right on D-90 (direction: Suzette) just before the gas station. After a few minutes you'll approach a pass. Look for signs on the left to Le Col de la Chaîne (Chain Pass). From this point on, the scenery gets better fast.*

❹ Le Col de la Chaîne Mountain Pass

Get out of your car at the pass (elevation: about 1,500 feet) and enjoy the breezy views. Wander about. The peaks in the distance—thrusting up like the back of a stegosaurus or a bad haircut (you decide)—are the Dentelles de Montmirail, a small range running just nine miles basically north to south and reaching 2,400 feet in elevation. This region's land is constantly shifting. Those rocky tops were the result of a gradual uplifting of the land, then were blown bald by the angry mistral wind. Below, pine and oak trees mix with the shrub Scotch broom, which blooms brilliant yellow in May and June. You may see rich yellow-to-reddish patches of land—the result of deposits of ochre located deep below. The village below the peaks is Suzette (you'll be there soon). The yellow-signed hiking-only trail leads to the castle-topped village of Le Barroux (3.5 miles, mostly downhill).

The scene is gorgeous and surprisingly undeveloped. You can thank the lack of water for the absence of more homes or farms in this area. Water is everything in this parched region, and if you don't have ready access to it, you can't build or cultivate the land. (Some farmers have drilled as far as 1,300 feet down to try to find water.) With no water at hand, farmers here lie awake at night worrying about fire. Hot summers, dry pines, and windy days make a scary recipe for fast-traveling fires.

Now turn around and face Mont Ventoux. Are there clouds on the horizon? You're looking into the eyes of the Alps (behind Ventoux), and those "foothills" help keep Provence sunny.

• *Time to push on. You'll pass yellow trail signs along this drive. (The Dentelles provide fertile ground for walking trails.) To sleep nearby, try* **La Ferme Dégoutaud**, *just ahead (described on page 214). With the medieval castle of Le Barroux topping the horizon in the distance (off to the left), drive on to little...*

❺ Suzette

Tiny Suzette floats on its hilltop, with a small 12th-century chapel, one café, a handful of residents, and the gaggle of houses where they live. Park in Suzette's lot, below, then find the big orientation board above the lot (Rome is 620 kilometers—385 miles—away). Look out to the broad shoulders of Mont Ventoux. At 6,000 feet, it always seems to have some clouds hanging around. If it's clear, the top looks like it's snow-covered; if you drive up there, you'll see it's actually white stone (see the Mont Ventoux drive on page 214). If it's very cloudy, the mountain takes on a dark, foreboding appearance.

Look to the village. A sign asks you to *Respectez son Calme* (respect its peace). Suzette's homes once lived in the shadow of an imposing castle, destroyed during the religious wars of the mid-

Cicadas (*Cigales*)

In the countryside, listen for *les cigales*. They sing in the heat and are famous for announcing the arrival of summer. (Locals say their song also marks the coming of the tourists...and more money.) People here love these ugly, long-winged bugs, an integral part of Provençal life. You'll see souvenir cicadas made out of every material possible. If you look closely—they are well-camouflaged—you can find live specimens on tree trunks and branches. Cicadas live for about two years, all but the last two weeks of which are spent quietly underground as larvae. But when they go public, their chirping begins with each sunrise and goes nonstop until sunset.

1500s. The recommended **Les Coquelicots** café makes a good lunch or drink stop (described on page 214). Good picnic tables lie just past Suzette on our route. Back across the road from the orientation table is a tasting room for **Château Redortier** wines (unreliable hours, English brochure and well-explained wine list provided).

• *Continue from Suzette in the direction of Beaumes de Venise. You'll drop down into the lush little village of La Fare. Here, joyriders can take a 20-minute detour into the mountains by taking a sharp right on entering the village, following* Dentelles de Montmirail *signs. The Domaine de Cassan winery (tastings possible, Mon–Sat 10:00–12:00 & 14:00–18:00, closed Sun, tel. 04 90 62 96 12) lies near the end of the road that also leads to the Col du Cayron hiking trail (to the village of Gigondas). Your partner could drop you off and meet you in Gigondas (it's a 1.5-hour walk over the pass).*

But La Fare's best wine-tasting opportunity is back on our route just after leaving the village, at...

❻ Domaine de Coyeux

A private road winds up and up to this impossibly beautiful

setting, with the best views of the Dentelles I've found. Olive trees frame the final approach, and *Le Caveau* signs lead to a modern tasting room (you may need to ring the buzzer). The owners and staff (mainly Marion) are formal but sincere, and take your interest in their wines seriously—pass on by if you only want a quick taste or are not interested in

CÔTES DU RHONE

buying. These wines have earned their excellent reputation (and are now available in the US). Let Marion guide you and make recommendations for the tasting. Afterward, take time to wander about the vineyards.

Cost and Hours: Wines-€7-14/bottle, Mon-Sat 10:00-12:00 & 14:00-18:00, no midday closure July-Aug and weekends in May, June, and Sept, closed Sun, tel. 04 90 12 42 42, some English spoken.

• *Drive on toward Beaumes de Venise. You'll soon pass the recommended* **Côté Vignes** *(described on page 214), a good stop place for lunch or dinner.*

You'll drop out of the hills as you approach Beaumes de Venise. To find the next winery, keep right at the first Centre-Ville *sign as the road bends left, then carefully track* Domaine de Durban *signs for three scenic miles to...*

❼ Domaine de Durban

This winery offers a stunning setting similar to Domaine de Coyeux, but has a less "engaged" staff—so for many, this place is skippable. But they do make a rosé and whites (Domaine de Coyeux doesn't) and the drive there is another doozy. You decide.

If you go, find the small tasting room and let your young hostess take your taste buds on a tour. This *domaine* produces appealing whites, reds, and Muscats. Start with the 100 percent Viognier (€4.50/bottle), then try their Viognier-Chardonnay blend. Their rosé is light and refreshing, and the three reds are very different from one another. Finish with their popular Muscat de Venise.

Picnics are not allowed at the winery, and the grass is off-limits, though strolling amid the gorgeous vineyards is OK.

Cost and Hours: Wines-€4-11/bottle, Mon-Sat 9:00-12:00 & 14:00-18:30, closed Sun, tel. 04 90 62 94 26.

• *Retrace your route to Beaumes de Venise, turn left at the bottom, then make a quick right and navigate through Beaumes de Venise, following signs for* Vacqueyras. *At a big roundabout, you'll pass Beaumes de Venise's massive* cave coopérative, *which represents many growers in this area (big selection, but too slick for my taste). Continue following signs for* Vacqueyras *(a famous wine village with a Thursday market and another* cave coopérative*), and then signs for* Gigondas *and* Vaison par la route touristique. *As you enter Gigondas, follow signs to the TI and park on or near the tree-shaded square.*

❽ Gigondas

This town produces some of the region's best reds and is ideally situated for hiking, mountain-biking, and driving into the mountains. The **TI** has a list of wineries, *chambres d'hôte,* and good hikes or drives (Mon-Sat 10:00-12:30 & 14:00-18:00, likely closed Sun, Place du Portail, tel. 04 90 65 85 46, www.gigondas-dm.fr). The €2.50 *Chemins et Sentiers du Massif des Dentelles* hiking map is helpful, though not critical, because routes are well-signed. The blue route makes a good one-hour round-trip high above Gigondas to superb views (walk up the steep road from the town hall—*mairie*—next to  the TI and follow blue markers toward the Dentelles). You can extend this hike into a three-hour loop (get directions from the TI). At the very least, take a short walk through the village lanes above the TI—the church is an easy destination with good views over the heart of the Côtes du Rhône vineyards.

You'll find several good tasting opportunities on the main square. **Le Caveau de Gigondas** is the best and the busiest, where Sandra and Barbara await your visit with a large and free selection of tiny bottles for sampling, filled directly from the barrel (daily 10:00-12:00 & 14:00-18:30, July-Aug until 19:00, close to the TI on the main town square, tel. 04 90 65 82 29, www.caveaudugigondas.com). They pride themselves on attentive service, so be patient if they are with someone when you arrive. Here you can compare wines from a variety of private producers in an intimate, low-key surrounding. The provided list of wines is helpful. A self-imposed gag rule (intended to keep staff from favoring the production of a single winery in this co-op showcase) makes it hard to get a strong recommendation here, so it's best to know what you want (see "French Wine Lingo" on page 65). You'll find a small grocery store and several eating options in the village. (See "Sleeping and Eating Near Vaison la Romaine," later.) To dine very well or sleep

nearby, find the recommended **Hôtel les Florets,** a half-mile above town (restaurant closed Wed, described on page 211).

• *From Gigondas, follow signs to the circular wine village of Sablet*—with generally inexpensive yet tasty wines (the TI and wine coopérative *share a space in the*

COTES DU RHONE

town center)—then past Séguret and back to Vaison la Romaine, where our tour ends.

   If you haven't had your fill, consider adding on some...

Villages North of the Côtes du Rhône

Cairanne, toward Orange from Vaison la Romaine, is a pleasant village producing fine wines with one of the largest and most respected wine *coopératives* in this region. The **Cave de Cairanne,** officially known as the **Maison Camille Cayran,** has been making wine for over 80 years with grapes from more than 100 different grape farmers. Start with the free museum-esque "sensory trail," which explores the five senses through interactive displays and prepares you to taste their large range of wines (free, daily wine tasting 9:00-18:30, museum closes at 17:30, lots of English spoken, on Route de Bollene—you can't miss the signs, tel. 04 90 65 98 15, www.maisoncamillecayran.com).

   Consider a meal afterward at the nearby wine-bar/restaurant **Le Tourne au Verre** (€16 three-course lunch *menu,* €27 dinner *menu,* closed Wed and Sun, Route de Sainte-Cécile, tel. 04 90 30 72 18, www.letourneauverre.com).

   Grignan, dramatically set on a rocky spur, is 30 minutes north of Vaison la Romaine, off the beaten path at the northern edge of Provence. Its cobbled village lanes peppered with cafés and shops make for pleasing wandering, but the reason most come here is to tour one of Provence's grandest châteaux. The **Château de Grignan** offers travelers a glimpse into 17th-century château life in Provence. Its most famous resident, Madame de Sévigné, was famous for her witty letters to friends and family, and remains a literary giant in France. The first floor has English explanations and can be toured on your own, but you must join a French-only tour to see the rest, except during July and August when English tours are available—call ahead for times (€4.50, daily 10:00-12:30 & 14:00-18:00, July-Aug 10:00-18:00, closed Tue Nov-March, tel. 04 75 91 83 55).

Sleeping and Eating near Vaison la Romaine

Drivers can enjoy a wealth of country-Provençal hotel and dining opportunities in rustic settings within 15 minutes of Vaison la Romaine. All accommodations and most of the eating suggestions listed are along the self-guided driving tour route described earlier. They offer a great opportunity for drivers who want to experience rural France and get better values. All restaurants listed have some outdoor seating and should be considered for lunch or dinner.

South of Vaison la Romaine, toward Gigondas
Sleeping
$$$ Domaine de Cabasse*** is a lovely spread flanked by vine-yards at the foot of Séguret (with a walking path to the village). Winemaking is their primary business—free tastings are offered every evening at 18:30 April-September (off-season weekends only, for non-guests too). Most of the 21 rooms have been renovated with modern decor, some with balconies. The four original rooms retain an Old World charm and come with terraces overlook-ing the vines (Db-€125-140, Wi-Fi, elevator, big pool, on D-23 between Sablet and Séguret, entry gate opens automatically...and slowly, tel. 04 90 46 91 12, www.cabasse.fr, hotel@cabasse.fr). The restaurant offers a fine, though limited, €34 dinner *menu*.

$$$ Hôtel les Florets**, with tastefully designed rooms, is a half-mile above Gigondas, buried in the foothills of the Dentelles de Montmirail. It comes with an excellent restaurant, a vast ter-race with views, and hiking trails into the mountains (standard Db-€115-135, superior Db-€145-175, annex rooms have front patios but I prefer rooms in main building, Wi-Fi, tel. 04 90 65 85 01, www.hotel-lesflorets.com, accueil@hotel-lesflorets.com).

Eating
The restaurant at **Hôtel les Florets** is a traditional, family-run place that's well worth the drive—particularly if you dine on the magnificent terrace. Dinners are a sumptuous blend of classic French cuisine and Provençal accents, served with class by English-speaking Thierry. The weighty wine list is literally encyclopedic (€34-53 *menus*, closed Wed, service can be slow). See listing under "Sleeping," earlier.

In Gigondas, the shaded red tables of **Du Verre à l'Assiette** ("From Glass to Plate") entice lunchtime eaters (also good interior ambience, €11 salads, €14-20 *plats*, closed Wed year-round, off-season open for lunch daily and Fri-Sat nights only, located diagonally across from TI, Place du Village, tel. 04 90 12 36 64).

East of Vaison la Romaine, toward Malaucène
Sleeping
$$$ La Madelène Chambres is a few miles off the road between Vaison la Romaine and Malaucène. This smartly restored ancient farmhouse comes with pleasant English owners (Jude and Philip) and complete isolation. Filled with nice touches, the place has meditative terraces, a view pool, and five very comfortable and spacious rooms (Db-€120-150, includes breakfast, a few bikes available for guests, Route d'Entrechaux 84340, Malaucène, tel. 06 75 78 84 97, www.bighouseinprovence.com). Ask about

Lavender

Whether or not you travel to Provence during the late-June and July lavender blossom, you'll see and smell examples of this particularly local product everywhere—in shops, on tables in restaurants, and in your hotel room. And if you come during lavender season, you'll experience one of Europe's great color events, where rich fields of purple lavender meet equally rich yellow fields of sunflowers. While lavender season is hot, you'll find the best fields in the cooler hills, because the flowers  thrive at higher altitudes. The flowers are harvested in full bloom (beginning in mid-July), then distilled to extract the oils for making soaps and perfume. For a good explanation of this process, visit the Museum of Lavender in Coustellet (see page 246).

And though lavender seems like an indigenous part of the Provence scene, it wasn't cultivated here until about 1920, when it was imported by the local perfume-makers. Because lavender is not native to Provence, growing it successfully requires great care. Three kinds of lavender are grown in Provence: true lavender (traditionally used by perfume-makers), spike lavender, and lavandin (a cloned hybrid of the first two). Today, a majority of Provence lavender fields are lavandin—which is also mass-produced at factories, a trend that is threatening to put true lavender growers out of business.

Some of the best lavender fields bloom near Vaison la Romaine. Lavender blooms later the higher you go; the ones described here are listed from lowest to highest elevations. For an impressive display, drive north of Vaison la Romaine and ramble the tiny road between Valréas and Vinsobres (D-190 and D-46). You'll see more beautiful fields along D-538 between Nyons and Dieulefit, and still more if you climb Mont Ventoux to Sault (described on page 214).

their wine-tasting packages (€300/person includes 3 meals, overnight accommodation, and wine tour with 3 tastings; €1,900/couple for 3-night stay with visits to several wineries, www.rhonewineholidays.com).

Eating

Auberge d'Anaïs, at the end of a dirt road 10 minutes from Vaison la Romaine, is another find—and a true Provençal experience. Outdoor tables gather under cheery lights with views and reliable

COTES DU RHONE

cuisine. Ask for a table *sur la terrasse* (€13 lunch *menu*, good three-course dinner *menus* from €18, closed Mon, tel. 04 90 36 20 06). From Vaison la Romaine, follow signs to *Carpentras*, then *St. Marcellin;* signs will guide you from there.

Le Panoramic, in hill-capping Le Crestet, serves average salads, crêpes, and *plats* at what must be Provence's greatest view tables. Drink in the view, but if cuisine is important, eat elsewhere (€12 *plats du jour,* April-Nov daily 10:30-22:00, closed in bad weather and Dec-March, tel. 04 90 28 76 42). Drivers should pass by the first parking lot in Le Crestet and keep climbing to park at Place du Château. The restaurant is well-signed at the top of the village.

North of Vaison la Romaine, toward Nyons
Sleeping
$$ L'Ecole Buissonnière Chambres is run by an engaging Anglo-French team, Monique and John, who share their peace and quiet 10 minutes from Vaison la Romaine. This creatively restored farmhouse has three character-filled half-timbered rooms, and convivial public spaces. Getting to know John, who has lived all over the south of France and even worked as a *gardian* (cowboy) in the Camargue, is worth the price of the room; he's also generous with his knowledge of the area. The outdoor kitchen allows guests to picnic in high fashion in the tranquil garden (Db-€62-74, Tb-€78-89, Qb-€94-99, cash only, includes breakfast, Wi-Fi; between Villedieu and Buisson on D-75—leave Vaison following signs to *Villedieu,* then follow D-51 toward Buisson and turn left onto D-75; tel. 04 90 28 95 19, www.buissonniere-provence.com, ecole.buissonniere@wanadoo.fr).

$$ Domaine le Puy du Maupas Chambres, three miles from Vaison la Romaine in the village of Puyméras, is a winery with five good-value B&B rooms, views over vineyards to Mont Ventoux, and a pool (Db-€68-80, Tb-€80, includes breakfast, cash only, Wi-Fi, on D-938, Route de Nyons, tel. 04 90 46 47 43, www.puy-du-maupas.com, sauvayre@puy-du-maupas.com).

Eating
La Girocedre, easiest for drivers, is an enchanting place to eat lunch or dinner if the weather's nice. Just three picturesque miles from Vaison la Romaine in adorable Puyméras, this eatery offers a complete country-Provençal package: outdoor tables placed just-so in a lush garden, warm interior decor, and real Provençal cuisine (€18-23 lunch *menus*, €23-28 dinner *menus*, closed all day Mon and for lunch Tue, off-season closed all day Tue, reservations smart, tel. 04 90 46 50 67, www.legirocedre.fr).

La Maison Bleue, about four miles from Vaison la Romaine on Villedieu's delightful little square, serves pizzas and salads with great outdoor ambience. Skip it if the weather forces you inside (March-Oct Thu-Sun open for lunch and dinner, closed Mon-Wed, except July-Aug closed Mon only, tel. 04 90 28 97 02).

Along the Self-Guided Driving Tour, near Suzette

Sleeping

$$ La Ferme Dégoutaud, a 20-minute drive from Vaison la Romaine, is a splendidly situated, roomy, and utterly isolated *chambre d'hôte* about halfway between Malaucène and Suzette (well-signed, a mile down a dirt road). Animated Véronique (speaks minimal English, her son Thibault more) rents three country-cozy rooms with many thoughtful touches, a view pool, table tennis, picnic-perfect tables, and a barbecue at your disposal (Db-€75, Tb-€85, Qb-€95, includes breakfast, tel. 04 90 62 99 29, www .degoutaud.fr, le.degoutaud@wanadoo.fr).

Eating

Les Coquelicots, a tiny eatery surrounded by vines and views in minuscule Suzette, is a sweet spot. The food is scrumptious (owner/chef Frankie insists on fresh products), and the setting is memorable. Try the *Assiette Provençale,* his omelets with herbs, or any of his grilled meats and fish (May-Sept usually closed Tue evening and all day Wed, Oct-April open weekends only, tel. 04 90 65 06 94).

　　Côté Vignes, off a short dirt road between Suzette and Beaumes de Venise, is a lighthearted wood-fired-everything place with outdoor tables flanked by fun interior dining. Young Corrine runs the restaurant with enthusiasm; try the Camembert cheese flambé with lettuce, potatoes, and ham (€10 salads and good pizza, *menus* from €18.50, closed Wed year-round, Oct-April also closed Mon-Tue evenings, tel. 04 90 65 07 16).

More Côtes du Rhône Drives

For further explorations of the Côtes du Rhône region, consider these suggestions: a scenic mountaintop, an off-the-beaten-path countryside ramble, and an impressive gorge.

▲Mont Ventoux and Lavender

The drive to Mont Ventoux is worth ▲▲▲ if the summit is open (see later) and skies are crystal-clear, or in any weather between late June and the end of July, when the lavender blooms. It also provides a scenic connection between the Côtes du Rhône villages and the Luberon. Allow an hour to drive to the top of this 6,000-

foot mountain, where you'll be greeted by cool temperatures, crowds of visitors, and acres of white stones. Most days you'll see any number of cyclists braving the long, grueling ascent, made famous by its annual inclusion in the Tour de France.

Mont Ventoux is Provence's rooftop, referred to as the "Giant of Provence" or "the Bald Mountain," with astonishing Pyrenees-to-Alps views when it's really clear (it usually isn't). But even under hazy skies, it's an interesting place. The top combines a barren and surreal lunar landscape with souvenirs, bikers, and hikers. All that chalky mess you see was once the bottom of a sea. Miles of poles stuck in the rock identify the route (the top is usually snowbound mid-Nov to April, sometimes May). **Le Vendran** restaurant (near the old observatory and Air Force control tower) offers snacks and meals with commanding views. An orientation board is available on the opposite side of the mountaintop.

Between Mont Ventoux and the Luberon, you'll duck into and out of several climate zones and remarkably diverse landscapes. The scene alternates between limestone canyons, lush meadows, and wildflowers. Forty-five minutes east of Mont Ventoux (about 16 miles), lavender fields forever surround the rock-top village of **Sault** (pronounced "soh"), which produces 40 percent of France's lavender essence.

Sault, a welcoming town in any season, goes unnoticed by most hurried travelers. It's a slow-down-and-smell-the-lavender kind of place, with a sociable "mountain market" on Wednesdays.

There's no reason to sleep in Sault, but it's a fine place for lunch or *un café*. **La Promenade** café has simple salads and grilled meats with territorial valley views (*plats* €9-14, daily mid-April-mid-Sept, closed Sun off-season, tel. 04 90 64 14 34). Or enjoy the same views with a picnic in the adjacent, tree-lined area, the "promenade."

Getting to Mont Ventoux: Two roads lead to the peak of Mont Ventoux, both of which have small ski stations at 4,600 feet (about 4 miles from the top); Mont Serein station is on the north and Chalet Reynard station is on the south. The mountain pass between these stations (Col de Mont Ventoux), including the summit, is closed annually due to snow and ice from mid-November to mid-April (sometimes later for the north road). Confirm that the pass is open before you leave.

To reach Mont Ventoux from Vaison la Romaine, drive to Malaucène (15 minutes), then wind up D-974 for 45 minutes to the top. Another option is to drive around the base of the Mont, over the Col de la Madeleine (follow signs from Maulaucène) and through the quaint village of Bédoin (good Monday market); from there D-974 leads to the south road and offers a much longer, but perhaps prettier route to the top). If continuing to

Sault (a worthwhile detour when the lavender blooms) or on to the Luberon (worthwhile anytime—see next chapter), follow signs to *Sault,* then *Gordes.* The *Les Routes de la Lavande* brochure suggests driving and walking routes in the area (available online at www .routes-lavande.com).

Drôme Provençale Loop Drive

This meander north into the Drôme Provençale is overkill for many, as the scenery is only subtly different than what you'll see closer to your hotel. But if you haven't had your fill of pretty vistas, this drive is away from popular tourist areas and combines rugged scenery with overlooked towns and villages (see map on page 178). I'd only do it on Thursdays, when it's market day in Nyons, or on Wednesdays, when it's market day in Buis-les-Barronies. Allow most of a day for this up-and-down, curve-filled drive, particularly if the market in Nyons is on. Or you can just do Nyons and call it a day.

From Vaison la Romaine, drive to **Nyons,** an attractive mid-size town set along a river and against the hills. Here you'll find a Roman bridge with views, an olive mill, a lavender distillery, a handful of walking streets, and an arcaded square—all with few tourists. Nyons is famous for its rollicking Thursday market (until 12:30) and for producing France's best olives, which you can taste at its well-organized *coopérative* (daily 9:00-12:30 & 14:00-19:00, closes at 18:00 on Sun, interesting museum about olives, on Place Olivier de Serres, tel. 04 75 26 95 00).

From Nyons, head for the hills following signs to Gap on D-94, then follow signs to St. Jalles on D-64. Little St. Jalles hovers above the road, with a pretty Romanesque church (usually closed), two cafés (Café de Lavande overhangs the river, providing a fine backdrop for a drink, lunch, or a snack), and a small winery making crisp whites and easy reds (Domaine de Rieu Frais, daily 10:00-12:00 & 14:00-18:00, closed Sun in winter, tel. 04 75 27 31 54, www.domaine-du-rieu-frais.com, jean-yves.liotaud@wanadoo .fr, best to call ahead and let them know you're coming).

From St. Jalles, cross the bridge following D-108 and *Buis-les-Barronnies* signs, and start your ascent over the rocky mountains. Prepare for miles of curves, territorial views, and no guardrails. Drop down (er, drive down) and meet the Ouvèze river, then follow it into bustling **Buis-les-Barronnies** (with all the services, including a slew of cafés and an attractive old town to stroll). Buis-les-Barronnies is the linden tree capital of France and hosts an earthy outdoor market on Wednesdays with produce and crafts.

From Buis-les-Barronnies, continue south on D-5, then turn left toward Eygaliers on D-72. Follow this slow, serpentine road along the back side of Mont Ventoux and go all the way to the jewel of this trip: **Brantes,** one of Provence's most spectacularly located villages. Stop here for some fresh air and a look at the local pottery.

Finally, follow signs back to Vaison la Romaine along the faster, less curvy D-40. A few minutes before Vaison la Romaine, you'll pass through pleasing little Entrechaux.

▲Ardèche Gorges (Gorges de l'Ardèche)

These gorges, which wow visitors with abrupt chalky-white cliffs, follow the Ardèche river through immense canyons and thick forests. To reach the gorges from Vaison la Romaine, drive west 1.5 hours, passing through Bollène and Pont Saint-Esprit to Vallon Pont d'Arc (the tourist hub of the Ardèche Gorges). From Vallon Pont d'Arc, you can canoe along the peaceful river through some of the canyon's most spectacular scenery and under the rock arch of Pont d'Arc (half-day, all-day, and 2-day trips possible; less appealing in summer, when the river is crowded and water levels are low), and learn about hiking trails that get you above it all (**TI** tel. 04 75 88 04 01, www.vallon-pont-darc.com). If continuing north toward Lyon, connect Privas and Aubenas, then head back on the autoroute. Endearing little **Balazuc**—a village north of the gorges, with narrow lanes, flowers, views, and a smattering of cafés and shops—makes a great stop.

HILL TOWNS
of the
LUBERON

France's Answer to Italy's Tuscany

Just 30 miles east of Avignon, the Luberon region hides some of France's most captivating hill towns and sensuous landscapes. Those intrigued by Peter Mayle's books love joyriding through the region, connecting I-could-live-here villages, crumbled castles, and meditative abbeys. Mayle's best-selling *A Year in Provence* marked its 20th anniversary in 2010. The book describes the ruddy local culture from an Englishman's perspective as he buys a stone farmhouse, fixes it up, and adopts the region as his new home. *A Year in Provence* is a great read while you're here—or, better, get it as an audiobook and listen while you drive.

The Luberon terrain in general (much of which is a French regional natural park) is as enticing as its villages. Gnarled vineyards and wind-sculpted trees separate tidy stone structures from abandoned buildings—little more than rock piles—that challenge city slickers to fix them up. Mountains of limestone bend along vast ridges, while colorful hot-air balloons survey the scene from above. The wind is an integral part of life here. The infamous mistral wind, finishing its long ride in from Siberia, hits like a hammer (see the sidebar on page 68).

Planning Your Time

There are no obligatory museums, monuments, or vineyards in the Luberon. Treat this area like a vacation from your vacation. Downshift your engine. Brake for the views, and lose your car to take a walk. Get on a first-name basis with a village.

To enjoy the ambience of the Luberon, you'll want at least one night and a car (only Isle-sur-la-Sorgue—and, to a lesser extent, Lourmarin—are accessible by train or bus). Allow a half-day for Isle-sur-la-Sorgue if it's market day (less time if not). Add more time if you want to paddle the Sorgue River or pedal between villages. You'll also want at least a full day for the Luberon villages.

For the ultimate Luberon experience, drivers should base themselves in or near Roussillon. To lose the tourists, set up in Oppède-le Vieux, St-Saturnin-lès-Apt, or Buoux.

If you lack wheels or prefer streams to hills and like a little more action, stay in Isle-sur-la-Sorgue, located within striking distance of Avignon and on the edge of the Luberon. Adequate train service from Avignon and Marseille, and some bus service, connect Isle-sur-la-Sorgue with the real world. Level terrain, tree-lined roads, and nearby villages make Isle-sur-la-Sorgue good for biking.

The village of Lourmarin works as a southern base for visiting Luberon sights, as well as Aix-en-Provence, Cassis, and Marseille. Determined travelers can take a bus from Avignon or Aix-en-Provence to reach Lourmarin.

Getting Around the Luberon

By Car: Luberon roads are scenic and narrow. With no major landmarks, it's easy to get lost in this area—and you will get lost, trust me—but getting lost is the point. Consider buying the Michelin map #332 or #527 to navigate, and look for a copy of the free *Carte Touristique du Pays d'Apt* at local TIs.

If connecting this region with the **Côtes du Rhône,** avoid driving through Carpentras (terrible traffic, confusing signage). If you're in a hurry, use the autoroute from Cavaillon and get off in Orange (if you plan to visit that town), or use the exit before *Orange Centre* (exit #22) to get to the villages. If time is not an issue, drive via Mont Ventoux—one of Provence's most spectacular routes (see end of previous chapter).

By Bus: Isle-sur-la-Sorgue is connected with Avignon's town center by the Raoux-TransVaucluse bus line #6 (€2 one-way, 6-8/day Mon-Sat, 3-4/day Sun, 45 minutes, central stop near post office in Isle-sur-la-Sorgue, ask for schedule info at TI or download French-only schedule from www.voyages-raoux.fr/lignes/index .php). Three to four buses daily connect the Avignon TGV station to Isle-sur-la-Sorgue (same line and prices). Buses link Lourmarin with Avignon (3/day, 1.5 hours, transfer in Cavaillon) and Aix-en-Provence (3/day, 1.25 hours, transfer in Pertuis), making it a workable village stop between these cities. Without a car or minivan tour, skip the more famous hill towns of the Luberon.

By Train: Trains get you to Isle-sur-la-Sorgue (station called "L'Isle-Fontaine de Vaucluse") from Avignon (10/day on weekdays, 5/day on weekends, 30 minutes) or from Marseille (8/day, 1-2 hours). If you're day-tripping by train, check return times before leaving the station.

By Minivan Tour: Dutchman Mike Rijken, who runs **Wine**

LUBERON

Luberon

To Carpentras
D-938
To Mont Ventoux
Murs
D-31
ABBEY DE SENANQUE
D-901
To Avignon
Isle-sur-la-Sorgue
Fontaine-de-Vaucluse
D-102
Joucas
D-31
Gordes
D-2
D-901
BORIES
Lagnes
St-Pantaléon
D-900
D-938
①
Coustellet
⑮ D-103
Goult
5 Kilometers
A-7
Cavaillon
D-2
D-3
Oppède-le-Vieux
⑩
Lacoste
5 Miles
D-973
Ménerbes
ABBEY ST. HILAIRE
A-7
To St-Rémy & Les Baux
D-99
To Aix & Marseille
To Aix & Marseille

① Chambres Sous l'Olivier	⑤ Hostellerie des Commandeurs
② Le Mas d'Estonge Chambres	⑥ La Ferme de la Huppe Hôtel
③ Le Clos des Cigales Chambres	⑦ Le Mas du Loriot Hôtel
④ Hôtel les Sables d'Ocre	⑧ Le Clos du Buis Chambres

Safari, offers tours of this area, as do several other Avignon-based companies (see "Tours of Provence" on page 56).

By Taxi: Contact **Luberon Taxi** (based in Maubec off D-3, mobile 06 08 49 40 57, www.luberontaxi.com, contact@luberon taxi.com).

By Bike: Hardy bikers can ride from Isle-sur-la-Sorgue to Gordes, then to Roussillon, connecting other villages in a full-day loop ride (30 miles round-trip to Roussillon and back, with lots of hills). Many appealing villages are closer to Isle-sur-la-Sorgue and offer easier biking options (described later, under "Sights—Near Isle-sur-la-Sorgue"). **Vélo Services** can help you plan a route and deliver a rental bike anywhere in the Luberon (see "Isle-sur-la-Sorgue—Helpful Hints," later).

Luberon Area Market Days

Monday: Cavaillon (produce and antiques/flea market)

Tuesday: Gordes, St-Saturnin-lès-Apt, and Lacoste (all small)

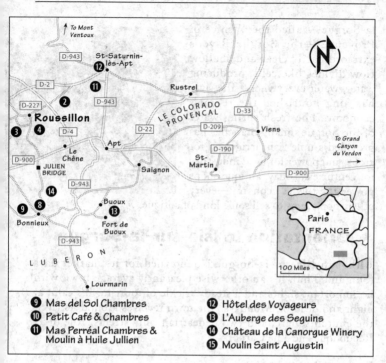

Wednesday: Sault (produce and antiques/flea market)
Thursday: Roussillon (cute) and Isle-sur-la-Sorgue (good, but smaller than its Sunday market)
Friday: Lourmarin (very good) and Bonnieux (pretty good)
Saturday: Apt (huge produce and antiques/flea market)
Sunday: Isle-sur-la-Sorgue (granddaddy of them all, produce and antiques/flea market) and Coustellet (very good and less touristy)

Isle-sur-la-Sorgue

This sturdy market town—literally, "Island on the Sorgue River"—sits within a split in its crisp, happy little river. It's a workaday town, with a gritty charm that feels refreshingly real after so many adorable villages. It also makes a good base for exploring the Luberon (15 minutes by car, doable by hardy bikers) and Avignon (30 minutes by car or train) and can work for exploring the Côtes du Rhône by car (allow an hour to Vaison la Romaine).

After the arid cities and villages elsewhere in Provence, the presence of water at every turn is a welcome change. In Isle-sur-

LUBERON

la-Sorgue—called the "Venice of Provence"—the Sorgue River's extraordinarily clear and shallow flow divides like cells, producing water, water everywhere. The river has long nourished the region's economy. The fresh spring water of the Sorgue's many branches has provided ample fish, irrigation for crops, and power for local industries for centuries. Today, antique shops power the town's economy—every other shop seems to sell some kind of antique.

Orientation to Isle-sur-la-Sorgue

Although Isle-sur-la-Sorgue is renowned for its market days (Sun and Thu), it's an otherwise pleasantly average town with no important sights and a steady trickle of tourism. It's calm at night and dead on Mondays. The town revolves around its river, the church square, and two pedestrian-only streets, Rue de la République and Rue Carnot.

Tourist Information
The TI has information on hiking, biking itineraries, and a line on rooms in private homes, all of which are outside of town (Mon-Sat 9:00-12:30 & 14:30-18:00, Sun 9:00-12:30, in town center next to church, tel. 04 90 38 04 78, www.oti-delasorgue.fr).

Arrival in Isle-sur-la-Sorgue
By Car: Traffic is a mess and parking is a headache on market days (all day Sun and Thu mornings). Circle the ring road and look for parking signs. There are several lots just west of the roundabout at Le Bassin (see map on page 224). You'll also pass freestyle parking on roads leaving the city. Don't leave anything visible in your car.

By Train: Remember that the train station is called "L'Isle-Fontaine de Vaucluse." To reach my recommended hotels, walk straight out of the station and turn right on the ring road.

By Bus: The bus from Avignon drops you near the post office (PTT, ask driver for "*luh pay-tay-tay*"), a block from the recommended Hôtel les Névons.

Helpful Hints
Shop Hours: The antique shops this town is famous for are open Saturday to Monday only.

Internet Access: Your best option is the centrally located **Cap**

LUBERON

Numérique (Mon-Sat 10:00-19:00, closed Sun, 40 Rue Carnot, tel. 04 90 15 40 16).

Laundry: A *laverie automatique* is on **Rue de la République** in the town center or, perhaps easier for drivers, at the **Centre Commercial Super U** supermarket, on the ring road at the roundabout, on Cours Fernande Peyre (daily 9:00-19:00).

Supermarket: A well-stocked **Spar** market is on the main ring road, near the Peugeot Car shop and the train station (Mon-Sat 8:30-12:30 & 15:00-19:30, Sun 15:00-19:30). A smaller, more central **Casino** market is on pedestrian Rue de la République (Tue-Sun 7:30-12:30 & 15:30-19:30, closed Mon).

Bike Rental: Vélo Services, run by helpful David Bollack, is at 3 Rue Docteur Tallet, but he can deliver bikes just about anywhere and help plan your trip. He also has dozens of free downloadable maps and route ideas in English (€10-20/day depending on bike, daily, tel. 06 38 14 49 50, http://veloservices .jimdo.com). **Luberon Biking,** in the nearby village of Velleron, can also deliver bikes (daily, tel. 04 90 90 14 62, www .luberon-biking.fr).

Taxi: Call 06 13 38 32 11 (mobile).

Public WC: A WC is in the parking lot between the post office (PTT) and the Hôtel les Névons.

Hiking: The TI has good information on area hikes; most trails are accessible by short drives, and you can use a taxi to get there.

Self-Guided Walk

Wandering Isle-sur-la-Sorgue

The town has crystal-clear water babbling under pedestrian bridges stuffed with flower boxes, and its old-time carousel is always spinning. For this walk (shown on the map in this chapter), navigate by the town's splintered streams and nine mossy waterwheels, which, while still turning, power only memories of the town's wool and silk industries.

• *Start your tour at the church next to the TI—where all streets seem to converge—and make forays into the town from there. Go first to the church.*

Notre-Dame des Anges: This 12th-century church has a festive Baroque interior and feels too big for today's town. Walk in. The curls and swirls and gilded statues date from an era that was all about Louis XIV, the Sun King. This is propagandist architecture, designed to wow the faithful into compliance. (It was made possible thanks to profits generated from the town's river-powered industries.) When you enter a church like this, the heavens should open up and assure you that whoever built it had

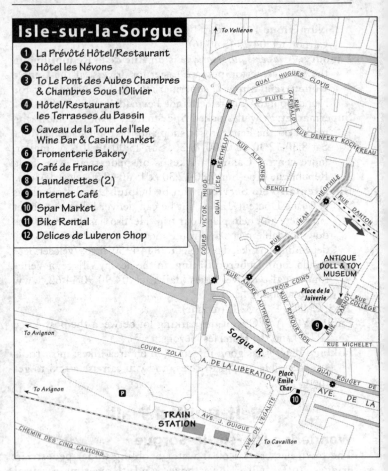

Isle-sur-la-Sorgue

1 La Prévôté Hôtel/Restaurant
2 Hôtel les Névons
3 To Le Pont des Aubes Chambres & Chambres Sous l'Olivier
4 Hôtel/Restaurant les Terrasses du Bassin
5 Caveau de la Tour de l'Isle Wine Bar & Casino Market
6 Fromenterie Bakery
7 Café de France
8 Launderettes (2)
9 Internet Café
10 Spar Market
11 Bike Rental
12 Delices de Luberon Shop

celestial connections (daily 10:00-12:00 & 15:15-17:00, Mass on Sun at 10:30).

Outside the church, notice the buildings' faded facades around you, recalling their previous lives (*fabrique de chaussures* was a shoemaker; *meubles* means furniture; *3 étages d'exposition* means 3 showroom floors). Admire Fauque Beyret's antique facade. Isle-sur-la-Sorgue retains a connection to its past uncommon in this renovation-happy region.

• *For a reality check, head into the town's historic (though less polished) side. Wander down Rue Danton, the narrow street to the right of the* meubles *sign, to lose the crowds and find...*

Three Waterwheels: These big, forgotten waterwheels have been in business here since the 1200s, when they were first used for grinding flour. Paper, textile, silk, and woolen mills would later find their power from this river. At its peak, Isle-sur-la-

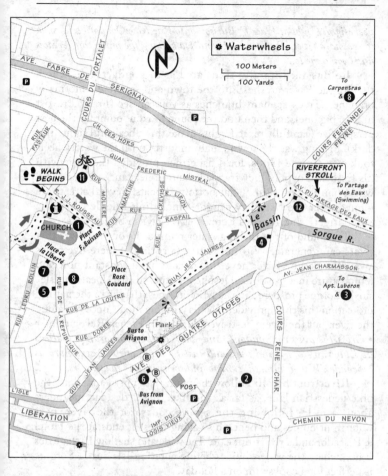

* Waterwheels

100 Meters

100 Yards

Sorgue had 70 waterwheels; in the 1800s, the town competed with Avignon as Provence's cloth-dyeing and textile center. Those stylish Provençal fabrics and patterns you see for sale everywhere were made possible by this river.

• *Double back to the church, turn left under the arcade, then find the small stream just past the TI. Breakaway streams like this run under the town like subways run under Paris. Take a right on the first street after the stream; it leads under a long arch (along Rue J. J. Rousseau). Look up for more faded facades (*bains, douches, *and* chambres meublées *means baths, showers, and furnished rooms). Follow this straight, and*

LUBERON

veer slightly right at Place F. Buisson onto Rue Rose Goudard and walk to the main river. Then turn left and walk along the many café terraces until you come to...

Le Bassin: Literally translated as a "pond," this is where the Sorgue River crashes into the town and separates into many branches. Track as many branches as you can see (Frank Provost hides a big one), and then find the round lookout point for the best perspective (carefully placed lights make this a beautiful sight after dark). Fishing was the town's main industry until the waterwheels took over. In the 1300s, local fishermen provided the pope with his fresh-fish quota. They trapped them in nets and speared them while standing on skinny, flat-bottomed boats. Several streets are named after the fish they caught—including Rue de l'Aiguille ("Eel Street") and Rue des Ecrevisses ("Crayfish Street").

The sound of the rushing water reminds us of the power that rivers can generate. With its source (a spring) a mere five miles away, the Sorgue River never floods and has a constant flow and temperature in all seasons. Despite its exposed (flat) location, Isle-sur-la-Sorgue prospered in the Middle Ages, thanks to the natural protection this river provided. Walls with big moats once ran along the river, but they were destroyed during the French Revolution.

• *Cross the busy roundabout, and walk to the neon orange* **Delices de Luberon** *store. Find the small tasting table with 12 scrumptious tapenades. Walk behind the store to find the river and take a refreshing...*

Riverfront Stroll: Follow the main river upstream, along the bike/pedestrian lane, as far as you like. The little road meanders about a mile, following the serene course of the river, past waterfront homes and beneath swaying trees. It ends at the Hôtel le Pescador and a riverfront café. The wide and shallow Partage des Eaux, where the water divides before entering Isle-sur-la-Sorgue, is perfect for a cool swim on a hot day.

Sights in Isle-sur-la-Sorgue

▲▲Market Days
The town erupts into a carnival-like market frenzy each Sunday and Thursday, with hardy crafts and local produce. The Sunday market is astounding and famous for its antiques; the Thursday market is more intimate (see market tips in the Shopping chapter). Find a table across from the church at the Café de France and enjoy the scene.

Antique Toy and Doll Museum
(Musée du Jouet et de la Poupée Ancienne)
The town's lone sight is a fun and funky toy museum with more than 300 dolls displayed in three small rooms.

Cost and Hours: €3.50, kids-€1.50; July-Sept Mon-Sat

10:30-18:30, Sun 11:00-18:00; Oct-June Tue-Fri 13:00-18:00, Sat-Sun 11:00-17:00, closed Mon; call ahead to confirm opening times, at 26 Rue Carnot down a short alley, mobile 06 09 10 32 66.

Near Isle-sur-la-Sorgue

Fontaine-de-Vaucluse

You'll read and hear a lot about this overrun village, impressively located at the source of the Sorgue River, where the medieval Italian poet Petrarch mourned for his love, Laura. The river seems to magically appear from nowhere (the actual source is a murky, green waterhole) and flows through the town past a lineup of cafés, souvenir shops, and wall-to-river tourists. The setting is beautiful—with cliffs jutting to the sky and a ruined castle above—but the trip is worth it only if the spring is flowing. *Sans* flowing spring, this is the most overrated sight in France. Ask your hotelier if the spring is active, and arrive early or late to avoid crowds. It's a good bike ride here from Isle-sur-la-Sorgue (about four miles).

Arriving by car, you'll pay to park (€3-4), and then walk about 20 minutes along the sparkling river to *la source* (the spring), located in a cave at the base of the cliff. (It's an uphill hike for the last part.) The spring itself is the very definition of anticlimactic, unless it's surging. At those times, it's among the most prolific water producers in the world, with a depth no one has yet been able to determine.

The path to the spring is lined with distractions. The only stops worth your time are the riverfront cafés and restaurants—**Philip's** offers the best seats—and the **Moulin à Papier,** a reproduction of a 17th-century paper mill. Here you'll see the value of harnessing the river's power. In the mill, a 22-foot-diameter paddle wheel turns five times a minute, driving hammers that pound paper for up to 36 hours (free, daily 9:00-19:00). As you watch the hammers pound away, imagine Isle-sur-la-Sorgue's waterwheels and the industries they once powered. The shop inside sells paper in every size.

Canoe Trips on the Sorgue

A better reason to travel to Fontaine-de-Vaucluse is to canoe down the river. If you're *really* on vacation, take this five-mile, two-hour trip. The guide escorts small groups in canoes (or you can go it alone), starting in Fontaine-de-Vaucluse and ending in Isle-sur-la-Sorgue; you'll return to Fontaine-de-Vaucluse by shuttle bus (call for departure times; ask about shuttle service from Isle-sur-la-Sorgue). The company, **Kayaks Verts,** is a family operation run by happy-go-lucky Michel, who speaks "small English" (late April-mid-Oct, €18/person, tel. 04 90 20 35 44, www.canoe-france.com /en/sorgue). To combine bike and boat, ask Michel about shuttling

LUBERON

your rental bikes back to Isle-sur-la-Sorgue while you float from Fontaine-de-Vaucluse (see suggested bike route below).

Biking

Isle-sur-la-Sorgue is ideally situated for short biking forays into the mostly level terrain. Pick up a biking itinerary at the TI, or consult with David at **Vélo Services** (see "Helpful Hints," earlier, for bike-rental info). These towns make easy biking destinations from Isle-sur-la-Sorgue: Velleron (5 flat miles north, a tiny version of Isle-sur-la-Sorgue with waterwheels, fountains, and an evening farmers' market Mon-Sat 18:00-20:00); Lagnes (3 miles east, a pretty and well-restored hill town with views from its ruined château); and Fontaine-de-Vaucluse (5 gently uphill miles northeast, described above). Allow 30 miles and many hills for the round-trip ride to Roussillon.

Sleeping in Isle-sur-la-Sorgue

Pickings are slim for good sleeps in Isle-sur-la-Sorgue, though the few I've listed provide solid values.

$$$ La Prévôté*** has the town's highest-priced digs. Its five meticulously decorated rooms—located above a classy restaurant—are decorated in earth tones, with high ceilings, a few exposed beams, and beautiful furnishings. Don't miss the before- and after-renovation photos in the hallways. Helpful Séverine manages the hotel while chef-hubby Jean-Marie controls the kitchen (standard Db-€160, larger Db-€185, suite Db-€220, cheaper for longer stays, air-con, no elevator, Wi-Fi, rooftop deck with Jacuzzi, no parking, one block from the church at 4 Rue J. J. Rousseau, tel. 04 90 38 57 29, www.la-prevote.fr, contact@la-prevote.fr).

$$ Hôtel les Névons**, two blocks from the center (behind the post office), is concrete motel-modern outside, but has comfortable rooms with eager-to-please staff within. The hotel also offers several family suites and a roof deck with 360-degree views around a small pool (standard Sb/Db-€69-80; Sb/Db with balcony-€79-90; huge Db with terrace-€98-120, Tb-€95-140 depending on size, Qb-€138-160; good but pricey breakfast, air-con, Wi-Fi, easy parking, 205 Chemin des Névons, push and hold the gate button a bit on entry, tel. 04 90 20 72 00, www.hotel-les-nevons.com, info@hotel-les-nevons.com).

$$ Le Pont des Aubes Chambres has two huggable rooms in an old green-shuttered farmhouse right on the river a mile from town. Borrow a bike or a canoe. From here you can cross a tiny bridge and walk 15 minutes along the river into Isle-sur-la-Sorgue. Charming Martine speaks English, while husband Patrice speaks smiles (Db-€75, Tb-€90, 1-room apartments-€390-500/week, cash only, a mile from town toward Apt, next to Pain d'Antan

Sleep Code

(€1 = about $1.30, country code: 33)
S = Single, **D** = Double/Twin, **T** = Triple, **Q** = Quad, **b** = bathroom, **s** = shower only, * = French hotel rating system (0-5 stars). Unless otherwise noted, credit cards are accepted and English is spoken.

To help you sort easily through these listings, I've divided the accommodations into three categories based on the price for a standard double room with bath:

$$$ Higher Priced—Most rooms €90 or more.
  $$ Moderately Priced—Most rooms between €60-90.
    $ Lower Priced—Most rooms €60 or less.

Prices can change without notice; verify the hotel's current rates online or by email. For the best prices, always book direct.

Boulangerie at 189 Route d'Apt, tel. 04 90 38 13 75, www.lepont desaubes.com, lepontdesaubes@yahoo.fr).

$$ Hôtel les Terrasses du Bassin's friendly owners Corinne and Gilles rent eight good-value rooms over a pleasant restaurant on Le Bassin, where the river waters separate before running through town. Several rooms look out over Le Bassin. Most have some traffic noise; a few have queen-size beds (Db-€60-82 depending on view and size, extra bed-€12, air-con, Wi-Fi in restaurant only, 2 Avenue Charles de Gaulle, tel. 04 90 38 03 16, www.les terrassesdubassin.com, corinne@lesterrassesdubassin.com).

Near Isle-sur-la-Sorgue

$$$ Chambres Sous l'Olivier, located five minutes east of Isle-sur-la-Sorgue, is well-situated for exploring the hill towns of the Luberon and Isle-sur-la-Sorgue. Its six lovely rooms are housed in a massive 150-year-old farmhouse with lounges that you and your entire soccer team could spread out in. Julien and Carole will take care of your every need, and will cook you an exquisite, full-blown dinner with wine for €31 per person (Db-€92-132, Tb-€122, 2-room Tb-€182, 3-room suite for up to 6 people-€230, prices include breakfast; credit cards not accepted—pay with cash, euro travelers checks, or bank transfer; heated pool; Route d'Apt, tel. 04 90 20 33 90, www.chambresdhotesprovence.com, souslolivier @orange.fr). It's below Isle-sur-la-Sorgue, about 25 minutes from Avignon toward Apt on D-900 (near Petit Palais—don't go to Lagnes by mistake). Look for signs 200 yards after the big sign to *le Mas du Grand Jonquier,* on the right.

LUBERON

Eating in Isle-sur-la-Sorgue

Inexpensive restaurants are easy to find in Isle-sur-la-Sorgue, but consistent quality is another story. The restaurants I list offer good value, but none of them is really "cheap." For inexpensive meals, troll the riverside cafés for today's catch. Dining on the river is a unique experience in this arid land, and shopping for the perfect table is half the fun. To assemble a riverside picnic, try the Fromenterie bakery, and head to Rue de la République, which has bakeries, butchers, a *traiteur* (deli), cheesemongers, a wine shop, and a supermarket.

Begin your dinner with a glass of wine (€3-5) at the cozy wine and cheese cellar **Caveau de la Tour de l'Isle**. Or for a light meal order a selection of cheeses (€10-16, great to share) with your wine and call it good (a few tables outside or find the bar hiding in the rear behind the cheese counter and wine shop, Tue-Sun 9:30-12:30 & 15:30-20:00, closed Mon except in July-Aug, 12 Rue de la République, tel. 04 90 20 70 25).

Les Terrasses du Bassin is your best riverfront option, with reasonable prices, great service, and tasty choices (eat on the terrace if weather allows). The hardworking owners are dedicated to providing a good value and welcoming service. Come for a full meal or just a *plat* (€13-17 lunch salads and starters, €20 dinner *plats*, €25-35 dinner *menu*, closed Tue-Wed Oct-May, 2 Avenue Charles de Gaulle, tel. 04 90 38 03 16, www.lesterrassesdubassin .com).

La Prévôté is a place to really do it up. Its dining room is covered in wood beams, the outdoor patio is peaceful, and the ambience is country-classy but not stuffy. A branch of the Sorgue runs under the restaurant, visible through glass windows (€50-80 *menus*, save room for amazing cheese platter, closed Tue-Wed, 4 Rue J. J. Rousseau, on narrow street that runs along left side of church as you face it, tel. 04 90 38 57 29, www.la-prevote.fr).

The **Fromenterie** bakery next to the post office (PTT) sells decadent quiche, monster sandwiches, prepared salads, desserts, wine and other drinks, and even plastic cutlery and cups—in other words, everything you need to picnic (open daily until 20:00, 19 Avenue des Quatre Otages).

The Heart of the Luberon

A 15-minute drive east of Isle-sur-la-Sorgue brings you to this protected area, where canyons and ridgelines rule, and land developers take a back seat. Still-proud hill towns guard access to winsome valleys, while carefully managed vineyards (producing inexpensive wines) play hopscotch with cherry groves, lavender fields, and cypress trees.

Two decades ago, Peter Mayle's *A Year in Provence* nudged tourism in this area into overdrive. A visit to Mayle's quintessential Provence includes many of the popular villages and sights described in this chapter. While the hill towns can be seen as subtly different variations on the same theme, each has a distinct character. Look for differences: the color of shutters, the pattern of stones, the way flowers are planted, or the number of tourist boutiques. Every village has something to offer—it's up to you to discover and celebrate it.

Stay in or near Roussillon. By village standards, Roussillon is always lively, and it struggles to manage its popularity. When restaurant-hunting, read descriptions of the villages in this chapter—many good finds are embedded in the countryside. For aerial views high above this charmed land, consider a hot-air balloon trip.

Planning Your Time

With a car and one full day, I'd linger in Roussillon in the morning, visit the Julien Bridge, then have lunch nearby in Lacoste or Bonnieux. After lunch, continue the joyride past Ménerbes to Oppède-le-Vieux, then return through Coustellet and Gordes. With a second full day, I'd start by climbing the Fort de Buoux, then lunch nearby. After lunch, continue to Saignon and Viens, then loop back via Le Colorado Provençal and St-Saturnin-lès-Apt.

I've described sights at each stop, but you'll need to be selective—you can't (and don't need to) see them all. Read through your options and choose the ones that appeal most. Slow down and get to know a few places well, rather than dashing between every stop you can cram in. The best sight is the dreamy landscape between the villages.

LUBERON

Roussillon

With all the trendy charm of Santa Fe on a hilltop, photogenic Roussillon requires serious camera and café time. Roussillon has been a protected village since 1943 and has benefited from a com-

plete absence of modern development. An enormous deposit of ochre, which gives the earth and its buildings that distinctive red color, provided this village with its economic base until shortly after World War II. This place is popular; it's best to visit early or late in the day.

Orientation to Roussillon

Roussillon sits atop Mont Rouge ("Red Mountain") at about 1,000 feet above sea level, and requires some uphill walking to reach. Exposed ochre cliffs form the village's southern limit.

Tourist Information
The little TI is in the center, across from the Chez David restaurant. If in need of accommodations, leaf through their informative binders describing area hotels and *chambres d'hôte*. Walkers should get info on trails from Roussillon to nearby villages (TI hours are unreliable, usually April-Oct Mon-Sat 9:30-12:00 & 13:30-18:00, closed Sun except afternoons in July-Aug; Nov-March Mon-Sat 14:00-17:30, closed Sun; Place de la Poste, tel. 04 90 05 60 25, www.roussillon-provence.com).

Arrival in Roussillon
Parking lots are available at every entry to the village (all €3/day, free if you're staying overnight and have arranged it with your hotel). Parking Sablons is near the recommended Hôtel Rêves d'Ocres. Parking Pasquier is closest to the village center, but has only 16 spots. Parking des Ocres (also called "P2") is the large lot on the hill toward the entrance to the ochre cliffs. Day-trippers should head straight here, as it's easier to find spots and comes with the best view of Roussillon. If you approach from Gordes or Joucas, you'll pass Sablons first. If you're coming from D-900 and the south, you'll land at Ocres/P2 or Pasquier (but don't park at Pasquier on Wednesday night, because Thursday is Roussillon's market day). Leave nothing valuable visible in your car.

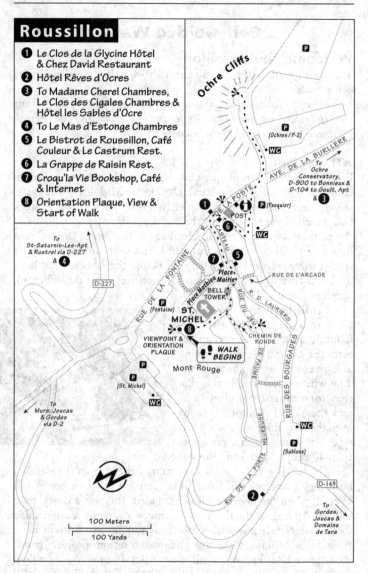

Roussillon

1 Le Clos de la Glycine Hôtel
   & Chez David Restaurant
2 Hôtel Rêves d'Ocres
3 To Madame Cherel Chambres,
   Le Clos des Cigales Chambres &
   Hôtel les Sables d'Ocre
4 To Le Mas d'Estonge Chambres
5 Le Bistrot de Roussillon, Café
   Couleur & Le Castrum Rest.
6 La Grappe de Raisin Rest.
7 Croqu'la Vie Bookshop, Café
   & Internet
8 Orientation Plaque, View &
   Start of Walk

Helpful Hints

An **ATM** is next to the TI. **Internet access** and a modest selection of English books are available at the delightful **Croqu'la Vie** bookshop on the main square (€2/30 minutes, free for customers, daily 10:00-18:00, later July-Sept, has recommended view café on top floor, Place de la Mairie, tel. 04 90 71 55 72). **Public WCs** are uphill toward the ochre cliffs.

Self-Guided Walk

Welcome to Roussillon

This quick walk will take you through Roussillon's village to its ochre cliffs.

• *To begin the walk, climb a few minutes from any parking lot (passing the Hollywood set-like square under the bell tower and the church). Continue past the church to the summit of...*

▲The Village

Find the orientation plaque and the dramatic **viewpoint,** often complete with a howling mistral. During the Middle Ages, a castle stood where you are, on the top of Red Mountain (Mont Rouge), and watched over the village below. Though nothing remains of the castle today, the strategic advantage of this site is clear. Count how many villages you can identify, and then notice how little sprawl there is in the valley below. Because the Luberon has been declared a natural reserve (Parc Naturel Régional du Luberon), development is strictly controlled.

Stroll back to the **church.** Duck into the pretty 11th-century Church of St. Michel, and appreciate the natural air-conditioning and the well-worn center aisle. The white interior tells you that the stone came from elsewhere, and the WWI memorial plaque over the side door suggests a village devastated by the war (more than 40 people from little Roussillon died).

On leaving the church, look across the way to the derelict building, a reminder of Roussillon's humble roots. After World War II, when the demand for ochre faded, this was a dusty, poor village. Adding to the town's economic woes, many residents fled for an easier life below, with level streets and modern conveniences. Abandoned buildings like this presented a serious problem (common throughout France)...until the tourists discovered Roussillon, and folks began reinvesting in the village. This building is still looking for a buyer. Detour behind the building to the left down a small lane to find the Chemin de Ronde, with terrific views of the Luberon and Gordes from atop the medieval walls.

• *Return to the church and continue down to the village.*

Notice the clamped-iron beams that shore up old walls. Examine the different hues of yellow and orange. These lime-finished exteriors, called *chaux* (literally, "limes"), need to be redone about every 10 years. Locals choose their exact color...

but in this town of ochre, it's never white. The church tower that you walk under once marked the entrance to the fortified town. Just before dropping down to the square, turn right and find the gigantic 150-year-old grapevine that decorates Restaurant la Treille. This is what you get when you don't prune.

Linger over *un café,* or—if it's later in the day—*un pastis,* in what must be the most picturesque village square in Provence

(Place de la Mairie). Watch the stream of shoppers. Is anyone playing *boules* at the opposite end? You could paint the entire town without ever leaving the red-and-orange corner of your palette. Many do. While Roussillon receives its share of day-trippers, mornings and evenings are romantically peaceful on this square. The Croqu'la Vie bookshop on the square's corner deserves a visit (nice top-floor café, see page 240).

• *With the cafés on your right, drop downhill past the lineup of shops and turn right past the TI to find the parking lot just beyond. Animals grazed here for centuries. It was later turned into a school playground. When tourists outnumbered students, it became a parking lot. Walk past the parking lot and head left uphill, hugging the cliffs to find the...*

▲▲Ochre Cliffs

Roussillon was Europe's capital for ochre production until World War II. A stroll to the south end of town, beyond the upper parking lot, shows you why: Roussillon sits on the world's largest known ochre deposit. A radiant orange path leads through the richly colored ochre cliffs, explaining the hue of this village.

Ochre is made of iron oxide and clay. When combined with sand, it creates the yellowish-red pigments you see in the buildings around you. Although ochre is also produced in the US and Italy, the quality of France's ochre is considered *le best.*

The value of Roussillon's ochre cliffs was known even in Roman times. Once excavated, the clay ochre was rinsed with water to separate it from sand, then bricks of the stuff were dried and baked for deeper hues. The procedure for extracting the ochre did not change much over 2,000 years, until ochre mining became industrialized in the late 1700s. Used primarily for wallpaper and linoleum, ochre use reached its zenith just before World War II. (After that, cheaper substitutes took over.)

Cost and Hours: €2.50, €7 combo-ticket with Ochre Conservatory—described next; March-April and Oct 10:00-17:30, May-June and Sept 9:30-18:30, July-Aug 9:00-19:30,

LUBERON

Nov-Dec 11:00-15:30, closed Jan-Feb. Beware: Light-colored clothing (especially shoes) and orange powder don't mix.

Sights near Roussillon

▲Ochre Conservatory
(Conservatoire des Ocres et Pigments Appliqués)

For a terrific introduction to the history and uses of ochre, visit this intriguing reconstructed ochre factory. Grab a pamphlet to follow their well-done self-guided tour, which shows how ochre is converted from an ore to a pigment (allow 45 minutes). Save the oven (#6) for later when it'll make more sense. Your visit ends with a great bookshop and a chance to try your hand at ochre painting.

Cost and Hours: €6, €7 combo-ticket with ochre cliffs, daily 9:00-18:00, July-Aug until 19:00, until 13:00-14:00 in low season, about a half-mile below Roussillon toward Apt on D-104, tel. 04 90 05 66 69, www.okhra.com.

Domaine de Tara

Just below Roussillon, on the road to Joucas, this welcoming winery has been making excellent wines for about 15 years. Pascale runs the tasting room and her husband makes wines to please every palate: red, white, rosé, sparkling, and sweet. Pop into the barrel room where they occasionally exhibit local artists' work. They don't mind if you picnic on the property afterward.

Cost and Hours: Prices vary by wine, daily April-Oct 10:00-19:30, Nov-March and Wed until 18:00, tel. 04 90 05 74 87, www.domainedetara.com.

Hot-Air Balloon Flight

Ply the calm morning air above the Luberon in a hot-air balloon. The **Montgolfières-Luberon** outfit has two flight options: the Four-Star Flight (€235, 1.5 hours in balloon, allow 3 hours total, includes picnic and champagne, reserve a few days ahead, maximum 12 passengers, mobile 06 03 54 10 92, www.montgolfiere-luberon.com).

Goult

Bigger than its sister hill towns, this surprisingly quiet village seems content to be away from the tourist path. Explore the small lanes and wander up the hill to the panoramic view and windmill. Notice how many of the historic buildings are built right on top of thick rock strata. Consider having a nice meal in one of Goult's many good restaurants—where you won't have to compete with tourists for a table. Small and well-run, **Aux Fines Herbes** is ideally situated just off the main square, and its food is affordable and as fresh as it gets (*menus* from €27, closed all day Wed, closed Sat for lunch, Rue de la République, tel. 04 32 50 23 54). Trendier

La Bartavelle is *the* place in town to dine, but is darn popular (book a table a week in advance, *menus* from €42, closed Tue-Wed, Rue du Cheval Blanc, tel. 04 90 72 33 72). **Le Carillon,** on the main square across from the church tower, is the new kid in town and gets good reviews from locals. Chef Bruce likes spices and herbs (€19-24 lunch *menus*, €34-46 dinner *menus*, closed Wed, Avenue du Luberon, tel. 04 90 72 15 09).

Sleeping in Roussillon

The TI posts a list of hotels and *chambres d'hôte*. Parking is free if you sleep in Roussillon; ask your hotelier where to park. The village offers three acceptable-value accommodations—conveniently, one for each price range.

$$$ Le Clos de la Glycine*** provides Roussillon's plushest accommodations, with formal staff and nine gorgeous rooms located dead-center in the village (Db-€145-160, big Db-€180, loft suite with deck and view-€275, guest computer, Wi-Fi, air-con, located at the recommended refined restaurant Chez David, so they prefer you pay for half-pension, across from the TI on Place de la Poste, tel. 04 90 05 60 13, www.luberon-hotel.com, le.clos .de.la.glycine@wanadoo.fr).

$$ Hôtel Rêves d'Ocres** is well-located but basic, with worn rooms and disinterested owners. Still, it works if you want to sleep in the village and not pay a fortune. Eight smaller rooms under the roof have low ceilings and small terraces; I prefer the larger rooms on the second floor (Sb-€60-70, Db without balcony-€85, Db with balcony-€90, Tb-€110, Qb-€135, musty bathrooms, meek air-con, Wi-Fi, Route de Gordes, tel. 04 90 05 60 50, www.hotel -revesdocres.com, hotelrevesdocres@wanadoo.fr). Coming from Gordes and Joucas, it's the first building you pass in Roussillon.

$ Madame Cherel rents bare-bones rooms with firm beds and a shared view terrace at fair rates (D-€46, family suite available, cash only, includes basic breakfast, Wi-Fi, access to kitchenette, 3 blocks from upper parking lot, between Casino store and school, La Burlière, tel. 04 90 05 71 71, mulhanc@hotmail.com). Chatty and sincere Cherel speaks English and is a wealth of regional travel tips.

Near Roussillon

These listings are for drivers only. The last two are most easily found by turning north off D-900 at the *Roussillon/Les Huguets* sign (the second turnoff to Roussillon coming from Avignon). Joucas and St-Saturnin-lès-Apt (both described later) also have good beds near Roussillon.

LUBERON

$$$ At Le Mas d'Estonge, charming Christiane and Robert welcome you into their little Provençal paradise. Their four well-furnished and cozy rooms share a sweet patio and a pool (Db-€95-135, suites-€165-190, 10 minutes from Roussillon on D-227, tel. 04 90 05 63 13, www.destonge.com).

$$ Le Clos des Cigales is a fine refuge run by friendly Philippe and his wife Brigitte. Of their five blue-shuttered, stylish bungalows, two are doubles and three are two-room suites with tiny kitchenettes; all have private patios facing a big pool. When you arrive, you'll understand the name—the cacophony from the *cigales* (cicadas) is deafening (Db-€80-90, Tb/Qb suite-€100-120, includes breakfast, Wi-Fi, table tennis, hammock, 5 minutes from Roussillon toward Goult on D-104, tel. 04 90 05 73 72, www.leclosdescigales.com, philippe.lherbeil@wanadoo.fr).

$$ Hôtel les Sables d'Ocre** offers 22 meticulously maintained, motelesque rooms, a big pool, the greenest grass around, air-conditioning, and fair rates (only 4 rooms are simple Sb/Db-€85-95, spring for the "supérieur" Db with garden balcony-€110-120, Db with private terrace-€110-135, half-pension available for €38/person, a half-mile from Roussillon toward Apt at intersection of D-108 and D-104, tel. 04 90 05 55 55, www.sablesdocre.com, sablesdocre@orange.fr).

Eating in Roussillon

Choose ambience over cuisine if dining in Roussillon, and enjoy any of the eateries on the main square. It's a festive place, where children twirl while parents dine, and dogs and cats look longingly for leftovers. Restaurants change with the mistral here—what's good one year disappoints the next. Consider my suggestions and go with what looks best (or look over my recommendations in other Luberon villages, like Goult, just a few minutes away by car). Look also at the hotels listed in Joucas (see "Sleeping and Eating in Joucas," later)—all offer quality cuisine at fair prices, just a few minutes' drive from Roussillon.

On Place de la Poste: **Chez David,** at the recommended hotel Le Clos de la Glycine (described earlier), is *the* place to splurge. You can enjoy a fine meal on the terrace or from an interior window table with point-blank views over the ochre cliffs. The Provençal cuisine is as fabulous as the scenery (€32-52 *menus,* closed all day Wed and Sun evening, Place de la Poste, tel. 04 90 05 60 13).

La Grappe de Raisin serves a house specialty of a simple but tasty plate of vegetables and fish served with aioli, a garlic-mayonnaise-based sauce (€15-aioli plate, lunch daily, dinner only in July-Aug, next door to TI, tel. 04 90 71 38 06).

On Place de la Mairie: The following places share the same

Luberon Restaurants that Justify the Trip

Many of the restaurants in the countryside around Roussillon are worth a detour. Use the list below as a quick reference, then flip to the full descriptions of those that sound most appealing. All of these are within a 20-minute drive from Roussillon. Remember that Isle-sur-la-Sorgue is a manageable 30-minute drive from Roussillon.

Ideal for Dinner

Chez David, in Roussillon, offers cuisine as terrific as its views (closed all day Wed and Sun evening; see page 238).

Hôtel des Voyageurs, located in St-Saturnin-lès-Apt, is another local favorite (closed all day Wed and Thu until 18:00, 15-minute drive from Roussillon; see page 252).

L'Auberge de la Loube is the ultimate country/Provençal experience. Located in Buoux, it makes for a long after-dinner drive, so many prefer it for lunch (closed Sun eve and all day Mon and Thu; see page 256).

Hostellerie des Commandeurs is inexpensive, traditional, friendly, and a solid value that's good for families (closed Wed, in Joucas—a 5-minute drive from Roussillon; see page 240).

Le Bistrot de Roussillon, on Roussillon's village square with a terrace out back, has excellent salads and *plats* priced just right (open daily; see next page).

Aux Fines Herbes and Le Carillon, both in overlooked Goult, offer fresh and fairly priced food (Aux Fines Herbes closed all day Wed and Sat for lunch, Le Carillon closed Wed, see page 236).

Best Places to Lunch

Chez David, L'Auberge de la Loube, and **Le Bistrot de Roussillon** are all listed for dinner, above—but are also top lunch stops. Here are some others to consider:

Le Terrail, in Bonnieux, serves fresh fish and produce on an outside terrace with stunning vistas (daily, see page 248).

Bar/Restaurant de France, in Lacoste, is an easygoing eatery with sensational view tables and good *plats*, omelets, and salads (daily, lunch only off-season; see page 249).

Le Petit Jardin Café, in remote Viens, offers an unpretentious lunch or dinner stop, with cozy interior tables, a garden terrace, and reasonable prices (closed Tue eve and all day Wed; see page 253).

square, and offer similar values. At least one should be open.

At **Le Bistrot de Roussillon,** Johan offers the most consistent value on the square, with excellent salads (try the *salad du bistrot*) and *plats* for the right price. There's a breezy terrace in back and a comfy interior (€16 for a filling salad and dessert, €13-18 *plats*, €12 shareable plates of cheese or meat, daily, tel. 04 90 05 74 45).

Café Couleur and **Le Castrum** flank Le Bistrot de Roussillon, offering similar atmosphere and prices, but less-steady quality.

Croqu'la Vie, opposite the above-listed restaurants on the square, hides a top-floor view café/*salon de thé* above its book-store (best for lunch, €19 *plats*, restaurant closed Mon, tel. 04 90 71 55 72).

Joucas

This understated, quiet, and largely overlooked village slumbers below the Gordes buzz. Vertical stone lanes with carefully  arranged flowers and well-restored homes play host to aspiring Claude Monets and a smattering of locals. There's not much to do or see here, except eat, sleep, and just be. Joucas has one tiny grocery, a view café, one pharmacy, a good kids' play area, and one good-value accommodation option. Sleep here for a central location and utter silence. For views, walk past the little fountain in the center and up the steep lanes as high as you want.

Several **hiking** trails leave from Joucas. Gordes and Roussillon are each three miles away, uphill. The three-mile hike up to the attractive village of Murs (which has several cafés/restaurants) is more scenic, though it's easier in the other direction (yellow signs point the way from the top of the village). You don't have to go far to enjoy the natural beauty on this trail.

Sleeping and Eating in Joucas

$$ Hostellerie des Commandeurs**, run by a young couple, Stéphane and Gaëlle, has simple, good-value rooms in the center of Joucas. It's kid-friendly, with a big pool and a sports field/play area next door. Ask for a south-facing room (*coté sud*) for the best views, or a north-facing room (*coté nord*) if it's hot. All rooms have showers (Db-€68-74, extra bed-€16, Wi-Fi, mini-fridges, above park at village entrance, hotel open March-Oct, tel. 04 90 05 78

01, www.lescommandeurs.com, hostellerie@lescommandeurs
.com). The simple restaurant offers tasty cuisine at fair prices
(three-course *menus* from €23, succulent lamb, memorable crème
brûlée with lavender, restaurant closed Wed). Village kids like to
hang out around the bar's pool table.

Near Joucas

$$$ **La Ferme de la Huppe***** has a Gordes address, but it's closer,
physically and spiritually, to Joucas. This small, farmhouse-elegant

hacienda makes an excellent
mini-splurge. Eleven rooms
gather on two levels behind the
stylish pool. The decor is tasteful,
understated, and rustic (Db-€170,
much bigger Db-€215, includes
good breakfast buffet, mini-
fridges, air-con, Wi-Fi; between
Joucas and Gordes on D-156 road
to Goult, just off D-2; tel. 04 90
72 12 25, www.lafermedelahuppe.com, info@lafermedelahuppe
.com). The restaurant has an excellent reputation (notice the
shelf of French cookery books at reception). Dine poolside or in
the smart dining room (lunch-€17-28, dinner-€42 seasonal ever-
changing three-course *menu* or €62 five-course tasting *menu*,
closed all day Sun and Mon at lunch).

$$$ **Le Mas du Loriot**, a 10-minute drive up from town, is
another worthwhile value near Joucas. Gentle owners Alain and
Christine have carved the ideal escape out of an olive grove, with
eight soothing rooms, private terraces, a generous pool, and home-
cooked dinners—all at fair prices and with a view to remember
(Sb/Db with view and terrace-€135-150, Sb/Db *sans* view and
smaller terrace-€135, request a view room, Nov-March-€70-115,
pricey breakfast-€13, €40 four-course dinners available 4 nights a
week—when half-pension is a smart idea, guest computer, Wi-Fi;
on D-102 between Joucas and Murs, turn left onto dirt road and
another left at yellow wall with sign; tel. 04 90 72 62 62, www
.masduloriot.com, hotel@masduloriot.com).

More Luberon Towns

Le Luberon is packed with appealing villages and beautiful scenery, but it has only a handful of must-see sights. I've grouped them by area to make your sightseeing planning easier (see the Luberon map at the beginning of this chapter). The D-900 highway cuts the Luberon in half like an arrow. The more popular and visited section lies above D-900 (with Roussillon and Gordes), while the villages to the south seem a bit less trampled.

The busiest sights are in and near Gordes; I've listed those first, to encourage you to avoid afternoon crowds. Beyond that, you're free to connect the stops however you please. Rambling the Luberon's spaghetti network of small roads is a joy, and getting lost comes with the territory—go with it. None of the sights listed below is a must-see, but all are close to each other. Pick up a good map (Michelin maps #332 and #527 work for me).

Gordes and Nearby Sights

Gordes

In the 1960s, Gordes was a virtual ghost town of derelict buildings. But now it's thoroughly renovated and filled with people who live in

a world without calluses. Many Parisian big shots and wealthy foreigners have purchased and restored older homes here, putting property values out of sight for locals—and creating gridlock and parking headaches (come early).

Ponder a region that in the last 40 years has experienced such a dramatic change. Post-World War II, the Luberon was mired in poverty. By 1970, the Luberon had recovered, but was still unknown to most travelers. Locals led simple lives and had few ambitions. Then came the theater festival in Avignon, bringing directors who wanted to re-create perfect Provençal villages on film. Parisians, Swiss, Brits, and a few Americans followed, willing to pay any price for their place in the Provençal sun. Property taxes increased—as did the cost of *une bière* at the corner café—and all too soon, villagers found themselves with few affordable options.

The village's setting is striking. As you approach Gordes, make a hard right at the impressive viewpoint (you'll find some parking along the small road). Beyond here, the village has little of interest, except its many boutiques and its Tuesday market (which ends at 13:00). The town's 11th-century castle houses contemporary art exhibits.

Near Gordes

The first two sights—the Abbey Notre-Dame de Sénanque and the Village des Bories—are both well-marked from Gordes.

Abbey Notre-Dame de Sénanque

This still-functioning and beautifully situated Cistercian abbey was built in 1148 as a back-to-basics reaction to the excesses of

Benedictine abbeys. The Cistercians strove to be separate from the world and to recapture the simplicity, solitude, and poverty of the early Church. To succeed required industrious self-sufficiency—a skill these monks excelled at. Their movement spread and colonized Europe with a new form of Christianity. By 1200 there were more than 500 such monasteries and abbeys in Europe.

The abbey is best appreciated from the outside, and is worth the

trip for its splendid and remote setting alone. Come early or late, stop at a pullout for a bird's-eye view as you descend, then wander the abbey's perimeter. The abbey church (Eglise Abbatiale) is always open (except during Mass, but you're welcome to attend) and highlights the utter simplicity sought by these monks. In late June through much of July, the lavender fields that surround the abbey make for breathtaking pictures and draw loads of visitors.

Most of the time, visiting the abbey itself requires a 50-minute, French-only tour with an English handout. You'll spend lots of time standing and waiting unless you are practicing your French comprehension skills. But the abbey allows unguided entry from February to October, Monday to Saturday from 9:45-11:00, when you can go at your own pace (Nov-Jan the abbey is closed in

the morning and allows unguided visits all afternoon). The tour covers Sénanque's church, the small cloisters, the refectory, and a *chauffoir*, a small heated room where monks could copy books year-round. The interior, which doesn't measure up to the abbey's spectacular setting, is not worth it for most people.

Medieval Monasteries

France is littered with medieval monasteries, and Provence is no exception. Most have virtually no furnishings (they never had many), which leaves the visitor with little to reconstruct what life must have been like in these cold stone buildings a thousand years ago. A little history can help breathe life into these important yet underappreciated monuments.

After the fall of the Roman Empire, monasteries arose as refuges of peace and order in a chaotic world. While the pope got rich and famous playing power politics, monasteries worked to keep the focus on simplicity and poverty. Throughout the Middle Ages, monasteries were mediators between Man and God. In these peacefully remote abbeys, Europe's best minds struggled with the interpretation of God's words. Every sentence needed to be understood and applied. Answers later debated in universities were once contemplated in monasteries.

St. Benedict established the Middle Ages' most influential monastic order (Benedictine) in Monte Cassino, Italy, in A.D. 529. He scheduled a rigorous program of monastic duties that combined manual labor with intellectual tasks. His movement spread north and took firm root in France, where the abbey of Cluny (Burgundy) eventually controlled more than 2,000 dependent abbeys and vied with the pope for control of the Church. Benedictine abbeys grew dot-com rich, and with wealth came excess (king-size beds and Wi-Fi). Monks lost sight of their purpose and became soft and corrupt. In the late 1100s, the determined and charismatic St. Bernard rallied the Cistercian order by going back to the original rule of St. Benedict. Cistercian abbeys thrived as centers of religious thought and exploration from the 13th through the 15th centuries.

A small monastic community still resides here. For more on monasteries, see the sidebar.

Cost and Hours: €7, with or without the French-only tour (mandatory Feb-Oct after 11:00), tours offered Mon-Sat usually at 10:10, 10:30, 14:30, 15:30, and 16:30; Sun at 14:30, 15:30, and 16:30; more tours June-Sept; tel. 04 90 72 05 72, www.senanque.fr. Appropriate clothing is required for entry—shoulders and knees must be covered. You can also attend Mass (Mon-Sat at 11:45, Sun at 10:00, check website or call to confirm).

Leaving the Abbey: If your next destination is near Roussillon, Bonnieux, or Apt, leave the abbey opposite the way you arrived, following signs to *Gordes*, then *Roussillon*, then follow *Murs* and *Joucas*...and enjoy the ride.

Village des Bories

A twisting, mile-long, stone-bordered dirt road sets the mood for this mildly entertaining open-air museum of stone huts *(bories).*

Cistercian abbots ran their abbeys like little kingdoms, doling out punishment and food to the monks, and tools to peasant farmers. Abbeys were occupied by two groups: the favored monks from aristocratic families (such as St. Bernard) and a larger group of lay brothers from peasant stock, who were given the heaviest labor and could join only the Sunday services.

Monks' days were broken into three activities: prayer, reading holy texts, and labor. Monks lived in silence and poverty, with few amenities—meat was forbidden, as was cable TV. In summer, they ate two daily meals—in winter, just one. Monks slept together in a single room on threadbare mats covering solid-rock floors.

With their focus on work and discipline, Cistercian abbeys became leaders of the medieval industrial revolution. Among the few literate people in Europe, monks were keepers of technological knowledge—about clocks, waterwheels, accounting, foundries, gristmills, textiles, and agricultural techniques. Abbeys became economic engines that helped drive France out of its Middle Aged funk.

As France (and Europe) slowly got its act together in the late Middle Ages, cities re-emerged as places to trade and thrive. Abbeys gradually lost their relevance in a brave new humanist world. Universities became the new center of intellectual development. Kings took over abbot selection, further degrading the abbeys' power, and Gutenberg's movable type made monks obsolete. The French Revolution closed the book on abbatial life, with troops occupying and destroying many abbeys. The still-functioning Abbey Notre-Dame de Sénanque, near Gordes, is a rare survivor.

The vertical stones you see on the walls as you approach the site were used as counterweights to keep these walls, built without mortar, intact. The "village" you tour is made up of dry-laid stone structures, proving that there has always been more stone than wood in this rugged region. Stone villages like this predated the Romans—some say by 2,000 years. This one was inhabited for 200 years (from about 1600 to 1800). *Bories* can still be seen in fields throughout the Luberon; most are now used to store tools or hay. A look around these hills confirms the supply of building materials: The trees are small and gnarled (not good for construction), but white stone grows everywhere.

The Village des Bories is composed of five "hamlets." Start with the short film (English subtitles), then duck into several homes and see animal pens, a community oven, and more (identified in English). Study the "beehive" stone-laying method and imagine the time it took to construct. The villagers had no scaffolds or support arches—just hammers and patience.

Cost and Hours: €6, buy €4 booklet of English translations to learn more, daily June-Sept 9:00-20:00, Oct-May 9:00-17:30, tel. 04 90 72 03 48.

Olive-Oil Mills with Tastings

The following two places give quick and free tastings with basic explanations, but are only really worth the time if you pass them en route to something else.

Moulin à Huile Jullien is a small, family operation making *"bio"* (organic) oils using modern equipment. Chantal speaks some English, and the hand-drawn signs do a good job of explaining the machinery (April-June 10:00-12:00 & 14:00-18:00, July-Aug 10:00-12:00 & 15:00-19:00, Sept-March 14:00-18:00; tel. 04 90 75 56 24, www.moulin-huile-jullien.com, near recommended Mas Perréal, a half-mile downhill from St-Saturnin-lès-Apt, on Route d'Apt).

Moulin Saint Augustin, originally a 16th-century flour mill, on the busy D-900 just east of Coustellet, is a property with centuries of history, but you can only enter the shop. Laure explains the qualities of the native olive varieties—yes, just like grapes, there are specific olive varieties that fare better locally (May-Sept Mon-Sat 10:00-19:00, Oct-April Mon-Sat 9:00-12:00 & 14:00-18:00, closed Sun year-round, 2800 Route d'Apt, tel. 04 90 72 43 66, www.moulin-saintaugustin.com).

St. Pantaléon

This postage-stamp-sized village feels lost in the valley below Gordes. It comes with an adorable 12th-century Romanesque church that has a remarkable necropolis around back, with tombs—many in the distinct shape of a human body—carved right out of the rock on which the church was built. It's a peaceful, moving site. To visit the interior of the church, you'll need the key: Cross the street to the Mas des Arts guesthouse—where you see the tables outside—owned by two likeable artists (who have a gallery in Roussillon) and ask for the key (*clé*, pronounced "clay"); you're on your own in the church. If they aren't home, try the café downhill, Le Chauvre Sourit, which also has a key and makes a nice spot to stop for a cheap drink (free Wi-Fi; open daily).

Museum of Lavender (Musée de la Lavande)

Located in Coustellet, halfway between Gordes and Isle-sur-la-Sorgue, this "museum" charges top dollar for a subtitled film and mediocre exhibits about the process of lavender production (plenty of English explanations). It's popular with tour groups, but the overwhelming scent of lavender gives many a headache. You can skip the tour and enter the ultimate "if they made it with lavender, we sell it" gift shop for free. For more on this fragrant flower, see page 212.

Cost and Hours: €7, daily May-Sept 9:00-19:00, Oct-April 9:00-12:00 & 14:00-18:00, in Coustellet just off D-900 toward Gordes, tel. 04 90 76 91 23, www.museedelalavande.com.

Villages and Sights South of Roussillon

These villages and sights below Roussillon and D-900 feel less visited than places north of this busy road. You'll need a good half-day to visit them all (see the map on page 220 to get oriented). They work well in the order described below, with lunch in Bonnieux or Lacoste (for recommendations, see sidebar on page 239). The first sight is situated south of Roussillon, where D-108 crosses D-900.

Julien Bridge (Pont Julien)

This delicate three-arched bridge, named for Julius Caesar, survives as a testimony to Roman engineers—and to the importance of

this rural area 2,000 years ago. It's the only surviving bridge on what was the main road from northern Italy to Provence—the primary route used by Roman armies. The 215-foot-long Roman bridge was under construction from 27 B.C. to A.D. 14. Mortar had not yet been invented, so (as with Pont du Gard) stones were carefully set in place. Amazingly, the bridge survives today, having outlived Roman marches, hundreds of floods, and decades of automobile traffic. A new bridge finally rerouted traffic from this beautiful structure in 2005.

Walk below the bridge. Notice how thin the layer of stone seems between the arch tops and the road. Those open niches weren't for statues, but instead allowed water to pass through when the river ran high. (At its current trickle, that's hard to fathom.) Walk under an arch and examine the pockmarks in the side—medieval thieves in search of free bronze stole the clamps.

Château de la Canorgue Winery

Well-signed halfway between the Julien Bridge and Bonnieux, this is a pretty winery; the film *A Good Year*, with Russell Crowe and French actress Marion Cotillard, was filmed here in 2006. A welcoming tasting room offers the full range of wines—from Viognier and Chardonnay whites to rosés and rich reds—with owner-in-waiting and winemaker Nathalie greeting guests on weekdays. For a good contrast in reds, compare the *Vendanges de Nathalie* with the *vin du pays*. Château de la Canorgue was one of the first wineries in the area to make organic wines, and they have reasonable prices.

Cost and Hours: Average bottle costs €10, Mon-Sat 9:00-12:00 & 14:00-18:00, closed Sun, tel. 04 90 75 81 01.

Bonnieux

Spectacular from a distance, this town disappoints me up close. It lacks a pedestrian center, though the Friday-morning market briefly creates one. The main reason to visit here is to enjoy the views from a well-positioned restaurant.

Sleeping in and near Bonnieux: **$$$ Le Clos du Buis** is an eight-room *chambres d'hôte* in Bonnieux's center, run by eager-to-please Lydia and Pierre. Their veranda makes a great place to sip a glass of rosé while taking in views over the Luberon (Db-€129-147, includes breakfast, less off-season, in the middle of town on Rue Victor Hugo, tel. 04 90 75 88 48, www.leclosdubuis.fr, le-clos-du-buis@wanadoo.fr).

The country-elegant *chambre d'hôte* **$$$ Mas del Sol,** between Bonnieux and Lacoste, is perfect for connoisseurs of the Luberon. Young Lucine and Richard Massol rent five bright, spacious rooms that come with views, vines, olives, and a big breakfast. The setting is unbeatable, and the stylish pool and gardens will calm your nerves (Db-€100-180, lower prices are for longer stays and off-season, tel. 04 90 75 94 80, www.mas-del-sol.com, lemasdelsol @gmail.com). From D-900, take the D-36 turnoff to Bonnieux and look for *Mas del Sol* signs after about three kilometers (two miles).

Eating in Bonnieux: **Le Terrail** is a local hangout where dogs are welcome and the humans enjoy an outside terrace with great views (or at least those lucky enough to land an end table). Owner Nicolas makes a point of using fresh fish and produce—the only frozen food here is his fantastic homemade ice cream (€11 lunch *plats,* try the aioli, dinner *menus* from €22, open daily, Place Gambetta, tel. 04 90 75 93 73). If you'd prefer your ice cream to go, pick some up across the street.

Lacoste

Little Lacoste slumbers across the valley from Bonnieux in the shadow of its looming castle. Climb through this photogenic village of arches and stone paths, passing American art students (from the Savannah College of Art and Design) showing their work. Support an American artist, learn about the art, and then keep climbing and climbing to the ruined castle base. The view of Bonnieux from the base of Lacoste's castle is as good as it gets.

The Marquis de Sade (1740-1814) lived in this **castle** for more than 30 years. Author of dirty novels, he was notorious for hosting orgies behind these walls, and for kidnapping peasants for scandalous purposes. He was eventually arrested and imprisoned for 30 years, and thanks to him, we have a word to describe his favorite hobby—sadism. Today, fashion designer Pierre Cardin lives in the lower part of the castle, having spent a fortune shoring up the protective walls and sponsoring a high-priced summer opera series. Some locals are critical of Cardin, claiming that he is buying up the town to create his own "faux-Provence." Could "Cardism" be next?

Eating in Lacoste: If it's time for lunch, find the **Bar/Restaurant de France**'s outdoor tables overlooking Bonnieux and savor the view (inexpensive, good omelets, daily, lunch only off-season, tel. 04 90 75 82 25).

Abbey St. Hilaire

A dirt road off D-103 between Lacoste and Ménerbes leads down to this long-forgotten and pint-size abbey. There's not much to see here—it's more about the experience. The tranquility and isolation sought by monks 800 years ago are still palpable in the simple church and modest cloisters. Once a Cistercian outpost for the bigger abbey at Sénanque, Abbey St. Hilaire is now owned by Carmelite Friars. The lone stone bench in front is picnic-ready, and a rugged WC is cut into the rock (across the courtyard). For a pleasing loop walk, start at the abbey and cross over the D-3 road to a path running along the base of the Luberon range (details available at the abbey). Leave nothing valuable in your car at this remote site.

Ménerbes

Ménerbes, now (in)famous as the village that drew author Peter Mayle's attention to this region, is also noteworthy for its truffle center and a smattering of scenic buildings. To explore Ménerbes, stash your car, then follow *Eglise* signs to the end of the village.

Sights in Ménerbes: At the end of Rue Corneille you'll pass the **citadel,** built in 1584 (after the Protestants of Ménerbes were defeated in the religious wars of 1577)—and never tested. The citadel is privately owned today, but from the outside you can still enjoy the impressive facade, which spans the width of the rock. Nearby, the ancient stone prison tower is also worth a look.

At the village's end, find the heavy Romanesque church (closed and under renovation) and **graveyard** (good views in all directions). You're face-to-face with the Grand Luberon ridge. Notice the quarry carved into its side, where the stone for this village came from.

On the way back, foodies can duck into the snazzy **Maison de la Truffe et du Vin,** which offers "truffle discovery workshops" (call for schedule, tel. 04 90 72 38 37, www.vin-truffe-luberon .com), a fine little *jardin à la française* (more great views), and a cute tasting room serving Luberon wines. All 180 of the Luberon's wines are sold here for the same price you'd pay at the winery. Their small restaurant serves a killer €24 *truffe d'été menu* (summer truffle, available June-Sept), best enjoyed in the garden's lovely setting (daily 12:30-17:00).

The **Corkscrew Museum** (Musée du Tire-Bouchon) is actually part of the **Domaine de la Citadelle** winery, a half-mile below Ménerbes. It is worth a stop if you're a corkscrew enthusiast or want to taste their very good wines. They have 1,200 corkscrews on display in glass cases and a well-stocked gift shop (€4 for the "museum," includes tasting, daily 10:00-12:00 & 14:00-19:00, tel. 04 90 72 41 58).

▲Oppède-le-Vieux

This windy barnacle of a town clings with all its might to its hillside. There are a handful of businesses and a dusty little square

at the base of a short, ankle-twisting climb to a pretty little church and ruined castle. This off-the-beaten-path fixer-upper of a village was completely abandoned in 1910, and today has a ghost town-like feel (it once housed 200 people). The inhabited village below has a rugged character and shows little inclination for boutiques and smart hotels. It's ideal for those looking to perish in Provence.

Sights in Oppède-le-Vieux: Plan your ascent to the **castle.** It's 20 minutes straight up, but the Luberon views justify the effort. (After making this walk, you'll understand why locals abandoned it for more level terrain.) Small information panels provide a worthwhile background in English as you climb, and the new paving and floodlighting will enhance your appreciation of the lovely setting. Walk under the central arch of the building across from Le Petit Café and climb. After walking under the arch, look back to notice the handsome building it supports. At the fork, you can go either way (though the path to the right is easier). Find the little church terrace. From here, tiled rooftops paint a delightful picture with the grand panorama; the flat plain of the Rhône delta is visible off to the left.

The colorful **Notre-Dame d'Alidon church** (1588) is generally open 9:30-18:30 (depending on availability of village volunteers, who are eager to answer questions). There's been a church on this site for 1,000 years. Pick up the English text and imagine having to climb this distance at least every Sunday—for your entire life. Notice the pride locals have for their church: You'll see new gold-leaf accents and other efforts to spruce up the long-abandoned building. The steps to chapels on the right were necessary, thanks to the church's hillside setting.

Unfortunately, what remains of the castle is now off-limits—it's too dangerous. But the views are worth the climb.

Eating and Sleeping in Oppède-le-Vieux: Once you're back down, consider a meal with views of the castle ruins at **Petit Café,** where friendly Jean-Marie is in charge (€12-15 salads, €25-lunch *menu,* €40-dinner *menu,* closed Tue-Wed eves, all day Thu, and mid-Dec-April). **$$ Petit Café** also offers simple but comfy rooms, all with nice views (Db-€65-75, big Db-€95, extra bed-€15, includes breakfast, air-con, €10-indoor Jacuzzi and sauna, rooftop terrace, tel. 04 90 76 74 01, www.petitcafe.fr).

Getting There: To find Oppède-le-Vieux from D-900, follow signs to *Oppède* and *Oppède le Village,* then *Oppède-le-Vieux,* and drive toward le Petit Luberon massif. You'll follow a long, one-way loop and be forced to park a few hundred yards from the village (unless you're sleeping there), for which you'll get to pay €3.

Villages and Sights East of Roussillon: La Provence Profonde

Provence is busy with tourists, but there are still plenty of characteristic and less-discovered places to explore. The area east of Roussillon feels quieter and less touristed—come here to get a sense of how most villages were before they became "destinations." Here are the key sights in the order that you'll pass them coming from Roussillon or Joucas. Allow a full day to complete this loop. If all you have is a half-day, head straight for Fort de Buoux (see map on page 220).

St-Saturnin-lès-Apt

Most tourists pass by this pleasant town (with a lively Tuesday market) on their way to more famous destinations. I couldn't find a souvenir shop. Ditch your car below the main entry to the town (just below the old city) and walk up the main drag past the Hôtel

Saint Hubert (Rue de la République). You'll come to a striking church that's a fine example of Provençal Romanesque, with a tall, rounded spire (the interior is often closed). From here, find the ramp with *Le Château* signs and climb. The ruined "château" grows right out of the rock, making it difficult to tell the man-made from the natural. Go left as you enter and hike as high as the sun allows with no shade—faded green dots guide you up. It's a scamperer's paradise, with views that rank among the best village-top vistas I've found in Provence. Find your way through the small opening to the little dam. On the opposite side of the reservoir is a shaded picnic table. The small chapel at the very top is only open on Sunday mornings in summer, but at any time you can take the path to the right of the chapel back down the hill to the village, where you'll see a lovely medieval gate.

Sleeping and Eating in or near St-Saturnin-lès-Apt: For a warm welcome, stay at **$$$ Mas Perréal** just outside St-Saturnin-lès-Apt. American Kevin and his Parisian wife, Elisabeth, left no stone unturned as they restored their lovely farmhouse. Elisabeth teaches French—that's how Kevin met her—and still gives lessons (book in advance). This place features sumptuous rooms (each with its own terrace), beds you won't want to get out of, a pool, 360-degree views (they own the vineyards and orchards around you), elaborate American-size breakfasts that change daily, and no language barrier (Db-€130-145, includes big breakfast, tel. 04 90 75 46 31, www.masperreal.com, elisabeth-kevin@masperreal .com). Mas Perréal is off D-943, between St-Saturnin-lès-Apt and D-900. Coming from D-900, turn left at Moulin à Huile Jullien (the olive-oil mill listed earlier), continue three-quarters of a mile, cross one "major" road, and have faith until you see the signs—it will be on your right.

$$ Hôtel des Voyageurs*, with amiable owners Nadine and Alain (who speak no English), is a time warp that has survived many Provençal trends without  changing its look or product. The basic accommodations gather around uneven floors and a frumpy upstairs terrace that only an artist could love (modest but nice Db-€60-68, big Db-€75, tel. 04 90 75 42 08, http://voyageurs enprovence.fr, hotel.rest.voyageur @orange.fr). The Old World restaurant, with vintage floor tiles, serves traditional cuisine that locals adore (*menus* from €20). Both the hotel and the restaurant are closed all day Wednesday and Thursday until 18:00. It's at the base of the old village—look for signs.

Le Colorado Provençal

This park has ochre cliffs similar to Roussillon's, but they're spread over a larger area, with well-signed trails. If hiking through soft, orange sand and Bryce Canyon-like rocks strikes your fancy, make time for Le Colorado Provençal.

For the best walk, cross the little footbridge to follow either the Cheminée de Fée ("Fairy Chimney") or the Sahara trail. Trails are color-coded and easy to follow. The Sahara offers a wider spectrum of colors and provides views of the chimney formations. Forgo light-colored clothing and allow about 40 minutes to walk this trail. Signs remind you to remain on the trails and not climb the cliffs.

Cost and Hours: Park is free and always open; located a half-mile below Rustrel off D-22, between Apt and Gignac—follow signs toward the village of *Rustrel*, the gateway to Le Colorado Provençal. A large, clearly marked parking lot on D-22 has snack stands and WCs (€4 for parking or park along the main road for free). Parking attendants are available from about 9:00 until 17:00 or 18:00.

Viens

Located about 15 minutes uphill and east of Le Colorado Provençal (turn right when leaving Colorado), this village is where Luberon

locals go to get away. With a setting like this, it's surprising that modest Viens is not more developed. The panoramas are higher and more vast than around Roussillon (with some lavender fields), and the vegetation is more raw. Walk the streets of the old town (bigger than it first appears) and visit the few shops scattered about. Uphill, find the courtyard of the old château, then walk to the end of the village and relax at a picnic table to enjoy the grand view. This is how Gordes must have looked before it became chic.

Eating in Viens: **Le Petit Jardin Café,** just below the town's only phone booth, fits perfectly in this unpretentious town where tourists are viewed as curiosities. Come for a drink and rub

LUBERON

shoulders with locals (notice the photos on the walls); or, better, have a meal. Dine in the small traditional interior, or outside on a garden terrace (€14 *menu du jour* on weekdays, more elaborate €24 *menu* on weekends, lunch served 12:00-14:30, closed Tue eve and all day Wed, Wi-Fi, tel. 04 90 75 20 05). A small **grocery store** (Tue-Sat 8:00-12:30 & 16:00-19:30, closed Sun afternoon and all day Mon) and a **bakery** (closed Mon) are a few blocks past the café, toward St. Martin de Castillon.

To reach the next village (Saignon), follow signs to *St. Martin de Castillon*, then turn right on D-900 toward Apt.

Saignon

Sitting high atop a rock spur, this village looks down onto Apt, a city of only 11,500—which from here looks like a megalopolis after all these tiny villages. You can peek into the too-big-for-this-village Romanesque church (Notre-Dame de la Pitié) and admire its wood doors and tympanum, then follow *Le Rocher* signs through the village up to the "ship's prow." If you need to see it all, climb to the Le Rocher Bellevue for grand views over lavender fields (about three stories of stairs to the top). There are a handful of cafés and a grocery store in the linear village's center. Parking is best just above the town (hike or drive farther above town for sensational views over Saignon).

La Maison de Solveig, a tiny, simple place just under the fountain square, is ideal for a light meal. Make a plate from the €12 starter buffet with salads, sliced meats, and marinated Provençal vegetables (for €22 combine the buffet with the *plat du jour*, tel. 04 90 04 68 33).

BUOUX

Buoux (pronounced "by-oox"), a way-off-the-beaten-path village, is home to two memorable restaurants and Provence's without-a-doubt best ruined castle. A trip to this far-flung corner rewards with rocky canyons, acres of lavender, and few tourists. Start early and climb to the castle before the heat rises, then have a long, well-earned lunch nearby. If you liked Les Baux but weren't so fond of the crowds and don't need an audioguide, you'll love it here.

Buoux is south of Apt on D-113 between Saignon and Lourmarin. Ambitious travelers can combine a visit to Buoux with Lourmarin and Bonnieux.

Sights in Buoux

▲▲Fort de Buoux

The remains of this remote ridgetop castle are a playground for energetic lovers of crumbled ruins and grand views. You need good

legs and stable shoes to navigate the steep, uneven footing.

Floating like a cloud above the valleys below, the fort is easy to miss—it blends with the lime-stone rock cliffs that dominate the landscape. The long, rocky outcrop has been inhabited since prehistoric times. In the Middle Ages, it was home to hundreds of residents and a powerful castle that controlled a vast area. Like Les Baux, the fort was destroyed in the 1500s during the wars of religion (it was a Protestant base) and again in the 1600s by a paranoid King Louis XIII (see sidebar on page 202).

Madame la Caretaker, Henriette, lives with her husband in the flowery house where you buy your ticket. (If you want to make her day, bring down any trash you find on the site, as she and her husband maintain the grounds themselves). Get the English map and start climbing. The map suggests a one-way route through the rocky ruins. You'll start with what's left of the village, then scramble around rock piles along the long outcrop to the castle remains, once home to hundreds of residents. You'll also climb around the remains of homes, a church, cisterns, and medieval storage silos.

The unforgettable highlight of this castle is a three-story stone spiral staircase, which would never in a million years be open to the public in the US. Cut into the cliffs, it leads back down to the base. At #36, near the grain silos (the many holes in the ground), walk under the archway and follow the faded white arrows as you leave the ruins (you'll walk uphill at first). The staircase is steep and has no handrails and big steps, so be very careful—or return the way you came. Allow one hour round-trip for this hike.

Cost and Hours: €4, open from sunrise to sunset, closed in bad weather when it's slippery and dangerous, tel. 04 90 74 25 75.

Getting There: The fort is 10 minutes by car from the village of Buoux. To reach the fort from Apt and the north, drive through Buoux on D-113, pass the recommended L'Auberge de la Loube, drop down, and be on the lookout for small signs to *Fort de Buoux* (and *L'Auberge des Seguins*). Slow down and expect sharp turns. If coming from the south, follow signs to *Apt*, then *L'Auberge des Seguins* and *Fort de Buoux*. You can use one of several dirt parking areas; you'll find the closest lot after passing two others. Once parked, walk through the green gate and then about 15 minutes up a dirt road to the foot of the fort.

Sleeping in Buoux

$$ L'Auberge des Seguins is a stone's throw from the parking area for the fort and draws a hiking crowd. It's a lush, if modest, Shangri-la kind of place at the end of the valley, with confident young Amélie (and hound Jules) in charge. The rambling old farm is completely isolated and purposefully unmanicured—guests are encouraged to enjoy the natural beauty. The 27 rooms are monk-like simple, clean, and squirreled about the place: Some require a dirt path to reach, some are built into the rocky cliff, and most could use some work. Kids love it (there's also a big pool, but it's not heated). This place is a good value for unpicky types (half-pension with dinner-€65/person, €40/person if you sleep in the cool 20-bed dorm room; not always well-signed—coming from Fort de Buoux, take your first possible right, which turns into a dirt road; tel. 04 90 74 16 37, www.aubergedesseguins.com, aubergedesseguins@gmail.com). See also "Eating in Buoux," next.

Eating in Buoux

L'Auberge de la Loube ("Inn of the Wolf") is up the road from the fort in Buoux village and delivers the ultimate in Provençal country-coziness. Plan to stay awhile and enjoy the superb cuisine and setting (indoors or out) and eccentric owner, Monsieur Leporati, who loves to sing while cooking. You'll understand why it was one of Peter Mayle's favorites—order the Provençal hors d'oeuvres for a true taste of the region. Call a day ahead to secure a table (allow €24 for lunch—more on Sun, €33 for dinner, cash only, reasonable wine list, closed Sun eve and all day Mon and Thu, tel. 04 90 74 19 58).

L'Auberge des Seguins (see "Sleeping in Buoux," earlier) has an OK restaurant and a small café with bar food and snacks. The choices are limited, but the produce is usually fresh (€10-15 lunch options, €25 dinner *menu*, indoor and outdoor seating, closed weekdays for lunch).

Lourmarin

The southernmost Luberon village of Lourmarin has a good Friday market, a beautiful Renaissance château on its fringe, and an enchanting town center. Lourmarin sits on a level plane and feels strangely peaceful and happy, away from the more-visited

villages in the heart of the Luberon. This self-assured and lovely town accommodates a healthy tourist demand without feeling overrun. It's the best Luberon village to enjoy in the winter when other, better-known towns rattle about with few residents and little commercial activity.

Existentialist writer Albert Camus *(The Stranger)* lived in Lourmarin in the 1950s and is buried here, lending it a certain fame that persists today. Author Peter Mayle moved here not so long ago, adding to the village's cachet... and now you're here, too. Lourmarin makes a good base for touring the southern Luberon, Aix-en-Provence, and even Marseille and maybe Cassis. From here you can tour big cities, beaches, and castles, returning every night to the comfort of your village.

Getting There: Three buses per day link Lourmarin to Avignon (1.5 hours) and to Aix-en-Provence (1.25 hours, bus to Pertuis leaves 3/day, transfer there to bus bound for Aix-en-Provence, 2/hour).

Orientation to Lourmarin

Tourist Information

The TI is located on Place Henri Barthélémy (Mon-Sat 10:00-12:30 & 15:00-18:00, closed Sun, tel. 04 90 68 10 77). Free public WCs are located to the right as you exit the TI, halfway down the stairs on the left.

Theft Alert: Lourmarin has experienced a rash of break-ins at its parking lots. Park centrally, and leave nothing visible in your car.

Sights in Lourmarin

Château de Lourmarin

This Renaissance château, impressive from the outside but with a skippable inside, looks across a grassy meadow at the village. If you tour the mildly interesting château, you'll see a few well-furnished rooms, a nice kitchen, fine exterior galleries, and a slick double spiral

LUBERON

staircase in stone.

Cost and Hours: €6.50, daily June-Aug 10:00-18:00, May and Sept 10:00-12:00 & 14:30-17:30, March-April and Oct until 16:30, Nov-Dec and Feb until 16:00, weekends only in Jan, decent English handout and posted explanations, tel. 04 90 68 15 23.

Market

Little Lourmarin erupts into a market frenzy every Friday until 13:00. Sleep here Thursday night and awake to the commotion, arrive early, or prepare for a good walk from your car.

Sleeping in Lourmarin

Try to sleep here on a Thursday, so you can be here for Friday's market. The good-value Villa St. Louis and Les Chambres de la Cordière sit across from each other at the very eastern end of the town center.

$$$ At Les Olivettes, Americans Joseph and Elizabeth DeLiso rent five apartments just a five-minute walk from the village center. The apartments are well-furnished and very comfortable, with kitchens, living rooms, CD players, and guest computers. They are rentable by the week or half-week in the off-season (1-bedroom unit-€430/3 nights, 2-bedroom unit-€842/3 nights, ask about special Rick Steves rates, Avenue Henri Bosco, tel. 04 90 68 03 52, www.olivettes.com, lourmarin@olivettes.com). As it's tricky to find this place even with a GPS, ask for directions when you make a reservation.

$$ Villa St. Louis is a splendid place. It's a cross between a museum, a grand old manor home, and a garage sale. The fun and slightly eccentric owner, Madame Bernadette, adds charm to a house packed with character. The dreamy backyard is ideal for a siesta (hammock provided) and picnics. The rooms are like Grandma's, and there's a common room with a fridge (Db-€65-80, cash only, Wi-Fi, secure parking, loaner bikes, 35 Rue de Henri Savournin, tel. 04 90 68 39 18, www.villasaintlouis.com, villa saintlouis@wanadoo.fr).

$$ Les Chambres de la Cordière is a cool getaway. Owner Françoise's goal is to make you feel at home. Six cozy rooms are tucked into one of the village's oldest buildings (c. 1582), with a tiny courtyard and welcoming cats (Db-€65-75, Tb-€85, Qb-€100, 4 rooms come with mini-kitchens—the 2 *gîtes* with full kitchens are usually rented only by the week for about €450, cash only, Rue Albert Camus, tel. 04 90 68 03 32, www.cordiere.com, cordiere luberon@aol.com).

Eating in Lourmarin

All roads seem to converge on the postcard-perfect intersection near **La Maison Café,** where you can enjoy a light meal or snack

inside or outside on their perched terrace (closed Mon-Tue, Rue du Galinier, tel. 04 90 09 54 01). The following listings are within a block of this intersection.

Restaurant l'Antiquaire, with stylish decor, is *the* place to eat well in Lourmarin (€32 *menu,* €40 bouillabaisse possible if ordered ahead, closed at lunch Mon-Tue and off-season all day Sun, only indoor seating but has air-con, a block up from La Maison Café on 9 Rue du Grand Pré, tel. 04 90 68 17 29, http://restaurant-antiquaire.com).

Le Bistrot de Lourmarin cooks up modern Provençal fare at fair prices in a welcoming, relaxed atmosphere (€15 *plats,* €28 *menu,* closed all day Thu and at lunch Fri, 2 Avenue Philippe de Girard, tel. 04 90 68 29 74).

At **La Récré,** across the street, owner Jean-Louis and his bright smile have been welcoming guests for 33 years. You'll find an inviting terrace and regional cuisine with vegetarian options (€16-20 *plats,* €28-35 *menus,* closed Wed except in summer, next to TI on Avenue Philippe de Girard, tel. 04 90 68 23 73, http://la-recre-lourmarin.com).

MARSEILLE, CASSIS, and AIX-EN-PROVENCE

In the rush to get between Avignon and the Riviera, most travelers zip through the eastern fringe of Provence. That's a shame, as this area nurtures compelling cities and a strikingly beautiful coastline, all in a tight package. I cover three different-as-night-and-day places, each worthy of a slice of your time. Marseille is an untouristy, semi-seedy-but-vibrant port city with 2,600 years of history. The nearby coastal village of Cassis offers the perfect antidote to the big city. And just inland, popular and polished Aix-en-Provence is the yin to Marseille's yang, with beautiful people to match its lovely architecture. Aix-en-Provence makes a good and easy first- or last-day stop for those using Marseille's airport.

For good regional guides who specialize in this area, see page 56.

Marseille

Those who think of Marseille as the "Naples of France"—a big, gritty, dangerous port—are missing the boat. Today's Marseille (mar-say), though hardly pristine, is closer to the "Barcelona of France." It's a big, gritty port, *sans* question, but it has a distinct culture, a proud spirit, and a populace determined to clean up its act. That's a tall order, but they're off to a fair start. Over the last few years, dozens of Marseille's historic buildings

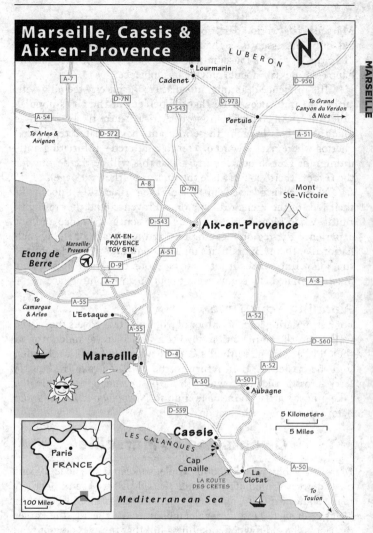

have been renovated and several new public buildings and exhibition spaces have been constructed (three of which are described in this book). The pedestrian zone around the Old Port was redesigned, and is now as wide as the Champs-Elysées. A new tramway system is up and running. This massive facelift was all in preparation for a year-long program as the European Capital of Culture in 2013, which attracted more than 10 million visitors to the city and cost roughly €3.5 billion. Marseille is on the move.

France's oldest (600 B.C.) and second-biggest city (and Europe's third-largest port) owns a history that goes back to ancient Greek times—and challenges you to find its charm.

MARSEILLE

Marseille is a world apart from France's other leading cities, and has only one essential sight to visit—Notre-Dame de la Garde. Here the city is the museum, the streets are its paintings, and the happy-go-lucky residents provide its ambience.

The influence of immigrants matters in this city teeming with authentic ambience. More than 25 percent of the city's population came from countries in North Africa. You're likely to hear as much Arabic as French. These migrants have created residential ghettos where nary a word of French is uttered—infuriating anti-immigrant French people certain that this will be the destiny for the rest of "their" country (see the sidebar on the next page).

Most tourists leave Marseille off their itinerary—it doesn't fit their idea of the French Riviera or of Provence (and they're right). But it would be a shame to come to the south of France and not experience the region's leading city and namesake of the French national anthem. By train, it's made-to-order for a half-day visit—the TGV line makes it just a three-hour trip from Paris. This much-maligned city seems eager to put on a welcoming face.

Planning Your Time

For a stimulating four-hour tour of Marseille that covers the basics, walk from the train station down La Canebière, wander around the Old Port, climb to the La Charité Museum (ideal lunch café), find the cathedral, then return to the port and take the shuttle ferry across to the new town (with the best eating options). Finally, take a bus, tourist train, or taxi up to Notre-Dame de la Garde before returning to the station.

Orientation to Marseille

Marseille is big, with 860,000 people, so keep it simple and focus on the area immediately around the Old Port (Vieux Port). A main boulevard (La Canebière) meets the colorful Old Port near a cluster of small (and skippable) museums and the TI. The Panier district is the old town, blanketing a hill that tumbles down to the port. Marseille's three new museums, anchored between the port and the cathedral, are impossible to miss. The harborside is a lively, broad promenade lined with inviting eateries, amusements, and a morning fish market. Everything described here (except Notre-Dame de la Garde) is within a 30-minute walk of the train station.

A few years ago the city unveiled both a smart new tramway line and

Vive la Différence

Marseille is one of Europe's greatest cultural melting pots. An important trading center since ancient times, Marseille has long been defined by the waves of immigrant peoples who have called this beautiful setting home. Accessible by land and sea to North Africa, Spain, Italy, and Greece, Marseille once attracted Phoenicians, Greeks, and Romans. Today, Marseille houses France's largest concentration of immigrants: 200,000 of its 860,000 residents are Muslim; 80,000 are Jewish (Marseille has had a large Jewish population since the Jews were expelled from Spain in 1492); 80,000 are Armenian Orthodox (escaping Ottoman injustices); and there are 70,000 Comorans (from a group of islands in the Indian Ocean).

There's a spirit of cooperation among Marseille's immigrants, who understand that what benefits one group helps them all. While anti-Semitic and anti-government riots have disrupted other parts of France in recent years (Paris in particular), gritty Marseille has remained relatively quiet. Unlike in Paris, immigrants in Marseille live in the city center, not the suburbs, so they are more visible and harder to ignore. And though unemployment is high among immigrants, it is not as high as in Parisian suburbs. The commercial port, a thriving high-tech industry, and tourism (mostly from cruise ships) fuel Marseille's economy. The city also has invested mightily in jobs programs and city-center renovation projects that have benefited its lower-income residents.

Marseille engenders a strong sense of identity apart from France (and the French language) that unites this city's diverse population. Locals see themselves as *Marseillais* (marsay-ay) first, and as French second (or third, after their native country). Locals' fierce pride is manifested in their passion for Olympique de Marseille, the city's soccer team. Since 1899 *Marseillais* have lived and died with the fate of their team. (A few years ago, I was here the day that 30,000 *Marseillais* fans were boarding trains to Paris for the France finals.) Olympique de Marseille has made a point of creating a team that looks like the city by recruiting players from North African countries (Zinédine Zidane is the most famous example). The strategy seems to have worked—Marseille has won the French Cup more than any other team in France.

Immigrant populations are booming in cities throughout Europe, challenging local governments to accommodate them. Many would do well to study Marseille.

a cheap public bike system called *le Vélo* (similar to Vélib' bikes in Paris)—though visitors won't find much use for either.

Tourist Information

The main TI is two blocks up from the Old Port on La Canebière (Mon-Sat 9:00-19:00, Sun 10:00-17:00, 11 La Canebière, toll tel. 08 26 50 05 00—€0.15/minute, www.marseille-tourisme.com). In summer, two satellite offices are open: One's at the St. Charles train station (see next) and a kiosk is at the Old Port. Pick up the good city map, the flier with a self-guided walk through the old town, and information on museums and the weekly walking tours.

Arrival in Marseille

By Train

St. Charles Station (Gare St. Charles) is busy, modern, and user-friendly. Many services are along track A, including WCs and baggage storage (daily). In summer you should find a TI sharing space with the Train Information Office opposite track C (open Mon-Fri only). The Ibis hotel and car rental are outside track A at its far end. If you exit the station at track A to Square Narvik, you'll see

Hôtel Ibis on your left (car rental is behind it); access to the old city by foot is to the right. With your back to the tracks, you'll find a veritable shopping extravaganza, lots of food options (including McDonald's), and the bus station and its ticket office (with airport buses and more) to the far right, past track N.

Getting from the Train Station to the Old Port: To reach the Old Port, you can walk, take the Métro, or catch a taxi. On **foot** it's an exhilarating 15-minute downhill gauntlet along grimy streets. Leave the station through the exit at track A (past the big departure board), veer right, and admire the view from atop the stairs (Toto, we're not in Cassis anymore). That's Notre-Dame de la Garde overlooking the city—pretty cool. Walk down the stairs and straight on Boulevard d'Athènes, which becomes Boulevard Dugommier. Turn right at McDonald's onto the grand boulevard, La Canebière, which leads directly to the main TI and the old port.

By **Métro** it's an easy subterranean trip from the train station to the Old Port: Go down the escalator opposite track E and then take a longer escalator to your left. Buy a ticket from the machines (look for the ones that accept coins, some take only credit cards) or the *Accueil* office (closed 12:40-13:40). Your €1.50 ticket is good for one hour of travel on Métro; buses and all-day passes cost €5

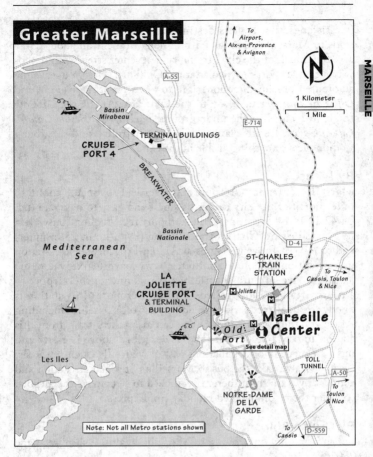

Greater Marseille

To Airport, Aix-en-Provence & Avignon

A-55

1 Kilometer

1 Mile

N

Bassin Mirabeau

TERMINAL BUILDINGS

E-714

CRUISE PORT 4

BREAKWATER

Bassin Nationale

D-4

Mediterranean Sea

ST-CHARLES TRAIN STATION

To Cassis, Toulon & Nice

LA JOLIETTE CRUISE PORT & TERMINAL BUILDING

M Joliette

Marseille Center

Old Port

M

See detail map

Les Iles

TOLL TUNNEL

A-50

To Toulon & Nice

NOTRE-DAME DE LA GARDE

To Cassis

D-559

Note: Not all Metro stations shown

(www.rtm.fr). At the turnstile, touch your ticket to the yellow pads to get the green light, and walk through. Take blue line 1 (direction: La Fourragère) two stops to Vieux Port (Old Port). Following *Sortie* signs, then *la Canebière* exit signs, you'll pop out within sight of the TI (and not far from the smell of the fish market). To return to the station from here, take blue line 1 (direction: La Rose) two stops and get off at Gare St. Charles.

Taxis are out the front doors of the station, down the escalator opposite track E. Allow €15 to the port and €20 to Notre-Dame de la Garde—though train station cabbies may refuse these short trips if business is hopping (tel. 04 91 02 20 20). Taxis along the port will take you on shorter rides.

By Car

Even drivers who are good in big, crazy cities will be frustrated in Marseille. There's always bad traffic here. If coming from the east

(Cassis and other Riviera destinations), opt for the A-50, which leads to Marseille's famous 1.5-mile-long tunnel (toll about €3)—avoiding much of the city's traffic-ridden center streets—and pops you out under Fort St. Nicolas at the Old Port. After you leave the autoroute from any direction, signs to *Vieux Port, Centre-Ville,* and *Office du Tourisme* take you to the Old Port. At the port, follow the blue *P* signs to the underground *Parking Charles de Gaulle-Canebière* lot. Locals claim pay lots are patrolled and safe, but I wouldn't leave anything visible in the car.

By Plane

Marseille's airport (Aéroport Marseille-Provence), about 16 miles north of the city center, is small and easy to navigate (tel. 04 42 14 14 14, www.marseille.aeroport.fr). Frequent buses run to Marseille's St. Charles train station (€9, 3/hour, 25 minutes) and to Aix-en-Provence (stops at Aix-en-Provence's TGV station or bus station, 2/hour, 35 minutes, www.navetteaixtgvaeroport .com). A five-minute shuttle bus trip connects the airport to a nearby train station, called Vitrolles Aéroport. This station is handy for its direct service to cities west of Marseille, including Arles, Avignon, and Nîmes. (You can also take a train from this station into Marseille, but the bus described above is easier and more frequent.) For destinations east of Marseille (such as Cassis, Nice, or Italy), take the bus to Marseille's St. Charles Station and connect by train from there. If you need to sleep near the airport, consider the recommended Holiday Inn Express.

By Cruise Ship

For information on arriving in Marseille by cruise ship, see page 280.

Helpful Hints

Pickpockets: As in any big city, thieves thrive in crowds and target tourists. Wear your money belt, and assume any commotion is a smokescreen for theft.

Car Rental: All the major companies are represented at St. Charles Station (see "Arrival in Marseille," earlier).

Bus #60 to the Basilica: This handy bus scoots you from the Old Port up to Notre-Dame de la Garde in 10 minutes for €1.50 round-trip (ticket is good for one hour, pay driver, 3/hour). Ask the driver for the Notre-Dame de la Garde stop (where most are going). To return to the port, you can board the bus at this same stop. You can also catch this bus on the north side of the port, along the Quai du Port terminal (see "From the Old Port to the New Town" later).

Bike Cabs: In summer, look for advertisement-slathered bicycle cabs that will zip you up and down the Old Port for free (tip optional).

Local Guide: Pascale Benguigui is a terrific guide for Marseille, Aix-en-Provence, St-Tropez, and anything in between (€156/half-day, €248/day, tel. 06 20 80 07 51, macpas@club -internet.fr).

Soccer Matches: *Le football* is to Marseille what American football is to Green Bay: Frenzied fans go crazy, and star worship is always temporary. One of the best-ever soccer players was raised here: Zinédine Zidane (known to Americans mostly for his notorious head-butt of an opponent during the 2006 World Cup Final). If you're here during soccer season (end of July to mid-May), consider getting tickets to a match (every other Sat, tickets start at about €15, ask at the TI or at the **FNAC** store in La Centre Bourse behind the Chamber of Commerce Building—see page 272). To get to the soccer stadium (Stade Vélodrome), take the Métro's red line 2 (direction: Ste. Marguerite-Dromel) to the stop called Rond-Point du Prado.

Tours in Marseille

Ask at the TI about occasional **walking tours** conducted in English and French (usually Sat afternoons, about €7, covers the Panier district).

Le Petit Train's helpful little tourist trains make two routes through town. Both leave at least hourly from the northeast corner of the Old Port, and have skimpy recorded information. The more interesting Notre-Dame de la Garde route (#1) saves you the 30-minute climb to the basilica's fantastic view and runs along a nice section of Marseille's waterfront (€7; allow 80 minutes for round-trip, including 20-30 minutes to visit the church; runs daily, April-Nov usually every 20 minutes 10:00-12:20 & 13:40-18:20, Dec-March every 40 minutes, 10:00-12:00 & 14:00-16:00; tel. 04  91 25 24 69, www.petit-train-marseille.com). I'd skip the Vieux Marseille route (#2), which toots you through the Panier district— better done on foot (€6, 65 minutes, includes one 30-minute stop, April-Oct only).

Marseille at a Glance

▲▲Notre-Dame de la Garde Marseille's landmark sight: a huge Romanesque-Byzantine basilica, towering above everything, with panoramic views. **Hours:** Daily April-Sept 7:00-20:00, until 19:00 Oct-March. See page 277.

▲Chamber of Commerce Building and Marine Museum Grandiose building with small exhibit on the city's maritime history. **Hours:** Daily 10:00-18:00. See page 272.

▲Old Port Economic heart of town, featuring lots of boats and a fish market, all protected by two impressive fortresses. **Hours:** Port—always open; fish market—daily until 13:00. See page 273.

▲La Charité Museum Housed in a beautiful building with Celtic, Greek, Roman, and Egyptian artifacts, plus temporary exhibits. **Hours:** Tue-Sun June-Sept 11:00-18:00, Oct-May 10:00-17:00, closed Mon year-round. See page 274.

Marseille History Museum Shows off the city's remarkable history with artifacts from Caesar to today in 13 multimedia "time sequences." **Hours:** Tue-Sun 10:00-18:00, closed Mon. See page 272.

Cathédrale de la Nouvelle Major Impressive striped cathedral

Two companies run pricey **big bus tours** that I don't recommend. **L'Open Tour**'s double-decker buses with open seating up top offer a 13-stop, hop-on, hop-off route that is very similar to Le Petit Train's routes. The buses depart from next to the Petit Train stop and run only every 45 minutes, leaving you too long at most stops, and there's a 1.5-hour gap in service at lunch (€18 for one-day pass, 70 minutes round-trip). Alternatively, the **City Tour** red buses do a longer route, including La Canebière, in a two-hour round-trip (€18, departures at 10:30, 14:30, and 18:00 July-Sept, same stop locations at the Old Port).

Sights in Marseille

I've listed these sights in roughly the order that you come to them as you approach the Old Port on La Canebière. I've also included some commentary to help you connect the dots (see the map on pages 270-271).

• *Start by the McDonald's at the corner of La Canebière and Boulevard Dugommier.*

with floor and wall mosaics. **Hours:** Tue-Sun 10:00-19:00, closed Mon. See page 275.

Arab Markets Taste of North Africa in downtown Marseille. **Hours:** Open long hours daily. See page 269.

Château d'If Island with fortress-turned-prison, featured in Alexandre Dumas' *The Count of Monte Cristo*. **Hours:** Boats depart daily from Quai des Belges, usually on the hour 9:00-17:00, last departure to visit château is 15:15. See page 277.

Musée Regards de Provence Mediterranean-centric art and media from the 18th to 21st centuries. **Hours:** Daily 10:00-18:00. See page 275.

Villa Méditerranée Rotating exhibitions, lectures, films, and forums focused on inspiring understanding between Mediterranean cultures. **Hours:** Tue-Thu 12:00-19:00, Fri 12:00-22:00, Sat-Sun 10:00-19:00, closed Mon. See page 275.

Museum of European and Mediterranean Civilizations (MuCEM) Art and artifacts from cultures surrounding the Mediterranean Sea. **Hours:** May-Oct Wed-Mon 11:00-19:00, Nov-April Wed-Mon 11:00-18:00, Fri until 22:00, closed Tue. See page 276.

Along La Canebière

The Boulevard La Canebière (pronounced "can o' bee-air") with its recent facelift—and classy tramway—is the celebrated main drag of Marseille. Strolling this stubby thoroughfare, you feel surrounded by a teeming, diverse city. Two blocks before the harbor, you'll find two museums, the TI, and a stylish shopping district. The boulevard dead-ends at the Old Port's fish market.

Arab Markets

Marseille's huge Moroccan, Algerian, and Tunisian populations give the city a special spice. For a taste of Africa, leave La Canebière by turning left at the second street onto Rue Longue des Capucins. Suddenly you're immersed in an exotic and fragrant little medina filled with commotion—and no one's speaking French. Stop by

MARSEILLE

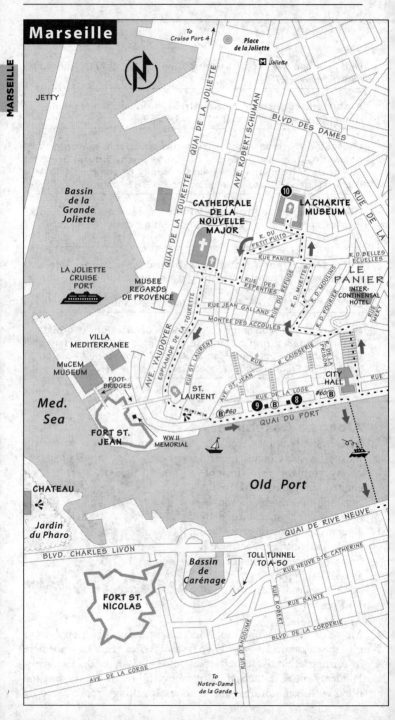

Marseille

To Cruise Port 4

Place de la Joliette

Ⓜ Joliette

JETTY

Bassin de la Grande Joliette

QUAI DE LA JOLIETTE

AVE. ROBERT SCHUMAN

BLVD. DES DAMES

RUE DE LA

CATHEDRALE DE LA NOUVELLE MAJOR

❿ LA CHARITE MUSEUM

R. DU PETIT PUITS

RUE PANIER

R.D. BELLES ECUELLES

LE PANIER

LA JOLIETTE CRUISE PORT

MUSEE REGARDS DE PROVENCE

QUAI DE LA TOURETTE

RUE DES REPENTIES

RUE DU REFUGE

RUE DES MUETTES

R.D. MOULINS

R.D. POIRIER

INTER-CONTINENTAL HOTEL

VILLA MEDITERRANEE

RUE JEAN GALLAND

MONTEE DES ACCOULES

AVE. VAUDOYER

ESPLANADE DE LA TOURETTE

RUE ST. LAURENT

RUE

R. CAISSERIE

R. DE LA PRISON

R. MERY

MuCEM MUSEUM

FOOT-BRIDGES

Med. Sea

ST. LAURENT

AVE. ST. JEAN

RUE DE LA LOGE

CITY HALL

RUE

#60 Ⓑ

⑨ Ⓑ ⑧

#60 Ⓑ

FORT ST. JEAN

WW II MEMORIAL

QUAI DU PORT

Old Port

CHATEAU

Jardin du Pharo

QUAI DE RIVE NEUVE

BLVD. CHARLES LIVON

Bassin de Carénage

TOLL TUNNEL TO A-50

RUE NEUVE STE. CATHERINE

RUE ROBERT

RUE SAINTE

FORT ST. NICOLAS

BLVD. DE LA CORDERIE

AVE. DE LA CORSE

RUE ENDOUME

To Notre-Dame de la Garde

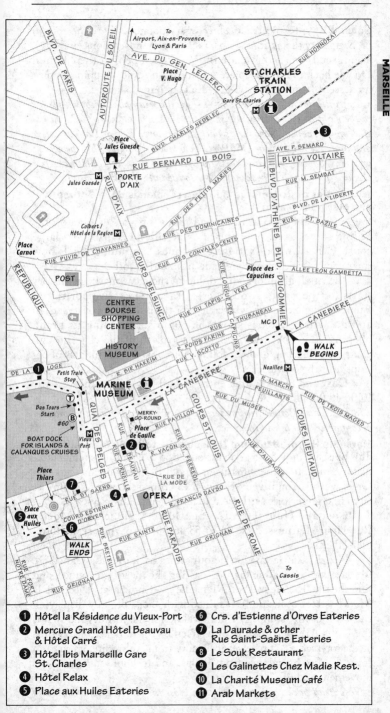

1 Hôtel la Résidence du Vieux-Port
2 Mercure Grand Hôtel Beauvau & Hôtel Carré
3 Hôtel Ibis Marseille Gare St. Charles
4 Hôtel Relax
5 Place aux Huiles Eateries
6 Crs. d'Estienne d'Orves Eateries
7 La Daurade & other Rue Saint-Saëns Eateries
8 Le Souk Restaurant
9 Les Galinettes Chez Madie Rest.
10 La Charité Museum Café
11 Arab Markets

Soleil d'Egypte and try a *bourek* wrap (potato and ground round) or, better, try the *pastilla* wrap (chicken, almonds, onions, and egg). You'll see them being made in the kitchen behind the counter. Double back to La Canebière on Rue d'Aubagne, stopping to pick up dessert (Tunisian pastries) at **La Carthage** bakery.

• *Continue down La Canebière. The grand triumphal arch you see far to the right at Cours Belsunce marks the historic gateway to the city of Aix-en-Provence. Now, cross back to the north side of La Canebière and continue toward the Old Port. Two blocks before you hit the water, on the right side, you can't miss the spacious Office de Tourisme. After checking in at the TI, head next door to the tall, grandiose building.*

▲Chamber of Commerce Building (Le Palais de la Bourse) and Marine Museum

Step inside and take in the grand 1860s interior. A relief on the ceiling shows great moments in Marseille's history and a large court with a United Nations of plaques, reminding locals how their commerce comes from trade around the world.

The small ground-floor exhibit on the city's maritime history starts (to the right as you enter) with an impressive portrait of Emperor Napoleon III (who called for the building's construction) and his wife. Sketches show the pomp surrounding its grand opening. The next room traces the growth of the city through charts of its harbor, and the following rooms display models of big ships over the centuries.

Cost and Hours: Free entry to building, museum-€2, daily 10:00-18:00, tel. 04 91 39 33 33.

• *In La Centre Bourse, the modern shopping center behind the chamber of commerce, you'll find the...*

Marseille History Museum (Musée d'Histoire de Marseille)

This museum provides a good introduction to Marseille's remarkable history, including the remains of an old Roman ship and bits of a Greek vessel. You'll walk through 13 "time sequences," from the city's first prehistoric settlement to its contemporary cityscape.

Cost and Hours: €5, Tue-Sun 10:00-18:00, closed Mon, 2 Rue Henri-Barbusse, tel. 04 91 55 36 00, http://musee-histoire.marseille.fr.

Nearby: For a fashion detour, cross back over La Canebière to Place du Général de Gaulle (passing the merry-go-round), and find the tiny Rue de la Tour, Marseille's self-proclaimed "Rue de la Mode" (street of fashion). It's lined with shops proudly displaying the latest fashions, mostly from local designers. Just beyond that is the 1920s Art Deco facade of Marseille's opera house. The words at the top read: "Art receives its beauty from Aphrodite, its rhythm from Apollo, its balance from Pallas, and to Dionysus it owes its movement and life."

• *Now head back the way you came, cross the major intersection and get close to the Old Port. From this view, the first thing you'll notice is Notre-Dame de la Garde Basilica perched high on the hill above—we will save this for the end of this tour. For now, let's admire the...*

Old Port (Vieux Port)

Protected by two impressive fortresses at its mouth, Marseille's Vieux Port has long been the economic heart of town. These

citadels were built in the 17th century under Louis XIV, supposedly to protect the city. But locals figured the forts were actually designed to keep an eye on Marseille—a city that was essentially autonomous until 1660—and challenge Marseille to thoroughly incorporate into the growing kingdom of France.

Today, the serious shipping is away from the center, and the Old Port is the happy domain of pleasure craft. The fish market along Quai des Belges (where you're standing) thrives each morn-

ing (unless the wind kept the boats home the day before). The stalls are gone by 13:00, but the smells linger. Looking out to sea from here, Le Panier (the old town) rises to your right. The harborfront below Le Panier was destroyed in 1943 by

the Nazis, who didn't want a tangled refuge for resistance fighters so close to the harbor. It's now rebuilt with modern condos and trendy restaurants.

• *Walk around the port with the water on your left and find the small ferry dock (La Ligne du Ferry Boat) that crosses the port. You'll be back here soon. But for now, turn around and find City Hall.*

Le Panier District (Old Town)

Until the mid-19th century, Marseille was just the hill-capping old town and its fortified port. Today, it's the best place to find the town's soul—but not at lunchtime, when everything is closed (except cafés). The ornate **City Hall** (Hôtel de Ville) stands across from the three-masted sailboat and the little shuttle ferry. Its bust of Louis XIV overlooks the harbor. Rue de la Mairie (which turns into Rue de la Guirlande) leads behind the City Hall and up the hill (where we're headed shortly). At the crest of the hill—the highest point in the old town—is the peaceful Place des Moulins, named for the 15 windmills that used to spin and grind from this windy summit. (Today, only the towers of three windmills remain.)

• *Walk up the broad stairway, passing City Hall. At the top is the shiny, just-restored 18th-century Hôtel Dieu (formerly a hospital), now an Intercontinental Luxury Hotel with 194 rooms, most with view terraces over the port, starting at €320 per night. Turn left at the hotel, then track the brown signs up—and up some more—to la Vieille Charité. As you walk, read the thoughtful English-information plaques (posted on iron stands at points of historic interest) and listen for the sounds of local life being played out, on the streets and in the rooms just above.*

▲La Charité Museum (Centre de la Vieille Charité)

Now a museum, this was once a poorhouse. In 1674 the French king decided that all the poor people on the streets were bad news. He built a huge triple-arcaded home to take in a thousand needy subjects. In 1940 the famous architect Le Corbusier declared it a shame that such a fine building was so underappreciated. Today, the striking building—wonderfully renovated and beautiful in its arcaded simplicity—is used as a collection of art galleries surrounding a Pantheonesque church. You can stroll around the courtyard for free. (Good WCs are in the far-left corner.)

The pediment of the church features the figure of Charity taking care of orphans (as the state did with this building). She's flanked by pelicans (symbolic of charity, for the way they were said to pick flesh from their own bosom to feed their hungry chicks, according to medieval legend). The ground floor outside the church houses temporary exhibits. Upstairs you'll find rooms with interesting collections of Celtic (c. 300 B.C.), Greek, and Roman artifacts from this region. There's also a surprisingly good Egyptian collection, along with masks from Africa and the South Pacific.

Cost and Hours: €3-6 depending on exhibits, Tue-Sun June-Sept 11:00-18:00, Oct-May 10:00-17:00, closed Mon year-round, no English information, idyllic café/bar, tel. 04 91 14 58 80.

• *From La Charité, cross the small cobbled triangular square, turn right on Rue du Petit Puits, and walk all the way to the end, where you'll run into a charming square with Le Bar des 13 Coins (open daily, free Wi-Fi, tel. 04 91 91 56 49). Have a drink at this eclectic little bar— the inspiration for the main setting of France's most famous soap opera, Plus Belle La Vie. Take the stairs to Rue de l'Evêché, go left and walk downhill, then take your first right to find...*

Cathédrale de la Nouvelle Major

Bam. This huge, striped cathedral seems lost out here, away from the action and above the nondescript cruise-ship port. The cathedral was built in the late 1800s to replace the old cathedral that the city had outgrown. It's more impressive from the outside, but worth a quick peek inside for its floor and wall mosaics over the nave.

Cost and Hours: Free, Tue-Sun 10:00-19:00, closed Mon.

• *Return to the Old Port by walking up the tree-lined Esplanade de la Tourette. Marseille's sprawling modern port is behind you and becomes visible as you climb.*

The Great Maritime Port of Marseille (GPMM)

The economy of Marseille is driven by its modern commercial ports, which extend 30 miles west from here (a nearby canal links Marseille inland via the Rhône River, adding to the port's importance). Over 100 million tons of freight pass through this port each year (60 percent of which is petroleum), making this one of Europe's top three ports. Container traffic is significant but is hampered by crippling strikes for which the left-leaning city is famous. By contrast, cruise-ship tourism has taken off in a big way, bringing more than 550,000 passengers to Marseille each year.

• *From this street you can also see three of Marseille's newest sights, built for the European Culture Capital city program in 2013, but remaining as permanent additions to the city.*

Musée Regards de Provence

Next to the cathedral, this new museum has a colorful collection of art and media from the 18th to 21st centuries, devoted to life along the Mediterranean. Don't miss the rooftop restaurant with sensational views over the cathedral. The building housing the museum was formerly the sanitary building for immigration, where immigrants were inspected and their clothing was disinfected.

Cost and Hours: €3.50 for permanant collection, more for temporary exhibits, daily 10:00-18:00, tel. 04 96 17 40 40, www.museeregardsdeprovence.com.

Villa Méditerranée

This center hosts rotating exhibitions, lectures, films, and forums all focused on inspiring peace, brotherhood, and understanding between Mediterranean cultures. Its building, with a cantilevered top floor, was designed by Milanese architect Stefano Boeri. With the goal of "bringing a part of the Mediterranean sea into the building," the entire basement floor is below sea level.

Cost and Hours: €7, Tue-Thu 12:00-19:00, Fri 12:00-22:00, Sat-Sun 10:00-19:00, closed Mon, tel. 04 95 09 42 52, www.villa-mediterranee.org.

Museum of European and Mediterranean Civilizations

This national museum, in a lacework-covered building, houses art and artifacts from cultures surrounding the Mediterranean Sea. It's known as MuCEM to locals (Musée des Civilisations de l'Europe et de la Méditerranée). This "vertical casbah," as the architect calls it, is connected by a rooftop footbridge to the Fortress St. Jean, where the exhibition space continues.

Cost and Hours: €8, more for special events and performances, May-Oct Wed-Mon 11:00-19:00, Nov-April Wed-Mon 11:00-18:00, Fri until 22:00, closed Tue, tel. 04 84 35 14 00, www.mucem.org.

• *Keep walking uphill. A fabulous view awaits you at the bend.*

View Terrace

Voilà! This is one of the best views of Marseille, with Notre-Dame de la Garde presiding above, and twin forts below protecting the entrance to the Old Port. The ugly, boxy building marked "Memorial" at the base of the fort (below and to your right) is a memorial to those lost during the Nazi occupation of the city in World War II. The small church to your left is the Church of St. Laurent, which once served as a parish church for sailors and fishermen—notice the lighthouse-like tower.

• *After you've soaked it all in, continue down the steps back to the Old Port.*

From the Old Port to the New Town

From the bottom of the stairs, you have options. If you are pressed for time or want to save some steps, hop on bus #60 here (€1.50, direction: Nôtre-Dame de la Garde). In 20 minutes, you'll circle around the Old Port and head directly up to the basilica. Or you can walk 10 minutes, halfway along the promenade (Quai du Port) to the City Hall, where you'll see the fun little **ferry boat** that shuttles locals across the harbor to the new town (free, every 10 minutes 8:00-17:00, lunch break from about 12:30-13:15). Note the unusual two-way steering wheel as you sail. You'll dock in the new town—which, because of the 1943 bombings, is actually older than the "old" town along the harborfront.

Directly in front of the ferry landing across the port, you'll find popular bars and brasseries, good for a quick meal or memorable drink. Wander in along Place aux Huiles, make your way left, and find a smart pedestrian zone crammed with cafés and restaurants (see "Eating in Marseille," later).

• *Don't miss a trip up to Notre-Dame de la Garde, described next.*

Overlooking the Old Port
▲▲Notre-Dame de la Garde

Crowning Marseille's highest point, 500 feet above the harbor, is the city's landmark sight. This massive Neo-Romanesque-

Byzantine basilica, built in the 1850s during the reign of Napoleon III, is a radiant collection of domes, gold, and mosaics. The monumental statue of Mary and the Baby Jesus towers above everything (Jesus' wrist alone is 42 inches around, and the statue weighs 9 tons). And though people come here mostly for the commanding city view, the interior will bowl you over. This hilltop has served as a lookout, as well as a place of worship, since ancient times. Climb to the highest lookout for an orientation table and the best views. Those islands straight ahead are the Iles du Frioul, including the island of If—where the Count of Monte Cristo spent time (described next).

Cost and Hours: Free, daily April-Sept 7:00-20:00, until 19:00 Oct-March, last entry 45 minutes before closing, cafeteria and WCs are just below the view terrace.

Getting There: To reach the church, you can hike 30 minutes straight up from the harbor. To save some sweat, catch a taxi (about €10), hop on bus #60, or ride the tourist train—all stop on the harborfront near the fish market (see map on page 270 and "Helpful Hints" on page 266).

Offshore Islands and *Calanques*
Château d'If

When King François I visited Marseille in the 16th century, he realized the potential strategic importance of a fort on the uninhabited island of If (one of the Islands of Frioul), just outside the harbor. His château was finished in 1531. The impregnable fortress, which never saw battle, became a prison—handy for locking up Protestants during the Counter-Reformation. Among its illustrious inmates was José Faria, a spiritualist priest who was the idol of Paris and whom Alexandre Dumas immortalized in *The Count of Monte Cristo*. Since 1890 the château has been open to the public. Tour boats take tourists to this French Alcatraz, where the required two-hour stay will leave you sensitive to the count's predicament. I'd bypass this prison.

Cost and Hours: €10.50 round-trip, €6 château entry (château info tel. 04 91 59 02 30), boats usually depart daily at least every hour 9:00-17:00, last departure to visit château is 15:15, 20-minute trip to château, one-hour round-trip if you don't get off the boat, get the latest schedule at the TI, tel. 04 96 11 03 50, www.frioul-if -express.com.

Islands of Frioul (Îles du Frioul)

These islands, which offer a nature break from the big city with a few hiking paths and cafés, are another 15 minutes away (next stop after Château d'If, included in round-trip ticket, get the latest schedule at the TI).

Calanques Cruises

For those who won't get to Cassis, **Croisières Marseille Calanques** offers day trips to the dramatic fjord-like inlets known as *calanques,* east of Marseille (€22/2.5 hours, €28/3.5 hours, tel. 04 91 58 50 58, www.croisieres-marseille -calanques.com). Boats depart from the northeast corner of the Old Port—look for the ticket kiosk. To read up on *calanques,* see page 288.

Sleeping in Marseille

Stay in Marseille only if you want a true urban experience. Hotel values and ambience are better 20 minutes away in Cassis (see page 291).

$$$ Hôtel la Résidence du Vieux-Port**,** pricey but superbly located on the Old Port, offers retro-modern rooms filled with bright colors. Most rooms face the port, have balconies with breathtaking views, and are worth the splurge (Db-€180-400 depending on view, season, and room size, look for deals on website, 18 Quai du Port, tel. 04 91 91 91 22, www.hotel-residence -marseille.com, info@hrvpm.com).

$$$ Mercure Grand Hôtel Beauvau**** lets you buy away the gritty reality outside your door with business-class comfort (Db-€190, Db with port view-€270, rates are frequently reduced, Wi-Fi in little lobby, 4 Rue Beauvau, tel. 04 91 54 91 00, www .accorhotels.com, h1293@accor.com).

$$ Hôtel Carré,** a block off the port, offers good rooms at good rates (Db-€90-140, air-con, elevator, Wi-Fi, 6 Rue Beauvau, tel. 04 91 33 02 33, www.hvpm.fr, carre@hvpm.fr).

$$ Hôtel Ibis Marseille Gare St. Charles,** with 170 rooms (which are often fully booked), is a worthwhile value because it's right at the train station—on the left as you exit—and has all the services, including a restaurant, café, and bar (Db-€95-110, €15 less on weekends, extra bed-€10, check for deals on website, air-

Sleep Code

(€1 = about $1.30, country code: 33)
S = Single, **D** = Double/Twin, **T** = Triple, **Q** = Quad, **b** = bathroom,
s = shower only, * = French hotel rating system (0-5 stars).
Unless otherwise noted, credit cards are accepted and
English is spoken.

To help you sort easily through these listings, I've divided
the accommodations into three categories based on the price
for a standard double room with bath:

$$$ Higher Priced—Most rooms €100 or more.
$$ Moderately Priced—Most rooms between €70-100.
$ Lower Priced—Most rooms €70 or less.

Prices can change without notice; verify the hotel's current rates online or by email. For the best prices, always book
direct.

con, elevator, Square Narvik, tel. 04 91 95 62 09, www.ibishotel
.com, h1390@accor.com).

$ Hôtel Relax*, humble and homey, is run by sweet Houria
(pronounced "oo-ree-ah," which means "Liberty" in Arabic—she's
Algerian) and her husband, Ali. Despite its downtown location, it
has little traffic noise and a lobby any poodle would love. Book this
place ahead. Half of the simple rooms overlook a classy square—
worth requesting, as the back-side rooms can be gloomy (back-side
Db-€62, Db on square-€67, no triples or quads, rooms have tight
bathrooms with step-up showers, air-con, Wi-Fi, just 2 blocks off
harbor on Place de l'Opéra at 4 Rue Corneille, tel. 04 91 33 15 87,
www.hotelrelax.fr, hotelrelax@free.fr).

Near the Airport: **$$ Holiday Inn Express** has easy train
connections to Marseille. If you have an early flight, consider
bedding down here (Db-€80; Impasse Pythagore, Z.I. de
Couperigne, 13127 Vitrolles; tel. 04 42 15 09 30, www.holidayinn
.com).

Eating in Marseille

In the New Town: For the best combination of trendiness, variety,
and a fun people scene, eat in the new town, on or near Quai de
Rive-Neuve (on the left side of the Old Port as you look out to
sea). Look for Place aux Huiles, Cours d'Estienne d'Orves, and
Rue Saint-Saëns for a melting pot of international eateries ranging
from giant salads and fresh seafood to crêpes, Vietnamese dishes,
Belgian waffles, and Buffalo wings. Come here for ambience,

not for top cuisine. **La Daurade** is worth considering, with fresh seafood at fair prices served in a classy setting (€18 *menus*, €30 bouillabaisse—requires two orders, closed Wed, 8 Rue Fortia, tel. 04 91 33 82 42).

Near the Old Port: For good views *en terrasse*, go to the quieter, other side of the port. Have a real Moroccan dinner at **Le Souk** (€18-20 couscous and *tajine* dishes, €29 three-course *menu*, vegetarian options, intimate and authentic interior, closed Mon, 100 Quai du Port, tel. 04 91 91 29 29, http://lesouk.idhii.net). If you want bouillabaisse, try **Les Galinettes Chez Madie** (€35/ person for bouillabaisse, €25 *menu*, €17 lunch *menu*, closed Sun, 138 Quai du Port, tel. 04 91 90 40 87, http://chezmadie.idhii.net).

At La Charité Museum: The lovely, quiet courtyard has a kiosk-café with a few tables (lunch only).

Marseille Connections

By Train and Bus

Marseille is well-served by TGV and local trains, and is the hub for many smaller stations in eastern Provence.

From Marseille by Train to: Cassis (20/day, 25 minutes), **Aix-en-Provence Centre-Ville** (2/hour, 45 minutes), **Antibes** (16/ day, 2.5 hours), **Nice** (18/day, 2.5 hours), **Arles** (11/day, 1.5 hours), **Avignon TGV** (10/day, 35 minutes), **Paris** (hourly, 3.25 hours), **Isle-sur-la-Sorgue** (8/day, 1-2 hours).

From Marseille's Train Station by Bus to: Marseille Airport (3/hour, 25 minutes), **Aix-en-Provence** (4/hour, 30-50 minutes).

By Cruise Ship

If your cruise visits Provence, you'll arrive either at Marseille or at nearby Toulon.

Marseille's Cruise Port

Marseille's enormous port sprawls for miles beneath a bluff west of downtown. In this gritty industrial zone, most cruise ships tuck themselves in between cargo vessels at the main port (Porte 4), which has several terminals (called *poste,* or "dock"). On busy days, a few cruises anchor offshore and tender passengers to the La Joliette pier, which is much closer to the town center (just below the cathedral). Smaller ships may even dock here.

Getting from the Ports to the City Center: Taxis meet arriving cruise ships at either dock, but rates are high (€15-20 to Old Port, Notre-Dame de la Garde, or train station; one-way to Aix-en-Provence-€55; all-day round-trip to Arles/Avignon area including stops at several sites-€175-220). More cost-effective options are explained next. If you do take a taxi, try to agree on a fixed rate up front, or make sure the meter is set to the correct rate.

From the **main port (Porte 4),** most cruise lines offer a convenient **shuttle bus** that takes you directly to downtown Marseille's Old Port in 15-20 minutes (around €7-14 round-trip, departs every 20 minutes). Skip the overly complicated public-transportation trip—it's worth springing for the shuttle.

From **La Joliette,** you can **walk** to the Old Port in just 15 minutes (simply walk with the port area on your right).

Getting from the Old Port to the Train Station: From the Old Port, you can walk to many of the sights in town or head up to St. Charles Station to catch a train to outlying destinations. To reach the train station, **walk** straight uphill on the main drag called La Canebière, then turn left up Boulevard Dugommier, which becomes Boulevard d'Athènes (about a 20-minute walk). Or, to save time and sweat, zip to the station on the **Métro:** Find the entrance to the Vieux Port Métro stop (there are several; a handy one is on the Old Port). Go down into the Métro, buy a €1.50 ticket at the machine, and get on a train going toward La Rose, to the stop called St. Charles, and escalate up into the station.

Toulon's Cruise Port

The pleasant if unspectacular city of Toulon, about 40 miles east of Marseille, is situated between mountains and a large bay. There's not much to see in Toulon itself; the best plan is to join a cruise-line excursion, rent a car, or head immediately to the train station to visit nearby towns on your own. The easiest side-trips by train are to **Cassis** (about hourly, 35 minutes) and **Marseille** (hourly, 45-60 minutes). For points beyond Marseille (most of them too far to be advisable on a short port visit), see "By Train and Bus," earlier.

Getting from the Port to the Train Station: To make a beeline to the train station, pay €7-10 for a **taxi** (if there are no taxis waiting, you can call one at tel. 04 94 93 51 51).

Otherwise, you can walk to the small old town market square called Place Louis Blanc (with TI, a pharmacy, and ATMs), then take a bus or walk to the station (10-minute walk to Place Louis Blanc, 30-minute walk to train station). To reach Place Louis Blanc from the port, walk toward the row of apartment blocks that line the top of the harbor. When you reach this embankment, swing left and walk alongside the apartments until you reach the big gap in the buildings. Hook right between the buildings; Place Louis Blanc is straight ahead.

Bus #7 departs from just a few steps off Place Louis Blanc; look for the bus stop alongside the church, on Avenue de la République (€1.40, buy ticket from driver, 4/hour Mon-Fri, 3-4/hour Sat, 1-2/hour Sun, 10-15-minute trip depending on traffic).

Get off at the Gare stop and walk two blocks up Avenue Vauban to the station.

The **walk** to the station from Place Louis Blanc takes about 25 minutes: With your back to the square, turn right onto busy Avenue de la République, and follow it for a few blocks until it runs into a major intersection. Head right with the road up Rue Henri Pastoureau, and continue straight up to the big square called Place de la Liberté. Cross diagonally through this square and out the top-left corner, on Rue Dumont d'Urville. You'll pop out on Boulevard de Tessé, with the train station just to your left.

Cassis

Hunkered below impossibly high cliffs, Cassis (kah-see) is an unpretentious port town that gives travelers a sunny time-out from their busy vacation. Two hours away from the fray of the Côte d'Azur, Cassis is a prettier, poor man's St-Tropez. Outdoor cafés line the small port on three sides, where boaters clean their crafts as they chat up café clients. Cassis is popular with the French and close enough to Marseille to be busy on weekends and all summer. Come to Cassis to dine portside, swim in the glimmering-clear water, and explore its rocky *calanques* (inlets).

Orientation to Cassis

The Massif du Puget mountain hovers over little Cassis, with hills spilling down to the port. Cap Canaille cliff rises from the southeast, and the famous *calanques* inlets hide along the coast northwest of town. Hotels, restaurants, and boats line the attractive little port.

Tourist Information

The TI is in the modern building in the middle of the port among the boats. They have free Wi-Fi, good maps for sale, and the latest information on the conditions of the *calanques* (May-Sept Mon-Sat 9:00-18:30, until 19:00 July-Aug, Sun 9:30-12:30 & 15:00-18:00; Oct-April Mon-Sat 9:30-12:30 & 14:00-18:00, Sun 10:00-12:30, Quai des Moulins, toll tel. 08 92 39 01 03-€0.34/minute, www.ot-cassis.fr, info@ot-cassis.com). If you're going to Marseille, pick up a map here.

Arrival in Cassis

By Train: Cassis' hills forced the train station to be built two miles away, and those last two miles can be a challenge. It's a small station with limited hours (no baggage storage, ticket windows open Mon-Fri 6:15-13:15 & 13:45-20:45, Sat-Sun 9:50-12:45 & 13:45-17:55). If you need to buy tickets when the station is closed, use the machines (coins only).

A **taxi** into town costs €12 with baggage and is well worth the expense unless a Marcouline bus is soon to arrive (see below). If there's no taxi waiting, call 04 42 01 78 96 (a pay phone is outside the train station). Otherwise, it's a 50-minute walk into town (turn left out of the station and follow signs).

Marcouline **buses** link the station with the town center, but service is spotty (€1, about hourly with longer intervals in the afternoon, schedule posted at all stops). Call the TI in advance to get the schedule (or check online at www.ot-cassis.com/fr/bus-intra-urbain-la-marcouline.html) and plan your arrival accordingly—but be ready to take a taxi. The bus drops you at the Casino stop in Cassis: From here, turn right on Rue de l'Arène and walk downhill five minutes to reach the port.

By Bus: Regional buses (including those from Marseille) run limited hours (check with the TI before taking one). The bus stop is a five-minute walk from the port on Avenue du 11 Novembre (stop is labeled Gendarmerie).

By Car: There are two exits from the autoroute for Cassis; the second (coming from Aix-en-Provence, exit #8) costs €1 more in tolls but saves you 10 minutes, provides easy access to La Route des Crêtes (described later, under "Sights in Cassis"), and offers memorable views.

The hills above Cassis can make it difficult to navigate. Hotels are signed, though the blue signs can be tricky to follow, so pay attention. Hotel parking is minimal (carefully read each hotel's listing in this book as some have more parking than others), and the traffic thickens the closer you get to the port.

No matter where you end up parking, leave nothing of value in your car. Outside of summer, drivers arriving by 10:00 usually can find curbside parking (about €1/hour, free 18:00-9:00); late-comers will likely need to park in one of the well-marked pay lots above the port (Parking de la Viguerie is closest but often full, and their *Abonnés* entrance is for locals only). Parking Daudet, up the road from Parking de la Viguerie, usually has better availability, as does La Madie up the road from the Casino bus stop.

If you're driving here on weekends, holidays, during school vacation periods (April-June and Sept-Oct), or any day in July and August, Cassis will be packed. So take advantage of the free parking at les Gorguettes, high above the town (well-signed), and use the *navettes* shuttle-bus service into town (€1.50 round-trip, 9:00-20:00, July-Aug daily until 1:00 in the morning).

A second *navette* bypasses the town center with stops at

CASSIS

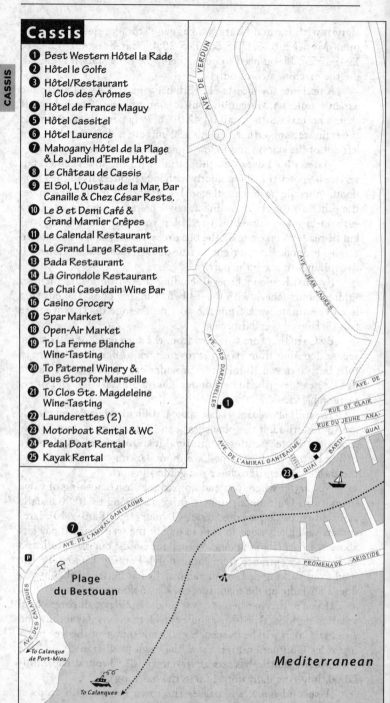

Cassis

1. Best Western Hôtel la Rade
2. Hôtel le Golfe
3. Hôtel/Restaurant le Clos des Arômes
4. Hôtel de France Maguy
5. Hôtel Cassitel
6. Hôtel Laurence
7. Mahogany Hôtel de la Plage & Le Jardin d'Emile Hôtel
8. Le Château de Cassis
9. El Sol, L'Oustau de la Mar, Bar Canaille & Chez César Rests.
10. Le 8 et Demi Café & Grand Marnier Crêpes
11. Le Calendal Restaurant
12. Le Grand Large Restaurant
13. Bada Restaurant
14. La Girondole Restaurant
15. Le Chai Cassidain Wine Bar
16. Casino Grocery
17. Spar Market
18. Open-Air Market
19. To La Ferme Blanche Wine-Tasting
20. To Paternel Winery & Bus Stop for Marseille
21. To Clos Ste. Magdeleine Wine-Tasting
22. Launderettes (2)
23. Motorboat Rental & WC
24. Pedal Boat Rental
25. Kayak Rental

AVE. DE VERDUN

AVE. JEAN JAURES

AVE. DES DARDANELLES

AVE. DE

RUE ST. CLAIR

RUE DU JEUNE ANA-

QUAI

AVE. DE L'AMIRAL GANTEAUME

QUAI BARTH.

AVE. DE L'AMIRAL GANTEAUME

PROMENADE ARISTIDE

Plage du Bestouan

AVE. DES CALANQUES

To Calanque de Port-Miou

To Calanques

Mediterranean

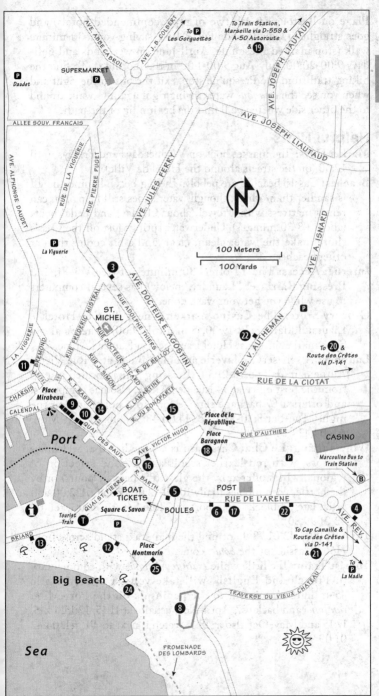

CASSIS

To Train Station , Marseille via D-559 & A-50 Autoroute & ⑲

AVE. J. B. COLBERT

AVE. ABBE CABROL

To ⓟ Les Gorguettes

AVE. JOSEPH LIAUTAUD

SUPERMARKET ⓟ

ⓟ *Daudet*

ALLEE SOUV. FRANCAIS

AVE. JOSEPH LIAUTAUD

AVE. ALPHONSE DAUDET

RUE DE LA VIGUERIE

RUE PIERRE PUGET

AVE. JULES FERRY

AVE. A. ISNARD

ⓟ *La Viguerie*

N

100 Meters
100 Yards

❸

AVE. DOCTEUR E. AGOSTINI

RUE ADOLPHE THIERS

ST. MICHEL

RUE FREDERIC MISTRAL

RUE DOCTEUR S. SICARD

RUE J. SIMON

R. DE BELLOY

❷❷

RUE V. AUTHEMAN

ⓟ

To ⑳ & Route des Crêtes via D-141

RUE DE LA CIOTAT

LA VIGUERIE

R. BREMOND

R. RASTIT

RUE LAMARTINE

R. DU BONAPARTE

⓫

CHARSIS

Place Mirabeau

CALENDAL

❾ ❿ ⓮

QUAI DES BAUX

❶❺

Place de la République

Place Baragnon

⓲

RUE D'AUTHIER

CASINO

Port

AVE. VICTOR HUGO

ⓣ ⓰

R. BARTH

BOAT TICKETS

QUAI ST. PIERRE

Square G. Savon

❺

BOULES

POST

ⓟ

Marcouline Bus to Train Station

Ⓑ

RUE DE L'ARENE

❻ ⓱

❷❷

AVE. REV.

❹

ⓘ

Tourist Train ⓣ

ⓟ

To Cap Canaille & Route des Crêtes via D-141 & ㉑

BRIAND

⓭

⓬

Place Montmorin

㉕

To ⓟ La Madie

Big Beach

㉔

❽

TRAVERSE DU VIEUX CHATEAU

Sea

PROMENADE DES LOMBARDS

CASSIS

Plage du Bestouan (with two of my recommended hotels) and goes straight to Calanque de Port-Miou, saving you a 30-minute walk (stop marked Presqu'ile, April-June on weekends and holidays 9:00-20:00; July-Aug 9:00-1:00 in the morning). To find the hiking trail from the Presqu'ile stop, exit the bus to the right and when you see the *calanque* water, swing right again to walk around to the other side where you'll find the beginning of the path.

Helpful Hints

Market Days: The market hops on Wednesdays and Fridays until 12:30 (on the streets around the Hôtel de Ville).

Beaches: Cassis' beaches are pebbly. The big beach behind the TI is sandier than others, though water shoes still help. You can rent a mattress with a towel (about €17/day) and pedal boats (about €8/30 minutes). Underwater springs just off the Cassis shore make the water clean, clear, and a bit cooler than at other beaches.

Internet Access: The TI offers 30 minutes of free Wi-Fi, and **Pressing Rairi** (see "Laundry," below) has several computers to use while you get your wash done.

Grocery Store: The **Casino** market is next door to Hôtel le Liautaud (daily 8:30-19:30, Sun until 19:00). There's also a **Spar** market just past Hôtel Laurence on Rue de l'Arène.

Laundry: A self-service **laverie automatique** is at 9 Rue Victor Autheman (daily 6:30-21:30). **Pressing Rairi,** located just up from the post office at 34 Rue de l'Arène, also has computers, and offers a €7 baggage service for those not spending the night (Tue-Sat 8:30-13:30 & 14:00-18:30, closed Sun-Mon, tel. 04 42 01 10 36).

Wine Tasting: Le Chai Cassidain is a wine bar that welcomes visitors, with red-leather stools and a good selection of regional wines offered by the glass (€5, healthy pours) or by the bottle, with nibbles (daily 10:00-13:00 & 15:00-22:00 and often later, 4 blocks from port at 6 Rue Séverin Icard, tel. 04 42 01 99 80).

Taxi: Call 04 42 01 78 96 or find the main taxi stand across from Hôtel Cassitel by the *boules* court.

Tourist Train: The little white *train touristique,* with commentary in French and English, will take you on a worthwhile 45-minute circuit out to the peninsula on the Port-Miou *calanque* and back (€7, April-Nov, usually at 11:15, 12:15, 14:15, 17:15 and May-Oct also at 18:15, catch it next to TI, tel. 04 42 01 09 98).

Self-Guided Tour

Cassis Visual Tour from the Port

Find a friendly bench in front of Hôtel le Golfe—or, better, enjoy a drink at their café—and read this quick town intro.

Cassis was born more than 2,500 years ago (on the hill with the castle ruins, across the harbor). Ligurians, Phoenicians, maybe Greeks, certainly Romans, and plenty of barbarians all found this spot to their liking. Parts of the castle date from the 8th century, and the **fortress walls** were constructed in the 13th century to defend against seaborne barbarian raids. The Michelin family sold the fortress to investors who turned it into a luxury five-suite *chambres d'hôtes,* where celebrities often hole up looking for peace and quiet (see "Sleeping in Cassis," later).

In the 18th century life became more secure, and people moved their homes back to the waterfront. Since then, Cassis has made its living through fishing, quarrying its famous white stone, and producing well-respected white wines—which, conveniently, pair well with the local seafood dishes, and *bien sûr,* with tourists like us.

With improvements in transportation following the end of World War II, tourism rose gradually in Cassis, though crowds are still sparse by Riviera standards. While foreigners overwhelm nearby resorts, Cassis is popular mostly with the French and still feels unspoiled. The town's protected status limits the height of the buildings along the waterfront. Cassis' port is home to some nice boats...but they're dinghies compared to those in the glitzier harbors farther east.

The big cliff towering above the castle hill is **Cap Canaille.** Europe's highest maritime cliff, it was sculpted by receding glaciers (wrap your brain around that concept), and today drops 1,200 feet straight down. You can—and should—drive or taxi along the top for staggering views (see "Above Cassis: La Route des Crêtes," later). Return to this bench at sunset, when the Cap glows a deep red.

If you can overcome your inertia, walk to your right, then veer left on top of the short wall in front of the public WCs. The rocky shore over your right shoulder looks cut away just for sunbathers. But Cassis was once an important **quarry,** and stones were sliced right out of this beach for easy transport to ships. The Statue of Liberty's base sits on this rock, and even today, Cassis

CASSIS

stone remains highly valued throughout the world...but yesterday's quarrymen have been replaced by today's sunbathers.

Sights in Cassis

▲▲▲The *Calanques*

Until you see these exotic Mediterranean fjords—with their translucent blue water, tiny intimate beaches, and stark cliffs plunging into the sea or forming rocky promontories—it's hard to understand what all the excitement is about.

Calanques (kah-lahnk) are narrow, steep-sided valleys partially flooded by the sea, surrounded by rugged white cliffs usually made of limestone (quarries along the *calanques* have provided building stone for centuries). The word comes from the Corsican word *calanca*, meaning "inlet"—the island of Corsica also has *calanques*. These inlets began as underwater valleys carved by the seaward flow of water at river mouths, and were later gouged out deeper by glaciers. About 12,000 years ago, when the climate warmed and glaciers retreated at the end of the last Ice Age, the sea level rose partway up the steep rocky sides of the *calanques*. Today the cliffs harbor a unique habitat that includes rare plants and nesting sites for unusual raptors.

The most famous inlets are in the Massif des Calanques, which runs along a 13-mile stretch of the coast from Marseilles to Cassis. This area and part of the surrounding region became a national park in 2012.

You can hike, or cruise by boat or kayak, to many *calanques*. Bring plenty of water, sunscreen, and anything else you need for the day, as there's nary a baguette for sale. Don't dawdle—to limit crowds and because of fire hazards, the most popular *calanques* can be closed to visitors between 11:00 and 16:00 in high season (mid-June-mid-Sept) and on weekends. When they are "closed," the only way to see the *calanques* is by boat or kayak. The TI can give you plenty of advice.

Cruising the *Calanques*: Several boats offer trips of various lengths (3 *calanques*-€15, 2/hour, 45 minutes; 5 *calanques*-€18, 3/day, 1 hour; 8-10 *calanques*-€25, 1-3/day, 1.5 hours, cash only; tel. 04 42 01 90 83, www.calanques-cassis.com). The three-*calanques* tour is the most popular. Tickets are sold (and boats depart) from a small booth on the port opposite the Hôtel Lieutaud.

Prochain départ means "next departure." Boats vary in size (some seat up to 100).

Hiking to the *Calanques*: Plan ahead. From June to September, many of the *calanques* are closed in certain weather conditions due to the high risk of brush fires. For information, check with the TI or call toll tel. 08 11 20 13 13; wait 30 seconds for English instructions. Conditions and closures are announced starting at 18:00 the day before.

Drivers can save 30 minutes of hiking by driving to Calanque de Port-Miou and paying €6 to park (described below). Anyone can take the *navette* shuttle bus directly from les Gorguettes parking lot to Port-Miou; it runs on weekends (April-June), holidays, and during July and August (see "Arrival by Car," earlier, for hours, www.ot-cassis.com/fr/la-navette-port-miou.html).

The trail lacing together *calanques* Port-Miou, Port-Pin, and d'En-Vau will warm a hiker's heart. Views are glorious, and the trail is manageable if you have decent shoes (though shade is minimal).

For most, the best *calanque* by foot is **Calanque Port-Pin,** about an hour from Cassis (30 minutes after the linear, boat-lined Calanque Port-Miou, which also works as a destination if time is short). Calanque Port-Pin is intimate and well-forested, with a small beach.

The most spectacular *calanque* is **Calanque d'En-Vau,** but it's a two-hour hike one-way from Cassis with a steep descent to the beach at the end. In summer (mid-June-mid-Sept), access is strictly controlled, and this *calanque* is closed by 11:00.

The TI's map of Cassis gives a general idea of the *calanques* trail, though you don't really need a map. Start along the road behind Hôtel le Golfe and walk past Plage du Bestouan, then look for green hiker signs to *Calanque Miou* (pay attention to your route for an easier return). You'll climb up, then drop down residential streets, eventually landing at the foot of Calanque de Port-Miou, where the dirt trail begins. Follow signs to *Calanques Port-Pin* and *d'En-Vau,* walking 500 yards along a wide trail and passing through an old quarry.

You're now on the *GR (Grande Randonnée)* trail, indicated by red, white, and green markers painted on rocks, trees, and other landmarks. Follow those markers as they lead uphill (great views at top), then connect to a rough stone trail leading down to Calanque Port-Pin (nice beach, good scampering). The trail continues from here back up and on to Calanque d'En-Vau. *Bonne route!*

Other Ways to Reach the *Calanques*: From about mid-April to mid-October, you can rent a **kayak** in Cassis—or in nearby Port-Miou, which is closer to the *calanques.* In Cassis, try Club Sports Loisirs Nautiques on Place Montmorin, behind the merry-go-round (one-seater-€30/4 hours, two-seater-€45/4 hours, tel. 04 42 01 80 01). In Port-Miou, call mobile 06 75 70 00 73. The TI has brochures for more kayak companies. You can also take a **kayak tour** (€35/half-day, €55/day, €30/sunset tour, depart from nearby town of La Ciotat, advance reservations smart, mobile 06 12 95 20 12, www.provencekayakmer.fr). If the hiking trails are closed, this is the only way you'll be able to get to those *calanques* beaches.

You can rent a small **motorboat** without a special boating license (€100/half-day, €140/day, €700 cash or credit-card imprint as deposit; at Loca'Bato office, a few steps away from Hôtel le Golfe; mobile 06 89 53 15 62 or 06 43 88 19 07). Another option is a **skippered boat rental** with JCF Boat Services (up to 8 people, about €350/half-day, €410/day, English-speaking captains, mobile 06 75 74 25 82 or 06 62 46 73 16, www.jcf-boat-services.com, contact@jcf-boat-services.com).

▲▲Above Cassis: La Route des Crêtes

If you have a car, or are willing to spring for a taxi (€30 for a 30-minute trip, 4 people per taxi), you must take this remarkable drive. Ride straight up to the top of Cap Canaille and toward the next town, La Ciotat. It's a twisty road, providing access to numbingly high views over Cassis and the Mediterranean. From Cassis, follow signs to *La Ciotat/Toulon*, then *La Route des Crêtes*. The towns just east of Cassis (La Ciotat, Bandol, etc.) do not merit a detour. This road is occasionally closed (because of strong winds or the high risk of brush fires June to September), though you can usually get partway up—before investing time and money in this trip, check at the TI.

Wine-Tasting in the Hills Behind Cassis

The following places offer good opportunities to taste the famous (mostly white) Cassis wine with the folks who make it (remember, if it's a *free* tasting, it's polite to buy a bottle or two).

The most reputable winery, and easiest to reach without a car, is the **Clos Ste. Magdeleine.** English tours of the vineyard and cellar are offered Monday-Saturday usually at 11:00 and 16:00, finishing with a tasting (€14, 45 minutes, tel. 04 42 01 70 28, confirm times in advance with the TI).

The following places offer tastings only (no tours): At **La Ferme Blanche**, right on D-559 above town, you'll find English-speaking Jeromine, who likes to explain what makes Cassis wine so special, but it's just a tasting room on a busy, noisy road (daily 9:00-12:00 & 14:00-19:00, tel. 04 42 01 00 74). You can practice your French at the modern, cool tasting room in **Paternel Winery,** where nobody speaks English (Mon-Sat 11:00-12:30 & 14:00-

18:00, closed Sun; follow signs out of town toward La Ciotat, it's a half-mile after the turn-off for La Route des Crêtes).

Sleeping in Cassis

Cassis hotels are laid-back places with less polish but lower rates than those on the Riviera (rooms average about €85). Some close from November to March, but those that stay open offer good discounts. All are busy on weekend and summer nights, when many can come with late-night noise (though most hotels have effective double-paned windows). Book early for sea views. Most hotels have free Wi-Fi and a few invaluable parking spots that you can reserve when booking your room. None of the places I list has an elevator. Skip your hotel breakfast and head to the port for café au lait with a view.

Near the Port or in Town

$$$ Best Western Hôtel la Rade*, a 10-minute walk uphill from the port, has good views from its lovely poolside deck and welcoming lounge, for which you'll pay *cher*. The two "standard" rooms are tiny; pay the extra €10 for a "classique," but skip the "comfort" rooms which promise balconies and views on the pines, but actually look onto a street (standard Db-€120, classique Db-€130, comfort Db-€200, suites-€280, extra bed-€15, free guest computer and Wi-Fi, parking-€15, Route des Calanques, 1 Avenue de Dardanelles, tel. 04 42 01 02 97, www.hotel-cassis.com, larade@hotel-cassis.com).

$$$ Hôtel le Golfe, over an easygoing (but not late-night) café, has good rates, air-conditioning, and the best views of the port. Half of its basic and slightly worn rooms come with port views and small balconies—these are worth booking ahead. Sleep elsewhere if you can't get a view (Sb/Db with view and some noise-€115, Sb/Db without view-€95, Tb-€115-130, Qb-€130-150, unreliable Wi-Fi, dim lighting, 3 parking spaces-€8/day, nearby garage-€10/day, 3 Place Grand Carnot, tel. 04 42 01 00 21, www .legolfe-cassis.fr, contact@legolfe-cassis.fr).

$$ Hôtel le Clos des Arômes is a simple, quiet retreat. This place has appealing ambience with public spaces you can stretch out in. *Très provençal*, it has a big courtyard terrace and a good restaurant. The rooms have old furnishings, so-so beds, poor lighting, church-bell noise (rooms on the front are quieter), and no air-conditioning (some have ceiling fans), but the place works in spite of these things (standard Db-€75, bigger Db-€85, Tb/Qb-€99, Wi-Fi in reception area only, parking-€14/day, near Parking la Viguerie at 10 Rue Abbé Paul Mouton, tel. 04 42 01 71 84, www.le-clos-des-aromes.com, closdesaromes@orange.fr). It's best to book by phone.

$$ Hôtel de France Maguy** is a good 10-room place for drivers on a budget (plenty of parking) or those without wheels (friendly owner Franck will pick you up at the station if you book ahead). It's a few blocks up from the port, so it's fairly quiet. Rooms are small, but air-conditioned and well-maintained. More expensive rooms are slightly larger, have tiny balconies or terraces, and come with mini-fridges (Db-€90-125, Tb/Qb-€140-150, includes breakfast and parking, free Wi-Fi, above the Casino on Avenue du Revestel, tel. 04 42 01 72 21, www.hoteldefrancemaguy.com, hoteldefrancemaguy@gmail.com).

$ Hôtel Cassitel**, located on the harbor over a lively café (noisy on weekends) has comfortable rooms with air-conditioning and Wi-Fi. In some rooms the shower and sink are open to the room (offering little privacy within the room), and in all rooms the double-paned windows filter most portside noise (standard Db-€75-85, large Db-€95-105, Tb-€105, Qb-€135, parking garage-€12/day, Place Clemenceau, tel. 04 42 01 83 44, www.hotel-cassis.com, cassitel@hotel-cassis.com).

$ Hôtel Laurence** offers good budget beds, in small but air-conditioned and relatively clean rooms (ashtrays by the beds) with friendly staff. Back rooms are quieter and some have views of the château. You must call a few days ahead to confirm your reservation (Db-€55-70, Db with balcony-€75-90, Db with view terrace-€85-100, extra bed-€13, Wi-Fi in reception only, closed in winter, 2 blocks off the port beyond Hôtel Cassitel at 8 Rue de l'Arène, no parking—drop bags in load zone and head to La Madie lot, tel. 04 42 01 88 78, www.cassis-hotel-laurence.com, contact@cassis-hotel-laurence.com). Animated Nadia runs the reception.

On Plage du Bestouan

The next two hotels are a 10-minute walk from the port on the next beach west, Plage du Bestouan. Easy parking makes them good for drivers.

$$$ Mahogany Hôtel de la Plage** faces the beach with a concrete exterior and mod interior, generous public spaces, and 30 well-conceived, quite comfortable, and mostly spacious rooms at acceptable rates (same price for Db with modern decor, deck, and sea view as for bigger suite-like Db with Provençal decor but no view-€165-185, Db suite with view-€220-280, includes breakfast, air-con, Wi-Fi, parking-€15, tel. 04 42 01 05 70, www.hotelmahogany.com, info@hotelmahogany.com).

$$$ Le Jardin d'Emile** is a villa-hotel located below the Mahogany Hôtel de la Plage. It's a charming little refuge with rich colors inside and out, plush rooms, and a green garden. Six of the seven rooms have decks, and three have sea views (Db-€140-160, extra bed-€30, air-con, free and secure parking, tel. 04 42 01 80 55, www.lejardindemile.fr, provence@lejardindemile.fr).

High Above the Port

$$$ Le Château de Cassis, privately owned and closed to the public for many years, recently opened its doors to visitors, renting five luxurious suites as *chambres d'hôtes*. Celebrities are often in residence, so access is strictly forbidden unless you have a reservation (suites-€300-690, spacious pool, gardens, views galore, all the amenities you can imagine, book well in advance, tel. 04 42 01 63 20, www.chateaudecassis.com, contact@chateaudecassis.com).

Eating in Cassis

Peruse the lineup of tempting restaurants along the port, window-shop the recommended places below, and then decide for yourself (all have good interior and exterior seating). You can have a ham-and-cheese crêpe or go all-out for bouillabaisse with the same great view. Arrive by 19:30 for the view tables. Picnickers can enjoy a beggars' banquet at the benches at Hôtel le Golfe or on the beach, or discover your own quiet places along the lanes away from the port (small grocery stores open until 19:30). Local wines are terrific: red from Bandol and whites/rosés from Cassis.

Dining Portside

The first four places are ideally situated side by side, allowing diners to comparison shop. I've enjoyed good meals at each of them.

El Sol is sharp and popular with discerning diners (*menus-*€21-30, closed Sun eve off-season, all day Mon year-round, and sometimes Tue for lunch, 20 Quai des Baux, tel. 04 42 01 76 10, www.restaurant-el-sol.fr).

L'Oustau de la Mar has a loyal following and fair prices (*menu-*€22, closed Mon eve and all day Tue, 20 Quai des Baux, tel. 04 42 01 78 22).

Bar Canaille specializes in fresh seafood platters, oysters, and other shellfish (open daily in summer, closed Wed off-season, 22 Quai des Baux, tel. 04 42 01 72 36).

Chez César was most popular with locals on my last visit, with good prices and selection (€26 *marmite de pêcheur*—a poor man's bouillabaisse, €12.50 *plats*, *menus* from €23, closed Sun-Mon, 21 Quai des Baux, tel. 04 42 01 75 47).

Le 8 et Demi serves crêpes, pizza, salads, and good Italian gelato on plastic tables with front-and-center portside views (closed Thu off-season, 8 Quai des Baux, tel. 04 42 01 94 63).

The **Grand Marnier crêpe stand** cooks delicious dessert crêpes to go for €3—the Grand Marnier crêpe rules. This is ideal for strollers (next to Le 8 et Demi, daily April-Sept 15:00-23:30).

Dining Away from the Port

Le Clos des Arômes, listed earlier under "Sleeping in Cassis," is the place to come for a refined, candlelit dinner. Dine on a lovely enclosed terrace (€26 *menu*, closed all day Wed and Thu for lunch, tel. 04 42 01 71 84, www.le-clos-des-aromes.com).

Le Calendal serves up *menus* that feature local dishes in a warm, charming, and cozy setting. Don't be surprised if the chef visits your table (indoor or terrace seating available). If you want bouillabaisse, you must order it a day ahead of time (€33 *menu*, closed Sun for lunch and all day Mon, 3 Rue Brémond, tel. 04 42 01 17 70).

Le Grand Large is indeed large and owns the scenic beachfront next to the TI. Come here for a quiet drink before dinner, or to dine seaside rather than portside (€32 *menu* with good choices, open daily, Plage de Cassis, tel. 04 42 01 81 00, www .cassis-grand-large.com).

Bada is a trendy beachfront place right behind the TI, serving breakfast with the sounds of crashing waves, and €14-17 salads at lunch (no dinner service). It's open only in good weather since it's not covered and the wind can be strong (Promenade Aristide Briand, tel. 04 42 83 70 09).

La Girondole is an easy place for families, with cheap pizza, pasta, and salads. It's a block off the port (open daily in summer, take-away also possible, closed Tue off-season, 1 Rue Thérèse Rastit, tel. 04 42 01 13 39).

Cassis Connections

Cassis' train station is two miles from the port. Shuttle buses meet some trains on weekdays, and taxis are reasonable (for details, see "Arrival in Cassis," earlier). All destinations below require a transfer in Marseille.

From Cassis by Train to: Marseille (20/day, 25 minutes), **Aix-en-Provence Centre-Ville** (12/day, 1.5 hours), **Arles** (7/day, 2 hours), **Avignon TGV** (7/day, 2 hours), **Nice** (14/day, 3 hours, transfer in Marseille or Toulon), **Paris** (7/day, 4 hours).

Aix-en-Provence

Aix-en-Provence is famous for its outdoor markets and handsome pedestrian lanes, as well as its cultivated residents and their ability to embrace the good life. Nowhere else in France is *l'art de vivre* (the art of living) so stylishly displayed. It was that way when the French king made the town his administrative capital of Provence, and it's that way today. For a tourist, Aix-en-Provence (the "Aix" is pronounced "X") is happily free of any obligatory turnstiles. And there's not a single ancient site to see. It's just a wealthy town filled with 140,000 people—most of whom, it seems, know how to live well and look good. Aix-en-Provence's 40,000 well-dressed students (many from other countries) give the city a year-round youthful energy, and its numerous squares, lined with cafés and fine shops, allow everyone a comfortable place to pose.

Orientation to Aix-en-Provence

With no "must-see" sights, Aix works well as a day trip, and is best on days when the most markets thrive (Tue, Thu, and Sat). The city can be seen in a 1.5-hour stroll from the TI or train station, though connoisseurs of southern French culture will want more time to savor this lovely place. Aix makes a good base for day-tripping to Marseille, Cassis, and southern villages of the Luberon (such as Lourmarin).

Cours Mirabeau (the grand central boulevard) divides the stately, quiet Mazarin Quarter from the lively old town (where all the action is). In the old half, picturesque squares are connected by fine pedestrian shopping lanes, many of which lead to the cathedral. Right-angle intersections are rare in the old half—expect to get turned around regularly.

Tourist Information

The TI, France's grandest, is located at La Rotonde traffic circle. Get the walking-tour brochure *In the Footsteps of Cézanne,* with the best city-center map and a good overview of excursions in the area. The TI has other maps that cover areas beyond old Aix (Mon-Sat 8:30-19:00, Sun 10:00-13:00 & 14:00-18:00, longer hours in the summer, shorter hours in the winter, 300 Avenue Giuseppe Verdi, tel. 04 42 16 11 61, www.aixenprovencetourism.com).

English-language **walking tours** (shown on monitors in the TI) of the old town are offered at 10:00 on Tuesdays; Cézanne walking tours leave at 10:00 on Thursdays and Saturdays (€8, two hours, depart from the TI).

Daily **excursions** into the countryside—Luberon villages, Pont du Gard, Les Baux, wineries, Mt. Ste. Victoire, and more—are also available from the TI (figure on per-person costs of €60/half-day and €115-135/day).

Arrival in Aix-en-Provence

By Train: Aix-en-Provence has two train stations: Centre-Ville, near the city center, and the faraway TGV station. Neither has baggage storage.

Arrival at the Centre-Ville Station: It's a breezy 10-minute stroll to the TI and pedestrian area. Cross the boulevard in front of the station and walk up Avenue Victor Hugo; turn left at the first intersection (you're still on Victor Hugo). At the large fountain (La Rotonde), turn left and go about a quarter of the way around the fountain to find the TI.

Arrival at Aix-en-Provence TGV Station: Shuttle buses

(navettes) connect the distant TGV station with Aix-en-Provence's city-center bus station, described below (€4, 4/hour, 20 minutes). From the tracks, follow signs for *Navette-Direction Aix-en-Provence* to the end of the hall and downstairs (buses leave from an underpass below the tracks).

By Bus: Aix-en-Provence's bus station is located on Avenue de l'Europe near its intersection with Avenue des Belges (tel. 08 21 20 22 03). From the bus station, it's a 10-minute walk to the TI. Head slightly uphill to the flowery roundabout, turn left on Avenue des Belges, and walk to the splashing fountain (La Rotonde, the big traffic circle by the TI).

By Plane: Buses link Marseille's airport with the bus station in Aix-en-Provence (2/hour, 30 minutes, www.navetteaix tgvaeroport.com).

By Car: The city is well-signed (yellow for hotels, green for parking). First, follow signs to *Centre-Ville*, then the yellow signs to your hotel. If your hotel has parking, use it. Otherwise, once you've spotted your hotel sign, follow green signs to park in the first pay lot you see (I've noted the closest parking to each hotel under "Sleeping in Aix-en-Provence," later). Day-trippers should look for the La Rotonde parking area (near the TI) or park in any pay lot near the old city. Allow €14 for 24 hours of parking.

Helpful Hints

Markets: Aix-en-Provence bubbles over with photogenic open-air morning markets in several of its squares: **Richelme** (produce daily, my favorite), **Palace of Justice** (produce and flea market Tue, Thu, and Sat), **L'Hôtel de Ville** (flower market Tue, Thu, and Sat; book market first Sun of each month), and along **Cours Mirabeau** (textiles and crafts, Tue and Thu morning). Most pack up at 13:00, except the book market, which runs all day. Saturday market days are the biggest. It's well worth planning your visit for a market day, as these markets are the sightseeing highlights of the town. Jennifer Dugdale leads market tours (see "Tours in Aix-en-Provence," later).

Internet Access: There are many options; ask your hotelier or the TI for suggestions.

Services: Public WCs, as they're not stylish, are nonexistent in Aix. Take advantage of WCs in every restaurant, museum, or other stop you make.

English Bookstore: Located on the quiet side of Aix-en-Provence, the atmospheric **Book in Bar** has a great collection of adult and children's books, and a good selection of tourist guides (Cassis, Arles, Avignon, and so on). It's a good way to connect with the expat community; events such as author lectures and book-club meetings are held regularly. They also serve fine coffee and scones (Mon-Sat 9:00-19:00, closed Sun, 4 Rue Joseph Cabassol, where it crosses Rue Goyrand, tel. 04 42 26 60 07).

Laundry: Launderettes are scattered throughout the city. The best is **Ecolav'**, with free Wi-Fi, just behind the TI on Square Narvik at 3 Rue Lapierre (daily 7:00-21:00). Others are at 11 Rue des Bernardines and at 3 Rue Fernand Dol (both daily 8:00-19:00).

Supermarket: Monoprix, on Cours Mirabeau, two long blocks up from La Rotonde, has a grocery store in the basement (Mon-Sat 8:30-21:30, closed Sun), but you'll find small ones all over the city.

Taxi: Call 04 42 27 71 11 or mobile 06 16 23 82 39.

Car Rental: Avis and **Hertz** are at the Centre-Ville train station (43 Avenue Victor Hugo, tel. 04 42 27 91 32), and **Europcar** is near La Rotonde (55 Boulevard de la République, toll tel. 08 25 89 69 76). All major companies have offices at the TGV station.

Famous Local Product: Signs at fancy bakeries advertise *calissons*

Aix-en-Provence

200 Meters
200 Yards

1. Hôtel/Rest. Cézanne
2. To Chambre d'Hôte Pavillon de la Torse
3. L'Epicerie Chambres
4. Grand Hôtel Negre Coste
5. Hôtel Saint Christophe
6. Hôtel le Manoir
7. Hôtel Cardinal
8. Hôtel des Quatre Dauphins
9. Chez Feraud Restaurant
10. Pasta Cosy Restaurant
11. Chez Mitch Restaurant
12. Chez Charlotte Restaurant
13. Le Papagayo Café
14. Juste en Face Restaurant
15. Le Poivre d'Ane Restaurant
16. L'Epicurien Restaurant
17. Aux Deux Garçons Rest.
18. Le Grillon Restaurant
19. La Brochurie Restaurant
20. Boulangerie La Varenne
21. O'Shannon's Pub
22. Pub O'Sullivan
23. Café l'Unic & Brûlerie Richelme
24. Book In Bar Bookshop
25. Monoprix (Groceries)
26. Car Rentals (3)
27. Launderettes (3)

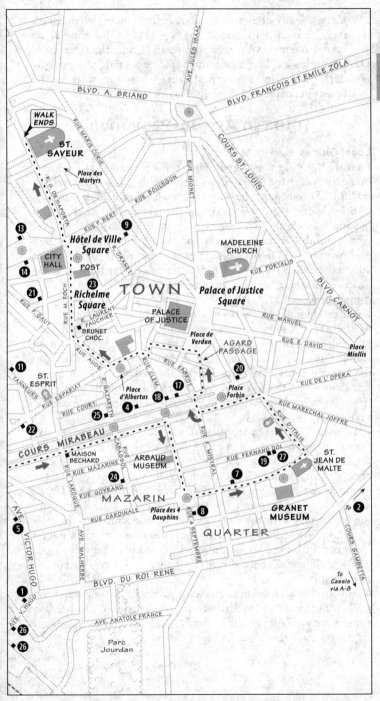

d'Aix, the city's homemade candy (which doesn't do much for me). It's made with almond paste—kind of like a marzipan cake—and makes a pleasing souvenir. I prefer the *macarons.*

Dark Sunglasses: You may want to pick up a pair of especially dark glasses (to be more discreet when appreciating the beautiful people of Aix-en-Provence).

Tours in Aix-en-Provence

Local Guides

Pascale Benguigui is a good choice for this area (also recommended earlier for Marseille; €156/half-day, €248/day, tel. 06 20 80 07 51, macpas@club-internet.fr). **Catherine d'Antuono** is a smart, capable guide for Aix-en-Provence, the Luberon, and beyond (mobile 06 17 94 69 61, tour.designer@provence-travel .com). **Sarah Pernet** is English born and bred but lives in Aix-en-Provence and offers enjoyable excursions within and from her adopted city (€80/half-day, €140/day, priced per person, www .discover-provence.net, discoverprovence@hotmail.com).

Culinary Tours

Jennifer Dugdale at **Tastes of Provence** introduces her clients to the art of living in Aix, with informative and delicious walking tours of the city's farmers' markets and specialty food stores. She offers two different three-hour tours that include top food destinations, intriguing shops, and tastings of local treats. Excursions into the Aix countryside are also available on request (€60/person, mobile 06 33 69 42 95, www.tastesofprovence.com).

Electric Minibus Joyride

For a mere €0.50, take an orientation ride on a *Diabline*—a six-seater electric-powered minibus. It leaves every 10 minutes from the La Rotonde fountain, opposite the TI (Mon-Sat 8:30-19:30, none on Sun, 40 minutes round-trip). You can also wave down the young drivers anywhere and hop on. There are three routes (A, B, and C); ask the driver for a map when you board. Line A gives you the best overview of the city and runs a route similar to the self-guided walk described later. It also gets you near Cézanne's studio. Designed with local seniors in mind, the minibus provides a fun (and less glamorous) slice-of-life experience in Aix-en-Provence.

Petit Train

Rest your feet and discover Aix-en-Provence's historic center on a 50-minute tour on the little train, while listening to English commentary (€7, departs from La Rotonde fountain). Ask about the longer tours that cover Cézanne's steps.

Aix-en-Provence History

Aix-en-Provence was founded in about 120 B.C. as a Roman military camp on the site of a thermal hot spring (in France, "Aix" refers to a city built over a hot spring). The Romans' mission: to defend the Greek merchants of Marseille against the local Celts. Strategically situated Aix-en-Provence was the first Roman base outside Italy—the first foreign holding of what would become a vast empire. (The region's name—Provence—comes from its status as the first Roman province.) But Rome eventually fell, and the barbarians destroyed Aix-en-Provence in the fourth century.  Through the Dark Ages, Aix-en-Provence's Roman buildings were nibbled to nothing by people needing the pre-cut stone. No buildings from Roman Aix-en-Provence survive.

Aix-en-Provence was of no importance through the Middle Ages. Because the area was once owned by Barcelona, Provence has the same colors as Catalunya: gold and red. In 1481 the Count of Provence died. He was hairless (according to my guide). Without a hair, Provence was gobbled up by France. When Aix-en-Provence was made the district's administrative center, noble French families moved in, kicking off the city's beautiful age (belle époque). They built about 200 *hôtels particuliers* (private mansions)—many of which survive today—giving Aix-en-Provence its classy look. As you wander around the town, look up, peek in, and notice the stately architecture with its grandiose extra touches.

Aix-en-Provence thrived thanks to its aristocratic population. But when the Revolution made being rich dicey, Aix-en-Provence's aristocracy and clergy fled. Aix-en-Provence entered the next stage of its history as the "Sleeping Beauty city." Later in the 19th century, the town woke up and resumed its familiar, pretentious ways. In Aix-en-Provence, the custom of rich people being bobbed along in sedan chairs survived longer than anywhere else in France. After the Revolution, you couldn't have servants do it—but you could hire pallbearers in their off-hours to give you a lift. If being ostentatious ever became the norm...it happened in Aix-en-Provence.

Self-Guided Walk

Welcome to Aix-en-Provence

I've listed these streets, squares, and sights in the order of a handy, lazy orientation stroll. This walk is highlighted on the map on page 298.

• *Start on Cours Mirabeau at La Rotonde, near the statues on either side of the street, and face...*

La Rotonde: In the 1600s, the roads from Paris and Marseille met just outside the Aix-en-Provence town wall at a huge roundabout called La Rotonde. From here locals enjoyed a sweeping view of open countryside before entering the town. As time passed, Aix-en-Provence needed space more than fortifications. The wall was destroyed and replaced by a grand boulevard (Cours Mirabeau). A modern grid-plan town, the Mazarin Quarter, arose across the boulevard from the medieval town (to the right as you look up Cours Mirabeau). In 1860, to give residents water and shade, the town graced La Rotonde with a fountain and a grand boulevard lined with trees. The three figures on top of the fountain represent Justice, Agriculture, and Fine Arts. *Voilà:* The modern core of Aix-en-Provence was created. The new Apple store facing La Rotonde is the latest feather in Aix's style cap, assuring locals that they are still among the chosen few.

• *Saunter slowly up the right side of Cours Mirabeau.*

Cours Mirabeau: This "Champs-Elysées of Provence" divides the higgledy-piggledy old town and the stately Mazarin Quarter. Designed for the rich and famous to strut their fancy stuff, Cours Mirabeau survives much as it was: a single lane for traffic and an extravagant pedestrian promenade, shaded by plane trees (see sidebar) and lined by 17th- and 18th-century mansions for the nobility. Rich folks lived on the right side (in the Mazarin Quarter); common folk lived on the left side (in the old town). Cross-streets were gated to keep everyone in their place. Which side are you sleeping on?

The street follows a plan based on fours: 440 meters long,

Plane Trees

Stately old plane trees line roads and provide canopies of shade for town squares all over southern France. These trees are a part of the local scene.

The plane tree is a hybrid of the Asian and American sycamores—created accidentally in a 16th-century Oxford botanical garden. The result was the perfect city tree: fast-growing, resistant to urban pollution, and hearty (it can survive with little water and lousy soil). The plane tree was imported to southern France in the 19th century to replace the traditional elm trees. Napoleon planted them along roads to give his soldiers shade for their long marches. Plane trees were used to leaf up grand boulevards as towns throughout France—including Aix-en-Provence—built their Champs-Elysées wannabes.

44 meters wide, plane trees (originally elms) 4 meters apart, and decorated by 4 fountains. The "mossy fountains," covered by 200 years of neglect, trickle with water from the thermal spa that gave Aix its first name (and make steamy sights on cold winter days).

Cours Mirabeau was designed for showing off. Today, it remains a place for *tendance* (trendiness)—or even *hyper-tendance*. Show your stuff and strut the broad sidewalk. As you stroll up the boulevard, stop in front of Aix's oldest and most venerated *patisserie,* **Maison Béchard** (on the right side at 12 Cours Mirabeau) and get a whiff coming from the vent under the entry.

• *Keep on strutting. From the mossy fountain at Rue du 4 Septembre, turn right onto Aix-en-Provence's quiet side, the pleasing little Place des Quatre Dauphins. This marks the center of the...*

Mazarin Quarter (Quartier Mazarin): Built in a grid plan during the reign of King Louis XIV, the Mazarin Quarter remains a peaceful, elegant residential neighborhood—although each of its mansions now houses several families rather than just one. Study the quarter's Baroque and Neoclassical architecture (from the 17th and 18th centuries). The square's Fountain of the Four Dolphins, inspired by Bernini's fountains in Rome, dates from an age when Italian culture set the Baroque standard across Europe. Appreciate how calm this half of the city feels.

Wander up Rue Cardinale to the vertical church, St. Jean-de-Malte, which faces a handsome square. The **Musée Granet** sits next door and features Aix's homegrown artists (including several "lesser" paintings by Cézanne—see sidebar). The museum is most popular for its selection of works from the Planque Collection, often including some by Picasso, Dufy, Monet, Van Gogh, and Braque. Check its website to see what works are on display and to learn about current exhibits, or ask at the TI (museum open June-Sept Tue-Sun 10:00-19:00, Oct-May Tue-Sun 12:00-18:00, closed Mon year-round, www.museegranet-aixenprovence.fr).

• *Turn left on Rue d'Italie behind the church and return to Cours Mirabeau. At the top of the boulevard, a statue celebrates the last count of Provence, during whose rule this region joined France. Stroll down the right side of the street to #53, and spot the venerable...*

Aux Deux Garçons: This café, once frequented by Paul Cézanne, is now popular with—and controlled by—the local mafia. Don't take photos here (and don't open a competing café—the mafia is a serious problem for many independent restaurateurs in Aix). Still, it's worth a peek for its beautiful circa-1790 interior and, for many, worth the higher (mafia-inflated) prices for the sidewalk setting. The Cézanne family hat shop was next door (#55). Cézanne's dad must have been some hatter. He parlayed that successful business into a bank, then into greater wealth, setting up his son to be free to enjoy his artistic pursuits.

• *From here we'll enter the lively Old Town, where pedestrian streets are filled with fine food stores and boutiques, and romantic street musicians. This is the place in Aix-en-Provence for shopping. Leave Cours Mirabeau at #55, through the tiny Passage Agard. It leads to the* **Palace of Justice Square,** *which hosts a bustling flea market (Tue, Thu, and Sat mornings). If the market is on, dally awhile. Leave this square heading left along the first street you crossed as you came into the square. The street you're on, Rue Marius Reinaud, hosts the top designer shops in town. Pause several blocks down when you hear the gurgling of water at the peaceful courtyard square called...*

Place d'Albertas: This sweet little square was created by the guy who lived across the street. He hated the medieval mess of buildings facing his mansion, so he drew up a harmonious facade with a fountain, and hired an architect to build his ideal vision and mask the ugly neighborhood. The neighbors got a nice new facade, and the rich guy got the view of his dreams. The long-overdue restoration of this once run-

down square is making a remarkable difference. But since only two-thirds of the property owners agreed to help fund the work, one-third remains undone.

With your back to the fountain, find the large wooden door on the building across the street. Take a look at the names on the door buzzers—the Albertas family still lives here. Behind this door is one of the most beautiful private courtyards in Aix.

• *From here turn right on Rue Aude, the main street of medieval Aix-en-Provence (which turns into Rue du Maréchal Foch). Notice the side streets, with their traffic-barrier stumps that lower during delivery hours. Turn right at Rue Laurent Fauchier, and detour down a few steps for a decadent* macaron *sensation at...*

Brunet Chocolatier and Macarons (closed Sun-Mon): Here you'll find *macarons*, those wonderful cookies made of cloud-like almond meringue sandwiched between luscious butter creams. They're the rage throughout France, nowhere more than here in Aix. You'll find them in every color and flavor imaginable. Try the caramel with salted butter, pistachio, or black-current violet. Though this confection's origins are vague (some claim they came from Italy in the 16th century), what matters is that they're delicious.

• *Try one or two, then continue on to...*

Richelme Square (Place Richelme): This wonderful square hosts a lively market, as it has since the 1300s (daily 8:00-13:00). It's the perfect Provençal scene—lovely buildings, plane trees, and farmers selling local produce. You'll also find two famous goat-cheese merchants. Bruno is a former marketing executive who purchased goats rather than a Ferrari during his midlife crisis. You can find his cheese (as well as pictures of his herd) on Tuesdays, Thursdays, and Saturdays on the Rue Maréchal Foch side of the market. The other famous goat-cheese stall is near the Bar de l'Horloge; the owner looks just like Paul Cézanne—or Jerry Garcia, if that's more your style. (He works Saturdays only and is fully aware of his special good looks; drop by for a sample and a photo if you like.) The cafés at the end of the square are ideal for market observation. To savor the market scene, pause for a drink at Café l'Unic (also draws a lively and young pre-dinner crowd). To experience the best coffee and hot chocolate in Aix, grab an outdoor stool and go local at Brûlerie Richelme (Tue-Sat 8:30-19:00, closed Sun-Mon).

• *One block uphill is the stately...*

L'Hôtel de Ville Square (Place de l'Hôtel de Ville): This square, also known as Place de la Mairie, is anchored by a Roman column. Stand with your back to the column and face the Hôtel de Ville. The center niche of this 17th-century City Hall once featured a bust of Louis XIV. But since the Revolution, Marianne (the Lady of the Republic) has taken his place. As throughout Europe, the three flags represent the region (Provence), country (France), and the European Union. Provence's flag carries the red and yellow of Catalunya (the region in Spain centered on Barcelona) because the counts of Provence originated there. Aix-en-Provence's coat of arms over the doorway combines the Catalan flag and the French fleur-de-lis.

The 18th-century building on your left was once the town's corn exchange (today it's a letter exchange). Its exuberant pediment features figures representing the two rivers of Provence: old man Rhône and madame Durance. While the Durance River floods frequently (here depicted overflowing its frame), it also brings fertility to the fields (hence the cornucopia).

Back toward Hôtel de Ville, the 16th-century bell tower was built in part with stones scavenged from ancient Roman buildings—notice the white stones at the tower's base. The niche above the arch once displayed the bust of the king. Since the Revolution, it has housed a funerary urn that symbolically honors all who gave their lives for French liberty. Walk under the arch to see a small plaque honoring the American 3rd Division that liberated the town in 1944 (with the participation of French troops; Aix-en-Provence got through World War II relatively unscathed).

History aside, the square is a delight for its vintage French storefronts and colorful morning markets: flowers (Tue, Thu, and Sat) and old books (first Sun of the month). On non-market days and each afternoon, café tables replace the market stalls.

• Stroll under the bell tower and up Rue Gaston de Saporta to the...

Cathedral of the Holy Savior (Saint-Sauveur): This church was built atop the Roman forum—likely on the site of a pagan temple. As the cathedral grew with the city, its interior became a parade of architectural styles. The many-faceted interior is at once confusing and fascinating, with three distinct sections: Standing at the entrance, you face the Romanesque section; to the left are the Gothic and then the Baroque sections. We'll visit each in turn (church open Mon-Sat 8:00-12:00 & 14:00-18:00, Sun 9:00-12:00 & 14:00-19:00).

In the **Romanesque section,** step down to the right to find the baptistery, with its early Christian (fourth-century) Roman font. It was located outside the church until the 14th century, when the church was expanded to house the baptistery. The font is big enough for immersion, which was the baptismal style in Roman times. Also notice that it's eight-sided, symbolizing eternity: one side more than the seven days it took God to create everything.

Paul Cézanne in Aix-en-Provence

Post-Impressionist artist Paul Cézanne (1839-1906) loved Aix-en-Provence. He studied law at the university (opposite the cathedral), and produced most of  his paintings in and around Aix-en-Provence—even though this conservative town didn't understand him or his art. Today the city fathers milk anything remotely related to his years here. But because the conservative curator of the town's leading art gallery, the Granet Museum, decreed "no Cézannes," you can see only some of Cézanne's lesser original paintings in Aix-en-Provence. Bad curator.

Instead, fans of the artist will want to pick up the *In the Footsteps of Cézanne* self-guided-tour flier at the TI, and follow the bronze pavement markers around town.

Atelier Cézanne, the artist's last studio, has been preserved as it was when he died and is open to the public. It's a 30-minute walk from the TI, or you can get there on electric minibus A (see "Tours in Provence," earlier). Although there is no art here, his tools and personal belongings make it almost interesting for enthusiasts—I'd skip it. If you must go, it's best (and essential in high season) to reserve a visit time in advance at the TI or at www.aixenprovencetourism.com.

Cost and Hours: €6, daily July-Aug 10:00-18:00, April-June and Sept 10:00-12:00 & 14:00-18:00, Oct-March until 17:00, English-language tours usually at 17:00, 2 miles from TI at 9 Avenue Cézanne, tel. 04 42 16 10 91, www.atelier-cezanne.com.

The font is surrounded by ancient columns with original fourth-century capitals below a Renaissance cupola.

Farther down is the door to the 12th-century cloister (visits on the half-hour except 12:00-14:00). After passing a side chapel, find the closet-sized architectural footprint of the original Christian chapel from the Roman era several feet below floor level. Like the baptistery, this would have been outside the current church walls until the 14th century.

In the **Gothic section,** two organs flank the nave: One works, but the other is a prop, added for looks...an appropriately symmetrical Neoclassical touch, as was the style in the 18th century (notice the lack of depth in one of them). The precious door (facing the street from this section) is carved of chestnut wood, with a Gothic top (showing sibyls, or ancient female prophets) and Renaissance lower half (depicting prophets). Because it faces the street, it's covered by a second, protective door (viewable on request).

In the **Baroque section,** don't miss the three-paneled altar painting of the burning bush (Buisson Ardent, 15th century, by Nicolas Froment). This finely detailed painting was rescued from a convent that was flattened during the French Revolution. The central panel shows the Virgin and Child on the burning bush as Moses looks on in amazement.

• *Your tour is over. Walking back through town, drop by a designer bakery to try a* calisson, *Aix-en-Provence's local candy (see "Helpful Hints," earlier). Or, for fewer calories and just as much fun, marvel at a town filled with people who seem to be living life very, very well.*

Sleeping in Aix-en-Provence

Hotel rooms, starting at about €70, are surprisingly reasonable in this highbrow city. Reserve ahead, particularly on weekends. Hotel stars have less meaning here. The best values are on the quiet side of Cours Mirabeau in the Mazarin Quarter.

$$$ Hôtel Cézanne****, a block up from the Centre-Ville train station, delivers professional service with a smile. The lobby and 55 plush, spacious rooms are *très* modern, with all the comforts. This stylish place pampers guests with an efficient, English-speaking staff (including your chef, adorable Christianne) and amenities like a daily champagne "brunch" that comes with French toast, omelets, fresh fruit, and smoked salmon (€20, served until noon, try the French toast with honey and the truffle omelet) and free nonalcoholic drinks from your minibar (standard Db-€250, deluxe Db-€350, some king-size beds, air-con, elevator, free parking if you book ahead, free and easy guest computer and Wi-Fi, 40 Avenue Victor Hugo, tel. 04 42 91 11 11, www.hotelaix .com, hotelcezanne@hotelaix.com).

$$$ Chambre d'Hôte Pavillon de la Torse is an upscale B&B in a park-like setting. A line of plane trees escorts you down a private lane into this urban retreat. Pass the 25-meter lap pool surrounded by gardens that Louis would appreciate, then get to know eager-to-help American Mary and Frenchman François, who offer every ame- nity (Db-€160-200, €20 less Nov and March; extra bed-€20 for kids who must be 5 or older, €50

for adults; 2-night minimum, includes breakfast, guest computer and Wi-Fi, easy parking, 20-30-minute walk south of the old city at 69 Cours Gambetta, tel. 09 50 58 49 96, www.latorse.com, contact@latorse.com).

$$$ L'Epicerie Chambres is an unusual place owned by an avid collector. The reception is a nostalgic general store, and the five rooms are well-conceived and very comfortable (Db-€100-130, Tb suite-€150, includes breakfast, air-con, limited check-in hours, a block off Forum des Cardeurs at 12 Rue du Cancel, mobile 06 08 85 38 68, www.unechambreenville.eu).

$$ Grand Hôtel Negre Coste** occupies a privileged position at the center of Cours Mirabeau. This once grand, now not-so-grand hotel houses a formal staff and traditional if unimaginative rooms, and may have rooms when others don't (Db-€100-115, big Db-€165, air-con, guest computer and Wi-Fi, private garage-€10, 33 Cours Mirabeau, tel. 04 42 27 74 22, www.hotelnegrecoste.com, contact@hotelnegrecoste.com).

$$ Hôtel Saint Christophe**, an impersonal business hotel with acceptable rates, is located just off La Rotonde and above a swanky brasserie. It has 58 tight but well-equipped rooms, some with small terraces (Db-€118-140, mezzanine sleeps up to 4-€170-185, air-con, elevator, parking garage-€14, 2 Avenue Victor Hugo, tel. 04 42 26 01 24, www.hotel-saintchristophe.com, saint christophe@francemarket.com).

$$ Hôtel le Manoir***, built on the heavy arches of a medieval monastery, is modest, peaceful, and central. The decor is simple and traditional, the staff is laid-back, and the setting is ideal (smallish Db-€80, standard Db-€100-120, Tb-€120, elevator, Wi-Fi, limited free parking, 8 Rue d'Entrecasteaux, tel. 04 42 26 27 20, www.hotelmanoir.com, resa@hotelmanoir.com).

$$ Hôtel Cardinal** is a top value on Aix-en-Provence's classy side, across Cours Mirabeau from the pedestrian zone. It's a homey, shy, rose-colored hotel with 29 wonderfully traditional rooms with many personal touches and a modern elevator and air-conditioning. The paintings hanging on the walls in public spaces were done by the owner Nathalie's papa (Sb-€69, Db-€79, cavernous Db suite in nearby annex-€117, Wi-Fi, closest parking is Mignet, 24 Rue Cardinale, tel. 04 42 38 32 30, www.hotel-cardinal -aix.com, hotel.cardinal@wanadoo.fr).

$$ Hôtel des Quatre Dauphins** is a simple and sweet little place in the quiet quarter with soft rooms, Old World decor, and excellent rates (Db-€70-85, bigger Db-€90-105, Tb-€105-120, air-con, no elevator, three floors, Wi-Fi, closest parking is Mignet, 54 Rue Roux Alphéran, tel. 04 42 38 16 19, www.lesquatredauphins .fr, lesquatredauphins@wanadoo.fr).

Eating in Aix-en-Provence

In Aix-en-Provence, you can dine on bustling squares, along a grand boulevard, or in little restaurants on side streets (where you'll find the best values). Cours Mirabeau is good for desserts and drinks, as are many of the outdoor places lining leafy squares. Aix is filled with tempting but mediocre restaurants. To eat higher on the food chain, try one of the following places.

In the Old Town

Chez Feraud, in a lovely vine-covered building that requires some extra time to find, is a good choice for a traditional dinner of authentic Provençal dishes. While maybe past its prime, this Old World place features a mother-son team: Mama serves with formal grace while son handles the grill (€30 *menu*, 8 Rue du Puits Juif, tel. 04 42 63 07 27).

Pasta Cosy is unique, serving a Franco-Italian fusion of original dishes in a small, cozy setting (inside and out). It's also family- and tourist-friendly, thanks to welcoming owner Fabien. He greets every client with the same enthusiasm—and with fluent English—and loves taking care of his guests. Split the antipasta-tapas appetizer (up to nine items), and be tempted by his rich Pastacosy dish (pasta cooked inside a wheel of parmesan cheese). Try the *fiocchetti* (pasta cooked with pears and gorgonzola) or the gourmet white truffle pasta. Desserts are homemade and delicious. The reasonably priced wine list features wines from Burgundy and Provence (closed Sun-Mon except open Mon in summer, across from Hôtel le Manoir at 5 Rue d'Entrecasteaux, tel. 04 42 38 02 28).

Chez Mitch is a fine choice for classic French cuisine with modern flair. Overlook the trendy decor, and savor the seasonal dishes, excellent wine list, and top-notch service that Mitch assures. Book ahead for weekends (€30-50 *menus*, closed Sun, vaulted dining room downstairs, 26 Rue des Tanneurs, tel. 04 42 26 63 08, www.mitchrestaurant.com).

Chez Charlotte is Aix's low-key, down-and-dirty diner, where old-school residents come for a good meal at a good price. A young couple, Laurent and Nathalie, are your hosts (he cooks, she makes pastry). The dining area is simple and convivial; come early to snag a cheery garden table (€19 three-course *menu* only, no à la carte, closed Sun-Mon, 32 Rue des Bernardines, tel. 04 42 26 77 56).

The recommended **Hôtel Cézanne** serves up a gourmet champagne brunch *à la française*. For €20 you can feast on a great selection of omelets (made with caramelized goat cheese or truffles) and sample real French toast (brunch served daily 7:00-12:00, 40 Avenue Victor Hugo, www.hotelaix.com).

On Forum des Cardeurs: Just off L'Hôtel de Ville Square, the Forum des Cardeurs is café-crammed. Browse the selection from

top to bottom, then decide. At the top, **Le Papagayo** has a good selection of salads and a quiche of the day (big €14 salads, open daily for lunch and dinner, 22 Forum des Cardeurs, tel. 04 42 23 98 35). **Juste en Face,** facing Papagayo, features grilled meats (the duck and rabbit are tasty) and Mediterranean cuisine, specializing in North African *tajine*—a vegetable-based stew usually served with meat (€16-20 *plats*, open daily, 6 Rue Verrerie, tel. 04 42 96 47 70).

Discerning diners should try one of these two places that face each other at the lower end of the big square. These restaurants are the talk of the city, so book ahead on weekends:

Le Poivre d'Ane has a stylish interior and good terrace tables. *Le chef* describes his cuisine as inventive and audacious (€30 three-course *menu*, €45 five-course *menu*, 40 Forum des Cardeurs, tel. 04 42 21 32 66, www.restaurantlepoivredane.com).

L'Epicurien has just eight tables, allowing the chef to maintain his top-quality standards. The cuisine is elegant and creatively Provençal (*menus* from €33-46, open Wed-Sat for dinner and Mon-Sat for lunch, closed Sun, 13 Forum des Cardeurs, tel. 06 89 33 49 83).

Along Cours Mirabeau

If you're interested in a delicious view more than delicious food, eat with style on Cours Mirabeau.

Aux Deux Garçons has always been the place to see and be seen: a vintage brasserie with door-to-door waiters in aprons, a lovely interior, and well-positioned outdoor tables with properly placed silverware on white tablecloths. It's busy at lunch but quiet for dinner (€20-30 *plats,* three-course *menus* from €25, great steak tartare, open daily, 53 Cours Mirabeau, tel. 04 42 26 00 51, www .les2garcons.fr). Even if you're not eating here, pop in to see the decor (see page 304).

Le Grillon is a younger, more boisterous choice for dinner on Cours Mirabeau (white tablecloths, €20 *plats*, €15-30 *menu*). Its bar is a hit with locals for the prime seating: front and center on the boulevard's strolling fashion show (open daily for lunch and dinner, corner of Rue Clémenceau and Cours Mirabeau, tel. 04 42 27 58 81, http://cafelegrillon.free.fr).

In the Mazarin Quarter

La Brocherie dishes up French rather than Provençal cuisine. Its stone-rustic, indoors-only ambience is best for cooler days. This family-owned bistro—run by Messieurs Soudain and Tourville—is deep in the Mazarin Quarter and highlights food from the farm (it's about beef). Dig into the hearty self-service salad buffet (all you can eat, €12) and meats grilled over a wood fire (skip the fish options). The €20 *menu* includes the salad bar (closed Sat for lunch and Sun all day, indoor seating only, 5 Rue Fernand Dol, tel. 04 42 38 33 21).

Le Late-Night

Aix is the only French city I know of with a 24/7 bakery. Find **Boulangerie La Varenne** at the non-Rotonde end of Cours Mirabeau (around the left side of the building that seals the street's upper end, across from #6, Rue la Tournefort). Their chocolate-chip cookies are a rare treat.

    Bar Hopping: For the young—and young at heart—the best action centers on Rue de la Verrerie. **O'Shannon's Pub** (#30) makes a great starting point for your evening out, as does **Pub O'Sullivan**, near La Rotonde, next to Hôtel de France on Place des Augustins.

Aix-en-Provence Connections

Remember, Aix-en-Provence has both a TGV station and a Centre-Ville train station (see "Arrival in Aix-en-Provence," earlier). In some cases, destinations are served from both stations; I've listed the station with the best connection. And for some destinations, the bus is a faster option than the train (these are noted at the end of this section).

    From Aix-en-Provence's Center to the TGV Station by Bus or Car: Buses from Aix-en-Provence to the TGV station depart from the bus station (on Avenue de l'Europe, near intersection with Avenue des Belges, tel. 08 21 20 22 03). To find the TGV by car from Aix-en-Provence, get on the A-51 autoroute toward *Marseille*, get off at the first exit (Les Milles), and follow signs for another 10 minutes. There's a small kiosk café in front of the TGV station with sandwiches, drinks, and such.

    From Aix-en-Provence's Centre-Ville Station by Train to: Marseille (2/hour, 45 minutes), **Cassis** (12/day, 1.5 hours, transfer in Marseille), **Arles** (10/day, 2.25 hours, transfer in Marseille; train may separate midway—be sure you're in section going to Arles).

    From Aix-en-Provence's TGV Station by Train to: Avignon TGV (10/day, 25 minutes), **Nice** (10/day, 2-3.5 hours, usually change in Marseille), **Paris** (14/day, 3 hours, may require transfer in Lyon).

From Aix-en-Provence by Bus to: Marseille (4/hour, 35 minutes), **Marseille's airport** (2/hour, 35 minutes), **Avignon** (6/day Mon-Sat, 2/day Sun, 75 min, faster and easier than train), **Arles** (faster than trains, 5/day Mon-Sat, 2/day Sun, 1.5 hours), **Lourmarin** (1.25 hours, 3/day, may require transfer in Pertuis), **Nice** (4/day, 2 hours—this is a cheaper and quicker option than taking the train).

THE FRENCH RIVIERA

THE FRENCH RIVIERA

La Côte d'Azur

A hundred years ago, celebrities from London to Moscow flocked to the French Riviera to socialize, gamble, and escape the dreary weather at home. Today, budget vacationers and heat-seeking Europeans fill belle-époque resorts at France's most sought-after fun-in-the-sun destination.

The region got its nickname from turn-of-the-20th-century vacationing Brits, who simply extended the Italian Riviera west to France to include Nice. Today, the Riviera label stretches even farther westward, running (for our purposes) from the Italian border to St-Tropez. To the French, this summer fun zone is known as *La Côte d'Azur*. All my French Riviera destinations are on the sea, except for a few hill towns and the Gorges du Verdon.

This sunny sliver of land has been inhabited for more than 3,000 years. Ligurians were first, then Greeks, then Romans—who, as usual, had the greatest impact. After the fall of Rome, Nice became an important city in the Kingdom of Provence (along with Marseille and Arles). In the 14th century Nice's leaders voted to throw their beach towel in with the duke of Savoy's mountainous kingdom (also including several regions of northern Italy), which would later evolve into the Kingdom of Sardinia. It was not until 1860 that Nice (and Savoy) became a part of France—the result of a citywide vote made possible by Napoleon III and the king of Sardinia.

Nice has world-class museums, a splendid beachfront promenade, a seductive old town, and all the drawbacks of a major city (traffic, crime, pollution, and so on). The day-trip possibilities are easy and exciting: Monte Carlo welcomes everyone with money to spend and will happily take your cash; Antibes has a thriving port and silky sand beaches; and image-conscious Cannes is the Riviera's self-appointed queen, with an elegant veneer hiding...very

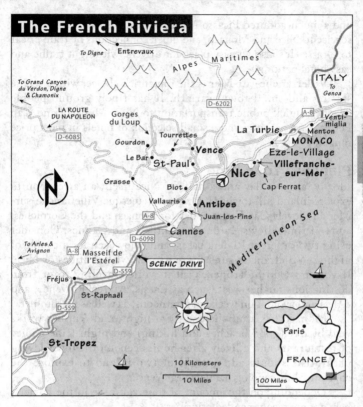

little. Yacht-happy St-Tropez swims alone an hour west (halfway to Cassis and Marseille). The Riviera's overlooked interior transports travelers to a world apart, with cliff-hanging villages, impossibly steep canyons, and alpine scenery—a refreshing alternative to the beach scene.

Choose a Home Base

My favorite home bases are Nice, Antibes, and Villefranche-sur-Mer.

Nice is the region's capital and France's fifth-largest city. With convenient train and bus connections to most regional sights, this is the most practical base for train travelers. Urban Nice also has a full palette of museums (most of which are free), a beach scene that rocks, the best selection of hotels in all price ranges, and good nightlife options. A car is a headache in Nice, though it's easily stored at one of the many pricey parking garages or for free at an outer tram station.

Nearby **Antibes** is smaller, with a bustling center, a lively night scene, great sandy beaches, grand vistas, good walking trails, and a much-admired Picasso Museum. Antibes has frequent train service to Nice and Monaco, and quick connections by train or car to Grasse. It's also an easy place for drivers, with light traffic and easy hotel parking.

Villefranche-sur-Mer is the romantic's choice, with a serene setting and small-town warmth. It has finely ground pebble beaches; quick public transportation to Nice, Monaco, and Cap Ferrat; easy parking; and a small selection of hotels in most price ranges.

Planning Your Time

Ideally, allow a day and a half for Nice itself, an afternoon to explore inland hill towns, a day for Italianesque Villefranche-sur-Mer and lovely Cap Ferrat, a day for Monaco and the Corniches, and—if time allows—a day for Antibes and Cannes. Consider using two different Riviera bases, and enjoy each for a couple of nights—Villefranche-sur-Mer pairs well with Antibes or Nice. If you must do St-Tropez, visit it while traveling to or from destinations farther west (such as Cassis, Aix-en-Provence, and Arles) and avoid it on weekend afternoons, as well as all summer.

Monaco has a unique energy at night, and Antibes works well by day (good beaches and hiking) and night (fine choice of restaurants and a lively after-hours scene). Hill-town-loving naturalists should add a night or two inland to explore the charming hill-capping hamlets near Vence.

Depending on the amount of time you have in the Riviera, here are my recommended priorities:

3 days:	Nice, Villefranche-sur-Mer with Cap Ferrat, and Monaco
5 days, add:	Antibes and maybe Cannes, and hill towns near Vence
7 days, add:	Grand Canyon du Verdon and St-Tropez

Helpful Hints

Medical Help: Riviera Medical Services has a list of English-speaking physicians all along the Riviera. They can help you make an appointment or call an ambulance (tel. 04 93 26 12 70, www.rivieramedical.com).

Closed Days: The following sights are closed on Mondays: the Modern and Contemporary Art Museum, Fine Arts Museum, Russian Cathedral, and Cours Saleya market in Nice, along with Antibes' Picasso Museum and Marché Provençal market (Sept-June). On Tuesdays these museums are closed: the Chagall, Matisse, Masséna, and Archaeological museums in Nice; the Renoir Museum in Cagnes-sur-Mer; and the Museum of the Annonciade in St-Tropez. On Fridays

Matisse's Chapel of the Rosary in Vence is closed.

Events: The Riviera is famous for staging major events. Unless you're actually taking part in the festivities, these occasions give you only room shortages and traffic jams. Here are the three biggies: **Nice Carnival** (Feb 14-March 4 in 2014, www.nicecarnaval.com), Festival de Cannes, better known as the **Cannes Film Festival** (May 14-24 in 2014, www.festival-cannes.com), and the **Grand Prix of Monaco** (May 22-25 in 2014, May 21-24 in 2015, www.acm.mc).

Local Guides: Agnès Dumartin, a top guide for the region, is a good teacher who understands Nice particularly well and loves all forms of art (€205/half-day, €295/day, mobile 06 81 82 17 67, agnes.dumartin@orange.fr). **Sylvie Di Cristo** offers terrific full-day tours throughout the French Riviera in a car or minivan. She adores educating people about this area's culture and history, and loves adapting her tour to your interests, from overlooked hill towns to wine, cuisine, art, or perfume (€200-250/person for 2-3 people, €120-150/person for 4-6 people, €90-100/person for 7-8 people, 2-person minimum, mobile 06 09 88 83 83, www.frenchrivieraguides.net, dicristosylvie@gmail.com). **Sofia Villavicencio** is a pleasant guide who makes the Riviera's art come alive (€145/half-day, €200/day, mobile 06 68 51 55 52, sofia.villavicencio@laposte.net). **Boba Vukadinovic** enjoys sharing her passion for her adoptive home. Her good tours of Nice and the Riviera are tailored to the sights and topics that appeal to you (€250/half-day, €350/day, mobile 06 27 45 68 39, www.yourguideboba.com, boba@yourguideboba.com).

Cooking Tour and Classes: Charming Canadian Francophile Rosa Jackson, a food journalist, Cordon Bleu-trained cook, and longtime resident of France, runs **Les Petits Farcis**, which offers three-hour "Taste of Nice" food tours for €90. She also teaches popular cooking classes in Vieux Nice, which include a morning trip to the open-air market on Cours Saleya to pick up ingredients, and an afternoon session spent creating an authentic Niçois meal from your purchases (€195/person, mobile 06 81 67 41 22, www.petitsfarcis.com).

Minivan Tours: The TI and most hotels have information on minivan excursions from Nice (roughly €50-70/half-day, €80-110/day). **Revelation Tours** takes pride in its guides (mobile 06 27 05 67 77, www.revelation-tours.com). **Med-Tour** is one of many (tel. 04 93 82 92 58, mobile 06 73 82 04 10, www.med-tour.com); **Tour Azur** is another (tel. 04 93 44 88 77, www.tourazur.com). All also offer private tours by the day or half-day (check with them for their outrageous prices, about €100/hour).

Cruise-Ship Sightseeing: The French Riviera is a popular cruise destination. Arriving ships are divided about evenly between three ports: Nice, Villefranche-sur-Mer, and Monaco. I've provided arrival instructions in the "Connections" section at the end of each of those destination chapters. Because these three ports line up conveniently along a 10-mile stretch of coast—easily connected by train or bus—from any of them, you'll have the Riviera by the tail. Consider hiring a local guide to help make the most of your limited time in port (listed earlier). A few smaller ships also call at Cannes, farther west. If your cruise includes destinations beyond the French Riviera, consider my guidebook, *Rick Steves' Mediterranean Cruise Ports.*

Getting Around the Riviera

If taking the train or bus, have coins handy. Ticket machines don't take US credit cards or euro bills, smaller train stations may be unstaffed, and bus drivers can't make change for large bills.

By Public Transportation: Trains and buses do a good job of connecting places along the coast, with bonus views along many routes. Buses also provide reasonable service to some inland hill towns. Choose the bus for convenience and economy, or the pricier but faster train when you want to save time.

Buses are an amazing deal. The Côte d'Azur has a single regional transportation network—Lignes d'Azur (www.lignes dazur.com). Any one-way bus or tram ride costs €1.50 (€10 for 10 tickets) whether you're riding 20 minutes to Villefranche-sur-Mer, 45 minutes to Monaco, or an hour to Antibes. The €1.50 ticket is good for 74 minutes of travel in one direction anywhere within the bus system except for airport buses (and can't be used  for a round-trip). Buy your bus ticket from the driver (be sure to carry small bills or coins) or from the machines at stops, and validate your ticket in the machine on board. You can even transfer between the buses of the Lignes d'Azur and the smaller TAM (Transports Alpes-Maritimes) system; if you board a TAM bus and need a transfer, ask for *un ticket correspondance.* A €6 all-day ticket is good on Nice's city buses, tramway, and airport express bus, plus selected buses serving nearby destinations (such as Villefranche, Cap Ferrat, and Eze-le-Village).

The **train** is more expensive, but there's no quicker way to move about the Riviera (http://en.voyages-sncf.com/en). Speedy trains link the Riviera's beachfront destinations—Cannes, Antibes, Nice, Villefranche-sur-Mer, Monaco, Menton, and the inland perfume town of Grasse. If in Nice, Villefranche, or Monaco, you can assume trains marked for *Vintimille* or *Menton* are going east, and those marked for *Grasse, Cannes,* or *Nice* are going west. Never board a train without a ticket or valid pass— fare inspectors don't accept any excuses, and the minimum fine is €70.

Nice makes the most convenient base for day trips, though public transport also works well from smaller Riviera towns such as Antibes and Villefranche-sur-Mer. St-Tropez is remote, requiring a bus or boat connection. Details are provided under each destination's "Connections" section. For a scenic inland train ride, take the narrow-gauge train into the Alps (see page 348).

And a final tip: No matter where you go, bring along a swimsuit if the weather's sunny—good beaches are plentiful.

For an overview of many Riviera train and bus connections, see the "Public Transportation in the French Riviera" chart on the next spread. The bus frequencies given are for Monday-Saturday (Sunday often has limited or no bus service)—confirm all connections and last train/bus times locally. I've listed some connections as "not recommended" due to the amount of time spent in transit and/or the number of transfers required.

By Car: After Paris, this is France's most challenging region to drive in. Beautifully distracting vistas (natural and human), loads of Sunday-driver tourists, and an overabundance of cars make for a dangerous combination; pay extra attention while driving down here. Parking can be tricky for the same reasons, so bring your patience. Have lots of coins ready for parking and for autoroute tolls.

The Riviera is awash with scenic roads. To sample some of the Riviera's best scenery, drivers should find the splendid coastal road between Cannes and Fréjus (D-6098 from Cannes/D-559 from Fréjus), which works well when connecting the Riviera with Provence. If it weren't for the Mediterranean sea below, you'd swear you were in Arizona (in Fréjus, follow signs to *Centre-Ville*, then *Cannes par la Bord de la Mer;* from Cannes, drive to the western end of town and follow *La Napoule* signs to reach the road).

Drivers should also scour the three coastal roads—called "corniches"—between Nice and Monaco (see page 407) and take my recommended inland hill-towns drive (on page 477). Farther inland, the Grand Canyon du Verdon patiently awaits, with breathtaking gorges and alpine scenery. But even if you have a car, consider the convenience that trains and buses offer for basic sightseeing between Monaco and Cannes.

FRENCH RIVIERA

Public Transportation in the French Riviera

From	To Cannes	To Antibes	To Nice
Cannes by Train	N/A	2/hr, 15 min	2/hr, 30-40 min
Cannes by Bus	N/A	#200, 2-4/hr, 35 min	#200, 2-4/hr, 1.5-1.75 hrs
Antibes by Train	2/hr, 15 min	N/A	2/hr, 15-30 min
Antibes by Bus	#200, 2-4/hr, 35 min	N/A	#200, 2-4/hr, 1-1.5 hrs
Nice by Train	2/hr, 30-40 min	2/hr, 15-30 min	N/A
Nice by Bus	#200, 2-4/hr, 1.5-1.75 hrs	#200, 2-4/hr, 1-1.5 hrs	N/A
Villefranche-sur-Mer by Train	2/hr, 50 min	2/hr, 40 min	2/hr, 10 min
Villefranche-sur-Mer by Bus	Not recommended	Not recommended	#100, 3-5/hr, 20 min; also #81, 2-4/hr, 20 min

Note: Bus frequencies are given for Monday-Saturday (Sunday often has limited or no bus service).

To Villefranche-sur-Mer	To Cap Ferrat	To Eze-le-Village	To Monaco
2/hr, 50 min	2/hr, 1 hr to Beaulieu-sur-Mer, then bus #81 to Cap Ferrat (2-4/hr, 10 min)	2/hr, 1 hr to Eze-Bord-de-Mer, then bus #83 to Eze (8/day, 15 min)	2/hr, 70 min
Not recommended	Not recommended	Not recommended	Not recommended
2/hr, 40 min	2/hr, 40 min to Beaulieu-sur-Mer, then bus #81 to Cap Ferrat (2-4/hr, 10 min)	2/hr, 45 min to Eze-Bord-de-Mer, then bus #83 to Eze (8/day, 15 min)	2/hr, 50 min
Not recommended	#200 to Nice (2-4/hr, 1-1.5 hrs), then #81 to Cap Ferrat (2-4/hr, 35 min)	Not recommended	Not recommended
2/hr, 10 min	Not recommended	2/hr, 15 min to Eze-Bord-de-Mer, then bus #83 to Eze (8/day, 15 min)	2/hr, 20 min
#100, 3-5/hr, 20 min; also #81, 2-4/hr, 20 min	#81, 2-4/hr, 35 min	#82/#112, 8-16/day, 40 min	#100, 3-5/hr, 45 min
N/A	N/A	2/hr, 10 min to Eze-Bord-de-Mer, then bus #83 to Eze (8/day, 15 min)	2/hr, 10 min
N/A	#81, 2-4/hr, 20 min	#80 to upper Villefranche (hourly), then bus #82/#112, 8-16/day, 20 min	#100, 3-5/hr, 25 min

(continued on next page)

(continued from previous page)

Public Transportation in the French Riviera

From	To Cannes	To Antibes	To Nice
Cap Ferrat by Train	Bus #81 to Beaulieu-sur-Mer (2-4/hr, 10 min), then train to Cannes (2/hr, 1 hr)	Bus #81 to Beaulieu-sur-Mer (2-4/hr, 10 min), then train to Antibes (2/hr, 40 min)	N/A
Cap Ferrat by Bus	Not recommended	#81 to Nice (2-4/hr, 35 min), then #200 to Antibes (3-4/hr, 1-1.5 hrs)	#81, 2-4/hr, 35 min
Eze-le-Village by Train	Bus #83 to Eze-Bord-de-Mer, 8/day, 15 min, then train to Cannes (2/hr, 1 hr)	Bus #83 to Eze-Bord-de-Mer, 8/day, 15 min, then train to Antibes (2/hr, 45 min)	Bus #83 to Eze-Bord-de-Mer, 8/day, 15 min, then train to Nice (2/hr, 15 min)
Eze-le-Village by Bus	Not recommended	Not recommended	#82/#112, 8-16/day, 40 min
Monaco by Train	2/hr, 70 min	2/hr, 50 min	2/hr, 20 min
Monaco by Bus	Not recommended	Not recommended	#100, 3-5/hr, 45 min

Note: Bus frequencies are given for Monday-Saturday (Sunday often has limited or no bus service).

To Villefranche-sur-Mer	To Cap Ferrat	To Eze-le-Village	To Monaco
N/A	N/A	N/A	N/A
#81, 2-4/hr, 20 min	N/A	#100 direction: Monaco to Gare d'Eze stop (3-5/hr, 30 min), then bus #83 to village (8/day, 15 min)	#100, 3-5/hr, 20 min
Bus #83 to Eze-Bord-de-Mer, 8/day, 15 min, then train to Villefranche (2/hr, 10 min)	N/A	N/A	N/A
#82/#112 to upper Villefranche (8-16/day, 20 min), then bus #80 to Villefranche (hourly)	#83 to Gare d'Eze stop (8/day, 15 min), then bus #100 direction: Nice (3-5/hr, 30 min)	N/A	#112, 6/day Mon-Sat, none on Sun, 20 min
2/hr, 10 min	N/A	N/A	N/A
#100, 3-5/hr, 25 min	#100, 3-5/hr, 20 min	#112, 6/day Mon-Sat, none on Sun, 20 min	N/A

Top Art Sights of the Riviera

These are listed in order of importance.

Fondation Maeght (St-Paul-de-Vence)

Chagall Museum (Nice)

Picasso Museum (Antibes)

Matisse Museum (Nice)

Museum of the Annonciade (St-Tropez)

Chapel of the Rosary (Vence)

Modern and Contemporary Art Museum (Nice)

Renoir Museum (Cagnes-sur-Mer)

Fine Arts Museum (Nice)

By Boat: Trans Côte d'Azur offers boat service from Nice to Monaco or to St-Tropez from June into September, as well as between Cannes and St-Tropez (tel. 04 92 98 71 30, www.trans-cote-azur.com). For details, see "Getting Around the Riviera from Nice" (page 336).

The Riviera's Art Scene

The list of artists who have painted the Riviera reads like a Who's Who of 20th-century art. Pierre-Auguste Renoir, Henri Matisse, Marc Chagall, Georges Braque, Raoul Dufy, Fernand Léger, and Pablo Picasso all lived and worked here—and raved about the region's wonderful light. Their simple, semi-abstract, and—most importantly—colorful works reflect the pleasurable atmosphere of the Riviera. You'll experience the same landscapes they painted in this bright, sun-drenched region, punctuated with views of the "azure sea." Try to imagine the Riviera with a fraction of the people and development you see today.

But the artists were mostly drawn to the uncomplicated lifestyle of fishermen and farmers that has reigned here since time began. As the artists grew older, they retired in the sun, turned their backs on modern art's "isms," and painted with the wide-eyed wonder of children, using bright primary colors, basic outlines, and simple subjects.

A dynamic concentration of well-organized modern- and contemporary-art museums (many described in this book) litter the Riviera, allowing art-lovers to appreciate these masters' works while immersed in the same sun and culture that inspired them.

Many of the museums were designed to blend pieces with the surrounding views, gardens, and fountains, thus highlighting that modern art is not only stimulating, but sometimes simply beautiful.

Entire books have been written about the modern-art galleries of the Riviera. If you're a fan, do some studying before your visit to be sure you know about that far-out museum of your dreams. Even if you aren't usually turned on by modern art, take the opportunity to experience the region's brilliant display of it by visiting the Fondation Maeght in St-Paul-de-Vence, and the Chagall and Matisse museums in Nice.

The Riviera's Cuisine Scene

The Riviera adds an Italian-Mediterranean flair to the food of Provence. While many of the same dishes served in Provence are available throughout the Riviera (see "Provence's Cuisine Scene" on page 61), there are differences, especially if you look for anything Italian or from the sea. The proximity to the water and historic ties to Italy are clear in this region's dishes.

La salade niçoise is where most Riviera meals start. A true specialty from Nice, this salad has many versions, though most include a base of green salad topped with green beans, boiled potatoes (sometimes rice), tomatoes (sometimes corn), anchovies, olives, hard-boiled eggs, and lots of tuna. Every café and restaurant adds its own twist to this filling dish that goes down well on sultry days.

For lunch on the go, look for a *pan bagnat* (like a *salade niçoise* stuffed into a hollowed-out soft roll). Other tasty bread treats include *pissaladière* (bread dough topped with onions, olives, and anchovies), *fougasse* (a spindly, lace-like bread sometimes flavored with nuts, herbs, olives, or ham), and *socca* (a thin chickpea crêpe, seasoned with pepper and olive oil and often served in a paper cone by street vendors).

Invented in Nice, ravioli and potato gnocchi can be found on menus everywhere (ravioli can be stuffed with a variety of fillings, but it's best with seafood). Thin-crust pizza and *pâtes fraîches* (fresh pasta) are generally a good value throughout the Riviera.

Bouillabaisse is the Riviera's most famous dish; look for it in any seafront village or city. It's a spicy fish stew based on recipes handed down from sailors in Marseille. It must contain at least four types of fresh fish, though most have five to twelve kinds. A true bouillabaisse never has shellfish. The fish—cooked in a tomato-based stock and flavored with saffron (and sometimes anise and orange)—is separated from the stock before serving. The cook then heightens the flavor of the stock by adding toasted croutons and a dollop of *rouille* sauce (a thickened reddish mayonnaise heady with garlic and spicy peppers). This dish often requires a minimum order of two and can cost up to €40-60 per person.

Those on a budget can enjoy other seafood soups and stews. Far less pricey than bouillabaisse and worth trying is the local *soupe de poisson* (fish soup). It's a creamy soup flavored like bouillabaisse, with anise and orange, and served with croutons and *rouille* sauce (but has no chunks of fish). For a less colorful but still tasty soup, look for *bourride*, a creamy fish concoction thickened with an aioli sauce instead of the red *rouille;* or *baudroie*, a fishy soup cooked with vegetables and garlic.

The Riviera specializes in all sorts of fish and shellfish. Other options include *fruits de mer,* or platters of seafood (including tiny shellfish, from which you get the edible part only by sucking really hard); herb-infused mussels; stuffed sardines; squid (slowly simmered with tomatoes and herbs); and tuna *(thon).* The popular *loup flambé au fenouil* is grilled sea bass, flavored with fennel and torched with *pastis* prior to serving.

Cheese and dessert dishes of the Riviera are indistinguishable from those in Provence. Refer to "Provence's Cuisine Scene" (page 61) for suggestions.

You're better off avoiding fixed-price *menus* at most places and just ordering a first course and a main course, or a main course and dessert. I prefer licking my dessert on an after-dinner waterfront stroll (works great in all three home bases I recommend).

Unfortunately, memorable restaurants that showcase the Riviera's cuisine are more difficult to find than in neighboring Provence. Because most visitors come more for the sun than the food, and because the clientele is predominantly international, many restaurants aim for the middle and are hard to tell apart. When dining on the Riviera, I look for views and ambience more than top-quality cuisine.

Wines of the Riviera

Do as everyone else does: Drink wines from Provence. Bandol (red) and Cassis (white) are popular and from a region nearly on the Riviera. The only wines made in the Riviera are Bellet rosé and white, the latter often found in fish-shaped bottles. For more on Provençal wine, see page 66.

NICE

Nice (sounds like "niece"), with its spectacular Alps-to-Mediterranean surroundings, is an enjoyable big-city highlight of the Riviera. Its traffic-free old town mixes Italian and French flavors to create a spicy Mediterranean dressing, while its big squares, broad seaside walkways, and long beaches invite lounging and people-watching. Nice may be nice, but it's hot and jammed in July and August—reserve ahead and get a room with air-conditioning *(une chambre avec climatisation)*. Everything you'll want to see in Nice is either within walking distance, or a short bus or tram ride away.

Orientation to Nice

The main points of interest lie between the beach and the train tracks (about 15 blocks apart—see map on page 330). The city revolves around its grand Place Masséna, where pedestrian-friendly Avenue Jean Médecin meets Vieux (Old) Nice and the Albert 1er parkway (with quick access to the beaches). It's a 20-minute walk (or a €15 taxi ride) from the train station to the beach, and a 20-minute walk along the promenade from the fancy Hôtel Negresco to the heart of Vieux Nice.

A 10-minute ride on the smooth-as-silk tramway through the center of the city connects the train station, Place Masséna, Vieux Nice, and the port (from nearby Place Garibaldi). The tram and all city and regional buses cost only €1.50 per trip, making this one

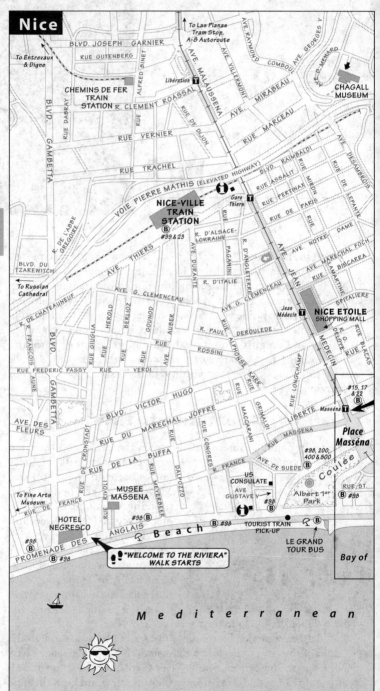

Nice

To Entrevaux
& Digne

BLVD. JOSEPH GARNIER
RUE GUTENBERG

To Las Planas
Tram Stop,
A-8 Autoroute

AVE. RAYMOND

AVE. VILLERMONT

AVE. MIRABEAU

COMBOUL

AVE. GEORGES V

AVE. D-MÉNARD

CHAGALL
MUSEUM

Libération T

CHEMINS DE FER
TRAIN
STATION

R. CLEMENT ROASSAL

ALFRED BINET

AVE. MALAUSSENA

RUE DE DIJON

AVE. MARCEAU

BLVD. DABRAY

RUE DABRAY

RUE VERNIER

RUE TRACHEL

BLVD. RAIMBALDI

RUE ASSALIT

RUE MIRON

RUE DE LEPANTE

RUE DES AMBROIS

VOIE PIERRE MATHIS (ELEVATED HIGHWAY)

NICE-VILLE
TRAIN
STATION

Gare
Thiers

RUE PERTINAX

RUE DE PARIS

RUE

R. D'ALSACE-
LORRAINE

#99 & 23

R. DE L'ABBE GREGOIRE

BLVD. DU
TZAREWITCH

AVE. THIERS

R. DURANTE

R. PAGANINI

R. D'ANGLETERRE

AVE. JEAN

AVE. NOTRE DAME

AVE. MARECHAL FOCH

RUE LAMARTINE

RUE BISCARRA

To Russian
Cathedral

R. DE CHATEAUNEUF

AVE. G. CLEMENCEAU

R. D'ITALIE

AVE. G. CLEMENCEAU

Jean
Médecin

NICE ETOILE
SHOPPING MALL

SPITALIERE

RUE

R. G. DELOYE

RUE BLACAS

R. DE CHATEAUNEUF

R. FRANCOIS AUNE

BLVD. GAMBETTA

RUE GIUGLIA

RUE GOUNOD

RUE HEROLD

RUE BERLIOZ

RUE AUBER

R. PAUL DEROULEDE

RUE

ROSSINI

MEDECIN

RUE FREDERIC FASSY

RUE VERDI

AVE.

KARR

RUE

GRIMALDI

RUE LONGCHAMP

#15, 17
& 22
B

Masséna T

AVE. DES
FLEURS

BLVD. VICTOR HUGO

RUE DU MARECHAL JOFFRE

RUE MACCARANI

LIBERTE

RUE MASSENA

Place
Masséna

RUE DE CRONSTADT

RUE CONGRES

RUE DE LA BUFFA

RUE MEYERBEER

RUE DALPOZZO

AVE. DE SUEDE

R. FRANCE

#98, 200,
400 & 500
B

Coulée

To Fine Arts
Museum

RUE DE
FRANCE

MUSEE
MASSENA

US
CONSULATE

AVE
GUSTAVE V

#98
B

Albert 1er
Park

RUE ST.

B #98

HOTEL
NEGRESCO

RUE RIVOLI

ANGLAIS

#98 B

Beach

B #98

TOURIST TRAIN
PICK-UP

LE GRAND
TOUR BUS

B

Bay of

#98
B

PROMENADE DES

"WELCOME TO THE RIVIERA"
WALK STARTS

M e d i t e r r a n e a n

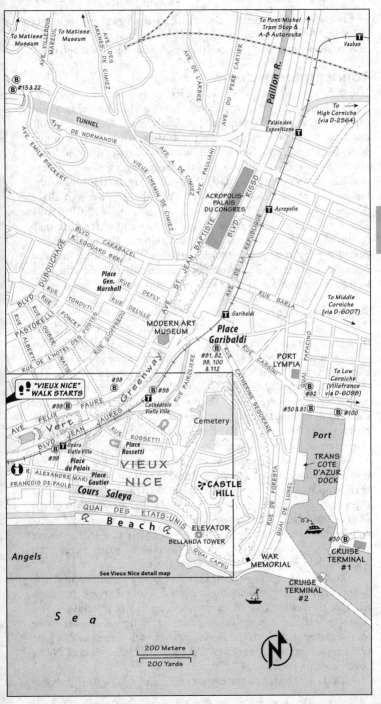

of the cheapest and easiest cities in France to get around in (see "Getting Around Nice," later). In 2014, work should begin on a new tramway line along (or under) the Promenade des Anglais.

Tourist Information

Nice's helpful TIs share a phone number and website (tel. 08 92 70 74 07, www.nicetourisme.com). There are TI branches at the **airport** (desks in both terminals, typically quiet, daily 9:00-18:00, until 20:00 April-Sept); next to the **train station** (busy, summer Mon-Sat 8:00-20:00, Sun 9:00-19:00, rest of year Mon-Sat 9:00-19:00, Sun 10:00-17:00); facing the **beach** at 5 Promenade des Anglais (moderately busy, daily 9:00-18:00, until 20:00 July-Aug, closed Sun off-season); and in a kiosk at the south end of **Place Masséna** (less busy, mid-June-Sept, typically daily 10:00-19:00). Pick up the thorough *Practical Guide to Nice* and a free Nice map (or find a better one at your hotel), but skip the Riviera Pass. You can also get day-trip information at any TI (including maps of Monaco or Antibes, details on boat excursions, and bus schedules to Eze-le-Village, La Turbie, Vence, and other destinations).

Arrival in Nice

By Train: All trains stop at Nice's main station, Nice-Ville (baggage storage at the far right with your back to the tracks, lockers open daily 8:00-21:00). Don't get off at the suburban Nice Riquier station, which is one stop east of the main station. The station area is gritty and busy: Never leave your bags unattended and don't linger here longer than necessary. The area in front of the station was under construction in 2013, but should be looking sharp by the time you visit. Because of this work, bus and taxi stops may be different from what I've described here.

Turn left out of the station to find a **TI** next door. Continue a few more blocks down Avenue Jean Médecin for the Gare Thiers **tram stop** (this will take you to Place Masséna, the old city, and the port). Board the tram heading toward the right, direction: Pont Michel (see "Getting Around Nice," later). You'll find many recommended city-center and Vieux Nice hotels a 10- to 20-minute walk down the same street, though for most it's easier to take the tram to Place Masséna and walk from there.

To walk to recommended hotels near the station or near the beach opposite Promenade des Anglais, cross Avenue Thiers in front of the station, go down the steps by Hôtel Interlaken, and continue walking down Avenue Durante. Follow this same route for the fastest path from the station to the beach—Avenue Durante turns into Rue des Congrés. You'll soon reach the heart of Nice's beachfront promenade.

Taxis and **buses to the airport** (#23 and #99) wait in front of the train station. **Car rental** offices are to the right as you exit the station.

By Bus: Nice's bus station was demolished as part of a major project to expand the city's central parkway (see the Vieux Nice Walk chapter for more on this green project). Most stops for bus routes important to travelers (those serving Antibes, the airport, Vence, Villefranche-sur-Mer, Monaco, and St-Jean-Cap-Ferrat) have been moved to other locations (see map on page 330). As work continues along the parkway, bus stop locations are subject to change; confirm locally.

By Car: To reach the city center on the autoroute from the west, take the first Nice exit (for the airport—called *Côte d'Azur, Central*) and follow signs for *Nice Centre* and *Promenade des Anglais* (expect detours if tramway construction is under way). Avoid arriving at rush hour (usually Mon-Fri 8:00-9:30 & 17:00-19:30), when Promenade des Anglais grinds to a halt. Hoteliers know where to park (allow €15-26/day; some hotels offer special deals but space is limited, so reserve ahead). The parking garage at the Nice Etoile shopping center on Avenue Jean Médecin is pricey but near many recommended hotels (ticket booth on third floor, about €20/day, €13/overnight—18:00-8:00). Other garages, like the one next to the recommended Hôtel Ibis at the train station, have similar rates. All on-street parking is metered (9:00-18:00 or 19:00), but usually free all day Sunday.

You can avoid driving in the center—and park for free during the day (no overnight parking)—by ditching your car at a parking lot at a remote tram stop (Las Planas is best) and taking the tram into town (10/hour, 15 minutes, €1.50, don't leave anything in your car; tramway described later, under "Getting Around Nice"). To find the Las Planas tram station from the A-8 autoroute, take the *Nice Nord* exit (see map on page 330).

By Plane or Cruise Ship: For information on Nice's airport and cruise-ship port, see "Nice Connections," at the end of this chapter.

Helpful Hints

Theft Alert: Nice has its share of pickpockets. Thieves target fanny packs: Have nothing important on or around your waist, unless it's in a money belt tucked out of sight. Don't leave things unattended on the beach while swimming, and stick to main streets in Vieux Nice after dark.

US Consulate: You'll find it at 7 Avenue Gustave V (tel. 04 93 88 89 55, fax 04 93 87 07 38, http://marseille.usconsulate.gov /nice.html).

Canadian Consulate: It's at 2 Place Franklin (tel. 04 93 92 93 22, fax 04 93 92 55 51).

NICE

Medical Help: Riviera Medical Services has a list of English-speaking physicians. They can help you make an appointment or call an ambulance (tel. 04 93 26 12 70, www.rivieramedical .com).

Sightseeing Tips: The following sights are closed on Mondays: the Modern and Contemporary Art Museum, the Fine Arts Museum, the Russian Cathedral, and the Cours Saleya market. On Tuesdays the Chagall, Matisse, Masséna, and Archaeological museums are closed. All of the sights in Nice—except the Chagall Museum—are free to enter, making rainy-day options a swinging deal here.

Internet Access: There's no shortage of places to get online. Almost all of the hotels I list have free Wi-Fi, and some have guest computers. For other access points, ask at your hotel or look for one of these establishments, all with free Wi-Fi: Quick Hamburger, Häagen Dazs, and McDonald's (multiple locations), or the Nice Etoile Shopping Center and Virgin Megastore (on Avenue Jean Médecin).

Laundry: You'll find launderettes everywhere in Nice—ask your hotelier for the nearest one.

Grocery Store: The big **Monoprix** on Avenue Jean Médecin and Rue Biscarra has it all, including a deli counter, bakery, and cold drinks (Mon-Sat 8:30-21:00, closed Sun, see map on page 362). You'll also find many small grocery stores (some open Sun and/or until late hours) near my recommended hotels.

Boutique Shopping: The chic streets where Rue Alphonse Karr meets Rue de la Liberté and then Rue de Paradis are known as the "Golden Square." If you need pricey stuff, shop here.

SNCF Boutique: There's a handy French rail ticket office a half-block west of Avenue Jean Médecin at 2 Rue de la Liberté (Mon-Fri 10:00-17:50, closed Sat-Sun).

Renting a Bike (and Other Wheels): Roller Station rents bikes (*vélos,* can be taken on trains, €5/hour, €10/half-day, €15/day), rollerblades, skateboards, and Razor-style scooters (*trotinettes,* €7/half-day, €9/day). You'll need to leave your ID as a deposit (daily March-May and Sept-Oct 10:00-19:00, June-Aug 10:00-20:30, Nov-Feb 10:00-18:00, next to yellow awnings of Pailin's Asian restaurant at 49 Quai des Etats-Unis—see map on page 356, tel. 04 93 62 99 05, owner Eric). If you need more power, the TI has a list of places renting electric scooters.

You'll notice blue bikes **(Vélos Bleu)** stationed at various points in the city. A thousand of these bikes, available for locals to use when running errands, rent cheaply for short-term use (first 30 minutes free, European-style chip-and-PIN credit card or American Express card required).

Car Rental: Renting a car is easiest at Nice's airport, which has offices for all the major companies. You'll also find most companies represented at Nice's train station and near Albert 1er Park.

English Radio: Tune in to Riviera-Radio at FM 106.5.

Views: For panoramic views, climb Castle Hill (see page 347), or take a one-hour boat trip (described later, under "Tours in Nice").

Beach Gear: To make life tolerable on the rocks, swimmers should buy a pair of the cheap plastic beach shoes sold at many shops (flip-flops fall off in the water). **Go Sport** at #13 on Place Masséna sells beach shoes, flip-flops, and cheap sunglasses (Mon-Sat 9:30-19:30, Sun 10:30-19:00—see map on page 356).

Updates to this Book: For news about changes to this book's coverage since it was published, see www.ricksteves.com/update.

NICE

Getting Around Nice

Although you can walk to most attractions in Nice, smart travelers make good use of the buses and tram. Both are covered by the same €1.50 single-ride ticket (€10 for 10 tickets that can be shared, good for 74 minutes in one direction, including transfers between bus and tram; can't be used for a round-trip or airport express bus). The **bus** is particularly handy for reaching the Chagall and Matisse museums and the Russian Cathedral. Pick up timetables at Nice's TIs (or view them online at www.lignesdazur.com) and buy tickets from the driver. Make sure to validate your ticket in the machine just behind the driver—watch locals do it and imitate.

The €6 all-day pass is valid on city buses and trams, as well as buses to some nearby destinations. The all-day ticket makes sense if you plan to take the bus to museums, use the tramway several times, or are going to the airport (you must validate your ticket on every trip). Express buses to and from the airport (#98 and #99) require the all-day pass, so savvy riders pack in other bus and/or tram rides on the day of their flight.

Nice's **tramway** makes an "*L*" along Avenue Jean Médecin and Boulevard Jean Jaurès, and connects the main train station (Gare Thiers stop), Place Masséna (Masséna stop, near many regional bus stops and a few blocks' walk from the sea), Vieux Nice (Opéra-Vieille Ville, Cathédrale-Vieille Ville), and the Modern

and Contemporary Art Museum and port (Place Garibaldi). It also comes within a few blocks of the Chemins de Fer de Provence train station (Libération stop)—the departure point for the scenic narrow-gauge rail journey (see page 348).

Boarding the tram in the direction of Pont Michel takes you from the train station toward the beach and Vieux Nice (direction: Las Planas goes the other way). Buy tickets at the machines on the platforms (coins only, no credit cards). Choose the English flag to change the display language, turn the round knob and push the green button to select your ticket, press it twice at the end to get your ticket, or press the red button to cancel. Once you're on the tram, validate your ticket by inserting it into the top of the white box, then reclaiming it (http://tramway.nice.fr).

Taxis are useful for getting to Nice's less-central sights, and worth it if you're nowhere near a bus or tram stop (figure €15 from Promenade des Anglais). Cabbies normally only pick up at taxi stands *(tête de station)*, or you can call 04 93 13 78 78.

The hokey **tourist train** gets you up Castle Hill (see "Tours in Nice," later).

Getting Around the Riviera from Nice

By Train and Bus: Nice is perfectly situated for exploring the Riviera by public transport. Monaco, Eze-le-Village, Villefranche-sur-Mer, Antibes, Vence, and St-Paul-de-Vence are all within about a one-hour bus or train ride. The train is pricier (fares range from €2 to nearby Villefranche-sur-Mer to €8.50 to farther-away Grasse) than the bus (€1.50 for most destinations), but will often save you time. You make the call—both modes of transportation work well.

All trains serving Nice arrive at and depart from Nice-Ville Station. Most regional buses stop near Boulevard Jean Jaurès, on Avenue de Verdun near Albert 1er Park, or near Place Garibaldi (near Vieux Nice; see maps on pages 352 and 356 for stop locations, www.lignesdazur.com).

With a little planning, you can link key destinations in an all-day circuit. For example, you can triangulate Nice, Monaco, and Eze-le-Village or La Turbie in a loop that ends up back in Nice (see page 431 for details). For a summary of train and bus connections, see the "Public Transportation in the French Riviera" sidebar on page 322; see also "Nice Connections" at the end of this chapter.

By Boat: From June to mid-September, Trans Côte d'Azur offers scenic trips several days a week from Nice to Monaco and Nice to St-Tropez. Boats leave in the morning and return in the evening, giving you all day to explore your destination. Drinks and WCs are available on board.

Boats to **Monaco** depart at 9:30 and 16:00, and return at 11:00 and 18:00 (€35 round-trip, €29 if you don't get off in Monaco, 45 minutes each way, June-mid-Sept Tue, Thu, and Sat only).

Boats to **St-Tropez** depart at 9:00 and return at 19:00 (€61 round-trip, 2.5 hours each way; mid-July-Aug Tue-Sun, no boats Mon; June-mid-July and Sept Tue, Thu, and Sat-Sun only).

Reservations are required for both boats, and tickets for St-Tropez often sell out, so book a few days ahead (tel. 04 92 98 71 30 or 04 92 00 42 30, www.trans-cote-azur.com, croisieres @trans-cote-azur.com). The boats leave from Nice's port, Bassin des Amiraux, just below Castle Hill—look for the ticket booth *(billeterie)* on Quai de Lunel (see map on page 330). The same company also runs one-hour round-trip cruises along the coast to Cap Ferrat (see "Tours in Nice," next).

Tours in Nice

Bus Tour

Le Grand Tour Bus provides an 11-stop, hop-on, hop-off service on an open-deck bus with headphone commentary (2/hour, 1.5-hour loop) that includes the Promenade des Anglais, the old port, Cap de Nice, and the Chagall and Matisse museums on Cimiez Hill (€21/1-day pass, €23/2-day pass, cheaper for seniors and students, €12 for last tour of the day at about 18:00, some hotels offer small discounts, buy tickets on bus, main stop is near where Promenade des Anglais and Quai des Etats-Unis meet, across from the Plage Beau Rivage lounge, tel. 04 92 29 17 00, www.nicelegrandtour .com). This tour is a pricey way to get to the Chagall and Matisse museums, but it's an acceptable option if you also want a city overview. Check the schedule if you plan to use this bus to see the Russian Cathedral, as it may be faster to walk there.

Tourist Train

For €8 (€4 for children under age 9), you can spend 45 embarrassing minutes on the tourist train tooting along the promenade, through the old city, and up to Castle Hill. This is a sweat-free way to get to the top of the hill—but so is the elevator, which is free (train runs every 30 minutes, daily 10:00-18:00, June-Aug until 19:00, recorded English commentary, meet train near Le Grand Tour Bus stop on Quai des Etats-Unis, tel. 02 99 88 47 07, www .ttdf.com).

▲Boat Cruise

Here's your chance to view Nice from the water. On this one-hour star-studded tour run by Trans Côte d'Azur, you'll cruise in a comfortable yacht-size vessel to Cap Ferrat and past Villefranche-sur-Mer, then return to Nice with a final lap along Promenade des Anglais. It's a scenic trip (the best views are from the seats on top), and worthwhile if you won't be hiking along the Cap Ferrat trails

Nice at a Glance

▲▲▲**Chagall Museum** The world's largest collection of Marc Chagall's work, popular even with people who don't like modern art. **Hours:** Wed-Mon 10:00-17:00, May-Oct until 18:00, closed Tue year-round. See page 341.

▲▲▲**Promenade des Anglais** Nice's four-mile sun-struck seafront promenade. **Hours:** Always open. See page 339.

▲▲**Vieux Nice** Charming old city offering enjoyable atmosphere and a look at Nice's French-Italian cultural blend. **Hours:** Always open. See page 340.

▲**Matisse Museum** Small but worthwhile collection of Henri Matisse's paintings, sketches, paper cutouts, and more. **Hours:** Wed-Mon 10:00-18:00, closed Tue. See page 341.

▲**Modern and Contemporary Art Museum** Ultramodern museum with enjoyable collection from the 1960s-1970s, including Warhol and Lichtenstein. **Hours:** Tue-Sun 10:00-18:00, closed Mon. See page 345.

▲**Russian Cathedral** Finest Orthodox church outside of Russia; may be closed in 2015. **Hours:** Tue-Sat 9:00-12:00 & 14:00-19:00, Sun 9:00-12:00, closed Mon. See page 346.

▲**Castle Hill** Site of an ancient fort boasting great views—especially in early mornings and evenings. **Hours:** Park closes at 20:00 in summer, earlier off-season. Elevator runs daily 10:00-19:00, until 20:00 in summer. See page 347.

Fine Arts Museum Lush villa shows off impressive paintings by Monet, Sisley, Bonnard, and Raoul Dufy. **Hours:** Tue-Sun 10:00-18:00, closed Mon. See page 345.

Masséna Museum Lavish beachfront mansion houses museum of city history, including exhibits of Napoleonic paraphernalia and images of Nice over the years. **Hours:** Wed-Mon 10:00-18:00, closed Tue. See page 347.

Molinard Perfume Museum Two-room museum in a storefront boutique tracing the history of perfume. **Hours:** Daily April-Sept 10:00-19:00, Oct-March 10:00-13:00 & 14:00-18:00, sometimes closed Sun off-season. See page 345.

that provide similar views.

French (and sometimes English-speaking) guides play Robin Leach, pointing out mansions owned by some pretty famous people, including Elton John (just as you leave Nice, it's the soft-yellow square-shaped place right on the water), Sean Connery (on the hill above Elton, with rounded arches and tower), and Microsoft co-founder Paul Allen (in the saddle of Cap Ferrat hill—look above the umbrellas of Plage de Passable beach and find the house with a sloping red-tile roof). I wonder if this gang ever hangs out together. Guides also like to point out the mansion between Villefranche-sur-Mer and Cap Ferrat where the Rolling Stones recorded *Exile on Main Street*. (€17; April-Oct Tue-Sun 2/day, usually at 11:00 and 15:00, no boats Mon or in off-season; call ahead to verify schedule, arrive 30 minutes early to get best seats, drinks and WCs available.) For directions to the dock and contact information, see "Getting Around the Riviera from Nice—By Boat," earlier.

Walking Tours

The TI on Promenade des Anglais organizes weekly walking tours of Vieux Nice in French and English (€12, May-Oct only, usually Sat morning at 9:30, 2.5 hours, reservations necessary, depart from TI, tel. 08 92 70 74 07). They also have evening art walks on Fridays at 19:00.

Local Guides and Cooking Classes

See page 319 of the French Riviera chapter for a list of guides for Nice and other regional destinations, plus "Taste of Nice" food tours and Vieux Nice cooking classes.

Sights in Nice

Walks and Beach Time

▲▲▲Promenade des Anglais and Beach

Meandering along Nice's four-mile seafront promenade on foot or by bike is an essential Riviera experience. From the days when wealthy English tourists filled the grand seaside hotels, this stretch has always been *the* place to be in Nice. Europeans still flock here to seek fun in the sun.

For a self-guided walk of this strip, see the Welcome to the Riviera Walk chapter. To rev up the pace of your promenade saunter, rent a bike and glide along the coast in either or both directions (about 30 minutes each way; for rental info see "Helpful Hints," earlier). Both of the

following paths start along Promenade des Anglais.

The path to the **west** stops just before the airport at perhaps the most scenic *boules* courts in France. Pause here to watch the old-timers while away the afternoon tossing shiny metal balls (for more on this game, see page 10). If you take the path heading **east,** you'll round the hill—passing a scenic cape and the town's memorial to both world wars—to the harbor of Nice, with a chance to survey some fancy yachts. Walk or pedal around the harbor and follow the coast past the Corsica ferry terminal (you'll need to carry your bike up a flight of steps). From there the path leads to an appealing tree-lined residential district.

And of course, there's the **beach.** Settle in on the smooth rocks or find a section with imported sand, and consider your options: You can play beach volleyball, table tennis, or *boules;* rent paddleboats, personal watercraft, or windsurfing equipment; explore ways to use your zoom lens for some revealing people-watching; or snooze on a comfy beach bed.

To rent a spot on the beach, compare rates, as prices vary—beaches on the east end of the bay are usually cheaper (chair and mattress—*chaise longue* and *transat*—about €15, umbrella-€5, towel-€4). Some hotels have special deals with certain beaches for discounted rentals (check with your hotel for details). Have lunch in your bathing suit (€12 salads and pizzas in bars and restaurants all along the beach). Or, for a peaceful café au lait on the Mediterranean, stop here first thing in the morning before the crowds hit. *Plage Publique* signs explain the 15 beach no-nos (translated into English).

▲▲Wandering Vieux Nice (Old Nice)

Offering an intriguing look at Nice's melding of French and Italian cultures, the old city is a fine place to linger. Enjoy its narrow lanes, bustling market squares, and colorful people.

For details on this neighborhood, see the Vieux Nice Walk chapter.

Museums and Monuments

To bring culture to the masses, the city of Nice has nixed entry fees to all municipal museums—so it's free to enter all the following sights except the Chagall Museum and the Russian Cathedral. Cool.

The first two museums (Chagall and Matisse) are a long walk northeast of Nice's city center. Because they're in the same direction and served by the same bus line (buses #15 and #22 stop at both museums), it makes sense to visit them on the same trip. From Place Masséna, the Chagall Museum is a 10-minute bus ride or a 30-minute walk, and the Matisse Museum is a 20-minute bus ride or a one-hour walk.

▲▲▲Chagall Museum (Musée National Marc Chagall)

Inspired by the Old Testament, modern artist Marc Chagall custom-painted works for this building, which he considered a "House of Brotherhood." In typical Chagall style, these paintings

are lively, colorful, and simple (some might say simplistic). The museum is a can't-miss treat for Chagall fans, and a hit even for people who usually don't like modern art.

Cost and Hours: €7.50, €1-2 more with (frequent) special exhibits, free first Sun

of the month (but crowded), open Wed-Mon 10:00-17:00, May-Oct until 18:00, closed Tue year-round, Avenue Docteur Ménard, tel. 04 93 53 87 20, www.musees-nationaux-alpesmaritimes.fr/chagall/.

For a complete self-guided tour of the museum, and directions on how to get here, see the Chagall Museum Tour chapter.

▲Matisse Museum (Musée Matisse)

This small museum contains a sampling of works from the various periods of Henri Matisse's long artistic career. The museum offers a painless introduction to the artist's many styles and materials, both shaped by Mediterranean light and by fellow Côte d'Azur artists Pablo Picasso and Pierre-Auguste Renoir. The collection is scattered throughout several rooms with a few worthwhile works, though it lacks a certain *je ne sais quoi* when compared to the Chagall Museum.

Cost and Hours: Free, Wed-Mon 10:00-18:00, closed Tue, 164 Avenue des Arènes de Cimiez, tel. 04 93 81 08 08, www.musee-matisse-nice.org. The museum is housed in a beautiful Mediterranean mansion set in an olive grove amid the ruins of the ancient Roman city of Cemenelum, a military camp that housed as many as 20,000 people.

Getting There: It's a long uphill walk from the city center. Take the bus (details follow) or a cab (€20 from Promenade des Anglais). Once here, walk into the park to find the pink villa. **Buses #15, #17,** and **#22** offer regular service to the Matisse Museum from just off Place Masséna on Rue Sacha Guitry (Masséna Guitry stop, at the east end of the Galeries Lafayette department store—see map on page 356, 20 minutes; note that bus #17 does not stop at the Chagall Museum). **Bus #20** connects the

Henri Matisse
(1869-1954)

Here's an outline of Henri Matisse's busy life:

1880s and 1890s—At age 20, Matisse, a budding lawyer, is struck down with appendicitis. Bedridden for a year, he turns to painting as a healing escape from pain and boredom. After recovering, he studies art in Paris and produces dark-colored, realistic still lifes and landscapes. His work is exhibited at the Salons of 1896 and 1897.

1897-1905—Influenced by the Impressionists, he experiments with sunnier scenes and brighter colors. He travels to southern France, including Collioure (on the coast near Spain), and seeks still more light-filled scenes to paint. His experiments are influenced by Vincent van Gogh's bright, surrealistic colors and thick outlines, and by Paul Gauguin's primitive visions of a Tahitian paradise. From Paul Cézanne, he learns how to simplify objects into their basic geometric shapes. He also experiments (like Cézanne) with creating the illusion of 3-D not by traditional means, but by using contrasting colors for the foreground and background.

1905—Back in Paris, Matisse and his colleagues (André Derain and Maurice de Vlaminck) shock the art world with an exhibition of their experimental paintings. The thick outlines, simple forms, flattened perspective, and—most of all—bright, clashing, unrealistic colors seem to be the work of "wild animals" (fauves). Fauvism is hot, and Matisse is instantly famous. (Though notorious as a "wild animal," Matisse himself was a gentle, introspective man.)

1906-1910—After just a year, Fauvism is out, and African masks are in. This "primitive" art form inspires Matisse to simplify and distort his figures further, making them less realistic but more expressive.

1910-1917—Matisse creates his masterpiece paintings. Cubism is the rage, pioneered by Matisse's friend and rival for the World's

port to the museum. On any bus, get off at the Arènes-Matisse bus stop (look for the crumbling Roman wall; for bus tips on leaving the museum, see the end of this listing.)

Background: Henri Matisse, the master of leaving things out, could suggest a woman's body with a single curvy line—letting the viewer's mind fill in the rest. Ignoring traditional 3-D perspective, he expressed his passion for life through simplified but

Best Painter award, Pablo Picasso. Matisse dabbles in Cubism, simplifying forms, emphasizing outline, and muting his colors. But ultimately it proves to be too austere and analytical for his deeply sensory nature. The Cubist style is most evident in his sculpture.

1920s—Burned out from years of intense experimentation, Matisse moves to Nice (spending winters there from 1917, settling permanently in 1921). Luxuriating under the bright sun, he's reborn, and he paints colorful, sensual, highly decorative works. Harem concubines lounging in their sunny, flowery apartments epitomize the lush life.

1930s—A visit to Tahiti inspires more scenes of life as a sunny paradise. Matisse experiments with bolder lines, swirling arabesques, and decorative patterns.

1940s—Duodenal cancer (in 1941) requires Matisse to undergo two operations and confines him to a wheelchair for the rest of his life. Working at an easel becomes a struggle for him, and he largely stops painting in 1941. But as World War II ends, Matisse emerges with renewed energy. Now in his 70s, he explores a new medium: paper cutouts pasted onto a watercolored surface (découpage on gouache-prepared surface). The technique plays to his strengths—the cutouts are essentially blocks of bright color (mostly blue) with a strong outline. Scissors in hand, Matisse says, "I draw straight into the color." (His doctor advises him to wear dark glasses to protect his weak eyes against the bright colors he chooses.) In 1947, Matisse's book *Jazz* is published, featuring the artist's joyful cutouts of simple figures. Like jazz music, the book is a celebration of artistic spontaneity. And like music in general, Matisse's works balance different tones and colors to create a mood.

1947-1951—Matisse's nurse becomes a Dominican nun in Vence. To thank her for her care, he spends his later years designing a chapel there. He oversees every aspect of the Chapel of the Rosary (Chapelle du Rosaire) at Vence, from the stained glass to the altar to the colors of the priest's robe (see page 484). Though Matisse is not a strong Christian, the church exudes his spirit of celebrating life and sums up his work.

1954—Matisse dies.

recognizable scenes in which dark outlines and saturated, bright blocks of color create an overall decorative pattern. You don't look "through" a Matisse canvas, like a window; you look "at" it, like wallpaper.

Matisse understood how colors and shapes affect us emotionally. He could create either shocking, clashing works (early Fauvism) or geometrical, balanced, harmonious ones (later cutouts).

Whereas other modern artists reveled in purely abstract design, Matisse (almost) always kept the subject matter at least vaguely recognizable. He used unreal colors and distorted lines not just to portray what an object looks like, but to express its inner nature (even inanimate objects). Meditating on his paintings helps you connect with life—or so Matisse hoped.

As you tour the museum, look for Matisse's favorite motifs—including fruit, flowers, wallpaper, and sunny rooms—often with a window opening onto a sunny landscape. Another favorite subject is the *odalisque* (harem concubine), usually shown sprawled in a seductive pose and with a simplified, masklike face. You'll also see a few souvenirs from his travels, which influenced much of his work.

Visiting the Museum: Enter the museum at park level from the door opposite the olive grove (not the basement entry). The museum features temporary exhibits about Matisse that change frequently.

Rooms on the entry level usually house paintings from Matisse's formative years as a student (1890s). Notice how quickly his work evolves: from dark still lifes *(nature mortes),* to colorful Impressionist scenes, to more abstract works, all in a matter of a few years. A beige banner describes his "Découverte de la Lumière" (discovery of light), which the Riviera (and his various travels to sun-soaked places like Corsica, Collioure, and Tahiti) brought to his art. You may see photographs of his apartment on Cours Saleya, which is described in my Vieux Nice Walk chapter.

Other rooms on this floor highlight Matisse's fascination with dance and the female body (these subjects may be upstairs). You'll see pencil and charcoal drawings, and a handful of bronze busts; he was fascinated by sculpture. *The Acrobat*—painted only two years before Matisse's death—shows the artist at his minimalist best. A room devoted to two 25-foot-long watery cutouts for an uncompleted pool project *(La Piscine)* for the city of Nice shows his abiding love of deep blue.

The floor above features sketches and models of Matisse's famous Chapel of the Rosary in nearby Vence (see page 484) and related religious works. On the same floor, you may find paper cutouts from his *Jazz* or *Dance* series, more bronze sculptures, various personal objects, and linen embroideries inspired by his travels to Polynesia.

The bookshop, WCs, and additional temporary exhibits are in the basement level. The fantastic wall-hanging near the bookshop—Matisse's colorful paper cutout *Flowers and Fruits*—shouts, "Riviera!"

Leaving the Museum: When leaving the museum, find the stop for buses #15 and #22 (frequent service to downtown, stops en route at the Chagall Museum): Turn left from the Matisse

Museum into the park and keep straight on Allée Barney Wilen, exiting the park at the Archaeological Museum, then turn right. Pass the bus stop across the street (#17 goes to the city center but not the Chagall Museum, and #20 goes to the port), and walk to the small roundabout. Cross the roundabout to find the shelter (facing downhill) for buses #15 and #22.

▲Modern and Contemporary Art Museum (Musée d'Art Moderne et d'Art Contemporain)

This ultramodern museum features an explosively colorful, far-out, yet manageable collection focused on American and European-American artists from the 1960s and 1970s (Pop Art and New Realism styles are highlighted). The exhibits cover three floors and include a few works by Andy Warhol, Roy Lichtenstein, and Jean Tinguely, and small models of Christo's famous wrappings. You'll find rooms dedicated to Robert Indiana, Yves Klein, and Niki de Saint Phalle (my favorite). The temporary exhibits can be as appealing to modern-art lovers as the permanent collection: Check the museum website for what's playing. Don't leave without exploring the rooftop terrace.

For a succinct introduction to modern art on the Riviera, see the French Riviera chapter.

Cost and Hours: Free, Tue-Sun 10:00-18:00, closed Mon, about a 15-minute walk from Place Masséna, near Vieux Nice on Promenade des Arts, tel. 04 93 62 61 62, www.mamac-nice.org.

Fine Arts Museum (Musée des Beaux-Arts)

Housed in a sumptuous Riviera villa with lovely gardens, this museum holds 6,000 artworks from the 17th to 20th centuries. Start on the first floor and work your way up to experience an appealing array of paintings by Monet, Sisley, Bonnard, and Raoul Dufy, as well as a few sculptures by Rodin and Carpeaux.

Cost and Hours: Free, Tue-Sun 10:00-18:00, closed Mon; inconveniently located at the western end of Nice, take bus #12 or #23 from the train station to the Rosa Bonheur stop and walk to 3 Avenue des Baumettes; tel. 04 92 15 28 28, www.musee-beaux -arts-nice.org.

Molinard Perfume Museum

The Molinard family has been making perfume in Grasse (about an hour's drive from Nice—see page 491) since 1849. Their Nice store has a small museum in the rear that illustrates the story of their industry. Back when people believed water spread the plague (Louis XIV supposedly bathed less than once a year), doctors advised people to rub fragrances into their skin and then powder their bodies. At that time, perfume was a necessity of everyday life.

The tiny first room shows photos of the local flowers, roots, and other plant parts used in perfume production. The second, main room explains the earliest (18th-century) production method.

Petals were laid out in the sun on a bed of animal fat, which would absorb the essence of the flowers as they baked. For two months, the petals were replaced daily, until the fat was saturated. Models and old photos show the later distillation process (660 pounds of lavender produced only a quarter-gallon of essence). Perfume is "distilled like cognac and then aged like wine." The bottles on the tables demonstrate the role of the "blender" and the perfume mastermind called the "nose" (who knows best); clients are allowed to try their hand at mixing scents. Of the 150 real "noses" in the world, more than 100 are French. Notice the photos of these lab-coat-wearing perfectionists. You are welcome to enjoy the testing bottles.

Cost and Hours: Free, daily April-Sept 10:00-19:00, Oct-March 10:00-13:00 & 14:00-18:00, sometimes closed Sun off-season, just between beach and Place Masséna at 20 Rue St. François de Paule, see map on page 356, tel. 04 93 62 90 50, www.molinard.com.

▲Russian Cathedral (Cathédrale Russe)

Nice's Russian Orthodox church—claimed by some to be the finest outside Russia—is worth a visit. Five hundred rich Russian

families wintered in Nice in the late 19th century, and they needed a worthy Orthodox house of worship. Czar Nicholas I's widow provided the land (which required tearing down her house), and Czar Nicholas II gave this church to the Russian community in 1912. (A few years later, Russian comrades who *didn't* winter on the Riviera assassinated him.) Here in the land of olives and anchovies, these proud onion domes seem odd. But, I imagine, so did those old Russians.

Cost and Hours: Free; Tue-Sat 9:00-12:00 & 14:00-19:00, Sun 9:00-12:00, closed Mon; chanted services Sat at 17:30 or 18:00, Sun at 10:00; may be closed during 2015, no shorts allowed, 17 Boulevard du Tzarewitch, tel. 04 93 96 88 02, www.acor-nice.com. The park around the church stays open at lunch and makes a fine setting for picnics.

Getting There: It's a 10-minute walk from the train station. Head west on Avenue Thiers, turn right on Avenue Gambetta, go under the freeway, and turn left following *Eglise Russe* signs. Or, from the station, take any bus heading west on Avenue Thiers and get off at Avenue Gambetta (then follow the previous directions).

Visiting the Cathedral: Step inside (pick up English info sheet). The one-room interior is filled with icons and candles, and traditional Russian music adds to the ambience. The wall of icons (iconostasis) divides the spiritual realm from and the temporal world of the worshippers. Only the priest can walk between the two worlds, by using the "Royal Door."

Take a close look at items lining the front (starting in the left corner). The angel with red boots and wings—the protector of the Romanov family—stands over a symbolic tomb of Christ. The tall black hammered-copper cross commemorates the massacre of Nicholas II and his family in 1918. Notice the Jesus icon to the right of the Royal Door. According to a priest here, as worshippers meditate, staring deep into the eyes of Jesus, they enter a lake where they find their soul. Surrounded by incense, chanting, and your entire community...it could happen. Farther to the right, the icon of the unhappy-looking Virgin and Child is decorated with semiprecious stones from the Ural Mountains. Artists worked a triangle into each iconic face—symbolic of the Trinity.

▲Castle Hill (Colline du Château)

Nice was first settled on this hill, which offers sweeping views over the city—best by far in the early morning or late in the day (park closes at 20:00 in summer, earlier off-season). You can get to the top by foot, by elevator (free, daily 10:00-19:00, until 20:00 in summer, next to beachfront Hôtel Suisse), or by pricey tourist train (described under "Tours in Nice" on page 337). Up top you'll find cafés and an extensive play area for kids.

For more on Castle Hill, see the Welcome to the Riviera Walk chapter.

Other Nice Museums

Both of these museums are acceptable rainy-day options, and free to enter.

Archaeological Museum (Musée Archéologique)

This museum displays various objects from the Romans' occupation of this region. It's convenient—just below the Matisse Museum—but has little of interest to anyone but ancient Rome aficionados. You also get access to the Roman bath ruins...which are, sadly, overgrown with weeds.

Cost and Hours: Free, very limited information in English, Wed-Mon 10:00-18:00, closed Tue, near Matisse Museum at 160 Avenue des Arènes de Cimiez, tel. 04 93 81 59 57.

Masséna Museum (Musée Masséna)

Like Nice's main square, this museum was named in honor of Jean-André Masséna, a highly regarded commander during France's Revolutionary and Napoleonic wars. The beachfront mansion is worth a gander for its lavish decor and lovely gardens alone (pick up your free ticket at the boutique just outside; no English information available).

NICE

Cost and Hours: Free, Wed-Mon 10:00-18:00, closed Tue, last entry 30 minutes before closing, 35 Promenade des Anglais, tel. 04 93 91 19 10, www.massena-nice.org.

Visiting the Museum: There are three levels. The elaborate reception rooms on the ground floor host occasional exhibits and give the best feeling for aristocratic Nice at the turn of the 19th century (find Masséna's portrait to the right after entering). The first floor up, offering a folk-museum-like look at Nice through the years, deserves most of your time. Moving counterclockwise around the floor, you'll find Napoleonic paraphernalia, Josephine's impressive cape and tiara, and Napoleon's vest (I'd look good in it). Next, antique posters promote vacations in Nice—look for the model and photos of the long-gone La Jetée Promenade and its casino, Nice's first. You'll see paintings of Russian nobility who appreciated Nice's climate, images of the city before its river was covered over by Place Masséna, and paintings honoring Italian patriot and Nice favorite Giuseppe Garibaldi. The top-floor painting gallery is devoted to the Riviera before World War II, with scenes of rural Villefranche-sur-Mer and other bucolic spots showing how the area looked before the tourist boom.

Near Nice: Scenic Railway
Narrow-Gauge Train into the Alps
(Chemins de Fer de Provence)

Leave the tourists behind and take the scenic train-bus-train combination that runs between Nice and Digne through canyons, along whitewater rivers, and through many tempting villages (4/day, 25 percent discount with railpass, departs Nice from Chemins de Fer de Provence Station—about 10 blocks behind the main train station, two blocks from the Libération tram stop, 4 Rue Alfred Binet, tel. 04 97 03 80 80, www.trainprovence.com).

Ongoing track work may affect the schedule; be sure to double-check all departures, arrivals, and connections.

Start with an early morning departure (look for an 8:30 train) and go as far as you want. Little **Entrevaux** is a good destination that feels forgotten and still stuck in its medieval shell (€10, 1.5 scenic hours from Nice). Climb high to the citadel for great views and appreciate the unspoiled character of the town. The train ends in **Digne-les-Bains** (a.k.a. simply Digne; €19, 3.5 hours), where you can catch a bus (covered by railpasses) to other destinations such as Aix-en-Provence (6/day, 2 hours). Mainline rail service to

Digne was recently eliminated, leaving travelers with few options other than limited bus connections. Most return to Nice, making a round-trip on the narrow-gauge train.

Nightlife in Nice

Promenade des Anglais, Cours Saleya, and Rue Masséna are all worth an evening walk. Nice's bars play host to a happening late-night scene, filled with jazz, rock, and trolling singles. Most activity focuses on Vieux Nice. Rue de la Préfecture and Place du Palais are ground zero for bar life, though Place Rossetti and Rue Droite are also good targets. **Distilleries Ideales** is a good place to start or end your evening, with a lively international crowd and a fun interior (where Rue de la Poissonnerie and Rue Barillerie meet, happy hour 18:00-21:00). **Wayne's Bar** is a happening spot for the younger, English-speaking backpacker crowd (15 Rue Préfecture). Along the Promenade des Anglais, the plush bar at **Hôtel Negresco** is fancy-cigar old English.

Plan on a cover charge or expensive drinks where music is involved. If you're out very late, avoid walking alone. Nice is well known for its lively after-dark action, but if you need even more action, head for the town of Juan-les-Pins (page 457). For more relaxed and accessible nightlife, consider nearby Antibes (page 443).

Sleeping in Nice

Don't look for charm in Nice. Go for modern and clean, with a central location and, in summer, air-conditioning. The rates listed here are for April through October. Prices generally drop €15-30 November through March, but go sky-high during the Nice Carnival (Feb 12-March 4 in 2014, www.nicecarnaval.com), the Cannes Film Festival (May 14-24 in 2014, www.festival-cannes .com), and Monaco's Grand Prix (May 22-25 in 2014, May 21-24 in 2015, www.acm.mc). Between the film festival and the Grand Prix, the second half of May is very tight every year. Nice is also one of Europe's top convention cities, and June is convention month here. Reserve early if visiting from May through August, especially during these times. For parking, ask your hotelier (several hotels offer deals for stashing your car or have limited private parking; reserve early), or see "Arrival in Nice—By Car" on page 333.

I've divided my sleeping recommendations into three areas: in the city center, between the train station and Place Masséna (easy access to the train station and Vieux Nice via the tramway, 20-minute walk to Promenade des Anglais); in the heart of Vieux Nice between Nice Etoile and the sea (east of Avenue Jean

Sleep Code

(€1 = about $1.30, country code: 33)

S = Single, **D** = Double/Twin, **T** = Triple, **Q** = Quad, **b** = bathroom, **s** = shower only, ***** = French hotel rating (0-5 stars). Hoteliers speak English; the hotels have elevators and accept credit cards unless otherwise noted.

To help you sort easily through these listings, I've divided the accommodations into three categories based on the price for a standard double room with bath:

$$$ Higher Priced—Most rooms €200 or more.
$$ Moderately Priced—Most rooms between €100-200.
$ Lower Priced—Most rooms €100 or less.

Prices can change without notice; verify the hotel's current rates online or by email. For the best prices, always book direct.

Médecin, good access to the sea at Quai des Etats-Unis); and near the beach, between Boulevard Victor Hugo and the sea (a somewhat classier and quieter area, offering better access to the Promenade des Anglais but longer walks to the train station and Vieux Nice. I've also listed hotels and a hostel on the outskirts. Before reserving, check hotel websites for deals (more common at larger hotels). Book directly with the hotel to get any special discounts for Rick Steves readers.

In the City Center

The train station area offers Nice's cheapest sleeps, though most hotels near the station ghetto are overrun, overpriced, and loud. The following hotels are the pleasant exceptions (most are near Avenue Jean Médecin).

$$$ Hôtel Masséna****, in a classy building two blocks from Place Masséna, is a "professional" hotel (popular with tour groups) with 110 rooms and way-mod public spaces. It's worth it only if you get a discounted rate (small Db-€199, larger Db-€289, still larger Db-€339, skip the €17 breakfast, call same-day for special rates—prices drop big time when hotel is not full, sixth-floor rooms have balconies, parking-€25/day—book ahead, 58 Rue Gioffredo, tel. 04 92 47 88 88, www.hotel-massena-nice.com, info@hotel-massena-nice.com).

$$ At Hôtel Durante***, you know you're on the Mediterranean as soon as you enter this cheery, way-orange building with rooms wrapped around a flowery courtyard. Every one of its quiet rooms overlooks a spacious, well-maintained patio/garden with an American-style Jacuzzi. The rooms are good enough (mostly big beds), the price is right enough, and the parking (limited spaces) is free (Sb-€85-105, Db-€100-115, Tb-€150-175, Qb-€180-200, breakfast-€10, air-con, Wi-Fi, 16 Avenue Durante, tel. 04 93 88 84 40, www.hotel-durante.com, info@hotel-durante .com).

$$ Hôtel Lafayette*, in a handy location a block behind the Galeries Lafayette department store, is a good value. It's comfortable, homey, and modest, with 17 mostly spacious rooms (some with thin walls), all one floor up from the street. It's family-run by Kiril, George, and young Victor. Rooms not overlooking Rue de l'Hôtel des Postes are quieter and worth requesting (standard Db-€105-120, spacious Db-€115-130, preferential rates for Rick Steves readers if booked directly with hotel, breakfast-€10, in-room coffee service, air-con, no elevator, guest computer and Wi-Fi, 32 Rue de l'Hôtel des Postes, tel. 04 93 85 17 84, www .hotellafayettenice.com, info@hotellafayettenice.com).

$$ Hôtel St. Georges, five blocks from the station toward the sea, offers fair rates, a backyard patio, and friendly Houssein at the reception. All rooms should be freshly renovated by the time you visit (Sb-€90, Db-€120, Tb with 3 beds-€140, extra bed-€20, breakfast-€9, air-con, free Wi-Fi, 7 Avenue Georges Clemenceau, tel. 04 93 88 79 21, www.hotelsaintgeorges.fr, contact@hotelsaint georges.fr).

$$ Hôtel Vendôme* gives you a whiff of the belle époque, with pink pastels, high ceilings, and grand staircases in a mansion set off the street. Its public spaces are delightful. The rooms are modern and come in all sizes; the best have balconies (on floors 4 and 5)—request *une chambre avec balcon* (Sb-€115-135, Db-€150-180, Tb-€180-200, prices vary with demand, check website for deals, breakfast-€15, air-con, guest computer and Wi-Fi, limited parking-€15/day—book ahead, 26 Rue Pastorelli at the corner of Rue Alberti, tel. 04 93 62 00 77, www.hotel-vendome-nice.com, contact@vendome-hotel-nice.com).

$ Hôtel Ibis Nice Centre Gare*, 100 yards to the right as you leave the station, gives those in need of train station access a secure refuge in this seedy area. It's big (200 rooms) and modern, but a good value with well-configured rooms, a refreshing pool, and cheap €9 parking (Db-€93, big "Club" Db-€125, breakfast-€9, air-con, guest computer and Wi-Fi, bar, café, 14 Avenue Thiers, tel. 04 93 88 85 85, www.ibishotel.com, h1396@accor.com).

$ Hôtel Belle Meunière*, in a fine old mansion built for Napoleon III's mistress, offers cheap beds and private rooms a block below the train station. Lively and youth hostel-esque, this simple

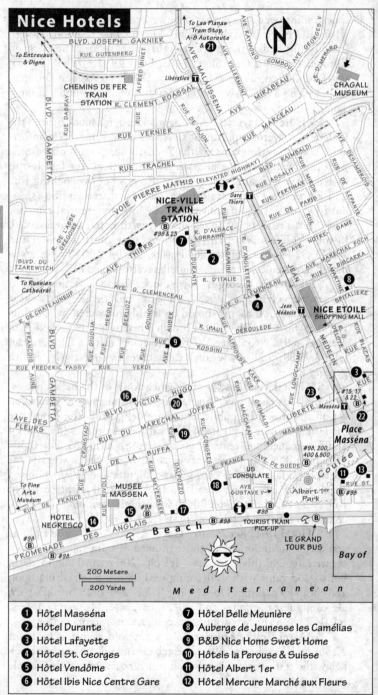

Nice Hotels

NICE

1 Hôtel Masséna
2 Hôtel Durante
3 Hôtel Lafayette
4 Hôtel St. Georges
5 Hôtel Vendôme
6 Hôtel Ibis Nice Centre Gare
7 Hôtel Belle Meunière
8 Auberge de Jeunesse les Camélias
9 B&B Nice Home Sweet Home
10 Hôtels la Perouse & Suisse
11 Hôtel Albert 1er
12 Hôtel Mercure Marché aux Fleurs

NICE

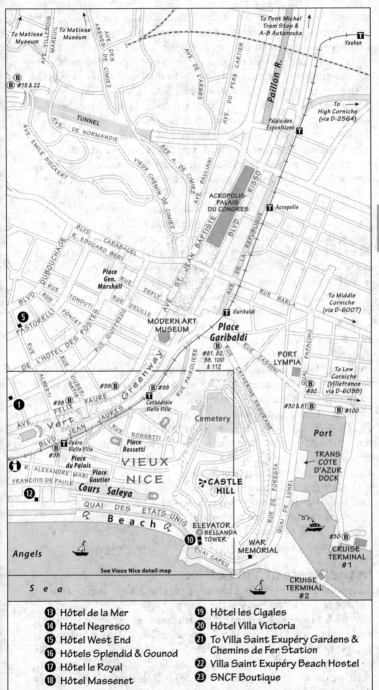

To Matisse Museum
To Matisse Museum
To Pont Michel Tram Stop & A-8 Autoroute

AVE. VILLEROIS
MAREUIL
AVE. DES ARÈNES DE CIMIEZ
AVE. DE L'ARBRE
AVE. DU PÈRE CARTIER
Vauban

#15 & 22
AVE. EMILE BIECKERT
TUNNEL DE NORMANDIE
VIEUX CHEMIN DE CIMIEZ
AVE. A. DE CIMIEZ
AVE. PAULIANI
Palais des Expositions
To High Corniche (via D-2564)

Paillon R.

ACROPOLIS-PALAIS DU CONGRÈS
Acropolis

BLVD. CARABACEL
BLVD. RISSO
BLVD. DE LA RÉPUBLIQUE

R. ÉDOUARD BERI
RUE DEFLY
RUE DELILLE
ST. JEAN BAPTISTE
RUE BARLA
To Middle Corniche (via D-6007)

Place Gen. Marshall
BLVD. DUBOUCHAGE
RUE TONDUTI
RUE FONCET
RUE GIOFFREDO

MODERN ART MUSEUM
Garibaldi
Place Garibaldi
#81, 82, 98, 100 & 112
PORT LYMPIA
QUAI PAPACINO
To Low Corniche (Villefranche via D-6098)

BLVD. PASTORELLI
RUE DE L'HOTEL DES POSTES
RUE CASSINI
RUE CATHERINE SÉGURANE
#82
#30 & 81
#100

❺

Greenway
#98
RUE PAIROLIÈRE
Cathédrale Vieille Ville

❶
AVE. ALBERTI
RUE GUBERNATIS
RUE FÉLIX FAURE
#98
#98
Port
TRANS CÔTE D'AZUR DOCK

Vert
BLVD. JEAN JAURÈS
RUE ROSSETTI
Place Rossetti

Opéra Vieille Ville
#98
VIEUX
Cemetery
RUE DE FORESTA

❶
R. ALEXANDRE MARI
Place du Palais
Place Gautier
NICE
RUE DE LUNEL

FRANCOIS DE PAULE
Cours Saleya
CASTLE HILL

❶❷
QUAI DES ETATS-UNIS
ELEVATOR
BELLANDA TOWER
#30
CRUISE TERMINAL #1

Beach
❶⓪
QUAI CAPEU
WAR MEMORIAL

Angels
See Vieux Nice detail map

S e a
CRUISE TERMINAL #2

⓭ Hôtel de la Mer
⓮ Hôtel Negresco
⓯ Hôtel West End
⓰ Hôtels Splendid & Gounod
⓱ Hôtel le Royal
⓲ Hôtel Massenet

⓳ Hôtel les Cigales
⓴ Hôtel Villa Victoria
㉑ To Villa Saint Exupéry Gardens & Chemins de Fer Station
㉒ Villa Saint Exupéry Beach Hostel
㉓ SNCF Boutique

but well-kept place attracts budget-minded travelers of all ages with basic-but-adequate rooms and charismatic Mademoiselle Marie-Pierre presiding (with perfect English). Tables in the front yard greet guests and provide opportunities to meet other travelers. Air-conditioning may be installed by 2014 (bunk in 4-bed dorm-€24-28 with private bath, €18-22 with shared bath; Db-€68-78, Tb-€84-93, Qb-€116-124; includes breakfast, Wi-Fi, laundry service, limited parking-€9/day, 21 Avenue Durante, tel. 04 93 88 66 15, www.bellemeuniere.com, hotel.belle.meuniere@cegetel.net).

$ Auberge de Jeunesse les Camélias is a fun, laid-back youth hostel with a great location, modern facilities, and a fun evening atmosphere. Rooms accommodate between four and eight people of all ages in bunk beds (136 beds in all) and come with showers and sinks—WCs are down the hall. Reservations must be made on the website at least three days in advance. If you don't have a reservation, call by 10:00—or, better, try to snag a bunk in person. The place is popular but worth a try for last-minute availability (€28/bed, one-time €18 extra charge without hostel membership, includes breakfast, maximum 6-night stay, rooms closed 11:00-15:00 but can leave bags, guest computer, laundry, kitchen, safes, bar, 3 Rue Spitalieri, tel. 04 93 62 15 54, www.hihostels.com, nice-camelias@fuaj.org).

$ B&B Nice Home Sweet Home is a great value if you have patience. Genevieve (a.k.a. Jennifer) Levert rents out three large rooms and one small single in her home. Her rooms are simply decorated, with high ceilings, big windows, lots of light, and space to spread out. One room comes with private bath; otherwise, it's just like at home...down the hall (S-€35-44, D-€61-75, Db-€65-78, Tb-€75-85, Q-€80-110, includes breakfast, elevator, one floor up, washer/dryer-€6, kitchen access, 35 Rue Rossini at intersection with Rue Auber, mobile 06 19 66 03 63, www.nicehomesweethome.com, glevert@free.fr).

Hostel: **$ Villa Saint Exupéry Beach,** run by the same owners as the Villa Saint Exupéry Gardens outside of town, is a new hostel in the center of Nice with a friendly vibe and reasonable rates (behind the Galleries Lafayette at 6 Rue Sacha-Guitry; see Villa Saint Exupéry Gardens listing on page 359 for contact info).

In the Heart of Vieux Nice

These Vieux Nice hotels are either on the sea or within an easy walk of it. For locations, see the map on page 356.

$$$ Hôtel la Perouse********, built into the rock of Castle Hill at the east end of the bay, gets my vote for Nice's best splurge. This refuge-hotel is top-to-bottom flawless in every detail—from its elegant rooms (satin curtains, velour headboards) and attentive staff to its rooftop terrace with Jacuzzi, sleek pool, and lovely garden restaurant. Sleep here to be spoiled and escape the big city (garden-view Db-€380, seaview Db-€480, good family options and Web deals, free Wi-Fi, 11 Quai Rauba Capeu, tel. 04 93 62 34 63, www.hotel-la-perouse.com, lp@hotel-la-perouse.com).

$$$ Hôtel Suisse**, below Castle Hill, has Nice's best sea and city views for the money, and is surprisingly quiet given the busy street below. Rooms are quite comfortable, the decor is tasteful, and the staff is helpful. There's no reason to sleep here if you don't land a view, so I've listed prices only for view rooms— many of which have balconies (Db-€200-285, extra bed-€36, breakfast-€17, book far in advance for better rates, Wi-Fi, 15 Quai Rauba Capeu, tel. 04 92 17 39 00, www.hotels-ocre-azur.com, hotel.suisse@hotels-ocre-azur.com).

$$ Hôtel Albert 1er* is a good value, located on Albert 1er Park, two blocks from the beach and Place Masséna. Rooms are bright and well appointed. Some come with views of the bay, while others overlook the park (standard Db-€169-189, sea- or park-view Db-€179-199, Tb-€189-209, breakfast-€12, air-con, Wi-Fi, 4 Avenue des Phocéens, tel. 04 93 85 74 01, www.hotelalbert-1er .com, info@hotel-albert1er.com).

$$ Hôtel Mercure Marché aux Fleurs** is ideally situated across from the sea and behind Cours Saleya. Rooms are tastefully designed and well-maintained (some with beds in a loft). Prices are reasonable, though rates vary dramatically depending on demand—check their website for deals. Don't confuse this Mercure with the four other branches in Nice (standard Db-€172, superior Db-€200 and worth the extra euros, sea view-€50 extra, breakfast-€8, air-con, 91 Quai des Etats-Unis, tel. 04 93 85 74 19, www.hotelmercure.com, h0962@accor.com).

$$ Hôtel de la Mer is a tiny place with an enviable position overlooking Place Masséna, just steps from Vieux Nice (it's among the closest of my listings to the old town). The majority of the rooms are smartly renovated and worth the higher price; the remaining few are "old school" and priced that way (older Db-€110, newer Db-€140, Tb-€160, breakfast-€7, air-con, Wi-Fi, 4 Place Masséna, tel. 04 93 92 09 10, www.hoteldelamernice.com, hotel.mer@wanadoo.fr).

Near the Beach

These hotels are close to the Promenade des Anglais (and most are far from Vieux Nice). The Negresco, West End, and le Royal are big, vintage Nice hotels that open onto the sea from the heart of the Promenade des Anglais.

$$$ Hôtel Negresco*** owns Nice's most prestigious address on Promenade des Anglais and knows it. Still, it's the kind of place that if you were to splurge just once in your life...

Vieux Nice Hotels & Restaurants

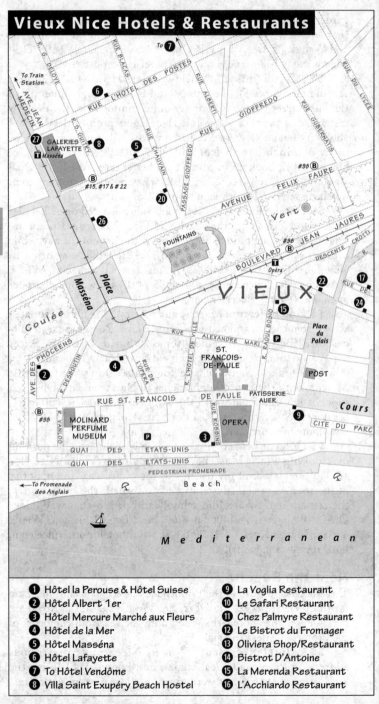

NICE

1 Hôtel la Perouse & Hôtel Suisse
2 Hôtel Albert 1er
3 Hôtel Mercure Marché aux Fleurs
4 Hôtel de la Mer
5 Hôtel Masséna
6 Hôtel Lafayette
7 To Hôtel Vendôme
8 Villa Saint Exupéry Beach Hostel
9 La Voglia Restaurant
10 Le Safari Restaurant
11 Chez Palmyre Restaurant
12 Le Bistrot du Fromager
13 Oliviera Shop/Restaurant
14 Bistrot D'Antoine
15 La Merenda Restaurant
16 L'Acchiardo Restaurant

NICE

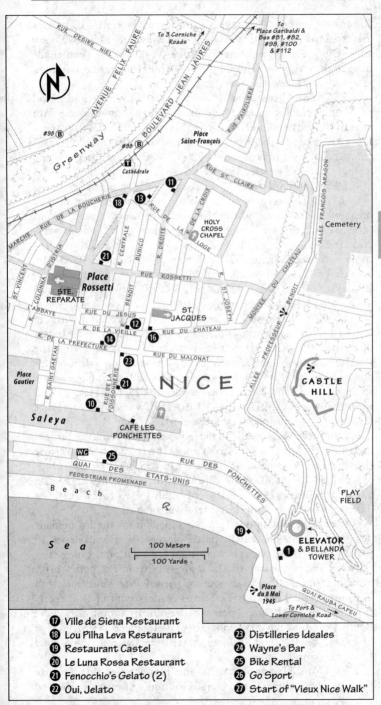

17 Ville de Siena Restaurant
18 Lou Pilha Leva Restaurant
19 Restaurant Castel
20 Le Luna Rossa Restaurant
21 Fenocchio's Gelato (2)
22 Oui, Jelato

23 Distilleries Ideales
24 Wayne's Bar
25 Bike Rental
26 Go Sport
27 Start of "Vieux Nice Walk"

Rooms are opulent (see page 372 for more description), and tips are expected (viewless Db-€380-560, seaview Db-€450-680, view suite-€890-2,700, breakfast-€30, Old World bar, 37 Promenade des Anglais, tel. 04 93 16 64 00, www.hotel-negresco-nice.com, reservations@hotel-negresco.com).

$$$ Hôtel West End**** delivers formal service and décor, polished public spaces, and high prices. Its chic rooms come with effective blinds and all the comforts (viewless Db-€300, seaview Db-€350, check website for deals, guest computer and Wi-Fi, 31 Promenade des Anglais, tel. 04 92 14 44 00, www.hotel-westend .com, reception@westsend3ahotels.com).

$$$ Hôtel Splendid**** is a worthwhile splurge if you miss your Marriott. The panoramic rooftop pool, bar/restaurant, and breakfast room almost justify the cost...but throw in plush rooms (all seven floors are non-smoking), a free gym, spa services, and air-conditioning, and you're as good as home (Db-€230— some with decks, deluxe Db with terrace-€270, suites-€355-410, breakfast-€19, better prices available on website, parking-€24, 50 Boulevard Victor Hugo, tel. 04 93 16 41 00, www.splendid-nice .com, info@splendid-nice.com).

$$ Hôtel le Royal*** is an old-school resort hotel with big lounges, long hallways, and 140 rooms that have seen better days. But the prices are close to acceptable, considering the terrific location—and sometimes they have rooms when others don't (viewless Db-€155-170, seaview Db-€195-215, bigger view room-€215-235 and worth it, extra person-€25, breakfast-€14, 23 Promenade des Anglais, tel. 04 93 16 43 00, www.hotel-royal-nice .cote.azur.fr, royal@vacancesbleues.com).

$$ Hôtel Massenet*** is tucked away a block off the Promenade des Anglais in a pedestrian zone. It has 29 tidy rooms (love the shag carpet) at good rates (small Db-€95, standard Db-€140-155, larger Db-€160, some rooms with decks, breakfast-€10, parking-€10/day, 11 Rue Massenet, tel. 04 93 87 11 31, www .hotelmassenet.com, hotelmassenet@wanadoo.fr).

$$ Hôtel les Cigales***, a few blocks from the Promenade des Anglais, is a smart little pastel place with tasteful decor, 19 sharp rooms (those with showers are a tad small, most have tub-showers and are standard size), air-conditioning, and a nifty upstairs terrace, all well managed by friendly Mr. Valentino, with Veronique and Elaine. Rick Steves readers who book directly through the hotel get a 7 percent discount by typing this code: RICK (standard Db-€110-160, Tb-€130-180, free Wi-Fi, 16 Rue Dalpozzo, tel. 04 97 03 10 70, ww.hotel-lescigales.com, info@hotel -lescigales.com).

$$ Hôtel Gounod*** is behind Hôtel Splendid. Because the two share the same owners, Gounod's guests are allowed free access to Splendid's pool, Jacuzzi, and other amenities. Most rooms are comfortable and quiet, with high ceilings and appealing decor (Db-€160, palatial 4-person suites-€260, breakfast-€11, air-con, parking-€18/day, 3 Rue Gounod, tel. 04 93 16 42 00, www .gounod-nice.com, info@gounod-nice.com).

$$ Hôtel Villa Victoria**** is a fine place managed by cheery Marlena, who welcomes travelers into her spotless, classy old building with an open, attractive lobby overlooking a sprawling garden-courtyard. Rooms are comfortable and well kept, with space to stretch out (streetside Db-€160, garden-side Db-€175, Tb-€190, suites-€210, breakfast-€15, air-con, minibar, Wi-Fi, parking-€18/day, 33 Boulevard Victor Hugo, tel. 04 93 88 39 60, fax 04 93 88 07 98, www.villa-victoria.com, contact@villa-victoria .com).

Barely Beyond Nice

$ Villa Saint Exupéry Gardens, a service-oriented hostel (they answer the phone in English), is a haven two miles north of the city center. Its amenities and 60 comfortable, spick-and-span rooms create a friendly climate for budget-minded travelers of any age. Often filled with energetic youth, the place can be noisy. There are units for one, two, and up to six people. Many have private bathrooms and views of the Mediterranean—some come with balconies. You'll also find a laundry room, complete kitchen facilities, and a lively bar. There's easy Internet access with a wall of guest computers in the lobby and Wi-Fi in all the rooms (bed in dorm-€20-40/person, S-€50-70, Db-€60-110, Tb-€110-150, includes big breakfast, discounts in low season, no curfew, 22 Avenue Gravier, tel. 04 93 84 42 83, toll-free tel. 08 00 30 74 09—works only within France, fax 04 92 09 82 94, www.villahostels .com, reservations@vsaint.com). From the center of town, ride the tram (direction: Las Planas) to the Compte de Falicon stop, then either walk 10 minutes or take the free shuttle from the Casino supermarket by the tram stop (no service 12:00-17:00).

Near the Airport

Several airport hotels offer a handy and cheap port-in-the-storm for those with early flights or who are just stopping in for a single night: Hôtel Première Classe (www.premiereclasse.com), and Hôtel Ibis Nice Aéroport (www.ibisnice.com). Free shuttles connect these hotels with both airport terminals.

You'll find greater comfort at the airport for a bit more (and free private shuttle vans) at these hotels: Novotel (www.novotel .com), Holiday Inn (www.holidayinn.com), and Campanile (www .campanile.fr).

Longer-Stay Rentals

Renting an apartment, house, or villa can be a cost-effective way to explore the Côte d'Azur. Rentals are typically by the week, giving you time to take advantage of day-trip possibilities.

Riviera Pebbles offers a wide range of rental apartments throughout the Riviera and gets good reviews from happy clients (www.rivierapebbles.com).

VRBO, an international network of vacation rentals (houses, apartments, and *gîtes*), cuts out the middleman and puts you directly in touch with the owner (www.vrbo.com).

Eating in Nice

Remember, you're in a resort. Seek ambience and fun, and lower your palate's standards. Italian is a low-risk and regional cuisine. The listed restaurants are concentrated in neighborhoods close to my recommended hotels. Promenade des Anglais is ideal for picnic dinners on warm, languid evenings. Vieux Nice has the best and busiest dining atmosphere (and best range of choices), while the Nice Etoile area is more local, convenient, and also offers a good range of choices. To feast cheaply, check out my suggestions in Vieux Nice, or explore the area around the train station. For a more peaceful meal, head for nearby Villefranche-sur-Mer (see page 404). Allow yourself one dinner at a beachfront restaurant in Nice, and for terribly touristy trolling, wander the wall-to-wall eateries lining Rue Masséna. Yuck.

In Vieux Nice

Nice's dinner scene converges on Cours Saleya (koor sah-lay-yuh), which is entertaining enough in itself to make the generally mediocre food a good deal. It's a fun, festive spot to compare tans and mussels. Even if you're eating elsewhere, wander through here in the evening. For locations, see the map on page 356.

La Voglia has figured out a winning formula: Good food + ample servings + fair prices = good business. Come here early for top-value Italian cuisine, or plan on waiting for a table. There's fun seating inside and out (€12-14 pizza and pasta, €15-25 *plats*, open daily, at the western edge of Cours Saleya at 2 Rue St. Francois de Paule, tel. 04 93 80 99 16).

Le Safari is a fair option for outdoor dining on Cours Saleya, with a few more locals than tourists. The cuisine is Niçois, and the service is professional (€18-30 *plats*, open daily, 1 Cours Saleya, tel. 04 93 80 18 44, www.restaurantsafari.fr).

Chez Palmyre is the place to eat on a budget in the old town. It's popular, so book this one ahead. The ambience is rustic but intimate, and the menu changes every two weeks. The three-course *menu* is only €15, and the food could not be more homemade (closed Sun, cash only, 5 Rue Droite, tel. 04 93 85 72 32).

Le Bistrot du Fromager's owner, Hugo, is crazy about cheese and wine. Come here to escape the heat and dine in cozy, cool, vaulted cellars surrounded by shelves of wine. All dishes use cheese as their base ingredient, although you'll also find pasta, ham, and salmon (with cheese, of course). This is a good choice for vegetarians (€10-14 starters, €15-21 *plats*, €6 desserts, closed Sun, just off Place du Jésus at 29 Rue Benoît Bunico, tel. 04 93 13 07 83).

Oliviera venerates the French olive. This shop/restaurant sells a variety of oils, offers free tastings, and serves a menu of dishes paired with specific oils (think of a wine pairing). Welcoming owner Nadim, who speaks excellent English, knows all his producers, and provides "Olive Oil 101" explanations with his tastings (best if you buy something afterward or have a meal). You'll learn how passionate he is about his products, and once you've had a taste, you'll want to stay and eat—so go early (or reserve ahead), as tables fill fast (allow €40 with wine, €16-24 main dishes, Tue-Sat 10:00-22:00, closed Sun-Mon, indoor seating only, 8 bis Rue du Collet, tel. 04 93 13 06 45).

Bistrot D'Antoine is a welcoming, vine-draped option whose delightful menu emphasizes Niçois cuisine and good grilled selections. The food is delicious and the prices are reasonable, so call ahead to reserve a table (€7-10 starters, €13-18 *plats*, €6 desserts, closed Sun-Mon, 27 Rue de la Préfecture, tel. 04 93 85 29 57).

La Merenda is a tiny place on the edge of the old town. Dine on simple, home-style dishes in a communal environment. The menu, presented tableside on a small blackboard, changes with the season. This place fills fast, so go early (opens at 19:00) or, since they don't have a phone, drop by during the day to reserve (€10-12 starters, €12-20 *plats*, €6 desserts, closed Sat-Sun, cash only, 4 Rue Raoul Bosio, www.lamerenda.net).

L'Acchiardo, hidden away in the heart of Vieux Nice, is a homey eatery that does a good job mixing a loyal clientele with hungry tourists. Its simple, hearty Niçois cuisine is served at fair prices by gentle Monsieur Acchiardo. The small plaque under the menu outside says the restaurant has been run by father and son since 1927 (€8 starters, €15-20 *plats,* €7 desserts, cash only, closed Sat-Sun, indoor seating only, 38 Rue Droite, tel. 04 93 85 51 16).

Ville de Siena draws young travelers who dig this place for its big portions, open kitchen, and raucous atmosphere, with tables crammed outside on a narrow lane. The food is Italian and hearty (€12-17 *plats*, closed Sun, 10 Rue St. Vincent, tel. 04 93 80 12 45).

Lou Pilha Leva delivers fun and cheap lunch or dinner options with Niçois specialties and always busy outdoor-only picnic-table dining (daily, located where Rue de la Loge and Rue

NICE

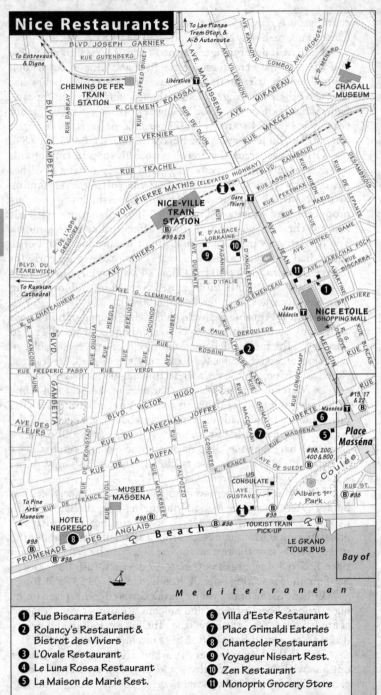

Nice Restaurants

1. Rue Biscarra Eateries
2. Rolancy's Restaurant & Bistrot des Viviers
3. L'Ovale Restaurant
4. Le Luna Rossa Restaurant
5. La Maison de Marie Rest.
6. Villa d'Este Restaurant
7. Place Grimaldi Eateries
8. Chantecler Restaurant
9. Voyageur Nissart Rest.
10. Zen Restaurant
11. Monoprix Grocery Store

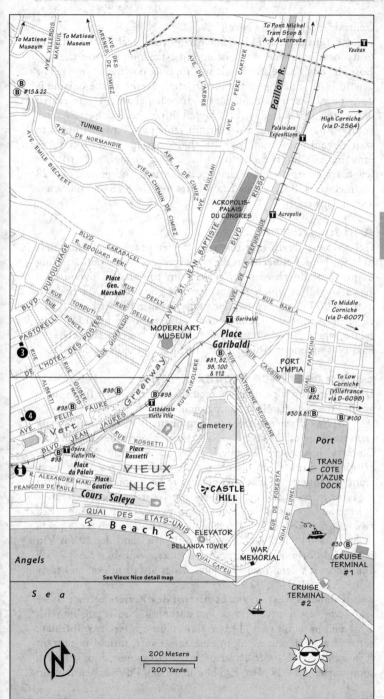

NICE

Centrale meet in Vieux Nice).

Restaurant Castel is a fine eat-on-the-beach option, thanks to its location at the very east end of Nice looking over the bay. Lose the city hustle and bustle by dropping down the steps below Castle Hill. The views are unforgettable even if the cuisine is not; you can even have lunch at your beach chair if you've rented one here (€15/half-day, €18/day). Dinner here is best: Arrive before sunset and find a waterfront table perfectly positioned to watch evening swimmers get in their last laps as the sky turns pink and city lights flicker on. Linger long enough to justify the few extra euros the place charges (€18 salads and pastas, €20-28 main courses, 8 Quai des Etats-Unis, tel. 04 93 85 22 66, www .castelplage.com).

And for Dessert...

Gelato lovers should save room for the tempting ice-cream stands in Vieux Nice. **Fenocchio** is the city's favorite, with mouthwatering displays of 86 flavors ranging from tomato to lavender to avocado—all of which are surprisingly good (daily March-Nov, until 24:00 in summer, two locations: 2 Place Rossetti and 6 Rue de la Poissonnerie). Gelato connoisseurs should head for **Oui, Jelato,** where the selection may be a fraction of Fenocchio's but the quality is superior (5 Rue de la Préfecture, on the Place du Palais).

Eating near Nice Etoile

If you're not up for eating in Vieux Nice, try one of these spots around the Nice Etoile shopping mall.

On Rue Biscarra: An appealing lineup of bistros overflowing with outdoor tables stretches along the broad sidewalk on Rue Biscarra (just east of Avenue Jean Médecin behind Nice Etoile, all closed Sun). Come here to dine with area residents away from the tourists. These two places are both good choices, with pleasant interior and exterior seating: **L'Authentic** has creative cuisine and comes with a memorable owner, burly Philippe (€23 two-course *menus,* €27 three-course *menus,* reasonable pasta dishes, tel. 04 93 62 48 88, www.lauthentic.com). **Le 20 sur Vin** is a neighborhood favorite with a cozy, wine-bar-meets-café ambience. It offers *(bien sûr)* good wines at fair prices, and tasty bistro fare (tel. 04 93 92 93 20).

Rolancy's Restaurant & Bistrot des Viviers attract those who require attentive service and authentic Niçois cuisine with a big emphasis on fish. This classy splurge offers two intimate settings as different as night and day: a soft, formal restaurant (€58 *menu,* €28-38 *plats*), and a relaxed *bistrot* next door (€10 fish soup starter, €24-35 *plats,* €45 bouillabaisse). I'd reserve a table in the atmospheric *bistrot,* where some outdoor seating is available (restaurant closed Sun, *bistrot* open daily, 5-minute walk west of Avenue Jean Médecin at 22 Rue Alphonse Karr, tel. 04 93 16 00 48, http://restaurant-gastronomique.fr).

L'Ovale takes its name from the shape of a rugby ball. This welcoming, well-run bistro has quality food at respectable prices, with an emphasis on the cuisine of southwestern France. Dine inside on big *plats* for €12-16; consider their specialty, *cassoulet* (€17), or the *salade de manchons* (€13), with duck and walnuts (excellent €18 three-course *menu,* €13 big salads, daily, air-con, 29 Rue Pastorelli, tel. 04 93 80 31 65).

Le Luna Rossa is *molto* Italian, with a smart setting inside and out. It's also *molto* popular with locals. Come early or book ahead (€10 starters, €20-27 *plats,* just north of the parkway at 3 Rue Chauvain, tel. 04 93 85 55 66).

La Maison de Marie is a surprisingly good-quality refuge off touristy Rue Masséna, where most other restaurants serve mediocre food to tired travelers. Enter through a deep-red arch to a bougainvillea-draped courtyard, and enjoy the fair prices and excellent cuisine that draw neighborhood regulars and out-of-towners alike. The interior tables are as appealing as those in the courtyard, but expect some smokers outside. The €23 *menu* is a terrific value (€12-18 starters and €20-30 *plats,* open daily, look for the square red sign at 5 Rue Masséna, tel. 04 93 82 15 93).

Villa d'Este has the same owners as the recommended La Voglia (listed earlier, under "In Vieux Nice"). The portions are big, the price is right, and the quality is tops (daily, on a busy pedestrian street at 6 Rue Masséna, tel. 04 93 82 47 77).

Near Promenade des Anglais

Worthwhile restaurants are few and far between in this area. Either head for Vieux Nice or try one of these good places.

On Place Grimaldi: This square nurtures a lineup of appealing restaurants with good indoor and outdoor seating along a broad sidewalk under tall, leafy sycamore trees. **Crêperie Bretonne** is the only *crêperie* I list in Nice (€11 dinner crêpes, closed Sun, 3 Place Grimaldi, tel. 04 93 82 28 47). **Le Grimaldi** delivers basic café fare (€17 pasta, €15-25 *plats,* closed Sun, 1 Place Grimaldi, tel. 04 93 87 98 13).

Chantecler has Nice's most prestigious address—inside the Hôtel Negresco. This is everything a luxury restaurant should be: elegant, soft, and top quality. If your trip is ending in Nice, call or email for reservations—you've earned this splurge (*menus* from €100, closed Mon-Tue, 37 Promenade des Anglais, tel. 04 93 16 64 00, chantecler@lenegresco.com).

NICE

Near the Train Station

Both of the following restaurants, a block below the train station, provide good indoor and outdoor seating as well as excellent value.

Voyageur Nissart has blended good-value cuisine with cool Mediterranean ambience and friendly service since 1908. Current owner Max is a great host, and the quality of his cuisine makes this a good choice for travelers on any budget—try the wonderful €14 *filet de rouget à la niçoise* or the fine €8 *salade niçoise* (€16 three-course *menus*, good *plats* from €11, inexpensive wines, closed Mon, 19 Rue d'Alsace-Lorraine, tel. 04 93 82 19 60).

Zen provides a Japanese break from French cuisine. Interior seating is arranged around the chef's stove, and the tasty specialties draw a strong following (€16 three-course *menu*, €8-15 sushi, open daily, 27 Rue d'Angleterre, tel. 04 93 82 41 20).

Nice Connections

By Train and Bus

For a comparison of train and bus connections from Nice to nearby coastal towns, see the "Public Transportation in the French Riviera" sidebar on page 322.

Note that most long-distance train connections to other French cities require a change in Marseille. The Grande Ligne train to Bordeaux (serving Antibes, Cannes, Toulon, and Marseille—and connecting from there to Arles, Nîmes, and Carcassonne) requires a reservation. Remember that on regional buses (except on express airport buses), many one-way rides cost €1.50—regardless of length (the €1.50 ticket is good for up to 74 minutes of travel in one direction, including transfers).

From Nice by Train to: Cannes (2/hour, 30-40 minutes), **Antibes** (2/hour, 15-30 minutes), **Villefranche-sur-Mer** (2/hour, 10 minutes), **Eze-le-Village** (2/hour, 15 minutes to Eze-Bord-de-Mer, then bus #83 to Eze, 8/day), **Monaco** (2/hour, 20 minutes), **Menton** (2/hour, 25 minutes), **Grasse** (15/day, 1.25 hours), **Marseille** (18/day, 2.5 hours), **Cassis** (14/day, 3 hours, transfer in Toulon or Marseille), **Arles** (11/day, 3.75-4.5 hours, most require transfer in Marseille or Avignon), **Avignon** (20/day, most by TGV, 4 hours, most require transfer in Marseille), **Paris'** Gare de Lyon (hourly, 5.75 hours, may require change; 11.5-hour night train goes to Paris' Gare d'Austerlitz), **Aix-en-Provence** TGV Station (10/day, 2-3.5 hours, usually changes in Marseille), **Chamonix** (4/day, 10 hours, many change in St-Gervais and Lyon), **Beaune** (7/day, 7 hours, 1-2 changes), **Munich** (4/day, 12.5-14 hours with 2-4 transfers, longer night trains possible, some via Italy), **Interlaken** (6/day, 9-10 hours, 2-5 transfers), **Florence** (6/day, 7-9 hours, 1-3 transfers), **Milan** (7/day, 5-5.5 hours, all require transfers), **Venice**

(5/day, 8-9 hours, all require transfers), **Barcelona** (1/day via Montpellier, 10 hours, more with multiple changes).

From Nice by Bus to: **Cannes** (#200, 4/hour Mon-Sat, 2-3/hour Sun, 1.5-1.75 hours), **Antibes** (#200, 4/hour Mon-Sat, 2-3/hour Sun, 1-1.5 hours), **Villefranche-sur-Mer** (#100, 4-5/hour Mon-Sat, 3-4/hour Sun, 20 minutes; or #81, 2-4/hour, 20 minutes), **St-Jean-Cap-Ferrat** (#81, 2-4/hour, 35 minutes), **Eze-le-Village** (#82 or #112, 16/day Mon-Sat, 8/day Sun, 40 minutes), **La Turbie** (#116 or #T-66, 5/day Mon-Sat, 7/day Sun, 45 minutes), **Monaco** (#100, 4-5/hour Mon-Sat, 3-4/hour Sun, 45 minutes), **Menton** (#100, 4-5/hour Mon-Sat, 3-4/hour Sun, 1.25 hours), **St-Paul-de-Vence** (#400, every 30-45 minutes, 45 minutes), **Vence** (#400, every 30-45 minutes, 50 minutes), **Grasse** (#500, every 30-45 minutes, 1.25 hours).

By Plane

Nice's easy-to-navigate airport (Aéroport de Nice Côte d'Azur, airport code: NCE) is on the Mediterranean, a 20- to 30-minute drive west of the city center. Planes leave roughly hourly for Paris (one-hour flight, about the same price as a train ticket, check www.easyjet.com for the cheapest flights to Paris' Orly airport). The two terminals (Terminal 1 and Terminal 2) are connected by frequent shuttle buses *(navettes)*. Both terminals have TIs (and Terminal 1 has an info desk just for Monaco), banks, ATMs, taxis, baggage storage (€6.50/day per piece, open daily 5:45-23:00), and buses to Nice (tel. 04 89 88 98 28, www.nice.aeroport.fr).

Getting from the Airport to the City Center

Taxis into the center are expensive considering the short distance (figure €35 to Nice hotels, €60 to Villefranche-sur-Mer, €70 to Antibes, 10 percent more 19:00-7:00 and all day Sun). Taxis stop outside door *(Porte)* A-1 at Terminal 1 and outside *Porte* A-3 at Terminal 2. Notorious for overcharging, Nice taxis are not always so nice. If your fare for a ride into town is much higher than €35 (or €40 at night or on Sun), refuse to pay the overage. If this doesn't work, tell the cabbie to call a *gendarme* (police officer). It's always a good idea to ask for a receipt *(reçu)*.

Airport shuttle vans work with some of my recommended hotels, but they only make sense when going *to* the airport, not when arriving on an international flight. Unlike taxis, shuttle vans offer a fixed price that doesn't rise on Sundays, early mornings, or evenings. Prices are best for groups (figure €30 for one person, and only a little more for additional people; keep in mind that taxis to the airport cost roughly €35, so be wary of services that charge much more). **Nice Airport Shuttle** is one option (1-2 people-€32, additional person-€14, mobile 06 60 33 20 54, www.nice-airport-shuttle.com). **Med-Tour**, in addition to sightseeing tours, also offers airport transfers (1-4 people-€29, €10 extra before 7:00 or after 21:00, tel. 04 93 82 92 58, mobile 06 73 82 04 10, www.med-tour.com). Ask your hotelier for other recommendations.

Three bus lines connect the airport with the city center, offering good alternatives to high-priced taxis. **Bus #99** (airport express) runs from both terminals to Nice's main train station (€6, 2/hour, 8:00-21:00, 30 minutes, drops you within a 10-minute walk of many recommended hotels). To take this bus *to* the airport, catch it right in front of the train station (departs on the half-hour). If your hotel is within walking distance of the station, #99 is a breeze.

Bus #98 serves both terminals, and runs along Promenade des Anglais to the edge of Vieux Nice (€6, 3/hour, from the airport 6:00-23:00, to the airport until 21:00, 30 minutes, see map on page 356 for stops). The slower, cheaper local **bus #23** serves only Terminal 1, and makes every stop between the airport and train station (€1, 5/hour, runs 6:00-20:00, 40 minutes, direction: St. Maurice).

For all buses, buy tickets in the information office just outside either terminal, or from the driver. To reach the bus information office and stops at Terminal 1, turn left after passing customs and exit the doors at the far end. Buses serving Terminal 2 stop across the street from the airport exit (information kiosk and ticket sales to the right as you exit).

Getting from the Airport to Nearby Destinations

To get to **Villefranche-sur-Mer** from the airport, take bus #98 to Place Garibaldi, then use the same ticket to transfer to bus #81 or #100 (4-5/hour Mon-Sat on #100, 3-4/hour Sun; 2-4/hour on #81; 20 minutes; see map on page 330 for stop location).

To reach **Antibes,** take bus #250 from either terminal (about 2/hour, 40 minutes, €9). For **Cannes,** take bus #210 from either terminal (2/hour, 50 minutes on freeway, €18). Pricey express bus #110 runs from the airport directly to **Monaco** (2/hour, 50 minutes, €20); it's cheaper (€6)—but more time-consuming—to take bus #99 or #98 to Nice, then transfer to a Monaco-bound bus or train.

By Cruise Ship

Nice's port is at the eastern edge of the town center, separated from the old town and best beaches by Castle Hill. Cruise ships dock at

either end of the mouth of this port: **Terminal 1** to the east (along the embankment called Quai du Commerce), or **Terminal 2** to the west (along Quai Infernet). At both terminals, TI kiosks (under pointy white tents) are timed to be open when cruises arrive.

A street called Place Ile de Beauté runs along the top of the port; here you'll find bus stops (including stops for the bus to Villefranche-sur-Mer and Monaco) and easy access to Place Garibaldi, where you can hop on Nice's tramway (which you can ride to the train station). From either terminal, it's about a 10-minute walk to the top of the port, or you can ride the free shuttle bus *(navette)*.

Taxis at the terminals charge about €25-30 to points within Nice (for example, the train station, or the Matisse or Chagall museums), €35-40 one-way to Villefranche-sur-Mer, or €80-90 one-way to Monaco. **Le Grand Tour Bus** hop-on, hop-off bus circuit has a stop at the top of the port (see "Tours in Nice," earlier).

Getting from the Port to the City Center

Nice's main promenade and old town are just on the other side of Castle Hill from the port. If your ship docks at Terminal 2, just walk around the base of the castle-topped hill (with the sea on your left), and you'll be at Vieux Nice in about 10-15 minutes. Terminal 1 is at the far end of the port from the old town. If you arrive here, it's slightly faster to circle around the back of Castle Hill: Walk or ride the shuttle bus to the top of the port, take the angled Rue Cassini to Place Garibaldi (described next), then walk into the old town from there (total walk: about 20-25 minutes).

The square called **Place Garibaldi** serves as a gateway between the port of Nice and the rest of the city. It's about a 15- to 20-minute walk from either cruise terminal: First, walk (or ride the shuttle bus) to the top-left corner of the port area, and head up the angled Rue Cassini toward the square with the palm trees. After three short blocks, you'll pop out at Place Garibaldi.

Once in Place Garibaldi, to reach Vieux Nice, walk straight through the middle of the square and out the other side, then turn left and walk down the broad Boulevard Jean Jaurès; the old town sprawls to your left. To reach the tram stop from Place Garibaldi, walk along the right side of the square, then turn right on Avenue de la République and walk a half-block. From here, you can ride the tram to Place Masséna (where you can catch bus #15 or #22 to the Chagall or Matisse museums, or #17 to the Matisse Museum) and the train station (Gare Thiers stop).

Getting from the Port to Nearby Destinations

To go from Nice to Villefranche-sur-Mer, Monaco, or other destinations, you can take either a train or a bus. The train is faster, but the bus stop is closer to Nice's port. For specifics on bus and train connections, see the "Public Transportation in the French Riviera" sidebar on page 322.

From Nice's cruise port, you can get to the **train station** by bus (#30, 2/hour, 15 minutes to Gare SNCF stop; catch it at the top-left corner of the port along Place Ile de Beauté; from Terminal 1, you can also catch it along Boulevard de Stalingrad, up the stairs) or by tram (follow directions to Place Garibaldi, previous page, then ride the tramway to the Gare Thiers stop, cross the tracks, and walk straight one long block on Avenue Thiers).

Handy **bus #100**—which connects to points eastward including Villefranche-sur-Mer and Monaco—stops along the top of the port (near the right end of Place Ile de Beauté).

In summer, a **boat** to Monaco departs from near the cruise terminals, but it's slow and inconvenient if you're short on time (see page 336).

NICE

WELCOME to the RIVIERA WALK

*From the Promenade des Anglais
to Castle Hill*

This leisurely, level walk begins on the Promenade des Anglais (near the landmark Hôtel Negresco) and ends on Castle Hill above Vieux Nice. While the entire walk is enjoyable at any time, the first half makes a great pre- or post-dinner stroll. Timing your stroll to end up on Castle Hill (this walk's grand finale) at sunset is ideal. Allow one hour at a promenade pace to reach the elevator up to Castle Hill (which stops running at 20:00 in summer). A quick visit to the Masséna Museum (free, Wed-Mon 10:00-18:00, closed Tue; see page 347), next to the starting point of this walk, sets the Riviera stage for this stroll.

The Walk Begins

Promenade des Anglais

Welcome to the Riviera. There's something for everyone along this four-mile-long seafront circus. Watch Europeans at play, admire

the azure Mediterranean, anchor yourself on a blue seat, and prop your feet up on the made-to-order guardrail. Later in the day, come back to join the evening parade of tans along the promenade.

For now, stroll like the belle-époque English aristocrats for whom the promenade was paved (see map on page 356). The broad sidewalks of the Promenade des Anglais ("Walkway of the English") were financed by upper-crust English tourists who wanted a secure and comfortable place to stroll and admire the view. The walk was done in marble in 1822 for aristocrats who didn't want to dirty their shoes or smell the fishy gravel. This grand promenade leads to the old city and Castle Hill.

• *Start at the pink-domed...*

Hôtel Negresco

Nice's finest hotel is also a historic monument, offering up the city's most expensive beds (see page 355) and a museum-like interior that,

sadly, has been made off-limits to non-guests—at least in high season. But, it's worth a try to enter—dress well, appear confident, and march in. (Or, you can always get in by patronizing the hotel's Le Relais bar, which opens at 15:00.)

The exquisite **Salon Royal** lounge is an elegant place for a drink and frequently hosts modern art exhibits (opens at 11:00). The chandelier hanging from the Eiffel-built dome is made of 16,000 pieces of crystal. It was built in France for the Russian czar's Moscow palace...but thanks to the Bolshevik

Revolution in 1917, he couldn't take delivery (portraits of Czar Alexander III and his wife, Maria Feodorovna—who returned to her native Denmark after the revolution—are to the right, under the dome). Saunter around the perimeter counterclockwise.

If the **Le Relais bar** door is open (after about 15:00), wander up the marble steps for a look. Farther along, nip into the toilets for either an early 20th-century powder room or a Battle of Waterloo experience. The chairs nearby were typical of the age (cones of silence for an afternoon nap sitting up).

The hotel's **Chantecler restaurant** is one of the Riviera's best (allow €100 per person before drinks; described on page 365). In France, big-time chefs are like famous athletes: People know about them and talk about who's hot and who's not. Cooking is serious business—about 10 years ago, a famous Burgundian chef lost a star and committed suicide. On your way out, pop into the **Salon Louis XIV** (right of entry lobby as you leave), where the embarrassingly short Sun King models his red platform boots (English descriptions explain the room).

Outside, walk away from the sea with the hotel to your left to find the hotel's original **entrance** on Rue Berretta (grander than today's)—in the 19th century, classy people stayed out of the sun, and any posh hotel that cared about its clientele would design its entry on the shady north side.

• *Cross the Promenade des Anglais, and—before you begin your seaside promenade—grab a blue seat and gaze out to the...*

Bay of Angels (Baie des Anges)

Face the water. The body of Nice's patron saint, Réparate, was supposedly escorted into this bay by angels in the fourth century. To your right is where you might have been escorted into France—Nice's airport, built on a massive landfill. On that tip of land way beyond the runway is Cap d'Antibes. Until 1860, Antibes and Nice were in different countries—Antibes was French, but Nice was a protectorate of the Italian kingdom of Savoy-Piedmont, a.k.a. the Kingdom of Sardinia. (During that period, the Var River—just west of Nice—was the geographic border between these two peoples.) In 1850 the people here spoke Italian and ate pasta. As Italy was uniting, the region was given a choice: Join the new country of Italy or join good old France (which was enjoying prosperous times under the rule of Napoleon III). The vast majority voted in 1860 to go French...and *voilà!*

The lower green hill to your left (Castle Hill) marks the end of this walk. Farther left lies Villefranche-sur-Mer (marked by the tower at land's end, and home to lots of millionaires), then Monaco (which you can't see, with more millionaires), then Italy (with lots of, uh, Italians). Behind you are the foothills of the Alps (Alpes-Maritimes), which trap threatening clouds, ensuring that the Côte d'Azur enjoys sunshine more than 300 days each year. While half a million people live here, pollution is carefully treated—the water is routinely tested and is very clean.

· *With the sea on your right, begin...*

Strolling the Promenade

The block next to Hôtel Negresco houses a lush park and the Masséna Museum of city history (described on page 347 and worth a short detour). Nearby sit two other belle-époque establishments: the West End and Westminster **hotels,** both boasting English names to help those original guests feel at home (the West End is now part of the Best Western group...to help American guests feel at home). These hotels symbolize Nice's arrival as a tourist mecca a century ago, when the combination of leisure time and a stable economy allowed visitors to find the sun even in winter. Hotel rooms back then were much larger than they are now—today, even the grandest hotels have sliced and diced floor plans to create more rooms.

As you walk, be careful to avoid the green bike lane. The promenade you're walking on was originally much narrower. It's been widened over the years to keep up with tourist demand, including increased bicycle use. You'll pass a number of separate **beaches**—some private, others public. In spite of the rocks, they're still a popular draw. You can go local and rent gear—about €15 for a *chaise longue* (long chair) and a *transat* (mattress), €5 for an

umbrella, and €4 for a towel. You'll
also pass several beach restaurants
(a highly recommended experience).
Some of these eateries serve breakfast, all serve lunch, some do dinner,
and a few have beachy bars...tailor-
made for a break from this walk (the
coolest lounge is Plage Beau Rivage,
farther along on Quai des Etats-
Unis). A few promote package deals,

including a lounge chair, an umbrella, a locker, and a meal, all for
about €28. Why all this gear rental? In Europe, most beach-going
families take planes or trains, since parking and gas are très pricey,
and traffic is ugly. So, unlike my family on a beach trip, they can't
stuff chairs, coolers, and the like in the trunk of their car and park
right near the beach.

Even a hundred years ago, there was sufficient tourism in
Nice to justify building its first **casino** (a leisure activity imported
from Venice). Part of an elegant casino, La Jetée Promenade stood
on those white-covered pilings just offshore, until the Germans
destroyed it during World War II. (The Masséna Museum has
images and models of the elaborate building.) When La Jetée was
thriving, it took gamblers two full days to get to the Riviera by
train from Paris—so if you had a week off, four of those days were
spent getting to and from this Promised Land.

Although La Jetée Promenade is gone, you can still see the
striking 1927 Art Nouveau facade of the Palais de la Méditerranée,
a grand casino, hotel, and theater. This intimidating edifice was
built during the Great Depression by American financier Frank
Jay Gould, who was looking for a better return on his investments
when America's economy was tanking. It soon became the
grandest casino in Europe, and today it is one of France's most
exclusive hotels, though the casino feels cheap and cheesy.

The unappealing Casino Ruhl stands in the next block.
Anyone can drop in for some one-armed-bandit fun, but to play
the tables at night you'll need to dress better and bring your
passport. **Albert 1er Park** is named for the Belgian king who
enjoyed wintering here—these were his private gardens. While
the English came first, the Belgians and Russians were also big
fans of 19th-century Nice. That tall statue at the edge of the park
commemorates the 100-year anniversary of Nice's union with
France.

Continue along the promenade, past the park. You're now on
Quai des Etats-Unis ("Quay of the United States"). This name
was given as a tip-of-the-cap to the Americans for finally entering
World War I in 1917. Check out the laid-back couches at the Plage

Beau Rivage lounge, and look for sections of public beach with imported sand (and be amazed that most locals still prefer lying on the rocks—I don't get it). The tall, rusted steel girders reaching for the sky (across the street, to the left) were designed to celebrate the 150th anniversary of Nice's union with France. The same artist created the Arc of the Riviera sculpture in the parkway near Place Masséna.

Five minutes past the Hôtel Suisse (brilliant views as you walk), there's a monumental **war memorial** sculpted from the rock in honor of the thousands of local boys who died serving their country in World Wars I and II.

• *Take the elevator next to the Hôtel Suisse up to Castle Hill (free, elevator runs daily 10:00-19:00, until 20:00 in summer).*

Castle Hill (Colline du Château)

This hill—in an otherwise flat city center—offers sensational views over Nice, the port (to the east), the foothills of the Alps, and the Mediterranean. The views are best early or at sunset, or whenever the weather's clear (park closes at 20:00 in summer, earlier off-season). Nice was founded on this hill. Its residents were crammed onto the hilltop until the 12th century, as it was too risky to live in the flatlands below. Today you'll find a waterfall, a playground, two cafés (with fair prices), and a cemetery—but no castle—on Castle Hill.

• *Your tour is finished. Enjoy the vistas. To walk down to Vieux Nice, follow signs from just below the upper café to Vieille Ville (not Le Port), turn right at the cemetery, and then look for the walkway down on your left. If you're planning a boat tour (see page 337 for details), follow the Le Port signs down the other side of the hill to the Bassin des Amiraux.*

VIEUX NICE WALK

From Place Masséna to Place Rossetti

This self-guided walk gives you a helpful introduction to Nice's bicultural heritage and its most interesting neighborhoods. Allow about an hour at a leisurely pace for this level walk, including a stop for coffee and *socca* (chickpea crêpe). It's best done in the morning (while the outdoor market thrives and the *socca*'s hot), and preferably not on a Sunday, when many shops are closed. This ramble is also a joy at night, when fountains glow and pedestrians control the streets.

The Walk Begins

• *Start on Avenue Jean Médecin, at the corner of Rue de l'Hôtel des Postes, a block north of the Galeries Lafayette department store (see map on page 378).*

Avenue Jean Médecin

Nice's "main street," once crammed with cars, buses, and delivery vehicles tangling with pedestrians, was turned into a walking and cycling nirvana in 2007. As you amble along this major street, notice how peaceful it is. Now think of a thoroughfare like this in your city, teeming with vehicles; then imagine it without the cars and trucks. Bravo, Nice. I used to avoid this street at all costs. Now I can't get enough of it. Places like the Café Ritz flourish in an environment of generous sidewalks and no traffic.

• *Stroll under pastel arches toward Place Masséna and drink in the*

Italianesque colors and street theater that surround you. Find a bench on Place Masséna.

Place Masséna

This vast square dates from 1848 and pays tribute to Jean-André Masséna, a French military leader during the Revolutionary and Napoleonic wars. He's not  just another pretty face in a long lineup of French military heroes, but is considered among the greatest commanders in history—anywhere, anytime. Napoleon thought of him as "the greatest name of my military Empire." No wonder this city is proud of him.

A huge casino was built on this square in 1884. Nice residents came to hate it and succeeded in getting it demolished in 1983, returning open space to the square.

The grand *place* is Nice's drawing room, where old meets new, and where the tramway bends between Vieux Nice and the train station. The square's black-and-white pavement feels like an elegant outdoor ballroom, with the sleek tram waltzing across its dance floor. The men on pedestals high above you are modern-art additions that arrived with the tram. For a mood-altering experience, return after dark and watch the illuminated figures float above. Place Masséna is at its sophisticated best after the sun goes down.

There's also no better place than Place Masséna to appreciate the city's Italian heritage (standing here makes me feel as if I'm in Venice's St. Mark's Square). The rich colors of the buildings reflect the taste of previous Italian rulers, back when Nice's residents rooted for Italian soccer teams.

Look west across Place Masséna and down the grassy parkway (toward the sea). You're standing on Nice's historic river, the Paillon. Covered since the late 1800s, it runs under Place Masséna and the parkway on its way to the sea. For centuries this river was Nice's natural defense to the north and west (the sea protected the south, and Castle Hill defended the east). A fortified wall once ran along the river's length, from the hills behind you to the sea.

With the arrival of tourism in the 1800s, Nice spread north, beyond the river to your right (where your hotel is probably located). The modern can't-miss-it sculpture in the parkway is meant to represent the "curve of the French Riviera"—the arc of the bay—but looks more like an answer to local skateboarders' prayers to me. The tramway here is the first of three planned routes

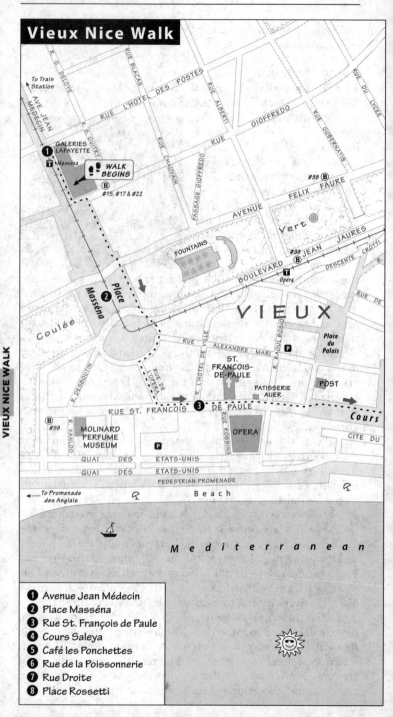

Vieux Nice Walk

To Train Station

R. G. DELOYE

R. BLASCAS

RUE L'HOTEL DES POSTES

RUE ALBERTI

GIOFFREDO

RUE GUBERNATIS

RUE DU LYCEE

AVE JEAN MEDECIN

R. ST G GUIRY

RUE CHAUVAIN

RUE GIOFFREDO

PASSAGE GIOFFREDO

GALERIES LAFAYETTE

1 Masséna

WALK BEGINS

B #15, #17 & #22

#98 **B**

FELIX FAURE

AVENUE

Vert

JEAN JAURES

#98 **B** JEAN JAURES

DESCENTE CROTTI

R.

FOUNTAINS

Opéra

BOULEVARD

RUE DE

2

Place Masséna

V I E U X

Coulée

RUE ALEXANDRE MARI

RUE DE L'OPERA

RUE

R. L'HOTEL DE VILLE

RAOUL BOSIO

P

Place du Palais

R. DESBOUTIN

ST. FRANCOIS-DE-PAULE

PATISSERIE AUER

POST

3 RUE ST. FRANCOIS DE PAULE

Cours

B #98

R. VANLOO

MOLINARD PERFUME MUSEUM

P

RUE ROBBINS

OPERA

CITÉ DU

QUAI DES ETATS-UNIS

QUAI DES ETATS-UNIS

PEDESTRIAN PROMENADE

To Promenade des Anglais

Beach

M e d i t e r r a n e a n

1 Avenue Jean Médecin
2 Place Masséna
3 Rue St. François de Paule
4 Cours Saleya
5 Café les Ponchettes
6 Rue de la Poissonnerie
7 Rue Droite
8 Place Rossetti

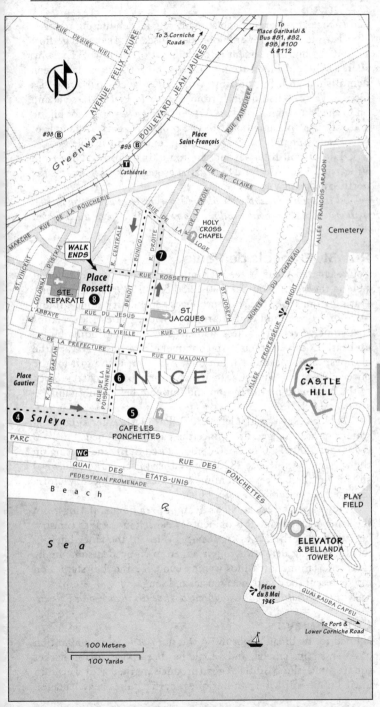

and is Nice's first serious stab at managing its debilitating traffic.

Turn to your right and look east to see Nice's ongoing effort to "put the human element into the heart of the town." Eyesores such as the old bus station and parking structures have been demolished and, by the time you visit, a green parkway—La Coulée Verte—should reach from the sea to Place Masséna and on to the Museum of Modern Art. Forming a key spine for biking and walking, this ambitious 30-acre project is another example of Nice's determination to make its urban center more livable.

The distant hills beyond the fountains separate Nice from Villefranche-sur-Mer, and that Italianesque clock tower marks the northern edge of Vieux Nice.

• Cross the square toward the Caisse d'Epargne Côte d'Azur bank, and walk between the curved buildings along Rue de l'Opéra, turning left on...

Rue St. François de Paule

You've entered Vieux Nice. Peer into the **Alziari** olive-oil shop at #14 (on the right, Mon-Sat 8:30-12:30 & 14:15-19:00, closed Sun). Dating from 1868, the shop produces top-quality stone-ground olive oil. The proud and charming owner, Gilles Piot, claims that stone wheels create less acidity (since metal grinding builds up heat). Locals fill their own containers from the huge vats (the cheapest one is peanut oil, not olive oil). Consider a gift for the olive-oil lover on your list. (Some may want to backpedal one block to the **Molinard** perfume shop and museum before continuing—see page 345.)

A block down on the left (at #7), **Pâtisserie Auer's** grand old storefront has changed little since the pastry shop opened in 1820 (Mon-Sat 9:00-13:30 & 14:30-18:00, closed Sun). The writing on the window says, "Since 1820 from father to son." The gold royal shields on the back wall remind shoppers that Queen Victoria indulged her sweet tooth here.

Across the street is Nice's grand **opera house,** dating from the same era. Imagine this opulent jewel back in the 19th century, buried deep in the old town of Nice. With all the fancy big-city folks wintering here, this rough-edged town needed some high-class entertainment (casinos weren't enough). The four statues on top represent theater, dance, music, and song.

• Continue on, sifting your way through souvenirs to the Cours Saleya.

Cours Saleya

Named for its broad exposure to the sun *(soleil)*, this commotion of color, sights, smells, and people has been Nice's main market square since the Middle Ages (produce market held Tue-Sun until 13:00—on Mon, an antiques market takes center stage).

Amazingly, part of this square was a parking lot until 1980, when the mayor of Nice had an underground garage built.

The first section is devoted to the Riviera's largest flower market (all day Tue-Sun and in operation since the 19th century). Here you'll find plants and flowers that grow effortlessly and ubiquitously in this climate, including the local favorites: carnations, roses, and jasmine. Not long ago, this region supplied all of France with its flowers; today, many are imported from Africa (the glorious orchids are from Kenya). Still, fresh flowers are perhaps the best value in this city.

The boisterous produce section trumpets the season with mushrooms, strawberries, white asparagus, zucchini flowers, and more—whatever's fresh gets top billing. Find your way down the center and buy something healthy.

The market opens up at Place Pierre Gautier (also called Plassa dou Gouvernou—bilingual street signs include the old Niçois language, an Italian dialect). This is where farmers set up stalls to sell their produce and herbs directly. For a great rooftop view of the market, climb the steps by Le Grand Bleu restaurant (you may have to step over the trash sacks, but it's allowed). As part of their goal to humanize Nice, the city is considering turning the rooftops of this long lineup of two-story buildings into an elevated pedestrian walkway.

Look up to the **hill** that dominates to the east. The city of Nice was first settled up there by Greeks (circa 400 B.C.). In the Middle Ages, a massive castle stood there with soldiers at the ready. Over time, the city grew down to where you are now. With the river guarding one side and the sea the other, this mountain fortress seemed strong—until Louis XIV leveled it in 1706. Nice's medieval seawall ran along the line of two-story buildings where you're standing.

Now, look across Place Pierre Gautier to the large "palace." The **Ducal Palace** was where the kings of Sardinia, the city's Italian rulers until 1860, resided when in Nice. (Today, it's police headquarters.) The land under the Cours Saleya was once the duke's gardens and didn't become a market until Nice's union with France.

Resume your stroll down the center of Cours Saleya, stopping when you see La Cambuse restaurant on your left. In front, hovering over the black-barrel fire with the paella-like pan on top, is the self-proclaimed **Queen of the Market,** Thérèse cooking *socca*, Nice's chickpea crêpe specialty (until about 13:00); spend €3

VIEUX NICE WALK

for a wad (careful—it's hot, but good). If Thérèse doesn't have a pan out, it's on its way (watch for the frequent scooter deliveries). Wait in line...or else it'll be all gone when you return.

• *Continue down Cours Saleya. The fine golden building that seals the end of the square is where Henri Matisse spent 17 years with a brilliant view onto Nice's world. The Café les Ponchettes is perfectly positioned for a people-watching break. Turn at the café onto...*

Rue de la Poissonnerie

Look up at the first floor of the first building on your right. **Adam and Eve** are squaring off, each holding a zucchini-like gourd. This scene (post-apple) represents the annual rapprochement in Nice to make up for the sins of a too-much-fun Carnival (Mardi Gras, the pre-Lenten festival). Residents of Nice have partied hard during Carnival for more than 700 years. The **spice shop** below offers a fine selection of regional herbs (usually outside).

Now, walk a few doors down to #6 (right side). That filthy **iron grille** above the door allows air to enter the building, but keeps out uninvited guests. You'll see lots of these open grilles in Vieux Nice. They were part of a clever system that sucked in cool air from the sea, circulating it through homes and blowing it out through vents in the roof.

A few steps ahead, check out the small **Baroque church** (Notre-Dame-de-l'Annonciation) dedicated to Ste. Rita, the patron saint of desperate causes. She holds a special place in locals' hearts, making this the most popular church in Nice. Drop in for a whiff of Baroque. The first chapel on the right is dedicated to St. Erasmus, protector of mariners.

• *Turn right on the next street, where you'll pass Vieux Nice's most happening café/bar (**Distilleries Ideales**), with a lively happy hour (18:00-21:00) and a* Pirates of the Caribbean-*style interior. Now turn left on "Right" Street (Rue Droite), and enter an area that feels like a Little Naples.*

Rue Droite

In the Middle Ages, this straight, skinny street provided the most direct route from wall to wall, or river to sea. Stop at **Espuno's bakery** (at Place du Jésus, closed Mon-Tue) and say *bonjour* to the friendly folks. Decades ago, this baker was voted the best in France—the trophies you see were earned for bread-making, not bowling. His son now runs the place. Notice the firewood stacked behind the oven. Try the house specialty, *tourte aux blettes*—a Swiss chard tart. It's traditionally made with jam (a sweet, tasty breakfast treat), but there's also a savory version, stuffed with pine nuts, raisins, and white beets (my favorite for lunch).

Pop into the Jesuit **Eglise St-Jacques** (also called Eglise du

Gésu) for a glorious explosion of Baroque exuberance hidden behind that plain façade. The interior of this place swirls up and over the top. Find the wooden pulpit and the crucifix extending from it—held by a sculpted arm. This clever support allowed the priest to focus on his sermon while reminding the congregation that Christ died for their sins.

Farther along, at #28, Thérèse (whom you met earlier) cooks her *socca* in the wood-fired oven before she carts it to her barrel on Cours Saleya. The balconies of the mansion in the next block mark the **Palais Lascaris** (c. 1647, gorgeous at night), a rare souvenir from one of Nice's most prestigious families. It's worth popping inside (handy WCs) for its Baroque Italian architecture and terrific collection of antique musical instruments—harps, guitars, violins, and violas (good English explanations). You'll also find elaborate tapestries and a few well-furnished rooms. The palace has four levels: the ground floor was used for storage, the first floor was devoted to reception rooms (and musical events), the owners lived a floor above that, and the servants lived at the top—with a good view but lots of stairs (free, Wed-Mon 10:00-18:00, closed Tue). Look up and make faces back at the guys under the balconies.

• *Turn left on the Rue de la Loge then left again on Rue Benoît Bunico.*

In the 18th century, the street you're walking on served as a **ghetto** for Nice's Jews. At sunset, gates would seal the street at either end, locking people in until daylight. To identify them as non-Christians, rich and poor Jewish men were forced to wear yellow stars and berets. The women wore yellow scarves.

• *Rue Benoît Bunico leads to...*

Place Rossetti

The most Italian of Nice's piazzas, Place Rossetti feels more like Rome than Nice. Named for the man who donated his land to create this square, Place Rossetti comes alive after dark. The recommended Fenocchio gelato shop is popular for its many flavors, ranging from classic to innovative.

Walk to the fountain and stare back at the church. This is the **Cathedral of St. Réparate**—an unassuming building for a major city's cathedral. It was relocated here in the 1500s, when Castle Hill was temporarily converted to military use only. The name comes from Nice's patron saint, a teenage virgin named Réparate, whose martyred body floated to Nice in the fourth century accompanied by angels (remember the Bay of Angels?). The interior of the cathedral gushes Baroque, a response to the Protestant Reformation. With the Catholic Church's Counter-Reformation, the theatrical energy of churches was cranked up with re-energized, high-powered saints and eye-popping decor.

• *Our tour is over. If you're re-energized, take a walk up **Castle Hill**.*

To get there, cross Place Rossetti and follow the lane leading uphill (see Castle Hill description at the end of the previous chapter, Welcome to the Riviera Walk). If it's early enough and you're up for a day trip, take a left outside the church—you're not far from bus stops to Monaco, Villefranche-sur-Mer, and Eze-le-Village (see map on page 352).

CHAGALL MUSEUM TOUR

Musée Chagall

Even if you're suspicious of modern art, this museum—with the world's largest collection of Marc Chagall's work in captivity—is a delight. After World War II, Chagall returned from the United States to settle in Vence, not far from Nice. Between 1954 and 1967 he painted a cycle of 17 large murals designed for, and donated to, this museum. These paintings, inspired by the biblical books of Genesis, Exodus, and the Song of Songs, make up the "nave," or core, of what Chagall called the "House of Brotherhood."

Orientation

Cost: €7.50, €1-2 more during frequent special exhibits, free first Sun of the month (but crowded).

Hours: Wed-Mon 10:00-17:00, May-Oct until 18:00, closed Tue year-round.

Getting There: You can reach the museum, located on Avenue Docteur Ménard, by bus or on foot.

    Buses #15 and #22 serve the Chagall Museum from the Masséna Guitry stop, near Place Masséna (5-7/hour Mon-Sat, 3/hour Sun, €1.50, immediately behind Galeries Lafayette department store—see map on page 330). The museum's bus stop (called Musée Chagall, shown on the bus shelter) is on Boulevard de Cimiez (walk uphill from the stop and cross the street to find the museum).

    To **walk** from central Nice to the Chagall Museum (30 minutes), go to the train-station end of Avenue Jean Médecin and turn right onto Boulevard Raimbaldi. Walk four long blocks along the elevated road, then turn left onto Avenue Raymond Comboul, and follow *Musée Chagall* signs.

Information: The free *Plan du Musée* helps you locate the rooms, though you can do without it as the museum is pretty simple. Tel. 04 93 53 87 20, www.musees-nationaux-alpesmaritimes.fr/chagall.

Audioguide: Although Chagall would suggest that you explore his art without help, the free audioguide gives you detailed explanations of his works and covers temporary exhibits.

Length of This Tour: Allow one hour.

Services: A spick-and-span WC is next to the ticket desk. Another WC is inside.

Cuisine Art: An idyllic café (€10 salads and *plats*) awaits in the corner of the garden.

Leaving the Museum: To take **buses** #15 or #22 back to downtown Nice, turn right out of the museum, then make another right down Boulevard de Cimiez, and catch the bus heading downhill. To continue on to the Matisse Museum, catch buses #15 or #22 using the uphill stop located across the street. **Taxis** usually wait in front of the museum. It's about €12 for a ride to the city center.

To **walk** to the train station area from the museum (20 minutes), turn left out of the museum grounds on Avenue Docteur Ménard, and follow the street to the left at the first intersection, continuing to hug the museum grounds. Where the street curves right (by #32), take the ramps and staircases down on your left, turn left at the bottom, cross under the freeway and the train tracks, then turn right on Boulevard Raimbaldi to reach the station.

The Tour Begins

This small museum consists of six rooms: two rooms with the 17 large murals, two rooms for special exhibits, an auditorium with stained-glass windows, and a mosaic-lined pond (viewed from inside). In the main hall you'll find the core of the collection (Genesis and Exodus scenes). The adjacent octagonal room houses five paintings—the Song of Songs room.

• *Buy your ticket, pass through the garden, and enter the museum at the baggage-check counter (daypacks must be checked). Find the main hall filled with Chagall's colorful paintings of...*

Old Testament Scenes

Each painting is a lighter-than-air collage of images that draws from Chagall's Russian folk-village youth, his Jewish heritage, biblical themes, and his feeling that he existed somewhere between heaven and earth. He believed that the Bible was a synonym for nature, and that color and biblical themes were key

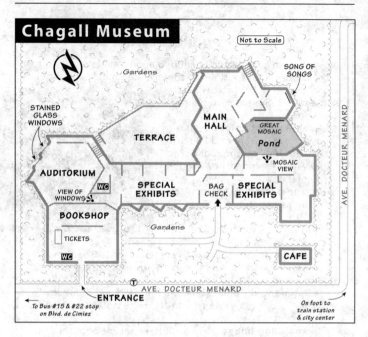

for understanding God's love for his creation. Chagall's brilliant blues and reds celebrate nature, as do his spiritual and folk themes. Notice the focus on couples. To Chagall, humans loving each other mirrored God's love of creation.

The paintings are described below in the order you should see them, going counterclockwise around the room (some paintings might be on loan to other museums). Look for posted explanations of each work in English.

Abraham and the Three Angels

In the heat of the day, Abraham looked up and saw three men. He said, "Let a little food and water be brought, so you can be refreshed..." (Genesis 18:1-5)

Abraham refreshes God's angels on this red-hot day and, in return, they promise Abraham a son (in the bubble, at right), thus making him the father of the future Israelite nation.

The Sacrifice of Isaac

Abraham bound his son Isaac and laid him on the altar. Then he took the knife to slay his son. But the angel of the Lord called out to him from heaven, "Abraham!" (Genesis 22:9-11)

Tested by God, Abraham prepares to kill his only son, but the angel stops him in time. Notice that Isaac is posed exactly as Adam is in *The Creation* (described next). Abraham's sacrifice

Chagall's Style

Chagall uses a deceptively simple, almost childlike style to paint a world that's hidden to the eye—the magical, mystical world below the surface. Here are some of the characteristics of his paintings:

- **Deep, radiant colors,** inspired by Expressionism and Fauvism (an art movement pioneered by Matisse and other French painters).
- **Personal imagery,** particularly from his childhood in Russia— smiling barnyard animals, fiddlers on the roof, flower bouquets, huts, and blissful sweethearts.
- **A Hasidic Jewish perspective,** the idea that God is every-where, appearing in everyday things like nature, animals, and humdrum activities.
- **A fragmented Cubist style,** multifaceted and multidimen-sional, a perfect style to mirror the complexity of God's creation.
- **Overlapping images,** like double-exposure photography, with faint imagery that bleeds through, suggesting there's more to life under the surface.
- **Stained-glass-esque technique** of dark, deep, earthy, "potent" colors, and simplified, iconic, symbolic figures.
- **Gravity-defying compositions,** with lovers, animals, and angels twirling blissfully in midair.
- **Happy (not tragic) mood** depicting a world of personal joy, despite the violence and turmoil of world wars and revolution.
- **Childlike simplicity,** drawn with simple, heavy outlines, filled in with Crayola colors that often spill over the lines. Major characters in a scene are bigger than the lesser characters. The grinning barnyard animals, the bright colors, the magical events presented as literal truth...Was Chagall a lightweight? Or a lighter-than-air-weight?

echoes three others: the sacrifice all men must make (Adam, the everyman), the sacrifice of atonement (the goat tied to a tree at left), and even God's sacrifice of his own son (Christ carrying the cross, upper right).

The Creation

God said, "Let us make man in our image, in our likeness..." (Genesis 1:26)

A pure-white angel descends through the blue sky and carries a still-sleeping Adam from radiant red-yellow heaven to earth. Heaven is a whirling dervish of activity, spinning out all the events of future history, from the tablets of the Ten Commandments to the Crucifixion—an overture of many images that we'll see in later paintings. (Though not a Christian, Chagall saw the Crucifixion as a universal symbol of man's suffering.)

Moses Receives the Ten Commandments
The Lord gave him the two tablets of the Law, the tablets of stone inscribed by the finger of God... (Exodus 31:18)

An astonished Moses is tractor-beamed toward heaven, where God reaches out from a cloud to hand him the Ten Commandments. While Moses tilts one way, Mount Sinai slants the other, leading our eye up to the left, where a golden calf is being worshipped by the wayward Children of Israel. But down to the right, Aaron and the menorah assure us that Moses will set things right. In this radiant final panel, the Jewish tradition—after a long struggle—is finally established.

Driven from Paradise
So God banished him from the Garden of Eden...and placed cherubim and a flaming sword to guard the way... (Genesis 3:23-24)

An angel drives them out with a fire hose of blue (there's Adam still cradling his flaming-red *coq*), while a sparkling yellow sword prevents them from ever returning. Deep in the green colors, the painting offers us glimpses of the future—Eve giving birth (lower-right corner) and the yellow sacrificial goat of atonement (top right).

Paradise
God put him in the Garden of Eden...and said, "You must not eat from the tree of the knowledge of good and evil..." (Genesis 2:15-17)

Paradise is a rich, earth-as-seen-from-space pool of blue, green, and white. Amoebic, still-evolving animals float around Adam (celibately practicing yoga) and Eve (with lusty-red hair). On the right, an angel guards the tempting tree, but Eve offers an apple, and Adam reaches around to sample the forbidden fruit.

The Rainbow
God said, "I have set my rainbow in the clouds as a sign of the covenant between me and the earth." (Genesis 9:13)

A flaming angel sets the rainbow in the sky, while Noah rests beneath it and his family offers a sacrifice of thanks. The pure-white rainbow's missing colors are found radiating from the features of the survivors.

Marc Chagall
(1887-1985)

1887-1910: Russia
Chagall is born in the small town of Vitebsk, Belarus. He's the oldest of nine children in a traditional Russian Hasidic Jewish family. He studies realistic art in his hometown. In St. Petersburg, he is first exposed to the Modernist work of Paul Cézanne and the Fauves.

1910-1914: Paris
A patron finances a four-year stay in Paris. Chagall hobnobs with the avant-garde and learns technique from the Cubists, but he never abandons painting recognizable figures or his own personal fantasies. (Some say his relative poverty forced him to paint over used canvases, which gave him the idea of overlapping images that bleed through. Hmm.)

1914-1922: Russia
Returning to his hometown, Chagall marries Bella Rosenfeld (1915), whose love will inspire him for decades. He paints happy scenes despite the turmoil of wars and the Communist Revolution. Moving to Moscow (1920), he paints his first large-scale works, sets for the New Jewish Theater. These would inspire many of his later large-scale works.

1923-1941: France and Palestine
Chagall returns to France. In 1931 he travels to Palestine, where the bright sun and his Jewish roots inspire a series of gouaches (opaque watercolor paintings). These gouaches would later inspire 105 etchings to illustrate the Bible (1931-1952), which would eventually influence the 17 large canvases of biblical scenes in the Chagall Museum (1954-1967).

1941-1947: United States/World War II
Fearing persecution for his Jewish faith, Chagall emigrates to New York, where he spends the war years. The Crucifixion starts to appear in his paintings—not as a Christian symbol, but as a representation of the violence mankind perpetrates on itself. In 1947 his beloved Bella dies, and he stops painting for months.

1947-1985: South of France
After the war, Chagall returns to France, eventually settling in St-Paul-de-Vence. In 1952 he remarries. His new love, Valentina Brodsky, plus the southern sunshine, brings Chagall a revived creativity—he is extremely prolific for the rest of his life. He experiments with new techniques and media—ceramics, sculpture, book illustrations, tapestry, and mosaic. In 1956 he's commissioned for his first stained-glass project. Eventually he does windows for cathedrals in Metz and Reims, and a synagogue in Jerusalem (1960). The Chagall Museum opens in 1973.

Jacob's Ladder

He had a dream in which he saw a ladder resting on the earth with its top reaching to heaven, and the angels of God were ascending and descending on it... (Genesis 28:12)

In the left half, Jacob (Abraham's grandson) slumps asleep and dreams of a ladder between heaven and earth. On the right, a spinning angel with a menorah represents how heaven and earth are bridged by the rituals of the Jewish tradition.

Jacob Wrestles with an Angel

So Jacob wrestled with him till daybreak. Jacob said, "I will not let you go unless you bless me..." (Genesis 32: 24, 26)

Jacob holds on while the angel blesses him with descendants (the Children of Israel) and sends out rays from his hands, creating, among others, Joseph (stripped of his bright-red coat and sold into slavery by his brothers).

Noah's Ark

Then he sent out a dove to see if the water had receded... (Genesis 8:8)

Adam and Eve's descendants have become so wicked that God destroys the earth with a flood, engulfing the sad crowd on the right. Only righteous Noah (center), his family (lower right), and the animals (including our yellow goat) are spared inside an ark. Here Noah opens the ark's window and sends out a dove to test the waters.

Moses Brings Water from the Rock

The Lord said, "Strike the rock, and water will come out of it for the people to drink..." (Exodus 17:5-6)

In the brown desert, Moses nourishes his thirsty people with water miraculously spouting from a rock. From the (red-yellow) divine source, it rains down actual (blue) water, but also a gush of spiritual yellow light.

Moses and the Burning Bush

The angel of the Lord appeared to him in flames of fire from within a bush... (Exodus 3:2)

Horned Moses—Chagall depicts him according to a medieval tradition—kneels awestruck before the burning bush, the event that calls him to God's service. On the left, we see Moses after the call, his face radiant, leading the Israelites out of captivity across the Red Sea, while Pharaoh's men drown (lower half of Moses' robe). The Ten Commandments loom ahead.

• *Return to* Moses Receives the Ten Commandments, *then walk past a stained-glass window on your way to the octagonal room.*

Song of Songs

Song of Solomon 7:11
Come, my lover, let us go to the countryside,
let us spend the night in the villages.
Song of Solomon 5:2
I slept but my heart was awake.
Song of Solomon 2:17
Until the day breaks and the shadows flee,
turn, my lover, and be like a gazelle or
like a young stag on the rugged hills.
Song of Solomon 3:4
I held him and would not let him go.
Song of Solomon 7:7
Your stature is like that of the palm, and your
breasts like clusters of fruit.

Song of Songs

Chagall wrote, "I've been fascinated by the Bible ever since my earliest childhood. I have always thought of it as the most extraordinary source of poetic inspiration imaginable. As far as I am concerned, perfection in art and in life has its source in the Bible, and exercises in the mechanics of the merely rational are fruitless. In art as well as in life, anything is possible, provided there is love."

Chagall enjoyed the love of two women in his long life—his first wife, Bella, then Valentina, who gave him a second wind as he was painting these late works. Chagall was one of the few "serious" 20th-century artists to portray unabashed love. Where the Bible uses the metaphor of earthly, physical, sexual love to describe God's love for humans, Chagall uses unearthly colors and a mystical ambience to celebrate human love. These red-toned canvases are hard to interpret on a literal level, but they capture the rosy spirit of a man in love with life. The sidebar above reflects the order of the verses displayed in the paintings.

• *Head back toward the entry and turn left at* The Sacrifice of Isaac *to find...*

The Pond

The great mosaic reflected in the pond evokes the prophet Elijah in his chariot of fire (from the Second Book of Kings)—with Chagall's addition of the 12 signs of the zodiac, which he used to symbolize Time.

• *Return to the main hall, veer left, and exit the hall to the right. Pass through the exhibition room with temporary displays. At the end, you'll find...*

The Auditorium

This room is worth a peaceful moment to enjoy three Chagall stained-glass windows: the creation of light, elements, and planets (a visual big bang that's four "days" wide); the creation of animals, plants, man and woman, and the ordering of the solar system (two "days" wide, complete with fish and birds still figuring out where they belong); and the day of rest, with angels singing to the glory of God (the narrowest—only one "day" wide). If you like these windows, make sure to visit the cathedral in Reims on a future trip.

VILLEFRANCHE-SUR-MER, CAP FERRAT, and EZE-LE-VILLAGE

Between Nice and Monaco lies the Riviera's richest stretch of real estate, paved with famously scenic roads (called the Three Corniches) and peppered with cliff-hanging villages, million-dollar vistas, and sea-splashed walking trails connecting beach towns. Fifteen minutes from Nice, little Villefranche-sur-Mer stares across the bay to woodsy and exclusive Cap Ferrat. The eagle's-nest Eze-le-Village and the Corniche-topping La Trophée des Alpes (in La Turbie) survey the scene from high above.

Villefranche-sur-Mer

In the glitzy world of the Riviera, Villefranche-sur-Mer offers travelers an easygoing slice of small-town Mediterranean life.

From here convenient day trips allow you to gamble in style in Monaco, saunter the Promenade des Anglais in Nice, or drink in immense views from Eze-le-Village. Villefranche-sur-Mer feels Italian, with soft-orange buildings; steep, narrow streets spilling into the sea; and pasta on most menus. Luxury sailing yachts glisten in the bay—an inspiration to those lazing along the harborfront to start saving when their trips are over. Cruise ships make occasional calls to Villefranche-sur-Mer's famously deep harbor, creating periodic rush hours of frenetic shoppers and happy boutique owners. Sand-pebble beaches, a handful of interesting

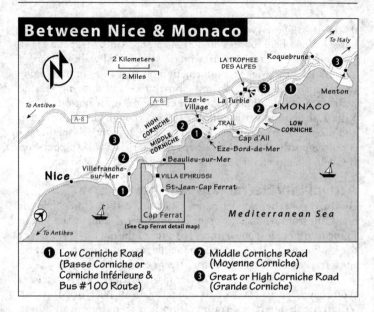

Between Nice & Monaco

2 Kilometers

2 Miles

To Antibes

A-8

A-8

To Italy

Roquebrune

LA TROPHEE
DES ALPES

Menton

MONACO

Eze-le-
Village

La Turbie

HIGH
CORNICHE

MIDDLE
CORNICHE

TRAIL

LOW
CORNICHE

Cap d'Ail

Eze-Bord-de-Mer

Beaulieu-sur-Mer

Nice

Villefranche-
sur-Mer

VILLA EPHRUSSI

St-Jean-Cap Ferrat

Mediterranean Sea

Cap Ferrat

To Antibes

(See Cap Ferrat detail map)

❶ Low Corniche Road
(Basse Corniche or
Corniche Inférieure &
Bus #100 Route)

❷ Middle Corniche Road
(Moyenne Corniche)

❸ Great or High Corniche Road
(Grande Corniche)

sights, and quick access to Cap Ferrat keep other visitors just busy enough.

Originally a Roman port, Villefranche-sur-Mer was overtaken by fifth-century barbarians. Villagers fled into the hills, where they stayed and farmed their olives. In 1295 the Duke of Provence—like many in coastal Europe—was threatened by the Saracen Turks. He asked the hillside olive farmers to move down to the water and establish a front line against the invaders, thus denying the enemy a base from which to attack Nice. In return for tax-free status, they stopped farming, took up fishing, and established a *Ville-* (town) *franche* (without taxes). Since there were many such towns, this one was specifically "Tax-free town on the sea" *(sur Mer)*. In about 1560, the Duke of Savoy built an immense, sprawling citadel in the town (which you can still tour). And today, while the town has an international following (including Tina Turner), two-thirds of its 8,000 people call it their primary residence. That makes Villefranche-sur-Mer feel more like a real community than many neighboring Riviera towns.

Orientation to Villefranche-sur-Mer

Tourist Information

The main TI is in the park named Jardin François Binon, below the main bus stop, labeled *Octroi* (mid-June-mid-Sept daily 9:00-18:00; mid-Sept-mid-June Mon-Sat 9:00-12:00 & 14:00-17:00, closed Sun; 20-minute walk or €10 taxi ride from train station, tel.

04 93 01 73 68, www.villefranche-sur-mer.com). Pick up regional bus schedules here (buses #80, #81, #82, #83, #100, #112, and #114). Also ask for the brochure detailing a self-guided walking tour of Villefranche-sur-Mer and information on boat rides (usually mid-June-Sept). The TI has a simple brochure-map showing seaside walks around neighboring Cap Ferrat and information on the Villa Ephrussi de Rothschild's gardens, though this book's map and directions are sufficient (see "Cap Ferrat," later). A smaller TI is on the port (mid-May-mid-Sept Mon-Fri 10:00-17:00, Sat-Sun 10:00-16:00, closed off-season).

Arrival in Villefranche-sur-Mer

By Bus: Whether you've taken bus #100 or #81 from Nice, or bus #100 from Monaco, hop off at the Octroi stop, at the Jardin François Binon, just above the TI. To reach the old town, walk past the TI down Avenue Général de Gaulle, take the first stairway on the left, then make a right at the street's end.

  By Train: Not all trains stop in Villefranche-sur-Mer (you may need to transfer to a local train in Nice or Monaco). Villefranche-sur-Mer's train station is a 15-minute walk along the water from the old town and many of the hotels listed in this chapter. Find your way down toward the water, and turn right to walk into town. Taxis to my recommended hotels cost €15, but they don't wait here, and they prefer longer trips, so call instead, and—if you don't have a mobile phone—pray that the pay phone outside the station is working (for taxi telephone numbers, see the next page).

  By Car: From Nice's port, follow signs for *Menton, Monaco,* and *Basse Corniche*. In Villefranche-sur-Mer, turn right at the TI (first signal after Hôtel la Flore) for parking and hotels. For a quick visit to the TI, park at the pay lot just below the TI. A bit farther down, you may find free parking in the small lot off Avenue Verdun; otherwise, look elsewhere and pay the meter. There's a secure pay lot on the water across from Hôtel Welcome, and some hotels have their own parking.

  By Plane: Allow an hour from Nice's airport to Villefranche-sur-Mer (for details on this connection, see page 368).

  By Cruise Ship: For information on arrival by cruise ship, see "Villefranche-sur-Mer Connections" on page 405.

Helpful Hints

Market Day: A fun bric-a-brac market enlivens Villefranche-sur-Mer on Sundays (on Place Amélie Pollonnais by Hôtel Welcome, and in Jardin François Binon by the TI). On Saturday mornings, a small food market sets up near the TI (only in Jardin François Binon). A small trinket market springs to action on Place Amélie Pollonnais whenever cruise ships grace the harbor.

Last Call: Villefranche-sur-Mer makes a great base for day trips, but the last bus back from Nice or Monaco is at about 20:00. After that, take the train or a cab.

Internet Access: Two options sit side by side on Place du Marché. **Chez Net,** an "Australian International Sports Bar Internet Café," has American keyboards, whereas **L'X Café** has French keyboards. Both are open daily, have Wi-Fi, and let you enjoy a late-night drink while surfing the Internet.

Laundry: The town has two launderettes, both owned by Laura and located just below the main road on Avenue Sadi Carnot. At the upper *pressing moderne,* Laura does your wash for you—for a price (Tue-Sat 9:00-12:30 & 15:00-19:00, closed Sun-Mon, next to Hôtel Riviera, tel. 04 93 01 73 71). The lower *laverie* is self-service only (daily 7:00-20:00, opposite 6 Avenue Sadi Carnot).

Electric Bike Rental: If you plan to explore Cap Ferrat but don't feel like walking, consider renting an electric bike from Henri at **Eco-Loc.** The adventurous can also try this as an alternative to taking the bus to Cap Ferrat, Eze-le-Village, or even Nice (although the road to Nice is awfully busy). You get about 25 miles on a fully charged battery (less on hilly terrain—after that you're pedaling; €15/half-day, €25/day, early April-Sept daily 9:00-17:00, deposit and ID required, best to call for reservations 24 hours in advance; helmets, locks, baskets, and child seats available; pick up bike across from small TI on the port, mobile 06 66 92 72 41, www.ecoloc06.fr).

Taxi: For a reliable taxi in Villefranche-sur-Mer, call or email **Didier** (mobile 06 15 15 39 15, taxididier.villefranchesurmer @orange.fr). If he's busy, beware of taxi drivers who overcharge—the normal weekday, daytime rate to central Nice is about €40; to the airport, figure €60; one-way to Cap Ferrat is about €25, to Eze-le-Village is about €40, and to Monaco is €60. The five-minute trip from the waterfront up to the main street level (to bus stops on the Low Corniche) should be less than €10. Ask your driver to write down the price before you get in, and get a receipt when you pay (general taxi tel. 04 93 55 55 55).

Minibus: Little **minibus #80** will save you the sweat of going from the harbor up the hill, but it only runs once per hour (daily 7:00-19:00, €1.50, schedule posted at stops and on www.lignedazur.com). It travels from the port to the top of the hill, stopping near Hôtel la Fiancée du Pirate and the Col de Villefranche stop for buses #82 and #112 to Eze-le-Village, before going to the outlying suburban Nice Riquier train

Villefranche-sur-Mer

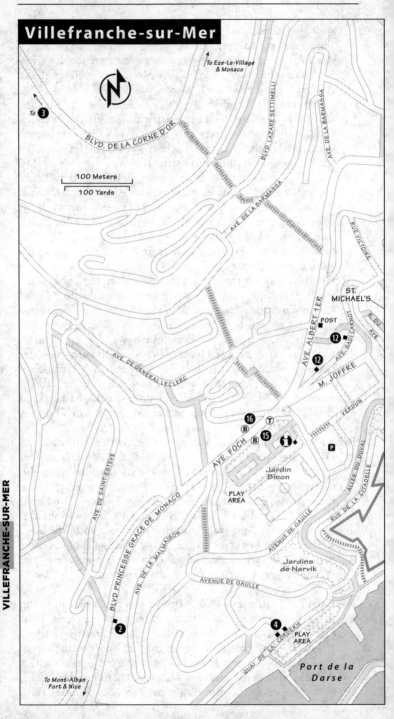

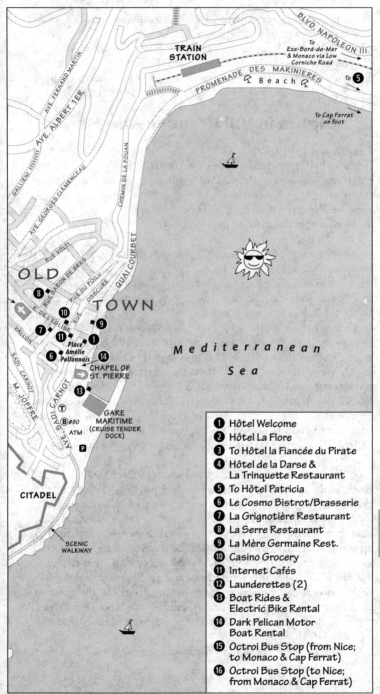

1 Hôtel Welcome
2 Hôtel La Flore
3 To Hôtel la Fiancée du Pirate
4 Hôtel de la Darse &
   La Trinquette Restaurant
5 To Hôtel Patricia
6 Le Cosmo Bistrot/Brasserie
7 La Grignotière Restaurant
8 La Serre Restaurant
9 La Mère Germaine Rest.
10 Casino Grocery
11 Internet Cafés
12 Launderettes (2)
13 Boat Rides &
   Electric Bike Rental
14 Dark Pelican Motor
   Boat Rental
15 Octroi Bus Stop (from Nice;
   to Monaco & Cap Ferrat)
16 Octroi Bus Stop (to Nice;
   from Monaco & Cap Ferrat)

station (only convenient if you're already on minibus, must transfer to train to downtown Nice).

Tourist Train: Skip the useless white **Petit Train,** which goes nowhere interesting (€7, 20-minute ride).

Spectator Sports: Lively *boules* action takes place each evening just below the TI and the huge soccer field (see page 10).

Sights in Villefranche-sur-Mer

The Harbor

Browse Villefranche-sur-Mer's minuscule harbor. Although the town was once an important fishing community, only a few families still fish here to make money. Find the footpath that leads beneath the citadel to the sea (by the port parking lot). Stop where the path hits the sea and marvel at the scene: a bay filled with beautiful sailing yachts. (You might see well-coiffed captains being ferried in by dutiful mates to pick up their statuesque call girls.) Local guides keep a list of the world's 100 biggest yachts and talk about some of them as if they're part of the neighborhood.

Looking far to the right, that last apartment building on the sea was the headquarters for the US Navy's Sixth Fleet following World War II, and remained so until 1966, when de Gaulle pulled France out of the military wing of NATO. (The Sixth Fleet has been based in Naples ever since.) A wall plaque at the bottom of Rue de l'Eglise commemorates the US Navy's presence in Villefranche-sur-Mer.

The peninsula across the bay is Cap Ferrat. You can't miss Rothschild's pink mansion, the Villa Ephrussi, slightly left of center hugging the top (worth visiting; see page 411). To its right, in the saddle of the hill, the next home, with big red-tiled roof, belongs to Paul Allen (not open for visits). Now look far to the left up to the dramatic cliffs and notice the impressive arch-supported Low Corniche road, which leads to Monaco. Until that road was built in 1860, those hills were free of any development...all the way to Monaco. Drop your gaze down to the water. On the point of land between you and Cap Ferrat, behind the large cedar trees, is the Villa Nellcote, where the Rolling Stones recorded *Exile on Main Street* (oh, yeah!).

• *You are standing at the base of Villefranche-sur-Mer's massive...*

Citadel

The town's mammoth castle was built in the 1500s by the Duke of Savoy to defend against the French. When the region joined France in 1860, it became just a barracks. In the 20th century, the city had no military use for the space, and started using the citadel to house its police station, city hall, a summer outdoor theater, and two art galleries. There's still only one fortified entry to this huge complex.

• *To continue along this footpath, see "Seafront Walks," later; otherwise, wander back along the harbor toward the Hôtel Welcome and find the...*

Chapel of St. Pierre (Chapelle Cocteau)

This chapel, decorated by artist Jean Cocteau, is the town's cultural highlight. Cocteau was a Parisian transplant who adored little Villefranche-sur-Mer and whose career was distinguished by his work as an artist, poet, novelist, playwright, and filmmaker. Influenced by his pals Marcel Proust, André Gide, Edith Piaf, and Pablo Picasso, Cocteau was a leader among 20th-century avant-garde intellectuals. At the door, Marie-France—who is passionate about Cocteau's art—collects a €2.50 donation for a fishermen's charity. She then sets you free to enjoy the chapel's small but intriguing interior. She's happy to give some explanations if you ask.

In 1955 Jean Cocteau covered the barrel-vaulted chapel with heavy black lines and pastels. Each of Cocteau's surrealist works—the Roma (Gypsies) of Stes-Maries-de-la-Mer who dance and sing to honor the Virgin, girls wearing traditional outfits, and three scenes from the life of St. Peter—is explained in English. Is that Villefranche-sur-Mer's citadel in the scene above the altar?

Cost and Hours: Wed-Mon 10:00-12:00 & 15:00-19:00, usually closed Tue (varies with cruise-ship traffic) and when Marie-France is tired, below Hôtel Welcome, tel. 04 93 76 90 70.

Nearby: A few blocks north along the harbor (past Hôtel Welcome), Rue de May leads to the mysterious **Rue Obscure**—a covered lane running 400 feet along the medieval rampart. This street served as an air-raid shelter during World War II. Much of the lane is closed indefinitely for repair.

Boat Rides (Promenades en Mer)

Consider treating yourself to a seaborne perspective of this beautiful area. A relatively inexpensive option is to take a **cruise** (€18 for 2-hour cruise as far as Monaco—but doesn't actually stop there, departs at 15:00, June-Sept Wed and Sat, also Thu in July-Aug, no trips Oct-May, boats depart from the harbor across from Hôtel Welcome, call to confirm ever-changing schedule, reservations a must, tel. 04 93 76 65 65, www.amv-sirenes.com). Or, to be your own skipper, rent a **motor boat** through Dark Pelican (€100/half-day, €165/day, deposit required, on the harbor at the Gare Maritime, tel. 04 93 01 76 54, www.darkpelican.com).

St. Michael's Church

The town church, a few blocks up Rue de l'Eglise from the harbor, features an 18th-century organ and a fine statue of a recumbent Christ—carved, they say, from a fig tree by a galley slave in the 1600s.

Seafront Walks

A seaside walkway originally used by customs agents to patrol the harbor leads under the citadel and connects the old town with the workaday harbor (Port de la Darse). At the port you'll find a few cafés, France's Institute of Oceanography (an outpost for the University of Paris oceanographic studies), and an 18th-century dry dock. This scenic walk turns downright romantic after dark. You can also wander the other direction along Villefranche-sur-Mer's waterfront and continue beyond the train station for postcard-perfect views back to Villefranche-sur-Mer (ideal in the morning—go before breakfast). You can even extend your walk to Cap Ferrat (see "Getting to Cap Ferrat" on page 411).

Hike up to Mont-Alban Fort

This fort, with a remarkable setting on the high ridge that separates Nice and Villefranche-sur-Mer, is a good destination for hikers needing to stretch their legs (also accessible by car). Get information at the Villefranche TI, then walk on the main road toward Nice about 200 yards past Hôtel Versailles. Look for wooden trail signs labeled *Escalier de Verre* and climb about 45 minutes as the trail makes long switchbacks through the woods up to the ridge. Find your way to Mont-Alban Fort and its view terrace (though it's not possible to enter the fort). Bus #30 from Nice gets close, as does bus #80 from Villefranche-sur-Mer's port. The views west over Nice, east over Villefranche, and north to the mountains are mesmerizing. There's talk of turning the fort into an exhibition hall for modern art.

Sleeping in Villefranche-sur-Mer

You have a handful of good hotels to choose from in Villefranche-sur-Mer. The ones I list have sea views from at least half of their rooms—well worth paying extra for.

$$$ Hôtel Welcome**** easily has the best location in Villefranche-sur-Mer, anchored right on the water in the old town, with all 35 balconied rooms overlooking the harbor. The lobby opens to the water, and the mellow wine bar lowers my pulse. You'll pay top price for all the comforts in this smart hotel (standard Db-€218, "comfort" Db-€275, "superior" Db-€340, suites-€340 and up, breakfast-€17, air-con, elevator, parking garage-€45/day with reservation, 3 Quai Amiral Courbet, tel. 04 93 76 27 62, www.welcomehotel.com, resa@welcomehotel.com).

Sleep Code

(€1 = about $1.30, country code: 33)
S = Single, **D** = Double/Twin, **T** = Triple, **Q** = Quad, **b** = bathroom, **s** = shower only, * = French hotel rating (0-5 stars). Unless otherwise noted, credit cards are accepted and English is spoken.

To help you sort easily through these listings, I've divided the accommodations into three categories based on the price for a standard double room with bath:

$$$ **Higher Priced**—Most rooms €150 or more.
$$ **Moderately Priced**—Most rooms between €90-150.
$ **Lower Priced**—Most rooms €90 or less.

Prices can change without notice; verify the hotel's current rates online or by email. For the best prices, always book direct.

$$ Hôtel La Flore*** is a fair value if your idea of sightseeing is to enjoy the view from your spacious bedroom deck (most rooms have one) or the pool. It's a 15-minute uphill hike from the old town, but the parking is free, and the bus stops for Nice and Monaco are close (Db with no view-€100-145, Db with view and deck-€140-160, larger Db with even better view and bigger deck-€170-212, Db mini-suite-€220, Qb loft with huge terrace-€220, extra bed-€34, breakfast-€12, 15 percent cheaper Oct-March, check website for deals, air-con, elevator; just off main road high above harbor—go 2 blocks from TI toward Nice to 5 Boulevard Princesse Grace de Monaco; tel. 04 93 76 30 30, www.hotel-la-flore.fr, infos@hotel-la-flore.fr).

$$ Hôtel la Fiancée du Pirate*** is a family-friendly refuge that's best suited for drivers, as it's high above Villefranche-sur-Mer on the Middle Corniche (although it is on bus lines #82 and #112 to Eze-le-Village and Nice, and also served by minibus #80 from the harbor). Don't let the streetside appearance deter you: Serious owners Eric and Laurence offer 15 bright and comfortable rooms, along with a large pool, a pleasant garden, a roomy lounge area (with board games), and a breakfast terrace with partial views of Cap Ferrat and the sea. Choose between rooms in the main building or below on the garden patio. Parking and Wi-Fi are free, the beds are firm, all rooms are air-conditioned, and the big breakfast features homemade crêpes. Light lunches, salads, and snacks are available during the day (Db-€128-148, Tb-€140-160, Qb-€185-205, breakfast-€12, laundry-€10/load, 8 Boulevard de la Corne d'Or, Moyenne Corniche/N-7, tel. 04 93 76 67 40, www.fianceedupirate.com, info@fianceedupirate.com).

$ Hôtel de la Darse** is a shy, unassuming little hotel burrowed in the shadow of its highbrow neighbors. This low-profile alternative on the water at Villefranche-sur-Mer's old port is a great budget option. It's less central—figure 10 minutes of level walking to the harbor, but a steep 15-minute walk up to the main road and buses. The rooms facing the sea are worth the extra few euros for their million-dollar-view balconies (view Db-€95, view Tb-€120, Qb-€120, almost all with air-con and some noise on weekend nights, book well ahead for these). Rooms on the quieter garden side are sharp and have air-con, but no view (Sb-€71, Db-€79, extra bed-€14, breakfast-€9, no elevator; from TI walk or drive down Avenue Général de Gaulle; walkers should turn left on Allée du Colonel Duval into the Jardins de Narvik and follow steps to bottom, then turn right at the old Port de la Darse; parking usually available nearby, tel. 04 93 01 72 54, www .hoteldeladarse.com, info@hoteldeladarse.com).

Eating in Villefranche-sur-Mer

Comparison-shopping is half the fun of dining in Villefranche-sur-Mer. Make an event out of a pre-dinner stroll through the old city. Check what looks good on the lively Place Amélie Pollonnais (next to Hôtel Welcome), where the whole village seems to converge at night; saunter the string of pricey candlelit places lining the waterfront; and consider the smaller, wallet-friendlier eateries embedded in the old city's walk-

ing streets. Arm yourself with a gelato from any ice-cream shop and enjoy a floodlit, post-dinner stroll along the sea.

Le Cosmo Bistrot/Brasserie takes center stage on Place Amélie Pollonnais with a great setting—a few tables have views to the harbor and to the Chapel of St. Pierre's facade (after some wine, the Cocteau art really pops). This tight but friendly place offers well-presented, tasty meals with good wines (I love their red Bandol). Ask for the daily suggestions and consider the €13 *omelette niçoise* (€16 fine salads and pastas, €16-29 *plats*, daily, Place Amélie Pollonnais, tel. 04 93 01 84 05, www.restaurant -lecosmo.fr).

Disappear into Villefranche-sur-Mer 's walking streets and find cute little **La Grignotière,** serving generous and delicious €21 *plats*, and plenty of other options. Gregarious Michel speaks English fluently and runs the place with his sidekick Brigitte.

The mixed seafood grill is a smart order, as are the spaghetti and *gambas* (shrimp), and Michel's personal-recipe bouillabaisse (€23). They also offer a hearty €33 *menu*, but good luck finding room for it. Dining is primarily inside, making this a good choice for cooler days (daily April-Oct, closed Wed Nov-April, 3 Rue du Poilu, tel. 04 93 76 79 83).

La Serre, nestled in the old town below St. Michael's Church, is a simple place with a hardworking owner. Sylvie serves well-priced dinners to a loyal local clientele, always with a smile. Choose from the many pizzas (all named after US states and €10 or less), salads, and meats; or try the good-value, €17 three-course *menu* (open daily, evenings only, cheap house wine, 16 Rue de May, tel. 04 93 76 79 91).

La Mère Germaine, right on the harbor, is the only place in town classy enough to lure a yachter ashore. It's dressy, with formal service and a price list to match. The name commemorates the current owner's grandmother, who fed hungry GIs during World War II. Try the bouillabaisse, served with panache (€79/person with 2-person minimum, €51 mini-version for one, €45 *menu*, open daily, reserve harborfront table, 9 Quai de l'Amiral Courbet, tel. 04 93 01 71 39, www.meregermaine.com).

La Trinquette is a relaxed, low-key place away from the fray on the "other port," next to the recommended Hôtel de la Darse (a lovely 10-minute walk from the other recommended restaurants). The cuisine is good and weekends bring a cool live music scene (€11-20 *plats,* daily in summer, closed Wed off-season, 30 Avenue Général de Gaulle, tel. 04 93 16 92 48).

There's a handy **Casino supermarket/grocery store** a few blocks above Hôtel Welcome at 12 Rue du Poilu (Mon-Tue and Thu-Sat 7:30-12:30 & 15:30-19:00, Sun 7:30-12:30 only, closed Wed).

Dinner Options for Drivers: If you have a car and are staying a few nights, take the short drive up to Eze-le-Village or, better still, La Turbie. If it's summer (June-Sept), the best option of all is to go across to one of Cap Ferrat's beach restaurants for a before-dinner drink or a dinner you won't soon forget (recommendations listed under each destination later in this chapter).

Villefranche-sur-Mer Connections

For a comparison of connections by train and bus, see the "Public Transportation in the French Riviera" sidebar on pages 322-325.

By Train

Trains run later than buses (until 24:00).

From Villefranche-sur-Mer by Train to: Monaco (2/hour,

10 minutes), **Nice** (2/hour, 10 minutes), **Antibes** (2/hour, 40 minutes).

By Bus

All buses in this area cost €1.50 per ride, regardless of your destination (buy ticket from driver). Tickets are good for 74 minutes in one direction and for transfers, but not round-trips. In Villefranche-sur-Mer, all bus stops are along the main drag; the most convenient is the Octroi stop, just above the TI.

These are the key routes: **Bus #81** follows a circular route from Nice through Villefranche-sur-Mer, Beaulieu-sur-Mer, then to all Cap Ferrat stops, ending at the port in the village of St. Jean (2-4/hour daily 6:35-20:15 from Nice, last return trip from St. Jean at 20:50, earlier on Sun). **Bus #100** runs along the coastal road between Nice and Menton, just beyond Monaco (4-5/hour Mon-Sat, 3-4/hour Sun). The last bus leaves Nice for Villefranche-sur-Mer at about 20:00; the last bus from Villefranche-sur-Mer to Nice departs at about 20:45.

From Villefranche-sur-Mer by Bus to: St-Jean-Cap-Ferrat (#81, 20 minutes; for other transportation options, see "Getting to Cap Ferrat," later), **Beaulieu-sur-Mer** (#81 or #100, 10 minutes), **Monaco** (#100, 25 minutes), **Nice** (#81 or #100, 20 minutes).

By Cruise Ship

Villefranche-sur-Mer hustles to impress its cruise passengers. Tenders deposit passengers at a slick terminal building (Gare Maritime) at the Port de la Santé, right in front of Villefranche-sur-Mer's old town. At the terminal TI, pick up the free town map that's tailor-made for arriving cruise passengers. The main road (with the main TI and bus stop) is a steep hike above, and the train station is a short stroll along the beach.

Taxis wait in front of the cruise terminal. Their exorbitant rates start with a minimum €10-20 charge for a ride to the train station, but many drivers will flat-out refuse such a short ride. For farther-flung trips, see the price estimates on page 397. For an all-day trip, you can try negotiating a flat fee (e.g., €300 for a 4-hour tour).

It's easy to **walk** to various points in Villefranche-sur-Mer. If you want to see the town itself, just walk straight ahead from the terminal into Villefranche-sur-Mer's charming restaurant-lined square and start poking into its twisty back lanes.

Little **minibus #80,** which departs from in front of the cruise terminal, saves you some hiking up to the main road and bus stop (see page 397).

To connect to other towns, choose between the **bus** (slower but more scenic) or **train** (fast). Leaving the terminal, you'll

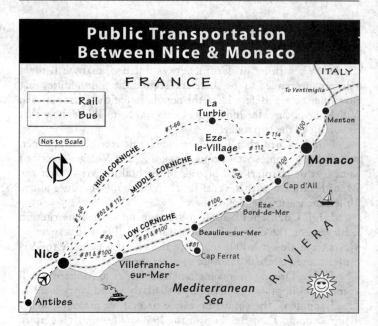

Public Transportation Between Nice & Monaco

ITALY

To Ventimiglia →

FRANCE

— Rail
- - - Bus

Not to Scale

La Turbie

Menton

#T-66

#100

Eze-le-Village

#114

HIGH CORNICHE

MIDDLE CORNICHE

#112

Monaco

#82 & #112

#100

#T-66

Cap d'Ail

#100

Eze-Bord-de-Mer

LOW CORNICHE

#80

#81 & #100

Beaulieu-sur-Mer

Nice

#81 & #100

Cap Ferrat

#81

Villefranche-sur-Mer

RIVIERA

Antibes

Mediterranean Sea

---

see directional sights pointing left, to *Town center/bus* (a 10- to 15-minute, steeply uphill walk to the Octroi bus stop with connections west to Nice or east to Monaco, both on bus #100 or #81); and right, to *Gare SNCF/train station* (a 10-minute, mostly level stroll with some stairs up at the end—just turn right and walk along the beach, with the sea on your right, until you see stairs up to the station on your left).

The Three Corniches

Nice, Villefranche-sur-Mer, and Monaco are linked by three coastal routes: the Low, Middle, and High Corniches. The roads are nicknamed after the decorative frieze that runs along the top of a building (cornice). Each Corniche (kor-neesh) offers sensational views and a different perspective. You can find the three routes from Nice by driving up Boulevard Jean Jaurès past Vieux Nice. For the Low Corniche, follow signs to N-98 *(Monaco par la Basse Corniche)*, which leads past Nice's port. Shortly after the turnoff to the Low Corniche, you'll see signs for N-7 *(Moyenne Corniche)* leading to the Middle Corniche. Signs for the High *(Grande)* Corniche appear a bit after that; follow D-2564 to *Col des 4 Chemins* and the *Grande Corniche*.

Low Corniche: The Basse Corniche (also called "Corniche

Inférieure") strings ports, beaches, and seaside villages together for a traffic-filled ground-floor view. It was built in the 1860s (along with the train line) to bring people to the casino in Monte Carlo. When this Low Corniche was finished, many hill-town villagers descended to the shore and started the communities that now line the sea. Before 1860, the population of the coast between Villefranche-sur-Mer and Monte Carlo was zero. Think about that as you make the trip today.

Middle Corniche: The Moyenne Corniche is higher, quieter, and far more impressive. It runs through Eze-le-Village (described later in this chapter) and provides breathtaking views over the Mediterranean, with several scenic pullouts. (The ones above Villefranche-sur-Mer are the best.)

High Corniche: Napoleon's crowning road-construction achievement, the Grande Corniche caps the cliffs with staggering views from almost 1,600 feet above the sea. It is actually the Via Aurelia, used by the Romans to conquer the West.

Villas: Driving from Villefranche-sur-Mer to Monaco, you'll come upon impressive villas. A particularly grand entry leads to "La Leopolda," the sprawling estate named for previous owner King Leopold II of Belgium in the 1930s. Those driving up to the Middle Corniche from Villefranche-sur-Mer can look down on this yellow mansion and its lush garden, which fill an entire hilltop. The property was later owned by the Agnelli family (of Fiat fame and fortune), and then by the Safra family (Brazilian bankers). Its current value is somewhere north of $500 million.

The Best Route: For a ▲▲▲ route, **drivers** should take the Middle Corniche from Nice or Villefranche-sur-Mer to Eze-le-Village; from there, follow signs to the *Grande Corniche* and *La Turbie (La Trophée des Alpes)*, then finish by dropping down into Monaco. **Buses** travel each route; the higher the Corniche, the less frequent the buses (4/hour on Low, 12/day on Middle, and 5/day on High; get details at TIs, or check www.lignedazur.com). There are no buses between Eze-le-Village and La Turbie (45-minute walk), though buses do connect Nice and Monaco with La Turbie.

If traveling by bus, follow my self-guided bus tour to Monaco (at the end of this chapter), then consider returning to Nice or Villefranche-sur-Mer by bus via Eze-le-Village, or to Nice via La Turbie (see "Monaco Connections" on page 439).

The following villages and sights are listed from west to east, in order of how you'll reach them when going from Villefranche-sur-Mer to Monaco.

Cap Ferrat

This exclusive peninsula, rated ▲▲, decorates Villefranche-sur-Mer's bay views. Cap Ferrat is a peaceful eddy off the busy Nice-Monaco route (Low Corniche). You could spend a leisurely day on this peninsula, wandering the sleepy port village of St-Jean-Cap-Ferrat (usually called "St. Jean"), touring the Villa Ephrussi de Rothschild mansion and gardens and the nearby Villa Kérylos, and walking on sections of the beautiful trails that follow the coast. If you have a house here, former Microsoft mogul Paul Allen is your neighbor.

Tourist Information: The main TI is between the port and the Villa Ephrussi (Mon-Fri 9:00-16:00, closed Sat-Sun, 59 Avenue Denis Séméria, bus #81 stops here at the *office du tourisme*). A smaller TI is in the village of St. Jean (unpredictable hours, likely Mon-Sat 10:00-17:00, closed Sun, 5 Avenue Denis Séméria). The two TIs share a phone number and email address (tel. 04 93 76 08 90, office-tourisme@saintjeancapferrat.fr).

Planning Your Time

Here's how I'd spend a day on the Cap: From Nice or Villefranche-sur-Mer, take the bus (#81) to the Villa Ephrussi de Rothschild stop (called Passable), then visit the villa. Walk 30 minutes, mostly downhill, to St. Jean for lunch (many options, including grocery shops for picnic supplies) and poke around the village. Consider the 45-minute walk on the Plage de la Paloma trail (ideal for picnics). After lunch, follow a beautiful 30-minute trail to the Villa Kérylos in Beaulieu-sur-Mer and tour that villa. Return to Villefranche-sur-Mer, Nice, or points beyond by train or bus. (If you have a car, skip the loop drive around the peninsula; there's nothing to see from the road.)

You can add Eze-le-Village to this day if you skip the small town of St. Jean and walk directly from the Villa Ephrussi de Rothschild to the Villa Kérylos. To get to Eze-le-Village, take bus #100 (direction: Monaco) from the stop near the Villa Kérylos and get off at the Gare d'Eze stop, where you meet bus #83, which shuttles up and up to the village (one €1.50 ticket covers both buses, get #83 schedule at a TI or check online at www.lignedazur.com).

Warning: Late-afternoon buses back to Villefranche-sur-Mer or Nice along the Low Corniche can be slammed (worse on weekends), potentially leaving passengers stranded at stops for long periods. To avoid this, either take the train or board bus #81 on the Cap itself (before it gets crowded).

CAP FERRAT

Cap Ferrat

To Villefranche-sur-Mer & Nice

To Monaco & Eze-le-Village

TRAIN STATION

LOW CORNICHE

Beaulieu-sur-Mer

l'Ange Gardien Stop

Bus #100 (Nice-to-Monaco) Stops

VILLA KERYLOS

Hôtel Royal Riviera

400 Meters
400 Yards

AVE. DURANDY

AVE. DE GRASSEUIL

Golfe de St-Hospice

VILLA EPHRUSSI DE ROTHSCHILD

#81

Plage de Passable

CHEMIN DU ROY

ALBERTO 1

St-Jean-Cap-Ferrat

#81

Plage de la Paloma

BLVD. GENERAL DE GAULLE

BLVD. GENERAL DE GAULLE

AVE. BELLEVUE

CORNICHE

LIGHTHOUSE

Mediterranean Sea

Hotels/Restaurants

1. Hôtel Brise Marine
2. Hôtel Oursin & Le St. Jean Pizzeria/Rest.
3. Hôtel Patricia
4. Captain Cook Restaurant
5. Restaurant de la Plage de Passable
6. Plage de la Paloma Restaurant

Trails

A. St. Jean to Beaulieu-sur-Mer (30 min)
B. Plage de la Paloma Loop (45 min)
C. Plage de Passable to St. Jean (2-3 hrs)
D. Walk to Villefranche-sur-Mer (1 hr)

Getting to Cap Ferrat

From Nice or Villefranche-sur-Mer: Bus #81 runs to all Cap Ferrat stops (see "Villefranche-sur-Mer Connections," earlier). For the Villa Ephrussi de Rothschild, get off at the Passable stop (allow 30 minutes from Nice and 10 minutes from Villefranche-sur-Mer's Octroi stop). Schedules are posted at stops, or get one from a TI. The times listed for *Direction Le Port/Cap Ferrat* are when buses depart from Nice—allow about 10 minutes after that for Villefranche-sur-Mer. The return bus (direction: Nice) begins in St. Jean.

Cap Ferrat is quick by **car** (take the Low Corniche) or **taxi** (allow €20 one-way from Villefranche-sur-Mer, €50 from Nice).

You can also **walk** 50 minutes from Villefranche-sur-Mer to Cap Ferrat: Go past the train station along the small beach lane, then climb the steps at the far end of the beach and walk parallel to the tracks on Avenue Louise Bordes. Continue straight past the mansions (with ornate gates) and take the first right on Avenue de Grasseuil. You'll see signs to *Villa Ephrussi de Rothschild*, then to Cap Ferrat's port.

Sights on Cap Ferrat

▲Villa Ephrussi de Rothschild

In what seems like the ultimate in Riviera extravagance, Venice, Versailles, and the Côte d'Azur come together in the pastel-pink Villa Ephrussi. Rising above Cap Ferrat, this 1905 mansion has views west to Villefranche-sur-Mer and east to Beaulieu-sur-Mer.

Cost and Hours: Palace and gardens-€13 (second child free with 2 adults), includes audioguide, combo-ticket with Villa Kérylos-€19—valid for one week; mid-Feb-Oct daily 10:00-18:00, July-Aug until 19:00; Nov-mid-Feb Mon-Fri 14:00-18:00, Sat-Sun 10:00-18:00; tel. 04 93 01 33 09, www.villa-ephrussi.com. Kids will enjoy the free treasure-hunt booklet.

Getting There: Parking is tricky; there's a small turnaround at the top. The nearest bus stop is Passable, just a few minutes after turning onto Cap Ferrat—be ready (bus #81, 10-minute walk uphill to the villa). If returning to Nice or Villefranche-sur-Mer by bus, check the posted schedule, and keep in mind that you're only a minute from the time-point listed for Port le St. Jean.

Visiting the Villa: Pick up the audioguide and garden map as you enter, then start with the well-furnished belle époque **interior** (well-described by the audioguide). Upstairs, an 18-minute film (with English subtitles) gives you good background on the life of rich and eccentric Beatrice, Baroness de Rothschild, the French banking heiress who built and furnished the place. Don't miss the view over the gardens from the terrace. As you stroll through the rooms, you'll pass royal furnishings and personal possessions, including the baroness's porcelain collection, and her bathroom case for cruises. An appropriately classy garden-tearoom serves drinks and lunches with a view (€16 *plats*, 12:00-17:30).

But the gorgeous **gardens** are why most come here (pick up the garden map when you get your audioguide). Designed in the shape of a ship, the gardens were inspired by Beatrice's many ocean-liner trips. Her small army of gardeners even dressed like sailors. Behind the mansion, stroll through the seven lush gardens re-created from locations all over the world. The sea views from here are jaw-dropping. Don't miss the Jardin Exotique's wild cactus, the rose garden at the far end, and the view back to the house from the "Temple of Love" gazebo.

Walks from the Villa Ephrussi: It's a lovely 30-minute stroll, mostly downhill and east, from the Villa Ephrussi to the Villa Kérylos in Beaulieu-sur-Mer (described later) or to the port of St. Jean. To get to either, make a hard left at the stop sign below the Villa Ephrussi and follow signs along a small road toward the Hôtel Royal Riviera on Avenue Henri Honoré Sauvan (see Cap Ferrat map). When the road comes to a T, keep going straight, passing a green gate down a pedestrian path, which ends at a trail—go left to reach the Villa Kérylos, or head right to get to St. Jean (be careful to follow the path left at the Villa Sonja Rello). It's about 15 minutes to either destination once you join this path.

To get to Plage de Passable from the Villa Ephrussi, turn left along the main road just below the villa; after 30 yards you'll find signs leading down to the beach.

Plage de Passable

This little beach, located below the Villa Ephrussi, comes with great views of Villefranche-sur-Mer and a rough, pebbly surface. It's a peaceful beach, popular with families. Half is public (free, with shower), and the other half is run by a small restaurant (€22 includes changing locker, lounge chair, and shower; reserve ahead in summer or on weekends as this is a prime spot, tel. 04 93 76 06 17). If ever you were to do the French Riviera rent-a-beach ritual, this would be the place.

To park near the beach (figure about €8/day), grab a curbside spot, or follow signs past the beach and go around the bend to a surprise lot. If it's full, follow signs over the hill and around to Lido Parking, a few steps from Plage de Passable.

For me, the best reason to come here is for dinner (see "Eating on Cap Ferrat," later). Beg, borrow, or steal a way to arrive here before sunset, then watch as darkness descends and lights flicker over Villefranche-sur-Mer's heavenly setting. At the recommended **Restaurant de la Plage de Passable,** enjoy a surprisingly elegant dining experience to the sounds of children still at play on the beach. Notice the streetlights that illuminate the path of the Low and Middle Corniches.

St-Jean-Cap-Ferrat

This quiet village port lies in Cap Ferrat's center, yet off most tourist itineraries. St. Jean houses yachts, boardwalks, views, and bou-

tiques packaged in a "take your time, darling" atmosphere. It's a few miles off the busy Nice-to-Monaco road—convenient for drivers, yet it feels overlooked. A string of restaurants line the port, with just enough visitors to keep them in business. St. Jean is especially peaceful at night.

There's a small TI in the village center with limited hours (described earlier). The bus stop back to Villefranche-sur-Mer is a block above the port near Hôtel la Frégate (if you need a taxi, call 04 93 76 86 00). The hiking trail to Beaulieu-sur-Mer (with access to the Villa Ephrussi and Villefranche-sur-Mer for hard-core walkers) begins past the beach, to the left of the port as you look out to the water (details follow).

▲▲Walks Around Cap Ferrat

The Cap is perfect for a walk, as you'll find well-maintained foot trails covering most of its length. You have three easy, mostly level options: 30 minutes, 45 minutes, or 2-3 hours. The TIs in Villefranche-sur-Mer and St. Jean have maps of Cap Ferrat with walking paths marked, or you can use the following itineraries with this book's map. During segments of all of the hikes, you can make out

the three Corniche roads cut into the side of the massive cliffs.

Between St. Jean and Beaulieu-sur-Mer (30 minutes): A level walk takes you past sumptuous villas, great views, and fun swimming opportunities. From St. Jean's port, walk along the harbor with the water on your right, and work your way past the beach. Head up the steps to Promenade Maurice Rouvier and continue; before long you'll see smashing views of the whitewashed Villa Kérylos (and you might be able to make out the hill town of Eze-le-Village crowning the last peak on the right across the bay).

To get from Beaulieu-sur-Mer to St. Jean or the Villa Ephrussi, start at the Villa Kérylos (with the sea on your left), walk toward the Hôtel Royal Riviera, and find the trail. If going to St. Jean, be careful to stay left at the Villa Sonja Rello (about halfway down); if going to the Villa Ephrussi, look for signs leading uphill before Villa Aurora (walk up the path to Avenue Henri Honoré Sauvan, then keep going). If you're walking from St. Jean to the Villa Ephrussi, turn left off the trail about 50 yards after passing the Villa Aurora.

Plage de la Paloma Loop Trail (45 minutes): Just east of St. Jean's port, a sea-soaked, view-loaded trail offers a terrific sampling of Cap Ferrat's beauty for a modest effort. From the port, walk or drive about a quarter-mile east (with the port on your left, passing Hôtel La Voile d'Or); parking is available at the port or on streets near Plage de la Paloma. You'll find the trailhead where the road comes to a T—look for a *Plage Paloma* sign pointing left, but don't walk left. Cross the small dirt park to start the trail, and do the walk counterclockwise. The trail is level and paved, yet uneven enough that good shoes are helpful. Plunk your picnic on one of the benches along the trail, or eat at the restaurant on Plage de la Paloma at the end of the walk (sandwiches and salads for lunch, elegant dinners in the evening—see "Eating on Cap Ferrat," later). If time is tight, walk up the road toward *Plage Paloma* signs and find the trail to enjoy the great views.

Plage de Passable to St. Jean (2-3 hours): For a longer hike that circles the Cap, follow the signs below the Villa Ephrussi marked *Plage Passable* (10 minutes downhill on foot from the villa, parking available near the trailhead). Walk down to the beach (you'll find a good café that's ideal for lunch), turn left, and cross the beach. Go along a paved road behind the apartment building, and after about 60 yards, take the steps down to the trail *(Sentier Littoral)*. Near the end of the trail, you'll pass by the port of St. Jean, where you have three options: Take bus #81 back to Villefranche-sur-Mer, walk back to the Villa Ephrussi and Plage de Passable via the shorter inland route (by reversing the directions under "Walks from the Villa Ephrussi," earlier), or continue on to Beaulieu-sur-Mer and take a bus to Monaco or Nice.

Sleeping on Cap Ferrat

In St. Jean

The sleepy village of St. Jean offers surprisingly good values, probably because it's off the main route (and less convenient if you don't have a car).

$$$ Hôtel Brise Marine*, flanked by tall palm trees and graced with gardens and a view terrace, is a peaceful retreat. Run by the gentle Monsieur Maître-Henri, this aged mansion—with faded, Old World character—feels lost in a time warp. Many of its spacious rooms come with sensational views, and some have small balconies (view Db with balcony-€200, view Db without balcony-€175, breakfast-€15, air-con, Wi-Fi, minibar, secure parking-€15/day with reservation, ideally located between the port and Plage de la Paloma at 58 Avenue Jean Mermoz, tel. 04 93 76 04 36, www.hotel-brisemarine.com, info@hotel-brisemarine.com).

$$ Hôtel Oursin** is central to the port, with 14 respectably priced and surprisingly well-appointed rooms all on one floor. Run by mother-and-son team Chantal and Aubrey, it's a welcoming, humble place with white walls, and feels more like a B&B than a hotel (small Ds-€45, smaller Db without air-con-€75, bigger Db with air-con and upgraded bathroom-€90-110, larger Db with port views-€125, €20 less Oct-April, 1 Avenue Denis Séméria, tel. 04 93 76 12 55, www.hoteloursin.com, reception@hoteloursin.com).

Between St. Jean and Villefranche-sur-Mer

$ Hôtel Patricia* sits across from Villefranche-sur-Mer, at the start of Cap Ferrat. It's a 20-minute walk to Villefranche or the Villa Ephrussi, and 10 minutes by foot into Beaulieu-sur-Mer. Helpful owners Joelle and Franck provide 11 central, simple, homey, and reasonably priced rooms (Db-€63-83, Wi-Fi, parking available, near l'Ange Gardien bus stop at 310 Avenue de l'Ange Gardien, tel. 04 93 01 06 70, www.hotel-patricia.riviera.fr, hotelpatricia@free.fr).

Eating on Cap Ferrat

For **picnics,** the short pedestrian street in St. Jean has all you need (grocery store, bakery, charcuterie, and pizza to go), and you'll have no trouble finding portside or seaside seating. Plage de la Paloma is a 10-minute walk away.

Le St. Jean Pizzeria/Restaurant is central, easygoing, and cheap (€10 pizzas, closed Wed, Avenue Denis Séméria, tel. 04 93 76 04 75).

Captain Cook is sweet little eatery that takes its fish seriously. There's a small patio in front, a bigger one out back (no view), and a cozy interior between (good €26 *menu,* ask about bouillabaisse, closed Wed, a few steps past the port toward Plage de la Paloma at 11 Avenue Jean Mermoz, tel. 04 93 76 02 66).

Restaurant de la Plage de Passable is your chance to dine on the beach with romance and class, while enjoying terrific views (€12-16 starters, €18-27 *plats,* open for dinner daily late May-early Sept, tel. 04 93 76 06 17, www.plage-de-passable.com).

Plage de la Paloma Restaurant is a 15-minute walk from the village of St. Jean, with classier ambience (€15 starters, €20-30 *plats,* closed late Sept-mid-April, route de St. Hospice, for directions see "Plage de la Paloma Loop Trail," earlier, tel. 04 93 01 64 71, www.paloma-beach.com). Call ahead to ask what time dinner service begins (can be as late as 20:00).

Near Cap Ferrat: Villa Kérylos

Beaulieu-sur-Mer, right on the Low Corniche road (just after Cap Ferrat), is perennially busy with traffic. It's a good place to pick up the hiking trail to St. Jean, and to visit the unusual **Villa Kérylos.** In 1902, an eccentric millionaire modeled his new mansion after a Greek villa from the island of Delos from about 200 B.C. No expense was spared in re-creating this Greek fantasy, from the floor

mosaics to Carrara marble columns to exquisite wood furnishings. The rain-powered shower is fun, and the included audioguide will increase your Greek IQ. The ceramics workshop—open only high season and weekend afternoons—offers a chance to test your talents.

Cost and Hours: €11, €19 combo-ticket with Villa Ephrussi de Rothschild—valid for one week; mid-Feb-Oct daily 10:00-18:00, July-Aug until 19:00; Nov-mid-Feb Mon-Fri 14:00-18:00, Sat-Sun 10:00-18:00; tel. 04 93 01 47 29, www.villa-kerylos.com.

Getting to and from the Villa Kérylos

Drivers should park near the casino in Beaulieu-sur-Mer, not on the villa's access road. Monaco-Nice bus #100 drops you at the Eglise stop at the Hôtel Metropole in Beaulieu (turn right off the bus and find signs to the Villa Kérylos), while bus #81 from Villefranche-sur-Mer and Nice stops at the villa's access road (for details on these buses, see page 406). Trains (2/hour, 10 minutes from Nice or Monaco) leave you a 10-minute walk away: Turn left out of the train station and left again down the main drag. Walk to the end, turn right, then find signs to the Villa Kérylos. The walking trail from the Villa Kérylos to Cap Ferrat and the Villa Ephrussi de Rothschild begins on the other side of the bay, beneath Hôtel Royal Riviera.

Eze-le-Village

Floating high above the sea, flowery and flawless Eze-le-Village (don't confuse it with the seafront town of Eze-Bord-de-Mer) is

entirely consumed by tourism. This *village d'art et de gastronomie* (as it calls itself) nurtures perfume outlets, stylish boutiques, steep cobbled lanes, and magnificent views. Touristy as this place certainly Eze, its stony state of preservation and magnificent hilltop setting over the Mediterranean may lure you away from the beaches. Day-tripping by

bus to Eze-le-Village from Nice, Monaco, or Villefranche-sur-Mer works well, provided you know the bus schedules (ask at TIs or check www.lignedazur.com; Villefranche-sur-Mer requires a transfer).

Getting to Eze-le-Village

There are two Ezes: Eze-le-Village (the spectacular hill town) and Eze-Bord-de-Mer (a modern beach resort far below Eze-le-Village). Eze-le-Village is about 20 minutes east of Villefranche-sur-Mer on the Middle Corniche.

From Nice and upper Villefranche-sur-Mer, buses #82 and #112 provide 16 buses per day to Eze-le-Village (8 on Sun, 20 minutes from Villefranche). Take hourly minibus #80 from the center of Villefranche-sur-Mer uphill to the Col de Villefranche stop near Hôtel la Fiancée du Pirate to make this connection.

From Nice, Villefranche-sur-Mer, or Monaco, you can also take the train or the Nice-Monaco bus to Eze-Bord-de-Mer, getting off at the Gare d'Eze stop. From here, take the #83 shuttle bus straight up to Eze-le-Village (8/day, daily 9:55-18:15, schedule is posted at the stop but it's best to know schedule before you go). From Monaco, it's best to connect by direct bus (described next).

To connect Eze-le-Village directly with Monte Carlo in Monaco, take bus #112 (6/day Mon-Sat, none on Sun, 20 minutes).

There are no direct buses from Villefranche-sur-Mer's center to Eze-le-Village, and there are no buses between La Turbie (La Trophée des Alpes) and Eze-le-Village (40-minute walk).

EZE-LE-VILLAGE

You could take a pricey taxi between the two Ezes or from Eze-le-Village to La Turbie (allow €25 one-way, mobile 06 09 84 17 84).

Tourist Information

The helpful TI is adjacent to Eze-le-Village's main parking lot, just below the town's entry. Ask here for bus schedules. Call in advance to arrange €8 English-language tours of the village and its gardens (TI open April-Oct daily 9:00-18:00, July-Aug until 19:00; Nov-March Mon-Sat 9:00-17:00, closed Sun; Place de Gaulle, tel. 04 93 41 26 00, www.eze-tourisme.com).

Helpful Hints

Bus Stops: The stop for buses to Nice is across the road by the Avia gas station, and the stops for buses to Eze-Bord-de-Mer and Monaco are on the village side of the main road, near the Casino grocery.

Services: Public WCs are just behind the TI and in the village behind the church, though the cleanest and best-smelling are at the perfume showrooms.

Self-Guided Walk

Welcome to Eze-le-Village

• *From the TI and parking lot, wander uphill into the town. You'll come to an exclusive hotel gate and the start of a steep trail down to the beach, marked* Eze/Mer. *For a panoramic view and an ideal picnic perch, walk 80 steps down this path (for more details, see "Trail to Eze-Bord-de-Mer," later). Continuing up into the village, find the steps just after the ritzy hotel gate and climb to...*

Place du Centenaire: In this square, a stone plaque in the flower bed (behind the soap and spice displays) celebrates the 100th anniversary of the 1860 plebiscite, the time when all 133 Eze residents voted to leave the Italian Duchy of Savoy and join France. *Vive la France!* A town map here helps you get oriented.

• *Now pass through the once-formidable town gate (designed to keep the Ottomans out) and climb into the 14th-century village. You'll find occasional English information plaques on walls in the old city that together give a good history of the village. Wandering the narrow lanes, follow signs to the...*

Château Eza: This was the winter getaway of the Swedish royal family from 1923 until 1953; today it's a hotel. The château's tearoom (Salon de Thé), on a cliff overlooking the jagged Riviera and sea, offers you the most scenic coffee or beer break you'll ever enjoy—for a price. The sensational view terrace is also home to an expensive-but-excellent restaurant. Reserve well ahead for dinner

(€7 teas and beers, €10 glasses of wine, €59 lunch *menus,* allow €120 for dinner, open daily, tel. 04 93 41 12 24, www.chateaueza.com, info@chateau eza.com).

• *The uphill lanes end at the hilltop castle ruins—now blanketed by the...*

Jardins d'Eze: Here you'll find a prickly festival of cactus. Since 1949, these ruins have been home to 400 different plants 1,300 feet above the sea (€6, open daily, hours change frequently but usually May-Sept 9:00-19:00, Oct-April until dusk, well-described in English, tel. 04 93 41 10 30). At the top, you'll be treated to a commanding 360-degree view, with a helpful *table d'orientation.* On a crystal-clear day (they say...) you can see Corsica. The castle was demolished by Louis XIV in 1706. Louis destroyed castles like this all over Europe (most notably along the Rhine), because he didn't want to risk having to do battle with rebellious nobles inside them at some future date.

• *As you descend, drop by the...*

Eze Church: Though built during Napoleonic times, it has an uncharacteristic Baroque fanciness—a reminder that 300 years of Savoy rule left the townsfolk with an Italian savoir faire and a sensibility for decor.

Sights in Eze-le-Village

Fragonard Perfume Factory

This factory, with its huge tour-bus parking lot, lies on the Middle Corniche, 350 feet below Eze-le-Village. Designed for tour groups, it cranks them through all day long. If you've never seen mass tourism in action, this place will open your eyes. (The gravel is littered with the color-coded stickers each tourist wears so that the salespeople know which guide gets the kickback.) Drop in for an informative and free tour, which can last anywhere from 20 to 40 minutes depending on the walking ability of the group. You'll see how the perfume and scented soaps are made, before being herded into the gift shop.

Cost and Hours: Daily 8:30-18:30, Nov-Jan 8:30-12:00 & 14:00-16:30; best Mon-Fri 9:00-11:00 & 14:00-15:30, when the "factory" actually has people working; tel. 04 93 41 05 05.

Nearby: For a more personal and intimate (but unguided) look at perfume, cross the main road in Eze-le-Village to visit the **Gallimard** shop. Explore the small museum and let the lovely ladies show you their scents (daily 9:00-18:00, handy and free WCs).

Trail to Eze-Bord-de-Mer

This steep trail leaves Eze-le-Village from the foot of the hill-town entry, near the fancy hotel gate (60 yards up from the main road), and descends 1,300 feet to the sea along a no-shade, all-view trail. The trail is easy to follow, but uneven—allow 45 minutes at a steady but manageable pace (good walking shoes are essential; expect to use all fours in certain sections). Once in Eze-Bord-de-Mer, you can catch a bus or train to all destinations between Nice and Monaco. While walking this trail in the late 1800s, Friedrich Nietzsche was moved to write his unconventionally spiritual novel, *Thus Spoke Zarathustra*.

Eating in Eze-le-Village

To enjoy Eze-le-Village in relative peace, visit at sunset and stay for dinner. There's a handy **Casino** grocery at the foot of the village by the bus stop (Mon-Sat 8:00-19:30, Sun 8:00-19:00) and a sensational picnic spot at the beginning of the trail to Eze-Bord-de-Mer. **Le Cactus** serves cheap crêpes, salads, and sandwiches at outdoor tables near the entry to the old town (daily, tel. 04 93 41 19 02). For a real splurge, dine at **Château Eza** (described earlier).

La Trophée des Alpes

High above Monaco, on the Grande (High) Corniche in the overlooked village of La Turbie, lies one of this region's most evocative historical sights (with dramatic views over the entire country of Monaco as a bonus). Rising well above all other buildings, this massive Roman monument, rated ▲▲, commemorates Augustus Caesar's conquest of the Alps and its 44 hostile tribes. It's exciting to think that, in a way, La Trophée des Alpes celebrates a victory that kicked off the Pax Romana—joining Gaul and Germania, freeing up the main artery of the Roman Empire, and linking Spain and Italy. (It's depressing to think that it's closed on Mondays, if that's your only chance to visit.)

You'll enter through a small park that offers grand views over Monaco and allows you to appreciate the remarkable setting selected by the Romans for this monument. Walk around and notice how the Romans built a fine, quarried-stone exterior, filled in with rubble and coarse concrete. Flanked by the vanquished in chains, the towering inscription tells the story: It was erected "by the senate and the people to honor the emperor." The structure served no military purpose when built, though it was fortified in the Middle Ages (like the Roman Arena in Arles) as a safe haven for villagers. When Louis XIV ordered the destruction of the area's fortresses in the early 18th century, he sadly included this one. The monument later became a quarry before being restored in the 1930s and 1940s with money from the Tuck family of New Hampshire.

The one-room **museum** shows a reconstruction and translation of the dramatic inscription, which lists all the feisty alpine tribes that put up such a fight. Recently upgraded, it has good English explanations and modern exhibits (an audioguide is available). Escorts from the museum take people up to the monument, but they're not worth waiting for.

Cost and Hours: €5.50, audioguide-€3.50, Tue-Sun mid-May–mid-Sept 9:30-13:00 & 14:30-18:30, off-season 10:00-13:00 & 14:30-17:00, closed Mon year-round, tel. 04 93 41 20 84.

La Turbie: The sweet old village of La Turbie sees almost no tourists, but it has plenty of cafés and restaurants (see "Eating in La Turbie," later). To stroll the old village, park in the main lot on Place Neuve (follow *Monaco* signs one block from the main road to find it), then walk behind the post office and find brick footpaths—they lead through a village with nary a shop.

Getting to and from La Trophée des Alpes (in La Turbie)

By **car,** take the High Corniche to La Turbie, ideally from Eze-le-Village (La Turbie is 10 minutes east of, and above, Eze-le-Village), then look for signs to *La Trophée des Alpes*. Once in La Turbie, park in the lot in the center of town (Place Neuve, follow *Monaco* signs for a short block) and walk from there (walk 5 minutes around the old village, with the village on your right); or drive to the site by turning right in front of La Régence Café. Those coming from farther afield can take the efficient A-8 to the La Turbie exit. To reach Eze-le-Village from La Turbie, follow signs to *Nice*, and then look for signs to *Eze-le-Village*.

You can also get here on **bus** #T-66 from Nice's Pont St. Michel stop (7/day, 45 minutes, last bus returns to Nice at about 18:00). In Nice, take the tram to the Pont St. Michel stop. From Monaco, bus #114 connects to La Turbie (6/day Mon-Sat, 5/day Sun, 30 minutes). La Turbie's bus stop is across from the post office (PTT) on Place Neuve (to reach La Trophée des Alps from here, walk 5 minutes around the old village, with the village on your right).

On **foot,** Eze-le-Village is a 45-minute roadside walk downhill from La Turbie (no buses). There's a bike lane for half of the trip, but the rest is along a fairly quiet road with no shoulder. Follow D-2564 from La Turbie to Eze-le-Village, and don't miss the turnoff for D-45. The views of Eze-le-Village are magnificent as you get close.

Eating in La Turbie

To eat very well, find **La Terrasse,** the Riviera's most welcoming restaurant (I'm not kidding—free calls are encouraged from their phone anywhere, anytime; there's a computer at your disposal; and the Wi-Fi is complimentary). Tables gather under sunshades and everyone seems to be on a first-name basis. The sea lies miles below (that point of land is Cap Ferrat), but most diners are more interested in the meal than the view. Let Helen, Jacques, and Annette tempt you to return for dinner at sunset—book ahead for a table with a view (€8-12 salads, great €14 *plats du jour,* €20 three-course *menu* includes glass of wine, steak tartare is a specialty, daily, near the post office at the main parking lot, 17 Place Neuve, tel. 04 93 41 21 84).

Quickie Riviera Bus Tour from Nice to Monaco

Don't have a car? You can still enjoy the trip from Nice to Monaco (and on to Menton, described in following chapter). Although most travelers see the Riviera from their train window as they zoom along the coast, the public bus affords a far better view of the dramatic crags, dreamy villas, and much-loved beaches that make it Europe's coast with the most.

This tour works best if you take the bus from Nice, ride the entire Nice-Monaco-Menton route (one scenic hour), enjoy Menton, then see Monaco (or find time for another stop) on the way back to Nice. To minimize bus and sightseeing crowds, time it so that you're on the bus by 9:00, but beware: Monte Carlo's casino does not open until 14:00 most days. Alternatively, come for late-afternoon sightseeing and stay into the evening. (Keep in mind that afternoon buses back to Nice are often crammed and agonizingly slow after Villefranche-sur-Mer—at these times, the train is a better solution.)

Bus Tips: Riding the bus couldn't be easier. Bus #100 runs along the Low Corniche (daily 6:00-20:00, 4-5/hour Mon-Sat, 3-4/hour on Sun, stops in Nice just off Place Garibaldi). You're looking for bus #100 to *destination: Monaco/Menton* (avoid the occasional express bus that takes the freeway to Monaco).

One simple €1.50 ticket is good for 74 minutes, no matter how far you go (one-way only). Pay the driver as you get on, and be assertive with the crowds trying to board.

Riding from Nice toward Monaco, grab a seat on the right-hand side. It's easiest to get a good seat if you go before 9:00. If there's a long line, you could wait for the next bus to be assured of a view seat.

Since bus fares are cheap, consider hopping on and off at great viewpoints (the next bus will be by soon). All stops have names (usually posted on the shelter or bus stop sign)—I'll identify the ones that matter along this route. Keep your eyes peeled for town names and bus stops as we go.

Many bus drivers on this line seem to be in training for the Monaco Grand Prix—so hold on tight.

Self-Guided Bus Tour

This Nice-to-Monaco route along the Low Corniche was inaugurated with the opening of the Monte Carlo Casino in 1863. It was designed to provide easy and safe access from Nice (and the rest of France) to the gambling fun in Monaco. Here's what you'll see along the way:

In Nice: Shortly after the bus pulls out, you'll get a quick glimpse of Nice's snazzy Museum of Modern Art on the left before passing by Place Garibaldi (easy transfer to the tram on your way back), with its linden trees and statue of Giuseppe Garibaldi (one of the men credited with uniting Italy in the 1860s) at the center.

Nice Harbor: This harbor was built in the 1700s. Before then, boats littered Nice's beaches. You'll see some yachts, an occasional cruise ship, and the daily ferry to Corsica. The one-hour boat tour along Cap Ferrat and Villefranche-sur-Mer leaves from the right side, about halfway down (see page 337). If you get on or off here on your return, it's a pleasant 30-minute walk around the point to or from the Promenade des Anglais.

From Nice to Villefranche-sur-Mer: As you glide away from Nice, look back for views of the harbor, Castle Hill, and the sweeping Bay of Angels. Imagine the views from the homes below, and imagine 007 on his deck admiring a sunset (the soft, yellow, rounded tower ahead near the top of the hill is part of Sean Connery's property). Elton John's home is higher up the hill (and out of view).

You'll soon pass the now-closed Hôtel Maerterlinck, one of several luxury hotels to go belly-up in recent years (now slated for condo-conversion). Next, you'll come to the yacht-studded bay of Villefranche-sur-Mer and the peninsula called Cap Ferrat—playground of the rich and famous, marked by its lighthouse on the point just across the bay. This bay is a rare natural harbor along the Riviera. Since it's deeper than Nice's, it hosts the huge cruise ships.

Villefranche-sur-Mer: To see charming Villefranche-sur-Mer, get off at the stop labeled *Octroi*. After passing through Villefranche-sur-Mer, look for sensational views back over the town. Looking ahead, the Baroness Rothschild's pink Villa Ephrussi, with its red-tiled roof, breaks the horizon on Cap Ferrat's peninsula. Keep an eye out as the road arcs to the right—the Rolling Stones recorded 1972's *Exile on Main Street* (one of your co-author's favorites) in the basement of the Villa Nellcote, the mansion below where you see the *l'Ange Gardien* signs.

Cap Ferrat: This peninsula is home to the Villa Ephrussi de Rothschild, the port town of St. Jean, and some lovely seaside paths. As you leave Cap Ferrat on our bus tour, remember that this road was built in 1860 to bring customers to Monaco. Before then, there was no development along this route, all the way to Monaco.

Beaulieu-sur-Mer: To visit the Villa Kérylos or to take the seaside walk to St. Jean on Cap Ferrat, get off at the Eglise stop, in front of the Hôtel Metropole. Just after the town of Beaulieu-sur-Mer, the cliffs create a micro-climate and a zone nicknamed "Little Africa." (The bus stop is labeled *Petite Afrique*.) Exotic vegetation (including the only bananas on the Riviera) grows among private, elegant villas that made Beaulieu-sur-Mer *the* place to be in the 19th century.

Eze-Bord-de-Mer: A few minutes after leaving Beaulieu-sur-Mer, be ready for scant, short-lived views way up to the fortified town of Eze-le-Village. After passing through a rock arch, you'll swing around a big bend going left: Eze-le-Village crowns the ridge in front of you. (To reach Eze-le-Village, the #83 shuttle bus makes the climb from the Gare d'Eze stop in Eze-Bord-de-Mer—see page 417).

Cap d'Ail: After passing through several tunnels, you emerge at Cap d'Ail. The huge, yellowish, hospital-like building below (what color is that, anyway?) once thrived as a luxury hotel popular with the Russian aristocracy. Now it's popular with condo-commandos. At the first stop in the village of Cap d'Ail (labeled *Cap d'Ail-Edmonds*), look above at the switchbacks halfway up the barren hillside. It was at the bend connecting these two switchbacks that Princess Grace Kelly (the former American movie star) was killed in a car crash in 1982. You can get off here and walk a lovely beach trail that will take you to Monaco in roughly 30 minutes.

Monaco (three bus stops): Cap d'Ail borders Monaco—you're about to leave France. You'll pass by some pretty junky development along this no-man's-land stretch. Eventually, to the right, just before the castle-topped hill (Monaco-Ville), is Monaco's Fontvieille district, featuring tall, modern apartments all built on land reclaimed from the Mediterranean. The first Monaco stop (Place d'Armes) is best for visiting the palace and other old-town sights in Monaco-Ville.

If you stay on the bus, you'll pass through the tunnel, then emerge to follow the road that Grand Prix racers (like your driver) speed along. In late May you'll see blue bleachers and barriers set up for the big race.

You'll pass the second Monaco stop (Stade Nautique), then enjoy the harbor and city views as you climb to the last Monaco stop (Casino). Get off here (look for the Häagen Dazs) for a glimpse at the gambling action (a plush, terraced garden leads down to the casino). For information on Monaco, see the next chapter. If you stay on the bus for a few more minutes, you'll be back in France, and in 15 more minutes you'll reach the end of the line, **Menton** (described in the following chapter).

Bonne route!

MONACO

Despite high prices, wall-to-wall daytime tourists, and a Disney-esque atmosphere, Monaco is a Riviera must. Monaco is on the go. Since 1929, cars have raced around the port and in front of the casino in one of the world's most famous auto races, the Grand Prix de Monaco (see sidebar, later). The modern breakwater—constructed elsewhere and towed in by sea—enables big cruise ships to dock here. The district of Fontvieille, reclaimed from the sea, bristles with luxury high-rise condos. But don't look for anything too deep in this glittering tax haven. Two-thirds of its 30,000 residents live here because there's no income tax—leaving fewer than 10,000 true Monegasques.

This minuscule principality (0.75 square mile) borders only France and the Mediterranean. The country has always been tiny, but it used to be...less tiny. In an 1860 plebiscite, Monaco lost two-thirds of its territory when the region of Menton voted to join France. To compensate, France suggested that Monaco build a fancy casino and promised to connect it to the world with a road (the Low Corniche) and a train line. This started a high-class tourist boom that has yet to let up.

Although "independent," Monaco is run as a piece of France. A French civil servant appointed by the French president—with the blessing of Monaco's prince—serves as state min-ister and manages the place. Monaco's phone system, elec-tricity, water, and so on, are all French.

The glamorous romance and marriage of the American actress Grace Kelly to Prince

Monaco

MIDDLE CORNICHE
To Menton

#112 To Eze-le-Village
& #114 To La Turbie

BLVD. DE LA RÉPUBLIQUE

BLVD. DES MOULINS

To Villa Sauber & Menton

FRANCE

To Nice

#1 & #2 B

AVE. SPEL

BLVD. LARVOTTO

TRAIN STATION (UNDERGROUND)

BLVD. PRINCESSE CHARLOTTE

#100 to Nice

#1 & #2 B

#100 from Nice B

Place du Casino

AMERICAN-STYLE CASINO

M O N A C O

AVE. COSTA

MONTE CARLO

CASINO

AVE. D'OSTENDE

BLVD. DU JARDIN EXOTIQUE

VILLA PALOMA

Jardin Exotique

RUE GRIMALDI

BLVD. RAINIER III

R. PRIN. ANT.

BLVD. ALBERT I

LA CONDAMINE

R. SUFFREN-REYMOND

2

R. PRIN. CAR.

3

1

#100 to Nice B

#100 from Nice

RAMPE MAJOR

To Nice

PALAIS DES CONGRES & "Le Casino"

SHUTTLE BOAT

Port
LOTSA YACHTS!

CRUISE TENDER DOCK

Place d'Armes (Local Buses)

MONACO-VILLE

#1 & #2 B AVE. QUARANTINE

AVE. DE LA PORTE NEUVE

FORT ANTOINE

PRINCE'S PALACE & NAPOLEON COLLECTION

Place du Palais

4

Place de la Visitation

5

POST

MONTE CARLO STORY & "Le Palais"

#1 & #2 B

CATHEDRAL

Jardin Botanique

AQUARIUM

WALK BEGINS

FONTVIEILLE

Mediterranean Sea

T ACCESS TO TRAIN STATION

B BUS STOP

300 Meters

300 Yards

1 Hôtel de France
2 Huit et Demi Rest.
3 Crock'in Café
4 Boulangerie
5 U Cavagnetu Rest.

Rainier added to Monaco's fairy-tale mystique. Princess Grace (Prince Albert's mother) first came to Monaco to star in the 1955 Hitchcock movie *To Catch a Thief,* in which she was filmed racing along the Corniches. She married the prince in 1956 and adopted the country, but tragically, the much-loved princess died in 1982 after suffering a stroke while driving on one of those same scenic roads. She was just 52 years old.

The death of Prince Rainier in 2005 ended his 56-year career of enlightened rule. Today Monaco is ruled by Prince Rainier's unassuming son, Prince Albert Alexandre Louis Pierre, Marquis of Baux. Prince Albert had long been considered Europe's most eligible bachelor—until he finally married on July 2, 2011, at age 53. His bride, known as Princess Charlene, is a South African commoner 20 years his junior. Sadly for Monaco, this rare royal event was overshadowed by the London wedding of Prince William and Kate Middleton.

A graduate of Amherst College, Albert is a bobsled enthusiast who raced in several Olympics, and an avid environmentalist who seems determined to clean up Monaco's tarnished tax-haven, money-laundering image. (Monaco is infamously known as a "sunny place for shady people.") Monaco is big business, and Prince Albert is its CEO. Its famous casino contributes only 5 percent of the state's revenue, whereas its 43 banks—which offer an attractive way to hide your money—are hugely profitable. The prince also makes money with a value-added tax (19.6 percent, the same as in France), plus real estate and corporate taxes.

Monaco is a special place: There are more people in Monaco's philharmonic orchestra (about 100) than in its army (about 80 guards). The princedom is well-guarded, with police and cameras on every corner. (They say you could win a million dollars at the casino and walk to the train station in the wee hours without a worry...and I believe it.) Stamps are so few that they increase in value almost as soon as they're printed. And collectors snapped up the rare Monaco versions of euro coins (with Prince Rainier's portrait) so quickly that many Monegasques have never even seen one.

Orientation to Monaco

The principality of Monaco has three distinct tourist areas: Monaco-Ville, Monte Carlo, and La Condamine. **Monaco-Ville** fills the rock high above everything else and is referred to by locals as Le Rocher ("The Rock"). This is the oldest section, home to the Prince's Palace and all the sights except the casino. **Monte Carlo** is the area around the casino. **La Condamine** is the port (which lies between Monaco-Ville and Monte Carlo). From here it's a 25-minute walk up to the Prince's Palace or to

the casino, or three minutes by local bus (see "Getting Around Monaco," later). A fourth, less-interesting area, **Fontvieille,** forms the west end of Monaco and was reclaimed from the sea by Prince Rainier in the 1970s.

The surgical-strike plan for most travelers is to start at Monaco-Ville (where you'll spend the most time), wander down along the port area, and finish by gambling away whatever you have left in Monte Carlo (the casino doesn't open until 14:00). You can walk the entire route in about 1.5 hours, or take three bus trips and do it in 15 minutes.

Tourist Information

The main TI is at the top of the park, above the casino (Mon-Sat 9:00-19:00, Sun 11:00-13:00, 2 Boulevard des Moulins, tel. 00-377/92 16 61 16 or 00-377/92 16 61 66, www.visitmonaco.com). Branch TIs may be open in the train station (Tue-Sat 9:00-17:00, until 18:00 in summer, closed Sun-Mon except July-Aug). From June to September, you might find information kiosks at the west exit (Nice end) of the train station, in the Monaco-Ville parking garage, and on the port. There is also a TI desk for Monaco in Terminal 1 of Nice's airport.

Arrival in Monaco

By Bus from Nice and Villefranche-sur-Mer: See my "Quickie Riviera Bus Tour from Nice to Monaco" on page 422 to plan your route and for tips. Bus riders need to pay attention, since stops are not announced. Cap d'Ail is the town before Monaco, so be on the lookout after that (the last stop before Monaco is called Cimetière). You'll enter Monaco through the modern cityscape of high-rises of the Fontvieille district. When you see the rocky outcrop of old Monaco, be ready to get off.

There are three stops in Monaco. Listed in order from Nice, they are Place d'Armes (in front of a tunnel at the base of Monaco-Ville's rock), Stade Nautique (closest stop to Monaco-Ville on the port), and Office de Tourisme (near the casino and the TI on Avenue d'Ostende). The Place d'Armes stop is the best starting point, and is the only signed stop (otherwise, verify with locals that you're at the right stop). From the Place d'Armes stop, you can walk up to Monaco-Ville and the palace (10 minutes straight up), or catch a quick local bus (line #1 or #2—see "Getting Around Monaco," later). To reach the bus stop and steps up to Monaco-Ville, cross the street right in front of the tunnel and walk with the rock on your right for about 200 feet (good WCs at the local-bus stop). To begin at the Office de Tourisme stop, pass through the port, and get off the bus when you see the Häagen-Dazs, walk past it, and turn right.

For directions on returning to Nice by bus, see "Monaco Connections," near the end of this chapter.

By Train from Nice: This looooong underground train station is in central Monaco, about a 15-minute walk to the casino or to the port, and about 25 minutes to the palace. The station has no baggage storage.

MONACO

The TI and ticket windows are up the escalator at the Italy end of the station. There are three exits from the train platform level (one at each end and one in the middle).

To reach Monaco-Ville and the palace from the station, take the platform-level exit at the Nice end of the tracks (signed *Sortie Fontvieille/Monaco Ville*), which leads through a long tunnel (TI annex at end); as you emerge from the tunnel, turn right, turn left at the end of the walkway, and cross the busy intersection. From here, it's a 15-minute hike up to the palace, or take the bus (#1 or #2).

To reach Monaco's port and the casino, take the mid-platform exit, closer to the Italy end of the tracks. Follow *Sortie la Condamine* signs down the steps and escalators, then follow *Accès Port* signs until you pop out at the port, where you'll see the stop for buses #1 and #2. It's a 25-minute walk from the port to the palace (to your right) or 20 minutes to the casino (up Avenue d'Ostende to your left), or a short trip via buses #1 or #2 to either.

If you plan to return to Nice by train after 20:30, when ticket windows close, buy your return tickets now or be sure to have about €4 in coins (the ticket machines only take coins).

To take the short-but-sweet coastal **walking path** into Monaco via its Fontvieille district, get off the train at Cap d'Ail, which is one stop before Monaco. Turn left out of the little station and walk 50 yards up the road, then turn left again, going down the stairs and under the tracks. Turn left onto the coastal trail, and hike the 20 minutes to Fontvieille. You'll end up at Plage Marquet. Once there, it's a 20-minute uphill hike to Monaco's sights (or hop on bus #100—walk up Avenue Marquet past the stadium, and make a left on Avenue de Fontvieille).

By Car: Follow *Centre-Ville* signs into Monaco (warning: traffic can be a problem), then watch for the red-letter signs to parking garages at *Le Casino* (for Monte Carlo) or *Le Palais* (for Monaco-Ville). You'll pay about €10 for four hours.

By Cruise Ship: For information on arrival by cruise ship, see "Monaco Connections," near the end of this chapter.

Helpful Hints

Combo-Ticket: If you plan to see all three of Monaco's big sights (Prince's Palace, Napoleon Collection, and the Cousteau Aquarium), buy the €19 combo-ticket at the first sight you visit.

Telephone Tip: To call Monaco from France, dial 00, then 377 (Monaco's country code) and the eight-digit number. Within Monaco, simply dial the eight-digit number.

Minivan Tours from Nice: Several companies offer daytime and nighttime tours of Monaco, allowing you freedom to gamble

MONACO

without worrying about catching the last train or bus home (see "Helpful Hints" on page 319).

Loop Trip by Bus: You can visit Monaco by bus, then take a bus from Monaco directly to Eze-le-Village (#112, none on Sun) or La Turbie (#114), then return to Nice by bus from there. For details, see "Monaco Connections," near the end of this chapter.

Evening Events: Monaco's Philharmonic Orchestra (tel. 00-377/98 06 28 28, www.opmc.mc) and Monte Carlo Ballet (tel. 00-377/99 99 30 00, www.balletsdemontecarlo.com) offer performances at reasonable prices.

Getting Around Monaco

By Local Bus: Buses #1 and #2 link all areas with fast and frequent service (single ticket-€2, 6 tickets-€10, day pass-€5, pay driver, slightly cheaper if bought from machine, 10/hour, fewer on Sun, buses run until 21:00). You can split a six-ride ticket with your travel partners (which is handy, since you're unlikely to take more than two or three rides in Monaco). Bus tickets are good for a free transfer if used within 30 minutes.

By Open Bus Tour: You could pay €18 for a hop-on, hop-off open-deck bus tour that makes 12 stops in Monaco, but I wouldn't. This tour doesn't go to the best view spot in the Jardin Exotique (described on page 435) and, besides, most of Monaco is walkable. If you want a scenic tour of the principality that includes its best views, pay €2 to take local bus #2, and stay on board for a full loop (or hop on and off as you please).

By Tourist Train: "Monaco Tour" tourist trains are an efficient way to enjoy a blitz tour of Monaco. They begin at the aquarium and pass by the port, casino, and palace (€8, 2/hour, 40 minutes, recorded English commentary).

By Taxi: If you've lost all track of time at the casino, you can call the 24-hour taxi service (tel. 08 20 20 98 98)...provided you still have enough money to pay for the cab home.

Self-Guided Walk

Welcome to Monaco-Ville

All of Monaco's sights (except the casino) are in Monaco-Ville, packed within a few cheerfully tidy blocks. This walk makes a tight little loop, starting from the palace square.

• *To get from anywhere in Monaco to the palace square (Monaco-Ville's sightseeing center, home of the palace and the Napoleon Collection), take bus #1 or #2 to the end of the line at Place de la Visitation. Turn right as you step off the bus and walk five minutes down Rue Emile de Loth. You'll pass the post office, a worthwhile stop for its collection of valuable*

MONACO

Monegasque stamps (we'll go there later—to visit it now, see next page).

If you're walking up from the port, the well-marked lane leads you directly to the palace.

Palace Square (Place du Palais): This square is the best place to get oriented to Monaco. Facing the palace, go to the right and look out over the city (er... principality). This rock gave birth to the little pastel Hong Kong look-alike in 1215, and it's managed to remain an independent country for most of its nearly 800 years. Looking beyond the glitzy port, notice the faded green roof above and to the right: It belongs to the casino that put Monaco on the map. The famous Grand Prix runs along the port, and then up the ramp

to the casino. And Italy is so close, you can almost smell the pesto. Just beyond the casino is France again (which flanks Monaco on both sides)—you could walk one-way from France to France, passing through Monaco in about 60 minutes.

The odd statue of a woman with a fishing net is dedicated to **Prince Albert I's** glorious reign (1889-1922). Albert was a Renaissance man with varied skills and interests. He had a Jacques Cousteau-like fascination with the sea (and built Monaco's famous aquarium), and was a determined pacifist who made many attempts to dissuade Germany's Kaiser Wilhelm II from becoming involved in World War I. It was Albert I's dad, Charles III, who built the casino.

• *Now walk toward the palace and find the statue of the monk grasping a sword.*

Meet **François Grimaldi,** a renegade Italian dressed as a monk, who captured Monaco in 1297 and began the dynasty that still rules the principality. Prince Albert is his great-great-great... grandson, which gives Monaco's royal family the distinction of being the longest-lasting dynasty in Europe.

• *Walk to the opposite side of the square.*

At the Louis XIV cannonballs, look down at Monaco's newest area, the reclaimed-from-the-sea **Fontvieille** district, which has seen much of Monaco's post-WWII growth (residential and commercial—notice the lushly planted building tops). Prince Rainier continued—some say, was obsessed with—Monaco's economic growth, creating landfills (topped with apartments, such as Fontvieille), flashy ports, more beaches, a big sports stadium marked by tall arches, and a rail station. (An ambitious new landfill project is in the works that would add still more prime real estate to Monaco's portfolio.) Today, thanks to Prince Rainier's efforts, tiny Monaco is a member of the United Nations. (If you have kids with you, check out the nifty play area just below.)

• *If you're into stamps, detour down Rue Comte Félix Gastaldi, then follow the jog to the right onto Rue Emile de Loth to find the...*

Post Office: Philatelists and postcard-writers with panache can buy—or just gaze in awe at—this post office's impressive collection of Monegasque stamps (Mon-Fri 8:00-19:00, Sat 8:00-12:00, closed Sun).

• *Backpedal a few steps to the...*

Prince's Palace (Palais Princier): A medieval castle sat where Monaco's palace is today. Its strategic setting has had a lot to do with Monaco's ability to resist attackers. Today, Prince Albert and his bride live in the palace, while poor Princesses Stephanie and Caroline live down the street. The palace guards protect the prince 24/7 and still stage a **Changing of the Guard** ceremony with all the pageantry of an important nation (daily at 11:55, fun to watch but jam-packed). Audioguide tours take you through part of the prince's lavish palace in 30 minutes. The rooms are well-furnished and impressive, but interesting only if you haven't seen a château lately (€8 combo-ticket includes audioguide and Napoleon Collection, €19 combo-ticket also includes Cousteau Aquarium; hours vary but generally April-Oct daily 10:00-18:00, closed Nov-March, last entry 30 minutes before closing; tel. 00-377/93 25 18 31).

• *Next to the palace entry is the...*

Napoleon Collection: Napoleon occupied Monaco after the French Revolution. This is the prince's private collection of items Napoleon left behind: military medals, swords, guns, letters, and—best of all—his hat. I found this collection more interesting than the palace (€4 includes audioguide, €8 combo-ticket includes Prince's Palace, €19 combo-ticket also includes Cousteau Aquarium; same hours as palace).

• *With your back to the palace, leave the square through the arch to the right side of the square (under the most beautiful police station I've ever seen) and find the...*

Cathedral of Monaco (Cathédrale de Monaco): The somber but beautifully lit cathedral, rebuilt in 1878, shows that Monaco cared for more than just its new casino. It's where centuries of Grimaldis are buried, and where Princess Grace and Prince Rainier were married. Circle slowly behind the altar (counterclockwise). The second tomb is that of

Monaco at a Glance

▲**Casino of Monte Carlo** Classy casino that saved Monaco's economy. **Hours:** All gaming rooms open daily at 14:00, must have passport and adhere to dress code.

Stamp Shopping Collector's stamps sold at Monaco's post offices. **Hours:** Mon-Fri 8:00-19:00, Sat 8:00-12:00, closed Sun.

Prince's Palace Prince Albert's extravagant residence. **Hours:** May vary but generally April-Oct daily 10:00-18:00, closed Nov-March.

Changing of the Guard Big ceremony for a tiny nation. **Hours:** Daily at 11:55 on the palace square.

Napoleon Collection The prince's private collection of Napoleonic stuff, from medals, swords, and guns, to his cool *chapeau*. **Hours:** Same as Prince's Palace.

Cathedral of Monaco Final resting place for Princess Grace and Prince Rainier. **Hours:** Daily 8:30-19:15.

Cousteau Aquarium Jacques Cousteau's cliff-hugging aquarium. **Hours:** Daily July-Aug 10:00-19:30, April-June and Sept 10:00-19:00, Oct-March 10:00-18:00.

Monte Carlo Story **Film** Informative 35-minute film describing Monaco's sexy history. **Hours:** Showings usually at 14:00, 15:00, 16:00, and 17:00, morning showings possible—ask.

Jardin Exotique Cliffside botanical garden mixing thousands of cacti and fantastic views. **Hours:** Daily May-Sept 9:00-19:00, Oct-April 9:00-18:00 or until dusk.

New National Museum of Monaco Rotating exhibits in two villas covering Monaco's cultural heritage. **Hours:** Daily June-Sept 11:00-19:00, Oct-May 8:00-18:00.

Albert I, who did much to put Monaco on the world stage. The second-to-last tomb—inscribed *"Gratia Patricia, MCMLXXXII"*—is where Princess Grace was buried in 1982. Prince Rainier's tomb lies next to Princess Grace's (daily 8:30-19:15).

• *As you leave the cathedral, find the 1956 wedding photo of Princess Grace and Prince Rainier (keep an eye out for other photos of the couple as you walk), then dip into the immaculately maintained Jardin Botanique, with more fine views. In the gardens, turn left. Eventually you'll find the...*

Cousteau Aquarium (Musée Océanographique): Prince Albert I built this impressive, cliff-hanging aquarium in 1910 as a monument to his enthusiasm for things from the sea. The aquarium, which Captain Jacques Cousteau directed for 32 years, has 2,000 different specimens, representing 250 species. The bottom floor features Mediterranean fish and colorful tropical species (all nicely described in English). My favorite is the zebra lionfish, though I'm keen on eels, too. Rotating exhibits occupy the entry floor. Upstairs, the fancy Albert I Hall houses a museum (included in entry fee, very little English information) and features ship models, whale skeletons, oceanographic instruments and tools, and scenes of Albert and his beachcombers hard at work. Find the display on Christopher Columbus with English explanations.

Don't miss the elevator to the rooftop terrace view, where you'll also find convenient WCs and a reasonable café (aquarium-€14, kids-€7, €19 combo-ticket includes Prince's Palace and Napoleon Collection; daily July-Aug 10:00-19:30, April-June and Sept 10:00-19:00, Oct-March 10:00-18:00; down the steps from Monaco-Ville bus stop, at the opposite end of Monaco-Ville from the palace; tel. 00-377/93 15 36 00, www.oceano.mc).

• *The red-brick steps, across from the aquarium and a bit to the right, lead up to stops for buses #1 and #2, both of which run to the port, the casino, and the train station. To walk back to the palace and through the old city, turn left at the top of the brick steps. For a brief movie break, as you leave the aquarium, take the escalator to the right and drop into the parking garage, then take the elevator down and find the...*

Monte Carlo Story: This informative 35-minute film gives an entertaining and informative account of Monaco's fairy-tale history, from fishing village to jet-set principality, and offers a comfortable, soft-chair break from all that walking. The last part of the film was added to the original version after the death of Prince Rainier, which is why your sound stops early (€8, headphone commentary in English; daily showings usually at 14:00, 15:00, 16:00, and 17:00; there may be a morning showing for groups that you can join—ask, tel. 00-377/93 25 32 33).

Sights in Monaco

Above Monaco-Ville

Jardin Exotique

This cliffside municipal garden, located above Monaco-Ville, has eye-popping views from France to Italy. It's a fascinating home to more than a thousand species of cacti (some giant) and other succulent plants, but probably worth the entry only for view-loving botanists (some posted English explanations provided). Your ticket includes entry to a skippable natural cave and an anthropological museum, as well as a not-to-be-missed view snack bar/café. Bus #2 runs here from any stop in Monaco, and makes a worthwhile mini tour of the country, even if you don't visit the gardens. You can get similar views over Monaco for free from behind the souvenir stand at the Jardin's bus stop; or, for even grander vistas, cross the street and hike toward La Turbie.

Cost and Hours: €7.20, €10 combo-ticket with New National Museum of Monaco, daily May-Sept 9:00-19:00, Oct-April 9:00-18:00 or until dusk, tel. 00-377/93 15 29 80, www.jardin-exotique.com.

New National Museum of Monaco (Nouveau Musée National de Monaco)

This two-branch museum, which opened in 2011, hosts a series of rotating exhibits that highlight Monaco's cultural heritage, from works by famous artists to exhibits on the development of Monaco to current challenges facing the principality. The collection is split between two historic villas (ticket includes entrance to both): Villa Paloma (next to the Jardin Exotique at 56 Boulevard du Jardin Exotique) and Villa Sauber (17 Avenue Princesse Grace), east of the casino. To reach Villa Paloma, take bus #2 from any stop in Monaco; for Villa Sauber, take bus #6 from Place du Casino.

Cost and Hours: €6, €10 combo-ticket with Jardin Exotique, free first Sun of the month, daily June-Sept 11:00-19:00, Oct-May 8:00-18:00, Villa Paloma tel. 00-377/98 98 48 60, Villa Sauber tel. 00-377/98 98 91 26, www.nmnm.mc.

In Monte Carlo

▲Casino

Monte Carlo, which means "Charles' Hill" in Spanish, is named for the prince who presided over Monaco's 19th-century makeover.

Begin your visit opposite Europe's most famous casino, in the park above the pedestrian-unfriendly traffic circle. In the mid-1800s, olive groves stood here. Then, with the construction of casino and spas, and easy road and train access, one of Europe's poorest countries was on the Grand Tour map—*the* place for the vacationing aristocracy to play. Today, Monaco has the world's highest per-capita income.

The casino is intended to make you feel comfortable while losing money. Charles Garnier designed the

Le Grand Prix Automobile de Monaco

Each May, the Grand Prix de Monaco (May 22-25 in 2014, May 21-24 in 2015, www.acm.mc) focuses the world's attention on this little country. The race started as an enthusiasts' car rally by the Automobile Club of Monaco (and is still run by the same group, more than 80 years later). The first race, held in 1929, was won by a Bugatti at a screaming average speed of...48 mph (today's cars double that speed). To this day, drivers consider this one of the most important races on their circuits.

By Grand Prix standards, it's an unusual course, running through the streets of this tiny principality, sardined between mountains and sea. The hilly landscape means that the streets are narrow, with tight curves, steep climbs, and extremely short straightaways. Each lap is about two miles, beginning and ending at the port. Cars climb along the sea from the port, pass in front of the casino, race through the commercial district, and do a few dandy turns back to the port. The race lasts 78 laps, and whoever is still rolling at the end wins (most don't finish).

The Formula 1 cars look like overgrown toys that kids might pedal up and down their neighborhood street (if you're here a week or so before the race, feel free to browse the parking structure below Monaco-Ville, where many race cars are kept). Time trials to establish pole position begin three days before the race, which is always on a Sunday. More than 150,000 people attend the gala event; like the nearby film festival in Cannes, it's an excuse for yacht parties, restaurant splurges, and four-digit bar tabs at luxury hotels. During this event, hotel rates in Nice and beyond rocket up (even for budget places).

place (with an opera house inside) in 1878, in part to thank the prince for his financial help in completing Paris' Opéra Garnier (which the architect also designed). The central doors provide access to slot machines, private gaming rooms, and the opera house. The private gaming rooms occupy the left wing of the building.

Count the counts and Rolls-Royces in front of Hôtel de Paris (built at the same time, visitors allowed in the hotel, no shorts, www.montecarloresort.com), then strut inside the casino to the sumptuous atrium. This is the lobby for the 520-seat opera house (open Nov-April only for performances). A model of the opera

MONACO

house is at the far right side of the room, near the marble WCs.

If it's before 20:00, shorts are allowed in the atrium area, though you'll need decent attire to go any farther. After 20:00, shorts are off-limits everywhere.

The scene, flooded with camera-toting tourists during the day, is great at night—and downright James Bond-like in the private rooms. This is your chance to rub elbows with some high rollers—provided you're 18 or older (bring your passport as proof).

If paying an entrance fee to lose money is not your idea of fun, you can access all games for free in the plebeian, American-style casino, adjacent to the old casino. The park behind the casino offers a peaceful café with a good view of the building's rear facade, and of Monaco-Ville.

Cost and Hours: The casino opens daily at 9:30 and stays open until the wee hours (there is no official closing time), but gambling is not allowed until 14:00. The **first gaming rooms** (Salle Renaissance, Salon de l'Europe, and Salle des Amériques) are free to enter after 14:00, with European and English roulette, blackjack, craps, and slot machines. You can pay €10 to visit in the morning to gawk—but not gamble—in the same rooms (daily 9:00-12:30, no dress code). The more glamorous **private game rooms** (Salons Touzet, Salle Medecin, and Terrasse Salle Blanche) cost €10 to enter and have the same games as above, plus Trente et Quarante, Ultimate Texas Hold 'Em poker, and Punto Banco—a version of baccarat.

Information: Tel. 00-377/92 16 20 00, www.montecarlocasinos.com.

Dress Code: During gambling hours, men need to wear a jacket and slacks. Dress standards for women are more relaxed—only tennis shoes and beach attire are definite no-no's.

Take the Money and Run: The stop for buses returning to Nice and Villefranche-sur-Mer, and for local buses #1 and #2, is at the top of the park, above the casino on Avenue de la Costa (under the arcade to the left). To get back to the train station from the casino, take bus #1 or #2 from this stop, or walk about 15 minutes down Avenue d'Ostende (just outside the casino) toward the port, and follow signs to *Gare SNCF* (see map).

Sleeping in Monaco

(€1 = about $1.30, country code: 377)

$$ Hôtel de France**, run by friendly Sylvie, is a centrally located, reasonably priced place—for Monaco (Db-about €135, Tb-about €160, breakfast-€10, air-con, Wi-Fi, near west exit from train station at 6 Rue de la Turbie, tel. 00-377/93 30 24 64, www.monte-carlo.mc/france, hotel-france@monte-carlo.mc).

Eating in Monaco

On the Port

Several cafés serve basic, inexpensive fare (day and night) on the port. I prefer the eateries that line the flowery and traffic-free Rue de la Princesse Caroline, which runs between Rue Grimaldi and the port. The best this street has to offer is **Huit et Demi.** It has a white-tablecloth-meets-director's-chair ambience, mostly outdoor tables, and cuisine worth returning for (€15 salads, €15 pizzas, €18-24 *plats*, closed Sat for lunch and all day Sun, 7 Rue de la Princesse Caroline, tel. 00-377/93 50 97 02). For a simple and cheap salad or sandwich, find the **Crock'in** café farther down at 2 Rue de la Princesse Caroline (closed Sat, tel. 00-377/93 15 02 78).

In Monaco-Ville

You'll find incredible *pan bagnat* (*salade niçoise* sandwich), quiche, and sandwiches at the yellow-bannered **Boulangerie,** a block off Place du Palais (open daily until 21:00, 8 Rue Basse). Try a *barbajuan* (a spring roll-size beignet with wheat, rice, and Parmesan), the *tourta de bléa* (pastry stuffed with pine nuts, raisins, and white beets), or the focaccia sandwich (salted bread with herbs, mozzarella, basil, and tomatoes, all drenched in olive oil). For dessert, order the *fougasse monégasque* (a soft-bread pastry topped with sliced almonds and anise candies).

The best-value restaurant in Monaco-Ville is **U Cavagnetu**— and it's no secret. You'll dine very cheaply on specialties from Monaco just a block from Albert's palace (€13-18 *plats*, €26 *menu*, daily, 14 Rue Comte Félix Gastaldi, tel. 00-377/97 98 20 40). Monaco-Ville has other pizzerias, *crêperies,* and sandwich stands, but the neighborhood is dead at night.

Monaco Connections

By Train and Bus

For a comparison of train and bus connections, see the "Public Transportation in the French Riviera" sidebar on pages 322-325. Any train labeled *Grasse* is heading west and will stop in Villefranche-sur-Mer and Nice.

From Monaco by Train to: Nice (2/hour, 20 minutes), **Villefranche-sur-Mer** (2/hour, 10 minutes), **Antibes** (2/hour, 50 minutes), **Cannes** (2/hour, 70 minutes).

By Bus to: Nice (#100, 4-5/hour Mon-Sat, 3-4/hour Sun, 45 minutes), **Nice Airport** (#110 express on the freeway, 2/hour, 50 minutes, €20), **Villefranche-sur-Mer** (#100, 4-5/hour Mon-Sat, 3-4/hour Sun, 25 minutes), **Eze-le-Village** (#112, 6/day Mon-Sat, none on Sun, 20 minutes), **Cap Ferrat** (#100, 4-5/hour

Mon-Sat, 3-4/hour Sun, 20 minutes plus 20-minute walk), **La Turbie** (#114, 6/day Mon-Sat, 5/day Sun, 30 minutes), **Menton** (#100, 4-5/hour Mon-Sat, 3-4/hour Sun, 40 minutes).

The Monaco-to-Nice bus (#100) is not identified at most stops—verify with a local by asking, *"A Nice?"* A handy stop is below Monaco-Ville at Place d'Armes (on the main road to Nice in front of the Brasserie Monte Carlo). Another is a few blocks above the casino on Avenue de la Costa (under the arcade to the left of Barclays Bank).

Buses #112 (to Eze-le-Village) and #114 (to La Turbie) depart Monaco from Place de la Crémaillère, one block above the main TI and casino park. Walk up Rue Iris with Barclays Bank to your left, curve right, and find the bus shelter across the street at the green Costa à la Crémaillère café. Bus numbers for these routes are not posted, but this is the stop.

Last Call: The last bus leaves Monaco for Villefranche-sur-Mer and Nice at about 20:00; the last train leaves Monaco for Villefranche-sur-Mer and Nice at about 23:30. If you plan to leave Monaco by train after 20:30, buy your tickets in advance (since the window will be closed), or bring enough coins for the machines.

By Cruise Ship

Cruise ships tender passengers to the end of Monaco's yacht harbor, a short walk from downtown. *Très elegant!* A seasonal **TI** is right next to the tender dock (open on busy days May-Sept). To summon a **taxi** (assuming none are waiting when you disembark), look for the gray taxi call box near the tender dock—just press the button and wait for your cab to arrive.

Whether visiting the sights in Monaco, or heading to outlying destinations, your first step for most journeys is to walk from the cruise port to the little market square called **Place d'Armes**. It's an easy and level stroll: Head straight along the yacht harbor until you reach the busy street, which is Boulevard Albert 1er. Use the white overpass (with an elevator) to cross the street, then follow green *Gare S.N.C.F./Ferroviare* signs through a maze of skyscrapers, across the street, and up a charming lane lined with motorcycle shops. Continue straight into the peach-and-yellow building, and ride the free public elevator up to *Marché Place d'Armes* (level 0). You'll pop out into Place d'Armes. At the far end of this square is a roundabout and the busy Rue Grimaldi.

Getting into Town: To reach the cliff-top old town of **Monaco-Ville,** you can either hike steeply up to the top of the hill next to the harbor, or ride a bus up. By **foot,** the fastest, steepest ascent (with an elevator option partway) is near the tip of the Monaco-Ville peninsula, just above where the tenders arrive:

Climb up the stairs next to the Yacht Club de Monaco to the base of the hill, turn left, then curl around the tip of land (with the water on your left-hand side), following signs for *Palais/Musées*. At the parking garage, you can either keep hiking up through the manicured park, or enter the garage and ride up the elevator, then the escalator; either way, you'll emerge near the Cousteau Aquarium, close to the end of my self-guided walk. (It's a five-minute walk through town to Palace Square and the start of the walk.) To ride **bus #1 or #2** up to Monaco-Ville, first walk to the bus stop near Place d'Armes (described earlier). As you exit the elevator into Place d'Armes, turn left and cross the street, then continue up to the second, uphill street (which leads up to the hilltop). Cross this second street and bear right to find the bus stop.

The ritzy skyscraper zone of **Monte Carlo** is basically across the harbor from the tender dock (casino opens for gambling at 14:00). You can walk to the casino area in about 25 minutes—just go all the way around the harbor. To shave some time off the hike, ride the little "bateau bus" shuttle boat across the mouth of the harbor (to find the dock from your tender, walk toward town, then go right along the pier extending into the harbor; €2, €5/day pass, 3/hour). To reach the upper part of Monte Carlo—with the TI, views down over the casino gardens, and handy bus stops (including the one for Eze-le-Village)—catch bus #1 or #2 at the top of the yacht harbor, along Boulevard Albert 1er.

Getting to Sights Beyond Monaco: Monaco is connected to most nearby sights by both train and bus. Monaco's **train station** is about a 20-minute walk from the tender harbor. From Place d'Armes (described earlier), head up to the far end, cross the busy Rue Grimaldi, and take the narrow, angled, red-asphalt lane (Rue de la Turbie) in the middle of the block across the street. Go up the stairs (or ride the elevator) into the little plaza, where you'll see a small TI kiosk (open only in peak season). Turn left, walk up more stairs, and enter the train station (the big, pink building on your right; the easy-to-miss entrance is at the far end—look for *Acces Gare* signs).

The stop for **bus #100**—which conveniently connects Monaco along the Lower Corniche to Villefranche-sur-Mer, Nice, and more—is near Place d'Armes. From Place d'Armes, head up to the far end, along Rue Grimaldi. The bus stop is across the roundabout on the left, on the right-hand side of the street (to get there, cross the street two times in either direction). To ride **bus #112** along the scenic Upper Corniche to Eze-le-Village (6/day Mon-Sat, none on Sun, 20 minutes), first ride bus #1 or #2 to the TI and casino (explained earlier), then follow the directions to the Place de la Crémaillère stop on page 440 and see map on page 427.

MONACO

Near Monaco: Menton

If you wish the Riviera were less glitzy and more like a place where humble locals take their families to lick ice cream and make sand castles, visit Menton (15 minutes by bus beyond Monaco). Menton feels like a poor man's Nice. It's unrefined and unpretentious, with lower prices, fewer rentable umbrellas, and lots of Italians day-tripping in from just over the border (five miles away). There's not an American in sight.

Though a bit rough, the Menton beach is a joy. An inviting promenade lines the beach, and seaside cafés serve light meals and salads (much cheaper than in Nice). A snooze or stroll here is a lovely Riviera experience. From the promenade, a pedestrian street leads through town. Small squares are alive with jazz bands playing crowd-pleasers under palm trees.

Stepping into the old town—which blankets a hill capped by a fascinating cemetery—you're immersed in a pastel-painted, yet dark and tangled Old World scene with (strangely) almost no commerce. A few elegant restaurants dig in at the base of the towering centuries-old apartment flats. The richly decorated Baroque St. Michael's Church (midway up the hill, Mon-Fri 10:00-12:00 & 15:00-17:15, closed to visitors Sat-Sun) is a reminder that, until 1860, Menton was a thriving part of the larger state of Monaco. Climbing past sun-grabbing flower boxes and people who don't get out much anymore, the steep stepped lanes finally deposit you at the ornate gate of a grand cemetery that fills the old castle walls. Explore the cemetery, which is the final resting place of many aristocratic Russians (buried here in the early 1900s) and offers breathtaking Mediterranean views.

Getting to Menton: While trains serve Menton regularly, the station is a 15-minute walk from the action. Buses are more convenient, as they drop visitors right on the beach promenade (#100, 4-5/hour Mon-Sat, 3-4/hour Sun, 1.25 hours from Nice, 40 minutes past Monaco, €1). To return to Monaco or Nice, catch bus #100 on Avenue Thiers, just off Avenue de Verdun.

ANTIBES, CANNES, and ST-TROPEZ

The Riviera opens up west of Nice with bigger, sandier beaches and an overabundance of tasteless beachfront development. Ancient Antibes and superficial Cannes buck the slap-it-up high-rise trend, each with thriving centers busy with pedestrians and yachts. Glamorous St-Tropez, a scenic 1.5-hour drive from Antibes, marks the western edge of the French Riviera.

Antibes

Antibes has a down-to-earth, easygoing ambience that's rare in this area. Its old town is a maze of narrow streets and red-tile roofs rising above the blue Med, protected by twin medieval towers and wrapped in extensive ramparts. Visitors making the short trip from Nice can browse Europe's biggest yacht harbor, snooze on a sandy beach, loiter through an enjoyable old town, and hike along a sea-swept trail. The town's cultural claim to fame, the Picasso Museum, shows off its great collection in a fine old building.

Though much smaller than Nice, Antibes has a history that dates back just as far. Both towns were founded by Greek traders in the fifth century B.C. To the Greeks, Antibes was "Antipolis"— the town *(polis)* opposite *(anti)* Nice. For the next several centuries, Antibes remained in the shadow of its neighbor. By the turn of the 20th century, the town was a military base—so the rich and famous partied elsewhere. But when the army checked out after World War I, Antibes was "discovered" and enjoyed a particularly roaring '20s—with the help of party animals like Rudolph Valentino and the rowdy (yet silent) Charlie Chaplin. Fun-seekers even invented water-skiing right here in the 1920s.

Orientation to Antibes

Antibes' old town lies between the port and Boulevard Albert 1er and Avenue Robert Soleau. Place Nationale is the old town's hub of activity. The restaurant-lined Rue Aubernon connects the port and the old town. Stroll along the sea between the old port and Place Albert 1er (where Boulevard Albert 1er meets the water). The best beaches lie just beyond Place Albert 1er, and the walk is beautiful. Good play areas for children are along this path and on Place des Martyrs de la Résistance (close to recommended Hôtel Relais du Postillon).

Tourist Information

Antibes has two TIs: one in a kiosk across the street from the **train station** (May-Sept only, Mon-Sat 9:00-12:00 & 14:00-18:00, closed Sun), and the main TI on **Place Général de Gaulle** where the fountains squirt (July-Aug daily 9:00-19:00; Sept-June Mon-Fri 9:00-12:30 & 13:30-18:00, Sat 9:00-12:00 & 14:00-18:00, Sun 10:00-12:30 & 14:30-17:00; tel. 04 97 23 11 11, www .antibesjuanlespins.com). At either TI, pick up the excellent city map and the self-guided walking tour of old Antibes. The Nice TI has Antibes maps and the Antibes TI has Nice maps—plan ahead.

Arrival in Antibes

By Train: Bus #14 runs every 30 minutes from the train station (bus stop 50 yards to right as you exit station) to the *gare routière* (bus station; near the main TI and old town), and continues to the fine Plage de la Salis with quick access to the Phare de la Garoupe trail. **Taxis** are usually waiting in front of the train station.

To **walk** to the port, the old town, and the Picasso Museum (15-20 minutes), cross the street in front of the station, skirting left of Piranha's Café, and follow Avenue de la Libération downhill as it bends left. At the end of the street, head right along the port, and continue until you reach the end of the parking lots, then turn right into the old town.

To walk directly to my hotels and to the main TI (15-minute walk to TI), cross the street to Piranha's Café, turn right, and stay the course for about eight blocks on Avenue Robert Soleau until you reach the fountain-soaked Place Général de Gaulle.

The last train back to Nice leaves at about midnight.

By Bus: The airport bus (#250) drops you behind the train station (see "Helpful Hints," later). Buses from other destinations

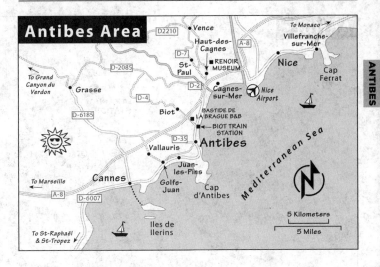

use the **bus station** at the edge of the old town on Place Guynemer, a block below the main TI on Place Général de Gaulle (info desk open Mon-Fri 7:30-19:00, Sat 8:30-12:00 & 14:30-17:30, closed Sun, www.envibus.fr).

By Car: Day-trippers follow signs to *Centre-Ville*, then *Port Vauban*, and park near the old town walls (first 30 minutes free, about €9/half-day). Walk into the old town through the last arch on the right. Street parking is free Monday through Saturday from 12:00-14:00 and 19:00-8:00, and all day Sunday. If you're sleeping here, follow *Centre-Ville* signs, then signs to your hotel, and get advice from your hotelier on where to park. (Most hotels have free parking.) The most appealing hotels in Antibes are easiest by car. Antibes works well for drivers—compared with Nice, parking is easy, it's a breeze to navigate, and it's a convenient springboard for the Inland Riviera. Pay parking is usually available at Antibes' train station, so drivers can ditch their cars here and day-trip from Antibes by train.

Helpful Hints

Monday, Monday: Avoid Antibes on Mondays, when all sights are closed.

Internet Access: Centrally located **l'Outil du Web** is two blocks from the Place Général de Gaulle TI—walk toward the train station (Mon-Fri 9:30-18:30, closed Sat-Sun, 11 Avenue Robert Soleau, tel. 04 93 74 11 86).

English Bookstore: **Heidi's English Bookshop** has a welcoming vibe and a great selection of new and used books, with many guidebooks—including mine (Tue-Sat 9:00-19:00, Sun-Mon 11:00-18:00, 24 Rue Aubernon, tel. 04 93 34 74 11).

ANTIBES

Antibes

1. Hôtel Pension le Mas Djoliba
2. To Hôtels la Jabotte & Beau-Site
3. To Bastide de la Brague
4. Modern Hôtel
5. Hôtel Relais du Postillon
6. La Marmite Restaurant
7. La Taverne du Safranier
8. L'Aubergine Restaurant
9. Le Broc en Bouche Rest.
10. Le Vauban Restaurant
11. Le Brulot & Le Brulot Pasta
12. Les Vieux Murs Restaurant
13. L'Épicerie du Marché Grocery
14. L'Épicerie de la Place Grocery
15. Monoprix
16. Internet Café
17. Heidi's English Bookshop
18. Launderette
19. Avis Car Rental
20. Hertz Car Rental
21. To Europcar Car Rental
22. Boat Rental

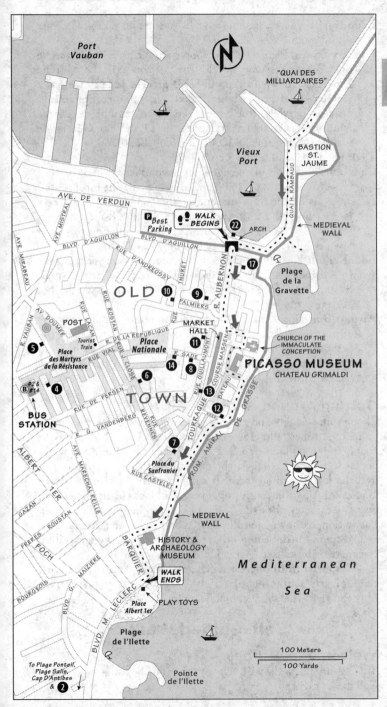

Port Vauban

"QUAI DES MILLIARDAIRES"

Vieux Port

BASTION ST. JAUME

QUAI H. RAMBAUD

MEDIEVAL WALL

AVE. DE VERDUN

AVE. MISTRAL

AVE. MIRABEAU

BLVD. D'AGUILLON

BLVD. D'AGUILLON

P Best Parking

WALK BEGINS

22 ARCH

Plage de la Gravette

RUE D'ANDREOSSY

THURET

R. AUBERNON

17

OLD

RUE LACAN

RUE ROSTAN

PALMIERS

10

9

RUE SADE

AV. DOUMER

POST

Tourist Trais

Place des Martyrs de la Résistance

MARKET HALL

11

CHURCH OF THE IMMACULATE CONCEPTION

RUE DE LA REPUBLIQUE

Place Nationale

RUE VIAL

RUE CLOSE

14

8

PICASSO MUSEUM

CHATEAU GRIMALDI

AV. VAUBAN

5

6

13

COURSE MASSENA

RUE GUILLAUMONT

BATEAU

R. AUBERNON

#2 & #14

B

4

TOWN

12

ROM. AMIRAL

DE GRASSE

BUS STATION

RUE DE FERSEN

AVE. MARECHAL REILLE

R. G. VANDENBERG

RUE REVENNES

TOURRAQUE

ALBERT 1ER

7

Place du Sanfranier

RUE CASTELET

GAZAN

FRERES ROUSTAN

FOCH

MEDIEVAL WALL

BARQUIER

Mediterranean Sea

BOURGEOIS

BLVD. G. MAIZIERE

HISTORY & ARCHAEOLOGY MUSEUM

WALK ENDS

BLVD. M. LECLERC

Place Albert 1er

PLAY TOYS

Plage de l'Ilette

To Plage Ponteil, Plage Salis, Cap D'Antibes & 2

Pointe de l'Ilette

100 Meters

100 Yards

Laundry: There's a launderette at 19 Avenue du Grand Cavalier (daily, mobile 06 47 88 12 97).

Grocery Stores: Picnickers will appreciate **L'Épicerie du Marché** on Cours Masséna, up the hill as you exit the Marché Provençal (daily until 23:00). **L'Épicerie de la Place** has a smaller selection (daily until 22:00 in summer, until 21:00 off-season, where Rue Sade meets Place Nationale). A large **Monoprix** is located next door to the TI on Place Général de Gaulle (Mon-Sat 8:30-20:30, Sun 9:00-12:30).

Taxi: For a taxi, call tel. 04 93 67 67 67.

Car Rental: The big-name agencies have offices in Antibes (all close Mon-Sat 12:00-14:00 and all day Sun). The most central are **Avis** (at the train station, tel. 04 93 34 65 15) and **Hertz** (across from the train station at 46 Avenue Robert Soleau, tel. 04 92 91 28 00). **Europcar** is about 1.5 miles northwest of town at 106 Route de Grasse (tel. 04 93 34 79 79).

Boat Rental: You can motor your own seven-person yacht thanks to **Antibes Bateaux Services** (€300/half-day, at the small fish market on the port, mobile 06 15 75 44 36, www.antibes -bateaux.com).

Airport Bus: Bus #250 runs from near the train station to Nice's airport (€9, 2/hour, 40 minutes; cross over the tracks on the pedestrian bridge—it's the last shelter to the right, stop from the airport is labeled *Vautrin,* stop going to the airport is labeled *Passerelle*).

Getting Around Antibes

Though most sights and activities are walkable, buses are a great value in Antibes, allowing one hour of travel for €1 (one-way or round-trip, unlimited transfers, www.envibus.fr). **Bus #2** provides access to the best beaches, the path to La Phare de la Garoupe, and the Cap d'Antibes trail. It runs from the bus station down Boulevard Albert 1er, with stops every few blocks (daily 7:00-19:00, every 40 minutes). **Bus #14** is also useful, linking the train station, bus station, old town, and Plage de la Salis. Pick up a schedule for return times for these and other regional buses at the bus station (for more on buses, see "Arrival in Antibes," earlier).

A **tourist train** offers circuits around old Antibes, the port, the ramparts, and to Juan-les-Pins (€8, departs from pedestrian-only Rue de la République, mobile 06 15 77 67 47).

Self-Guided Walk

Welcome to Antibes

This 40-minute walk will help you get your bearings, and works well day or night.

• *Begin at the old port (Vieux Port) at the southern end of Avenue de Verdun. Stand at the port, across from the archway with the clock.*

Old Port: Locals claim that this is Europe's first and biggest

pleasure-boat harbor, with 1,600 stalls. The port was enlarged in the 1970s to accommodate ever-expanding yacht dimensions. The work was financed by wealthy yacht owners (mostly Saudi Arabian) eager for a place to park their aircraft carriers. That old four-pointed structure crowning the opposite end of the port is **Fort Carré** (described later), which protected Antibes from foreigners for more than 500 years.

The pathetic remains of a once-hearty **fishing fleet** are moored in front of you. The Mediterranean is pretty much fished out. Most of the seafood you'll eat here comes from fish farms or the Atlantic.

• *With the port on your left, pass the sorry fleet and duck under the*

arches to the shell-shaped **Plage de la Gravette,** *a normally quiet public beach tucked right in the middle of old Antibes.*

Wander up the ramp to the round lookout to better appreciate the scale of the ramparts that protected this town. Because Antibes was the last fort before the Italian

border, the French king made sure the ramparts were top-notch. Those twin towers crowning the old town are the church's bell tower and the tower topping Château Grimaldi (today's Picasso Museum). As you face the old town, forested Cap d'Antibes is the point of land in the distance to the left, with a terrific sea-soaked walking trail (see "Cap d'Antibes Hike" on page 456). Looking east toward Nice, I'm not sure what the white mesh-man sculpture is all about, but I know it was created by the same artist who did the pedestal-top statues on Place Masséna in Nice (see page 377).

• *Admirers of mega-sized toys will want to wander farther out along the port (others can skip ahead to the old town).*

Continuing along the port leads you past historic maps and images of Antibes' port to a controlled entry point that pedestrians are welcome to enter (along the ochre path). Welcome to the **"Quai des Milliardaires"** (billionaires' dock), where yacht-length envy inspires unfathomable conspicuous consumption. The Union Jacks fluttering above most boats are the flag of the Cayman Islands—

can you say tax dodge? The people you see working on the boats are busy keeping them meticulously clean...for the 5-10 days a year these boats actually sail somewhere. That big tower, the Bastion Saint Jaume, houses special exhibits and events.

• *Now let's backtrack to where we started and enter Antibes' old town through the arch under the clock.*

Old Town: Today, the town is the haunt of a large community of English, Irish, and Aussie boaters who help crew those giant yachts in Antibes' port. (That explains the Irish pubs and English bookstores.) Continue straight and uphill (halfway up on the right, you'll pass Rue Clemenceau, which leads to the heart of the old town), and you'll arrive at Antibes' **market hall** (described later, under "Sights in Antibes"). This hall does double duty—market by day, restaurants by night (a fun place for dinner).

Go left where the market starts (Rue Chessel) and find Antibes' pretty pastel **Church of the Immaculate Conception,** built on the site of a Greek temple (worth a peek inside). A church has stood on this site since the 12th century. This one served as the area's cathedral until the mid-1200s. The stone bell tower stands apart from the church and predates it by 600 years, when it was part of the city's defenses. Those heavy stones were pillaged from Antibes' Roman monuments.

Looming above the church on prime real estate is the white-stone **Château Grimaldi,** where you'll find Antibes' prized **Picasso Museum** (for a self-guided tour, see page 451). This site has been home to the acropolis of the Greek city of Antipolis, a Roman fort, and a medieval bishop's palace (once connected to the cathedral below). Later still, the château was the residence of the Grimaldi family (which still rules Monaco; think Prince Rainier and now Prince Albert). Its proximity to the cathedral symbolized the sometimes too-cozy relationship between society's two dominant landowning classes: the Church and the nobility. (In 1789, the French Revolution changed all that.)

• *After visiting the Picasso Museum, exit it to the left. Work your way through a warren of pretty lanes, then head out to the water, turn right along the ramparts, and find a sweeping sea view. As you walk, notice the ground-floor level of the homes to your right (watch out for cars).*

The homes in this area make up a special Antibes community called **La Commune Libre du Safranier.** A group of public-spirited residents banded together in the 1960s to preserve this most traditional of Antibes neighborhoods, where small homes line narrow lanes and sidewalk plantings are meticulously maintained. To best explore this picturesque community, turn right just before the four large palm trees in the small parking lot, and find a tiny path tucked between thorny bushes. Head down the stairs to poke around.

• *To continue our walk, return to the path along the sea and find the* **History and Archaeology Museum** *(described later, under "Sights in Antibes").*

Before going in, stop on the terrace above the museum, where you'll get a clear view of **Cap d'Antibes,** crowned by its lighthouse and studded with mansions (see "Cap d'Antibes Hike," later). The Cap was long the refuge of Antibes' rich and famous, and a favorite haunt of F. Scott Fitzgerald and Ernest Hemingway.

After taking a quick spin through the museum, continue hugging the shore past Place Albert 1er until you see the views back to old Antibes. Benches and soft sand await (a few copies of famous artists' paintings of Antibes are placed on bronze displays along the beach walkway). You're on your own from here—energetic walkers can continue to the view from the Phare de la Garoupe (see page 456); others can return to old Antibes and wander around in its peaceful back lanes.

Sights in Antibes

▲▲Picasso Museum (Musée Picasso)

Sitting serenely where the old town meets the sea, this compact

three-floor museum offers a manageable collection of Picasso's paintings, sketches, and ceramics. Picasso lived in this castle for four months in 1946, when he cranked out an amazing amount of art. He was elated by the end of World War II, and his works show a celebration of color and a rediscovery of light after France's long nightmare of war. Picasso was also re-energized by his young and lovely companion, Françoise Gilot (with whom he would father two children). The resulting collection (donated by Picasso) put Antibes on the tourist map.

Cost and Hours: €6; mid-June–mid-Sept Tue–Sun 10:00-18:00, July–Aug Wed and Fri until 20:00; mid-Sept–mid-June Tue–Sun 10:00-12:00 & 14:00-18:00, closed Mon year-round, last entry 30 minutes before closing, tel. 04 92 90 54 20, www.antibes-juanlespins.com.

Visiting the Museum: After buying your ticket, go through the glass door. Before heading inside, pause in the sculpture

Pablo Picasso
(1881-1973)

Pablo Picasso was the most famous and—OK, I'll say it—the greatest artist of the 20th century. Always exploring, he became the master of many styles (Cubism, Surrealism, Expressionism, and so on) and of many media (painting, sculpture, prints, ceramics, and assemblages). He could make anything he touched look unmistakably like "a Picasso."

Born in Málaga, Spain, Picasso was the son of an art teacher. At a very young age, he quickly advanced beyond his teachers. Picasso's teenage works are stunningly realistic, with wise insight into the people he painted. As a youth in Barcelona, he fell in with a bohemian crowd that mixed wine, women, and art.

In 1900, at age 19, Picasso started making trips to Paris; at this time, he rejected the surname his father had given him (Ruiz) in favor of his mother's. Four years later, he moved to the City of Light and absorbed the styles of many painters (especially Henri de Toulouse-Lautrec) while searching for his own artist's voice. His paintings of beggars and other social outcasts show the empathy of a man who was himself a poor, homesick foreigner. When his best friend, Spanish artist Carlos Casagemas, committed suicide, Picasso plunged into a **Blue Period** (1901-1904)—so called because the dominant color in these paintings matches the melancholy mood and subject matter (emaciated beggars, hard-eyed pimps, and so on).

In 1904, Picasso got a steady girlfriend (Fernande Olivier) and suddenly saw the world through rose-colored glasses—the **Rose Period.** He was further jolted out of his Blue Period by the "flat" look of the Fauves. Not satisfied with their take on 3-D, Picasso played with the "building blocks" of line and color to find new ways to reconstruct the real world on canvas.

At his studio in Montmartre, Picasso and his neighbor Georges Braque worked together, in poverty so dire they often didn't know where their next bottle of wine was coming from. And then, at the age of 25, Picasso reinvented painting. Fascinated by the primitive power of African and Iberian tribal masks, he sketched human faces with simple outlines and almond eyes. Intrigued by the body of his girlfriend Fernande, he sketched it from every angle, then experimented with showing several different views on the same canvas. A hundred paintings and nine months later, Picasso gave birth to a monstrous canvas of five nude, fragmented prostitutes with mask-like faces—*Les Demoiselles d'Avignon* (1907).

This bold new style was called **Cubism.** With Cubism, Picasso shattered the Old World and put it back together in a new way. The subjects are somewhat recognizable (with the help of the titles), but they're built with geometric shards (let's call them "cubes")—like viewing the world through a kaleidoscope of brown and gray. Cubism gives us several different angles of the subject at once—say, a woman seen from the front and side angles simultaneously, resulting in two eyes on the same side of the nose. This involves showing the traditional three dimensions, plus Einstein's new fourth dimension—the time it takes to walk around the subject to see other angles.

In 1918, Picasso married his first wife, Olga Kokhlova, with whom he had a son. He then traveled to Rome and entered a **Classical Period** (the 1920s) of more realistic, full-bodied women and children, inspired by the three-dimensional sturdiness of ancient statues. While he flirted with abstraction, throughout his life, Picasso always kept a grip on "reality." His favorite subject was people. The anatomy might be jumbled, but it's all there.

Though he lived in France and Italy, Picasso remained a Spaniard at heart, incorporating Spanish motifs into his work. Unrepentantly macho, he loved bullfights, seeing them as a metaphor for the timeless human interaction between the genders. The horse—clad with blinders and pummeled by the bull—has nothing to do with the fight. To Picasso, the horse symbolizes the feminine, and the bull, the masculine. Spanish imagery—bulls, screaming horses, a Madonna—appears in Picasso's most famous work, *Guernica* (1937, on display in Madrid). The monumental canvas of a bombed village summed up the pain of Spain's brutal Civil War (1936-1939) and foreshadowed the onslaught of World War II.

At war's end, Picasso left Paris and all of his emotional baggage behind, finding fun in the sun in Antibes and other villages in the **South of France** (1948-1954). Sun! Color! Water! Spacious skies! Freedom! Sixty-five-year-old Pablo Picasso was reborn, enjoying worldwide fame and the love of a beautiful 23-year-old painter named Françoise Gilot. Dressed in rolled-up white pants and a striped sailor's shirt, bursting with pent-up creativity, Picasso often cranked out more than a painting a day. Picasso's Riviera works set the tone for the rest of his life—sunny, lighthearted, childlike, experimenting in new media and using motifs of the sea, of Greek mythology (fauns, centaurs), and animals (birds, goats, and pregnant baboons). His childlike doves became an international symbol of peace.

Picasso also made collages, built "statues" out of wood, wire, ceramics, papier-mâché, or whatever, and even turned everyday household objects into statues (like his famous bull's head made of a bicycle seat with handlebar horns). **"Multimedia"** works like these have become so standard today that we forget how revolutionary they were when Picasso invented them. His last works have the playfulness of someone much younger. As it is often said of Picasso, "When he was a child, he painted like a man. When he was old, he painted like a child."

garden to appreciate Picasso's working environment (and wonder why he only spent four months here).

Bottom Floors: The museum's interior is a calm place of white walls, soft arches, and ample natural light—a great space for exhibiting art. The ground floor houses a permanent collection of 20th-century works by Hans Hartung and his partner, Anna-Eva Bergman, who, like Picasso, both donated their paintings to the museum. Their work blends well with what you'll see by Picasso. The first floor up usually holds a small collection of works by Nicolas de Staël and temporary exhibits of other artists' work.

Picasso Collection: The museum's highlight is on the top floor, where you'll find the permanent collection of Picasso's works. Visitors are greeted by a large image of Picasso and a display of photographs of the artist at work and play during his time in Antibes. Tour the floor clockwise, noticing the focus on sea creatures, tridents, and other marine themes (*oursin* is a sea urchin, *poulpe* is an octopus, and *poisson* is, well, fishy). *Nature Morts* means still life, and you'll see many of these in this collection.

The first gallery room (up the small staircase to your left) houses several famous works, including the lively, frolicking, and big-breasted *La Joie de Vivre* painting (from 1946). This Greek bacchanal sums up the newfound freedom in a just-liberated France and sets the tone for the rest of the collection. You'll also see the colorless, three-paneled *Satyr, Faun and Centaur with Trident* and several ceramic creations (the bull rocks).

As you tour the collection, you'll see both black-and-white and colorful ink sketches that challenge the imagination—these show off Picasso's skill as a cartoonist and caricaturist. Look also for the Basque fishermen and several Cubist-style nudes *(nus couchés)*, one painted on plywood—Picasso loved experimenting with materials and different surfaces (I particularly like the crayon sketches).

Near the end, don't miss the wall devoted to his ceramic plates. Inspired by a visit to a ceramics factory in nearby Vallauris, Picasso was smitten by the texture of soft clay and devoted a great deal of time to exploring this medium—producing over 2,000 pieces in one year. In the same room, the wall-sized painting *Ulysses and the Sirens* screams action and anxiety.

History and Archaeology Museum (Musée d'Histoire et d'Archéologie)

More than 2,000 years ago, Antibes was the center of a thriving maritime culture. It was an important Roman city with aqueducts, theaters, baths, and so on. This museum—the only place to get a sense of the city's ancient roots—displays Greek, Roman, and Etruscan odds and ends in two simple halls (no English descriptions, though the small museum brochure offers some

ANTIBES

background in English). Your visit starts at an 1894 model of Antibes and continues past displays of Roman coins, cups, plates, and scads of amphorae. The lanky lead pipe connected to a center box was used as a bilge pump; nearby is a good display of Roman anchors.

Cost and Hours: €3; mid-June-mid-Sept Tue-Sun 10:00-12:00 & 14:00-18:00, July-Aug Wed and Fri until 20:00; mid-Sept-mid-June Tue-Sun 10:00-13:00 & 14:00-17:00, closed Mon year-round, on the water between Picasso Museum and Place Albert 1er, tel. 04 92 90 54 37.

▲Market Hall (Marché Provençal)

The daily market bustles under a 19th-century canopy, with flowers, produce, Provençal products, and beach accessories. The market wears many hats: produce daily until 13:30, handicrafts Thursday through Sunday in the afternoon, and fun outdoor dining in the evenings (Sept-June until 12:30, closed Mon, behind Picasso Museum on Cours Masséna).

Other Markets and Squares

Antibes' lively antiques/flea market fills Place Nationale and Place Audiberti (next to the port) on Thursdays and Saturdays (7:00-18:00). Its clothing market winds through the streets around the post office (Rue Lacan) on Thursdays (9:00-18:00). Place Général de Gaulle, a pleasing, palm-studded, and fountain-flowing square in Antibes' modern city, is the trendy place to be seen.

Fort Carré

This impressively situated citadel, dating from 1487, was the last fort inside France. It protected Antibes from Nice, which until 1860 was part of Italy. You can tour this unusual four-pointed fort for the fantastic views over Antibes, but there's little to see inside.

Cost and Hours: €3, includes tour in French, Tue-Sun mid-June-mid-Sept 11:00-17:30, mid-Sept-mid-June 10:00-16:00, closed Mon year-round, 30-minute walk from Antibes along Avenue du 11 Novembre, easy parking nearby.

▲Beaches (Plages)

The best beaches stretch between Antibes' port and Cap d'Antibes. The first you'll cross is Plage Publique (no rentals required). Next are the groomed Plage de la Salis and Plage du Ponteil (with mattress,

umbrella, and towel rental). All are busy but manageable in summer and on weekends, with cheap snack stands and exceptional views of the old town. The closest beach to the old town is at the port (Plage de la Gravette), which seems calm in any season.

Walks and Hikes

From Place Albert 1er (where Boulevard Albert 1er meets the beach), you get a good view of Plage de la Salis and Cap d'Antibes. That tower on the hill is your destination for the first walk listed. The longer Cap d'Antibes hike begins on the next beach, just over that hill. The two hikes are easy to combine by bus, bike, or car.

▲▲Chapelle et Phare de la Garoupe

The territorial views—best in the morning, skippable if hazy—from this viewpoint more than merit the 20-minute uphill climb from Plage de la Salis (a few blocks after Maupassant Apartments, where the road curves left, follow signs and the rough, cobbled Chemin du Calvaire up to lighthouse tower). An orientation table explains that you can see from Nice to Cannes and up to the Alps.

Getting There: Take bus #2 or bus #14 to the Plage de la Salis stop and find the trail a block ahead. By car or bike, follow signs for *Cap d'Antibes,* then look for *Chapelle et Phare de la Garoupe* signs.

▲Cap d'Antibes Hike
(Sentier Touristique Piétonnier de Tirepoil)

At the end of the mattress-ridden Plage de la Garoupe (over the hill from Phare de la Garoupe lighthouse) lies a terrific trail around

the tip of Cap d'Antibes. Use a map of Antibes from the TI to track this trail. The beautiful path undulates above a splintered coastline splashed by turquoise water and peppered with exclusive mansions. You'll walk for about two miles, then head inland, hooking up with Avenue Mrs. L.D. Beaumont, ending at the recommended Hôtel Beau-Site (and bus stop). You can walk as far as you'd like and then double back, or do the whole loop (allow 3 hours at most). Bring good shoes, as the walkway is uneven and slippery in places. Sundays are busiest.

Getting There: Take bus #2 (catch it at the bus station, along Boulevard Albert 1er, or at Plage de la Salis) for about 15 minutes to the La Fontaine stop at Hôtel Beau-Site (return stop is 50 yards away on opposite side, get return times at station). Walk 10 minutes down to Plage de la Garoupe and start from there. By car or bike, follow signs to *Cap d'Antibes,* then to *Plage de la Garoupe,* and park there. The trail begins at the far-right end of Plage de la Garoupe.

Near Antibes

Juan-les-Pins

The low-rise town of **Juan-les-Pins,** sprawling across the Cap d'Antibes isthmus from Antibes, is where the action is...after hours. It's a modern waterfront resort with good beaches, plenty of lively bars and restaurants, and a popular jazz festival in July. The town is also famous for its clothing boutiques that stay open until midnight in high season (people are too busy getting tanned to shop at normal hours). As locals say, "Party, sleep in, shop late, party more."

Getting There: Buses, trains, and even a tourist train (see "Getting Around Antibes" on page 448) make the 10-minute trip to and from Antibes constantly.

Marineland and Parc de la Mer

A few backstrokes from Antibes, Parc de la Mer is a world of waterslides, miniature golf, exhibits, and more. Marineland anchors this sea-park extravaganza with French-language shows featuring dolphins, sea lions, and killer whales.

Cost and Hours: Marineland only-€38, kids-€30; Aquasplash waterslide park-€26, kids-€20, closed in winter; various combo-tickets cover Aquasplash waterslides, miniature golf, and other attractions; daily 10:00-19:00, until 23:00 July-Aug, tel. 04 93 33 49 49, www.marineland.fr.

Getting There: The park is a short walk from the train station in nearby Biot (5 minutes from Antibes) and about 15 minutes from Antibes' bus station on buses #200 or #7. By car, the park is signed from RN-7, several miles from Antibes toward Nice.

Renoir Museum (Musée Renoir)

Halfway between Antibes and Nice, above Cagnes-sur-Mer, Pierre Auguste Renoir found his Giverny. Here, the artist spent

the last 12 years of his life (1907-1919) tending his gardens, painting, and even dabbling in sculpture (despite suffering from rheumatoid arthritis). His home was later converted into a small museum, which has been closed for renovation for two years but should be reopened by your visit (expect some changes). Visitors to the museum get a very personal look into Renoir's later years. You'll likely see his studio, wheelchair, and bedroom; take a stroll in his gardens; and enjoy several of his and other artists' paintings of people and places around Cagnes-sur-Mer. It's a pleasant place and a must-see for his fans.

Cost and Hours: Likely €4, Wed-Mon May-Sept 10:00-12:00 & 14:00-18:00, Oct-April until 17:00, closed Tue year-round, Chemin des Collettes, tel. 04 93 20 61 07.

Getting There: Take bus #200 to Cagnes-sur-Mer, and ask the driver for the stop closest to the museum: *"Musée Renoir? Quel arrêt?"* (mew-zay reh-nwah kehl ah-reh?). From there, it's a 20-minute walk uphill to the museum. The train stops downhill from the museum as well (40-minute uphill walk to the museum—take a cab). Drivers go to Cagnes-sur-Mer, then follow brown *Musée Renoir* signs.

More Day Trips from Antibes

Antibes is halfway between Nice and Cannes (easy train and bus service to both), and close to the artsy pottery and glassblowing village of **Biot,** home of the Fernand Léger Museum as well as Parc de la Mer (listed earlier). Biot village is easy to reach on bus #10 from Antibes' train station (daily, every 30-40 minutes). The Biot train station is a 45-minute walk below the village—take bus #10 from here. The best parking is just above the town, allowing direct access to its pretty pedestrian street.

Another pottery center, **Vallauris,** is a striking hill town and popular with lovers of blown glass. Picasso fans will enjoy his murals in the Chapel of War and Peace (bus #8 from Place de la Libération in Antibes, or take bus #200 or the train to Golfe-Juan-Vallauris—3/hour, 6 minutes, get details at local TIs).

Sleeping in Antibes

My favorite Antibes hotels are best by car or taxi, though walkers and bus users can manage as well. Pickings are slim when it comes to centrally located hotels in this city, where restaurants are a dime a dozen but hotels play hard to get. Air-conditioning is rare.

Outside the Town Center

$$$ Hôtel Pension le Mas Djoliba*** is a fair splurge that's better for drivers but also workable for walkers (10 minutes to Plage de la Salis, 15 minutes to old Antibes, 30 minutes to the train station). Reserve early for this traditional, bird-chirping, flower-filled manor house where no two rooms are the same. From May to September, they definitely prefer (but won't insist) that you dine here. It's hard to pass up once you see the setting: After a busy day of sightseeing, dinner by the pool is a treat. The cuisine is average but copious. Some rooms are small, the bigger rooms are well worth the additional cost, and several rooms come with small decks (Sb-€107, Db-€125-182 depending on size, several good family rooms-

---

Sleep Code

(€1 = about $1.30, country code: 33)
S = Single, **D** = Double/Twin, **T** = Triple, **Q** = Quad, **b** = bathroom,
s = shower only, * = French hotel rating (0-5 stars). Unless
otherwise noted, credit cards are accepted and English is
spoken.

To help you sort easily through these listings, I've divided
the accommodations into three categories based on the price
for a standard double room with bath:

$$$ **Higher Priced**—Most rooms €120 or more.
$$ **Moderately Priced**—Most rooms between €90-120.
$ **Lower Priced**—Most rooms €90 or less.

Prices can change without notice; verify the hotel's current rates online or by email. For the best prices, always book
direct.

€200-275, figure €95-120 per person with breakfast and dinner;
air-con, Wi-Fi, cool *boules* court and loaner balls; 29 Avenue de
Provence—from Boulevard Albert 1er, look for gray signs as you
approach the beach, turn right onto Boulevard Général Maizière,
then veer right again up Avenue Gaston Bourgeois; tel. 04 93 34
02 48, www.hotel-djoliba.com, contact@hotel-djoliba.com).

$$ Hôtel la Jabotte**, hidden along an ignored alley a block
from the famous beaches and a 15-minute walk from the old town,
is a cozy place that defies the rules. Nathalie and Pierre run this
small beach villa turned boutique hotel with personality: The
colors are rich, the decor shows a personal touch, and most rooms
have individual terraces facing a small, central garden where you'll
get to know your neighbor. Rooms are not air-conditioned, but
fans are provided (Db-€112-141, Db suite-€198, includes good
breakfast and a few parking spots, Wi-Fi, 13 Avenue Max Maurey,
take the third right after passing the big Hôtel Josse, tel. 04 93 61
45 89, www.jabotte.com, info@jabotte.com).

$$ Hôtel Beau-Site***, my only listing on Cap d'Antibes,
is a 10-minute drive from the old town. It's a terrific value if you
want to get away...but not *too* far away. (Without a car, you may
feel isolated.) This place is a sanctuary, with helpful Nathalie in
charge as well as a pool, a comfy patio garden, and free parking.
Rooms are spacious and comfortable, and several have balconies
(standard Db-€90-95, bigger Db-€105-130, even bigger Db-€140-
176, junior suites-€195-240; extra bed-€25, huge breakfast-€13,
continental breakfast-€8, air-con, Wi-Fi, secure parking, may have
a few bikes available, 141 Boulevard Kennedy, tel. 04 93 61 53 43,

www.hotelbeausite.net, hbeausit@club-internet.fr). From the hotel, it's a 10-minute walk down to Plage de la Garoupe and a nearby hiking trail (described earlier, under "Walks and Hikes").

$ Bastide de la Brague is an easygoing, seven-room bed-and-breakfast hacienda up a dirt road above Marineland (10-minute drive east of Antibes). It's run by a fun-loving family (wife Isabelle, who speaks English, hubby Franck, and Mama). Rooms are quite comfortable, air-conditioned, and affordable; several are made for families. Request the tasty €29 home-cooked dinner (less for kids; adult meal includes apéritif, wine, and coffee) and enjoy a family dining experience (Db-€85-105, Tb/Qb-€112-130, includes breakfast, free Wi-Fi and computer with printer for guests, 55 Avenue No. 6, tel. 04 93 65 73 78, www.bbchambreantibes.com, bastidebb06@gmail.com). Franck is happy to take guests on a private morning boat tour of the coast (allow €40/person, 4-person minimum). From Antibes, follow signs that read *Nice par Bord de la Mer,* turn left toward Brague and Marineland, then right at the roundabout (toward Groules), then take the first left and follow the signs. Antibes bus #10 drops you five minutes away, and the Biot train station and buses #200 or #250 are a 15-minute walk away (ask for details when you book). If arranged in advance, they can pick you up at the train station in Antibes or Biot.

In the Town Center

$ Modern Hôtel, in the pedestrian zone behind the bus station, is a solid value for budget-conscious travelers. The 17 standard-size rooms—each with air-conditioning, bright decor, and Wi-Fi—are simple, spick-and-span, and well-run by Laurence (Db-€75-85, breakfast-€7, 1 Rue Fourmillière, tel. 04 92 90 59 05, www.modernhotel06.com, modern-hotel@wanadoo.fr).

$ Hôtel Relais du Postillon is a mellow place on a central square above a peaceful café. There are a few cheap true singles and 13 well-designed doubles with small balconies. All have air-conditioning (Sb-€49-59, Db-€80-125, price varies with room size, most have tight bathrooms, Wi-Fi, 8 Rue Championnet, tel. 04 93 34 20 77, www.relaisdupostillon.com, relais@relaisdupostillon.com).

Eating in Antibes

Antibes is a fun place to dine out. You can eat on a budget, enjoy a good meal at an acceptable price, or join the party just inside the walls on Boulevard d'Aguillon, on Place Nationale, or—my favorite—under the festive Marché Provençal (all are filled with

tables and tourists). The options are endless. Take a walk and judge for yourself, and be tempted by these suggestions. Romantics should picnic at the beach (**L'Épicerie du Marché** is open late; see "Helpful Hints" on page 448). Everyone should stroll along the ramparts after dinner.

La Marmite owner Patrick offers diners an honest, unpretentious budget value in old Antibes, with eight tables, charming decor, helpful service, and delicious seafood choices but no air-conditioning (*menus* from €17, closed Mon, 20 Rue James Close, tel. 04 93 34 56 79).

La Taverne du Safranier, hiding in a small square a block from the sea, feels right out of a movie. It's a cheery place away from the rest, where you'll order from colorful chalkboard menus and dine under grapevines and happy lights (seafood is their forte, €11 pasta, €14-24 *plats*, €28 three-course *menu*, closed Mon, Place du Safranier, tel. 04 93 34 80 50, www.taverne-du-safranier.fr).

L'Aubergine delivers fine cuisine at fair prices—including good vegetarian options—served with no hurry in an intimate room rich with color. Arrive early to get a table (*menus* from €30, opens at 18:30, closed Wed, opens early for lunch on Sun only, 7 Rue Sade, tel. 04 93 34 55 93).

Le Broc en Bouche is part cozy wine bar, part bistro, and part collector's shop. Florence serves while her husband cooks. Come early to get a seat at this cool little place, where you'll enjoy well-prepared dishes from a selective list (€20-30 *plats*, closed Tue-Wed, 8 Rue des Palmiers, tel. 04 93 34 75 60).

Le Vauban is run by a young couple who draw a local following with their handsome interior, smart tableware, and reliable cuisine at fair prices (€29 three-course *menu*, closed for lunch Mon and Wed, closed all day Tue, opposite 4 Rue Thuret, tel. 04 93 34 33 05, www.levauban.fr).

Le Brulot is an Antibes institution with two restaurants—Le Brulot and Le Brulot Pasta—that sit almost side-by-side a short block below Marché Provençal on Rue Frédéric Isnard. Join Antibes residents at the very popular **Le Brulot,** known for its Provençal cuisine and meats cooked on an open fire. It's a small place, overflowing onto the street, with a few outside tables and a dining room below. Try the aioli (*menus* from €19, closed Sun, at #2, tel. 04 93 34 17 76). **Le Brulot Pasta** is family-friendly, with excellent pizza (the €11 *printanière* is tasty and huge) and big portions of pasta, served in air-conditioned comfort under stone arches (daily, at #3, tel. 04 93 34 19 19).

Les Vieux Murs is a romantic splurge with a candlelit, red-toned interior overlooking the sea. The outside tables are worth booking ahead—but pass on the upstairs room (€44 dinner *menu*, €30 lunch *menu*, closed Mon, also closed Sun evening off-season, valet parking available, along ramparts beyond Picasso Museum at 25 Promenade de l'Amiral de Grasse, tel. 04 93 34 06 73, www.lesvieuxmurs.com).

Antibes Connections

For a comparison of train and bus connections, see the "Public Transportation in the French Riviera" sidebar on pages 322-325.

From Antibes by Train: TGV and local trains serve Antibes' little station. Trains go to **Cannes** (2/hour, 15 minutes), **Nice** (2/hour, 15-30 minutes, €4), **Grasse** (1/hour, 40 minutes), **Villefranche-sur-Mer** (2/hour, 40 minutes), **Monaco** (2/hour, 50 minutes), and **Marseille** (16/day, 2.5 hours).

By Bus: Handy bus #200 ties everything together, but runs at a snail's pace when traffic is bad (Mon-Sat 4/hour, Sun 2-3/hour, any ride costs €1). This bus goes west to **Cannes** (35 minutes); and east to near **Biot** village (15 minutes—bus #10 is better, described on page 458), **Cagnes-sur-Mer** (and its Renoir Museum, 25 minutes), and **Nice** (1-1.5 hours). Bus #250 links to **Nice Airport** (2/hour, 40 minutes, €8).

Cannes

Cannes (pronounced "can"), famous for its film festival (May 14-24 in 2014), is the sister city of Beverly Hills. That says it all.

When I asked at the TI for a list of museums and sights, they just smiled. Cannes—with big, exclusive hotels lining mostly private stretches of perfect, sandy beach—is for strolling, shopping, dreaming of meeting a movie star, and lounging on the seafront. Cannes has little that's unique to offer the traveler...except a mostly off-limits film festival and quick access to two undeveloped islands. You can buy an ice-cream cone at the train station and see everything before you've had your last lick. Money is what Cannes has always been about—wealthy people come here to make the scene, so there's always enough *scandale* to go around. The king of Saudi Arabia purchased a serious slice of waterfront just east of town and built his compound with no regard to local zoning regulations. Money talks on the Riviera...and always has.

Orientation to Cannes

Don't sleep or drive in Cannes. Instead, day-trip here by train or bus. It's a breeze, as trains and buses run frequently along the Riviera, and they all stop in Cannes (train is faster, bus is cheaper). Buses arrive next to the train station. If you must drive, store your car at the parking garage next to the train station. For more specifics on buses, trains, and arrival by cruise ship, see "Cannes Connections," later.

Cannes' glamorously quiet **TI** is located in the Film Festival Hall at 1 Boulevard de la Croisette (daily July-Aug 9:00-20:00, Sept-June 10:00-19:00).

Self-Guided Walk

Do the Cannes Cancan

This self-guided walking tour will take you to Cannes' sights in a level, one-hour walk at a movie-star pace. Well-kept WCs are available in the lobbies of any large hotel you pass.

• *From the train station, cross the street and walk for five unimpressive minutes down Rue des Serbes to the beachfront. Cross the busy Boulevard de la Croisette and make your way past snack stands to the sea. Find the round lookout and get familiar with...*

The Lay of the Land: Cannes feels different from its neighbors to the east. You won't find the distinctive pastel oranges and pinks of Old Nice and Villefranche-sur-Mer. Cannes was never part of Italy—and through its architecture and cuisine, it shows.

Face the water. The land jutting into the sea on your left is actually two islands, St. Honorat and Ste. Marguerite. **St. Honorat** has been the property of monks for over 500 years; today its abbey,

vineyards, trails, and gardens can be visited by peace-seeking travelers. **Ste. Marguerite,** which you also can visit, is famous for the stone prison that housed the 17th-century Man in the Iron Mask (whose true identity remains unknown).

Now look to your right. Those striking mountains sweeping down to the sea are the Massif de l'Esterel. Their red-rock outcrops

CANNES

Handy Cannes and St-Tropez Phrases

Where is a movie star?	*Où est une vedette?*
I am a movie star.	*Je suis une vedette.*
I am rich and single.	*Je suis riche et célibataire.*
Are you rich and single?	*Etes-vous riche et célibataire?*
Are those real?	*Ils sont des vrais?*
How long is your yacht?	*Quelle est la longeur de votre yacht?*
How much did that cost?	*Combien coûtait-il?*
You can always dream...	*On peut toujours rêver...*

oversee spectacular car and train routes (see page 320). Closer in, the hill with the medieval tower caps Cannes' old town (Le Suquet). This hilltop offers grand views and pretty lanes, but little else. Below the old town, the port welcomes yachts of all sizes... provided they're big.

Face inland. On the left, find the modern, cream-colored building that's home to the famous film festival (we'll visit there soon). Back the other way, gaze up the boulevard. That classy building with twin black-domed roofs is Hôtel Carlton, our eventual target and as far as we'll go together in that direction.

• *Continue with the sea on your right and stroll the...*

Promenade (La Croisette): You're walking along Boulevard de la Croisette—Cannes' famed two-mile-long promenade. First popular with kings who wintered here after Napoleon fell, the elite parade was later joined by British aristocracy. Today, Boulevard de la Croisette is fronted by some of the most expensive apartments and hotels in Europe. If it's  lunchtime, you might try one of the beach cafés—Brad Pitt did. **Plage le Goéland's** café has fair-enough prices and appealing decor (daily, closest private beach to the Film Festival Hall, tel. 04 93 38 22 05).

• *Stop when you get to...*

Hôtel Carlton: This is the most famous address on Boulevard de la Croisette (allow €1,300-6,000 per night). Face the beach. The iconic Cannes experience is to slip out of your luxury hotel

(preferably this one), into a robe (ideally, monogrammed with your initials), and onto the beach—or, better yet, onto the pier (this avoids getting irritating sand on your carefully oiled skin). While you may not be doing the "fancy hotel and monogrammed robe" ritual on this Cannes excursion, you can—for about €25—rent a chair and umbrella and pretend you're tanning for a red-carpet premiere. Cannes does have a few token public beaches, but most beaches are private and run by hotels like the Carlton. You could save money by sunning among the common folk, but the real Cannes way to flee the rabble and paparazzi is to rent a spot on a private beach (best to reserve ahead in July-Aug).

Cross over and wander into the hotel—you're welcome to browse (except during the festival). Ask for a hotel brochure, verify room rates, check for availability. Can all these people really afford this? Imagine the scene here during the film festival (see anyone famous?). A surprisingly affordable café (considering the cost of a room) lies just beyond.

• *You can continue your stroll down La Croisette, but I'm doubling back to the cream-colored building that is Cannes'...*

Film Festival Hall: Cannes' film festival (Festival de Cannes), staged since 1946, completes the "Big Three" of Riviera events (with Monaco's Grand Prix and Nice's Carnival). The hall where the festival takes place—a busy-but-nondescript convention center that also hosts the town TI—sits like a plump movie star on the beach. You'll recognize the formal grand entryway—but

the red carpet won't be draped for your visit. Find the famous (Hollywood-style) handprints in the sidewalk all around. To get inside during the festival, you have to be a star (or a photographer—some 3,000 paparazzi attend the gala event, and most bring their own ladders to get above the crowds).

The festival originated in part as an anti-fascist response to Mussolini's Venice Film Festival. Cannes' first festival was due to open in 1939, on the very day Hitler invaded Poland. Thanks to what followed (World War II), the opening was delayed until 1946 (in 2002 they screened the films that would have been shown in 1939). Cannes' film festival is also famous as the first festival to give one vote per country on the jury (giving films from smaller countries a fighting chance).

Though off-limits to us, the festival is all that matters around here—and is worth a day trip to Cannes if you happen to be in the region when it's on. The town buzzes with mega-star energy, press passes, and revealing dresses. Locals claim that it's the world's third-biggest media event, after the Olympics and the World Cup (soccer). The festival prize is the Palme d'Or (like the Oscar for Best Picture). The French press can't cover the event enough, and the average Jean in France follows it as Joe would the World Series in the States. In 2008, the French surprised everyone by winning the prize for the first time in 21 years, for the unhyped, realistic drama *Entre les Murs (The Class*, about a teacher's struggles in a Paris middle school).

• Around the other side of the festival hall is the port (Gare Maritime).

The Port and Old Town (Le Suquet): The big-boy yachts line up closest to the Film Festival Hall. After seeing this yacht frenzy, everything else looks like a dinghy. Boat service to St-Tropez and the nearby islands of St. Honorat and Ste. Marguerite depart from the far side of the port (at Quai Laubeuf; for boat info, see "Sights in Cannes," next).

Cannes' oldest neighborhood, Le Suquet, crowns the hill past the port. Locals refer to it as their Montmartre. It's artsy and charming, but it's a steep 15-minute walk above the port, with little of interest except the panoramic views from its ancient church, Notre-Dame-de-l'Espérance (Our Lady of Hope).

• To find the views in Le Suquet, walk past the bus station at the northwest corner of the port and make your way up cobbled Rue Saint-Antoine (next to the Café St. Antoine). Turn left on Place du Suquet, and then follow signs to Traverse de la Tour *for the final leg.*

Cue music. Roll end credits. Our film is over. For further exploration, look for Cannes' "underbelly" between Le Suquet and the train station—narrow lanes with inexpensive cafés and shops that regular folks can afford.

Sights in Cannes

Shopping

Cannes is made for window-shopping (the best streets are between the station and the waterfront). For the trendiest boutiques, stroll down handsome Rue d'Antibes (it parallels the sea about three blocks inland). Rue Meynadier anchors a pedestrian zone with more affordable shops closer to the port. To bring home a real surprise, consider cosmetic surgery. Cannes is well-known as *the* place on the Riviera to have your face (or other parts) realigned.

Excursions to St. Honorat and Ste. Marguerite Islands

Boats ferry tourists 15 minutes to these twin islands just off Cannes' shore (€13 round-trip, daily 9:00-18:00, 1-2/hour, www.trans-cote  -azur.com, no ferry runs between the 2 islands). The islands offer a refreshing change from the frenetic mainland, with almost no development, good swimming, and peaceful walking paths. On Ste. Marguerite you can visit the castle and cell where the mysterious Man in the Iron Mask was imprisoned (good little museum with decent English explanations featuring cargo from a sunken Roman vessel). On St. Honorat you can hike seafront trails and visit the abbey where monks still live and pray.

Yachters' Itinerary

If you're visiting Cannes on your private yacht, here's a suggested itinerary:

1. Take in the Festival de Cannes and the accompanying social scene. Organize an evening party on your boat.
2. Motor over to Monte Carlo for the Grand Prix, scheduled—conveniently for yachters—just after the film festival.
3. On your way back west to St-Tropez, deconstruct events from the film festival and Grand Prix with Brigitte Bardot.
4. Drop down to Porto Chervo on Sardinia, one of the few places in the world where your yacht is "just average."
5. Head west to Ibiza and Marbella in Spain, where your friends are moored for the big party scene.

Eating in Cannes

For a tasty, easy lunch in Cannes, consider **Fournil St. Nicholas.** You'll get mouthwatering quiche and sandwiches and exquisite salads at affordable prices (leaving the train station, turn right and walk a few blocks to 5 Rue Venizelos, tel. 04 93 38 81 12).

Cannes Connections

TGV and local trains serve Cannes' station. Buses stop next to the train station.

From Cannes by Train to: Antibes (2/hour, 15 minutes), **Nice** (2/hour, 30-40 minutes, €6), **Grasse** (roughly 1/hour, 30 minutes), **Monaco** (2/hour, 70 minutes).

By Bus: Bus #200 heads east from Cannes along the Riviera

(Mon-Sat 3-4/hour, Sun 2-3/hour, €1.50 for any destination), stopping at **Antibes** (35 minutes) and **Nice** (1.5-1.75 hours). Trip duration depends on traffic. Bus #210 is an express on the freeway to **Nice Airport** (1-2/hour, 50 minutes).

By Boat: Trans Côte d'Azur runs boat excursions from Cannes to St-Tropez (€46 round-trip, 1.25 hours each way; July-Aug daily 1/day; June and Sept 1/day Tue, Thu, and Sat-Sun only; no service Oct-May; tel. 04 92 98 71 30, www.trans-cote-azur .com). This boat trip is popular—book a few days ahead from June to September.

By Cruise Ship: Ships tender passengers to the west side of Cannes' port. From here, it's an easy **walk into town:** Just head inland, with the port on your right-hand side. You'll see the Film Festival Hall across the port. (The tender dock is near the end of my self-guided walk; you can either start the walk here and do it in reverse; or you can stroll about 10 minutes around the port to the walk's starting point—in the park just beyond the festival hall.)

It's about a 15-minute walk from the tender dock to the **train station:** Go up to the square at the top of the port. Walk to the far end of the square, and exit at its top-right corner, onto Rue Maréchal. Bear right up Rue Vénizélos, and you'll pop out at the train station.

St-Tropez

St-Tropez is a busy, charming, and traffic-free port town smothered with fashion boutiques, elegant restaurants, and luxury boats. If you came here for history or quaintness, you caught the wrong yacht. But if you have more money than you know what to do with, you're home. There are 5,700 year-round residents...and more than 100,000 visitors daily in the summer. Come in the winter if you can.

As with many seaside villages in southern France, the pastel beauty of St-Tropez was first discovered by artists. Paul Signac introduced several of his friends to St-Tropez in the late 1800s, giving the village its first notoriety. But it wasn't until Brigitte Bardot made the scene here in the 1956 film ...*And God Created Woman* that St-Tropez became synonymous with Riviera glamour. Since then, it's the first place that comes to mind when people think of the jet set luxuriating on

Mediterranean beaches. For many, the French Riviera begins here and runs east to Menton, on the Italian border.

The village itself is the attraction, as the nearest big beach is miles away. Window-shopping, people-watching, tan maintenance, and savoring slow meals fill people's days, weeks, and, in some cases, lives. Here, people dress up, size up one another's yachts, and troll for a partner. While the only models you'll see are in the shop windows, Brigitte Bardot still hangs out on a bench in front of the TI signing autographs (Thu 15:00-17:30, and if you believe that...).

Wander the harborfront, where fancy yachts moor stern-in, their carefully coiffed captains and first mates enjoying *pu-pus* for happy hour—they're seeing and being seen. Take time to stroll the back streets (the small lanes below La Citadelle are St-Tropez's most appealing) while nibbling a chocolate-and-Grand Marnier crêpe. Find the big Place des Lices (good cafés and local hangout), and look for some serious games of *pétanque (boules)*.

Orientation to St-Tropez

St-Tropez lies between its famous port and the hilltop Citadelle (with great views). The network of lanes between the port and Citadelle are strollable in a Carmel-by-the-Sea sort of way.

Tourist Information

The main TI is on the starboard side of the port (to you landlubbers, that's to the right as you face the sea), where Quai Suffren and Quai Jean Jaurès meet (daily July-Aug 9:30-13:00 & 14:30-19:00, April-June and Sept-Oct 9:30-12:30 & 14:00-19:00, Nov-March until 18:00, tel. 08 92 68 48 28, www.ot-saint-tropez.com). Pick up their good, €2 walking tour brochure (in English, usually inserted into a larger tourist brochure), ask about events in town, and get maps and bus information if you plan to hike along the coast.

In summer, drivers will find a small TI at Parking du Port (July-Aug Tue-Sat 10:00-18:00, closed Sun-Mon and off-season; parking lot described below, under "By Car").

Arrival in St-Tropez

For bus and boat details, see "St-Tropez Connections," at the end of this chapter.

By Bus: Buses leave you a few minutes' walk to the port, near the parking lot—Parking du Vieux Port—on Avenue Général de Gaulle.

By Boat: Boats from St-Raphaël deposit you by the Parking du Vieux Port, a five-minute walk to the port.

By Car: Prepare for traffic in any season—worse on weekends

ST-TROPEZ

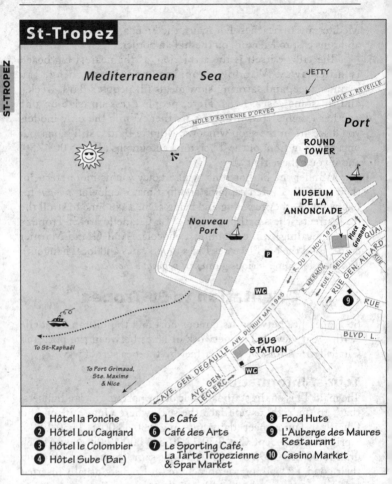

St-Tropez

Mediterranean   Sea

JETTY

MOLE J. REVEILLE

MOLE D'ESTIENNE D'ORVES

Port

ROUND TOWER

MUSEUM DE LA ANNONCIADE

Nouveau Port

R. DU 11 NOV. 1918

Place Gramont

QUAI

R. MERMOZ

RUE H. SEILLON

RUE GEN. ALLARD

P

WC

RUE

9

BLVD. L.

To St-Raphaël

AVE. DU HUIT MAI 1945

AVE. GEN. DEGAULLE

BUS STATION

WC

To Port Grimaud, Ste. Maxime & Nice

AVE. GEN. LECLERC

❶ Hôtel la Ponche
❷ Hôtel Lou Cagnard
❸ Hôtel le Colombier
❹ Hôtel Sube (Bar)

❺ Le Café
❻ Café des Arts
❼ Le Sporting Café, La Tarte Tropezienne & Spar Market

❽ Food Huts
❾ L'Auberge des Maures Restaurant
❿ Casino Market

(forget driving on Sunday afternoons), always ugly during summer, and downright impossible between St-Tropez and Ste. Maxime on weekends. You can avoid this bottleneck by taking the autoroute to Le Luc and following the windy D-558 to St-Tropez from here (via La Garde-Freinet and Port Grimaud).

The last few miles to St-Tropez are along a too-long, two-lane road with one way in, one way out, and too many people going exactly where you're going. There are two main parking lots (both about €2.50/hour): Parking des Lices (near all recommended hotels) and Parking du Port (best for day-trippers; small TI in summer). Signage from Parking du Port to the main TI is poor. To find it, face the boats, then head to the right of the boats for about five minutes to reach the old port. The main TI is on the opposite side of the port.

ST-TROPEZ

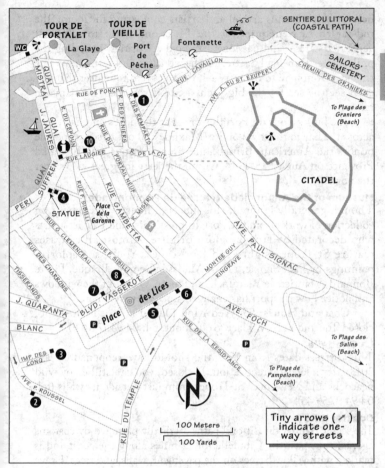

Sights in St-Tropez

The TI's self-guided walking tour brochure offers a worthwhile tour of St-Tropez's highlights. Use their tour to connect the following sights.

The Port

The port has played an important role in St-Tropez's economy since the 18th century, when it saw a brisk trade in wine, cork, and lumber. St-Tropez's shipyards were famous for their durably built three-mast ships, which could carry more than 1,000 barrels of wine. Today's port is known for its sailing regattas and oversized boats. There's something bizarre about the size of those boats, docked cheek-to-jowl in such a small harbor.

While strolling around, you'll see busy deckhands (hustling

before their captains arrive) and artists competing for room. The red-tabled **Le Sénéquier,** by the TI, is one of the town's most venerated cafés—and has long attracted celebrities, including the philosopher Jean-Paul Sartre. High-end cafés and restaurants line the port from here to the jetty—it doesn't seem to matter that you can't see the sea for the big yachts. See if you recognize anyone famous.

The bulky **Tour du Portalet** tower at the port's end has views across the bay to the town of Ste. Maxime and out to sea. A plaque honors the American, British, and French troops who liberated Provence on August 15, 1944. Climb the jetty for great views over the port.

Museum of the Annonciade (Musée de l'Annonciade)

Though generally ignored, this museum houses an enchanting collection of works from the Post-Impressionist and Fauvist artists who decorated St-Tropez before Brigitte. Almost all canvases feature St-Tropez sights and landscapes. You'll see colorful paintings by Paul Signac, Henri Matisse, Georges Braque, Pierre Bonnard, Maurice de Vlaminck, and more. Gaze out the windows and notice how the port has changed since they were here.

Cost and Hours: €5, Wed-Mon 10:00-12:00 & 14:00-18:00, closed Tue and in Nov, Place Grammont, tel. 04 94 17 84 10.

La Citadelle

This fortress dates from 1558 and should have reopened by late 2013 after a lengthy renovation. If closed, you can still enjoy wild peacocks and views over St-Tropez from just outside its walls (tel. 04 94 97 59 43).

Coastal Hike

The scenic Sentier du Littoral path, originally patrolled by customs agents, runs past the Citadelle for 12 miles along the coast and is marked with yellow dashes on the pavement, walls, and trees. Leave St-Tropez along the road below the Citadelle, pass the Sailors' Cemetery, and you'll join the path before long. If you're really into this, take the 20-minute bus *(la navette)* from Place des Lices in St-Tropez to the Capon/Pinet stop and walk three hours back to St-Tropez (bus only runs 2/day, taxi also works, get details at TI).

Boat Excursions

Several companies offer mildly interesting tours of the bay (paralleling the Sentier du Littoral described above). **Le Brigantin II** has reliable outings aboard a comfortable wooden vessel with personalized English commentary. You'll learn a smidgen about St-Tropez's history and a lot about villas of the rich and famous. Conrad Hilton and John Grisham both have little bungalows, and you'll sail right past Brigitte Bardot's surprisingly modest-looking home. Redhead Victoria (from Britain) staffs the information desk on the Quai Suffren and can explain the trip (one-hour tour-€9, kids age 5-10-€4.50, 6/day Feb-Nov, tel. 04 94 54 40 61, www .lebrigantin.com).

Boules

The vast *pétanque (boules)* court on Place des Lices is worth your attention. Have a drink at the recommended Le Café and take in the action. Study up on the sport (see page 10) and root for your hero.

Near St-Tropez

Port Grimaud

Although more modern than St-Tropez, Port Grimaud (located a few miles toward Ste. Maxime) is no less attractive or upscale. This "Venice of Provence" was reclaimed from a murky lagoon about 40 years ago, and is now lined with four miles of canals, lovely homes, and moorage for thousands of yachts. It's a fascinating look at what clever minds can produce from a swamp. Park at the lot across from the town entry (TI next to the parking lot, tel. 04 94 56 02 01, www.grimaud-provence.com), and cross the barrier and bridge into a beautiful world of privilege. Climb the church bell tower for a good panorama view.

Sleeping in St-Tropez

Though everything seems pricey in this golden town, I've uncovered a few jewels. Sleep only in the town center, as traffic makes coming and going a royal headache. High season in St-Tropez runs from June through September, and weekends are busy year-round.

$$$ Hôtel la Ponche**** offers a warm welcome and the most central, luxurious beds I could find (standard Db-€210-430 depending on season; Db with balcony, terrace, or sea view-€310-570; Db suites-up to €830; continental breakfast-€20, Wi-Fi, parking-€25/day, near the sea, several blocks behind the TI at 3 Rue des Remparts, tel. 04 94 97 02 53, www.laponche.com, hotel @laponche.com).

$$ Hôtel Lou Cagnard**, with a courtyard garden entrance and foliage crawling up the side, is a pretty, well-managed, and shockingly reasonable hotel (Ds-€80, bigger Db-€95-165, higher prices are for gardenside and larger rooms, 1-week minimum June-Sept, closed Nov-Jan, most rooms have air-con, free parking, follow signs to *Parking des Lices* and you'll pass the hotel, 18 Avenue Paul Roussel, tel. 04 94 97 04 24, www.hotel-lou-cagnard.com).

$$ Hôtel le Colombier**, little and adorable, is on a quiet street. Its 11 soft and comfortable rooms enclose a small, sweet garden patio. This is a solid value for St-Tropez (Ds-€105, Db-€105-130, bigger Db-€140-185, Tb/Qb-€230-280, no American Express, rates include easy parking nearby, air-con,

Wi-Fi, follow *Parking des Lices* signs and look for hotel signs on left, Impasse des Conquêtes, tel. 04 94 97 05 31).

Eating in St-Tropez

Dining out in St-Tropez is a rich man's hobby—you can spend *beaucoup* and get *rien* in return. Picnics are a good option, with several grocery stores in the old city and plenty of scenic places to set up. A **Casino** market is a block off the port, up Rue V. Laugier, and a **Spar** market is on Place des Lices.

Start or end your evening with St-Tropez's best port-view seats on the small deck at **Hôtel Sube's** second-floor bar on Quai Suffren, near the TI (drinks only, fine interior).

Place des Lices, where locals eat and relax, has several appealing and reasonably priced places to choose from, and offers a great opportunity to watch *pétanque* matches from your café table. **Le Café** serves reasonably good cuisine and has long been *the* place to park your beret on this square. Stroll inside past the soft chairs and old wooden floor, and find one of the best zinc counters in France, complete with an atmospheric bar (daily, €20-30 *menus*, €18 *plats*, tel. 04 94 97 44 69, www.lecafe.fr). **Café des Arts,** at the end of the square, has good ambience inside and out, and serves pizza, salads, and *plats* for €10-20 (daily, tel. 04 94 97 02 25). Don't confuse this restaurant with the ultra-swanky and overpriced Brasserie des Arts two doors down.

On the opposite side of the *place*, **Le Sporting** serves up standard café-brasserie fare at reasonable prices and is always packed with locals, especially at lunch (daily, good salads, €14 *plats du jour*, 42 Place des Lices, tel. 04 94 97 00 65). Nearby, **La Tarte Tropezienne** is half bakery, half café, selling sandwiches, quiches, salads, and pastries (take-away or sit down, daily 6:30-20:00, tel. 04 94 97 04 69). A number of **food huts** are clustered around the north side of the *place* if you want to eat and stroll (sandwiches, crepes, pizza, and more). Here, locals stand at counters to eat.

L'Auberge des Maures has a rich, lively decor, indoor and outdoor tables, a fine reputation, and a welcoming staff. It's a good place to go for quality Provençal cuisine (€54 *menus,* open daily for dinner only, 4 Rue du Docteur Boutin, tel. 04 94 97 01 50, www .aubergedesmaures.fr).

St-Tropez Connections

With no trains to St-Tropez, buses and boats are your only options.

By Bus: Bus #7601 serves St-Tropez from behind St-Raphaël's train station via Ste. Maxime to the east (almost hourly, 1.5 hours to **St-Raphaël**, 30 minutes to **Ste. Maxime**). Bus #7801 and #7802 run from **Toulon**'s train station to the west (7/day, 2 hours). If you're arriving in St-Raphaël or Toulon by train, check the bus schedules to St-Tropez in advance at www.varlib.fr to be sure you will make the connection.

By Boat: Boats make the one-hour trip between St-Tropez and **St-Raphaël** twice daily (€15 one-way, €30 round-trip, departs St-Tropez at 10:30 and 17:15, departs St-Raphaël at 9:30 and 14:30, tel. 04 94 95 17 46, www.bateauxsaintraphael.com, or call the TI). Boats between St-Tropez and **Ste. Maxime** run about every hour (€7, 15 minutes, tel. 04 94 49 29 39, www.bateauxverts.com, info @bateauxverts.com). For boats connecting St-Tropez with Nice, see page 336; with Cannes, page 467.

INLAND RIVIERA

*St-Paul-de-Vence • Vence •
Grasse • Le Grand Canyon
du Verdon*

For a verdant, rocky, fresh escape from the beaches, head inland
and upward. Some of France's most perfectly perched hill towns
and splendid scenery hang overlooked in this region that's more
famous for beaches and bikinis. A short car or bus ride away from
the Mediterranean reaps big rewards: lush forests, deep canyons,
and swirling hilltop villages. A longer drive brings you to Europe's
greatest canyon, the Grand Canyon du Verdon.

Getting Around the Inland Riviera

By Car: Driving is the most flexible way to tour this area
(particularly in the off-season)—though summer and weekend
traffic and parking challenges will test your patience. Car rental
is worth considering (see the "Helpful Hints" sections in the Nice
and Antibes chapters). I describe the best route later.

By Bus: Buses get you to many of the places in this chapter.
Vence, St-Paul-de-Vence, and Grasse are well-served by bus from
Nice about every 30-45 minutes, and Grasse has train service
from Nice, Antibes, and Cannes. A few buses to Tourrettes-sur-
Loup, Le Bar-sur-Loup, and Grasse leave from Vence daily except
Sunday (7/day, 15 minutes to Tourrettes-sur-Loup, 35 minutes to
Le Bar-sur-Loup; 4/day to Grasse, 50 minutes). Bus connections
for the Gorges du Loup, the village of Gourdon, or the Gorges du
Verdon are either too complicated or nonexistent.

With a Local Guide: Informative and enjoyable guides **Sylvie
Di Cristo** and **Boba Vukadinovic** both live in inland villages and
can show you around their backyards. See page 319 for contact
information.

Benôit and Corinne, owners of the recommended Frogs'
House in St-Jeannet, are happy to organize cooking classes, wine

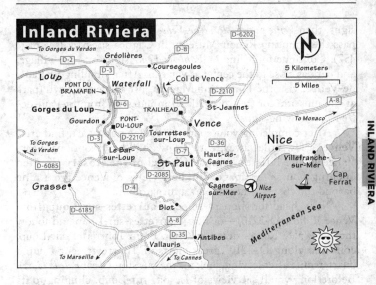

tastings, hiking trips, and other excursions around their native area (see page 487).

Self-Guided Driving Tour

The Inland Riviera:
From St-Paul-de-Vence to Grasse

This splendid loop drive connects St-Paul-de-Vence, Vence, Tourrettes-sur-Loup, and Grasse. It's best done by car as a day trip from the Nice/Antibes area (allow all day), though it could be done en route to the Gorges du Verdon (the most impressive part of the Grand Canyon du Verdon area). Some of the villages can be linked by bus, but a car is essential to do the loop as described. Each stop is only minutes away from the next by car or bus, but allow 45 minutes to drive from Nice or Antibes to the first stop, St-Paul-de-Vence. Start early if you want to see St-Paul-de-Vence without the mobs (have breakfast at St-Paul-de-Vence's Café de la Place). If you won't be visiting the Gorges du Verdon (or if you care more about nature than art), take the exceptionally beautiful long way around from Vence to Gourdon (described later, under "Alternate Route"), and skip Tourrettes-sur-Loup and the Gorges du Loup (you won't miss them, trust *moi*).

The bolded stops below are explained in detail later in this chapter.

The Drive Begins

Let's get started. From Nice, leave along the promenade des Anglais and head toward Cannes and Antibes. Follow *Grasse* signs, then *Vence* and *St-Paul-de-Vence* signs. On this route, you'll pass the tempting Renoir Museum in Cagnes-sur-Mer (see page 457). Continue following *St-Paul-de-Vence* signs into the village, and park as close to the center as you can. After sampling **St-Paul-de-Vence**, visit the **Fondation Maeght** just above the town (park at the museum for free, or walk 20 minutes up from St-Paul-de-Vence, following signs).

After completing your course in contemporary art, find artsy **Vence**, a few miles away, with many good lunch options. From Vence visit Matisse's famous **Chapel of the Rosary** (limited opening hours—see page 484; best views of Vence are a mile beyond the chapel, where there's a turnaround).

Next, head for slippery-sloped **Tourrettes-sur-Loup** (from Vence, follow D-2210)—or skip Tourrettes-sur-Loup and follow the "Alternate Route" described later. From Tourrettes-sur-Loup, continue along D-2210 (great views of Tourrettes-sur-Loup a quarter-mile after leaving, look for the bus stop *Chemin de la Gare*). Before long you'll see views of Le Bar-sur-Loup, clinging to its hillside in the distance. Just before the tiny village of Pont-du-Loup, you'll arrive at the junction of the roads to Gourdon/Gorges du Loup (D-6) and Le Bar-sur-Loup (D-2210), look way up to your destination—the tiny soaring village of Gourdon. Sugar addicts can detour quickly down to Pont-du-Loup and visit the small candied-fruit factory of **Confiseries Florian.**

Follow *Gourdon* and *Gorges du Loup* signs to the right along D-6 and climb into the teeth of a rocky canyon, the **Gorges du Loup.** It's a mostly second-gear road that winds between severe rock faces above a surging stream. (Buses cannot enter the Gorges du Loup, so non-drivers must continue on directly to Grasse.) Several miles into the gorge, you can visit the Cascades du Saut du Loup **waterfall**, which may have you thinking you've made a wrong turn into Hawaii (€1, easy walk down).

The drive passes all too quickly to where the road hooks back, crossing Pont du Bramafen and up toward Gourdon on D-3. Climb above the canyon you just drove through and watch the world below miniaturize. At the top, the village of **Gourdon**, known as the "Eagle's Nest" (2,400 feet), waits for tourists with shops, good lunch options, and grand panoramas.

From Gourdon, slide downhill—passing stone quarries—toward **Grasse**. Enjoy sensational views down to (literally) overlooked Le Bar-sur-Loup. Follow signs to *Grasse*, then *Centre-Ville*, and park at the first underground lot you come to (by the Grasse bus station). After mastering your scent in Grasse—the capital of perfume—return to your Riviera home base (allow 45 minutes to Nice or 30 minutes to Antibes via Cannes and the autoroute), or continue to the Gorges du Verdon.

Alternate Route

If you won't be visiting the Gorges du Verdon, consider this delicious detour, which takes you a bit farther inland (ideal if staying in Vence): Follow the route described above until Vence and complete your sightseeing there, then find D-2 just before the bridge that leads to St-Jeannet, and follow signs for *Col de Vence* (the Vence pass). This road switches up and up beyond the tree line into a stones-only landscape to the pass in about 15 minutes. Great views over Vence begin a few minutes after leaving the town. (For a 45-minute uphill hike to views over Vence and the Riviera, pass the Château St-Martin, drive another kilometer, then look for the brown trailhead sign to *Baous des Blancs*.) From the pass (3,000 feet), continue on D-2, trading rocky slabs for lush forests, pastures, and vast canyons. You'll pass the postcard-perfect village of Coursegoules (worth a photo but not a detour), then follow signs to *Gréolières*. At a roundabout just before Gréolières you'll find D-3, which leads to Nice, Gorges du Loup, and Gourdon. But first, continue a few minutes past Gréolières to the pullout barely above the village, with stirring views over the village and its ruined castle. Consider a coffee break in Gréolières before backtracking to the roundabout, following signs to *Gourdon*. After visiting Gourdon, you can continue to Grasse, or return to Nice or Antibes.

Shortcut from Vence to the Gorges du Verdon

To save time and add scenery, you can skip the town of Grasse and take D-2 from Vence toward Col de Vence (Vence pass), and climb above the tree line. Follow D-2 up and over, passing the photogenic villages of Coursegoules and Gréolières, and continue west following signs to *Thorenc*, *Valderoure*, and *Grasse*, to where the road eventually meets D-6085. From here, turn left, then shortly after follow signs to the right to *Draguignan* and *Gorges du Verdon*, and join the "Le Grand Canyon du Verdon" route described on page 496.

St-Paul-de-Vence

This most famous of Riviera hill towns is also the most-visited village in France. And it feels that way—like an overrun and over-restored artist-shopping-mall. Its attraction is understandable, as every cobble and flower seems just-so, and the setting is postcard-perfect. Avoid visiting between 11:00 and 18:00, particularly on weekends. Beat the crowds by skipping breakfast at your hotel and eating it in St-Paul-de-Vence, or come for dinner and experience the village at its tranquil best.

Orientation to St-Paul-de-Vence

Tourist Information

The helpful **TI,** just through the gate into the old city on Rue Grande, has maps with minimal explanations of key buildings (daily 10:00-18:00, until 19:00 June-Sept, closed some days 13:00-14:00). The TI offers five different themed walking tours with English translations, including tours focused on history, art, and *pétanque (boules).* Call or email in advance to reserve (€5, tel. 04 93 32 86 95, www.saint-pauldevence.com, serviceguide@saint-pauldevence.com).

Arrival in St-Paul-de-Vence

Arrive early to park near the village (cars are not allowed inside St-Paul). Bus #400 (connects with Nice and Vence) stops on the main road, a short walk from the village. If the traffic-free lane leading to the old city is jammed, walk along the road that veers up and left just after Café de la Place, and enter the town through its side door. Or, if it's really packed, consider walking outside the ramparts one way (from main entrance, find green gate downhill to the right, just beyond the *boules* court). The dirt path takes you through a playground and ends at the cemetery. From there, you can swim upstream through the crowds and back to the main entrance.

Sights in St-Paul-de-Vence

The Old Town

St-Paul's old city has no essential sights, though its lovely cobbled lanes and peekaboo views delight most who come. You'll pass the vintage **Café de la Place** on entering the village—a good place to have a coffee and croissant and watch as waves of tourists crash into the town (daily from 7:00, tel. 04 93 32 80 03). On the square, serious *boules* competitions take place all day long, rain or heat. Meander deep into St-Paul-de-Vence's quieter streets to find panoramic views. Visit Marc Chagall's grave in the cemetery at the opposite end of town (from the cemetery entrance, turn right, then left; it's the third gravestone). Walk up the stairs to the view platform and try to locate the hill town of Vence at the foot of an impressive mountain. Is the sea out there—somewhere?

Fondation Maeght

This inviting, pricey, and far-out private museum is situated a steep walk or short drive above St-Paul-de-Vence. Fondation Maeght (fohn-dah-shown mahg) offers an excellent introduction to modern Mediterranean art by gathering many of the Riviera's most famous artists under one roof.

Cost and Hours: €15, €5 to take photos (you'll get a small button to wear as proof of payment), daily July-Sept 10:00-19:00, Oct-June 10:00-18:00, tel. 04 93 32 81 63, www.fondation-maeght .com.

Getting There: The museum is a steep uphill-but-doable 20-minute walk from St-Paul-de-Vence and the bus stop. Signs indicate the way (parking is usually available at the upper lot). From the lower lot, signed *Parking Conseille*, a shortcut on a steep, dirt path through the trees leads directly to the green gate in front of the ticket booth.

Visiting the Museum: The founder, Aimé Maeght, long envisioned the perfect exhibition space for the artists he supported and befriended as an art dealer. He purchased this arid hilltop, planted more than 35,000 plants, and hired an architect (José Luis Sert) with the same vision.

A sweeping lawn laced with amusing sculptures and bending pine trees greets visitors. On the right, a chapel designed by

Georges Braque—in memory of the Maeghts' young son, who died of leukemia—features a moving purple stained-glass work over the altar. The unusual museum building is purposefully low profile, to let its world-class modern-art collection take center stage. Works by Fernand Léger, Joan Miró, Alexander Calder, Georges Braque, and Marc Chagall are thoughtfully arranged in well-lit rooms. The backyard of the museum has views, a Gaudí-esque sculpture labyrinth by Miró, and a courtyard filled with the wispy works of Alberto Giacometti. The only permanent collection in the museum consists of the sculptures, though the museum tries to keep a good selection of paintings by the famous artists here year-round. For a review of modern art, see "The Riviera's Art Scene" on page 326. There's also a great gift shop and cafeteria.

Eating in St-Paul-de-Vence

If you come late in the day and stay for dinner (smart plan, particularly if sleeping in Vence), go all out at **Le Tilleul** (www .restaurant-letilleul.com). Book ahead, as you'll be competing with locals for tables on the lovely terrace or in the cozy interior (à la carte only, allow €50/person for three courses, open daily, tel. 04 93 32 80 36).

To rub elbows with the wealthy, book a table well in advance at the historic **La Colombe d'Or,** where the menu hasn't changed in 50 years. Back when the town was teeming with artists, this restaurant served as their virtual clubhouse. The walls are covered with paintings by Picasso, Miró, Braque, Chagall, and others, who were often given free meals in exchange for pieces of their work. The terrace garden is lovely, but the true ambience is inside by the fire, which is best on bad-weather days or anytime in the winter (figure €60/person with wine, across from Café de la Place, closed Nov-Dec, tel. 04 93 32 80 02; for reservations, email contact @la-colombe-dor.com; www.la-colombe-dor.com).

Vence

Vence is a well-discovered yet appealing town set high above the Riviera. While growth has sprawled beyond Vence's old walls, and cars jam its roundabouts, the mountains are front and center and the breeze is fresh. Vence bubbles with workaday life and ample tourist activity in the day but is quiet at night, with few visitors and cooler temperatures than along the coast. Vence makes a handy base for travelers wanting the best of both worlds: a hill-town refuge near the sea. Some enjoy the Gorges du Verdon as a long day trip from Vence, though (see the route described on page 496).

Orientation to Vence

Tourist Information

Vence's fully loaded and eager-to-help TI faces the main square at 8 Place du Grand Jardin, across from the merry-go-round. It offers free Wi-Fi, bus schedules, brochures on the cathedral, and a city map with a well-devised self-guided walking tour (25 stops, incorporates informative wall plaques). The TI also publishes a list of Vence art galleries with English descriptions of the collections. To properly engage you in French culture, the staff can help you find French-language classes and—even better—*pétanque* instructions with *boules* to rent for €3 per person. Ask about guided walking tours in English (TI open July-Aug Mon-Sat 9:00-19:00, Sun 10:00-18:00; March-June and Sept-Oct Mon-Sat 9:00-18:00, Nov-Feb 10:00-17:00; closed Sun Sept-June; free Wi-Fi, tel. 04 93 58 06 38, www.ville-vence.fr).

Market day in the *cité historique* (old town) is on Friday mornings on Place Clemenceau. A big all-day antiques market is on Place du Grand Jardin every Wednesday. If you miss market day, a **Monoprix** is on Avenue de la Résistance, across from the entrance to the Marie Antoinette parking lot (grocery store upstairs, Mon-Sat 8:30-20:00, Sun 8:30-12:30).

Arrival in Vence

By Bus: Buses #94 and #400 (from Nice, Cagnes-sur-Mer, and St-Paul-de-Vence) drop you at the bus stop labeled *Halte Routière de l'Ara*, which is on a roundabout at Place Maréchal Juin. It's a 10-minute walk to the town center along Avenue Henri Isnard or Avenue de la Résistance.

By Car: Follow signs to *cité historique*, then look for blue *P* signs and park in one of two lots: **Marie Antoinette** or the underground **Grand Jardin**. Both are a five-minute walk from the town center and have the same rates (€15/day, €2/overnight 20:00-8:00). Some hotels offer discounted rates.

Sights in Vence

Explore the narrow lanes of the old town using the TI's worthwhile self-guided tour map. Connect the picturesque streets, enjoy a drink on a quiet square, inspect an art gallery, and find the small 11th-century cathedral with its colorful Chagall mosaic of Moses (for background, see the Chagall Museum Tour chapter). If you're here later in the day, enjoy the *boules* action across from the TI (rent a set from the TI and join in).

Château de Villeneuve

This 17th-century mansion, adjoining an imposing 12th-century watchtower, bills itself as "one of the Riviera's high temples of modern art," with a rotating collection. Check with the TI to see what's playing in the temple.

Cost and Hours: €5, Tue-Sun 10:00-12:30 & 14:00-18:00, closed Mon, tel. 04 93 58 15 78.

INLAND RIVIERA

Vence

1. La Maison du Frêne
2. To Hôtel Miramar
3. To Aux 3 Lits qui Chantent B&B
4. Auberge des Seigneurs
5. La Cassolette Restaurant
6. La Litote Restaurant
7. La Farigoule Restaurant
8. Bistro du Peyra & Le Pigeonnier Restaurant
9. Monoprix Grocery

AVENUE HENRI ISNARD

To **3**
Col de Vence via D-2
& Chapel of the Rosary

CHATEAU DE VILLENEUVE
MODERN ART MUSEUM

RUE DU DR. BINET

AVENUE DE LA RESISTANCE

To
Place M. Juin (Bus Stop),
Tourrettes-sur-Loup via D-2210
& St. Paul via D-7

TOWER

PORTE DU PEYRA

RUE DU DR. BINET

Place du Grand Jardin

Marie Antoinette

PLACE DU GRAND JARDIN

Grand Jardin

RUE DES ARCS

RUE MASSENA

RUE GAMBETTA

WC

▲Chapel of the Rosary (Chapelle du Rosaire)

The chapel, a short drive or 20-minute walk from town, was designed by an elderly and ailing Henri Matisse as thanks to the

Dominican sister who had taken care of him (he was 81 when the chapel was completed—see the timeline of Matisse's life on page 342). The modest chapel holds a simple series of charcoal black-on-white tile sketches and uses three symbolic colors as accents: yellow (sunlight and the light of God), green (nature), and blue (the Mediterranean sky). Bright sunlight filters through the stained-glass windows and does a cheery dance across the sketches. While the chapel is the ultimate pilgrimage for

INLAND RIVIERA

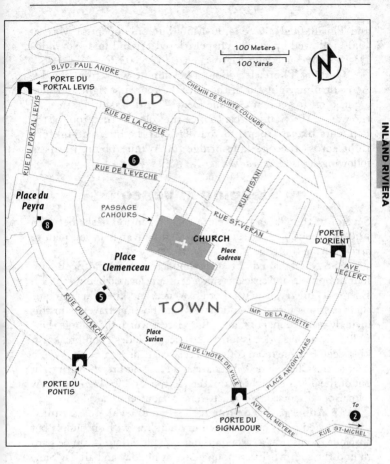

serious Matisse fans, the experience may underwhelm others. (If you've taken my self-guided tour of the Matisse Museum in Nice, you'll remember that he was the master of leaving things out.) Decide for yourself whether Matisse met the goal he set himself: "Creating a religious space in an enclosed area of reduced proportions and to give it, solely by the play of colors and lines, the dimension of infinity."

Your entry ticket includes a 20-minute tour from one of the kind nuns who speaks English. Downstairs you'll find displays of

the vestments Matisse designed for the priests, his models of the chapel, and sketches. Photography is not allowed.

Cost and Hours: €5; Mon, Wed, and Sat 14:00-17:30, Tue

and Thu 10:00-11:30 & 14:00-17:30, Sun only open for Mass at 10:00 followed by tour of chapel, closed Fri and mid-Nov-mid-Dec; 466 Avenue Henri Matisse, tel. 04 93 58 03 26.

Getting There: It's about a 20-minute walk from the TI. After turning right out of the TI, take your first right and then a quick left to get onto Avenue Henri Isnard. Take this street all the way to the traffic circle (notice the colorful tiled roof of the Pénitents Blancs Chapel to your left). At the intersection, turn right across the one-lane bridge on Avenue Henri Matisse, following signs to *St-Jeannet*.

Sleeping in Vence

Several of the places I list close their reception desks between 12:00 and 16:00. Make arrangements in advance if you plan to arrive during this time.

$$$ La Maison du Frêne is a modern, art-packed B&B with four sumptuous and spacious suites centrally located behind the TI. Energetic Thierry, who was born in Vence, and kind Guy combine their passions for contemporary art and hosting travelers in this lovingly restored manor house. This place is worth the splurge (Db-€150-185, higher price is for peak times, includes good breakfast, kids sleep free, in-room coffee/tea service, fridges, air-con, Wi-Fi; next to the Château de Villeneuve at 1 Place du Frêne—turn right out of the TI, then right again, then left; tel. 04 93 24 37 83, www .lamaisondufrene.com, contact@lamaisondufrene.com).

$$ Auberge des Seigneurs feels medieval. It's a funky, dark-wooded place in a 17th-century building with six simple but spacious rooms over a restaurant in a good location. It can be hard to find the staff when reception closes at midday and all day Sun-Mon (when the restaurant isn't open)—just ring the bell (small Db in back-€80, Db-€90, Wi-Fi in lobby only, includes €10 parking voucher, 1 Rue du Dr. Binet, tel. 04 93 58 04 24, www.auberge -seigneurs.com, sandrine.rodi@wanadoo.fr).

$$ Hôtel Miramar*** is a laid-back, 18-room Mediterranean villa perched on a ledge with grand panoramas, a 10-minute walk above the old town. Old World rooms come with soothing, Provençal colors, worn furnishings, and owners who could use a course in customer service. (Hint: Don't arrive at lunchtime.) The pool and view terrace could make you late for dinner, or seduce you into skipping it altogether—picnics are allowed. Access is a challenge for drivers (standard Db-€78-108, Db with balcony-€98-128, Db with great view and balcony-€160, family suite-€180, some rooms have air-con, bar, table tennis, parking, turn left out of the TI and follow the brown signs to 167 Avenue

---

Sleep Code

(€1 = about $1.30, country code: 33)
S = Single, **D** = Double/Twin, **T** = Triple, **Q** = Quad, **b** = bathroom,
s = shower only, * = French hotel rating (0-5 stars). Credit
cards are accepted and English is spoken unless otherwise
noted.

To help you sort easily through these listings, I've divided
the accommodations into three categories based on the price
for a standard double room with bath:

$$$ Higher Priced—Most rooms €110 or more.
$$ Moderately Priced—Most rooms between €70-110.
$ Lower Priced—Most rooms €70 or less.

Prices can change without notice; verify the hotel's current rates online or by email. For the best prices, always book
direct.

Bougearel—behind the soccer field, tel. 04 93 58 01 32, www
.hotel-miramar-vence.com, resa@hotel-miramar-vence.com).

$ Aux 3 Lits qui Chantent ("The Three Singing Beds") has
friendly hosts and an international vibe, and is easy for those
arriving by bus or car. Run by globetrotting couple Jean-Lucien
and Sarah-Jane, this cozy BB&B (bed, bike, and breakfast) has
simple yet comfortable rooms, and books and bicycles at your
disposal (Sb-€54, Db-€69-78 depending on size, bigger family
rooms-€99-123, includes hearty breakfast, Wi-Fi, Rue Elise, tel.
04 93 32 67 03, www.aux3litsquichantent.com).

Near Vence in St-Jeannet

To melt into the Inland Riviera's quiet side, drive 15 minutes
from Vence to the remarkably situated, no-tourist-in-sight hill
town of St-Jeannet. Views are endless and everywhere. It's so
quiet, it's hard to believe that the beach is only 10 miles away.
But the best reason to visit St-Jeannet is to stay at **$$ The Frogs'
House,** where Benôit and Corinne will eagerly welcome you to
this region, which they are both mad about. This young couple
offers a full menu of good rooms, fine meals, cooking lessons,
hikes in the area, and day trips to popular destinations. If you
don't have wheels, they'll happily pick you up at the train station
or airport. The hotel is freshly renovated, so everything feels new.
Rooms are small but sharp (Db-€89, Db with balcony-€99, family
suite with private salon-€159, €10 less for 3-night or longer stay,
includes breakfast, Corinne's 4-course dinner *menu*-€34, tel. 04

93 58 98 05, mobile 06 28 06 80 28, www.thefrogshouse.com, info @thefrogshouse.com). A parking lot is in the center of St-Jeannet, a few blocks from this small hotel.

Eating in Vence

Tempting outdoor eateries litter the old town. Lights embedded in the cobbles illuminate the way after dark. The first three restaurants serve tasty Provençal cuisine in the center of the old town and are my top choices.

La Cassolette, at 10 Place du Clemenceau, is an intimate place with reasonable prices and a romantic terrace across from the floodlit church (€32 *menus*, €14-17 *plats*, closed Tue-Wed except July-Aug, tel. 04 93 58 84 15, www.restaurant-lacassolette-vence .com).

Nearby, **La Litote** is lauded by locals as a good value, with outdoor tables on a quiet, hidden square (€25-30 two- and three-course meals, closed Mon-Tue and Sun evening, 7 Rue de l'Evêché, tel. 04 93 24 27 82).

Hiding just behind the TI, on an unassuming street, **La Farigoule** circles a flowery courtyard, and serves gourmet meals with limited choices. This is a good splurge (€30-45 *menus*, €23-28 *plats*, closed Tue, 15 Avenue Henri Isnard, tel. 04 93 58 01 27).

For less expensive, casual dining, head to Place du Peyra, where you'll find ample outdoor seating and early dinner service. At **Bistro du Peyra,** enjoy a relaxed dinner salad or pasta dish outdoors to the sound of the town's main fountain (€15-20 *plats*, daily April-Oct, off-season closed Wed-Thu at lunch, closed Jan-Feb, 13 Place du Peyra, tel. 04 93 58 67 63). Or try **Le Pigeonnier** next door for good omelets, salads, and pasta (€14 *plats*, daily mid-June-Sept, off-season closed Wed all day and Sun evening, 5-7 Place du Peyra, tel. 04 93 58 03 00).

Near Vence

In St-Jeannet: If you're looking to get away, the village of St-Jeannet offers several options. For a very personal experience, reserve ahead for a meal with Benôit and Corinne at **The Frogs' House,** their small hotel in St-Jeannet. You'll dine in their grand kitchen and learn about local produce and recipes (€34 for dinner with wine and the works, see listing under "Sleeping in Vence," earlier).

In St-Paul-de-Vence: For upscale dining, book a table at **Le Tilleul** or **La Colombe d'Or** (both described on page 482).

In **Tourrettes-sur-Loup**: For peace and quiet with a Michelin star, head to **Clovis**, 10 minutes away by car (see next section).

Hill Towns and Sights Between Vence and Grasse

The following sights are connected by the Inland Riviera self-guided driving tour (see page 477).

Tourrettes-sur-Loup

This unspoiled and picturesque town, hemmed in by forests, looks from afar like it's ready to skid down its hill. Tourrettes-sur-Loup is small, with no sprawl. The well-preserved, narrow medieval lanes will keep a photographer busy and make most visitors feel as if they've stepped onto a cobble-and-stone Hollywood movie set. Known as the *Cité des Violettes,* the village produces more violets than anywhere else in France, most of which get shipped off to end up in bottles that make you smell nice. On the first or second Sunday of March, this small village fills with almost 10,000 visitors (hard to imagine) for the annual Violet Festival (La Fête des Violettes).

Park in the lot at the village center (€.50/hour, first 30 minutes free), near the TI (Mon-Sat 9:30-13:00 & 14:00-18:00, closed Sun, maps sometimes left outside when closed—but you don't really need one, tel. 04 93 24 18 93, www.tourrettessurloup .com). Wednesday is market day (on Place de la Libération).

With your back to the TI, walk to the right and under the clock tower, and onto the Grande Rue. Stroll in a counterclockwise direction, eventually ending up back at the parking lot. Along the way you'll find a smattering of arts and crafts boutiques, though fewer than in the "Vence towns," and a handful of places to eat or take a break.

Tom's Ice Cream may entice you with its violet-flavored scoops or tasty coffee and free Wi-Fi (daily from 13:30, 25 Grand Rue, tel. 04 93 24 12 12). For a real culinary treat, book a table at **Clovis**, where Michelin-starred chef Julien Bousseau uses seasonal ingredients in his limited and ever-changing menu. Julien speaks English and helps his wife with the service—it's all part of the welcoming atmosphere in this cozy find tucked into tiny Tourrettes (€37-50 for 2-4 courses, €62-90 *menu*, indoor seating only, air-con, reservations smart, closed Mon-Tue, 21 Grande Rue, tel. 04 93 58 87 04).

Wine lovers should head to **La Cave de Tourrettes**, a small wine bar serving salads and quiches, with a daily by-the-glass selection and a vast cellar. The mini-balcony has a nice view (Tue-Sun for lunch, Thu-Sat for dinner, closed Mon, 8 Rue de la Bourgade, near the St. Grégoire Church on the parking lot, tel. 04 93 24 10 12).

More views of Tourrettes-sur-Loup await a minute away on the drive to Pont-du-Loup.

Confiseries Florian

The candied-fruit factory hides between trees down in Pont-du-Loup (though their big, bright sign is hard to miss). Ten-minute tours of their factory leave regularly, covering the candied-fruit process and explaining the use of flower petals (like violets and jasmine) in their products. Everything they make is fruit-filled—even their chocolate (with oranges). The tour ends with a tasting of the *confiture* in the dazzling gift shop.

Cost and Hours: Tours are free, request a tour with English commentary, daily 9:00-12:00 & 14:00-18:30, gift shop stays open during lunch in summer, tel. 04 93 59 32 91, www.confiserie florian.com.

Gorges du Loup

The Inland Riviera is crawling with spectacular canyons only miles from the sea. Slotted between Grasse and Vence, the Gorges du Loup is the easiest gorge to reach and works in well with a day trip from the Nice area. You can drive about five miles right up into the canyon (on D-6), passing waterfalls and sheer rock walls, then return on the gorge's rooftop (on D-3) to the "Eagle's Nest" village of Gourdon for magnificent vistas and a complete change of scenery.

Gourdon

This 2,400-foot-high, cliff-topping hamlet features grassy picnic areas, a short lineup of tourist shops, and a few good lunch options. The village's most famous building is its château, which is best enjoyed from the outside (infrequent, French-only tours of the interior). A well-marked trail (Chemin du Paradis) leads down the cliffs to Le Bar-sur-Loup (1 hour)—now *that's* steep. The far side of the village features fabulous vistas, a tiny Romanesque church, and a nice option for lunch with a view.

Eating in Gourdon: **La Taverne Provençale** boasts a popular spread of outdoor tables overlooking the grandeur (€10-12 omelets and pasta dishes, €18 *menu,* July-Aug daily lunch and dinner, Sept-June Thu-Tue lunch only, closed Wed, Place de l'Eglise, tel. 04 93 09 68 22).

Grasse

Both the historic and contemporary capital of perfume, Grasse offers a contrast to the dolled-up hill towns above the Riviera. Though famous for its pricey product, Grasse's urban center is an unpolished, intriguing collection of walking lanes, peekaboo squares, and vertical staircases. The place feels in need of a graffiti-facelift and a jobs program for its large immigrant population. Grasse is refreshingly real. Its historic alliance with Genoa explains the Italian-esque look of the old city. Still, the only good reasons to visit Grasse are if you care about perfume, or if you're heading to or from the Gorges du Verdon.

Orientation to Grasse

Tourist Information

All sights in Grasse cluster near the main TI in the Palais du Congrès—the stoic white building with peeling paint—on Cours Honoré Cresp, also referred to as Place du Cours (July-mid-Sept Mon-Sat 9:00-19:00, Sun 9:00-18:00; mid-Sept-June Mon-Sat 9:00-12:30 & 14:00-18:00, closed Sun; tel. 04 93 36 66 66, www.grasse.fr). A branch TI (Grasse Espace Accueil) is on Place de la Foux near the bus station. At either TI, pick up an English map with a self-guided tour of the old city (handy information plaques). If heading to the Gorges du Verdon, get specifics here.

Arrival in Grasse

By Train: Fifteen trains a day connect Grasse with Nice (1.25 hours), Antibes (40 minutes), and Cannes (30 minutes). A shuttle bus called FUNIX runs from the train station to the town center every 15 minutes (€1.50 round-trip, none on Sun). Ask the driver to let you off at the stop closest to *Parfumerie Fragonard;* for your return trip, find the shuttle stop at the bus station on Place de la Buanderie.

By Bus: Buses run to the bus station *(gare routière)* on Place de la Buanderie directly from Cannes in 40 minutes and Nice in 1.25 hours. From the bus station it's a five-minute walk to the sights (walk one block straight out of the station to Boulevard du Jeu de Ballon, turn left, and take the pleasant stroll downhill to Cours Honoré Cresp).

By Car: Grasse's size, hilly terrain, and inconsistent signage can confuse drivers. Those coming from Nice (via A-8), Antibes, and Cannes should follow signs to *Centre-Ville* and *Office du Tourisme* (follow *Peymeinade* signs if you lose *Centre-Ville* signs). Soon after passing the golden Fragonard perfume boutique, turn

INLAND RIVIERA

left into the Parking Honoré Cresp. This parking lot's *Sortie Parfumerie* leads you directly to the Fragonard perfume tour. Those arriving from Vence, Gourdon, and the Gorges du Verdon should follow signs to *Centre-Ville* until you see the Espace Napoleon building on your right (pay attention—it's easy to miss). Here, make a hard left and follow signs toward *Nice/Gare S.N.C.F.* and *N-85*), then make an immediate right and park in the underground lot called Nôtre Dame des Fleurs Martelly (€1.70/hour, next to the bus station). Follow the walking directions from the bus station described earlier.

Sights in Grasse

▲International Museum of Perfume
(Musée International de la Parfumerie)

This city museum is a magnificent tribute to perfume, providing a thorough examination of its history and production from ancient Greece to today. The museum is well-designed, with excellent English explanations, a good audioguide, and impressive multimedia exhibits that could keep a perfume fan busy for days. Start in the Sensorial Room, where you'll spend nine minutes getting mellow and preparing your senses for the visit. The three floors below teach you everything there is to know about perfume. Your visit ends with a cool display of perfume packages for every year since 1900 and a chance to sniff 32 key perfume ingredients. Allow at least an hour to see everything.

The museum also offers a self-guided visit to their gardens, Les Jardins du MIP, about five miles from Grasse. The gardens feature 8.5 acres of important plants and flowers used in perfume production (bus service available—schedules at museum).

Cost and Hours: museum—€3, includes audioguide; gardens—€3; €5 combo-ticket includes gardens and round-trip bus; museum—May-Sept daily 10:00-19:00, Sat until 21:00, Oct-April Wed-Mon 11:00-18:00, closed Tue, last entry 45 minutes before closing; gardens—daily May-Sept 10:00-19:00, April and Oct 11:00-18:00, closed Nov-March; museum located a block up from the main TI at 2 Rue Jeu de Ballon, museum tel. 04 97 05 58 00, garden tel. 04 92 98 92 69, www.museesdegrasse.com.

Fragonard Perfume Factory (Visite de l'Usine)

This well-run, functioning factory, located dead-center in Grasse, provides frequent, fragrant, informative 20-minute tours and an interesting "museum" to explore while you wait. Pick up the English brochure describing what's in the museum cases, then drop down to where the tour begins. On your tour you'll learn that the difference between perfume, eau de toilette, and cologne is only a matter of perfume percentages. You'll also learn how the product is

INLAND RIVIERA

Fragrant Grasse

Grasse has been at the center of the fragrance industry since the 1500s, when it was known for its scented leather gloves. The cultivation of aromatic plants around Grasse slowly evolved to produce ingredients for soaps and perfumes, and by the 1800s, Grasse was recognized as the center for perfume (thanks largely to its flower-friendly climate), making it a wealthy city.

It can take a ton of carefully picked petals (like jasmine)—that's about 10,000 flowers—to make about two pounds of essence. A damaged flower petal is bad news. Today, perfumes are made from as many as 500 different scents; most are imported to Grasse from countries around the world. The "blender" of these scents and the perfume mastermind is called the "nose" (who knows best). The five master "noses" who work here must study their profession longer than a doctor goes to med school (seven years). They have to show that they have the gift before entering "nose school" (in Versailles), and they cannot drink alcohol, ever.

Skip the outlying perfumeries with French-only tours. Only three factories out of forty open their doors to visitors, and only one is worth visiting: Fragonard Perfume in Grasse.

---

made today, as well as how they used to do it (by pressing flowers in animal fat). The tour ends with a whiff in the elegant gift shop.

Cost and Hours: Free guided tour, Feb-Oct daily 9:00-18:00 or 18:30, last tour at 17:00 or 18:00, Nov-Jan daily 9:00-12:30 & 14:00-18:00 or 18:30, just off Cours Honoré Cresp at 20 Boulevard Fragonard, tel. 04 93 36 44 65, www.fragonard.com.

Museum of Provençal Costume and Jewelry (Musée Provençal du Costume et du Bijou)

This dimly lit, small museum displays traditional dresses and jewelry from the 18th and 19th centuries. Upon leaving, you'll be given a card that you can exchange for a free gift at a shop next door.

Cost and Hours: Free, daily 10:00-13:00 & 14:00-18:30, closed Sun in winter, a block above the *parfumerie* on the pedestrian street at 2 Rue Jean Ossola, tel. 04 93 36 44 65, www.fragonard .com.

Fragonard Museum (Musée Fragonard)

This air-conditioned, free museum houses paintings by three of Grasse's most famous artists: Jean-Honoré Fragonard, Marguerite Gérard, and Jean-Baptiste Mallet. Ask for the English explanations at the welcome desk.

Cost and Hours: Free, daily 10:00-18:00, just a few doors down from the costume museum, 14 Rue Jean Ossola, tel. 04 93 36 02 07, www.fragonard.com.

Villa Jean-Honoré Fragonard

The home of the 18th-century Baroque painter of swirling big bodies (whose father started the smelly business) has a good collection of his paintings and reproductions.

Cost and Hours: Free, excellent English handout; June-Sept daily 10:00-18:00; Oct and Dec-May Wed-Mon 11:00-18:00, closed Tue and Nov; turn left out of Fragonard Perfume and walk downhill to 23 Boulevard Fragonard, tel. 04 93 36 52 98, www .museesdegrasse.com.

Old Grasse

Just above the Fragonard Perfume museum, Rue Jean Ossola leads into the labyrinthine ancient streets that form an intriguing pedestrian area. To get a good taste of old Grasse, you can follow the TI's minimalist self-guided tour with your map (takes an hour at a speedy pace) or, better, just wander and read the beige information plaques when you see them. Start by strolling up Rue Jean Ossola (just above Boulevard Fragonard), then turn right down Rue Gazan to find the Romanesque cathedral opposite an unusual WWI monument (it's worth peering into the cathedral to see its tree-trunk-like columns and austere decor). Find the view terrace behind the cathedral. From here you can descend many steps to the Italian-esque Place de l'Evêché (fun cafés) and work your way back up. Or skip the steps and double back to Rue Jean Ossola, turn right, then make a left up bohemian Rue de l'Oratoire and pop out onto a lively square, Place aux Aires (with more good eating options).

Le Grand Canyon du Verdon

Two hours north of Nice and three hours east of Avignon lies the Parc Naturel Régional du Verdon (a.k.a. Gorges du Verdon). This

immense area of natural beauty is worth ▲▲▲...even to Arizonans.

For millions of years, the region currently known as Provence-Alpes-Côte d'Azur was covered by the sea. Over time, sediments and the remains of marine animals were deposited here, becoming thick layers of limestone as they were buried. Later, earth movements uplifted and erosion exposed the limestone, and the Verdon River—with help from Ice Age glaciers—carved out the gorges and its side canyons. At their

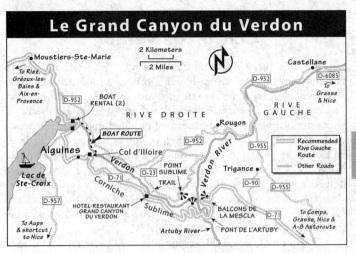

deepest points, the gorges drop 2,200 feet to the river. At the bottom, the canyons narrow to as little as 26 feet across, while at the top, the canyon walls spread as far as 4,700 feet apart.

The Verdon River is named for its turquoise-green hue. The striking color comes from very fine particles of rock suspended in the water, pulverized by glaciers high at the river's source. It's a sight that has inspired visitors since Ligurian Celts ruled the region.

Planning Your Time

The Grand Canyon du Verdon, Europe's greatest canyon, offers a dilly of a detour between the Riviera and Provence (figure seven hours with modest canyon time between Nice and the Luberon or Aix-en-Provence; see my self-guided driving tour of the Inland Riviera on page 477). I prefer to stop and smell the canyon, overnighting en route (suggestions later in this chapter). You can reach the canyon on a very long round-trip drive from the Nice area if you leave early (easier if staying in Vence or Antibes). Take the most direct route to or from the canyon and make it a one-way loop (from Nice take the route via Grasse, tour the canyon in the westbound direction, leave the route just before the Lac de Ste-Croix, and connect to the autoroute back to Nice near Draguignan; details below). The canyon can be overrun with cars in summer and on weekends, but is dead quiet any day in the off-season.

Here are some rough driving times: Riviera to Grasse—1 hour, Grasse to Balcon de la Mescla—1.5 hours, Balcon de la Mescla to Aiguines—1 hour with photo stops, Aiguines to Moustiers-Ste-Marie—20 minutes, Moustiers-Ste-Marie to Manosque (en route to Provence)—1 hour.

Orientation to Le Grand Canyon du Verdon

The Parc Naturel Régional du Verdon, far more than just its famous canyon, is an extensive area mixing alpine scenery with misty villages, meandering streams, and seas of gentle meadows. The canyon is the heart of the park, where overpowering slabs of white and salmon-colored limestone plunge impossible distances to the snaking Verdon River far below. You need a car, ample time, and a lack of vertigo to appreciate this area. If traveling in summer or on holiday weekends, go really early or skip it. Fill your tank before leaving Grasse or Moustiers-Ste-Marie, as gas is scarce. Roads crawl along the length of the canyon on both sides (Rive Gauche and Rive Droite); the Rive Gauche (left bank) works best for most, though both are spectacular.

The Grand Canyon du Verdon is located between the villages of Moustiers-Ste-Marie and Aiguines to the west and Castellane to the east. The most scenic driving segments are along the right (north) bank between Moustiers-Ste-Marie and the Point Sublime overlook, and along the left (south) bank between Aiguines and the Balcon de la Mescla. (Thrill-seekers head for the Castellane area, where the whitewater rafting, climbing, and serious hiking trails are best.) Picnickers will find endless choices for the perfect lunch stop.

The most photogenic stretch of the Grand Canyon's northern side (and arguably both sides) lies along the narrow 23-kilometer loop called the **Route des Crêtes.** It starts one kilometer (.6 miles) north of La Palud-sur-Verdon and does a one-way, clockwise loop back to the village.

Self-Guided Driving Tour

Grand Canyon du Verdon: Rive Gauche (Left Bank)

For drivers connecting the Riviera with Provence via the canyon, the Rive Gauche (left bank) offers the most accessible and most scenic tour of the gorges. Coming from the Riviera, you'll drive the canyon from east to west. The basic route: Drive through Grasse and Digne, then turn off to hit the canyon at the Balcon de la Mescla. After seeing the canyon's most scenic stretch, you can either split off (after Aiguines) to return to the Riviera, or continue through Moustiers-Ste-Marie and on to Provence. (For drivers coming *from* Provence, this tour can be done in reverse, west to east; see "Approaching from Provence," at the end of the tour.)

The Drive Begins

The most direct route from the Riviera follows D-6185, which starts near Cannes (A-8 autoroute from Nice to Cannes saves time) and passes through Grasse, changing to D-6085 and continuing north toward Digne and Castellane. You'll turn left off D-6085 about 20 kilometers before Castellane, following signs to the *Gorges du Verdon* and *Draguignan* (an impressive medieval bridge stands just north of the road, about 3 kilometers before Comps-sur-Artuby, signed *La Souche*). Turn right onto D-71 at Comps-sur-Artuby, following signs to *Gorges du Verdon, Rive Gauche* (not *Rive Droite*). In a few minutes, you'll reach a pullout with a good view of the village of Trigance.

Balcon de la Mescla to Aiguines: Driving along D-71, you'll soon find yourself upon the canyon rim at the Balcon de la Mescla. Stop at **Le Relais de Balcon** café, with a friendly shop that has a good selection of maps and books. The lookout on the lower side of the gift shop/café is best.

From here you'll follow the canyon lip for about 60 serpentine minutes (including stops). You'll drive at an escargot's pace, navigating hairpin turns along the Corniche Sublime while enjoying constant views of rocky masses and vanishing-point views up the canyon. Hikes into the canyon are too long and steep for most (I've described one good hike for determined hikers). Most travelers are better off walking along the main road for a bit or detouring down some of the short paths scattered alongside the road. There are many small pullouts along the route, so stop frequently and get out of that car to allow the driver a look at the views.

A little beyond the Balcon de la Mescla, you can amble across Europe's second highest bridge, the **Pont de l'Artuby,** and imagine working on its construction crew *(non, merci)*. About three kilometers past the bridge is a dirt pullout on the north side of the road. A 10-minute stroll along the path leads to sensational views of the canyon and acres of limestone to scramble over.

About halfway through the canyon is the recommended **Hôtel-Restaurant Grand Canyon du Verdon,** clinging to its cliff like a baby to its mother. This concrete, funky place looks slapped together, but the café terrace has a table for you with stupendous views (drinks, snacks, and meals available at fair prices).

A stone's throw beyond the hotel is your best option for a sturdy **hike:** A posted trail leads all the way down to the river (parking available by the trailhead). It's a steep, challenging, and visually interesting 30 minutes straight down and into the canyon to the Passerelle de l'Estellié, and at least twice that long back up (good shoes and strong ankles are essential, as the rocky trail can be slippery). Once down, you can explore along the river, or cross the footbridge and prowl the right bank. Do this hike earlier in the day—in the afternoon, the high canyon walls can make darkness set in quickly. Once back up, celebrate with a drink on the hotel's terrace café.

Back along the main road, the **Col d'Illoire**—the last pass before leaving the canyon—provides sweeping views from the western portal. Park in the large pullout, where you'll find a few picnic tables scattered above and some good rock-scampering just below.

Aiguines: Just west of the canyon, the small village of Aiguines squats below waves of limestone and overlooks the long turquoise Lac de Ste-Croix. This unspoiled village has a handful of shops, recommended hotels, and cafés. It's an outdoorsy, popular-with-hikers place that most canyon visitors cruise right through. Detour onto the grounds of the 15th-century *château* for the view over Aiguines

(with picnic benches and a fun play area for kids; *château* interior closed to the public). Aiguines' TI is on the main drag (July-Aug Mon-Sat 8:30-18:00, Sun 10:00-12:00 & 14:00-18:00; Sept-June Mon-Fri 9:00-12:00 & 14:00-17:00, closed Sat-Sun; Internet access, Allée des Tilleuls, tel. 04 94 70 21 64, www.aiguines.com).

For more views over Aiguines and the lake, stroll up one of the many staircases along the main drag to the small **Chapelle St. Pierre.** From here, you can walk up the small road five minutes to the campground café, with nice tables on its broad view terrace (ideal for a pre-dinner drink or morning coffee).

Back to the Riveria: If you're day-tripping from the Riviera, follow signs for *Aups* (D-957) as you leave Aiguines, then *Draguignan*, then *Nice* via A-8.

Aiguines to Moustiers-Ste-Marie: If you're continuing to Provençal destinations, head for Moustiers-Ste-Marie and continue the tour below.

Barely more than 30 years old, the man-made **Lac de Ste-Croix** is about six miles long and is the last stop for water flowing out of the Gorges du Verdon. For a fun lake/river experience, rent a canoe or a paddleboat at either side of the low bridge halfway between Moustiers and Aiguines. You can paddle under the bridge, then follow the aquamarine inlet upstream as far as 2.5 miles, tracing the river's route up the gorge on its final journey to the lake (€10/hour for paddle boat or canoe, figure 2 hours for a good trip).

Moustiers-Ste-Marie: Here's another pretty Provençal face lined with boutiques—though this one comes with an impressive setting straddling a small stream at the base of the limestone cliffs of the Gorges du Verdon (best views are from the road that approaches from the west—look for the pullout). The town is slammed with tourists clamoring for the locally famous china. The helpful **TI** is in the center, next to the church (daily 10:00-12:30 & 14:00-18:00, no midday break July-Aug, free Wi-Fi, Place de l'Eglise, tel. 04 92 74 67 84, www .moustiers.fr). Hotel and restaurant recommendations are listed later. Parking is limited and can be difficult, especially in high season. The supermarket **8 à Huit** is at the bottom of the town near the parking lots.

You can escape some of the crowds by climbing 20 minutes on a steep, ankle-twisting path (262 steps) to the **Chapelle Notre-Dame de Beauvoir**—a simple chapel that has attracted pilgrims for centuries. A notebook in the chapel allows travelers to pen a request for a miracle for a loved one. For most, the chapel does not warrant the effort, though you'll get great views over the village by walking a short way up the path.

Moustiers-Ste-Marie to Provence: From here it's another 1.5 to 2 hours to most Provençal destinations. From Moustiers-Ste-Marie, head for Riez, then Gréoux-les-Bains. From Gréoux-les-Bains, follow signs for *Manosque*, then *Apt* for Luberon and Avignon; or use A-51 south to reach Aix-en-Provence, Lourmarin in the Luberon, Cassis, Marseille, or Arles.

Approaching from Provence

Drivers coming from Provence can do the above tour from west to east (Moustiers-Ste-Marie to the Balcon de la Mescla).

All roads from Provence pass through Gréoux-les-Bains, which is about an hour northeast of Aix-en-Provence. Those coming from Cassis, Aix-en-Provence, the southern Luberon, and Arles will find A-51 north the fastest path; those coming from the central Luberon and Avignon should take D-900 via Apt (turns into D-4100), then follow signs for *Manosque*. From Gréoux-les-Bains, follow signs to *Riez, Moustiers-Ste-Marie*, and *Aiguines* before entering the Grand Canyon du Verdon (Rive Gauche).

Leave the canyon after the Balcon de la Mescla. To get to Nice, follow signs for *Comps-sur-Artuby* (and *Draguignan* for a short distance), then *Grasse* and *Nice*. The fastest way from Grasse to Nice is via Cannes and A-8.

If you are staying in or near Vence, or you just haven't had enough breathtaking views, take the shortcut drive up and over the Col de Vence to Vence (not recommended if your destination is Nice or another coastal city). See "Shortcut from Vence to the Gorges du Verdon" on page 479.

Sleeping and Eating near the Grand Canyon du Verdon

These places are listed in the order you'll reach them on the self-guided driving tour from east to west. Notice that, unlike in the rest of this book, some hotel rates in this remote area are for half-pension for two people (including breakfast and dinner for both). Hotels in this area always request that you take half-pension, but it is rarely required outside of high season; I've tried to list room-only prices when available. Budget-minded travelers will find lots of places to picnic in this region, but bring your groceries with you as stores are scarce (grocery stores and bakeries are in Gréoux and Moustiers if coming from the west, but there's not much if coming from the east—stock up before you head out).

Midway Through the Canyon

$$$ Hôtel-Restaurant Grand Canyon du Verdon** is housed in a funky structure that must have been grandfathered in to own such an unbelievable location—2,500 feet high on the Corniche Sublime. In addition to its incredible view terrace, the hotel rents 15 basic, alpine-modern rooms, half on the canyon side (worth reserving ahead) and six with view decks (no-view Db-€125 for 2 people with half-pension, view Db-€140 for 2 people with half-pension—easily worth the added cost; room only: view Db-€95, no-view Db-€85; open mid-April-mid-Oct, easy parking, tel. 04 94 76 91 31, www.hotel-canyon-verdon.com, hotel.gd.canyon.verdon@wanadoo.fr).

In Aiguines

$$$ Hôtel du Vieux-Château**, which has been in business for 200 years, is Aiguines' most characteristic hotel. Run by Frédéric, the hotel's 10 snug rooms are red-tiled, spotless, and cool—literally, as there's little direct light (Db-€110-132 for 2 people with half-pension, Db room only-€64-86, more expensive on weekends, cozy restaurant open daily with simple, hearty fare and good soups, Wi-Fi-€5, Place de la Fontaine, closed Nov-March, tel. 04 94 70 22 95, www.hotelvieuxchateau.fr, contact@hotelvieuxchateau.fr).

$$$ Hôtel Altitude 823**, just below, offers more predictable comfort with less character but better views, with lovely owners

Patrice and Rosélyne at the helm (Db-€120-144 for 2 people with half-pension, Db room only-€86-98, open March-Oct, no air-con, free Wi-Fi, tel. 04 98 10 22 17, www.hotel-altitude823-verdon .com, altitude823@laposte.net).

In Moustiers-Ste-Marie

$$$ La Bonne Auberge** has pastel, no-frills rooms, and a nice pool at the southern edge of the old town (Db-€130-140 for 2 people with half-pension, Db room only-€65-90, extra bed-€17, garage-€6, open April-Oct, route de Castellane, tel. 04 92 74 66 18, www.bonne-auberge-moustiers.com, contact@bonne-auberge -moustiers.com).

    $$ Auberge du Loup is a good value *chambres d'hôte,* a 10-minute walk outside of town. Spirited Edith welcomes guests to her five-bedroom *bastide,* where all rooms come with private patios and comfortable beds (Db-€70-80, extra bed-€20, cash only, includes breakfast, Wi-Fi, free parking, tel. 04 92 74 65 61, mobile 06 03 50 95 52, www.le-mas-du-loup.com, masduloup7 @hotmail.fr).

    $ Restaurant/Chambres Clerissy offers travelers four spacious and spotless rooms. It's good for families. The place has new owners, so prices may change from those listed here (Db-€47, Tb-€57, breakfast-€5, cash only, Place du Chevalier de Blacas, in the village center across from the left transept of the church, mobile 06 33 34 06 95, tel. 04 92 74 62 67, www.clerissy.fr, contact@clerissy.fr).

    Eating: There is no shortage of dining options in Moustiers-Ste-Marie. The simple **Restaurant Clerissy** (whose rooms are listed earlier) offers inexpensive and simple meals (crêpes and pizza) and appealing indoor and outdoor tables. **Côté Jardin** is a haven of quiet a few steps south of the old town, with a pleasing garden setting and good cuisine at fair prices (*menus* from €25, closed Mon evening and all day Tue, tel. 04 92 74 68 91).

INLAND RIVIERA

TRAVELING
with
CHILDREN

With relatively few must-see museums, plenty of outdoor activities, and cooperative weather, Provence and the French Riviera are practically made for kids. This part of France has beaches, fun canoeing on safe rivers, good biking, Roman ruins to scramble over, abundant sunshine, and swimming pools everywhere. Teenagers love the seaside resorts (Cassis is best) and enjoy the hustle and bustle of cities like Avignon, Arles, Aix-en-Provence, and Nice. Younger kids tend to prefer the rural areas, which offer more swimming pools, open spaces, and parks.

Before You Go

Get your kids into the spirit ahead of time using these tips:

- Pick up books at the library and rent videos. Watch or read the Madeline stories by Ludwig Bemelmans, *The Hunchback of Notre-Dame* by Victor Hugo, *The Three Musketeers* by Alexandre Dumas, or Dumas' *The Man in the Iron Mask*. *Anni's Diary of France*, by Anni Axworthy, is a fun, picture-filled book about a young girl's trip; it could inspire your children. *How Would You Survive in the Middle Ages?*, by Fiona MacDonald, is a worthwhile "guide" for kids. Serious kid-historians will devour *The Kingfisher History Encyclopedia*. For a fantastical visit to Avignon in the days of the pope, *The Lady and the Squire* by former Monty Python member Terry Jones is a fun read. If your children are interested in art, get your hands on *The History of Art for Young People* by Anthony Janson and *Discovering Great Artists: Hands-On Art for Children in the Styles of the Great Masters* by MaryAnn Kohl. (Also see the recommended books and movies list, which includes some good choices for teenagers, in this book's appendix.)
- Involve your kids in trip planning. Have them read about the

Parenting French-Style

Famous for their topless tanning, French women are equally comfortable with public breastfeeding of their babies: No need for shawls or "hooter hiders" here. Changing tables are nonexistent, so bring a roll-up changing mat and get comfortable changing your baby on your knees, on a bench, or wherever you find enough space.

French grandmothers take their role as community elders seriously and won't hesitate to recommend that you put more sunscreen on your child in the summer, or add a layer of clothing if it's breezy.

Rather than saying *bonjour* to French children, say *coucou* (coo-coo) if they are young and *salut* (sal-oo) if they are pre-teens or older.

For older kids, be aware that the drinking age is 16 for beer and wine and 18 for the hard stuff: Your waiter will assume that your teen will have wine with you at dinner. Teens are also welcome in most bars and lounges (there's no 21-and-older section).

places that you may include in your itinerary (even the hotels you're considering), and let them help with your decisions.

- Hotel selection is critical. In my recommendations, I've identified hotels that seem particularly kid-friendly (pools, table tennis, grassy areas, easygoing owners, etc.). If you're staying for a week or more in one place, one great option is to rent a *gîte* (see "*Gîtes* and Apartments" on page 36).

What to Bring

Consider packing the following items.

- Children's books in English are scarce and pricey in France. My children read much more when traveling in Europe than while at home, so don't skimp here (see the reading list, earlier). For more portability, consider an ereader.
- Bring peanut butter (hard to find in France)...or help your kids acquire a taste for Nutella, the tasty hazelnut-chocolate spread available everywhere. Look for organic *(bio)* stores in cities where you can find *Chocolade*, a less-sugary version of Nutella, and numerous nut butters.
- Choose items that are small and convenient for use on planes, trains, and in your hotel room: compact travel games, a deck of cards, a handheld video game, a portable media player, or a lightweight laptop, smartphone, or tablet. Bring your own drawing paper, pens, and crayons, as these supplies are pricey in France. A small travel journal and a glue stick make saving museum ticket stubs a fun activity.

- For younger kids, Legos are easily packed and practical (it's also fun to purchase kits in Europe, where the Legos are sometimes different from those in the US).
- Budding fashionistas enjoy traveling with—and buying new outfits for—a Corolle doll or another 16-inch doll. The French have wonderful doll clothes, with a much wider selection than typically found in the US.
- For traveling with younger kids, car-rental agencies usually rent car seats, though you must reserve one in advance (verify the price ahead of time—you may want to bring your own). And though most hotels have some sort of crib, I brought a portable crib and did not regret it.
- Cameras are a great investment to get your kids involved. Give younger kids an old digital camera that you don't use anymore.
- For longer drives, audio books can be fun for the whole family (if carefully chosen). I recommend Peter Mayle's *A Year in Provence*.

Tips

These tips will help your children—and you—have a better trip.

- Lower your sightseeing ambitions and prepare to savor fewer places for longer periods. Plan longer stays at fewer stops—you won't regret it.
- To make your trip fun for everyone in the family, mix heavy-duty sights with kids' activities, such as playing *mini-golfs* or *boules*, renting bikes or canoes, and riding the little tourist trains popular in many towns. Some kids also like audio-guides, available at important sights in many cities.
- Follow this book's crowd-beating tips to a T. Kids despise long lines more than you do.
- Eat dinner early (19:00-19:30 at restaurants, earlier at cafés). Skip romantic eateries. Try relaxed cafés (or fast-food restaurants) where kids can move around without bothering others. Picnics work well.
- For breakfast, croissants are a hit, though a good *pain au chocolat* (croissant with chocolate bits) will be appreciated even more. Hot chocolate, fruit, cereal, and yogurt are usually available. For lunch and dinner, it's easy to find fast-food places and restaurants with kids' menus, or *crêperies*, which have a wide variety of fillings for both savory and dessert crêpes. In the south of France, pizza is omnipresent. For food emergencies, I travel with a plastic container of peanut butter brought from home and smuggle small amounts of jam from breakfast.
- The best and cheapest toy selections are usually in department

stores, like Monoprix and Galeries Lafayette.

- Let kids help choose daily activities, lead you through ancient sights, and so on.
- Give your kids a business card from your hotel, along with your contact information and taxi fare, just in case you get separated.
- Minimize hotel changes by planning three-day stops. Aim for hotels with restaurants, so older kids can go back to the room while you finish a pleasant dinner.
- Homesick kids can keep in touch with friends with cheap international phone cards and email. Wi-Fi hotspots are a godsend for parents with teenagers—you'll find them at hotels, many TIs, some cafés, and all Starbucks and McDonalds. It makes bringing a laptop, smartphone, or tablet worthwhile. Some parents find buying a French mobile phone—or roaming with an American mobile phone—a helpful investment; adults can stay connected to teenagers while allowing them maximum independence (see page 529). If you and your teenager both have mobile phones that work in Europe, sending each other text messages can be a relatively inexpensive way to keep in touch (much cheaper than actual phone calls).
- Kids like the French adventure comics Astérix and Tintin (both available in English, sold in bigger bookstores with English sections).
- If you're in France near Bastille Day, remember that fireworks stands pop up everywhere on the days leading up to July 14. Putting on their own fireworks show can be a highlight for teenagers.
- Swap babysitting duties with your partner if one of you wants to take in an extra sight.
- For memories that will last long after the trip, keep a family journal. Pack a small diary and a glue stick. While relaxing at a café over a *citron-pressé* (lemonade), take turns writing about the day's events and include mementos such as ticket stubs from museums, postcards, or stalks of lavender.

Top Kids' Sights and Activities

Attractions

These are listed in no particular order:

- Pont du Gard. An entire wing of the museum is dedicated to kids, who can also swim or take a canoe trip on the river nearby (see page 169).
- Cassis. Boat trip to the *calanques* or the port and beaches for teenagers (see page 282).
- Monaco. Changing of the Guard in Monaco (11:55 daily, see

TRAVELING WITH CHILDREN

page 433) and Cousteau Aquarium (see page 435).

- Pedal boats on the Mediterranean (see page 286) and into the Gorges du Verdon (see page 498).
- Biking through vineyards to small villages, from Vaison la Romaine (see page 195).
- Les Baux's castle ruins, with medieval weaponry and great walls to climb (see page 106).
- Canoeing on the Ardèche River (see page 217), the Sorgue River (see page 227), or into the Gorges du Verdon (see page 498).
- Boat trips from Nice (see page 337), Villefranche-sur-Mer (see page 401), or St-Tropez (see page 472).
- Biking or in-line skating on the Promenade des Anglais in Nice (see page 334).
- Marineland near Antibes (see page 457).

Honorable mention goes to Arles' Ancient History Museum (see page 77), horseback riding and public beaches in the Camargue (see page 125), Roman arenas in Nîmes (see page 160) and Arles (see page 85), the beaches of Antibes (see page 455), and the narrow-gauge train ride from Nice (see page 348).

Activities

Movies

It's fun to take kids to movies (even if not in English) just to see how theaters work elsewhere. Movies shown in their original language—usually with subtitles—are listed as *v.o.* at the box office. (One showing could be *v.o.* and the next could be dubbed in French, labeled *v.f.*; be aware that *v.o.* movies are hard to find outside major cities.) *Dessin animé* means "cartoon." While many live-action movies can be found in their original language with French subtitles, cartoons and kids' movies (intended for an audience that doesn't read so well yet) are almost always dubbed.

Swimming

I've listed swimming pools in many places—they're great for kids. But be warned: Public pools in France commonly require a small, Speedo-like bathing suit for boys and men (American-style swim trunks won't do)—though they usually have these little suits to loan. At hotel pools, any type of swimsuit will do.

Rides

You'll find old-style merry-go-rounds in many cities, perfect for younger travelers (my daughter's goal was to ride a merry-go-round in every town...she came close). There are also little tourist trains in nearly every city.

Farms

Visits to local goat-cheese-makers in early spring yield good kid rewards (look for *fromage fermier de chèvre* signs along the country roads). Goats are social animals and goat-cheese makers will usually let your child hold or pet one. You can also pick up some superb fresh cheese for your picnic.

Boules

Consider buying a set of *boules* (a.k.a. *pétanque*, a form of outdoor bowling—for the rules, see sidebar on page 10). Play *boules* before dinner, side by side with real players on the village court. Get your *boules de pétanque* at sporting-goods stores or larger department stores. Since they're heavy, buy a set only if you'll be driving. The *boules* also make fun, if weighty, souvenirs, and are just as enjoyable to play back at home.

SHOPPING

Provence and the Riviera offer France's best shopping outside of Paris, with a great range of reasonably priced items ideal for souvenirs and gifts. And if approached thoughtfully, shopping in the south of France can be a culturally enlightening experience. There's no better way to mix serious shopping business with travel pleasure than at the weekly markets *(marchés)* in towns and villages throughout the region. These traditional market days offer far more than fresh produce and fish; in many cases, about half the market is devoted to durable goods (baskets, tablecloths, pottery, and fabrics)—*très* handy for gift-scavenging travelers. If you miss market day, most Provençal towns have more than enough small shops that sell local products—and more than enough kitschy souvenirs. (They're often selling the same items you can find more cheaply at weekly markets.) If you crave French fashion, the cities described in this book have unlimited boutique shopping for clothing.

In this chapter you'll find information on shopping for souvenirs, navigating market days, and browsing boutiques. For information on VAT refunds and customs regulations, see page 23. For a comparison of French to US clothing sizes, see the appendix.

What to Buy

Here's a shopping list of locally made goods in Provence and the Riviera. You'll find most of these items in tourist-oriented boutiques, though many of them can be had for less on market days. If you buy more expensive, nonperishable goods, most stores will work with you to send them home.

- **Jams** *(confiture)* containing lush and often exotic fruits, such as *fruits de passion* (passion fruit), *figues* (figs), and *pastèque* or *citre* (different types of watermelon).
- **Honey** *(miel)*, particularly lavender *(lavande)* or rosemary

(romarin). Stronger palates should try the chestnut *(châtaigne)* or even oak-flavored *(chêne)* honey.

- Tins of **tapenade** (olive paste) and all kinds of **olives:** black, green, and stuffed with garlic or anchovies.

- **Olive-wood products** such as utensils and bowls. Olives are not just for nibbling; in Provence, the entire tree is used.

- Canned **pâtés,** including the buttery, rich foie gras (its "home" is Périgord, but you'll also find it in the markets of Provence). Canned goose, duck, and pork pâté can be imported to the US, but not beef.

- Packets of **herbs** (including the famous *herbes de Provence*), **salt** from the Camargue (look for *Fleur de Sel* for the best, and use sparingly), and bottles or tins of **olive oil** from local trees (Nyons is France's olive capital, though Les Baux is rightly proud of its olives as well). Most of these items can be found in attractive packaging that can be saved and enjoyed long after the product itself is gone.

- Sweets, including the famous *nougat de Montélimar* (a rich, chewy confection made with nuts and honey and sometimes flavored with lavender or other fragrances), *calissons* (orange-and-almond-flavored candy, shaped like the nut and originally from Aix-en-Provence), and **chocolates** from the Provençal producer Puyricard.

- **Soaps and lotions,** particularly those "perfumed" with local plants such as lavender *(lavande)*, rosemary *(romarin)*, or linden *(tilleul)*. You'll also find colorful **sachets** containing the same fragrances.

- Brightly colored **table linens.** Souleiado and Les Olivades are the most famous local manufacturers, but good-quality knockoffs can be found in most any market or store.

- **Cloth bags** with French designs for grocery shopping (these pack easily and cost pennies).

- Local **pottery** (*poterie; faïence* is hand-painted *poterie*). Terre Provence is a well-known (and pricey) brand, but many other producers offer excellent quality, usually for less. Serious potters can plan ahead to visit a pottery fair featuring the best of the regions' potters (calendar at http://artceramistes.free.fr /marches/Provence).

- *Santons,* the tiny, brightly adorned clay or wood Provençal figurines. Originally designed for traditional Christmas crèche scenes, today's *santons* ("little saints") represent all walks of life—from the local *boulanger* to the woman sewing bright Provençal cloth to the village doctor. The most famous *santon* makers are in Séguret and Aubagne. All *santon* makers belong to the *santon*-maker guild (think medieval stonecutters or woodworkers), and each *santon* is handmade and signed.

Market Day *(Jour du Marché)*

Market days are a big deal throughout France, and in no other region are they more celebrated than in Provence and the Riviera.

Markets have been a central feature of life in rural areas since the Middle Ages. No single event better symbolizes the French preoccupation with fresh products, and their strong ties to the small farmer, than the weekly market. Many locals mark their calendars with the arrival of the new season's produce.

Provence is a Mediterranean melting pot, where Italy, Spain, and North Africa intersect with France to do business. Notice the ethnic mix of the vendors (and the products they sell). Spices from Morocco and Tunisia, fresh pasta from Italy, saffron from Spain, and tapenade from Provence compete for your attention at Provence's *marchés*.

There are two kinds of weekly open-air markets: *les marchés* and *les marchés brocantes*.

Les marchés are more general in scope, more common, and more colorful, featuring products from area farmers and artisans. These markets can offer a mind-boggling array of choices, from the perishable (produce, meats, cheeses, breads, and pastries) to the nonperishable (kitchen wares, inexpensive clothing, brightly colored linens, and pottery).

Les marchés brocantes specialize in quasi-antiques and flea-market bric-a-brac. *Brocantes* markets began in the Middle Ages, when middlemen would gather to set up small stalls and sell old, flea-infested clothes and the discarded possessions of the wealthy at bargain prices to eager peasants. Buyers were allowed to *rummage* through piles of aristocratic garbage.

Many *marchés* have good selections of produce and some *brocantes*. The best of all market worlds may rest in the town of Isle-sur-la-Sorgue, where, on Sunday mornings, a brilliant food *marché* tangles with an active flea market and a good selection of antiques.

I've listed days and locations for both market types throughout this book. Notice the signs as you enter towns indicating the *jours du marché* (essential information to any civilized soul, and a reminder not to park on the streets the night before—be on the lookout for *stationnement interdit* signs that mark "no parking" areas). Most *marchés* take place once a week in the town's main square; larger *marchés* spill into nearby streets.

Usually, the bigger the market, the greater the overall selection, particularly for nonperishable goods. Bigger towns (like Arles) may have two weekly markets, one a bit larger than the other, with more nonperishable goods; in other towns (including Isle-sur-la-Sorgue), the second weekly market simply may be a smaller version of the main market day. The biggest market days are usually on weekends, so that everyone can go. In the largest cities (such as Avignon and Nîmes), modern market halls have been established, with produce stands and meat counters selling fresh goods daily.

Market day is as important socially as commercially—it's a weekly chance for locals to resume friendships and get the current gossip. Here neighbors can catch up on Henri's barn renovation, see photos of Jacqueline's new grandchild, and relax over *un café*. Dogs are tethered to café tables while friends exchange kisses. Tether yourself to a table and observe: three cheek-kisses for good friends (left-right-left), a fourth for friends you haven't seen in a while. (The appropriate number of kisses varies by region—Paris, Lyon, and Provence have separate standards.)

Markets begin at about 8:00, with setup commencing in the predawn hours (for some, a reason not to stay in a main-square hotel the night before market day). They usually end by 13:00. Most perishable items are sold directly from the producers—no middlemen, no credit cards, just really fresh produce (*du pays* means "grown locally"). Sometimes you'll meet a widow selling a dozen eggs, two rabbits, and a wad of herbs tied with string. But most vendors follow a weekly circuit of markets they feel works best for them, showing up in the same spot every week, year in and year out. At a favorite market, my family has done business with the same olive vendor and "cookie man" for 20 years.

It's bad form to be in a hurry on market day. Allow the crowd to set your pace. Observe the interaction between vendor and client. Notice the joy they can find in chatting each other up. Wares are displayed with pride. Generally the rule is "don't touch"—instead, point and let them serve you. If self-serve is the norm, the seller will hand you a bag. Remember, they use metric weight. Ask for *un kilo* (about 2 pounds), *un demi-kilo* (about 1 pound—also called *une livre*), or *un quart-kilo* (pronounced "car-kilo," about half a pound). Many vendors speak enough English to assist you in your selection. Your total price will be hand-tallied on small scraps of paper and given to you. Vendors are normally honest. If you're struggling to find the correct change, just hold out your hand and they will take only what is needed. (Still, you're wise to double-check the amount you just paid for that olive tree.)

At the root of a good market experience is a sturdy shopping basket or bag. Find the vendor selling baskets and other wicker

Key Shopping Phrases

English	French	Pronounced
Just looking.	*Je regarde.*	zhuh ruh-garde
How much is it?	*Combien?*	kohm-bee-ehn
Too big / small / expensive	*Trop grand / petit/cher*	troh grahn / puh-tee/sher
May I try it on?	*Je peux l'essayer?*	zhuh puh luh-say-yay
Can I see more?	*Puis-je en voir d'autres?*	pweezh ehn vwahr doh-truh
I'll think about it.	*Je vais y penser.*	zhuh vayz-ee pahn-say
I'd like this.	*Je voudrais ça.*	zhuh voo-dray sah
on sale	*solde*	sold-ay
discounted price	*prix réduit*	pree ray-dwee
big discounts	*prix choc*	pree shock

items and go local (*osier* is the French name for wicker, *cade* is the Provençal name—from the basket-making Luberon village of Cadenet); you can also find plastic and nylon versions. Most baskets are inexpensive, make for fun and colorful souvenirs, and can come in handy for odd-shaped or breakable carry-ons for the plane trip home. With basket in hand, shop for your heaviest items first. (You don't want to put a kilo of fresh apples on top of the bread you bought for your picnic.)

Markets change seasonally. In April and May, look for asparagus (green, purple, or the prized white—after being cooked, these are dipped in vinegar or homemade mayonnaise and eaten by hand). In late spring, shop for strawberries, including the best: *fraises des bois* (wild strawberries). Almost equally prized are the strawberries called *gariguettes* and *maras des bois*. Soon after, you'll see cherries and other stone fruits, plus the famously sweet Cavaillon melons (resembling tiny cantaloupes, often served cut in half with a spoonful or two of the sweet Rhône white wine Beaumes de Venise). Don't worry if these are split open—the abundance of sugar and sunshine are the cause, and the *fendus* are considered the sweetest. In late June and early September, watch for figs (*figues*). From July through September, essential vegetables for the Provençal dish ratatouille—including eggplant, tomatoes, zucchinis, and peppers—come straight from the open fields. In the fall you'll see stands selling game birds, other beasts of the hunt, and a glorious array of wild mushrooms.

After November and throughout the winter, look for little (or big, depending on your wallet size) black truffles. Truffles preserved and sealed in jars can safely be brought back to the United States. The Luberon is one of Provence's largest truffle-producing areas. The town of Carpentras hosts a truffles-only market on Friday mornings in winter, off the main roundabout in front of a café. Listen carefully and you might hear the Provençal language being spoken between some vendors and buyers. Richerenches, Northern Provence's truffle capital, holds its own winter truffle market; during its annual truffle-themed Mass, many parishioners give a truffle as a small offering, instead of money. *Vive la France.*

For more immediate consumption, look for local cheeses (cow, called *vache;* sheep or ewe, called *brebis;* or the Provençal favorite: goat cheese, or chèvre, named *picodons*). Cheeses range from very fresh (aged one day) to aged for weeks. The older the cheese, the more dried and shrunken. Some may even be speckled with edible mold. Cheeses come in many shapes (round, logs, pyramids) and various sizes (from single-bite mouthfuls to wheels that will feed you for several meals). Some are sprinkled with herbs or spices. Others are more adorned, such as those rolled in ash *(à la cendre)* or wrapped in leaves *(banon)*. Watch for the locally produced *banon de banon,* a goat cheese soaked in *eau-de-vie* (the highly alcoholic "water of life"), then wrapped in chestnut leaves and tied with string—*ooh la la*.

Next, move on to the sausages (many also rolled in herbs or spices). Samples are usually free—try the *sanglier* (boar). Be on the lookout for locally produced wines or ciders (free tastings are standard) and find samples of foie gras (available in take-it-home tins), good with the sweet white wine of Beaumes de Venise. These items make perfect picnic fare when teamed with a crusty baguette.

Throughout Provence you'll see vendors selling paella made *sur place* (on the spot) in huge traditional round pans. Paella varies by area and chef, but most recipes include the traditional ingredients of fresh shellfish, chicken, and sausages mixed into saffron-infused rice. And throughout France you'll see vans selling sizzling, spit-roasted chicken (perfectly bagged for carrying-out) or pizza (made to your liking on the spot). *Bon appétit!*

Clothing Boutiques

Those preferring fashion over food will be happy to learn that they don't have to go to Paris to enjoy the latest trends. The stylish boutiques lining the shopping streets of Avignon, Nîmes, Aix-en-Provence, St. Rémy, Uzès, Nice, and the ultra-trendy Juan-les-Pins offer more than sufficient selection and style for the fashion-conscious. Still, they play by a different set of rules in France, and the better knowledge you have of the rules, the better player you'll be. While many shopkeepers speak some English, an effort to speak even a minimum of French earns better service. These tips should get you off on the right track:

- In small stores, always say, *"Bonjour, Madame* or *Mademoiselle* or *Monsieur"* when entering. And remember to say *"Au revoir, Madame/Mademoiselle/Monsieur"* when leaving.
- The customer is not always right; in fact, some clerks figure they're doing you a favor by waiting on you.
- Except in department stores, it's not normal for the customer to handle clothing. Ask first before you pick up an item: *"Je peux?"* (zhuh puh), meaning, "Can I?"
- By law the price of items in a window display must be visible, often written on a slip of paper set on the floor or framed on the wall. This gives you an idea of how expensive or affordable the shop is.
- For clothing-size comparisons between the US and France, see the appendix.
- Forget returns (and don't count on exchanges).
- Observe French shoppers, then imitate them.
- Saturday afternoons are *très* busy and not for the faint of heart.
- Stores are closed on Sunday and usually on Monday mornings.
- Don't feel obliged to buy. If a shopkeeper offers assistance, just say, *"Je regarde, merci,"* meaning, "Just looking, thanks."

SHOPPING

FRANCE: PAST and PRESENT

French History in an Escargot Shell

About the time of Christ, Romans "Latinized" the land of the Gauls. With the fifth-century A.D. fall of Rome, the barbarian Franks and Burgundians invaded. Today's France evolved from this unique mix of Latin and Celtic cultures.

While France wallowed with the rest of Europe in medieval darkness, it got a head start in its development as a nation-state. In 507, Clovis, the king of the Franks, established Paris as the capital of his Christian Merovingian dynasty. Clovis and the Franks would eventually become Louis and the French. The Frankish military leader Charles Martel stopped the spread of Islam by beating the Spanish Moors at the Battle of Poitiers in 732. And Charlemagne, the most important of the "Dark Age" Frankish kings, was crowned Holy Roman Emperor by the pope in 800. Charles the Great presided over the "Carolingian Renaissance" and effectively ruled an empire that was vast for its time.

The Treaty of Verdun (843), which divided Charlemagne's empire among his grandsons, marks what could be considered the birth of Europe. For the first time, a treaty was signed in vernacular languages (French and German), rather than in Latin. This split established a Franco-Germanic divide and heralded an age of fragmentation. While petty princes took the reigns, the Frankish king ruled only Ile de France, a small region around Paris.

Vikings, or Norsemen, settled in what became Normandy. Later, in 1066, these "Normans" invaded England. The Norman king, William the Conqueror, consolidated his English domain, accelerating the formation of modern England. But his rule also muddied the political waters between England and France, kicking off a centuries-long struggle between the two nations.

Typical Church Architecture

History comes to life when you visit a centuries-old church. Even if you wouldn't know your apse from a hole in the ground, learning a few simple terms will enrich your experience. Note that not every church has every feature, and a "cathedral" isn't a type of church architecture, but rather a designation for a church that's a governing center for a local bishop.

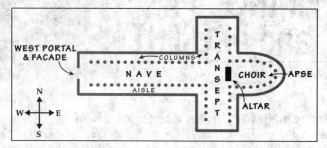

Aisles: The long, generally low-ceilinged arcades that flank the nave.

Altar: The raised area with a ceremonial table (often adorned with candles or a crucifix), where the priest prepares and serves the bread and wine for Communion.

Apse: The space beyond the altar, generally bordered with small chapels.

Barrel Vault: A continuous round-arched ceiling that resembles an extended upside-down U.

Choir: A cozy area, often screened off, located within the church nave and near the high altar where services are sung in a more intimate setting.

Cloister: Covered hallways bordering a (usually square-shaped) open-air courtyard, traditionally where monks and nuns got fresh air.

Facade: The exterior surface of the church's main (west) entrance, usually highly decorated.

Groin Vault: An arched ceiling formed where two equal barrel vaults meet at right angles. Less common usage: term for a medieval jock strap.

Narthex: The area (portico or foyer) between the main entry and the nave.

Nave: The long, central section of the church (running west to east, from the entrance to the altar) where the congregation sits or stands through the service.

Transept: In a traditional cross-shaped floor plan, the transept is one of the two parts forming the "arms" of the cross. The transepts run north-south, perpendicularly crossing the east-west nave.

West Portal: The main entry to the church (on the west end, opposite the main altar).

In the 12th century, Eleanor of Aquitaine (a separate country in southwest France) married Louis VII, king of France, bringing Aquitaine under French rule. They divorced, and she married Henry of Normandy, soon to be Henry II of England. This marital union gave England control of a huge swath of land, from the English Channel to the Pyrenees. For 300 years France and England would struggle for control of Aquitaine. Any enemy of the French king would find a natural ally in the English king.

In 1328, the French king Charles IV died without a son. The English king (Edward III), Charles IV's nephew, was interested in the throne, but the French resisted. This quandary pitted France, the biggest and richest country in Europe, against England, which had the largest army. They fought from 1337 to 1453 in what was modestly called the Hundred Years' War.

Regional powers from within France actually sided with England. Burgundy took Paris, captured the royal family, and recognized the English king as heir to the French throne. England controlled France from the Loire north, and things looked bleak for the French king.

Enter Joan of Arc, a 16-year-old peasant girl driven by religious voices. France's national heroine left home to support Charles VII, the dauphin (boy prince, heir to the throne but too young to rule). Joan rallied the French, ultimately inspiring them to throw out the English. In 1430 Joan was captured by the Burgundians, who sold her to the English, who convicted her of heresy and burned her at the stake in Rouen. But the inspiration of Joan of Arc lived on, and by 1453 English holdings on the Continent had dwindled to the port of Calais.

By 1500 a strong, centralized France had emerged, with borders similar to those of today. Its kings (from the Renaissance François I through the Henrys and all those Louises) were model divine monarchs, setting the standard for absolute rule in Europe.

Outrage over the power plays and spending sprees of the kings—coupled with the modern thinking of the Enlightenment (whose leaders were the French *philosophes*)—led to the French Revolution (1789). In France it was the end of the *ancien régime*, as well as its notion that some are born to rule, while others are born to be ruled.

The excesses of the Revolution in turn led to the rise of Napoleon, who ruled the French empire as a dictator. Eventually, *his* excesses ushered him into a South Atlantic exile, and after another half-century of monarchy and empire, the French settled on a compromise role for their leader. The modern French "king" is ruled by a constitution. Rather than dress in leotards and powdered wigs, the president goes to work in a suit and carries a briefcase.

The 20th century spelled the end of France's reign as a military

PAST AND PRESENT

Top French Notables in History

Madame and Monsieur Cro-Magnon: Prehistoric hunter-gatherers who moved to France (c. 30,000 B.C.), painted cave walls at Lascaux and Font-de-Gaume, and eventually settled down as farmers (c. 10,000 B.C.).

Vercingétorix (72-46 B.C.): This long-haired warrior rallied the Gauls against Julius Caesar's invading Roman legions (52 B.C.). Defeated by Caesar, France fell under Roman domination, resulting in 500 years of peace and prosperity. During that time, the Romans established cities, built roads, taught in Latin, and converted people to Christianity.

Charlemagne (742-814): For Christmas in 800, the pope gave King Charlemagne the title of Emperor, thus uniting much of Europe under the leadership of the Franks ("France"). Charlemagne stabilized France amid centuries of barbarian invasions. After his death, the empire was split, carving the outlines of modern France and Germany.

Eleanor of Aquitaine (c. 1122-1204): The beautiful, sophisticated ex-wife of the King of France married the King of England, creating an uneasy union between the two countries. During her lifetime, French culture was spread across Europe by roving troubadours, theological scholars, and skilled architects pioneering "the French style"—a.k.a. Gothic.

Joan of Arc (1412-1431): When France and England fought the Hundred Years' War to settle who would rule (1337-1453), teenager Joan of Arc—guided by voices in her head—rallied the French troops. Though Joan was captured and burned as a heretic, the French eventually drove England out of their country for good, establishing the current borders. Over the centuries, the church upgraded Joan's status from heretic to saint (canonized in 1920).

François I (1494-1547): This Renaissance king ruled a united, modern nation, making it a cultural center that hosted the Italian Leonardo da Vinci. François set the tone for future absolute monarchs, punctuating his commands with the phrase, "For such is our pleasure."

Louis XIV (1638-1715): Charismatic and cunning, the "Sun King" ruled Europe's richest, most populous, most powerful nation-state. Every educated European spoke French, dressed in Louis-style leotards and powdered wigs, and built Versailles-like palaces. Though Louis ruled as an absolute monarch (distracting the nobility with courtly games), his reign also fostered the arts and philosophy, sowing the seeds of democracy and revolution.

Marie Antoinette (1755-1793): As the Austrian-born wife of Louis XVI, she came to symbolize (probably unfairly) the decadence of France's ruling class. When the Revolution broke out (1789), she was arrested, imprisoned, and executed—one of thousands who were guillotined on Paris' Place de la Concorde as an enemy of the people.

Napoleon Bonaparte (1769-1821): This daring young military man became a hero during the Revolution, fighting Europe's royalty. He went on to conquer much of the Continent, become leader of France, and, eventually, rule as a dictator with the title of Emperor. In 1815 an allied Europe defeated and exiled Napoleon, reinstating the French monarchy—though future kings and emperors (including Napoleon's nephew, who ruled as Napoleon III) were somewhat subject to democratic constraints.

Claude Monet (1840-1926): Monet's Impressionist paintings captured the soft-focus beauty of the belle époque—middle-class men and women enjoying drinks in cafés, walks in gardens, and picnics along the Seine. At the turn of the 20th century, French culture reigned supreme while its economic and political clout was fading, soon to be shattered by the violence of World War I.

Charles de Gaulle (1890-1970): A career military man, de Gaulle helped France survive occupation by Nazi Germany during World War II with his rousing radio broadcasts and unbending faith in his countrymen. He left politics in the postwar period, but after France's divisive wars in Vietnam and Algeria, he came to the rescue, becoming president of the Fifth Republic in 1959. De Gaulle shocked supporters and allies by granting Algeria its independence, blocking Britain's entry into the Common Market, and withdrawing from the military wing of NATO. Turbulent student riots in the late 1960s eventually led to his resignation in 1969.

Contemporary French: Which recent French people will history remember? President François Mitterrand (1916-1996), the driving force behind Paris' La Grande Arche and Opéra Bastille? Marcel Marceau (1923-2007), white-faced mime? Chef Paul Bocuse (b. 1926), inventor of nouvelle cuisine? Brigitte Bardot (b. 1934), film actress, crusader for animal rights, and popularizer of the bikini? Yves Saint Laurent (1936-2008), one of the world's greatest fashion designers? Jean-Marie Le Pen (b. 1928), founder of the far-right National Front party, with staunch anti-immigration policies? Bernard Kouchner (b. 1939), co-founder of Doctors Without Borders and minister of foreign affairs under President Nicolas Sarkozy? Zinédine Zidane (b. 1972), France's greatest ever soccer player, whose Algerian roots helped raise the status of Arabs in France? Or Dominique Strauss-Kahn (b. 1949), disgraced International Monetary Fund chief? (I hope not.)

and political superpower. Devastating wars with Germany in 1870, 1914, and 1940—and the loss of her colonial holdings—left France with not quite enough land, people, or production to be a top player on a global scale. But the 21st century may see France rise again: Paris is a cultural capital of Europe, and France—under the EU banner—is a key player in unifying Europe as a single economic power. And when Europe becomes a superpower, Paris may yet be its capital.

Contemporary Politics in France

Today, the main political issue in France is—like everywhere— the economy. Initially, France weathered the 2008 downturn better than the US, because it was less invested in risky home loans and the volatile stock market. But France, along with the rest of Europe, is now struggling. French unemployment remains high (over 10 percent) and growth has flat-lined. France has not balanced its books since 1974, and public spending, at 56 percent of GDP, chews up a bigger chunk of output than in any other Eurozone country. Abroad, the entire Eurozone is being dragged down by countries heavily in debt—Greece, Spain, Portugal, Italy, and Ireland. The challenge for French leadership is to address its economic problems while maintaining the high level of social services that the French people expect from their government.

France has its economic strengths: a well-educated workforce, an especially robust services sector and high-end manufacturing industry, and more firms big enough to rank in the global *Fortune* 500 than any other European country. Ironically, while France's economy may be one of the world's largest, the French remain skeptical about the virtues of capitalism and the work ethic. Business conversation is generally avoided, as it implies a fascination with money that the French find vulgar. (It's considered gauche even to ask what someone does for a living.) In France, CEOs are not glorified as celebrities—chefs are.

The French believe that the economy should support social good, not vice versa. This has produced a cradle-to-grave social security system of which the French are proud. France's poverty rate is half of that in the US, proof to the French that they are on the right track. On the other hand, if you're considering starting a business in France, think again—taxes are formidable (figure a total small-business tax rate of around 66 percent) and likely to increase. French voters are notorious for their belief in the free market's heartless cruelty, and they tend to see globalization as a threat rather than a potential benefit. France is routinely plagued with strikes, demonstrations, and slowdowns as workers try to preserve their hard-earned rights in the face of a competitive global economy.

France is part of the 28-member European Union, a kind of "United States of Europe" that has dissolved borders and implemented a common currency, the euro. France's governments have been decidedly pro-EU. But many French are Euroskeptics, afraid that EU meddling threatens their job security and social benefits.

The French political scene is complex and fascinating. France is governed by a president (currently François Hollande) who is elected by popular vote every five years. The president then selects the prime minister, who in turn chooses the cabinet ministers. Collectively, this executive branch is known as the *gouvernement*. The parliament consists of a Senate (343 seats) and the 577-seat Assemblée Nationale.

In France, compromise and coalition-building are essential to keeping power. Unlike America's two-party system, France has a half-dozen major political parties, plus more on the fringes. A simple majority is rare. Even the biggest parties rarely get more than a third of the votes. Since the parliament can force the *gouvernement* to resign at any time, it's essential that the *gouvernement* work with them.

For a snapshot of the current political landscape, look no further than the 2012 presidential elections. The various parties all chose a candidate. Incumbent president Nicolas Sarkozy headed the center-right Popular Movement Union (UMP). He defended his tough-love, carrot-and-stick approach to dealing with the sluggish economy. During his tenure, he cut taxes, reduced the size of government, limited the power of unions, cut workers' benefits, and (most controversially) raised the retirement age from 60 to 62. He also offered tax incentives to those who worked overtime (above the current 35- to 39-hour workweek).

Opposing Sarkozy were a host of left-leaning candidates. François Hollande, of the center-left Socialist Party (PS), pointed out that Sarkozy's austerity policies were not working. The more-radical Left Front Party (which includes the once-powerful Communists) proposed raising the minimum wage to $2,200 a month and establishing a "maximum wage" of $500,000, beyond which you pay 100 percent taxes. The environmental Green Party (Les Verts) promised to stimulate the economy with half a million new green jobs.

On the far right was the National Front party (FN), led by Marine Le Pen, daughter of party founder Jean-Marie Le Pen. The FN campaigned on a "France for the French" platform, calling for expulsion of ethnic minorities, restoration of the French franc as the standard currency, secession from the EU, and broader police powers. Marine Le Pen studiously avoided the kind of anti-Semitic, racist rants that have made her father notorious in France.

Trouble in Paradise: Population Growth in Southern France

Life is not as perfect as it may appear amid the breezy, sun-kissed beaches, cities, and villages of Provence and the French Riviera. The south of France has become a bouillabaisse of people in search of their Provençal paradise. While some say the influx into this region has invigorated the culture, many residents are feeling growing pains. Two major trends are fueling the population boom in the south: northern Europeans looking for their place in the sun, and North African immigrants looking for a better life in France. These trends are converging in southern France.

Cheap flights and lightning-fast train service have enabled northern Europeans to experience the south of France as a weekend getaway...and a growing number are choosing to stay. Thanks to its sunny climate, relatively inexpensive homes (if you're from northern Europe), and plentiful transportation options, this region is an understandably big draw. Unfortunately, as wealthy northerners pick off local homes and inflate prices, the average Jean is losing out.

Immigration, particularly from North Africa, is another cause of the population boom. With the historic loss of able-bodied men from World Wars I and II, and native-French birth rates unable to replace those losses, France looked across the Mediterranean to its old colonies for cheap sources of manual labor. When these workers came, they brought their families, who stayed in France and had families of their own (sound familiar?). Today, France has Europe's second-largest Muslim population—only Russia's is greater.

Five million North Africans legally reside in France—and many more live here illegally. Around 100,000 illegal immigrants arrive in France each year, about half of whom are North African. Most live in the south (more than a quarter of Marseille's population is North African). This concentration of immigrants among a very Catholic French population (Muslims outnumber Protestants 2 to 1), combined with high unemployment (nearly 20 percent compared to a national average of around 10 percent), has led to the rise of racist politics. This anti-immigrant movement has been spearheaded by the National Front party, which wants to keep "France for the French." Its founder, Jean-Marie Le Pen, has referred to the growing numbers of North Africans in France as "the silent invasion." The National Front generally receives about 20 percent of this region's vote in national elections.

After several months and one TV debate (yes, the French election season is that short), François Hollande and the Socialists emerged victorious. And just one month after the presidential election, French voters returned to the polls to select all 577 seats of the Assemblée Nationale. Though it's almost unheard of for a single party to win an outright majority of seats, that's exactly what the Socialists did, eking out just over 50 percent. Other leftist parties also scored well, giving President Hollande a leftist mandate for change. Nevertheless, Hollande has to work closely with legislators, a strong minority of whom are from opposing parties.

François Hollande is politically moderate and personally modest, even boring. Raised in a middle-class home in suburban Paris, he rose quietly through the ranks: assemblyman from a nondescript *department*, small-town mayor, secretary of the Socialist Party. He's never before held a major elected office. Though Hollande is a "Socialist" (a word that spooks Rush Limbaugh), he's in the mainstream of the European political spectrum. France's "Première Dame" is Valerie Trierweiler, a well-known journalist who writes for the glossy magazine *Paris Match* (the French counterpart to *Time*). Trierweiler is the first unwed first lady to occupy the Elysée Palace (French White House). *Oh-la-la*—imagine that in the States.

Hollande faces huge challenges. On the sluggish economy, he favors government expansion and stimulus rather than austerity: hiring thousands of teachers, building hundreds of thousands of homes, and taxing all income above a million euros at 75 percent. Abroad, he's run into trouble working with Germany to shore up weaker members of the Eurozone. And he's had to abandon his promise to return the retirement age—at least for some workers—to 60.

France must also address immigration, which is shifting the country's ethnic and cultural makeup. Ten percent of France's population is of North African descent, mainly immigrants from former colonies. The increased number of Muslims raises more questions, particularly in tight economic times. The French have (quite controversially) made it illegal for women to wear a full, face-covering veil *(niqāb)* in public. They continue to debate whether banning the veil enforces democracy—or squelches diversity.

Finally, Hollande must deal with high-profile members of his own turbulent party. In the run-up to the 2012 election, the front-runner was former International Monetary Fund chief Dominique Strauss-Kahn. He was forced to drop out after being accused of sexual assault in New York City. All charges were later dropped, but he agreed to an out-of-court settlement with the hotel worker. Then he was investigated for a string of sex parties with prostitutes—one newspaper called him a "pimp daddy." (Strauss-Kahn has speculated he was framed by political rivals, and many in France would not find that too far-fetched.)

Another prominent Socialist is Ségolène Royal. She lost to Sarkozy in the 2007 presidential election, and lost to Hollande in the 2011 primary. As it happens, Royal and Hollande know each other well: They met in college, lived together for 30 years, and raised four children before splitting up in 2007. They never married. French politics makes strange bedfellows.

APPENDIX

Contents

Tourist Information

The French national tourist office **in the US** is a wealth of information. Before your trip, scan their website—www.franceguide.com. It has particularly good resources for special-interest travel and plenty of free-to-download brochures.

In France, your best first stop in a new city is generally the tourist information office; remember that these are abbreviated as **TI** in this book.

Throughout Provence and the French Riviera, you'll find TIs are well-organized, with English-speaking staff. They're good places to get a city map and information on public transit (including bus and train schedules), walking tours, special events, and nightlife. Many TIs have information on the entire country or at least the region, so try to pick up maps for destinations you'll be visiting later in your trip. If you're arriving in town after the TI closes, pick up a map in a neighboring town. Towns with a lot of tourism generally have English-speaking guides available for private hire (about $140 for a 2-hour guided town walk).

The French call TIs by different names: *Office de Tourisme* and *Bureau de Tourisme* are used in cities; *Syndicat d'Initiative* and *Information Touristique* are used in small towns. Also look for *Accueil* signs in airports and at popular sights. These information booths are staffed with seasonal helpers who provide tourists with limited, though generally sufficient, information. Smaller TIs are often closed from 12:00 to 14:00 and on Sundays.

While TIs are eager to book you a room, use their room-finding service only as a last resort. They are unable to give hard opinions on the relative value of one place over another. The accommodations stakes are too high to go potluck through the TI. Even if there's no "fee," you'll save yourself and your host money by going direct with the listings in this book.

Communicating

The Language Barrier and that French Attitude

You've probably heard that the French are "mean and cold and refuse to speak English." This is an out-of-date preconception left over from the days of Charles de Gaulle—and it's especially incorrect in this region. In these southern lands kissed by the sun and sea, you'll find your hosts more jovial and easygoing (like their Italian neighbors) than in the more serious north. Still, be reasonable in your expectations: Waiters are paid to be efficient, not chatty. And Provençal postal clerks are every bit as speedy, cheery, and multilingual as ours are back home.

The biggest mistake most Americans make when traveling in France is trying to do too much with limited time. This approach is a mistake in the bustling north, and a virtual sin in the laid-back south. Hurried, impatient travelers who miss the subtle pleasures of people-watching from a sun-dappled café often misinterpret French attitudes. By slowing your pace and making an effort to understand French culture by living it, you're far more likely to have a richer experience. With the five weeks of paid vacation and 35-hour work week that many French workers consider as nonnegotiable rights, your hosts can't fathom why anyone would rush through their vacation.

The French take great pride in their customs, clinging to the belief in their own cultural superiority despite the fact that they're no longer a world superpower. Let's face it: It's tough to keep on smiling when you've been crushed by a Big Mac, Mickey Moused by Disney, and drowned in Starbucks coffee. Your hosts are cold only if you decide to see them that way. Polite and formal, the French respect the fine points of culture and tradition. Here, strolling down the street with a big grin on your face and saying hello to strangers is a sign of senility, not friendliness (seriously). They think that Americans, though friendly, are hesitant to pursue more serious friendships. Recognize sincerity and look for kindness. Give them the benefit of the doubt.

Communication difficulties are exaggerated. To hurdle the language barrier, bring a small English/French dictionary, a phrase book (look for mine, which contains a dictionary and menu decoder), a menu reader (if you're a gourmet eater, get the pricey but thorough *A to Z of French Food, a French to English Dictionary of Culinary Terms*, by G. de Temmerman), and a good supply of patience (for a list of survival phrases, see page 571). In transactions, a small notepad and pen minimize misunderstandings about prices; have vendors write the price down.

Though many French people—especially those in the tourist trade, and in big cities—speak English, you'll get better treatment if you learn and use the French pleasantries. If you learn only five phrases, choose these: *bonjour* (good day), *pardon* (pardon me), *s'il vous plaît* (please), *merci* (thank you), and *au revoir* (good-bye). The French value politeness. Begin every encounter with *"Bonjour* (or *S'il vous plaît), madame* or *monsieur"* and end every encounter with *"Au revoir, madame* or *monsieur."*

The French are language perfectionists—they take their language (and other languages) seriously. Often they speak more English than they let on. This isn't a tourist-baiting tactic, but timidity on their part about speaking another language less than fluently. Start any conversation with, *"Bonjour, madame* or *monsieur. Parlez-vous anglais?"* and hope they speak more English than you speak French.

Telephones

Smart travelers use the telephone to reserve or reconfirm rooms, get tourist information, reserve restaurants, confirm tour times, or phone home. When spelling out your name on the phone, you'll find that most letters are pronounced very differently in French: *a* is pronounced "ah," *e* is pronounced "eh," and *i* is pronounced "ee." To avoid confusion, say *"a*, Anne," *"e*, euro," and *"i*, Isabelle."

This section covers dialing instructions, phone cards, and types of phones (for more in-depth information, see www.ricksteves .com/phoning).

How to Dial

Calling from the US to France, or vice versa, is simple—once you break the code. The European calling chart later in this chapter will walk you through it.

APPENDIX

Dialing Domestically Within France

The following instructions apply whether you're dialing from a landline (such as a pay phone or your hotel-room phone) or a French mobile phone.

France has a direct-dial 10-digit phone system (no area codes). To make domestic calls anywhere within France, just dial the number. For example, the number of one of my recommended hotels in Nice is 04 97 03 10 70. That's the number you dial whether you're calling it from across the street or across the country.

If you're dialing within France using your US mobile phone, you may need to dial as if it's a domestic call, or you may need to dial as if you're calling from the US (see "Dialing Internationally," next). Try it one way, and if it doesn't work, try it the other way.

Understand the various prefixes. All landlines in Provence and the Riviera begin with 04. Any number beginning with 06 or 07 is a mobile phone, and costs more to dial. France's toll-free numbers start with 0800 (like US 800 numbers, though in France you dial a 0 first rather than a 1). In France these 0800 numbers— called *numéro vert* (green number)—can be dialed free from any phone without using a phone card. But you can't call France's toll-free numbers from America, nor can you count on reaching US toll-free numbers from France.

Any 08 number that does not have a 00 directly following is a toll call, generally costing 10 to 50 cents per minute.

Dialing Internationally to or from France

If you want to make an international call, follow these steps:

• Dial the international access code (00 if you're calling from Europe, 011 from the US or Canada). If you're dialing from a mobile phone, you can replace the international access code with +, which works regardless of where you're calling from. (On many mobile phones, you can insert a + by pressing and holding the 0 key.)

• Dial the country code of the country you're calling (33 for France, or 1 for the US or Canada).

• Dial the local number. If you're calling France, drop the initial zero of the phone number (For specifics per country, see the European calling chart in this chapter).

Calling from the US to France: To call the recommended Nice hotel from the US, dial 011 (US access code), 33 (France's country code), then 4 97 03 10 70 (the hotel's number without its initial zero).

Calling from any European Country to the US: To call my office in Edmonds, Washington, from anywhere in Europe, I dial 00 (Europe's access code), 1 (US country code), 425 (Edmonds' area code), and 771-8303.

Mobile Phones

Traveling with a mobile phone is handy and practical. There are two basic options: roaming with your own phone (expensive but easy) or buying and using SIM cards with an unlocked phone (a bit more hassle, but potentially much cheaper).

Roaming with Your US Mobile Phone: This pricier option can be worthwhile if you won't be making or receiving many calls, don't want to bother with SIM cards, or want to stay reachable at your US number. Start by calling your mobile-phone service provider to ask whether your phone works in Europe and what the rates are (likely $1.29-1.99 per minute to make or receive calls, and 20-50 cents to send or receive text messages). Tell them to enable international calling on your account, and if you know you'll be making multiple calls, ask your carrier about any global calling deals to lower the per-minute costs. When you land in Europe, turn on your phone and—bingo!—you have service. Because you'll pay for receiving calls and texts, be sure your family knows to call only in an emergency. Note that Verizon and Sprint use a different technology than European providers, so their phones are less likely to work abroad; if yours doesn't, your provider may be able to send you a loaner phone before you leave for Europe (arrange in advance).

Buying and Using SIM Cards in Europe: If you're comfortable with mobile-phone technology, will be making lots of calls, and want to save some serious money, consider this very affordable alternative: Carry an unlocked mobile phone, and use it with a European SIM card to get much cheaper rates.

Getting an **unlocked phone** may be easier than you think. You may already have an old, unused mobile phone in a drawer somewhere. When you got the phone, it was probably "locked" to work only with one company—but if your contract is now up, your provider may be willing to send you a code to unlock it. Just call and ask. Otherwise, you can simply buy an unlocked phone: Search your favorite online shopping site for an "unlocked quad-band phone" before you go, or wait until you get to Europe and buy one at a mobile-phone shop there. Either way, a basic model costs less than $50.

Once in Europe, buy a **SIM card**—the little chip that inserts into your phone (either under the battery, or in a slot on the side)—to equip the phone with a European number. (Note that smaller "micro-SIM" or "nano-SIM" cards—used in some iPhones—are less widely available.) SIM cards are sold at mobile-phone shops, department-store electronics counters, and some newsstand kiosks for $5-10, and usually include about that much prepaid calling credit (making the card itself virtually free). In most places, buying a SIM card is as easy as buying a pack of gum—and almost as

Smartphones and Data Roaming

I take my smartphone to Europe, using it to make phone calls (sparingly) and send texts, but also to check email, listen to audio tours, and browse the Internet. You may have heard horror stories about people running up outrageous data roaming bills on their smartphones. But if you understand the options, it's easy to avoid these fees and still stay connected. Here's how.

For voice calls and text messaging, smartphones work like any mobile phone (as described under "Roaming with Your US Mobile Phone," earlier). To avoid roaming charges, connect to free Wi-Fi, and use Skype, FaceTime, or other apps to make cheap or free calls (see "Calling over the Internet," later).

To get online with your phone, you have two options: Wi-Fi and mobile data. Because free Wi-Fi hotspots are generally easy to find in Europe (at most hotels, many cafés, and even some public spaces), the cheap solution is to use Wi-Fi wherever possible.

But what if you just can't get to a hotspot? Fortunately, most providers offer an affordable, basic data-roaming package for Europe: $25 or $30 buys you about 100 megabytes—enough to view 100 websites or send/receive 1,000 emails. If you don't buy a data-roaming plan in advance, but use data in Europe anyway, you'll pay staggeringly high rates—about $20 per megabyte, or about 80 times what you'd pay with a plan.

While a data-roaming package is handy, your allotted megabytes can go quickly—especially if you stream videos or music. To keep a cap on usage and avoid incurring overage charges, I manually turn off data roaming on my phone whenever I'm not actively using it. (To turn off data and voice roaming, look in your phone's menu—try checking under "Cellular" or "Network," or ask your mobile-phone provider how to do it.) As I travel through Europe, I jump from hotspot to hotspot. But if I need to get online at a time when I can't easily access Wi-Fi—for example, to download driving directions when I'm on the road to my next hotel—I turn on data roaming just long enough for that task, then turn it off again. You can also limit how much data your phone uses by switching your email settings from "push" to "fetch" (you choose when to download messages rather than having them automatically "pushed" to your device). By carefully budgeting my data this way, my 100 megabytes last a long time.

If you want to use your smartphone exclusively on Wi-Fi—and not worry about either voice or data charges—simply turn off both voice and data roaming (or put your phone in "Airplane Mode" and then turn your Wi-Fi back on). By sticking with Wi-Fi wherever possible and budgeting your use of data, you can easily and affordably stay connected while you travel.

cheap. (In some countries—including Italy, Germany, and Hungary—it can take a bit longer, because you have to show your passport and be registered.) Because SIM cards are prepaid, there's no contract and no commitment (in fact, they expire after just a few months of disuse); I buy one even if I'm in a country for only a few days.

When using a SIM card in its home country, it's free to receive calls and texts, and it's cheap to make calls—domestic calls average 20-30 cents per minute (though toll lines can be substantially more). Rates are higher if you're roaming in another country, but as long as you stay within the European Union, these fees are capped (about 30 cents per minute for making calls or 10 cents per minute for receiving calls). Texting is cheap even if roaming in another country. Particularly inexpensive SIM card brands (such as Lebara) let you call either within Europe or to the US for less than 10 cents per minute.

When purchasing a SIM card, always ask about fees for domestic and international calls, roaming charges, and how to check your credit balance and buy more time. If text or voice prompts are in another language, ask the clerk whether they can be switched to English.

Mobile-Phone Calling Apps: If you have a smartphone, you can use it to make free or cheap calls in Europe by using a calling app such as Skype or FaceTime when you're on Wi-Fi; for details, see the next section.

Calling over the Internet

Some things that seem too good to be true...actually are true. If you're traveling with a smartphone, tablet, or laptop, you can make free calls over the Internet to another wireless device, anywhere in the world, for free. (Or you can pay a few cents to call from your computer or smartphone to a telephone.) The major providers are Skype, Google Talk, and (on Apple devices) FaceTime. You can get online at a Wi-Fi hotspot and use these apps to make calls without ringing up expensive roaming charges (though call quality can be spotty on slow connections). You can make Internet calls even if you're traveling without your own mobile device: Many European Internet cafés have Skype, as well as microphones and webcams, on their terminals—just log on and chat away.

Landline Telephones

Just like Americans, these days most Europeans make the majority of their calls on mobile phones. But you'll still encounter landlines in hotel rooms and at pay phones.

Hotel-Room Phones: Calling from your hotel room can be great for local calls and for international calls if you have an

European Calling Chart

Just smile and dial, using this key:
AC = Area Code, LN = Local Number.

European Country	Calling long distance within ...	Calling from the US or Canada to ...	Calling from a European country to ...
Austria	AC + LN	011 + 43 + AC (without initial zero) + LN	00 + 43 + AC (without initial zero) + LN
Belgium	LN	011 + 32 + LN (without initial zero)	00 + 32 + LN (without initial zero)
Bosnia-Herzegovina	AC + LN	011 + 387 + AC (without initial zero) + LN	00 + 387 + AC (without initial zero) + LN
Britain	AC + LN	011 + 44 + AC (without initial zero) + LN	00 + 44 + AC (without initial zero) + LN
Croatia	AC + LN	011 + 385 + AC (without initial zero) + LN	00 + 385 + AC (without initial zero) + LN
Czech Republic	LN	011 + 420 + LN	00 + 420 + LN
Denmark	LN	011 + 45 + LN	00 + 45 + LN
Estonia	LN	011 + 372 + LN	00 + 372 + LN
Finland	AC + LN	011 + 358 + AC (without initial zero) + LN	999 (or other 900 number) + 358 + AC (without initial zero) + LN
France	LN	011 + 33 + LN (without initial zero)	00 + 33 + LN (without initial zero)
Germany	AC + LN	011 + 49 + AC (without initial zero) + LN	00 + 49 + AC (without initial zero) + LN
Gibraltar	LN	011 + 350 + LN	00 + 350 + LN
Greece	LN	011 + 30 + LN	00 + 30 + LN
Hungary	06 + AC + LN	011 + 36 + AC + LN	00 + 36 + AC + LN
Ireland	AC + LN	011 + 353 + AC (without initial zero) + LN	00 + 353 + AC (without initial zero) + LN
Italy	LN	011 + 39 + LN	00 + 39 + LN

European Country	Calling long distance within ...	Calling from the US or Canada to ...	Calling from a European country to ...
Latvia	LN	011 + 371 + LN	00 + 371 + LN
Montenegro	AC + LN	011 + 382 + AC (without initial zero) + LN	00 + 382 + AC (without initial zero) + LN
Morocco	LN	011 + 212 + LN (without initial zero)	00 + 212 + LN (without initial zero)
Netherlands	AC + LN	011 + 31 + AC (without initial zero) + LN	00 + 31 + AC (without initial zero) + LN
Norway	LN	011 + 47 + LN	00 + 47 + LN
Poland	LN	011 + 48 + LN	00 + 48 + LN
Portugal	LN	011 + 351 + LN	00 + 351 + LN
Russia	8 + AC + LN	011 + 7 + AC + LN	00 + 7 + AC + LN
Slovakia	AC + LN	011 + 421 + AC (without initial zero) + LN	00 + 421 + AC (without initial zero) + LN
Slovenia	AC + LN	011 + 386 + AC (without initial zero) + LN	00 + 386 + AC (without initial zero) + LN
Spain	LN	011 + 34 + LN	00 + 34 + LN
Sweden	AC + LN	011 + 46 + AC (without initial zero) + LN	00 + 46 + AC (without initial zero) + LN
Switzerland	LN	011 + 41 + LN (without initial zero)	00 + 41 + LN (without initial zero)
Turkey	AC (if there's no initial zero, add one) + LN	011 + 90 + AC (without initial zero) + LN	00 + 90 + AC (without initial zero) + LN

- The instructions above apply whether you're calling to or from a European landline or mobile phone.

- If calling from any mobile phone, you can replace the international access code with "+" (press and hold 0 to insert it).

- The international access code is 011 if you're calling from the US or Canada.

- To call the US or Canada from Europe, dial 00, then 1 (country code for US and Canada), then the area code and number. In short, 00 + 1 + AC + LN = Hi, Mom!

international phone card (described later). Otherwise, hotel-room phones can be an almost criminal rip-off for long-distance or international calls. Many hotels charge a fee for local and sometimes even "toll-free" numbers—always ask for the rates before you dial.

Public Pay Phones: Coin-op phones are becoming extinct in Europe. To make calls from public phones, you'll need a prepaid phone card, described next.

Telephone Cards

There are two types of phone cards: insertable (for pay phones) and international (cheap for overseas calls and usable from any type of phone). A phone card works only in the country where you bought it, so if you have a live card at the end of your trip, give it to another traveler to use—most cards expire three to six months after the first use.

Insertable Phone Cards: Called a *télécarte* (tay-lay-kart), this type of card can be used only at pay phones. These cards are handy and affordable for local and domestic calls, but more expensive for international calls. They're sold in two denominations—*une petite* costs about €8; *une grande* about €15—at *tabacs* (tobacco shops), newsstands, post offices, and train stations. To use the card, insert it into a slot in the pay phone. Push the flag button on the phone to change the display until you see English and follow the instructions. Though you can use a *télécarte* to call anywhere in the world, it's only a good deal for making quick local calls from a phone booth.

International Phone Cards: With these "code cards" (*cartes à code*, cart-ah-code), phone calls from France to the US can cost less than a nickel a minute. They can also be used to make local calls, and they work from any type of phone, including a mobile phone with a European SIM card, and—usually—your hotel-room phone. To use the card, dial a local or toll-free access number, then enter your scratch-to-reveal PIN code. Note that some hoteliers block their phones from accepting access numbers; ask your hotelier about access and rates before you call.

You can buy cards at newsstand kiosks and *tabacs* (tobacco shops). Ask the clerk for a *carte à code pour les Etats-Unis* (for the US; cart-ah-code poor lay-zay-tah-oo-nee). Buy a lower denomination in case the card is a dud. Tell the vendor where you'll be making most calls (to the US), and he'll select the brand with the best deal. Some shops also sell cardless codes, printed right on the receipt.

To make a call, dial the free (usually 4-digit) access number. If the access code on the card doesn't work from your hotel-room phone, try the card's 10-digit, toll-free code that starts with 08.

Either way, a voice in French (followed by English) tells you to enter your (usually 12-digit) code. Before or after entering your code, you may need to press (or "*touche*," pronounced toosh) the pound key (#, *dièse*, dee-ehz) or the star key (*, *étoile*, eh-twahl). At the next message, dial the number you're calling (possibly followed by pound or star key; you don't have to listen through the entire sales pitch).

Since you don't need the actual card or receipt to use the account, you can write down the access number and code and share it with friends.

US Calling Cards: These cards, such as the ones offered by AT&T, Verizon, and Sprint, are a rotten value, and are being phased out. Try any of the options outlined earlier.

Useful Phone Numbers

For tips on making calls, including specifics on dialing toll-free service numbers, see "How to Dial" on page 527.

Emergency Needs
Police: Tel. 17
Emergency Medical Assistance (called "SAMU"): Tel. 15
Collect Calls to the US: Tel. 08 00 99 00 11
Riviera Medical Services: Tel. 04 93 26 12 70, www.riviera medical.com (has list of English-speaking physicians in the Riviera region and can help make an appointment or call an ambulance)

Embassies and Consulates
US Consulate in Nice: Tel. 04 93 88 89 55 (7 Avenue Gustave V, http://marseille.usconsulate.gov/nice.html; does *not* provide visa services—Paris is the nearest office for these services)
Canadian Consulate in Nice: Tel. 04 93 92 93 22 (2 Place Franklin). For emergency assistance, call collect, Canadian tel. 613/996-8885.
US Consulate in Marseille: Tel. 04 91 54 90 84 (Place Varian Fry, http://marseille.usconsulate.gov)
US Consulate and Embassy in Paris: Tel. 01 43 12 22 22, (4 Avenue Gabriel, to the left as you face Hôtel Crillon, Mo: Concorde, http://france.usembassy.gov)
Canadian Consulate and Embassy in Paris: Tel. 01 44 43 29 02, (35 Avenue Montaigne, Mo: Franklin D. Roosevelt, www.amb -canada.fr). For 24/7 emergency assistance, call collect to Canadian tel. 613/996-8885.
Australian Consulate in Paris: Tel. 01 40 59 33 00 (4 Rue Jean Rey, Mo: Bir-Hakeim, www.france.embassy.gov.au)

Travel Advisories
US Department of State: Tel. 888-407-4747, from outside US tel. 1-202-501-4444, www.travel.state.gov
Canadian Department of Foreign Affairs: Canadian tel. 800-387-3124, from outside Canada tel. 1-613-996-8885, www.travel.gc.ca
US Centers for Disease Control and Prevention: Tel. 800-CDC-INFO (800-232-4636), www.cdc.gov/travel

Airports
Nice: Aéroport de Nice—tel. 08 20 42 33 33, airport code NCE, http://en.nice.aeroport.fr
Marseille: Aéroport Marseille-Provence—tel. 04 42 14 14 14, airport code MRS, www.marseille.aeroport.fr
Paris: Aéroports Charles de Gaulle and Orly share the same numbers—toll tel. 3950 (€0.35/minute); from the US dial 011 33 1 70 36 39 50; airport codes CDG and ORV, www.adp.fr; Beauvais—tel. 08 92 68 20 66, airport code BVA, www.aeroportbeauvais.com
Lyon: Saint-Exupéry Airport—tel. 08 26 80 08 26, airport code LYS, www.lyon.aeroport.fr

Airlines
Note that airline websites have alternate numbers to call in the US or in other European countries.
Aer Lingus: Tel. 08 21 23 02 67, Mon-Fri 9:00-17:00
Air Canada: Tel. 08 25 88 08 81, daily 7:30-15:00
Air France: Tel. 3654, daily 6:30-22:00
Alitalia: Tel. 08 92 65 56 55, Mon-Fri 8:00-20:00, Sat-Sun 9:00-19:00
American Airlines: Tel. 08 26 46 09 50, Mon-Fri 8:00-20:00, Sat-Sun 9:30-18:00
Austrian Airlines: Tel. 08 20 81 68 16, daily 8:00-20:00
British Airways: Tel. 08 25 82 54 00, Mon-Fri 9:00-18:00, Sat 9:00-14:00, closed Sun
Delta: Tel. 08 92 70 26 09
easyJet: Tel. 08 20 42 03 15, Mon-Fri 8:00-20:00, Sat-Sun 9:00-17:00
Iberia: Tel. 08 25 80 09 65
Icelandair: tel. 01 44 51 60 51
KLM: Tel. 08 92 70 26 08
Lufthansa: Tel. 08 92 23 16 90
Royal Air Maroc: Tel. 08 20 82 18 21
SAS: Tel. 08 25 32 53 35, Mon-Fri 9:00-17:00
Swiss International: Tel. 08 92 23 25 01
United: Tel. 08 10 72 72 72, Mon-Fri 8:00-20:00, Sat-Sun 9:30-18:00

Hotel Chains

Accor Hotels (huge chain, including Ibis, Mercure, and Novotel): Tel. 08 25 88 00 00, US tel. 800-221-4542, www.accorhotels.com

Ibis Hotels: Tel. 08 92 68 66 86, US tel. 800-221-4542, www.ibishotel.com

Mercure Hotels: Tel. 08 25 88 33 33, US tel. 800-221-4542, www.mercure.com

Kyriad Hotels: Tel. 08 92 23 05 91, www.kyriad.com,

Best Western Hotels: US tel. 800-780-7234, www.bestwestern.com

Country Home Rental: www.gites-de-france.com or www.gite.com

Hostelling International, US Office: www.hiusa.org

Hostelling International, Canada Office: www.hihostels.ca

Cooking Schools

Cuisine de Provence: Charming, easygoing Barbara Schuerenberg leads reasonably priced cooking classes from her home in Vaison la Romaine (tel. 04 90 35 68 43, www.cuisinedeprovence.com, barbara@cuisinedeprovence.com, see page 193).

Jardin de Bacchus: Northwest of Avignon, in their Tavel bed-and-breakfast, Christine and Erik offer fun cooking classes (tel. 04 66 90 28 62, www.provence-escapade.fr, jardindebacchus@free.fr, see page 149).

Les Petits Farcis: In Old Nice, Rosa Jackson teaches a variety of cooking courses, some of which include visits to the city's markets (www.petitsfarcis.com, see page 319).

Internet Access

It's useful to get online periodically as you travel—to confirm trip plans, check train or bus schedules, get weather forecasts, catch up on email, blog or post photos from your trip, or call folks back home (explained earlier, under "Calling over the Internet").

Your Mobile Device: The majority of accommodations in France offer Wi-Fi (pronounced "wee-fee" in French), as do some cafés, making it easy for you to get online with your laptop, tablet, or smartphone. Access is often free, but sometimes there's a fee. At hotels that charge for a certain number of hours, save money by logging in and out of your account on an as-needed basis. You should be able to stretch a two-hour Wi-Fi pass over a stay of a day or two.

Public Internet Terminals: Many accommodations offer a guest computer in the lobby with Internet access. If you ask politely, smaller places may let you sit at their desk for a few minutes just to check your email. If your hotelier doesn't have access, ask to be directed to the nearest place to get online. In cities such as Nice and Avignon, you'll find plenty of cafés that offer Wi-Fi if you buy a drink. All Starbucks and McDonald's offer Wi-Fi for free. In smaller towns, post offices may offer Internet access *(cyberposte)*; buy a chip-card (about the same prices as phone cards) and you're in business.

Security: Whether you're accessing the Internet with your own device or at a public terminal, using a shared network or computer comes with the potential for increased security risks. If you're not convinced a connection is secure, avoid accessing any sites (such as online banking) that could be vulnerable to fraud.

Mail

You can mail one package per day to yourself worth up to $200 duty-free from Europe to the US (mark it "personal purchases"). If you're sending a gift to someone, mark it "unsolicited gift." For details, visit www.cbp.gov and search for "Know Before You Go."

The French postal service works fine, but for quick transatlantic delivery (in either direction), consider services such as DHL (www.dhl.com). French post offices are referred to as *la Poste* or PTT, for "Post, Telegraph, and Telephone." Hours vary, though most are open weekdays 8:00-19:00 and Saturday morning 8:00-12:00. Stamps and phone cards are also sold at *tabacs* (tobacco shops). It costs about €1 to mail a postcard to the US. One convenient, if expensive, way to send packages home is to use the PTT's Colissimo XL postage-paid mailing box. It costs €36-47 to ship boxes weighing 5-7 kilos (about 11-15 pounds).

Transportation

APPENDIX

By Car or Public Transportation?

If you're debating between public transportation and car rental, consider these factors: Cars are best for three or more traveling together (especially families with small kids), those packing heavy, and those scouring the countryside in search of the perfect hill town—a tempting plan for this region. Trains and buses are best for solo travelers, blitz tourists, city-to-city travelers, and those who don't want to drive in Europe. While a car gives you more freedom, trains and buses zip you effortlessly and scenically from city to city, usually dropping you in the center, often near a TI.

If you plan to focus on Arles, Avignon, Aix-en-Provence, and seaside destinations along the Riviera, go by train. Stations are centrally located in each city, which makes hotel-hunting and sightseeing easy. Buses and taxis pick up where trains leave off. While bus service can be sparse, taxis are generally available and reasonable. If relying on public transportation, focus on fewer destinations, or hire one of the excellent minivan tour guides I

French Train Terms and Abbreviations

SNCF (Société Nationale Chemins de Fer): This is the Amtrak of France, operating all national train lines that link cities and towns.

TGV (Train à Grande Vitesse): SNCF's network of high-speed trains (twice as fast as regular trains) that connect major cities in France. These trains always require a reservation.

Intercité: Compared to the TGV, these trains are the next best in terms of speed and comfort.

TER (Trains Express Régionale): These trains serve smaller stops within a region. For example, you'll find trains called TER de Bourgogne (trains operating only in Burgundy) and TER Provence (Provence-only trains).

---

recommend (see "Tours of Provence" on page 56).

I've included two sample itineraries—by car and by public transportation—to help you explore Provence and the French Riviera smoothly; you'll find these in the Introduction.

Trains

France's rail system (SNCF) sets the pace in Europe. Its super TGV (*train à grande vitesse;* tay zhay vay) system has inspired bullet trains throughout the world. The TGV runs at 170-220 mph. Its rails are fused into one long, continuous track for a faster and smoother ride. The TGV has changed commuting patterns in much of France and put most of the country within day-trip distance of Paris. TGV trains serve these cities in Provence and the Riviera: Avignon, Arles (very few trains), Nîmes, Marseille, Orange, Aix-en-Provence, Antibes, Cannes, and Nice. Avignon and Aix-en-Provence have separate TGV stations outside of town (with bus connections into the center)—note carefully which station your train serves (either "Centre-Ville" or "TGV"; if it's not specified, then it's the central station).

At any train station, you can get schedule information, make reservations, and buy tickets for any destination.

Schedules

Schedules change by season, weekday, and weekend. Verify train times shown in this book—check www.bahn.com (Germany's all-Europe schedule site) or locally at train stations. The French rail website is http://en.voyages-sncf.com/en; for info on getting deals on point-to-point tickets if you order in advance, see "Buying Tickets," later.

Bigger stations may have helpful information agents (wearing

APPENDIX

Key Travel Phrases

Bonjour, monsieur/madame, parlez-vous anglais?
Pron: bohn-zhoor, muhs-yur/mah-dahm, par-lay-voo ahn-glay?
Meaning: Hello, sir/madam, do you speak English?

Je voudrais un départ pour (destination), *pour le* (date), *vers* (general time of day), *la plus direct possible.*
Pron: zhuh voo-dray uhn day-par poor (destination), poor luh (date), vehr (time), lah ploo dee-rehk poh-see-bluh.
Meaning/Example: I would like a departure for Avignon, on 23 May, about 9:00, the most direct way possible.

red or blue vests) roaming the station and at *Accueil* offices or booths. They can answer schedule questions more quickly than staff at the ticket windows. Make use of their help; don't stand in a ticket line if all you need is a train schedule.

Railpasses

Long-distance travelers can save money with a France Railpass, sold only outside Europe (through travel agents or Europe Through the Back Door). For roughly the cost of a Paris-Avignon-Paris ticket, the France Railpass offers three days of travel (within a month) anywhere in France. You can add up to six more days for the cost of a two-hour ride each day. You'll save money by getting the second-class instead of the first-class version, but first class gives you more options when reserving popular TGV routes (seats are very limited for passholders, so reserving these fast trains at least several weeks in advance is recommended). The Saver Pass version gives two or more people traveling together a 15 percent discount.

Each day of use allows you to take as many trips as you want on one calendar day (you could go from Paris to Beaune in Burgundy, enjoy wine-tasting, then continue to Avignon, stay a few hours, and end in Nice—though I don't recommend it). Buy second-class tickets in France for shorter trips and spend your valuable railpass days wisely.

For a summary of railpass deals and the latest prices, check my Guide to Eurail Passes at www.ricksteves.com/rail. If you decide to get a railpass, this guide will help you know you're getting the right one for your trip.

Buying Tickets

While there's no deadline to buy any train ticket, the fast, reserved TGV trains get booked up. Reserve well ahead for any TGV you

Rail Passes

Prices listed are for 2014 and are subject to change. For the latest prices, details, and train schedules (and easy online ordering), see my comprehensive *Guide to Eurail Passes* at www.ricksteves.com/rail.

"Saver" prices are per person for two or more people traveling together. "Youth" means under age 26. The fare for children 4–11 is half the adult individual fare or Saver fare. Kids under age 4 travel free.

FRANCE PASS

	Adult 1st Class	Adult 2nd Class	Senior 1st Class	Youth 1st Class	Youth 2nd Class
3 days in 1 month	$306	$248	$273	$2221	$187
Extra rail days (max 6)	39-43	30-37	34-38	28-31	24-28

Senior = 60 and up.

FRANCE SAVERPASS

	1st Class	2nd Class
3 days in 1 month	$269	$218
Extra rail days (max 6)	34-38	25-31

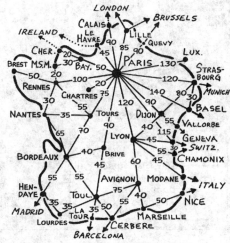

Map key:
Approximate point-to-point one-way second-class rail fares in US dollars. First class costs 50 percent more. Add up fares for your itinerary to see if a railpass will save you money.

APPENDIX

FRANCE–SPAIN PASS

	Individual 1st Class	Individual 2nd Class	Saver 1st Class	Saver 2nd Class	Youth 2nd Class
4 days in 2 months	$428	$365	$365	$311	$280
Extra rail days (max 6)	45-51	38-44	38-44	33-37	29-33

If you're only dipping into a bit of Spain, you may not need the France-Spain pass. A TGV reservation with a France (only), Spain (only) or France-Spain pass covers the whole trip to/from Barcelona.

Public Transportation in Provence

Legend:
- Rail
- TGV High Speed Rail
- Bus
- Boat
- ✈ Airports (Not All Shown)

Note: In some cases regular train lines and TGV lines share the same track

Not to Scale

Mediterranean Sea

cannot afford to miss. Tickets go on sale 90 days in advance, with a wide range of prices on any one route, and the cheapest tickets sell out early; reservations for railpass holders also go particularly fast. To buy the cheapest advance-discount tickets (50 percent less than full-fare), visit http://en.voyages-sncf.com/en about three months ahead of your travel date. The first time you visit and are faced with a map of the whole world, go to the "French" page, then change to "Other Countries/English language," and choose "Pick up in France." Select the cheapest, non-refundable category of tickets (such as "Prems"), choose the eticket delivery option (which

Public Transportation on the French Riviera

you can print at home), and pay using a PayPal account. These low-rate tickets are not available from Rail Europe or other US agents.

After the non-refundable rates are sold out, you currently can buy other fare types on the French site only if you have set up the "Verified by Visa" or "MasterCard SecureCode" program for your US credit card. Otherwise, US customers have to order from Rail Europe (www.raileurope.com), which offers both etickets and home delivery, but doesn't have access to some of the cheapest rates.

In France, you can buy tickets at SNCF Boutiques (small travel agencies located conveniently in the city center). If you need to get a ticket at the station, buy it from a staffed ticket window or from a machine (pay in cash as US credit cards normally do not work). You can buy tickets on the train for a €4-10 surcharge depending on the length of your trip, but you must find the conductor immediately upon boarding; otherwise it's a €35 minimum charge.

Train Ticket Machines

The ticket machines available at most stations are great time-savers for short trips when ticket-window lines are long. The machines won't accept your American credit card unless it has a chip, so you'll need euro coins instead. Some machines have English instructions, but for those that don't, here is what you are prompted to do. (The default is usually what you want; turn the dial or move the cursor to your choice, and press *Validez* to agree to each step.)

1. *Quelle est votre destination?* (What's your destination?)
2. *Billet Plein Tarif* (Full-fare ticket—yes for most.)
3. *1ère ou 2ème* (First or second class; normally second is fine.)
4. *Aller simple ou aller-retour?* (One-way or round-trip?)
5. *Prix en Euro* (The price should be shown if you get this far.)

Reservations

In Provence and the French Riviera, reservations are required for any TGV train, *couchettes* (sleeping berths) on night trains, and the Grande Ligne (mainline) train between Nice and Bordeaux (serves Antibes, Cannes, Toulon, Arles, Carcassonne, and other destinations en route). You can reserve any train at any station or through SNCF Boutiques (small travel agencies). If you're buying a point-to-point ticket for a TGV train, you'll reserve your seat when you purchase your ticket.

The fast and popular TGV trains usually fill up quickly, making it a challenge to get reservations (particularly for railpass-holders, who are allocated a limited number of seats). It's wise to book well ahead for any TGV, especially on the busy Paris-Avignon-Nice line. Reservations cost €3 (more during peak periods) and are possible up to 90 days in advance. If the TGV trains you wanted are fully booked, ask about TER trains serving the same destination as they do not require reservations. Railpass holders can't book TGV reservations at French stations within three days of departure, but can book reservations as etickets at www.raileurope.com, if reservations are still available.

If you're taking an **overnight train** and you need a *couchette* (overnight bunk), consider booking it in advance through a US agent (such as www.raileurope.com), even though it may cost more.

Although reservations are generally unnecessary for non-TGV trains (except the Nice-Bordeaux train mentioned above), they are advisable during busy times (e.g., Fri and Sun afternoons, Sat mornings, weekday rush hours, and particularly holiday weekends; see "Holidays and Festivals" on page 563).

Validating Tickets, Reservations, and Railpasses

You are required to validate (*composter*, kohm-poh-stay) all train

Coping with Strikes

Going on strike (en grève) is a popular pastime in this revolution-happy country. Because bargaining between management and employees is not standard procedure, workers strike to get attention. Truckers and tractors block main roads and autoroutes (they call it Opération Escargot—"Operation Snail's Pace"), baggage handlers bring airports to their knees, and museum workers make artwork off-limits to tourists. Métro and train personnel seem to strike every year—probably during your trip. What does the traveler do? You could jetter l'éponge (throw in the sponge) and go somewhere less strike-prone (Switzerland's lovely), or learn to accept certain events as out of your control. Strikes in France generally last no longer than a day or two, and if you're aware of them, you can usually plan around them. Your hotelier will know the latest (or can find out). Make a habit of asking your hotel receptionist about strikes, or check www.americansinfrance.net (look under "Daily Life").

tickets and reservations. Before boarding any SNCF train, look for a yellow machine nearby to stamp your ticket or reservation. (Do not composter your railpass, but do validate it at a ticket window before the first time you use it.)

Baggage Check

Baggage check (consigne, or Espaces Bagages) is available only at the biggest train stations (about €4-10/bag depending on size), and is noted where available in this book (depends on security concerns, so be prepared to keep your bag). For security reasons, all luggage must carry a tag with the traveler's first and last name and current address. This applies to hand luggage, as well as bigger bags that are stowed. Free tags are available at train stations.

Train Tips

• Arrive at the station with plenty of time before your departure to find the right platform, confirm connections, and so on. *Remember that Avignon and Aix-en-Provence have separate TGV stations that are outside the town center.*

• Small stations have minimal staff; if you can't find an agent at the station, go directly to the tracks and look for the overhead sign that confirms your train stops at that track.

• Larger stations have platforms with monitors showing TGV car layouts (numbered forward or backward) so you can figure out where your *voiture* (car) will stop on the long platform and where to board it.

• Try to check schedules in advance. Upon arrival at a station, find out your departure possibilities (don't trust rail website schedules too much; for instance, they may not reflect construction delays). Large stations have a separate information *(accueil)* window or office; at small stations, the regular ticket office gives information.

• If you have a rail flexipass, write the date on your pass each day you travel (before or immediately after boarding your first train).

• Validate tickets and reservations (not passes) in yellow machines before boarding. If you're traveling with a pass and have a reservation for a specific trip, you must validate the reservation.

• Before getting on a train, confirm that it's going where you think it is. For example, if you want to go to Antibes, ask the conductor or any local passenger, *"À Antibes?"* (ah ahn-teeb; meaning, "To Antibes?")

• If a non-TGV train seat is reserved, it will usually be labeled *réservé,* with the cities to and from which it is reserved.

• Some longer trains split cars en route. Make sure your train car is continuing to your destination by asking, for example, *"Cette voiture va à Avignon?"* (seht vwah-tewr vah ah ah-veen-yohn; meaning, "This car goes to Avignon?") On my last trip, the train from Marseilles to Arles split off some cars along the way—which was not mentioned when I asked the conductor if this train went to Arles.

• If you don't understand an announcement, ask your neighbor to explain, *"Pardon madame/monsieur, qu'est-ce qui se passe?"* (kehs kee suh pahs; meaning, "Excuse me, what's going on?").

• Verify with the conductor all of the transfers you must make: *"Correspondance à?"*; meaning, "Transfer to where?"

• To guard against theft, keep your bags in sight (directly overhead is ideal but not always possible—the early boarder gets the best storage space). If you must store them in the lower racks by the doors (available in most cars), pay attention at stops. Your bags are most vulnerable to theft before the train takes off and whenever it stops.

• Note your arrival time so you'll be ready to get off.

• Use the train's free WCs before you get off (but not while the train is stopped).

Low-Cost TGV Trains to Southern France

A new TGV train called OUIGO (pronounced "we go") offers a direct connection from Disneyland Paris to southern France. These trains leave from the Marne-la-Vallée TGV station, 45 minutes from Paris on RER-A. So you can hang at Disneyland Paris before (or after) your trip south and connect with a direct TGV. Fares are affordable and the service is no frills. You can't use a railpass, and only one carry-on-size bag plus one handbag are free. Larger or extra luggage costs €5 per bag if you pay when you buy your ticket. If you just show up without paying in advance, it's €40 per bag on the train—yikes! (http://ouigo.voyages-sncf.com).

Buses

You can get nearly anywhere in Provence and the Riviera by rail and bus...if you're well-organized, patient, and not in a hurry. Review my bus schedule information, and verify times at the local tourist office or bus station. Regional buses work well for some destinations not served by trains. A few bus lines are run by SNCF (France's rail system) and are included with your railpass (show railpass at station to get free bus ticket), but most bus lines are independent of the rail system and are not covered by railpasses. Train stations often have bus information where train-to-bus connections are important—and vice versa for bus companies. On Sunday, regional bus service virtually disappears.

Bus Tips

• Read the train tips described earlier, and use those that apply.

• Use TIs often to help plan your trip; they have regional bus schedules and are happy to assist you.

• Remember that service is sparse to nonexistent on Sunday. Wednesday bus schedules are often different during the school year, since school is out this day (and regional buses generally serve schools).

• Confirm a bus stop's location before you leave (rural stops are often not signed) and be at bus stops at least five minutes early.

• On schedules *(horaires)*, *en semaine* means Monday through Saturday, *dimanche* is Sunday, and *jours fériés* are holidays. *Année* means the bus runs all year on the days listed, *vac* means it runs only during summer vacations, and *scol (scolaire)* means it runs only when school is in session. *Ligne* means route (or bus line) and *réseau* means network (usually all routes).

Regional Minivan Excursions

Worthwhile day tours generally are available in regions where bus and train service is sparse. I list reliable companies that provide this helpful service at fair rates for most regions in this book. Some of these minivan excursions simply offer transportation between the sights; others add helpful commentary.

Renting a Car

If you're renting a car in France, bring your driver's license. It's recommended, but not required, that you also have an International

Driving Permit (sold at your local AAA office for $15 plus the cost of two passport-type photos; see www.aaa.com); however, I've frequently rented cars in France and traveled problem-free with just my US license.

Rental companies require you to be at least 21 years old and to have held your license for one year. Drivers under the age of 25 may incur a young-driver surcharge, and some rental companies do not rent to anyone 75 or older. If you're considered too young or old, look into leasing (covered later), which has less-stringent age restrictions.

Research car rentals before you go. It's cheaper to arrange most car rentals from the US. Call several companies and look online to compare rates, or arrange a rental through your hometown travel agent.

Most of the major US rental agencies (including Avis, Budget, Hertz, Enterprise, and Thrifty) have offices throughout Europe. Also consider the two major Europe-based agencies, Europcar and Sixt. It can be cheaper to use a consolidator, such as Auto Europe (www.autoeurope.com) or Europe by Car (www.ebctravel.com), which compares rates at several companies to get you the best deal. However, my readers have reported problems with consolidators, ranging from misinformation to unexpected fees; because you're going through a middleman, it can be more challenging to resolve disputes that arise with the rental agency.

Regardless of the car-rental company you choose, always read the fine print carefully for add-on charges—such as one-way drop-off fees, airport surcharges, or mandatory insurance policies—that aren't included in the "total price." You may need to query rental agents pointedly to find out your actual cost.

For the best deal, rent by the week with unlimited mileage. To save money on fuel, ask for a diesel car. I normally rent the smallest, least-expensive model with a stick shift (generally much cheaper than an automatic). Almost all rentals are manual by default, so if you need an automatic, request one in advance; be aware that these cars are usually larger models. Roads and parking spaces are narrow in France, so you'll do yourself a favor by renting the smallest car that meets your needs.

For a one-week rental, allow roughly $250-350 per week in summer. Allow extra for insurance, fuel, tolls, and parking. For trips of three weeks or more, look into leasing; you'll save money on insurance and taxes.

You can sometimes get a GPS unit with your rental car or leased vehicle for an additional fee (around $15/day; be sure it's set to English and has all the maps you need before you drive off). Or, if you have a portable GPS device at home, consider taking it with you to Europe (buy and upload European maps before your trip).

GPS apps are also available for smartphones, but downloading maps in Europe could lead to an exorbitant data-roaming bill (for more details, see the sidebar on page 530).

Big companies have offices in most cities; ask whether they can pick you up at your hotel. Small local rental companies can be cheaper but aren't as flexible.

Compare pick-up costs (downtown can be less expensive than the airport) and explore drop-off options. Always check the hours of the location you choose: Many rental offices close from midday Saturday until Monday morning and, in smaller towns, at lunchtime.

When selecting a location, don't trust the agency's description of "downtown" or "city center." In some cases, a "downtown" branch can be on the outskirts of the city—a long, costly taxi ride from the center. Before choosing, plug the addresses into a mapping website. You may find that the "train station" location is handier. But returning a car at a big-city train station or downtown agency can be tricky; get precise details on the car drop-off location and hours, and allow ample time to find it.

If you want a car for only a day or two (e.g., for the Côtes du Rhône wine route or Luberon villages), you'll likely find it cheaper to rent it in France—US-arranged rentals tend to make financial sense only for three days or more. You can rent a car on the spot just about anywhere. In many cases, this is a worthwhile splurge. All you need is your American driver's license and a major credit card (figure €65-85/day, including 100 kilometers, or 60 miles, per day).

When you pick up the rental car, check it thoroughly and make sure any damage is noted on your rental agreement. Find out how your car's lights, turn signals, wipers, and fuel cap function, and know what kind of fuel the car takes. When you return the car, make sure the agent verifies its condition with you.

A France Rail and Drive Pass allows you to mix car and train travel economically (sold only outside France, available from your travel agent). The basic version comes with two days of car rental and two days of rail in one month. Generally, big-city connections are best by train, and rural regions are best by car. With a France Rail and Drive Pass, you can take advantage of the speed and comfort of the TGV trains for longer trips, and rent a car for as little as one day at a time for day trips that can't be done without one. You can pick up a car in one city and drop it off in another. You must reserve each car pick-up and each TGV seat reservation at least three days in advance, and preferably much earlier, as vehicles are not always available on short notice and TGV trains limit the number of seats for railpass travelers.

Car Insurance Options

When you rent a car, you are liable for a very high deductible, sometimes equal to the entire value of the car. Limit your financial risk with one of these three options: Buy Collision Damage Waiver (CDW) coverage from the car-rental company, get coverage through your credit card (free, if your card automatically includes zero-deductible coverage), or buy coverage through Travel Guard.

CDW includes a very high deductible (typically $1,000-1,500). Though each rental company has its own variation, basic CDW costs $15-35 a day (figure roughly 30 percent extra) and reduces your liability, but does not eliminate it. When you pick up the car, you'll be offered the chance to "buy down" the basic deductible to zero (for an additional $10-30/day; this is sometimes called "super CDW").

If you opt for **credit-card coverage,** there's a catch. You'll technically have to decline all coverage offered by the car-rental company, which means they can place a hold on your card (which can be up to the full value of the car). In case of damage, it can be time-consuming to resolve the charges with your credit-card company. Before you decide on this option, quiz your credit-card company about how it works.

Finally, you can buy collision insurance from **Travel Guard** ($9/day plus a one-time $3 service fee covers you for up to $35,000, $250 deductible, tel. 800-826-4919, www.travelguard.com). It's valid everywhere in Europe except the Republic of Ireland, and some Italian car-rental companies refuse to honor it. Note that various states differ on which products and policies are available to their residents—check with Travel Guard *before* you rent your car.

For more on car-rental insurance, see www.ricksteves.com/cdw.

Leasing

For trips of three weeks or more, consider leasing (which automatically includes zero-deductible collision and theft insurance). By technically buying and then selling back the car, you save lots of money on tax and insurance. Leasing provides you a brand-new car with unlimited mileage and a 24-hour emergency assistance program. You can lease for as little as 21 days to as long as six months. Car leases must be arranged from the US.

Anyone age 18 or over with a driver's license is eligible. You can pick up or return cars in major cities outside of France, but you'll have to pay an additional fee.

Four reliable companies offer 21-day lease packages:

• **Auto France** (Peugeot cars only, US tel. 800-572-9655, www.autofrance.net)

• **Europe by Car** (Peugeot, Citroën, and Renault cars, US tel.

800-223-1516, www.ebctravel.com)

• **Idea Merge** (Volkswagen, Citroën, Renault, and Peugeot, US tel. 888-297-0001, www.ideamerge.com)

• **Kemwel** (Peugeot cars only, US tel. 877-820-0668, www .kemwel.com).

RV and Campervan Rental

Even given the extra fuel costs, renting your own rolling hotel can be a great way to save money, especially if you're sticking mainly to rural areas. Keep in mind that RVs in France are much smaller than those you see at home. Companies to consider:

• **Van It** (mobile 06 70 43 11 86, www.van-it.com)

• **Idea Merge** (see listing in "Leasing," above)

• **Origin** (current-model Volkswagen vans fully equipped for 2-3 people, rates less than RVs, mobile 06 80 01 72 77, www .origin-campervans.com).

Driving in Provence and the French Riviera

It's a pleasure to explore this region by car, but you need to know the rules.

Road Rules: Seat belts are mandatory for all, and children under age 10 must be in the back seat. In city and town centers, traffic merging from the right (even from tiny side streets) normally has the right-of-way *(priorité à droite)*. So even when you're driving on a major road, pay attention to cars merging from the right. In contrast, cars entering the many suburban roundabouts must yield *(cédez le passage)*. U-turns are illegal throughout France, and you cannot turn right on red lights.

Be aware of typical European road rules; for example, many countries require headlights to be turned on at all times, and it's generally illegal to drive while using your mobile phone without a hands-free headset. Ask your car-rental

STOP **AND LEARN THESE ROAD SIGNS**

Speed Limit (km/hr)

Speed Limit No Longer Applies

No Passing

End of No Passing Zone

One Way

Intersection

Main Road

Expressway

Danger

No Entry

Cars Prohibited

All Vehicles Prohibited

No Through Road

Restrictions No Longer Apply

Yield to Oncoming Traffic

No Stopping

Parking

No Parking

Customs

Yield

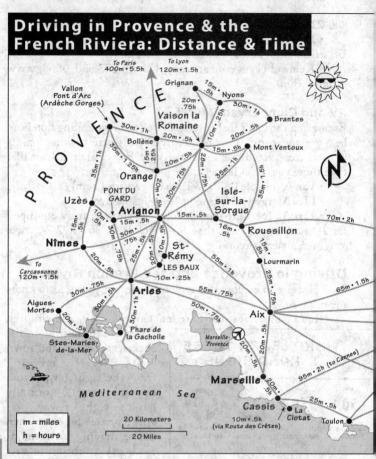

Driving in Provence & the French Riviera: Distance & Time

company about these rules, or check the US State Department website (www.travel.state.gov, click on "International Travel," then specify your country of choice and click "Traffic Safety and Road Conditions").

Speed Limits: Because speed limits are by road type, they typically aren't posted, so it's best to memorize them:
- Two-lane D and N routes outside cities and towns: 90 km/hour
- Divided highways outside cities and towns: 110 km/hour
- Autoroutes: 130 km/hour

If it's raining, subtract 10 km/hour on D and N routes and 20 km/hour on divided highways and autoroutes. Speed-limit signs have a red circle around a number; when you see that same number again in gray with a broken line diagonally across it, this means that limit no longer applies. Speed limits drop to 30-50 km/hour

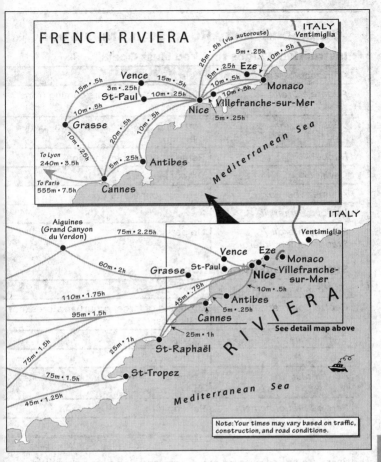

Note: Your times may vary based on traffic, construction, and road conditions.

in villages (always posted) and must be respected.

Road speeds are monitored regularly with camera boxes (a mere two kilometers over the limit gets a pricey ticket). The good news is that drivers are warned a few hundred yards before the camera with signs showing the proper speed, so you have no excuse for blowing it. Look for a sign with a radar graphic that says *Pour votre sécurité, contrôles automatiques.* Anyone caught driving over the limit will be fined a minimum of about $180, though the French use these cameras not to make money but to slow down traffic—and it works.

Don't Drink and Drive: The French are serious about curbing drunk driving. Soon all motorists, including those in rental cars, will be required to have a breath-testing instrument on hand so that the drivers themselves can tell if they're over the legal alcohol limit—which is lower in France than in the US (drinker beware).

Quick-and-Dirty Road Sign Translation

Instructional Signs that You Must Obey:

Cédez le Passage	Yield
Priorité à Droite	Right-of-way is for cars coming from the right
Vous n'avez pas la priorité	You don't have the right of way (when merging)
Rappel	Remember to obey the sign
Déviation	Detour
Allumez vos feux	Turn on your lights
Doublage Interdit	No passing
Parking Interdit / Stationnement Interdit	No parking

Signs for Your Information:

Route Barrée	Road blocked
Centre Commercial	Grouping of large, suburban stores (not city center)
Centre-Ville	City center
Feux	Traffic signals
Horadateur	Remote parking meter, usually at the end of the block
Parc de Stationnement	Parking lot

If drivers are pulled over for any reason and don't have the kit in their car, they'll be fined (driver beware). When you pick up your rental car, ask if it has a kit (if it doesn't, ask where you can get one, which should cost only around €3).

Fuel: Gas *(essence)* is expensive—about $8 per gallon. Diesel *(gazole)* is less—about $7 per gallon—and diesel cars get better mileage, so try to rent a diesel to save money. Be sure you know what type of fuel your car takes before you fill up. Gas is most expensive on autoroutes and cheapest at big supermarkets (closed at night and on Sun). Many gas stations close on Sunday. Your US credit and debit cards won't work at self-serve pumps; instead you can pay cash, find gas stations with attendants, or consider getting a card that works with the chip-and-PIN system (see page 21). Most drivers will spend about $150 per week on gas to prowl the roads in Provence and the French Riviera.

Rue Piétonne	Pedestrian-only street
Sauf Riverains	Local access only
Sortie des Camions	Work truck exit
Toutes Directions	All directions (passing through a city)
Autres Directions	Other directions (passing through a city)

Signs Unique to Autoroutes:

Aire	Rest stop with WCs, telephones, and sometimes gas stations
Bouchon	Traffic jam ahead
Fluide	No slowing ahead ("fluid conditions")
Péage	Toll
Télépéage	Toll booths—automatic toll payment only
Par temps de Pluie	When raining (modifies speed-limit signs)

Tolls: Four hours on the autoroute costs about €25 in tolls. American credit cards not accepted unless chip-and-PIN, but cash is—it's best to have smaller bills ready. Tolls are pricey, but the alternative to these super "feeways" usually means being marooned in countryside traffic—especially near the Riviera. Autoroutes save enough time, gas, and nausea to justify the splurge. Mix high-speed "autorouting" with scenic country-road rambling (be careful of sluggish tractors on country roads).

You'll usually take a ticket when entering an autoroute and pay when you leave. At pay points, avoid the Télepéage tollbooths and those with a credit-card icon. Look instead for green arrows above the tollbooth, which indicate they accept cash. Some exits are entirely automated, with machines taking all euro bill denominations. Shorter autoroute sections (including along the Riviera) have periodic toll booths, where you can pay by dropping coins into a basket (change given, but keep a good supply of coins handy to avoid waiting for an attendant). For more information, see www.autoroutes.fr.

Autoroute gas stations usually come with well-stocked mini-marts, clean restrooms, sandwiches, maps, local products, and cheap vending-machine coffee (€1.30—I dig the *cappuccino sucré*). Many have small cafés or more elaborate cafeterias with reasonable prices.

Highways: Roads are classified into departmental (D), national (N), and autoroutes (A). D routes (usually yellow lines on maps) are often slower but the most scenic. N routes and important D routes (red lines) are the fastest after autoroutes (orange lines). Green road signs are for national routes; blue are for autoroutes. Note that some key roads in France are undergoing letter designation and number changes (mostly N roads converting to D roads). If you are using an older map, the actual route name may differ from what's on your map. Navigate by destination rather than road name...or buy a new map. There are plenty of good facilities, gas stations (most closed Sun), and rest stops along most French roads.

Parking: Finding a parking place can be a headache in the larger cities. Ask your hotelier for ideas, and pay to park at well-patrolled lots (blue *P* signs direct you to parking lots in French cities). Parking structures usually require that you take a ticket with you and pay at a machine (called a *caisse*) on your way back to the car. Be aware that US credit cards probably won't work in these automated machines but euro bills will. Overnight parking (usually 19:00-8:00) is generally reasonable (except in Nice). Curbside metered parking also works (usually free 12:00-14:00 & 19:00-9:00, and all day and night in Aug). Look for a small machine selling time (called *horadateur*, usually one per block), plug in a few coins (€1.50 buys about an hour, varies by city), push the button, get a receipt showing the amount of time you have, and display it inside your windshield. For cheap overnight parking until the next afternoon, buy three hours' worth of time after 19:00. This gets you until noon the next day, after which two more hours are usually free (12:00-14:00), so you're good until 14:00.

Theft: Theft is a huge problem throughout southern France. Thieves easily recognize rental cars and assume they are filled with a tourist's gear. Try to make your car look locally owned by hiding the "tourist-owned" rental-company decals and putting a French newspaper in your back window. Be sure all of your valuables are out of sight and locked in the trunk—or, even better, with you or in your room. And don't assume that just because you're parked on a main street that you'll be fine. Thieves work fast.

Driving Tips

- Be ready for many roundabouts—navigating them is an art. The key is to know your direction and be ready for your turn-off. If you miss it, take another lap.

- At intersections and roundabouts, French road signs use the name of the next destination for directions—the highway number is usually missing. That next destination could be a major city, or it could be the next minor town up the road. Even if you rent a GPS system, it's a good idea to check your map ahead of time and get familiar with the names of towns and cities along your route—and even major cities on the same road beyond your destination.

- When navigating into cities, approach intersections cautiously, stow the map, and follow the signs to *Centre-Ville* (city center). From there, head to the TI *(Office de Tourisme)* or your hotel.

- When leaving or just passing through cities, follow the signs for *Toutes Directions* or *Autres Directions* (meaning "anywhere else") until you see a sign for your specific destination.

- Driving on any roads but autoroutes will take longer than you anticipate, so allow yourself plenty of time for slower traffic. (Tractors, trucks, traffic, and hard-to-follow signs all deserve blame.) First-timers should estimate how long they think a drive will take...then double it. I pretend that kilometers are miles (for distances) and base my time estimates accordingly. While locals are eating lunch (12:00-14:00), many sights (and gas stations) are closed, so you can make great time driving—but keep it slow when passing through villages.

- Be very careful when driving on smaller roads—many are narrow, flanked by little ditches that can lure inattentive drivers. I've met several readers who "ditched" their cars (and had to be pulled out by local farmers).

- On autoroutes, keep to the right lanes to let fast drivers by, and be careful when merging into a left lane, as cars can be coming at very high speeds. Cars and trucks commonly keep their left blinker on while in a passing lane, indicating that they plan to get back over to the right.

- Motorcycles will scream between cars in traffic. Be ready—they expect you to make space to let them pass.

- Gas is tricky to find in rural areas on Sunday, so fill up on Saturday. Autoroute filling stations are always open.

- Keep a stash of coins in your ashtray for parking and small autoroute tolls.

Biking

You'll find areas in Provence and the Riviera where public transportation is limited and bicycle touring might be a good idea. For many, biking is a romantic notion whose novelty wears off after the first hill or headwind—realistically evaluate your physical condition and be clear on the limitations bikes present. Start with an easy pedal to a nearby village or through the vineyards, then decide how ambitious you feel. Most find that two hours on a narrow, hard seat is enough. I've listed bike-rental shops where appropriate and suggested a few of my favorite rides. TIs always have addresses for bike-rental places. For a good touring bike, figure about €10 for a half-day and €16 for a full day. You'll pay more for better equipment; generally the best is available through bike shops, not at train stations or other outlets. French bikers often do not wear helmets, though most rental outfits have them (for a small fee).

Cheap Flights

If you're visiting one or more French cities on a longer European trip—or linking up far-flung French cities (such as Paris and Nice)—a flight may save you both time and money. When comparing your options, factor in the time it takes to get to the airport and how early you'll need to arrive to check in.

The best comparison search engine for both international and intra-European flights is www.kayak.com. For inexpensive flights within Europe, try www.skyscanner.com or www.hipmunk.com. If you're not sure who flies to your destination, check its airport's website for a list of carriers.

Well-known cheapo airlines include easyJet (www.easyjet .com) and Ryanair (www.ryanair.com). Be aware of the potential drawbacks of flying on the cheap: nonrefundable and nonchangeable tickets, minimal or nonexistent customer service, treks to airports far outside town, and stingy baggage allowances with steep overage fees. If you're traveling with lots of luggage, a cheap flight can quickly become a bad deal. To avoid unpleasant surprises, read the small print before you book.

Resources

Resources from Rick Steves

Rick Steves' Provence and the French Riviera is one of many books in my series on European travel, which includes country guidebooks, city guidebooks (Paris, Rome, Florence, London, etc.), Snapshot Guides (excerpted chapters from my country guides), Pocket Guides (full-color little books on big cities such as Paris), and my budget-travel skills handbook, *Rick Steves' Europe Through the*

Back Door. Most of my books are available as ebooks. My phrase books—for Italian, French, German, Spanish, and Portuguese—are practical and budget-oriented. My other books include *Europe 101* (a crash course on art and history designed for travelers); *Mediterranean Cruise Ports* and *Northern European Cruise Ports* (how to make the most of your time in port); and *Travel as a Political Act* (a travelogue sprinkled with tips for bringing home a global perspective). A more complete list of my titles appears near the end of this book.

Video: My public television series, *Rick Steves' Europe*, covers European destinations in 100 shows, with 10 episodes on France. To watch episodes online, visit www.hulu.com; for scripts and local airtimes, see www.ricksteves.com/tv.

Audio: My weekly public radio show, *Travel with Rick Steves*, features interviews with travel experts from around the world. All of this free audio content is available at Rick Steves Audio Europe, an extensive online library organized by destination. Choose whatever interests you, and download it via the Rick Steves Audio Europe smartphone app, www.ricksteves.com/audioeurope, iTunes, or Google Play.

Maps

The black-and-white maps in this book are concise and simple, designed to help you locate recommended places and get to local TIs, where you can pick up more in-depth maps of cities and regions (usually free). Better maps are sold at newsstands and bookstores. Before you buy a map, look at it to be sure it has the level of detail you want.

Michelin maps are available throughout France at bookstores, newsstands, and gas stations (about €5 each, cheaper than in the US). The orange Michelin map #527 (1:275,000 scale) covers this book's destinations with good detail for drivers. Michelin map #332 is good for the Luberon and the Côtes du Rhône, and map #340 is best for the Bouches-du-Rhône (the southern area around Arles). Train travelers will do fine with the maps provided in this book. Drivers going beyond Provence and the Riviera should consider the soft-cover Michelin France atlas (the entire country at 1:200,000, well-organized in a €20 book with an index and maps of major cities). Spend a few minutes learning the Michelin key to get the most sightseeing value out of these maps.

APPENDIX

Other Guidebooks

If you're like most travelers, this book is all you need. But if you're heading beyond my recommended destinations, $40 for extra maps and books can be money well spent. If you'll be traveling elsewhere in France, consider *Rick Steves' France* or *Rick Steves' Paris*.

The following books are worthwhile, though most are not updated annually; check the publication date before you buy.

Of the several guidebooks on Provence and the Riviera, many are high on facts and low on opinion, guts, or personality. For well-researched (though not annually updated) background information, try the Cadogan guide to Southern France. The colorful Eyewitness series, which focuses mainly on sights, has editions on France, including one for Provence. They're fun for their great graphics and photos, but they're relatively skimpy on content and weigh a ton. The popular, skinny green Michelin guides are dry but informative, especially for drivers. They're known for their city and sightseeing maps, and for their succinct, helpful information on all major sights. English editions, covering most of the regions you'll want to visit, are sold in France for about €14 (or $20 in the US).

Recommended Books and Movies

To learn more about France past and present, and specifically Provence and the French Riviera, check out a few of these books or films.

Nonfiction

For a good introduction to French culture and people, read *French or Foe* (Polly Platt) and *Sixty Million Frenchmen Can't Be Wrong* (Jean-Benoit Nadeau and Julie Barlow). The latter is a must-read for anyone serious about understanding French culture, contemporary politics, and what makes the French tick.

In *A Distant Mirror,* respected historian Barbara Tuchman takes readers back to medieval France. *The Course of French History* (Pierre Goubert) is a concise and readable summary. Ina Caro's *The Road from the Past* is filled with enjoyable essays on her travels through France, with an accent on history. And *The Yellow House* (Martin Gayford) vividly recounts Van Gogh and Gauguin's tumultuous stay in Arles.

Peter Mayle's bestselling memoirs, *A Year in Provence* and *Toujours Provence,* offer an evocative view of life in southern France. The travelogue *Portraits of France* (Robert Daley) includes chapters on Provence. In *At Home in France* (Ann Barry), an American author describes her visits to her country house. *Postcards from France* (Megan McNeill Libby) was written by an observant foreign exchange student. A mix of writers explores French culture in *Travelers' Tales: Provence* (edited by Tara Austen Weaver and James O'Reilly).

La Seduction: How the French Play the Game of Life (Elaine Sciolino) gives travelers a fun, insightful, and tantalizing peek into how seduction has been used in all aspects of French life from small villages to the halls of government.

A Goose in Toulouse (Mort Rosenblum) provides keen insights on rural France through its focus on cuisine. Foodies may also enjoy *From Here, You Can't See Paris* (Michael S. Sanders), about a local restaurant where foie gras is always on the menu.

Da Vinci Code fans will enjoy reading that book's inspiration, *Holy Blood, Holy Grail* (Michael Baigent, Richard Leigh, and Henry Lincoln), which takes place mostly in southern France.

APPENDIX

Labyrinth (Kate Mosse) is an intriguing tale partly set in medieval southern France during the Cathar crusade.

If you'll be enjoying an extended stay in France, consider *Living Abroad in France* (Terry Link) or *Almost French* (Sarah Turnbull), a funny take on living as a French native. The most complete (and priciest) menu reader around is *A to Z of French Food, a French to English Dictionary of Culinary Terms* (G. de Temmerman). Travelers seeking green and vegetarian options in France could consider *Traveling Naturally in France* (Dorian Yates).

Fiction

Written in the 1930s, *Joy of Man's Desiring* captures the charm of rural France. (The author, Jean Giono, also wrote the Johnny Appleseed eco-fable set in Provence, *The Man Who Planted Trees*.) *The Fly-Truffler* (Gustaf Sobin) features a character who studies the Provençal dialect. Peter Mayle, whose nonfiction books are recommended above, also writes fiction set in Provence, including *Hotel Pastis* and *A Good Year*. For a list of recommended books for children, see the chapter on Traveling with Children.

Films

Alfred Hitchcock's *To Catch a Thief* (1955) features both the French Riviera and crackling performances by Grace Kelly and Cary Grant. In *La Grande Vadrouille* (1966), set during World War II, two French civilians aid the crew of a downed Allied bomber in crossing the demarcation line into southern France. *The Return of Martin Guerre* (1982) takes place during the Middle Ages.

Jean de Florette (1986), a marvelous tale of greed and intolerance, is about a city hunchback who inherits a valuable piece of property in rural France, only to have his efforts thwarted by his villainous neighbor. Its sequel, *Manon des Sources* (1986), continues the story, focusing on the hunchback's beautiful daughter.

Two films based on the memoirs of writer/filmmaker Marcel Pagnol show his early life in Provence: *My Father's Glory* (1991) and *My Mother's Castle* (1991).

The crime-thriller *Ronin* with Robert De Niro (1998) was filmed in Nice, Villefranche-sur-Mer, and Arles, and the hilarious *Dirty Rotten Scoundrels*, with Steve Martin and Michael Caine (1988), was filmed in and around Villefranche-sur-Mer.

Cyrano de Bergerac (1990), about a romantic poet with a large nose, has scenes filmed at the Abbaye de Fontenay. *French Kiss* (1995) includes scenes in the French countryside and Cannes, as well as Paris. *Chocolat* (2000), which was filmed in the Dordogne region, shows Juliette Binoche opening a chocolate shop and stirring up a tiny town. (*The Horseman on the Roof*, from 1995, is also set in southern France and also features the beautiful Binoche.)

APPENDIX

The Chorus (2004), filled with angelic choir music, tells the story of a schoolteacher and the boys he brings together.

Holidays and Festivals

This list includes selected festivals in the Provence and French Riviera region, plus national holidays observed throughout France. Many sights and banks close down on national holidays—keep this in mind when planning your itinerary. Before planning a trip around a festival, verify its dates by checking the festival's website or the France TI (www.franceguide.com). Hotels get booked up on Easter weekend, Labor Day, Ascension Day, Pentecost, Bastille Day, and the winter holidays. For sports events, see www.sportsevents365.com for schedules and ticket information.

Jan 1	New Year's Day
Jan 6	Epiphany
Feb-March	Carnival-Mardi Gras, parades and fireworks, Nice (Feb 14–March 4 in 2014, www.nicecarnaval.com)
Easter Sunday	April 20 in 2014, April 5 in 2015
Easter Monday	April 21 in 2014, April 6 in 2015
May	Cannes Film Festival, Cannes (May 14-24 in 2014, www.festival-cannes.com)
May 1	Labor Day
May 8	V-E (Victory in Europe) Day
Ascension	May 29 in 2014, May 14 in 2015
Late May	Monaco Grand Prix, auto race, Monaco (May 22-25 in 2014, May 21-24 in 2015, www.acm.mc).
Pentecost	June 8 in 2014, May 24 in 2015
June 21	Fête de la Musique, free concerts and dancing in the streets throughout France
July	International Music and Opera Festival, Aix-en-Provence (www.festival-aix.com)
July	Avignon Festival, theater, dance, and music, Avignon (www.festival-avignon.com)
July	Tour de France, national bicycle race culminating on the Champs-Elysées in Paris (www.letour.fr)
July 14	Bastille Day, fireworks, dancing, and revelry

APPENDIX

Mid-July	"Jazz à Juan" International Jazz Festival, Antibes/Juan-les-Pins (www.jazzajuan.com)
Mid-July	Nice Jazz Festival, Nice (www.nicejazzfestival.fr)
Mid-July–early Aug	Chorégies d'Orange, music and opera performed in a Roman theater, Orange (www.choregies.asso.fr)
July-Aug	International Fireworks Festival, Cannes (www.festival-pyrotechnique-cannes.com)
Aug 15	Assumption of Mary
Nov 1	All Saints' Day
Nov 11	Armistice Day
Dec 25	Christmas Day
Dec 31	New Year's Eve

Conversions and Climate

Numbers and Stumblers

- Europeans write a few of their numbers differently than we do. 1 = 1, 4 = 4, 7 = 7.
- In Europe, dates appear as day/month/year, so Christmas 2014 is 25/12/14.
- Commas are decimal points and decimals are commas. A dollar and a half is $1,50, one thousand is 1.000, and there are 5.280 feet in a mile.
- When counting with fingers, start with your thumb. If you hold up your first finger to request one item, you'll probably get two.
- What Americans call the second floor of a building is the first floor in Europe.
- On escalators and moving sidewalks, Europeans keep the left "lane" open for passing. Keep to the right.

Metric Conversions

A kilogram is 2.2 pounds, and l liter is about a quart, or almost four to a gallon. A kilometer is six-tenths of a mile. I figure kilometers to miles by cutting them in half and adding back 10 percent of the original (120 km: 60 + 12 = 72 miles, 300 km: 150 + 30 = 180 miles).

1 foot = 0.3 meter	1 square yard = 0.8 square meter
1 yard = 0.9 meter	1 square mile = 2.6 square kilometers
1 mile = 1.6 kilometers	1 ounce = 28 grams
1 centimeter = 0.4 inch	1 quart = 0.95 liter
1 meter = 39.4 inches	1 kilogram = 2.2 pounds
1 kilometer = 0.62 mile	32°F = 0°C

Clothing Sizes

When shopping for clothing, use these US-to-European comparisons as general guidelines (but note that no conversion is perfect).

- Women's dresses and blouses: Add 30
  (US size 10 = European size 40)
- Men's suits and jackets: Add 10
  (US size 40 regular = European size 50)
- Men's shirts: Multiply by 2 and add about 8
  (US size 15 collar = European size 38)
- Women's shoes: Add about 30
  (US size 8 = European size 38-39)
- Men's shoes: Add 32-34
  (US size 9 = European size 41; US size 11 = European size 45)

Tire Pressure

In Europe tire pressure is measured in *bars* of pressure. To convert to PSI (pounds per square inch) the formula is: *bar* × 14.5 = PSI (so 2 *bars* would be 2 × 14.5, or 29 PSI). To convert to *bar* pressures from PSI, the formula is: PSI × 0.07 = *bar* (so 30 PSI × 0.07 would be 2.1 *bar*). Usually you can find your car's recommended tire pressure on a sticker mounted on the driver-side doorframe.

APPENDIX

Nice's Climate

First line, average daily high; second line, average daily low; third line, average days without rain. For more detailed weather statistics for destinations in this book (as well as the rest of the world), check www.wunderground.com.

J	F	M	A	M	J	J	A	S	O	N	D
50°	53°	59°	64°	71°	79°	84°	83°	77°	68°	58°	52°
35°	36°	41°	46°	52°	58°	63°	63°	58°	51°	43°	37°
23	22	24	23	23	26	29	26	24	23	21	21

Temperature Conversion: Fahrenheit and Celsius

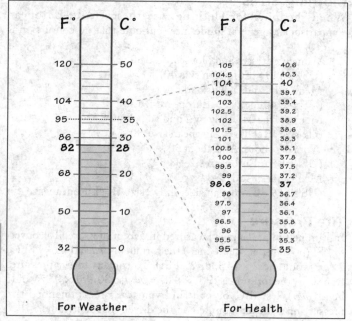

For Weather   For Health

Europe takes its temperature using the Celsius scale, while we opt for Fahrenheit. For a rough conversion from Celsius to Fahrenheit, double the number and add 30. For weather, remember that 28°C is 82°F—perfect. For health, 37°C is just right.

Packing Checklist

Whether you're traveling for five days or five weeks, here's what you'll need to bring. Pack light to enjoy the sweet freedom of true mobility. Happy travels!

- ❏ 5 shirts: long- & short-sleeve
- ❏ 1 sweater or lightweight fleece
- ❏ 2 pairs of pants
- ❏ 1 pair of shorts
- ❏ 5 pairs of underwear & socks
- ❏ 1 pair of shoes
- ❏ 1 rainproof jacket with hood
- ❏ Tie or scarf
- ❏ Swimsuit
- ❏ Sleepwear
- ❏ Money belt
- ❏ Money—your mix of:
  - ❏ Debit card
  - ❏ Credit card(s)
  - ❏ Hard cash ($20 bills)
- ❏ Documents plus photo-copies:
  - ❏ Passport
  - ❏ Printout of airline eticket
  - ❏ Driver's license
  - ❏ Student ID, hostel card, etc.
  - ❏ Railpass/train reservations/ car-rental voucher
  - ❏ Insurance details
- ❏ Guidebooks & maps
- ❏ Address list (for sending emails & postcards)
- ❏ Notepad & pen
- ❏ Journal
- ❏ Daypack
- ❏ Toiletries kit:
  - ❏ Toiletries
  - ❏ Medicines & vitamins
  - ❏ First-aid kit
  - ❏ Glasses/contacts/ sunglasses (with prescriptions)
- ❏ Small towel/washcloth
- ❏ Laundry supplies:
  - ❏ Laundry soap
  - ❏ Clothesline
- ❏ Sewing kit

- ❏ Electronics—your choice of:
  - ❏ Camera (& related gear)
  - ❏ Mobile phone
  - ❏ Portable media player (iPod or other)
  - ❏ Laptop/netbook/ tablet
  - ❏ Ebook reader
  - ❏ Headphones or earbuds
  - ❏ Chargers for each of the above
  - ❏ Plug adapter(s)
- ❏ Alarm clock
- ❏ Earplugs
- ❏ Sealable plastic baggies
- ❏ Empty water bottle
- ❏ Postcards & photos from home

If you plan to carry on your luggage, note that all liquids must be in 3.4-ounce or smaller containers and fit within a single quart-size sealable baggie. For details, see www.tsa.gov/travelers.

APPENDIX

Pronunciation Guide for Place Names

When using the phonetics: Try to nasalize the n sound (let the sound come through your nose). Note that the "ahn" combination uses the "ah" sound in "father," but the "an" combination uses the "a" sound in "sack." Pronounce the "ī" as the long "i" in "light." If your best attempt at pronunciation meets with a puzzled look, just point to the place name on the list.

Aigues-Mortes	ayg-mort
Aiguines	ayg-ween
Aix-en-Provence	ehks ahn proh-vahns
Antibes	ahn-teeb
Ardèche Gorges	ar-dehsh gorzh
Arles	arl
Avignon	ah-veen-yohn
Balazuc	bah-lah-zewk
Bedoin	buh-dwan
Biot	bee-oht
Bonnieux	bohn-yuh
Brantes	brahnt
Buis-les-Barronnies	bwee-lay-bah-roh-nee
Buoux	byoo
Cairanne	kay-rahn
Camargue	kah-marg
Cannes	kan
Cap Ferrat	kahp feh-rah
Cassis	kah-see
Cavaillon	kah-vī-yohn
Châteauneuf-du-Pape	shah-toh-nuhf-dew-pahp
Côte du Rhône	koht dew rohn
Eze-Bord-de-Mer	ehz-bor-duh-mehr
Eze-le-Village	ehz-luh-vee-lahzh
Gigondas	zhee-gohn-dahs
Gordes	gord
Gourdon	goor-dohn
Grasse	grahs
Grignan	green-yahn
Isle-sur-la-Sorgue	eel-sewr-lah-sorg
Joucas	zhoo-kahs
Juan-les-Pins	zhwahn-lay-pan
La Trophée des Alpes	lah troh-fay dayz ahlp
La Turbie	lah tewr-bee

Lacoste	lah-kohst
Le Bar-sur-Loup	luh bar-sewr-loo
Le Crestet	luh kruh-stay
Les Baux	lay boh
Lourmarin	loor-mah-ran
Luberon	lew-buh-rohn
Marseille	mar-say
Ménerbes	may-nehrb
Menton	mahn-tohn
Monaco	moh-nah-koh
Monte Carlo	mohn-tay kar-loh
Mont Ventoux	mohn vahn-too
Moustier-Ste-Marie	moost-yay-sahnt-mah-ree
Nice	nees
Nîmes	neem
Nyons	nee-yohns
Oppède-le-Vieux	oh-pehd-luh-vee-uh
Orange	oh-rahnzh
Pont du Gard	pohn dew gar
Port Grimaud	por gree-moh
Provence	proh-vahns
Roussillon	roo-see-yohn
Saignon	sayn-yohn
Séguret	say-gew-ray
St-Jalles	san-zhahl
St-Jean	san-zhahn
St-Paul-de-Vence	san-pohl-duh-vahns
St-Rémy-de-Provence	san-ray-mee-duh-pro-vahns
St-Saturnin-lès-Apt	san-sah-tewr-nan-lehz-ahpt
St-Tropez	san-troh-pay
Stes-Maries-de-la-Mer	sahnt-mah-ree-duh-lah-mehr
Suzette	sew-zeht
Tourrettes-sur-Loup	too-reht-sewr-loo
Uzès	ew-zehs
Vaison la Romaine	vay-zohn lah roh-mehn
Vallauris	vah-loh-rees
Vence	vahns
Viens	vee-ahn
Villa Kérylos	vee-lah kay-ree-lohs
Villefranche-sur-Mer	veel-frahnsh-sewr-mehr

French Survival Phrases

When using the phonetics, try to nasalize the n sound.

English	French	Pronunciation
Good day.	*Bonjour.*	bohn-zhoor
Mrs. / Mr.	*Madame / Monsieur*	mah-dahm / muhs-yur
Do you speak English?	*Parlez-vous anglais?*	par-lay-voo ahn-glay
Yes. / No.	*Oui. / Non.*	wee / nohn
I understand.	*Je comprends.*	zhuh kohn-prahn
I don't understand.	*Je ne comprends pas.*	zhuh nuh kohn-prahn pah
Please.	*S'il vous plaît.*	see voo play
Thank you.	*Merci.*	mehr-see
I'm sorry.	*Désolé.*	day-zoh-lay
Excuse me.	*Pardon.*	par-dohn
(No) problem.	*(Pas de) problème.*	(pah duh) proh-blehm
It's good.	*C'est bon.*	say bohn
Goodbye.	*Au revoir.*	oh vwahr
one / two	*un / deux*	uhn / duh
three / four	*trois / quatre*	twah / kah-truh
five / six	*cinq / six*	sank / sees
seven / eight	*sept / huit*	seht / weet
nine / ten	*neuf / dix*	nuhf / dees
How much is it?	*Combien?*	kohn-bee-an
Write it?	*Ecrivez?*	ay-kree-vay
Is it free?	*C'est gratuit?*	say grah-twee
Included?	*Inclus?*	an-klew
Where can I buy / find...?	*Où puis-je acheter / trouver...?*	oo pwee-zhuh ah-shuh-tay / troo-vay
I'd like / We'd like...	*Je voudrais / Nous voudrions...*	zhuh voo-dray / noo voo-dree-ohn
...a room.	*...une chambre.*	ewn shahn-bruh
...a ticket to ___.	*...un billet pour ___.*	uhn bee-yay poor
Is it possible?	*C'est possible?*	say poh-see-bluh
Where is...?	*Où est...?*	oo ay
...the train station	*...la gare*	lah gar
...the bus station	*...la gare routière*	lah gar root-yehr
...tourist information	*...l'office du tourisme*	loh-fees dew too-reez-muh
Where are the toilets?	*Où sont les toilettes?*	oo sohn lay twah-leht
men	*hommes*	ohm
women	*dames*	dahm
left / right	*à gauche / à droite*	ah gohsh / ah dwaht
straight	*tout droit*	too dwah
When does this open / close?	*Ça ouvre / ferme à quelle heure?*	sah oo-vruh / fehrm ah kehl ur
At what time?	*À quelle heure?*	ah kehl ur
Just a moment.	*Un moment.*	uhn moh-mahn
now / soon / later	*maintenant / bientôt / plus tard*	man-tuh-nahn / bee-an-toh / plew tar
today / tomorrow	*aujourd'hui / demain*	oh-zhoor-dwee / duh-man

In a French-Speaking Restaurant

English	French	Pronunciation
I'd like / We'd like...	Je voudrais / Nous voudrions...	zhuh voo-dray / noo voo-dree-ohn
...to reserve...	...réserver...	ray-zehr-vay
...a table for one / two.	...une table pour un / deux.	ewn tah-bluh poor uhn / duh
Non-smoking.	Non fumeur.	nohn few-mur
Is this seat free?	C'est libre?	say lee-bruh
The menu (in English), please.	La carte (en anglais), s'il vous plaît.	lah kart (ahn ahn-glay) see voo play
service (not) included	service (non) compris	sehr-vees (nohn) kohn-pree
to go	à emporter	ah ahn-por-tay
with / without	avec / sans	ah-vehk / sahn
and / or	et / ou	ay / oo
special of the day	plat du jour	plah dew zhoor
specialty of the house	spécialité de la maison	spay-see-ah-lee-tay duh lah may-zohn
appetizers	hors-d'oeuvre	or-duh-vruh
first course (soup, salad)	entrée	ahn-tray
main course (meat, fish)	plat principal	plah pran-see-pahl
bread	pain	pan
cheese	fromage	froh-mahzh
sandwich	sandwich	sahnd-weech
soup	soupe	soop
salad	salade	sah-lahd
meat	viande	vee-ahnd
chicken	poulet	poo-lay
fish	poisson	pwah-sohn
seafood	fruits de mer	frwee duh mehr
fruit	fruit	frwee
vegetables	légumes	lay-gewm
dessert	dessert	duh-sehr
mineral water	eau minérale	oh mee-nay-rahl
tap water	l'eau du robinet	loh dew roh-bee-nay
milk	lait	lay
(orange) juice	jus (d'orange)	zhew (doh-rahnzh)
coffee	café	kah-fay
tea	thé	tay
wine	vin	van
red / white	rouge / blanc	roozh / blahn
glass / bottle	verre / bouteille	vehr / boo-teh-ee
beer	bière	bee-ehr
Cheers!	Santé!	sahn-tay
More. / Another.	Plus. / Un autre.	plew / uhn oh-truh
The same.	La même chose.	lah mehm shohz
The bill, please.	L'addition, s'il vous plaît.	lah-dee-see-ohn see voo play
tip	pourboire	poor-bwar
Delicious!	Délicieux!	day-lee-see-uh

For more user-friendly French phrases, check out *Rick Steves' French Phrase Book and Dictionary* or *Rick Steves' French, Italian & German Phrase Book.*

INDEX

MAP INDEX

Explore Europe

At ricksteves.com you can browse through thousands of articles, videos, photos and radio interviews, plus find a wealth of money-saving travel tips for planning your dream trip. And with our mobile-friendly website, you can easily access all this great travel information anywhere you go.

TV Shows

Preview the places you'll visit by watching entire half-hour episodes of Rick Steves' Europe (choose from all 100 shows) on-demand, for free.

your travel dreams into affordable reality

Radio Interviews

Enjoy ready access to Rick's vast library of radio interviews covering travel

tips and cultural insights that relate specifically to your Europe travel plans.

Travel Forums

Learn, ask, share! Our online community of savvy travelers is a great resource

for first-time travelers to Europe, as well as seasoned pros. You'll find forums on each country, plus travel tips and restaurant/hotel reviews. You can even ask one of our well-traveled staff to chime in with an opinion.

Travel News

Subscribe to our free Travel News e-newsletter, and get monthly updates from Rick on what's happening in Europe.

Rick's Free Travel App

Get your FREE **Rick Steves Audio Europe**™ app to enjoy...

- Dozens of self-guided tours of Europe's top museums, sights and historic walks
- Hundreds of tracks filled with cultural insights and sightseeing tips from Rick's radio interviews
- All organized into handy geographic playlists
- For iPhone, iPad, iPod Touch, Android

With Rick whispering in your ear, Europe gets even better.

Find out more at ricksteves.com

Save time and energy

This guidebook is your independent-travel toolkit. But for all it delivers, it's still up to you to devote the time and energy it takes to manage the preparation and logistics that are essential for a happy trip. If that's a hassle, there's a solution.

Rick Steves Tours

A Rick Steves tour takes you to Europe's most interesting places with great

with minimum stress

guides and small groups of 28 or less. We follow Rick's favorite itineraries, ride in comfy buses, stay in family-run hotels, and bring you intimately close to the Europe you've traveled so far to see. Most importantly, we take away the logistical headaches so you can focus on the fun.

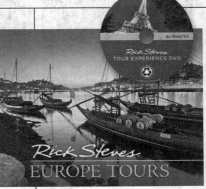

customers—along with us on 40 different itineraries, from Ireland to Italy to Istanbul. Is a Rick Steves tour the right fit for your travel dreams? Find out at ricksteves.com, where you can also get Rick's latest tour catalog and free Tour Experience DVD.

Join the fun

This year we'll take 18,000 free-spirited travelers— nearly half of them repeat

Europe is best experienced with happy travel partners. We hope you can join us.

See our itineraries at ricksteves.com

EUROPE GUIDES

Best of Europe
Eastern Europe
Europe Through the Back Door
Mediterranean Cruise Ports
Northern European Cruise Ports

COUNTRY GUIDES

Croatia & Slovenia
England
France
Germany
Great Britain
Ireland
Italy
Portugal
Scandinavia
Spain
Switzerland

CITY & REGIONAL GUIDES

Amsterdam, Bruges & Brussels
Barcelona
Budapest
Florence & Tuscany
Greece: Athens & the Peloponnese
Istanbul
London
Paris
Prague & the Czech Republic
Provence & the French Riviera
Rome
Venice
Vienna, Salzburg & Tirol

SNAPSHOT GUIDES

Berlin
Bruges & Brussels
Copenhagen & the Best of
 Denmark
Dublin
Dubrovnik
Hill Towns of Central Italy
Italy's Cinque Terre
Krakow, Warsaw & Gdansk
Lisbon
Madrid & Toledo
Milan & the Italian Lakes District
Munich, Bavaria & Salzburg
Naples & the Amalfi Coast
Northern Ireland
Norway
Scotland
Sevilla, Granada & Southern Spain
Stockholm

POCKET GUIDES

Amsterdam
Athens
Barcelona
Florence
London
Paris
Rome
Venice

Rick Steves guidebooks are published by Avalon Travel,
a member of the Perseus Books Group.